JOURNEYS

A Reading and Literature Program

Arrivals
Teacher's Manual
Test Booklet

Banner
Teacher's Manual
Test Booklet

Cascade
Teacher's Manual
Test Booklet

Delta
Teacher's Manual
Test Booklet

Emblem
Teacher's Manual
Test Booklet

Findings
Teacher's Manual
Test Booklet

JOURNEYS

A Reading and Literature Program

Findings

Curriculum and Writing

Richard J. Smith

Professor of Curriculum and Instruction,
University of Wisconsin.
Formerly, Director of Reading Development,
Public Schools of Madison, Wisconsin.
Formerly, Reading Coordinator, Public Schools
of Ripon, Wisconsin.

Max F. Schulz

Professor of English,
University of Southern California.

 HARCOURT BRACE JOVANOVICH, PUBLISHERS

New York   Chicago   San Francisco   Atlanta   Dallas   *and*   London

Acknowledgments

For permission to reprint copyrighted material, grateful acknowledgment is given to the following sources:

The American-Scandinavian Foundation: "The Brothers" from *Told in Norway* by Björnstjerne Björnson (American-Scandinavian Foundation: New York, 1927).

Atheneum Publishers: "Forsythia Bush" from *I Thought I Heard the City* by Lilian Moore. Text copyright © 1969 Lilian Moore. "Separation" from *The Moving Target* by W. S. Merwin. Copyright © 1962 W. S. Mervin.

Brandt & Brandt Literary Agents, Inc.: "An Underground Episode" by Edmund Ware Smith. An adapted version by special permission. Copyright 1934 by *Story* Magazine. Copyright renewed © 1962 by Edmund Ware Smith. "What Sort of Person is This Amanda Jones Anyway?" by Joan Aiken. Copyright © 1972 by Joan Aiken.

Curtis Brown Ltd., London: "Nearly Perfect" by A. A. Milne.

Curtis Brown Ltd., London and Simon & Schuster, a Division of Gulf & Western Corporation: "The Old Cat" (retitled) from *Particularly Cats* by Doris Lessing. Copyright © 1967 by Doris Lessing Productions, Ltd.

Curtis Brown Ltd., London and Doubleday & Company, Inc.: Text of "The Birds" from *Kiss Me Again, Stranger* by Daphne Du Maurier. Copyright 1952 by Daphne Du Maurier.

Coward, McCann & Geoghegan, Inc.: "Counters" from *Compass Rose* by Elizabeth Coatsworth. Copyright 1929; renewed © 1957 by Elizabeth Coatsworth.

Toby Cole-Abernethy: "War" from *The Medals and Other Stories* by Luigi Pirandello. © E. P. Dutton & Co., Inc. 1932, 1967. Reprinted by permission of the Pirandello Estate and Toby Cole, agent.

Joan Daves, 59 East 54 Street, New York, N.Y. 10022: "My Delicate Heart Condition" by Toni Cade Bambara. Copyright © 1965 by Toni Cade Bambara.

Doubleday & Company, Inc.: "The Singing Bell" from *Asimov's Mysteries* by Isaac Asimov. Copyright 1954 by Fantasy House, Inc. "Sasquatch Alias 'Bigfoot' " from *Strange Monsters and Great Searches* by George Laycock. Copyright © 1973 by George Laycock.

Norma Millay (Ellis): "Lament" from *Collected Poems* by Edna St. Vincent Millay, Harper & Row. Copyright 1921, 1948 by Edna St. Vincent Millay.

Farrar, Straus and Giroux, Inc.: "The Son from America" from *A Crown of Feathers* by Isaac Bashevis Singer. Copyright © 1970, 1971, 1972, 1973 by Isaac Bashevis Singer. "Gold" (retitled) from *Coming Into the Country* by John McPhee. Copyright © 1976, 1977 by John McPhee. This material originally appeared in *The New Yorker.*

Edward Field: "Frankenstein" from *Variety Photoplays* by Edward Field, published by Maelstrom Press, P.O. Box 4261, Long Beach, CA 90804.

Herbert Goldstone and The Magazine of Fantasy and

Critical Readers

We wish to thank the following people, who helped to evaluate materials for this book.

Steve Magocsi
Hughes High School, Cincinnati, Ohio

Michael J. Romeo
Kearny High School, Kearny, New Jersey

Robert C. Schappell
Conestoga Valley Schools, Lancaster, Pennsylvania

Shelley Umans
Columbia University, New York, New York
Formerly with New York City Public School System, New York, New York

CONTENTS

Impressions

Ventures

Quest

Poetry

Changes

Treasures

Drama

Turn to p. xiv **for Outline of Skills**

OUTLINE OF SKILLS

Literature Skills

Reading Skills

Word Attack Skills

Composition Skills

IMPRESSIONS

Cemetery Path

Leo Rosten

Ivan was a timid little man—so timid that the villagers called him "Pigeon" or mocked him with the title "Ivan the Terrible." Every night Ivan stopped in at the saloon which was on the edge of the village cemetery. Ivan never crossed the cemetery to get to his lonely shack on the other side. The path through the cemetery would save him many minutes, but he had never taken it—not even in the full light of the moon.

Late one winter's night, when bitter wind and snow beat against the saloon, the customers took up the familiar mockery.

Ivan's sickly protest only fed their taunts, and they jeered cruelly when the young Cossack[1] lieutenant flung his horrid challenge at him.

---

1. Cossack (kŏs′ăk) *adj.*: Pertaining to a Cossack, a native of the southeastern portion of the Soviet Union. Cossacks are known for their horsemanship and their bravery.

"You are a pigeon, Ivan. You'll walk all around the cemetery in this cold—but you dare not cross the cemetery."

Ivan murmured, "The cemetery is nothing to cross, Lieutenant. It is nothing but earth, like all the other earth."

The lieutenant cried, "A challenge, then! Cross the cemetery tonight, Ivan, and I'll give you five rubles[2]—five gold rubles!"

Perhaps it was the vodka. Perhaps it was the temptation of the five gold rubles. No one ever knew why Ivan, moistening his lips, said suddenly: "Yes, Lieutenant, I'll cross the cemetery!"

The saloon echoed with their disbelief. The lieutenant winked to the men and unbuckled his sword. "Here, Ivan. When you get to the center of the cemetery, in front of the biggest tomb, stick the sword into the ground. In the morning we shall go there. And if the sword is in the ground—five gold rubles to you!"

Ivan took the sword. The men drank a toast: "To Ivan the Terrible!" They roared with laughter.

The wind howled around Ivan as he closed the door of the saloon behind him. The cold was knife-sharp. He buttoned his long coat and crossed the dirt road. He could hear the lieutenant's voice, louder than the rest, yelling after him, "Five rubles, Pigeon! If you live!"

Ivan pushed the cemetery gate open. He walked fast. "Earth, just earth . . . like any other earth." But the darkness was a massive dread. "Five gold rubles . . ." The wind was cruel, and the sword was like ice in his hands. Ivan shivered under the long, thick coat and broke into a limping run.

He recognized the large tomb. He must have sobbed—that was drowned in the wind. And he kneeled, cold and terrified, and drove the sword into the hard ground. With his fist, he beat it down to the hilt. It was done. The cemetery . . . the challenge . . . five gold rubles.

Ivan started to rise from his knees. But he could not move. Something held him. Something gripped him in an unyielding hold. Ivan tugged and lurched and pulled—gasping in his panic, shaken by a monstrous fear. But something held Ivan. He cried out in terror, then made senseless gurgling noises.

They found Ivan, next morning, on the ground in front of the tomb that was in the center of the cemetery. His face was not that of a frozen man's, but of a man killed by some nameless horror. And the lieutenant's sword was in the ground where Ivan had pounded it—through the dragging folds of his long coat.

---

2. rubles (roo′bəlz) n.: Russian coins.

Close Up

1. (a) Why do the villagers call Ivan "Pigeon" and "Ivan the Terrible"? (b) What evidence in the first paragraph supports the villagers' low opinion of Ivan?

2. When the lieutenant taunts him, Ivan replies, "The cemetery is nothing to cross, Lieutenant. It is nothing but earth, like all the other earth." Do you think Ivan really believes this? Why or why not?

3. Why do you think Ivan accepts the lieutenant's challenge to cross the cemetery?

4. The next morning the villagers find Ivan dead, his face that "of a man killed by some nameless horror." What really killed Ivan?

The Short Story

A short story is a brief work of fiction that is meant to be read during a short period of time. It is imaginative writing; it is usually about made-up characters and events. A short story often centers on a struggle or problem that the characters must solve. The *climax* of the story is the point where the struggle comes to a head and is the most exciting or intense. The *resolution* is the point where the conflict, or struggle, ends, and the problem is resolved. Usually, the story ends when the conflict is resolved.

1. The main character, Ivan, has a serious problem. What is it?

2. When does Ivan's struggle to solve his problem become most intense?

3. (a) At what point does Ivan's struggle end? (b) Do you think he won or lost his struggle? Why?

4. Do you think the resolution of this story is believable; that is, do you think it is in keeping with Ivan's character?

Activities

1. **Composition.** Imagine you are Ivan. What do you think is holding on to you in the cemetery? Write a paragraph describing this "nameless horror."

2. Franklin Delano Roosevelt once said, "The only thing we have to fear is fear itself." Write a paragraph explaining what you think he meant.

SENTENCE MEANING

Identifying Core Parts

A sentence contains at least two core parts: the simple subject and the simple predicate, or verb. The simple subject is a noun or pronoun and answers the question "Who?" or "What?" The simple predicate answers the question "Did what?" or is a form of the verb *to be*. Look at the sentence below. The simple subject is underlined once and the simple predicate twice.

"The <u>saloon</u> <u>echoed</u> with their disbelief."

What? Saloon. Did what? Echoed.

Some sentences have three core parts. The third core part completes the meaning of the simple predicate. It answers the question "What?" in regard to the verb. Look at the sentences below. The third core part is underlined three times.

"<u>Ivan</u> <u>took</u> the <u>sword</u>."

Who? Ivan. Did what? Took. Took what? Sword.

"<u>He</u> <u>recognized</u> the large <u>tomb</u>."

Who? He. Did what? Recognized. Recognized what? Tomb.

---

1. Copy the following sentences on a piece of paper. Then underline the simple subject once and the simple predicate twice. Remember that the simple subject answers the question "Who?" or "What?" The simple predicate answers the question "Did what?" or is a form of the verb *to be*.
   a. Ivan walked slowly into the cemetery.
   b. The lieutenant laughed in Ivan's face.
   c. The other customers jeered at Ivan.
   d. The bitter wind beat against the saloon.
   e. In the center of the cemetery lay Ivan.

2. Copy the following sentences on a piece of paper. Then underline the simple subject once, the simple predicate twice, and the word that completes the meaning of the simple predicate three times.
   a. The soldiers drank a toast to Ivan.
   b. Ivan drove the sword into the ground.
   c. The lieutenant hurled his challenge at Ivan.
   d. Fearfully, Ivan crossed the cemetery, step by painful step.
   e. In the cemetery he felt a tug at his coat.

WORD ATTACK

Using a Glossary

You can find the pronunciation, part of speech, and meaning of many unfamiliar words used in the selections in the glossary at the back of this book. The glossary words are listed in alphabetical order. Guide words appear at the top of each page. They tell you the range of words appearing on that page.

Look at the word *mockery* in the following sentence.

> "Late one winter's night, when bitter wind and snow beat against the saloon, the customers took up the familiar *mockery*."

If you are not familiar with this word, you can look it up in the glossary, where you will find the following information.

> **mock er y** (mŏk′ ər-ē) *n*.: Ridicule; words used to make someone appear foolish or ridiculous.

The symbols in parentheses (mŏk′ ər-ē) tell you how to pronounce this word. A key to these symbols appears at the front of the glossary. The key tells you that ŏ is pronounced as the o in *pot*, k is pronounced as the consonant sounds in *kick*, and ə is pronounced as the e in *item*. An accent mark tells you which syllable to stress. When a word has more than one accent mark, the heavy accent mark (′) tells you which syllable gets the heavy stress. The light accent mark (′) tells you which syllable gets the lighter stress (sĕm′ ə-tĕr′ ē).

The abbreviation *n*. tells you that *mockery* is a noun. Other abbreviations you may see in the glossary are *adj.* for adjective, *v.* for verb, *adv.* for adverb, and *prep.* for preposition. After the colon (:) you will find the definition of the word.

---

1. Look up each of the following words in the glossary. On a piece of paper, copy each complete glossary entry.

   a. taunt   **f.** lurch

   b. jeer   **g.** monstrous

   c. temptation   **h.** panic

   d. lieutenant   **i.** gurgling

   e. unyielding   **j.** hilt

2. Write sentences using each word above.

The Rising of the Moon

Lady Augusta Gregory

Characters

Sergeant

Policeman X

Policeman B

A Ragged Man

(*Scene: Side of a wharf in a seaport town. Some posts and chains. A large barrel. Enter three Policemen. Moonlight.*

Sergeant, who is older than the others, crosses the stage to right and looks down steps. The others put down a pastepot and unroll a bundle of placards.)

Policeman B: I think this would be a good place to put up a notice. (*He points to barrel.*)

Policeman X: Better ask him. (*Calls to Sergeant.*) Will this be a good place for a placard?

(*No answer.*)

Policeman B: Will we put up a notice on the barrel?

(*No answer.*)

Sergeant: There's a flight of steps here that leads to the water. This is a place that should be minded well. If he got down here, his friends might have a boat to meet him; they might send it in here from outside.

Policeman B: Would the barrel be a good place to put up a notice?

Sergeant: It might; you can put it there.

(*They paste the notice up.*)

Sergeant (*reading it*): Dark hair—dark eyes, smooth face, height, five feet five—there's not much to take hold of in that—— It's a pity I had no chance of seeing him before he broke out of jail. They say he's a

wonder, that it's he makes all the plans for the whole organization. There isn't another man in Ireland would have broken jail the way he did. He must have some friends among the jailers.

Policeman B: A hundred pounds is little enough for the Government to offer for him. You may be sure any man in the force that takes him will get promotion.

Sergeant: I'll mind this place myself. I wouldn't wonder at all if he came this way. He might come slipping along there *(points to side of wharf)*, and his friends might be waiting for him there *(points down steps)*, and once he got away it's little chance we'd have of finding him; it's maybe under a load of kelp he'd be in a fishing boat, and not one to help a married man that wants it to the reward.

Policeman X: And if we get him itself, nothing but abuse on our heads for it from the people, and maybe from our own relations.

Sergeant: Well, we have to do our duty in the force. Haven't we the whole country depending on us to keep law and order? It's those that are down would be up and those that are up would be down, if it wasn't for us. Well, hurry on, you have plenty of other places to placard yet, and come back here then to me. You can take the lantern. Don't be too long now. It's very lonesome here with nothing but the moon.

Policeman B: It's a pity we can't stop with you. The Government should have brought more police into the town, with *him* in jail, and at assize[1] time too. Well, good luck to your watch.

(They go out.)

Sergeant *(walks up and down once or twice and looks at placard)*: A hundred pounds and promotion sure. There must be a

great deal of spending in a hundred pounds. It's a pity some honest man not to be the better of that.

(A Ragged Man appears at left and tries to slip past. Sergeant suddenly turns.)

Sergeant: Where are you going?

Man: I'm a poor ballad-singer, your honor. I thought to sell some of these *(holds out bundle of ballads)* to the sailors. *(He goes on.)*

Sergeant: Stop! Didn't I tell you to stop? You can't go on there.

Man: Oh, very well. It's a hard thing to be poor. All the world's against the poor.

Sergeant: Who are you?

Man: You'd be as wise as myself if I told you, but I don't mind. I'm one Jimmy Walsh, a ballad-singer.

Sergeant: Jimmy Walsh? I don't know that name.

Man: Ah, sure, they know it well enough in Ennis. Were you ever in Ennis, sergeant?

Sergeant: What brought you here?

Man: Sure, it's to the assizes I came, thinking I might make a few shillings here or there. It's in the one train with the judges I came.

Sergeant: Well, if you came so far, you may as well go farther, for you'll walk out of this.

Man: I will, I will; I'll just go on where I was going. *(Goes toward steps.)*

Sergeant: Come back from those steps; no one has leave to pass down them tonight.

Man: I'll just sit on the top of the steps till I see will some sailor buy a ballad off me that would give me my supper. They do be late going back to the ship. It's often I saw them in Cork carried down the wharf in a handcart.

Sergeant: Move on, I tell you. I won't have anyone lingering about the wharf tonight.

Man: Well, I'll go. It's the poor have the hard life! Maybe yourself might like one, sergeant. Here's the good sheet now. *(Turns one over.)* "Content and a Pipe"—that's not much. "The Peeler and the Goat"—you wouldn't like that. "Johnny Hart"—that's a lovely song.

---

1. assize (ə-sīz′) *adj.*: Pertaining to the regular court sessions held in each British county.

Sergeant: Move on.

Man: Ah, wait till you hear it. (*Sings.*)

There was a rich farmer's daughter lived
    near the town of Ross;
She courted a Highland soldier, his name
    was Johnny Hart;
Says the mother to her daughter, "I'll go
    distracted mad
If you marry that Highland soldier dressed
    up in Highland plaid."

Sergeant: Where are you going?

Man: Sure you told me to be going, and I am going.

Sergeant: Don't be a fool. I didn't tell you to go that way; I told you to go back to the town.

Man: Back to the town, is it?

Sergeant (*taking him by the shoulder and shoving him before him*): Here, I'll show you the way. Be off with you. What are you stopping for?

Man (*who has been keeping his eye on the notice, points to it*): I think I know what you're waiting for, sergeant.

Sergeant: What's that to you?

Man: And I knew well the man you're waiting for—I know him well—I'll be going. (*He shuffles on.*)

Sergeant: You know him? Come back here. What sort is he?

Man: Come back is it, sergeant? Do you want to have me killed?

Sergeant: Why do you say that?

Man: Never mind. I'm going. I wouldn't be in your shoes if the reward was ten times as much. (*Goes offstage to left.*) Not if it was ten times as much.

Sergeant (*rushing after him*): Come back here, come back. (*Drags him back.*) What sort is he? Where did you see him?

Man: I saw him in my own place, in the County Clare. I tell you you wouldn't like to be looking at him. You'd be afraid to be in the one place with him. There isn't a weapon he doesn't know the use of, and as to strength, his muscles are as hard as that board. (*Slaps barrel.*)

Sergeant: Is he as bad as that?

Man: He is then.

Sergeant: Do you tell me so?

Man: There was a poor man in our place, a sergeant from Ballyvaughan. —It was with a lump of stone he did it.

Sergeant: I never heard of that.

Man: And you wouldn't, sergeant. It's not everything that happens gets into the papers. And there was a policeman in plainclothes, too . . . It is in Limerick he was . . . It was after the time of the attack on the police barrack at Kilmallock . . . Moonlight . . . just like this . . . waterside. . . . Nothing was known for certain.

Sergeant: Do you say so? It's a terrible country to belong to.

Man: That's so, indeed! You might be standing there, looking out that way, thinking you saw him coming up this side of the wharf (*points*), and he might be coming up this other side (*points*), and he'd be on you before you knew where you were.

Sergeant: It's a whole troop of police they ought to put here to stop a man like that.

Man: But if you'd like me to stop with you, I could be looking down this side. I could be sitting up here on this barrel.

Sergeant: And you know him well, too?

Man: I'd know him a mile off, sergeant.

Sergeant: But you wouldn't want to share the reward?

Man: Is it a poor man like me, that has to be going the roads and singing in fairs, to have the name on him that he took a reward? But you don't want me. I'll be safer in the town.

Sergeant: Well, you can stop.

Man (*getting up on barrel*): All right, sergeant. I wonder, now, you're not tired out, sergeant, walking up and down the way you are.

Sergeant: If I'm tired I'm used to it.

Man: You might have hard work before you tonight yet. Take it easy while you can.

There's plenty of room up here on the barrel, and you can see farther when you're higher up.

Sergeant: Maybe so. (*Gets up beside him on barrel, facing right. They sit back to back, looking different ways.*) You made me feel a bit queer with the way you talked.

Man: Give me a match, sergeant. (*He gives it, and Man lights pipe.*) Take a draw yourself? It'll quiet you. Wait now till I give you a light, but you needn't turn round. Don't take your eye off the wharf for the life of you.

Sergeant: Never fear, I won't. (*Lights pipe. They both smoke.*) Indeed, it's a hard thing to be in the force, out at night and no thanks for it, for all the danger we're in. And it's little we get but abuse from the people, and no choice but to obey our orders, and never asked when a man is sent into danger, if you are a married man with a family.

Man (*sings*):

As through the hills I walked to view the
    hills and shamrock plain,
I stood awhile where nature smiles to view
    the rocks and streams,
On a matron fair I fixed my eyes beneath a
    fertile vale,
As she sang her song it was on the wrong of
    poor old Granuaile.[2]

Sergeant: Stop that; that's no song to be singing in these times.

Man: Ah, sergeant, I was only singing to keep my heart up. It sinks when I think of him. To think of us two sitting here, and he creeping up the wharf, maybe, to get to us.

Sergeant: Are you keeping a good lookout?

Man: I am; and for no reward too. Amn't I the foolish man? But when I saw a man in trouble, I never could help trying to get him out of it. What's that? Did something hit me?

Sergeant (*patting him on the shoulder*): You will get your reward in heaven.

Man: I know that, sergeant, but life is precious.

Sergeant: Well, you can sing if it gives you more courage.

Man (*sings*):

Her head was bare, her hands and feet
    with iron bands were bound,
Her pensive strain and plaintive wail min-
    gled with the evening gale,
And the song she sang with mournful air, I
    am old Granuaile.
Her lips so sweet that monarchs kissed . . .

Sergeant: That's not it . . . "Her gown she wore was stained with gore." . . . That's it—you missed that.

Man: You're right, sergeant, so it is; I missed it. (*Repeats the line.*) But to think a man like you knowing a song like that.

Sergeant: There's many a thing a man might know and might not have any wish for.

Man: Now, I daresay, sergeant, in your youth, you used to be sitting up on a wall, the way you are sitting up on this barrel now, and the other lads beside you, and you singing "Granuaile"?

Sergeant: I did then.

Man: And the "Shan Bhean Bhocht"?[3]

Sergeant: I did then.

Man: And the "Green on the Cape"?[4]

Sergeant: That was one of them.

---

2. Granuaile (grăn-yo͞o-āl'): A sixteenth century woman pirate who resisted Queen Elizabeth I's efforts to rule Ireland. The name Granuaile (Gaelic for Grace O'Malley) became a personification of Ireland and her fight for independence.

3. "Shan Bhean Bhoct" (shän vän vôKHt): An Irish liberation song. The literal translation, "poor old woman," refers to Ireland and the burden of British rule.

4. "Green on the Cape": An Irish liberation song. The title signifies Ireland's determination to gain independence (the traditional British uniform featured a red cape).

Man: And maybe the man you are watching for tonight used to be sitting on the wall, when he was young, and singing those same songs. . . . It's a queer world. . . .

Sergeant: Whisht! . . . I think I see something coming. . . . It's only a dog.

Man: And isn't it a queer world? . . . Maybe it's one of the boys you used to be singing with that time you will be arresting today or tomorrow, and sending into the dock. . . .

Sergeant: That's true indeed.

Man: And maybe one night, after you had been singing, if the other boys had told you some plan they had, some plan to free the country, you might have joined them . . . and maybe it is you might be in trouble now.

Sergeant: Well, who knows but I might? I had great spirit in those days.

Man: It's a queer world, sergeant, and it's a little any mother knows when she sees her child creeping on the floor what might happen to it before it has gone through its life, or who will be who in the end.

Sergeant: That's a queer thought now, and a true thought. Wait now till I think it out. . . . If it wasn't for the sense I have, and for my wife and family, and for me joining the force the time I did, it might be myself now would be after breaking jail and hiding in the dark, and it might be him that's hiding in the dark and that got out of jail would be sitting up where I am on this barrel. . . . And it might be myself would be creeping up trying to make my escape from himself, and it might be himself would be keeping the law, and myself would be breaking it, and myself would be trying maybe to put a bullet in his head, or to take up a lump of stone the way you said he did . . . no, that myself did. . . . Oh! (*Gasps. After a pause.*) What's that? (*Grasps Man's arm.*)

Man (*jumps off barrel and listens, looking out over water*): It's nothing, sergeant.

Sergeant: I thought it might be a boat. I had a notion there might be friends of his coming about the wharfs with a boat.

Man: Sergeant, I am thinking it was with the people you were, and not with the law you were when you were a young man.

Sergeant: Well, if I was foolish then, that time's gone.

Man: Maybe, sergeant, it comes into your head sometimes, in spite of your belt and your tunic, that it might have been as well for you to have followed Granuaile.

Sergeant: It's no business of yours what I think.

Man: Maybe, sergeant, you'll be on the side of the country yet.

Sergeant (*gets off barrel*): Don't talk to me like that. I have my duties and I know them. (*Looks round.*) That was a boat; I hear the oars. (*Goes to the steps and looks down.*)

Man (*sings*):

O, then, tell me, Shawn O'Farrell,
    Where the gathering is to be.
In the old spot by the river
    Right well known to you and me!

Sergeant: Stop that! Stop that, I tell you!

Man (*sings louder*):

One word more, for signal token,
    Whistle up the marching tune,
With your pike upon your shoulder,
    At the Rising of the Moon.

Sergeant: If you don't stop that, I'll arrest you.

(*A whistle from below answers, repeating the air.*)

Sergeant: That's a signal. (*Stands between him and steps.*) You must not pass this way. . . . Step farther back. . . . Who are you? You are no ballad-singer.

Man: You needn't ask who I am; that placard will tell you. (*Points to placard.*)

Sergeant: You are the man I am looking for.

Man (*takes off hat and wig; Sergeant seizes them*): I am. There's a hundred pounds on

my head. There is a friend of mine below in a boat. He knows a safe place to bring me to.

Sergeant: (*looking still at hat and wig*): It's a pity! It's a pity. You deceived me. You deceived me well.

Man: I am a friend of Granuaile. There is a hundred pounds on my head.

Sergeant: It's a pity, it's a pity!

Man: Will you let me pass, or must I make you let me?

Sergeant: I am in the force. I will not let you pass.

Man: I thought to do it with my tongue. (*Puts hand in breast.*) What is that?

Voice of Policeman X outside: Here, this is where we left him.

Sergeant: It's my comrades coming.

Man: You won't betray me . . . the friend of Granuaile. (*Slips behind barrel.*)

Voice of Policeman B: That was the last of the placards.

Policeman X (*as they come in*): If he makes his escape it won't be unknown he'll make it.

(*Sergeant puts hat and wig behind his back.*)

Policeman B: Did anyone come this way?

Sergeant (*after a pause*): No one.

Policeman B: No one at all?

Sergeant: No one at all.

Policeman B: We had no orders to go back to the station; we can stop along with you.

Sergeant: I don't want you. There is nothing for you to do here.

Policeman B: You bade us to come back here and keep watch with you.

Sergeant: I'd sooner be alone. Would any man come this way and you making all that talk? It is better the place be quiet.

Policeman B: Well, we'll leave you the lantern anyhow. (*Hands it to him.*)

Sergeant: I don't want it. Bring it with you.

Policeman B: You might want it. There are clouds coming up and you have the darkness of the night before you yet. I'll leave it over here on the barrel. (*Goes to barrel.*)

Sergeant: Bring it with you, I tell you. No more talk.

Policeman B: Well, I thought it might be a comfort to you. I often think when I have it in my hand and can be flashing it about into every dark corner (*doing so*) that it's the same as being beside the fire at home, and the bits of bogwood blazing up now and again. (*Flashes it about, now on the barrel, now on Sergeant.*)

Sergeant (*furious*): Be off the two of you, yourselves and your lantern!

(*They go out. Man comes from behind barrel. He and Sergeant stand looking at one another.*)

Sergeant: What are you waiting for?

Man: For my hat, of course, and my wig. You wouldn't wish me to get my death of cold?

(*Sergeant gives them.*)

Man (*going toward steps*): Well, good-night, comrade, and thank you. You did me a good turn tonight, and I'm obliged to you. Maybe I'll be able to do as much for you when the small rise up and the big fall down . . . when we all change places at the Rising (*waves his hand and disappears*) of the Moon.

Sergeant (*turning his back to audience and reading placard*): A hundred pounds reward! A hundred pounds! (*Turns toward audience.*) I wonder now, am I as great a fool as I think I am?

Close Up

1. In 1917 Irish volunteers organized to rid Ireland of British rule. They finally succeeded in 1949 when the Republic of Ireland became an independent state. In this play, the police hunt for a man who has escaped from prison. What makes you think he is a rebel fighting for Irish independence?

2. (a) Why does the sergeant sit by the steps leading to the docks? (b) Why does he allow the ragged man to stop there?

3. When the ragged man sings the wrong lyrics to "Granuaile," the sergeant corrects him. (a) What does this incident reveal about the sergeant's past? (b) How does the ragged man use this information to his advantage?

4. At first the sergeant wants only two things: the reward money and a promotion. Why does he decide to give up these things and let the ragged man escape?

5. The ragged man identifies himself as "a friend of Granuaile." Why do you think you are never told his name?

The Play

Most plays are written to be performed before an audience. Actors take the parts of the characters, or people in the play. The story is told chiefly through dialogue—what the characters say to each other. The dialogue and the characters' actions reveal the characters and their problems.

When you read a play, you will notice stage directions. (In this play, the stage directions are enclosed in parentheses and are printed in *italics*.) Stage directions help you to visualize how the play would look on stage. They describe the setting and suggest where the actors would stand and how they would speak their lines.

1. Look at the opening stage directions. (a) Where and when does this play take place? (b) How many people come on stage?

2. Through the police officers' conversation you learn something about the man they are trying to catch. (a) What does this man look like? (b) Why is the man considered "a wonder"?

3. The stage directions help you to visualize what is happening. (a) Why doesn't the sergeant realize who the ragged man is until near the end of the play? (b) Why don't the other officers discover the ragged man when they come back to the dock?

4. The sergeant asks the audience, "I wonder now, am I as great a fool as I think I am?" Why does he feel like a fool?

SENTENCE MEANING

Finding Compound Subjects and Compound Verbs

A sentence has at least two core parts—the simple subject and the simple predicate, or verb. The simple subject answers the question "Who?" or "What?" The simple predicate answers the question "Did what?" or is a form of the verb *to be*.

Some sentences have two or more subjects that take the same verb. These subjects are joined together by a conjunction (*and* or *or*). They are called *compound subjects*. For example:

<u>Policeman B</u> and the <u>sergeant</u> <u>entered</u>.

Who? *Policeman B* and *sergeant*. Did what? *Entered*.

Notice the compound subjects in the following sentences. In the second sentence, the subjects are separated by a group of words.

<u>Policeman B</u>, <u>Policeman X</u>, and the <u>sergeant</u> <u>display</u> the notice.

Suddenly the <u>sergeant</u> on the right side of the barrel and the <u>man</u> on the left side <u>heard</u> the sound of a boat.

Some sentences have two or more verbs that take the same subject. These verbs are joined together by a conjunction. They are called compound verbs. For example:

The <u>sergeant</u> <u>sat</u> on the barrel and <u>waited</u> for the escaped man.

Who? *Sergeant*. Did what? *Sat* and *waited*.

The <u>sergeant</u> <u>turns</u>, <u>sees</u> the stranger, and <u>shouts</u>.

That night <u>he</u> <u>sat</u> on the wall and <u>sang</u> patriotic songs.

1. Copy each of the following sentences on a piece of paper. Then underline the compound subjects once. Underline the simple predicate twice.
   a. The sergeant and the stranger talked about Ireland.
   b. The sergeant and the policemen hunted for the man.
   c. His wife and his children waited for him at home.
   d. After hearing the signal, the sergeant and the stranger confronted each other.
   e. Loyalty to his job and allegiance to his country fought within him.

2. Write each of the following sentences on a piece of paper. Underline the simple subject once. Underline the compound verbs twice.

a. He heard the boat and signaled his friends.
b. The man sat on the dock and waited for his friends.
c. After a while, he reappeared and thanked the sergeant for his help.
d. The stranger wore a hat and wig and carried a bundle of ballad sheets.

WORD ATTACK

Understanding Companion Forms

Many English words have companion forms. **Companion forms are words that are closely related in meaning.** However, they are spelled differently and may be different parts of speech.

Companion Form	Part of Speech	Meaning
note	noun or verb	short letter (n.); to jot down (v.)
notification	noun	formal letter or document
notify	verb	to inform someone or make someone aware

When you learn a new word, you can increase your vocabulary by learning its companion forms.

1. Look up each *italicized* word in a dictionary. On a piece of paper, write the part of speech and meaning of each word.
   a. Well, we have to do our *duty* in the force.
      The sergeant was a *dutiful* policeman.
   b. The whole country *depends* on us to keep order.
      One hundred pounds could certainly help a family man and his *dependents*.
   c. The Department surely will *promote* him.
      The sergeant hoped to receive a *promotion*.
   d. The sergeant thought he was a *fool*.
      The sergeant was afraid he had done a *foolhardy* thing.
   e. The sergeant complains that the police take much *abuse* from the people.
      The sergeant complains that the people are *abusive*.

2. Look up the word *certain* in a dictionary and find one companion form. Write an original sentence containing the word *certain* and one containing the companion form.

The Glory of the Day Was in Her Face

James Weldon Johnson

The glory of the day was in her face,
The beauty of the night was in her eyes.
And over all her loveliness, the grace
Of Morning blushing in the early skies.

5   And in her voice, the calling of the dove;
Like music of a sweet, melodious part.
And in her smile, the breaking light of love;
And all the gentle virtues in her heart.

And now the glorious day, the beauteous night,
10 The birds that signal to their mates at dawn,
To my dull ears, to my tear-blinded sight
Are one with all the dead, since she is gone.

Taught Me Purple

Evelyn Tooley Hunt

My mother taught me purple
Although she never wore it.
Wash-gray was her circle,
The tenement her orbit.

5 My mother taught me golden
And held me up to see it,
Above the broken molding,
Beyond the filthy street.

My mother reached for beauty
10 And for its lack she died,
Who knew so much of duty
She could not teach me pride.

Close Up

1. (a) In "The Glory of the Day Was in Her Face," to what does the poet compare the woman's face and eyes? (b) To what does he compare her voice and smile?

2. At the end of the poem, why can the poet no longer appreciate "the glorious day, the beauteous night"?

3. The color purple stands for high rank or royalty. In "Taught Me Purple," what does the poet mean when she says, "My mother taught me purple"?

4. (a) What color does the poet use to describe her mother's life? (b) Golden describes very valuable or precious things. Why does the mother have to hold the poet up to see golden?

5. Pride is a proper sense of your own worth. (a) Why was the poet's mother unable to teach her pride? (b) Do you think the poet regrets this? Why or why not?

The Lyric Poem

A lyric poem is a short work in verse that expresses the poet's emotional response to a person, place, object, or idea. Often a lyric poem contains both *rhythm* and *rhyme*. Rhythm, which is the pattern of stressed and unstressed syllables in a line, gives the poem its musical quality. In the following line, every other syllable is stressed. (The mark ′ tells you that the syllable is stressed and - tells you that it is unstressed.)

The glory of the day was in her face

Rhyme usually occurs at the end of lines. Rhyme is the repetition of sounds in different words. For example, *face* rhymes with *grace*.

1. In "The Glory of the Day Was in Her Face," how does the poet feel about the woman? Find evidence to support your answer.

2. This poem is divided into three groups of lines, or *stanzas*. Copy the first stanza on a piece of paper and write *a* over the end word of the first line ("face"). Then write *a* over any other end word in the stanza that rhymes with "face." Write *b* over each end word that does not rhyme with "face." What is the rhyme scheme of this poem: *abba, aabb,* or *abab*?

3. In "Taught Me Purple," the first line has the following rhythm: "My mother taught me purple." (a) Which four lines do not follow this exact pattern? (b) By changing the pattern of these lines, the poet emphasizes them. Why might she want to make these lines stand out?

SENTENCE MEANING

Using Punctuation Marks

Many poems are written to be read aloud. Punctuation marks are signals that tell you how to read the poem. They tell you when to pause and when to stop. Commas (,) tell you to pause briefly. Semicolons (;) tell you to pause slightly longer. Periods (.) tell you to stop before going on to the next sentence.

In a poem, the end of a line is not always the end of a sentence, even though the first word in every line begins with a capital letter. To find the end of a sentence, look for the period.

1. Answer the following questions about "The Glory of the Day Was in Her Face." Then read the poem aloud.
   a. Should you pause longer at the end of the first line or the second line? Why?
   b. At the end of which lines should you pause *slightly longer* than you would for a comma? Why?
   c. At the end of which lines should you not pause at all? Why?
   d. The first stanza contains how many sentences?
   e. The third stanza contains how many sentences?
   f. In the third stanza, how does the poet emphasize the word *dead?*

2. Answer the following questions about "Taught Me Purple." Then read the poem aloud.
   a. This poem contains how many sentences?
   b. What is the last word in the first sentence?
   c. What is the last word in the third sentence?
   d. The second stanza contains four lines. At the end of which lines should you pause briefly?
   e. In the third stanza, at the end of which lines should you not pause at all?

WORD ATTACK

Understanding Words That Have More Than One Meaning

Many words have more than one meaning. You can increase your vocabulary by learning several meanings for common words. For example, in the following lines, *grace* means "seemingly effortless beauty or elegance of movement or form." "And over all her loveliness, the *grace*/Of Morning blushing in the early skies." *Grace* can also mean (1) pleasant manners; (2) a short prayer of thanks; and (3) an extended period of time in which to do something.

1. Look up the following words in a dictionary. How many meanings do you find for each word?
   a. glory
   b. beauty
   c. sweet
   d. gentle
   e. dull
   f. pride
   g. purple
   h. filthy
   i. reach
   j. duty

2. Write a sentence for each word below in the way indicated. You may use a dictionary to help you.
   a. Use *pride* so that it means "conceit."
   b. Use *reach* so that it means "to arrive at."
   c. Use *sweet* so that it means "having a sugary taste."
   d. Use *gentle* so that it means "gradual."
   e. Use *pride* so that it means "a group of lions."

3. Often a poet uses a word to suggest several meanings. Look at the following line: "The glory of the day was in her face." Decide which dictionary definitions of *glory* fit this context.

4. Look at the following lines: "The birds that signal to their mates at dawn,/To my dull ears, to my tear-blinded sight/Are one with all the dead, since she is gone." Decide which dictionary definitions of *dull* fit this context.

The Listeners

Walter de la Mare

"Is there anybody there?" said the Traveler,
   Knocking on the moonlit door;
And his horse in the silence champed the grasses
   Of the forest's ferny floor:
5 And a bird flew up out of the turret,
   Above the Traveler's head:
And he smote upon the door again a second time;
   "Is there anybody there?" he said.
But no one descended to the Traveler;
10   No head from the leaf-fringed sill
Leaned over and looked into his gray eyes,
   Where he stood perplexed and still.
But only a host of phantom listeners
   That dwelt in the lone house then
15 Stood listening in the quiet of the moonlight
   To that voice from the world of men:
Stood thronging the faint moonbeams on the dark stair,
   That goes down to the empty hall,
Hearkening in an air stirred and shaken
20   By the lonely Traveler's call.
And he felt in his heart their strangeness,
   Their stillness answering his cry,
While his horse moved, cropping the dark turf,
   'Neath the starred and leafy sky;
25 For he suddenly smote on the door, even

Louder, and lifted his head:—
"Tell them I came, and no one answered,
  That I kept my word," he said.
Never the least stir made the listeners,
30   Though every word he spake
Fell echoing through the shadowiness of the still house
  From the one man left awake:
Ay, they heard his foot upon the stirrup,
  And the sound of iron on stone,
35 And how the silence surged softly backward,
  When the plunging hoofs were gone.

Close Up

1. This poem begins with a question: "Is there anybody there?" Who are the listeners who hear the Traveler's question?

2. Read again lines 29–32. (a) Who is "the one man left awake"? (b) *Awake* usually means "not asleep." What else might it mean in this poem?

3. Although this poem centers on the Traveler, it is called "The Listeners." Why do you think the poet chose this title?

4. The poet's choice of words contributes to the sense of strangeness and mystery. For example, the words "moonbeams on the dark stair" create a strong sense of mystery. Find five other examples of words that contribute to the sense of mystery.

The Narrative Poem

A narrative poem tells a story about characters and events. Often a narrative poem contains rhythm and rhyme. Many narrative poems are meant to be read aloud, and the rhythm and rhyme help listeners follow and remember the story. Rhythm is the pattern of stressed and unstressed sounds in a line. Rhyme, which usually occurs at the end of lines, is the repetition of the same sound in different words; for example, *run/fun* and *river/quiver*.

1. This poem suggests, more than it clearly tells, a story. The Traveler comes to the house, knocks but receives no response, and leaves. Why do you think the Traveler has come to the house? Find the lines that tell you.

2. Most of the lines in this poem have three accented syllables. Line 2 has the following pattern: "Knocking on the moonlit door." Find two other lines that follow this pattern.

3. Copy the first four lines of the poem on a piece of paper. Label *a* the word at the end of the first line. Label *b* the word at the end of the second line. (a) Does any other end word rhyme with *a*? If so, label it *a*. (b) Does any other end word rhyme with *b*? If so, label it *b*. (If there is an end word that does not rhyme with *a* or *b*, label it *c*.)

4. How would you describe the rhyme scheme of this poem: no rhyme, *abab*, *abcb*, or *aabb*?

Activity

▶ **Composition.** Imagine it is ten years in the future. You have returned to your school for a class reunion. As you sit in one of the empty rooms, what thoughts fill your mind?

SENTENCE MEANING

Reading Sentences with Unusual Structure

Sometimes sentences in poetry are difficult to read. The core parts may not appear in their natural order. For example, in the following sentence, the predicate appears before the subject.

Out of the turret <u>flew</u> the <u>bird</u>.

The core parts may be separated by a group of words. For example, in the following sentence, the words "standing in the moonlight" separate the subject and predicate.

The <u>traveler</u>, standing in the moonlight, <u>beat</u> upon the door.

The sentence may contain one or more negative words. If you overlook these words, you may miss the meaning of the sentence. For example:

He knocked on the door but **no one** answered.
Never was the silence broken.
It was **not unusual** for the man to keep his word.

▶ Read the following sentences and answer the questions that follow each sentence.

a. "No head from the leaf-fringed sill/Leaned over and looked into his gray eyes,/Where he stood perplexed and still."
  (1) Did anyone lean over the sill? Which two words tell you this?
  (2) Which group of words separates the subject from the verb *leaned*?
  (3) Did anyone look into his gray eyes?

b. "But only a host of phantom listeners/That dwelt in the lone house then/Stood listening in the quiet of the moonlight/To that voice from the world of men:/Stood thronging the faint moonbeams on the dark stair,/That goes down to the empty hall,/Hearkening in an air stirred and shaken/By the lonely Traveler's call."
  (1) Who stood listening?
  (2) To what did they listen?
  (3) Who stood thronging?

c. "Never the least stir made the listeners,/Though every word he spake/Fell echoing through the shadowiness of the still house/From the one man left awake:"

(1) Did the listeners ever stir?

(2) Look at the following group of words: "Never the least stir made the listeners." What is the subject? What is the predicate? (Hint: You may find it helpful to locate the predicate first.) Rewrite this sentence in natural word order; that is, put the subject first.

WORD ATTACK

Understanding Alliteration

Poets rely heavily on the sounds as well as on the meanings of words to communicate their ideas and feelings. One technique they use is called alliteration. **Alliteration is the repetition of initial (first) consonant sounds in two or more neighboring words.** For example, in the following line, the sound of /s/ is repeated: "For he suddenly smote on the door . . ." In the next line, the sounds of /l/ and /h/ are repeated: ". . . Louder, and lifted his head." Alliteration is pleasing to the ear. Poets also use it when they want to emphasize certain words.

1. Alliteration occurs in each of the lines below. On a piece of paper, write the words that show alliteration.
   a. "Of the forest's ferny floor:"
   b. "Leaned over and looked into his gray eyes,"
   c. "Hearkening in an air stirred and shaken"
   d. "And he felt in his heart their strangeness,"
   e. "Where he stood perplexed and still."

2. The sound that is repeated most often in this poem is /s/. Read aloud lines 29–36. (a) How many times do you hear the sound /s/ at the beginning of words? (b) Do you think this sound contributes to the eerie quality of this poem? Why or why not?

Stop Those Hiccoughs[1]

Robert Benchley

Anyone will be glad to admit that he knows nothing about beagling, or the Chinese stock market, or ballistics, but there is not a man or woman alive who does not claim to know how to cure hiccoughs. The funny thing is that the hiccoughs are never cured until they get darned good and ready.

The most modest and unassuming man in the world becomes an arrogant know-it-all in the presence of hiccoughs—in somebody else.

"Don't be silly," he says, patronizingly. "Just put your head under your arm, hold a glass of water against the back of your neck, and count to five hundred by fives without taking a breath. It never fails."

Then, when it *has* failed, he blames you. "It's absolutely surefire if you only follow my directions," he says. He also implies darkly that what is ailing you is not just merely hiccoughs.

To date, I have been advised to perform the following feats to cure hiccoughs:

Bend the body backward until the head touches the floor, and whistle in reverse.

Place the head in a pail of water and inhale twelve times deeply.

---

1. hiccoughs (hĭk′ŭpz′) n.: Also spelled hiccups. Involuntary gasps of breath which result in spasms in the throat.

Drink a glass of milk from the right hand with the right arm twisted around the neck until the milk enters the mouth from the left side.

Hop, with the feet together, up and down a flight of steps ten times, screaming loudly at each hop.

Roll down a long, inclined lawn, snatching a mouthful of grass up each time the face is downward.

I have tried them all, with resultant torn ligaments, incipient drowning, lockjaw, and arsenic poisoning, but each time, at the finish of the act, and a few seconds of waiting while my mentor[2] says, triumphantly: "See! What did I tell you?" that one, big hiccough always breaks the tension, indicating that the whole performance has been a ghastly flop.

My latest fiasco[3] came as the result of reading the prescription of a Boston doctor, and almost resulted in my being put away as an irresponsible person. "All that the sufferer has to do," wrote the doctor, "is to blow up an ordinary paper bag, as if to explode it, and then hold it over the mouth and nose tightly, breathing in and out of the bag instead of in and out of the open air."

This, according to the doctor, creates an excess of carbon monoxide gas in the bag, which is breathed over and over again, acting on a nervous center of the brain and curing the hiccoughs.

Being alone in the room at the time, I blew the bag up and held it tightly over my face, including not only my mouth and nose, but my eyes as well, like a gas mask. I subjected myself to this treatment for possibly three minutes, walking around the room at the same time to keep from getting bored.

When I removed the bag I found myself the object of the silent but terrified scrutiny of my wife, who had entered the room without my knowing it.

My explanation that I was curing hiccoughs did not go very big, as what I had obviously been doing was walking around the room alone with a paper bag over my head. This is not a good sign.

Incidentally, I still have my hiccoughs.

---

2. mentor (mĕn′tôr′) n.: A trusted adviser or teacher.
3. fiasco (fē-ăs′kō) n.: A total or complete failure.

1. According to Benchley, what is the one thing everyone assumes he or she can do?

2. (a) List three cures Benchley has tried. (b) List the results of these cures.

3. (a) Describe the paper bag cure. (b) How did this cure almost result in Benchley's "being put away as an irresponsible person"?

The Essay

An essay is a short composition about one topic. In an essay, the author expresses his or her thoughts and feelings about the topic and reaches certain conclusions.

Many essays are informal. An informal essay is a kind of "chat" with the reader. It has a casual style and often contains colloquial language (words and phrases used in everyday conversation but rarely used in formal writing). For example, in this essay, Benchley describes his performance as a "ghastly flop" and his friend tells him about a "surefire" cure.

Some informal essays are humorous. In them the author may include absurd or ridiculous situations and may exaggerate the facts to make you laugh.

1. The topic of this essay is "cures for hiccoughs." Benchley states his conclusion about this topic in the first paragraph of this essay. What is his conclusion?

2. Benchley claims that the most modest person "becomes an arrogant know-it-all in the presence of hiccoughs—in somebody else." (a) What example does he give to back up his claim? (b) Do you think Benchley is completely serious about this claim or is he exaggerating?

3. A *feat* is an outstanding deed or accomplishment requiring bravery or skill. (a) Why is calling an attempt to cure hiccoughs a *feat* an example of exaggeration? (b) Find two other examples of exaggeration.

Activity

▶ **Composition.** Write a paragraph describing your special cure for hiccoughs. Try to make this cure as ridiculous or nonsensical as you can.

SENTENCE MEANING

Understanding the Verb Phrase

A complete sentence always has two core parts—the simple subject and the simple predicate, or verb. In some sentences the simple predicate is a verb phrase. For example, *does know, has failed, was walking, has been singing.*

A verb phrase is made up of a main verb plus one or more helping verbs. The following are frequently used helping verbs:

am	will	does	could
is	shall	do	may
are	has	did	might
was	have	should	must
were	had	would	can

Look at the following sentence:

I *have tried* them all.

The simple predicate is the verb phrase *have tried.*

Sometimes the verb phrase is separated by another word or group of words. For example: *Have* **I** *tried* them all? Sometimes it is separated by negative words. Negative words such as *not* and *never* are not part of the verb phrase. For example: I *have* **not** *tried* them all.

▶ Copy the following items on a piece of paper. Then draw two lines under each verb phrase.

a. This will create an excess of carbon monoxide gas in the bag.

b. The carbon monoxide should act on the nervous center of the brain.

c. You can count to five hundred by fives.

d. His wife did not believe his explanation for his behavior.

e. In spite of these tactics, the hiccoughs are never cured.

f. We will not find a cure for hiccoughs.

g. Why did Benchley try these cures?

h. He had obviously been walking around with a bag over his head.

i. Never had she seen such a ridiculous sight.

j. Not in a million years would she laugh so hard again.

WORD ATTACK

Understanding Synonyms

A synonym is a word that has the same or almost the same meaning as another word. For example, the words *glad* and *happy* are synonyms, as are the words *funny* and *humorous*.

When you choose a synonym for a word, you must be certain it fits the context. For example, although *humorous* is a synonym for *funny* when *funny* means "amusing," it is not a synonym for funny when *funny* means "curious or odd."

> It was a very *funny* story. It made me laugh.
> It was a *funny* or curious event that has never been satisfactorily explained.

► Use a dictionary to find a synonym for each of the *italicized* words in the sentences below.

   a. "Then, when it has failed, he *blames* you."

   b. "It's *absolutely* surefire if you only follow my directions."

   c. "To date, I have been advised to perform the following *feats* to cure hiccoughs . . . ."

   d. "My latest *fiasco* came as the result of reading the prescription of a Boston doctor . . . ."

   e. " 'Don't be silly,' he says, *patronizingly*."

Shooting an Elephant

George Orwell

In Moulmein, in Lower Burma, I was hated by large numbers of people—the only time in my life that I have been important enough for this to happen to me. I was subdivisional police officer of the town, and in an aimless, petty kind of way anti-European feeling was very bitter. No one had the guts to raise a riot, but if a European woman went through the bazaars alone somebody would probably spit betel juice over her dress. As a police officer I was an obvious target and was baited whenever it seemed safe to do so. When a nimble Burman tripped me up on the football field and the referee (another Burman) looked the other way, the crowd yelled with hideous laughter. This happened more than once. In the end the sneering yellow faces of young men that met me everywhere, the insults hooted after me when I was at a safe distance, got badly on my nerves. The young Buddhist priests were the worst of all. There were several thousands of them in the town and none of them seemed to have anything to do except stand on street corners and jeer at Europeans.

All this was perplexing and upsetting. For at that time I had already made up my mind that imperialism was an evil thing and the sooner I chucked up my job and got out of it the better. Theoretically—and secretly, of course—I was all for the Burmese and all against their oppressors, the British. As for the job I was doing, I hated it more bitterly than I can perhaps make clear. In a job like that you see the dirty work of Empire at close quarters. The wretched prisoners huddling in the stinking cages of the lockups, the gray, cowed faces of the long-term convicts, the scarred buttocks of the men who had been flogged with bamboos—all these oppressed me with an intolerable sense of guilt. But I could get nothing into perspective. I was young and ill-educated and I had had to think out my problems in the utter silence that is imposed on every Englishman in the East. I did not even know that the British Empire is dying, still less did I know that it is a great deal better than the younger empires that are going to supplant it. All I knew was that I was stuck between my hatred of the empire I served and my rage against the evil-spirited little beasts who tried to make my job impossible. With one part of my mind I thought of the British Raj[1] as an unbreakable tyranny, as something clamped down, *in saecula saeculorum,*[2] upon the will of prostrate peoples; with another part I thought that the greatest joy in the world would be to drive a bayonet into a Buddhist priest's guts. Feelings like these are the normal byproducts of imperialism; ask any Anglo-Indian official, if you can catch him off-duty.

One day something happened which in a roundabout way was enlightening. It was a tiny incident in itself, but it gave me a better glimpse than I had had before of the real nature of imperialism—the real motives for which despotic governments act. Early one morning the subinspector at a police station the other end of the town rang me up on the phone and said that an elephant was ravaging the bazaar. Would I please come and do something about it? I did not know what I could do, but I wanted to see what was happening and I got onto a pony and started out. I took my rifle, an old .44 Winchester and much too small to kill an elephant, but I thought the noise might be useful *in terrorem.*[3] Various Burmans stopped me on the way and told me about the elephant's doings. It was not, of course, a wild elephant, but a tame one which had gone "must."[4] It had been chained up as tame elephants always are when their attack of "must" is due, but on the previous night it had broken its chain and escaped. Its mahout,[5] the only person who could manage it when it was in that state, had set out in pursuit, but he had taken the wrong direction and was now twelve

hours' journey away, and in the morning the elephant had suddenly reappeared in the town. The Burmese population had no weapons and were quite helpless against it. It had already destroyed somebody's bamboo hut, killed a cow and raided some fruit stalls and devoured the stock; also it had met the municipal rubbish van, and, when the driver jumped out and took to his heels, he turned the van over and inflicted violence upon it.

The Burmese subinspector and some Indian constables were waiting for me in the quarter where the elephant had been seen. It was a very poor quarter, a labyrinth of squalid bamboo huts, thatched with palm leaf, winding all over a steep hillside. I remember that it was a cloudy stuffy morning at the beginning of the rains. We began questioning the people as to where the elephant had gone, and, as usual, failed to get any definite information. That is invariably the case in the East; a story always sounds clear enough at a distance, but the nearer you get to the scene of events the vaguer it becomes. Some of the people said that the elephant had gone in one direction, some said that he had gone in another, some professed not even to have heard of any elephant. I had almost made up my mind that the whole story was a pack of lies, when we heard yells a little distance away. There was a loud, scandalized cry of "Go away, child! Go away this instant!" and an old woman with a switch in her hand came round the corner of a hut, violently shooing away a crowd of naked children. Some more women followed, clicking their tongues and exclaiming; evidently there was something there that the children ought not to have seen. I rounded the hut and saw a man's dead body sprawling in the mud. He was an Indian, a black Dravidian coolie, almost naked, and he could not have been dead many minutes. The people said that the elephant had come suddenly upon him round the corner of the hut, caught him with its trunk, put its foot on his back and ground him into

---

1. Raj (räj) *n.*: In India, government or rule.
2. *in saecula saeculorum* (ĭn sē′ kōō-lə sē′kōō-lôr′ əm): Latin phrase meaning "forever and ever."
3. *in terrorem* (ĭn tə-rôr′ əm): Latin phrase meaning "for terror."
4. "must" (mŭst) *n.*: A periodic state of frenzy in the male elephant.
5. mahout (mə-hout′) *n.*: Elephant-keeper.

the earth. This was the rainy season and the ground was soft, and his face had scored a trench a foot deep and a couple of yards long. He was lying on his belly with arms crucified and head sharply twisted to one side. His face was coated with mud, the eyes wide open, the teeth bared and grinning with an expression of unendurable agony. (Never tell me, by the way, that the dead look peaceful. Most of the corpses I have seen looked devilish.) The friction of the great beast's foot had stripped the skin from his back as neatly as one skins a rabbit. As soon as I saw the dead man I sent an orderly to a friend's house nearby to borrow an elephant rifle. I had already sent back the pony, not wanting it to go mad with fright and throw me if it smelled the elephant.

The orderly came back in a few minutes with a rifle and five cartridges, and meanwhile some Burmans had arrived and told us that the elephant was in the paddy fields below, only a few hundred yards away. As I started forward practically the whole population of the quarter flocked out of their houses and followed me. They had seen the rifle and were all shouting excitedly that I was going to shoot the elephant. They had not shown much interest in the elephant when he was merely ravaging their homes, but it was different now that he was going to be shot. It was a bit of fun to them, as it would be to an English crowd; besides, they wanted the meat. It made me vaguely uneasy. I had no intention of shooting the elephant—I had merely sent for the rifle to defend myself if necessary—and it is always unnerving to have a crowd following you. I marched down the hill, looking and feeling a fool, with the rifle over my shoulder and an ever-growing army of people jostling at my heels. At the bottom, when you got away from the huts, there was a metaled[6] road and beyond that a miry waste of paddy fields a thousand yards across, not yet plowed but soggy from the

first rains and dotted with coarse grass. The elephant was standing eighty yards from the road, his left side towards us. He took not the slightest notice of the crowd's approach. He was tearing up bunches of grass, beating them against his knees to clean them and stuffing them into his mouth.

I had halted on the road. As soon as I saw the elephant I knew with perfect certainty that I ought not to shoot him. It is a serious matter to shoot a working elephant—it is comparable to destroying a huge and costly piece of machinery—and obviously one ought not to do it if it can possibly be avoided. And at that distance, peacefully eating, the elephant looked no more dangerous than a cow. I thought then and I think now that his attack of "must" was already passing off; in which case he would merely wander harmlessly about until the mahout came back and caught him. Moreover, I did not in the least want to shoot him. I decided that I would watch him for a little while to make sure that he did not turn savage again, and then go home.

But at that moment I glanced round at the crowd that had followed me. It was an immense crowd, two thousand at the least and growing every minute. It blocked the road for a long distance on either side. I looked at the sea of yellow faces above the garish clothes—faces all happy and excited over this bit of fun, all certain that the elephant was going to be shot. They were watching me as they would watch a conjurer about to perform a trick. They did not like me, but with the magical rifle in my hands I was momentarily worth watching. And suddenly I realized that I should have to shoot the elephant after all. The people expected it of me and I had got to do it; I could feel their two thousand wills pressing me forward, irresistibly. And it was at this moment, as I stood there with the rifle in my hands, that I first grasped the hollowness, the futility of the white man's dominion in the East. Here was I, the white man with his gun, standing

---

6. metaled (mĕt′ld) *adj.*: Paved with broken stones.

in front of the unarmed native crowd—seemingly the leading actor of the piece; but in reality I was only an absurd puppet pushed to and fro by the will of those yellow faces behind. I perceived in this moment that when the white man turns tyrant it is his own freedom that he destroys. He becomes a sort of hollow, posing dummy, the conventionalized figure of a sahib.[7] For it is the condition of his rule that he shall spend his life in trying to impress the "natives" and so in every crisis he has got to do what the "natives" expect of him. He wears a mask, and his face grows to fit it. I had got to shoot the elephant. I had committed myself to doing it when I sent for the rifle. A sahib has got to act like a sahib; he has got to appear resolute, to know his own mind and do definite things. To come all that way, rifle in hand, with two thousand people marching at my heels, and then to trail feebly away, having done nothing—no, that was impossible. The crowd would laugh at me. And my whole life, every white man's life in the East, was one long struggle not to be laughed at.

But I did not want to shoot the elephant. I watched him beating his bunch of grass against his knees, with that preoccupied grandmotherly air that elephants have. It seemed to me that it would be murder to shoot him. At that age I was not squeamish about killing animals, but I had never shot an elephant and never wanted to. (Somehow it always seems worse to kill a *large* animal.) Besides, there was the beast's owner to be considered. Alive, the elephant was worth at least a hundred pounds; dead, he would only be worth the value of his tusks—five pounds, possibly. But I had got to act quickly. I turned to some experienced-looking Burmans who had been there when we arrived, and asked them how the elephant had been behaving. They all said the same thing: he took no notice of you if you left him alone, but he

---

7. sahib (sä′ĭb) n.: Indian title of respect applied to European gentlemen.

might charge if you went too close to him.

It was perfectly clear to me what I ought to do. I ought to walk up to within, say, twenty-five yards of the elephant and test his behavior. If he charged I could shoot; if he took no notice of me it would be safe to leave him until the mahout came back. But also I knew that I was going to do no such thing. I was a poor shot with a rifle and the ground was soft mud into which one would sink at every step. If the elephant charged and I missed him, I should have about as much chance as a toad under a steamroller. But even then I was not thinking particularly of my own skin, only the watchful yellow faces behind. For at that moment, with the crowd watching me, I was not afraid in the ordinary sense, as I would have been if I had been alone. A white man mustn't be frightened in front of "natives"; and so, in general, he isn't frightened.

The sole thought in my mind was that if anything went wrong, those two thousand Burmans would see me pursued, caught, trampled on and reduced to a grinning corpse like that Indian up the hill. And if that happened it was quite probable that some of them would laugh. That would never do. There was only one alternative. I shoved the cartridges into the magazine and lay down on the road to get a better aim.

The crowd grew very still, and a deep, low, happy sigh, as of people who see the theater curtain go up at last, breathed from innumerable throats. They were going to have their bit of fun after all. The rifle was a beautiful German thing with cross-hair sights. I did not then know that in shooting an elephant one should shoot to cut an imaginary bar running from earhole to earhole. I ought therefore, as the elephant was sideways on, to have aimed

Shooting an Elephant **45**

straight at his earhole; actually I aimed several inches in front of this, thinking the brain would be further forward.

When I pulled the trigger I did not hear the bang or feel the kick—one never does when a shot goes home—but I heard the devilish roar of glee that went up from the crowd. In that instant, in too short a time, one would have thought, even for the bullet to get there, a mysterious, terrible change had come over the elephant. He neither stirred nor fell, but every line of his body had altered. He looked suddenly stricken, shrunken, immensely old, as though the frightful impact of the bullet had paralyzed him without knocking him down. At last, after what seemed a long time—it might have been five seconds, I dare say—he sagged flabbily to his knees. His mouth slobbered. An enormous senility seemed to have settled upon him. One could have imagined him thousands of years old. I fired again into the same spot. At the second shot he did not collapse but climbed with desperate slowness to his feet and stood weakly upright, with legs sagging and head drooping. I fired a third time. That was the shot that did for him. You could see the agony of it jolt his whole body and knock the last remnant of strength from his legs. But in falling he seemed for a moment to rise, for as his hind legs collapsed beneath him he seemed to tower upwards like a huge rock toppling, his trunk reaching skyward like a tree. He trumpeted, for the first and only time. And then down he came, his belly towards me, with a crash that seemed to shake the ground even where I lay.

I got up. The Burmans were already racing past me across the mud. It was obvious that the elephant would never rise again, but he was not dead. He was breathing very rhythmically with long rattling gasps, his great mound of a side painfully rising and falling. His mouth was wide open—I could see far down into caverns of pale pink throat. I waited a long time for him to die, but his breathing did not weaken. Finally I fired my two remaining shots into the spot where I thought his heart must be. The thick blood welled out of him like red velvet, but still he did not die. His body did not even jerk when the shots hit him, the tortured breathing continued without a pause. He was dying, very slowly and in great agony, but in some world remote from me where not even a bullet could damage him further. I felt that I had got to put an end to that dreadful noise. It seemed dreadful to see the great beast lying there, powerless to move and yet powerless to die, and not even to be able to finish him. I sent back for my small rifle and poured shot after shot into his heart and down his throat. They seemed to make no impression. The tortured gasps continued as steadily as the ticking of a clock.

In the end I could not stand it any longer and went away. I heard later that it took him half an hour to die. Burmans were arriving with dahs[8] and baskets even before I left, and I was told they had stripped his body almost to the bones by the afternoon.

Afterwards, of course, there were endless discussions about the shooting of the elephant. The owner was furious, but he was only an Indian and could do nothing. Besides, legally I had done the right thing, for a mad elephant has to be killed, like a mad dog, if its owner fails to control it. Among the Europeans opinion was divided. The older men said I was right, the younger men said it was a damn shame to shoot an elephant for killing a coolie, because an elephant was worth more than any damn Coringhee coolie. And afterwards I was very glad that the coolie had been killed; it put me legally in the right and it gave me a sufficient pretext for shooting the elephant. I often wondered whether any of the others grasped that I had done it solely to avoid looking a fool.

---

8. dahs (däz) n.: Large knives.

1. (a) How do the Burmese regard the police officer? (b) What incident makes them consider the police officer "momentarily worth watching"?

2. The police officer finally spots the elephant in a paddy field. (a) Find three reasons why he doesn't want to shoot it. (b) What does he decide to do instead of shooting it?

3. The police officer says that he appears to be "the leading actor in the piece," although he really is "only an absurd puppet." (a) Why does he feel he has to do what the natives expect of him? (b) What decision does this force him to make?

4. Legally the police officer is justified in shooting the elephant. Why, then, does he doubt that he did the right thing?

The Personal Narrative

A personal narrative is a true story written by the person who had the experience. Usually it tells about one event or a series of events in this person's life. The author, who is also the narrator, often tells you his or her thoughts and feelings about the experience.

A personal narrative is told in the first person. This means that the narrator refers to himself or herself by the pronoun "I."

1. (a) Who is the author of this story? (b) Who is the narrator, the person telling the story?

2. The narrator says that secretly, he "was all for the Burmese and all against their oppressors." Why does he bitterly hate his job?

3. The narrator says that the incident with the elephant was enlightening since it helped him to see the emptiness of imperialism—the white man's control in the East. Why is the narrator forced to do what the natives expect him to do?

Activity

▶ Imagine you had the opportunity to interview George Orwell. What questions would you have asked him about his experiences in Burma?

SENTENCE MEANING

Understanding Compound Sentences

A compound sentence is made up of two complete sentences, or independent clauses. Sometimes these clauses are joined together by a conjunction *(and, but, or)*. Sometimes these clauses are separated by a semicolon. Each independent clause contains a simple subject and a simple predicate. For example, look at the following compound sentence:

> It was a tiny incident, but the shooting gave him a better understanding of imperialism.

The first independent clause is: *It was a tiny incident.* The subject of this clause is *it* and the predicate is *was.* The second independent clause is: *the shooting gave him a better understanding of imperialism.* The subject of this clause is *shooting* and the predicate is *gave.* Notice that the conjunction *but* joins these clauses.

---

1. Copy each compound sentence below on a piece of paper. Then underline the simple subject once and the simple predicate twice.
   a. "He wears a mask, and his face grows to fit it."
   b. "I was subdivisional police officer of the town, and in an aimless, petty kind of way anti-European feeling was very bitter."
   c. "They did not like me, but with the magical rifle in my hands I was momentarily worth watching."
   d. "The thick blood welled out of him like red velvet, but still he did not die."

2. Read the sentence below and answer the questions that follow.

   > He was oppressed by the wretched condition of the prisoners in their cages, the defeated faces of the long-term prisoners, and the scarred bodies of the tortured men; these things, as well as the hatred of the Burmese, made him detest imperialism.

   a. What is the first independent clause?
   b. What is the second independent clause?
   c. What three things oppressed him?
   d. What did these things finally make him do?

WORD ATTACK

Understanding Antonyms

Antonyms are words that have opposite or nearly opposite meanings. For example, *hate* and *love* are antonyms and *defend* and *attack* are antonyms.

▶ Match each *italicized* word in the left-hand column with its antonym in the right-hand column. Use your dictionary to help you.

a.	a *hideous* mask	(1)	ecstasy
b.	an *obvious* reason	(2)	arid
c.	an *oppressed* people	(3)	strong
d.	breathing *rhythmically*	(4)	unlikely
e.	a *resolute* action	(5)	irregularly
f.	*remote* from me	(6)	free
g.	*agony* of the jolt	(7)	uncertain
h.	a *perplexing* problem	(8)	clearcut
i.	*miry* wastes	(9)	beautiful
j.	a *feeble* person	(10)	close

REVIEW QUIZ

On the Selections

1. In "Cemetery Path," why does Ivan avoid the path through the cemetery?

2. In what country does this story take place?

3. In the beginning of "The Rising of the Moon," why does the sergeant send the other policemen away?

4. In what way is the sergeant like the ragged man?

5. In "The Glory of the Day Was in Her Face," how does the poet feel now that the woman is gone?

6. In "Taught Me Purple," what does the color purple represent?

7. In "The Listeners," at what time of day does the Traveler knock on the door?

8. To whom does the pronoun *they* refer: "Ay, *they* heard his foot upon the stirrup . . ."?

9. In "Stop Those Hiccoughs," why does Benchley call the last cure he tries a "fiasco"?

10. In "Shooting an Elephant," why does Orwell send for the rifle?

On Sentence Meaning

1. Find the two core parts in each of the following sentences. Write them on a piece of paper.
   a. Late that night Ivan walked swiftly through the cemetery.
   b. For many nights he had walked around it.

2. Find the three core parts in each of the following sentences. Write them on a piece of paper.
   a. On the dock that night the sergeant sang songs with the stranger.
   b. With the rifle, he shot the elephant.

3. Find the compound subject in the following sentence. Write it on a piece of paper.
   The Cossack and the villagers challenged Ivan to walk through the cemetery.

4. Find the compound verb in the following sentence. Write it on a piece of paper.
   The Cossack unbuckled his sword and gave it to Ivan.

5. The following sentences are not in natural word order. Rewrite each sentence so that the subject appears before the verb.
   a. From the window came their answer.
   b. Through the cemetery walked Ivan.
   c. An old ballad sang the sergeant.
   d. On the barrel sat the two men.

On Types of Literature

▶ Decide which of the following statements are true and which are false. Write your answers on a piece of paper.
   a. The climax of a story is the point at which the conflict is resolved.
   b. In most plays, the story is told chiefly through dialogue.
   c. The repetition of sounds at the end of words is called rhyme.
   d. An essay is a short composition about one topic.
   e. A personal narrative is told in the third person.

COMPOSITION

Sentence Combining

You can combine two closely related sentences about the same person by turning the second sentence into a clause beginning with the word *who*. Look at the following sentences:

> Orwell shot the elephant.
> He was a British official in Burma.
>
> *becomes*
>
> Orwell, who was a British official in Burma, shot the elephant.

Notice that you change the pronoun *he* in the second sentence to *who*. When you insert the clause "who was a British official in Burma" in the first sentence, you use commas to separate this clause from the rest of the sentence.

Now look at the next example:

> Ivan never walked through the cemetery to get to his shack.
> He was timid.
>
> *becomes*
>
> Ivan, who was timid, never walked through the cemetery to get to his shack.

▶ Combine each pair of sentences below by turning the second sentence into a clause beginning with the word *who*. Remember to use commas to separate the clause from the rest of the sentence. The caret (∧) tells you where to insert the second sentence.

a. Ivan ∧ accepted their challenge.
He was shamed by their taunts.

b. The sergeant ∧ watched for the escaped man.
He wanted the reward money.

c. Robert Benchley ∧ has written about many subjects.
He is an American humorist.

d. The narrator ∧ tried to calm the crowd.
He was a police officer in town.

BEFORE GOING ON

Reading for a Purpose

When you set a purpose for reading a selection you improve your comprehension, or understanding. The steps listed below tell you how to set a purpose for reading.

1. Study the title of the selection. Ask yourself what the selection is about. Then jot down several questions you hope the selection will answer. For example: Who is Amelia Earhart? Why is she a legend?
2. Read the first two or three paragraphs. Jot down several more questions. For example: How will Amelia's childhood affect her? What further adventures will she encounter as an adult?
3. Search for the answers to these questions as you read the rest of the selection.
4. As you read the selection, continue to ask questions and to search for answers.

---

1. Follow the steps above to set your own purpose for reading "The Legend of Amelia Earhart."

2. Find answers to the following questions.
   a. When did Amelia first become interested in flying?
   b. Who gave her her first flying lesson?
   c. Did she fly the plane on her first transatlantic flight?
   d. What were her "popping off" letters?
   e. Why did she want to make a transatlantic flight by herself?
   f. What events suggest that Amelia's last flight was really a secret reconnaissance trip?
   g. What did her mother think of the official version of Amelia's disappearance?
   h. How did the public react to Amelia's disappearance?

Further Reading

The Legend of Amelia Earhart

Pete Hamill

Amelia Earhart was born in Atchison, Kansas, on July 24, 1898. Her father Edwin was a railroad lawyer, a small, precise man with a streak of brooding melancholy that he often drowned in hard drinking. Her mother, Amy Otis Earhart, the daughter of the most prominent judge in town, was by all accounts a remarkable woman; influenced by the first wave of American feminism, but still a prisoner of the rigid social codes of her day.

The marriage was tense from the beginning, as Judge Otis attempted to impose his will on the lives of his daughter and her husband. Earhart was away a lot, in his work as a claims agent, and sometimes he took his wife along with him. The result was that Amelia and her younger sister Muriel spent much of their childhood living with their grandparents. Amelia had a rich fantasy life, and lived

adventurous summers exploring caves, playing baseball with equipment given to her by her father, reading Scott, Dickens, George Eliot; but she must have learned early on that she was essentially alone.

"I was a horrid little girl," she said later. "Perhaps the fact that I was exceedingly fond of reading made me endurable. With a large library to browse in, I spent many hours not bothering anyone after I once learned to read."

The family moved to Des Moines in 1907, apparently to escape the domination of the grandparents, and on her tenth birthday, Amelia saw her first airplane. That day, her father took her to the Iowa State Fair; it was only five years after the Wright Brothers had first flown at Kitty Hawk (incidentally, with money provided by a Wright sister) and airplanes were a great curiosity. Amelia, however, was not impressed.

"It was a thing of rusty wire and wood," she wrote in 1937. "I was much more interested in an absurd hat made of an inverted peach-basket which I had just purchased for fifteen cents. . . . Today I loathe hats for more than a few minutes on the head and am sure I should pass by the niftiest creation if an airplane were anywhere around."

She went through six schools before finally graduating from Hyde Park High School in Chicago in 1916. In the yearbook she was described as "the girl in brown, who walks alone." Her mother then insisted on sending her to the Ogontz finishing school in Philadelphia, and she was at Ogontz in 1917 when the Americans entered the First World War. At Christmas she traveled to Toronto to visit her sister Muriel, who was then attending St. Margaret's School.

"Canada had been in the war four weary years—years the United States will never appreciate," Amelia wrote later. "Four men on crutches, walking together on King Street in Toronto that winter, was a sight which changed the course of existence for me."

Amelia quit the Ogontz school, and went to work as a nurse's aide for the Canadian Red Cross, caring for shell-shocked veterans. Much of her work was routine and boring, but the impact of sustained intimate contact with these wounded men was clearly profound; in later life, Amelia was a pacifist.

Toronto was also the place where she saw her second airplane, and its impact was considerably different from the one she saw when she was ten.

"A young woman friend and I had gone to the fair grounds to see an exhibition of stunt-flying by one of the aces returned from the war," she remembered later. Amelia and her friend, dressed in their nurses' uniforms, moved to a clearing to get a better view. The pilot went through a repertory of stunts.

"After fifteen or twenty minutes of stunting, the pilot began to dive at the crowd," she wrote. "Looking back as a pilot I think I understand why. He was bored."

Then he saw Amelia and her friend in the open clearing, and started to swoop down on them, too. The friend broke and ran. Amelia stood still, watching the plane come at her.

"I remember the mingled fear and pleasure which surged over me as I watched that small plane at the top of its earthward swoop. Common sense told me that if something went wrong with the mechanism, or if the pilot lost control, he, the airplane, and I would be rolled up in a ball together. . . . I believe that little red airplane said something to me as it swished by."

The sensuality of that moment of embrace stayed with her all of her life. In the fall of 1919, she moved to New York and enrolled in a premed course at Columbia University, where she "started in to do the peculiar things they do who would be physicians. I fed orange juice to mice and dissected cockroaches." She took a heavy load of subjects, but she didn't forget flying.

In the summer of 1920, she went on vacation to California, where her parents had moved to start a new life after the death of her grandparents. On that trip, her father took her to an air meet. The planes were old wartime Jennies and Canucks, the pilots all members of that first swaggering generation of barnstormers. The commercial airline industry had not yet been established; the skies were still empty. Amelia was enthralled.

"One thing I knew that day," she wrote. "I wanted to fly." She decided not to return to the University.

At first, she was too shy to ask about flying lessons, afraid that the all-male world of aviation would snicker at the arrival of a woman in the ranks; she had her father ask on her behalf. He arranged for her to take a trial hop, as a passenger. "I am sure he thought one ride would be enough for me," she wrote later, "and he might as well act to cure me promptly."

The pilot was Frank Hawks, a slim, handsome man in the classic *macho* style, who was to become a famous aviator. Hawks insisted that another pilot accompany them on the flight in the event that Amelia turned out to be a "nervous lady." They flew out over the still smog-free green earth of Southern California, with the hills of Hollywood to one side and the vast blue Pacific on the other. Amelia was not a nervous lady. When the plane landed, she was determined to raise the five hundred dollars she would need for a twelve-hour course of instruction.

"Two things deterred me at that moment," she remembered. "One was the tuition fee to be wrung from my father, and the other the determination to look up a woman flier. . . . I felt I should be less self-conscious taking lessons with her, than with the men, who overwhelmed me with their capabilities."

The flier was Neta Snook, the first woman to graduate from the Curtiss School of Aviation, and a good instructor. Amelia took the first of twenty-eight jobs she was to hold in the next years—as a file clerk at the telephone company—in order to pay for her lessons, and Snook extended credit. Amelia, who had once taken a course in auto mechanics just to see what an automobile

engine was made of, found herself as interested in the aircraft engines and design as she was in flying itself. When the phone-company money did not cover her expenses, she took another job, driving a truck for a sand and gravel company.

It was an exhilarating time, and Amelia soon was deeply involved in the life of airports. She learned to play rummy with the mechanics. She chopped her hair short, so that her leather helmet fitted snugly.

"I remember so well my first leather coat," she said later. "It was 1922. Somehow I'd contrived to save twenty dollars. With it I bought—at a very special sale—an elegant leather coat. *Patent* leather! Shiny and lovely. But suddenly I saw that it looked *too* new. How were people to think that I was a flier if I was wearing a flying coat that was brand-new? Wrinkles! That was it. There just had to be wrinkles. So—I slept in it for three nights to give my coat a properly veteran appearance."

Meanwhile, Neta Snook had gone broke and was forced to sell her plane. Amelia finally soloed under the guidance of a veteran named John Montijo. But even with her license in her pocket, she still did not know what to do with her life: the commercial aviation business was very young and there was no room in it for women.

Amelia studied photography and worked in a professional darkroom. She had a few secretarial jobs. She plowed all this money into the world of flying. In 1922, in a small open-cockpit Kinner Canary, she flew to fourteen thousand feet, establishing her first world's record: highest altitude attained by a woman pilot.

Characteristically, she then tried to break her own record, and almost ended in disaster. "From the sight of cities and the glistening sea two miles below," she wrote about that dangerous attempt, "I plunged into a rolling bank of clouds. There was snow inside. It stung my face and plastered my goggles. At eleven thousand feet the snow

changed to sleet, and at about twelve thousand, dense fog enveloped me. Unbelievably—until you've tried it—human sensations fail when one is thus 'blind.' Deprived of a horizon, a flier may lose the feel of his position in space. Was I flying one wing high? Was I turning? I couldn't be sure. I tried to keep the plane in flying trim, with one wish growing stronger every moment—to see the friendly earth again. Spinning was the quickest way down my inexperience could suggest. And so I spun. Seconds seemed very long, until I saw clear weather several thousand feet above the world I knew."

On the ground, the man at the field was angry. "Show a little sense," he said. "Suppose the clouds had closed in until they touched the ground. We'd have had to dig you out in pieces."

"Yes," Amelia said, "I suppose you would."

Flying at last, but with no clear objective in sight, Amelia started feeling like "another sunkist victim of inertia." She had bought a small airplane, but in the spring of 1925, partly because of pressure from her parents and friends, she decided to sell it, buy a car, and drive back to the East Coast; perhaps to become a teacher. Her mother, whose marriage had not improved with a change of locale, went with her on the long drive across the country.

In 1927, after some study at Harvard and Columbia, she went to work as a sixty-dollars-a-month social worker at Denison House in Boston, one of the largest settlement houses in the country. Amelia plunged into the work, dealing with the educational and emotional problems of the immigrant kids who came there every day. But the period wasn't all work; she also bought herself a yellow Kissel convertible, and she would often load it up with the settlement-house kids for rides into the country, or take it out herself when she felt the need for solitude.

She kept up her interest in aviation, but

the crowded East Coast was still far behind the open places of the West. She joined the Boston chapter of the National Aeronautic Association, became one of the five board members of an early commercial aircraft concern, and had discussions with another great woman flier of the era, Ruth Nichols, about the need to establish a national association of women pilots. (These talks later led to the founding of the Ninety-Nines, an organization that still exists.) But the days of the flying circuses were fading, buried by a blizzard of new federal and state safety regulations, and the big-money people were moving into the business to ensure ownership of its future. By 1928, her aviation dream had so far receded that Amelia was reduced to being a judge of a model airplane contest sponsored by the Boston Playground Association.

Then one morning, Amelia Earhart received a phone call. "I remember when called to the phone I replied I couldn't answer unless the message was more important than entertaining many little Chinese and Syrian children. The word came assuring me that it was."

The voice on the other end belonged to a press agent named Hilton H. Railey, and he wanted to know whether Amelia was interested in becoming the first woman to fly the Atlantic. At first she thought it was either a joke or a more sinister proposition; on at least two occasions bootleggers had asked her to fly a certain cargo from a certain place to a certain other place. She asked Railey for references. He was legitimate; one of his clients was Commander Richard E. Byrd. She went to see Railey at his Boston office and started getting the full story.

He told her that a tri-motored Fokker, the same airplane that Byrd flew to the South Pole, had recently been purchased by Mrs. Amy Guest. At first Mrs. Guest said that she wanted to fly the Atlantic herself, but her family objected. In those days, even after Lindbergh's historic crossing, the flight was perilous; plane after plane had disappeared in the ocean. Radio equipment was primitive; so was weather information. De-icers had not been developed, so that some planes found themselves paralyzed with up to five hundred pounds of ice.

But Mrs. Guest was determined that a woman should fly the Atlantic. If she could not do it, then it should be someone else. She asked a friend, George Palmer Putnam, to find a suitable woman, and Putnam (whose family owned the publishing concern of G. P. Putnam's) had asked Railey to help. He poked around at Boston airports and was told about the young woman from Denison House named Amelia Earhart. He was very impressed when he saw her: not by her obvious intelligence, or her more than five hundred hours of flying time, but by her physical resemblance to Charles Lindbergh. Visions of "Lady Lindy" bounced in his head. He reported this to Putnam, and an anxious Amelia was summoned to New York.

"I was interviewed by David T. Laymen, Jr., and John S. Phipps," she wrote, "and found myself in a curious situation. If they did not like me at all, or found me wanting in too many respects, I would be deprived of the trip. If they liked me too well, they might be loath to drown me. It was, therefore, necessary for me to maintain an attitude of impenetrable mediocrity. Apparently I did, because I was chosen."

The weeks that followed were nerve-racking. Amelia, who was to be paid absolutely nothing for the flight, was going only as a passenger. The pilot, a hard-drinking veteran named Wilmer "Bull" Stultz, was being paid twenty thousand dollars; his mechanic, Lou "Slim" Gordon, was to receive five thousand dollars. But the Atlantic had already been flown; the true novelty of this flight was that its passenger was a woman. The sponsors did not want the rest of the world to know their plans, because someone carrying a woman might beat them across the Atlantic; the result was that Amelia was kept away from the airport, where Stultz and Gordon were working on the plane. Among other things, she wrote some "popping off" letters to her parents, in the event that the *Friendship,* as the plane was called, followed so many others into the Atlantic. The letters were sealed and not discovered until 1937.

"Dearest Dad:

"Hooray for the last grand adventure! I wish I had won, but it was worthwhile anyway. You know that. I have no faith we'll meet anywhere again, but I wish we might.

"Anyway, goodbye and good luck to you.

"Affectionately, your doter. Mill."

To her mother she wrote: "Even though I have lost, the adventure was worthwhile. Our family tends to be too secure. My life has really been very happy, and I don't mind contemplating its end in the midst of it."

There was a third letter—to her sister Muriel—which was opened and shown to the press on the morning that Amelia and the *Friendship* took off from Boston Harbor.

"Dear Scrappy," it began. "I have tried to play for a large stake and if I succeed all will be well. If I don't, I shall be happy to pop off in the midst of such an adventure. My only regret would be leaving you and mother stranded for a while. . . .

"Sam (Chapman) will tell you the whole story. Please explain all to mother. I couldn't stand the added strain of telling mother and you personally.

"If reporters talk to you, say you knew, if you like . . . Yours respectfully, Sister."

Throughout the days before departing Boston, the biggest problem was weather.

"When it was right in Boston, the mid-Atlantic was foreboding," Amelia wrote. "I have a memory of long gray days which had a way of dampening our spirits against our best efforts to be cheerful."

Finally, they departed Boston on June 3, 1928, only to find themselves bogged down for another two weeks in Trespassey, Newfoundland. Stultz could not eat fish, and existed on candy bars and booze; they wandered around the tiny town, examined and reexamined the engines and pontoons, and waited for the weather to break. On the morning of the 17th, they finally took off. Amelia began to keep a detailed log of the flight, which later became a book, *20 Hours, 40 Minutes*. Some excerpts:

"Marvelous shapes in white stand out, some trailing shimmering veils. The clouds look like icebergs in the distance. . . . I think I am happy—sad admission of scant intellectual equipment."

"I am getting housemaid's knee kneeling here gulping beauty."

"How marvelous is a machine and the mind that made it. I am thoroughly occidental[1] in this worship."

"Port motor coughing a bit. Sounds like water. We are going to go into, under, or over a storm. I don't like to, with one motor acting the way it is."

"Himmel! The sea! We are three thousand. Patchy clouds. We have been jazzing from one thousand to five thousand where we now are, to get out of clouds."

"Can't use radio at all. Coming down now in a rather clear spot. Twenty-five-hundred feet. Everything sliding forward."

"8:50. Two Boats!!!!"

"Try to get bearing. Radio won't. One hour's gas. Mess. All craft cutting our course. Why?"

The answer to the "Why?" was land. They had made it across the Atlantic, and came down over the harbor of Burry Port, Wales. Amelia Earhart was famous.

The fame was sudden and all-encompassing. She was on all the front pages of the world, posing in a borrowed dress, smiling and giving credit for everything to Stultz and Gordon. As Railey had hoped, the papers started to call her "Lady Lindy." She

was feted in London. Her arrival in New York brought the kind of ticker-tape parades reserved for heroes. She was interviewed, photographed, mauled for autographs and souvenirs.

And waiting for her was George Palmer Putnam. He was a promoter, a gifted writer, a bit of a con man, who had been a newspaperman, Mayor of Bend, Oregon, and soldier before joining the family publishing firm. That was the era of adventure, and Putnam concentrated on the great books of exploration. His greatest coup was in signing Lindbergh to write *We* for $100,000, after the famous solo flight. Now he wanted Lady Lindy. Brash, complex, irritating, driven, Putnam was by all accounts a remarkable character. They were married in February, 1931.

Most of her public life is a matter of record, and in the years after her marriage, she lived most of her life in public. She broke record after record; she campaigned for Franklin Roosevelt and once took Eleanor up for a midnight ride; she spoke out on women's issues, looking for "the day when women . . . will be individuals free to live their lives as men are free."

But Amelia always had something more personal to prove. "I wanted to make another flight alone," she wrote. "I wanted to justify myself to myself. I wanted to prove that I deserved at least a small fraction of the nice things said about me. . . . I already had the credit—heaped up and running over. I wanted to deposit a little security to make that credit good. Illogical? Perhaps. Most of the things we want are illogical."

The flight alone was to make up for the *Friendship*. She wanted to cross the Atlantic, flying the plane herself, with no one around to help. Again working in secret to avoid the added pressure of heavy publicity, she took a Lockheed from Teterboro airport in New Jersey to Harbor Grace, Newfoundland. And on Friday, May 20, 1932, she took off. The journey was rough. Her altimeter failed, so that

---

1. occidental (ŏk′sə-dĕn′təl) *adj.*: Western in attitude or outlook.

in fog she could not truly determine how close she was to the ocean. At one point, the plane iced up and went into a spin. "How long we spun I do not know . . . . As we righted and held level again, through the blackness below I could see the whitecaps too close for comfort."

Then a fire broke out in the manifold ring of her engine. "There was nothing to do about it," she said. "There was no use turning back, for I knew I couldn't land at Harbor Grace in the dark even if I could find my way. And I didn't want to roll up in a ball with all that gasoline . . . . So it seemed sensible to keep going."

The fire kept burning in the exhaust manifold, and she discovered she had a leaky fuel gauge. As the hours dragged on, she knew she would soon have to go down. And then she saw land. She circled over green hills and landed in a pasture. Cows scattered in all directions, and a man came rushing out of a farmhouse.

"I've come from America," Amelia said.

"Do ye be tellin' me that now?" said Dan McCallion, and she knew she was in Ireland. She was exuberant. For the first time, after everything else she had done, Amelia Earhart felt that her fame was for real.

As she moved deeper into her own and the century's thirties, Amelia started to feel that time was beginning to run out. The old flying-by-the-seat-of-the-pants days were clearly over; the commercial giants were beginning to eat up or eliminate their smaller competitors. Amelia continued to set records, from Hawaii to Oakland, from Mexico City to Newark and more. She campaigned for Roosevelt in the 1936 election. She took a job as counselor in careers for women at Purdue University, and, with the financial help of Purdue, began to plan one last flight, in a Lockheed Electra fitted out as a flying laboratory. She wanted to fly around the world at the equator, a distance of 27,000 miles. Others had flown around the world, but only via the shorter northern route.

"I have a feeling," she told a reporter in 1937, "that there is just about one more good flight left in my system, and I hope this trip is it."

The last flight remains mysterious to this day, shrouded in unsolved speculation. Was she on a secret reconnaissance trip for the government; an early intelligence pilot under orders from Roosevelt? Was she captured and imprisoned or killed by the Japanese? No one knows for sure. The first phase of this last adventure ended in March, 1937, when Amelia's overloaded Lockheed Electra crashed on the runway at Pearl Harbor. The plane was badly damaged, but Amelia was not injured. The plane was then taken apart by Lockheed engineers and shipped back to Burbank for repairs. It has never been determined exactly who paid for these repairs.

Between March and June, when the second phase started, a number of events took place. The route was altered, a fact noted by those who speculate about a reconnaissance mission. Instead of traveling around the world by going west, the route was changed to follow an Oakland-Miami-South America-Africa-Asia-Australia course, with the final 2,600-mile hop from Lae, New Guinea, to Howland Island in the mid-Pacific, the most dangerous part of the flight.

In addition, Fred Noonan became the sole navigator. Earlier, Amelia was helped by Paul Mantz on technical matters, and Captain Harry Manning was to be the navigator for part of the flight, with Noonan as his assistant. But Manning canceled after the Honolulu crash, and Mantz was busy on movie work.

Noonan was a legendary character in aviation. He had served as a maritime navigator, transport pilot, navigational instructor, manager of the Port-au-Prince airport in Haiti, and then inspector of all Pan Am airports. He had survived World War I torpedoing, and helped Pan Am map its routes across the Pacific. Nobody knew the Pacific better than Fred Noonan.

Noonan had lost his job with Pan Am because of his heavy drinking, but he had told friends that the flight with Amelia was to be a "second chance." And Amelia insisted she had faith in him.

The official story of the "Last Flight" is told in Amelia's book of that title (compiled by Putnam after her disappearance from letters, reports, and cables sent along the way). They took off from Miami on June 1 heading south to the equator and east around the world. After a month of grueling flight, they set out on the last lap of the journey. They never reached Howland Island.

There are many theories about the disappearance; writers have gone over the trail in considerable detail. Even Amelia's mother doubted the offical version of events. In 1949, she said: "Amelia told me many things, but there were some things she couldn't tell me. I am convinced she was on some sort of a government mission, probably on verbal orders."

If Amelia was on a spy mission, it is most likely that she changed planes in Port Darwin, Australia, picking up another Lockheed Electra specially fitted with cameras. The political rationale for this theory includes Roosevelt's position then: he was unable to end the Depression and wanted heavy defense spending, but faced a Congress reluctant to spend money on guns when there were millions of unemployed Americans walking the streets. If Roosevelt could prove through photographs that Japan was building major naval bases on Saipan and Truk, he would get his defense bill. And in the event that Amelia and Noonan did not make it back, their disappearance would justify a massive sea-and-air search and the Americans could get their photographs anyway.

This in fact is precisely what happened. After the disappearance, a massive sea-and-air search was conducted, covering 400,000 square miles of the Pacific; some sixty-five airplanes were used; American ships moved freely through areas that were previously off-limits. In January, Roosevelt got the largest peacetime naval spending bill of his first two administrations.

Meanwhile, there was genuine grief over Amelia's disappearance. Newspapers were full of the story. Tributes poured in. Statues were erected to her. Schools were named for her. After eighteen months, she was declared legally dead. Putnam married twice more, wrote some books, and died in 1950. The commercial airlines froze out women pilots, an event that might not have happened had Amelia still been around to lead a public fight. The old small planes went into the scrap heaps or the museums. Jets arrived. The DC-3 became the 707 which became the 747. Men landed on the moon. America had no women astronauts, and many years elapsed before there was even one woman pilot of a major airline.

And yet, Amelia Earhart seems more alive and more relevant now than she has been since the days of her glory. Perhaps that is why rumors still drift to the surface: she is living in Japan, having survived a wartime concentration camp; she is living in New Jersey, still guarding the secret of her wartime mission by allowing the public to believe her dead. Like male heroes who were thought to live on after death, from Alexander through Zapata,[2] she fulfilled some need in us for the heroic spirit, and so we cannot quite bear to believe that she is gone.

---

2. Alexander through Zapata: Alexander the Great (356–323 BC), king of Macedonia, conquered most of the known world from the Mediterranean Sea to India. Emiliano Zapata (sä-pä′tä) (1877?–1919), a famous Mexican revolutionist, fought for land reform.

VENTURES

Nearly Perfect

A. A. Milne

Can Julian commit the perfect crime?

Kindness doesn't always pay," said Coleby, "and I can tell you a very sad story that proves it."

"Kindness is its own reward," I said. I knew that somebody else would say it if I didn't.

"The reward in this case was the hangman's rope. Which is what I was saying."

"Is it a murder story?"

"Very much so."

"Good."

"What was the name of the kind gentleman?" asked Sylvia.

"Julian Crayne."

"And he was hanged?"

"Very unfairly, or so he thought. And if you will listen to the story instead of asking silly questions, you can say whether you agree with him."

"How old was he?"

"About thirty."

"Good-looking?"

"Not after he was hanged. Do you want to hear this story, or don't you?"

"Yes!" said everybody.

So Coleby told us the story.

Julian Crayne (he said) was an unpleasantly smooth young man who lived in the country with his Uncle Marius. He should have been working, but he disliked work. He disliked the country, too, but a suggestion that Julian should help the export drive in London—with the aid of a handsome allowance from Marius—met with an unenthusiastic response even when Julian threw in an offer to come down regularly for weekends and bring some of his friends with him. Marius didn't particularly like his nephew, but he liked having him about. Rich, elderly bachelors often become bores, and bores prefer to have somebody at hand who cannot escape. Marius did not intend to let Julian escape. To have nobody to talk to through the week, and then to have a houseful of rowdy young people at the weekend, none of whom wanted to listen to him, was not his idea of pleasure. He had the power over his nephew that money gives, and he preferred to use it.

"It will all come to you when I die, my boy," he said, "and until then you won't grudge a sick old man the pleasure of your company."

"Of course not," said Julian. "It was only that I was afraid you were getting tired of me."

If Marius had really been a sick old man, any loving nephew such as Julian might have been content to wait. But Marius was a sound sixty-five, and in that very morning's newspaper there had been talk of somebody at Runcorn who had just celebrated his hundred-and-fifth birthday. Julian didn't know where Runcorn was, but he could add forty years to his own age, and ask himself what the devil would be the use of this money at seventy; whereas now, with £150,000 in the bank, and all life to come—Well, you can see for yourself how the thing would look to him.

I don't know if any of you have ever wondered about how to murder an uncle—an uncle whose heir and only relation you are. As we all know, the motives for murder are many. Revenge, passion, gain, fear, or simply the fact that you have seen the fellow's horrible face in the paper so often that you feel it to be almost a duty to eliminate it. The only person I have ever wanted to murder is—— Well, I won't mention names, because I may do it yet. But the point is that the police, in their stolid, unimaginative way, always look first for the money motive, and if the money motive is there, you are practically in the bag.

So you see the very difficult position in which Julian was placed. He lived alone with his uncle, he was his uncle's heir, and his uncle was a very rich man. However subtly he planned, the dead weight of that £150,000 was against him. Any other man might push Marius into the river, and confidently wait for a verdict of accidental death; but not Julian. Any other man might place a tablet of some untraceable poison in the soda-mint bottle, and look for a certificate of "Death from Natural Causes"; but not Julian. Any other man might tie a string across the

top step of the attic stairs—— But I need not go on. You see, as Julian saw, how terribly unfair it was. The thing really got into his mind. He used to lie awake night after night thinking how unfair it was, and how delightfully easy it would be if it weren't for that £150,000.

The trouble was that he had nobody in whom to confide. He wished now, and for the first time, that he were married. With a loving wife to help him, how blithely they could have pursued, hand in hand, the search for the foolproof plan. What a stimulant to his brain would have been some gentle, fair-haired creature of the intelligence of the average policeman, who would point out the flaws and voice the suspicions the plan might raise. In such a delicate matter as this, two heads were better than one, even if the other head did nothing but listen with its mouth slightly ajar. At least he would then have the plan out in the open and be able to take a more objective view of it.

Unfortunately, the only person available was his uncle.

What he had to find—alone, if so it must be—was an alternative suspect to himself; somebody, in the eyes of the police, with an equally good motive. But what other motive could there be for getting rid of such an estimable man as Marius Crayne? A bore, yes; but would the average Inspector recognize boredom as a reasonable motive? Even if he did, it would merely be an additional motive for Julian. There was, of course, the possibility of "framing" somebody, a thing they were always doing in detective stories. But the only person in a position to be framed was old John Coppard, the gardener, and the number of footprints, fingerprints, blunt instruments, and blood-stained handkerchiefs with the initials J.C. on them that would be necessary to offset the absence of motive was more than Julian cared to contemplate.

I have said that Uncle Marius was a bore. Bores can be divided into two classes: those who have their own particular subject, and those who don't need a subject. Marius was in the former, and less offensive class. Shortly before his retirement (he was in the tea business), he had brought off a remarkable double. He had filled in his first football-pool form "just to see how it went," distributing the numbers and the crosses in an impartial spirit, and had posted it "just for fun." He followed this up by taking over a lottery ticket from a temporarily embarrassed but rather intimidating gentleman whom he had met on a train. The result being what it was, Marius was convinced that he had a flair—as he put it, "a nose for things." So when he found that through the long winter evenings—and, indeed, during most of the day—there was nothing to do in the country but read detective stories, it soon became obvious to him that he had a nose for crime.

Well, it was this nose poor Julian had had to face. It was bad enough, whenever a real crime was being exploited in the papers, to listen to his uncle's assurance that once again Scotland Yard was at fault, as it was obviously the mother-in-law who had put the arsenic in the gooseberry tart; it was much more boring when the murder had taken place in the current detective story, and Marius was following up a confused synopsis of the first half with his own analysis of the clues.

"Oh, I forgot to tell you, this fellow—I forget his name for a moment—Carmichael, something like that—had met the girl, Doris—I mean Phyllis—had met Phyllis accidentally in Paris some years before—well, a year or two, the exact time doesn't matter—it was just that she and this fellow, what did I call him, Arbuthnot? . . ."

And it was at just such a moment as this that Julian was suddenly inspired.

"You know, Uncle Marius," he said, "you ought to write a detective story."

Marius laughed self-consciously, and said he didn't know about that.

"Of course you could! You're just the man. You've got a flair for that sort of thing, and

you wouldn't make the silly mistakes all these other fellows make."

"Oh, I dare say I should be all right with the deduction and induction and so on—that's what I'm really interested in—but I've never thought of myself as a writer. There's a bit of a knack to it, you know. More in your line than mine, I should have thought."

"Uncle, you've said it!" cried Julian. "We'll write it together. Two heads are better than one. We can talk it over every evening and criticize each other's suggestions. What do you say?"

Marius was delighted with the idea. So, of course, was Julian. He had found his collaborator.

Give me a drink, somebody.

Yes (went on Coleby, wiping his mouth), I know what you are expecting. Half of you are telling yourselves that, ironically enough, it was Uncle who thought of the foolproof plan for murder that Nephew put into execution; and the rest of you are thinking what much more fun it would be if Nephew thought of the plan, and, somewhat to his surprise, Uncle put it into execution. Actually, it didn't happen quite like that.

Marius, when it came to the point, had nothing much to contribute. But he knew what he liked. For him, one murder in a book was no longer enough. There must be two, the first one preferably at a country house party, with plenty of suspects. Then, at a moment when he is temporarily baffled, the Inspector receives a letter inviting him to a secret rendezvous at midnight, where the writer will be waiting to give him important information. He arrives to find a dying man, who is just able to gasp out "Horace" (or was it Hoxton?) before expiring in his arms. The murderer has struck again!

"You see the idea, my boy? It removes any doubt in the reader's mind that the first death was accidental, and provides the detective with a second set of clues. By collating the two sets——"

"You mean," asked Julian, "that it would

be taken for granted that the murderer was the same in the two cases?"

"Well, of course, my dear boy, of course!" said Marius, surprised at the question. "What else? The poacher, or whoever it was, had witnessed the first murder but had foolishly given some hint of his knowledge to others—possibly in the bar of the local public house. Naturally the murderer has to eliminate him before the information can be passed on to the police."

"Naturally," said Julian thoughtfully. "Yes. . . . Exactly. . . . You know"—and he smiled at his uncle—"I think something might be done on those lines."

For there, he told himself happily, was a foolproof plan. First, commit a completely motiveless murder, of which he could not possibly be suspected. Then, which would be easy, encourage Uncle Marius to poke his "nose for things" into the case, convince him that he and he alone had found the solution, and persuade him to make an appointment with the local inspector. And then, just before the Inspector arrives, "strike again." It was, as he was accustomed to say when passing as a Battle of Britain pilot in Piccadilly bars, a piece of cake.

It may seem to some of you that in taking on this second murder Julian was adding both to his difficulties and his moral responsibility. But you must remember that through all these months of doubt he had been obsessed by one thing only, the intolerable burden of motive, so that suddenly to be rid of it, and to be faced with a completely motiveless killing, gave him an exhilarating sense of freedom in which nothing could go wrong. He had long been feeling that such a murder would be easy. He was now persuaded that it would be blameless.

The victim practically selected himself, and artistically, Julian liked to think, was one of whom Uncle Marius would have approved. A mile or two away at Birch Hall lived an elderly gentleman by the name of Corphew. Not only was he surrounded by greedy relations of both sexes, but in his younger days he had lived a somewhat mysterious life in the East. It did not outrage credibility to suppose that, as an innocent young man, he might have been mixed up in some Secret Society, or, as a more experienced one, might have robbed some temple of its most precious jewel. Though no dark men had been seen loitering in the neighborhood lately, it was common knowledge that Sir George had a great deal of money to leave and was continually altering or threatening to alter his will. In short, his situation fulfilled all the conditions Uncle Marius demanded of a good detective story.

At the moment Julian had no personal acquaintance with Sir George. Though, of course, they would have to be in some sort of touch with each other at the end, his first idea was to remain discreetly outside the family circle. Later reflection, however, told him that in this case he would qualify as one of those mysterious strangers who were occasionally an alternative object of suspicion for the police—quite effectively, because Julian was of a dark, even swarthy, complexion. It would be better, he felt, to be recognized as a friendly acquaintance; obviously harmless, obviously with nothing to gain, even something to lose, by Sir George's death.

In making this acquaintance with his victim, Julian was favored by fortune. Rejecting his usual method of approach to a stranger (an offer to sell him some shares in an oil well in British Columbia), he was presenting himself at the Hall as the special representative of a paper interested in Eastern affairs, when he heard a cry for help from a little coppice[1] that bordered the drive. Sir George, it seemed, had tripped over a root and sprained his ankle. With the utmost good will, Julian carried him up to the house. When he left an hour later, it was with a promise to drop in on a bedridden Sir George

---

1. coppice (kŏp′ĭs) n.: A thicket of small bushes or trees.

the next day, and play a game of chess with him.

Julian was no great chess player, but he was sufficiently intimate with the pieces to allow Sir George the constant pleasure of beating him. Between games, he learned all he could of his host's habits and the family's members. There seemed to him to be several admirable candidates for chief suspect, particularly a younger brother of sinister aspect called Eustace, who had convinced himself that he was to be the principal legatee. Indeed, the possibility of framing Eustace did occur to him, but he remembered in time that a second framing for the murder of Marius would then be necessary, and might easily be impracticable. Let them sort it out. The more suspects the better.

Any morbid expectations you may now have of a detailed account of the murder of Sir George Corphew will not be satisfied. It is enough to say that it involved the conventional blunt instrument, and took place at a time when at least some of the family would not be likely to have an alibi. Julian was not at this time an experienced murderer, and he would have been the first to admit that he had been a little careless about footprints, fingerprints, and cigarette ashes. But as he would never be associated with the murder, this did not matter.

All went as he had anticipated. A London solicitor[2] had produced a will in which all the family was heavily involved, and the Inspector had busied himself with their alibis, making it clear that he regarded each one with the liveliest suspicion. Moreover, Uncle Marius was delighted to pursue his own line of investigation, which, after hovering for a moment round the Vicar, was now rapidly leading to a denunciation of an undergardener called Spratt.

"Don't put anything on paper," said Julian kindly. "It might be dangerous. Ring up the Inspector, and ask him to come in and see you tonight. Then you can tell him all about it."

"That's a good idea, my boy," said Marius. "That's what I'll do."

But, as it happened, the Inspector was already on his way. A local solicitor had turned up with a new will, made only a few days before. "In return for his kindness in playing chess with an old man," as he put it, Sir George had made Julian Crayne his sole legatee.

---

2. solicitor (sə-lĭs′ə-tər) n.: A lawyer in England who can prepare cases or advise clients, but may plead cases only in the lower courts.

Close Up

1. Julian lives in the country with his rich Uncle Marius. (a) Why does Julian want to murder him? (b) How does this motive stand in the way of his committing the crime?

2. (a) How does Julian trick Marius into helping him plan his own murder? (b) What important contribution does Marius make to the plan?

3. (a) Why does Julian select Sir George Corphew as the perfect victim? (b) Why does he decide to make friends with Sir George instead of remaining outside the family circle?

4. (a) Why does Julian want Marius to call the Inspector? (b) Why is the Inspector already on his way?

5. At the beginning of the story, the narrator says, "Kindness doesn't always pay." How does Julian's "kindness" backfire on him?

Plot

Plot is the pattern of action or events in a story. Each event is connected to what happened before and what happens later. The events work together to lead to a satisfying conclusion.

Plot is made up of what the characters do and why they do it. Plot usually centers on a problem or conflict that the main character must resolve by the end of the story. The point at which the conflict becomes most exciting or intense is called the *climax*. The point at which the problem is resolved is called the *resolution*.

1. Julian has a problem: If he is to murder his Uncle Julius and not get caught, he needs to find "an alternative suspect to himself." Why does Julian decide against framing the gardener?

2. Julian thinks he has a solution to his problem. Why does he decide to commit two murders instead of one?

3. At first, Julian's plan seems to be working perfectly. Why does the Inspector suspect the family members?

4. The climax of the story occurs when Julian asks Uncle Marius to call the Inspector. (a) What are you lead to believe will happen next? (b) What is the resolution; that is, what really happens?

5. The opening paragraphs of this story tell you that Julian is caught and hanged. Did knowing this ruin the story for you or did it make the story more exciting? Why?

RELATIONSHIPS

Understanding Spatial Order

Spatial order tells you the location of objects in space. For example, it tells you whether one object is *in*, *close to*, *far from*, *above*, or *below* another.

When you read, you create mental pictures of objects in a story. You "see" each object in relation to other objects. For example, "But Marius was a sound sixty-five, and in that very morning's newspaper there had been talk of somebody at Runcorn who had just celebrated his hundred-and-fifth birthday." Where was the article? It was *in* the newspaper. Where did the 105-year-old live? He lived *at* Runcorn.

▶ Read each item below. Then answer the question or questions following each.

  a. "Any other man might push Marius into the river, and confidently wait for a verdict of accidental death; but not Julian."
  Where might someone push Marius?

  b. "Any other man might place a tablet of some untraceable poison in the soda-mint bottle, and look for a certificate of 'Death from Natural Causes'; but not Julian."
  Where might someone place the tablet?

  c. "Any other man might tie a string across the top step of the attic stairs . . ."
  Where might someone tie the string?

  d. "Not only was he surrounded by greedy relations of both sexes, but in his younger days he had lived a somewhat mysterious life in the East."
  Where had he lived a somewhat mysterious life?

  e. ". . . he was presenting himself at the Hall as a special representative of a paper interested in Eastern affairs, when he heard a cry for help from a little coppice that bordered the drive."
  Where was Julian presenting himself?
  From where did he hear the cry?
  Where was the coppice in relation to the drive?

WORD ATTACK

Using Context Clues

The context of a word is made up of all the words surrounding it. Sometimes, the context can help you determine the meaning of an unfamiliar word. For example, you may not know the meaning of *rendezvous* in the following sentence:

> "Then, at a moment when he is temporarily baffled, the Inspector receives a letter inviting him to a secret *rendezvous* at midnight, where the writer will be waiting to give him important information."

By looking at the words surrounding *rendezvous*, you should be able to guess that it means "an appointment or a prearranged meeting place."

▶ Use context to determine the meaning of each *italicized* word below. Then check your answers against a dictionary.

a. "It removes any doubt in the reader's mind that the first death was accidental, and provides the detective with a second set of clues. By *collating* the two sets——"

b. "A local solicitor had turned up with a new will, made only a few days before. 'In return for his kindness in playing chess with an old man,' as he put it, Sir George had made Julian Crayne his sole *legatee*."

c. "Moreover, Uncle Marius was delighted to pursue his own line of investigation, which, after hovering for a moment round the Vicar, was now rapidly leading to a *denunciation* of an undergardener called Spratt."

d. "Half of you are telling yourselves that, *ironically* enough, it was Uncle who thought of the foolproof plan for murder that Nephew put into *execution*; and the rest of you are thinking what much more fun it would be if Nephew thought of the plan, and, somewhat to his surprise, Uncle put it into execution."

The Sniper

Liam O'Flaherty

". . . he felt a sudden curiosity as to the identity of the enemy sniper whom he had killed."

The Long June twilight faded into night. Dublin lay enveloped in darkness but for the dim light of the moon that shone through fleecy clouds, casting a pale light as of approaching dawn over the streets and the dark waters of the Liffey.[1] Around the beleaguered Four Courts the heavy guns roared. Here and there through the city, machine guns and rifles broke the silence of the night, spasmodically, like dogs barking on lone farms. Republicans and Free Staters[2] were waging civil war.

On a rooftop near O'Connell Bridge, a Republican sniper lay watching. Beside him lay his rifle and over his shoulders were slung a pair of field glasses. His face was the face of a student, thin and ascetic, but his eyes had the cold gleam of the fanatic. They were deep and thoughtful, the eyes of a man who is used to looking at death.

He was eating a sandwich hungrily. He had eaten nothing since morning. He had been too excited to eat. He finished the sandwich, and, taking a flask of whiskey from his pocket, he took a short draft. Then he returned the flask to his pocket. He paused for a moment, considering whether he should

---

1. Liffey (lĭf'ē): A river in Ireland that runs through Dublin.
2. Republicans and Free Staters: Republicans were the faction in Ireland that advocated complete independence from England. Free Staters were the faction that opposed complete independence; instead, they advocated establishing Ireland as a free state within the British Commonwealth.

risk a smoke. It was dangerous. The flash might be seen in the darkness, and there were enemies watching. He decided to take the risk.

Placing a cigarette between his lips, he struck a match, inhaled the smoke hurriedly, and put out the light. Almost immediately, a bullet flattened itself against the parapet of the roof. The sniper took another whiff and put out the cigarette. Then he swore softly and crawled away to the left.

Cautiously he raised himself and peered over the parapet. There was a flash and a bullet whizzed over his head. He dropped immediately. He had seen the flash. It came from the opposite side of the street.

He rolled over the roof to a chimney stack in the rear, and slowly drew himself up behind it, until his eyes were level with the top of the parapet. There was nothing to be seen—just the dim outline of the opposite housetop against the blue sky. His enemy was under cover.

Just then an armored car came across the bridge and advanced slowly up the street. It stopped on the opposite side of the street, fifty yards ahead. The sniper could hear the dull panting of the motor. His heart beat faster. It was an enemy car. He wanted to fire, but he knew it was useless. His bullets would never pierce the steel that covered the gray monster.

Then round the corner of a side street came an old woman, her head covered by a tattered shawl. She began to talk to the man in the turret of the car. She was pointing to the roof where the sniper lay. An informer.

The turret opened. A man's head and shoulders appeared, looking toward the sniper. The sniper raised his rifle and fired. The head fell heavily on the turret wall. The woman darted toward the side street. The sniper fired again. The woman whirled round and fell with a shriek into the gutter.

Suddenly from the opposite roof a shot rang out and the sniper dropped his rifle with a curse. The rifle clattered to the roof.

The sniper thought the noise would wake the dead. He stopped to pick the rifle up. He couldn't lift it. His forearm was dead. "I'm hit," he muttered.

Dropping flat onto the roof, he crawled back to the parapet. With his left hand he felt the injured right forearm. The blood was oozing through the sleeve of his coat. There was no pain—just a deadened sensation, as if the arm had been cut off.

Quickly he drew his knife from his pocket, opened it on the breastwork of the parapet, and ripped open the sleeve. There was a small hole where the bullet had entered. On the other side there was no hole. The bullet had lodged in the bone. It must have fractured it. He bent the arm below the wound. The arm bent back easily. He ground his teeth to overcome the pain.

Then taking out his field dressing, he ripped open the packet with his knife. He broke the neck of the iodine bottle and let the bitter fluid drip into the wound. A paroxysm of pain swept through him. He placed the cotton wadding over the wound and wrapped the dressing over it. He tied the ends with his teeth.

Then he lay still against the parapet, and, closing his eyes, he made an effort of will to overcome the pain.

In the street beneath all was still. The armored car had retired speedily over the bridge, with the machine gunner's head hanging lifeless over the turret. The woman's corpse lay still in the gutter.

The sniper lay still for along time nursing his wounded arm and planning escape. Morning must not find him wounded on the roof. The enemy on the opposite roof covered his escape. He must kill that enemy and he could not use his rifle. He had only a revolver to do it. Then he thought of a plan.

Taking off his cap, he placed it over the muzzle of his rifle. Then he pushed the rifle slowly upward over the parapet, until the cap was visible from the opposite side of the street. Almost immediately there was a re-

port, and a bullet pierced the center of the cap. The sniper slanted the rifle forward. The cap slipped down into the street. Then catching the rifle in the middle, the sniper dropped his left hand over the roof and let it hang, lifelessly. After a few moments he let the rifle drop to the street. Then he sank to the roof, dragging his hand with him.

Crawling quickly to the left, he peered up at the corner of the roof. His ruse had succeeded. The other sniper, seeing the cap and rifle fall, thought that he had killed his man. He was now standing before a row of chimney pots, looking across, with his head clearly silhouetted against the western sky.

The Republican sniper smiled and lifted

his revolver above the edge of the parapet. The distance was about fifty yards—a hard shot in the dim light, and his right arm was paining him like a thousand devils. He took a steady aim. His hand trembled with eagerness. Pressing his lips together, he took a deep breath through his nostrils and fired. He was almost deafened with the report and his arm shook with the recoil.

Then when the smoke cleared he peered across and uttered a cry of joy. His enemy had been hit. He was reeling over the parapet in his death agony. He struggled to keep his feet, but he was slowly falling forward, as if in a dream. The rifle fell from his grasp, hit the parapet, fell over, bounded off the pole of a barber's shop beneath, and then clattered on the pavement.

Then the dying man on the roof crumpled up and fell forward. The body turned over and over in space and hit the ground with a dull thud. Then it lay still.

The sniper looked at his enemy falling and he shuddered. The lust of battle died in him. He became bitten by remorse. The sweat stood out in beads on his forehead. Weakened by his wound and the long summer day of fasting and watching on the roof, he revolted from the sight of the shattered mass of his dead enemy. His teeth chattered, he began to gibber to himself, cursing the war, cursing himself, cursing everybody.

He looked at the smoking revolver in his hand, and with an oath he hurled it to the roof at his feet. The revolver went off with the concussion and the bullet whizzed past the sniper's head. He was frightened back to his senses by the shock. His nerves steadied. The cloud of fear scattered from his mind and he laughed.

Taking the whiskey flask from his pocket, he emptied it at a draft. He felt reckless under the influence of the spirit. He decided to leave the roof now and look for his company commander, to report. Everywhere around was quiet. There was not much danger in going through the streets. He picked up his revolver and put it in his pocket. Then he crawled down through the skylight to the house underneath.

When the sniper reached the laneway on the street level, he felt a sudden curiosity as to the identity of the enemy sniper whom he had killed. He decided that he was a good shot, whoever he was. He wondered did he know him. Perhaps he had been in his own company before the split in the army. He decided to risk going over to have a look at him. He peered around the corner into O'Connell Street. In the upper part of the street there was heavy firing, but around here all was quiet.

The sniper darted across the street. A machine gun tore up the ground around him with a hail of bullets, but he escaped. He threw himself face downward beside the corpse. The machine gun stopped.

Then the sniper turned over the dead body and looked into his brother's face.

Close Up

1. The sniper and his enemy on the rooftop play a dangerous game of cat and mouse. (a) How is the enemy able to get a clear shot at the sniper? (b) How does the sniper convince his enemy that he is dead?

2. A fanatic is someone who is markedly and excessively devoted to a cause. (a) At what point in the story does the sniper waver in his devotion to the cause? (b) What event frightens him back to his senses?

3. Why does the sniper risk going over to look at the corpse?

4. Think about the ending of this story. What statement do you think the author wants to make about civil war?

Suspense

Suspense is the quality of a story that makes you want to read on to find out what will happen next. One method of building suspense is to make the reader worry about what will happen to one of the characters. For example, will this character live or die? Will this character succeed or fail? A second method is to introduce a situation for which the reader wants an explanation. For example, how did this situation come about? How will it turn out? What effect will it have on the main character?

1. The situation at the beginning of the story immediately sets up an atmosphere of suspense. (a) Why does the sniper hesitate to smoke? (b) What happens when he decides to take the risk anyway?

2. After their initial run-in, the sniper and the enemy each go under cover. (a) How does the arrival of the armored car add to the suspense? (b) How does the appearance of the informer further complicate the sniper's situation?

3. When the sniper is wounded, it looks as if the enemy will be victorious. (a) How does the sniper then get the upper hand? (b) The sniper has proven that he is a good marksman. Why can't you be sure that he will be able to kill the enemy, even though he has a clear shot at him?

4. Once the enemy dies, you can be relatively certain that the sniper will escape. (a) How does the author manage to keep you in suspense until the end of the story? (b) What effect did the ending of the story have on you?

RELATIONSHIPS

Understanding Simple and Significant Listing

A list is a collection of items that fit into a particular category, or group. For example, a list of weapons would include: revolver, rifle, bayonet, and hand grenade.

In simple listing, the items are not arranged in any particular order. In significant listing, the items are arranged in a particular order; for example, smallest to largest, least powerful to most powerful, lightest to heaviest, least important to most important.

---

1. Read the items below. Then divide these items into two lists. In one list, group all the items that fall under the category *military uniforms*. In the second list, group all the items that fall under the category *military machinery*.

   a. tank
   b. boots
   c. battleship
   d. jeep
   e. helmet

   f. shirt
   g. helicopter
   h. jacket
   i. bomber plane
   j. aircraft carrier

2. Which items do not belong in the following list? Tank, battleship, jeep, fighter plane, first-aid kit, helicopter, helmet.

3. Rearrange the following items from smallest to largest in order to make a significant listing.

   a. tank
   b. battleship
   c. jeep

   d. revolver
   e. rifle

WORD ATTACK

Using Context Clues

The context of a word consists of the other words in the sentence or sentences surrounding it. If you read carefully, you may find that the context provides enough clues to help you define an unfamiliar word. For example, look at the following passage.

> "Then round the corner of a side street came an old woman, her head covered by a tattered shawl. She began to talk to the man in the turret of the car. She was pointing to the roof where the sniper lay. An *informer*."

The woman is talking to the man in the enemy car and pointing to the sniper's hiding place. This information should help you to define "informer" as "one who reveals information about something; a betrayer or traitor."

▶ Use context to select the correct definition for each *italicized* word.

a. "He finished the sandwich, and, taking a flask of whiskey from his pocket, he took a short *draft*. Then he returned the flask to his pocket."
(1) air current (2) bank note (3) sip

b. "Suddenly from the opposite roof a shot rang out and the sniper dropped his rifle with a curse. The rifle *clattered* to the roof. The sniper thought the noise would wake the dead."
(1) fell silently (2) broke (3) fell noisily

c. "Crawling quickly to the left, he peered up at the corner of the roof. His *ruse* had succeeded. The other sniper, seeing the cap and rifle fall, thought he had killed his man."
(1) weapon (2) strategy or trick (3) costume

d. "The sniper looked at his enemy falling and he shuddered. The lust of battle died in him. He became bitten by *remorse*."
(1) self-reproach or bitter regret (2) fever (3) the inability to speak

e. "Almost immediately there was a *report*, and a bullet pierced the center of the cap."
(1) formal announcement (2) explosive noise (3) rumor or gossip

The Lady, or the Tiger?

Frank R. Stockton

In the very olden time, there lived a semi-barbaric king who was a man of exuberant fancy and of an authority so irresistible that, at his will, he turned his varied fancies into facts. He was greatly given to self-communing; and when he and himself agreed upon anything, the thing was done. When everything moved smoothly, his nature was bland and genial; but whenever there was a little hitch, he was blander and more genial still, for nothing pleased him so much as to make the crooked straight, and crush down uneven places.

Among his borrowed notions was that of the public arena, in which, by exhibitions of manly and beastly valor, the minds of his subjects were refined and cultured.

But even here the exuberant and barbaric fancy asserted itself. This vast amphitheater,[1] with its encircling galleries, its mysterious vault, and its unseen passages, was an agent of poetic justice, in which crime was punished, or virtue rewarded, by the decrees of an impartial and incorruptible chance.

When a subject was accused of a crime of sufficient importance to interest the king, public notice was given that on an appointed day the fate of the accused person would be decided in the king's arena.

When all the people had assembled in the galleries, and the king, surrounded by his court, sat high up on his throne of royal state on one side of the arena, he gave a signal, a door beneath him opened, and the accused subject stepped out into the amphitheater. Directly opposite him, on the other side of the enclosed space, were two doors, exactly alike and side by side. It was the duty and the privilege of the person on trial to walk directly to these doors and open one of them. He could open either door he pleased. He was subject to no guidance or influence but that of the aforementioned impartial and incorruptible chance. If he opened the one, there came out of it a hungry tiger, the fiercest and most cruel that could be procured, which immediately sprang upon him and tore him to pieces, as a punishment for his guilt. The moment that the case of the criminal was thus decided, doleful iron bells were clanged, great wails went up from the hired mourners posted on the outer rim of the arena, and the vast audience, with bowed heads and downcast hearts, wended slowly their homeward way, mourning greatly that one so

---

1. amphitheater (ăm′fə-thē′ə-tər) n.: An open arena surrounded by rising tiers of seats.

young and fair, or so old and respected, should have merited so dire a fate.

But if the accused person opened the other door, there came forth from it a lady, the most suitable to his years and station that His Majesty could select among his fair subjects; and to this lady he was immediately married, as a reward of his innocence. It mattered not that he might already possess a wife and family, or that his affections might be engaged upon an object of his own selection. The king allowed no such arrangements to interfere with his great scheme of punishment and reward. The exercises, as in the other instance, took place immediately, and in the arena. Another door opened beneath the king, and a priest, followed by a band of choristers, and dancing maidens blowing joyous airs on golden horns, advanced to where the pair stood, side by side; and the wedding was promptly and cheerily solemnized. Then the gay brass bells rang forth their merry peals, and the people shouted glad hurrahs, and the innocent man, preceded by children strewing flowers on his path, led his bride to his home.

This was the king's semibarbaric method of administering justice. Its perfect fairness is obvious. The criminal could not know out of which door would come the lady. He opened either he pleased, without having the slightest idea whether, in the next instant, he was to be devoured or married. On some occasions the tiger came out of one door, and on some, out of the other. The decisions were not only fair, they were positively decisive. The accused person was instantly punished if he found himself guilty; and, if innocent, he was rewarded on the spot, whether he liked it or not. There was no escape from the judgments of the king's arena.

The institution was a very popular one. When the people gathered together on one of the great trial days, they never knew whether they were to witness a bloody slaughter or a hilarious wedding. This element of uncertainty lent an interest to the occasion which it could not otherwise have attained. Thus, the masses were entertained and pleased, and the thinking part of the community could bring no charge of unfairness against this plan; for did not the accused person have the whole matter in his own hands?

This semibarbaric king had a daughter as blooming as his most florid fancies, and with a soul as fervent and imperious as his own. As is usual in such cases, she was the apple of his eye, and was loved by him above all humanity. Among his courtiers was a young man of that fineness of blood and lowness of station common to the heroes of romance who love royal maidens. This royal maiden was well satisfied with her lover, for he was handsome and brave to a degree unsurpassed in all this kingdom; and she loved him with an ardor that had enough of barbarism in it to make it exceedingly warm and strong. This love affair moved on happily for many months, until one day the king happened to discover its existence. He did not hesitate nor waver in regard to his duty. The youth was immediately cast into prison, and a day was appointed for his trial in the king's arena. This, of course, was an especially important occasion; and His Majesty, as well as all the people, was greatly interested in the workings and development of this trial. Never before had such a case occurred—never before had a subject dared to love the daughter of a king. In after years such things became commonplace enough; but then they were, in no slight degree, novel and startling.

The tiger cages of the kingdom were searched for the most savage and relentless beasts, from which the fiercest monster might be selected for the arena; and the ranks of maiden youth and beauty throughout the land were carefully surveyed by competent judges, in order that the young man might have a fitting bride in case fate did not determine for him a different destiny. Of course, everybody knew that the deed with which the accused was charged had been done. He had loved the princess, and neither he, she, nor anyone else thought of denying the fact. But the king would not think of allowing any fact of this kind to interfere with the workings of the court of judgment, in which he took such great delight and satisfaction. No matter how the affair turned out, the youth would be disposed of; and the king would take pleasure in watching the course of events, which would determine whether or not the young man had done wrong in allowing himself to love the princess.

The appointed day arrived. From far and near the people gathered, and thronged the great galleries of the arena; and crowds, unable to gain admittance, massed themselves against its outside walls. The king and his court were in their places, opposite the twin doors—those fateful portals, so terrible in their similarity.

All was ready. The signal was given. A door beneath the royal party opened, and the lover of the princess walked into the arena. Tall, beautiful, fair, his appearance was greeted with a low hum of admiration and anxiety. Half the audience had not known so grand a youth had lived among them. No wonder the princess loved him! What a terrible thing for him to be there!

As the youth advanced into the arena, he turned, as the custom was, to bow to the king. But he did not think at all of that royal personage; his eyes were fixed upon the princess, who sat to the right of her father. Had it not been for the barbarism in her nature, it is probable that lady would not have been there. But her intense and fervid soul would not allow her to be absent on an occasion in which she was so terribly interested. From the moment that the decree had gone forth that her lover should decide his fate in the king's arena, she had thought of nothing, night or day, but this great event and the various subjects connected with it. Possessed of more power, influence, and force of character than anyone who had ever before been interested in such a case, she had done what

no other person had done—she had possessed herself of the secret of the doors. She knew in which of the two rooms that lay behind those doors stood the cage of the tiger, with its open front, and in which waited the lady. Through these thick doors, heavily curtained with skins on the inside, it was impossible that any noise or suggestion should come from within to the person who should approach to raise the latch of one of them. But gold, and the power of a woman's will, had brought the secret to the princess.

And not only did she know in which room stood the lady, ready to emerge, all blushing and radiant, should her door be opened, but she knew who the lady was. It was one of the fairest and loveliest of the damsels of the court who had been selected as the reward of the accused youth, should he be proved innocent of the crime of aspiring to one so far above him; and the princess hated her. Often had she seen, or imagined that she had seen, this fair creature throwing glances of admiration upon the person of her lover, and sometimes she thought these glances were perceived and even returned. Now and then she had seen them talking together. It was but for a moment or two, but much can be said in a brief space. It may have been on most unimportant topics, but how could she know that? The girl was lovely, but she had dared to raise her eyes to the loved one of the princess; and, with all the intensity of the savage blood transmitted to her through long lines of wholly barbaric ancestors, she hated the woman who blushed and trembled behind that silent door.

When her lover turned and looked at her, and his eye met hers as she sat there paler and whiter than anyone in the vast ocean of anxious faces about her, he saw, by that power of quick perception which is given to those whose souls are one, that she knew behind which door crouched the tiger, and behind which stood the lady. He had expected her to know it. He understood her nature, and his soul was assured that she

would never rest until she had made plain to herself this thing, hidden to all other lookers-on, even to the king. The only hope for the youth in which there was any element of certainty was based upon the success of the princess in discovering this mystery; and the moment he looked upon her, he saw she had succeeded.

Then it was that his quick and anxious glance asked the question: "Which?" It was

before her. She raised her hand, and made a slight, quick movement toward the right. No one but her lover saw her. Every eye but his was fixed on the man in the arena.

He turned, and with a firm and rapid step he walked across the empty space. Every heart stopped beating, every breath was held, every eye was fixed immovably upon that man. Without the slightest hesitation, he went to the door on the right, and opened it.

Now, the point of the story is this: Did the tiger come out of that door, or did the lady?

The more we reflect upon this question, the harder it is to answer. It involves a study of the human heart which leads us through roundabout pathways of passion, out of which it is difficult to find our way. Think of it, fair reader, not as if the decision of the question depended upon yourself, but upon that hot-blooded, semibarbaric princess, her soul at a white heat beneath the combined fires of despair and jealousy. She had lost him, but who should have him?

How often, in her waking hours and in her dreams, had she started in wild horror and covered her face with her hands as she thought of her lover opening the door on the other side of which waited the cruel fangs of the tiger!

But how much oftener had she seen him at the other door! How in her grievous reveries had she gnashed her teeth and torn her hair, when she saw his start of rapturous delight as he opened the door of the lady! How her soul had burned in agony when she had seen him rush to meet that woman, with her flushing cheek and sparkling eye of triumph; when she had seen him lead her forth, his whole frame kindled with the joy of recovered life; when she had heard the glad shouts from the multitude, and the wild ringing of the happy bells; when she had seen the priest, with his joyous followers, advance to the couple, and make them man and wife

as plain to her as if he shouted it from where he stood. There was not an instant to be lost. The question was asked in a flash; it must be answered in another.

Her right arm lay on the cushioned parapet

before her very eyes; and when she had seen them walk away together upon their path of flowers, followed by the tremendous shouts of the hilarious multitude, in which her one despairing shriek was lost and drowned!

Would it not be better for him to die at once, and go to wait for her in the blessed regions of semibarbaric futurity?

And yet, that awful tiger, those shrieks, that blood!

Her decision had been indicated in an instant, but it had been made after days and nights of anguished deliberation. She had known she would be asked, she had decided what she would answer, and, without the slightest hesitation, she had moved her hand to the right.

The question of her decision is one not to be lightly considered, and it is not for me to presume to set up myself as the one person able to answer it. And so I leave it with all of you: Which came out of the opened door—the lady, or the tiger?

Close Up

1. (a) In what ways is the king's method of administering justice fair? (b) In what ways is it unfair?

2. (a) Why is this method popular with the people? (b) Why could the thinking part of the community "bring no charge of unfairness against this plan"?

3. The youth is guilty of loving the king's daughter. Why is the king certain to be rid of the youth even if the arena proves him innocent?

4. (a) Why is the princess able to learn the secret of the doors? (b) What other secret does she know?

Dilemma

A dilemma is a situation in which a character must choose between two unpleasant alternatives. By placing a character in a dilemma, the author is able to build suspense. The author makes you wonder what choice the character will make and what the consequence will be.

1. The princess must make a difficult choice. She can either send the youth to his death or let him live. (a) What is unpleasant about each alternative? (b) What is pleasant about each?

2. The narrator says that the princess' heart contains "the combined fires of despair and jealousy." (a) What does her despair make her want to do? (b) What does her jealousy make her want to do?

3. Based on what you have learned about the princess, which do you think comes out of the open door—the lady, or the tiger? Why?

Activity

▶ **Composition.** Imagine you are either the youth or the princess. When the door on the right opens, a beautiful maiden walks out. Write a paragraph expressing your feelings.

RELATIONSHIPS

Understanding Time Order

Time order is the sequence in which events happen. It tells you which event happens first, second, third, etc. For example, in "The Lady, or the Tiger?" first the king establishes his system of justice. Second, he discovers that the youth has dared to love the princess. Third, he places the youth on trial.

1. Place the events below in the correct time order. Begin with the event that happens first.
   a. The youth steps into the arena.
   b. The princess raises her right hand.
   c. The fiercest tiger is found for the youth's trial.
   d. The eyes of the princess meet the eyes of her lover.
   e. The youth opens the door on the right.

2. Choose five events from this story not mentioned in Exercise **1.** Then draw a horizontal line across a piece of paper. On the left side of this line, write the event that happened first. On the right side, write the event that happened last. Then place the three other events on the line in the order in which they occurred.

WORD ATTACK

Understanding When Context Helps and When It Doesn't

The context of a word consists of the words surrounding it. Sometimes context helps you define an unfamiliar word. For example,

> The youth showed great *valor* in the face of death. He turned, and with a firm and rapid step, he went to meet his fate. Without the slightest hesitation, he approached the door on the right and opened it.

The context suggests that *valor* means "great courage or bravery."

Sometimes, though, the context does not help. For example,

> The priest, followed by a band of *choristers*, walked toward the happy couple.

The other words in the sentence do not suggest what *choristers* means. You have to look it up in a dictionary.

---

1. Copy each of the following items on a piece of paper. Write *Yes* by each item where context helps you define the *italicized* word. Write *No* by each item where context does not help.
   a. "The king and his court were in their places, opposite the twin doors—those fateful *portals*, so terrible in their similarity."
   b. "He was greatly given to *self-communing*; and when he and himself agreed upon anything, the thing was done."
   c. "This royal maiden was well satisfied with her lover, for he was handsome and brave to a degree unsurpassed in all this kingdom; and she loved him with an ardor that had enough of *barbarism* in it to make it exceedingly warm and strong."
   d. "This semibarbaric king had a daughter as blooming as his most florid fancies, and with a soul as *fervid* . . . as his own."

2. Reread the sentences in Exercise **1.** For each item you labeled *Yes,* use context to write the meaning of the *italicized* word. Check your answers against the glossary. For each item you labeled *No,* use your glossary to find the meaning of the *italicized* word.

The Lady, or the Tiger? **95**

What Sort of Person Is This Amanda Jones Anyway?

Joan Aiken

"I didn't remember tying those laces. I didn't remember putting on the shoes. I had forgotten who I was."

The train was somewhere north of London when the rucksack[1] fell on my head. My own fault, of course. It was insecurely perched and when we came to one of those sudden stops it bounced down and beaned me.

The only other person in the carriage was an elderly man, rather prissy-looking, folded into an evening paper. He put it down and came along and picked the rucksack off my feet, as I wasn't doing anything but sitting and looking at it vacantly.

"Are you all right?" he asked. He glanced toward the communication cord, but there didn't seem much sense in pulling it, as we were stationary anyway.

"Yes thanks," I answered automatically. I nodded to show how okay I was, and put up a tentative hand to the back of my neck,

---

1. rucksack (rŭk′săk′) n.: A canvas bag worn on the back and used for carrying supplies.

which felt as if I had been sandbagged. I certainly didn't intend to tell this fellow the embarrassing thing that had happened to me, and, after another doubtful survey, he went back to his corner and his paper.

I stared at my feet. Size three, or thereabouts, in suede shoes with laces. I didn't remember tying those laces. I didn't remember putting on the shoes. I had forgotten who I was.

We were still at a standstill, so I had time to take stock before flying into a panic. I'm female, I thought, he called me miss. I'm English. People in stories can always tackle this sort of situation, so I should be able to.

Furtively glancing at the man out of the corner of my eye, I began excavating my handbag, which must surely contain plenty of clues.

Evidently I had a sweet tooth—three packets of buttermints and half a bar of chocolate—I was over twenty-one, or, at any rate, owned a latchkey; I also had a checkbook and a return half from Edinburgh to King's Cross. Aha! Now I knew where to get out.

There were some postcards of Scottish lochs and a sprig of heather; it seemed fair to assume I'd been on holiday in Scotland.

Beneath these things was a letter addressed to Miss Amanda Jones, Flat F, Noble Crescent, N.6:

Honey Darling,

How wonderful that you've actually *sold a story,* and are rushing off to Scotland for ten days. Mind you take plenty of spare socks and sweaters—*it always rains in Scotland.*

Father is well and sends love; he has just gone off with the parish magazines after telling me not on any account to weed the front border. *He doesn't trust me an inch.*

Honey dear, don't forget, will you, that Aunt Leonie is coming to see you on the twentieth and do please try, chickie, to make a good impression. I know she is an old Tartar but she is Father's only sister. And she's fond of you—only the other day she was saying what a pity it was that you'd never married!

Have a wonderful holiday. I'll send a cake and some eggs to greet you when you get back.

Love and hugs from Mother

The letter made me chuckle, and gave me a vivid picture of Mother's face as she sat writing, a smudge of flour on her nose, a rose-cutting tangled in her cardigan sleeve, and a lock of untidy gray-fair hair falling over her eyes. Surreptitiously I peered into my compact mirror and confirmed that I was just like her—straight nose, same gray eyes, same untidy fair hair. And, darn it, what did Aunt Leonie mean by *never married?*—I couldn't be a day over twenty! I began to feel rather indignant toward the old trout.

But I still couldn't remember anything about myself—except for some dim childhood recollections of having tea on the rectory lawn and Father in his surplice going off for evensong.[2] What kind of a person was this Amanda Jones?

The train had started again and now began to slow down, pulling in to King's Cross. The elderly man got out, giving me a last disapproving glance. He left his evening paper behind and I pounced on it as I followed him. Saturday September 20. That meant Aunt Leonie was coming this evening—I hadn't left myself much time for giving a good impression.

There were five ten-penny pieces in my purse and I decided this was definitely an occasion for a taxi. Sitting in it, I began to feel sorry for myself. Aunt Leonie had started it off. Here I am, I thought, going back to a lonely, empty flat, after a sad, solitary holiday walking about a Scottish moor. There won't be a soul to welcome me, and I don't know a thing about myself.

I paid off the cab outside a big house in a

---

2. evensong (ē′ vən-sông′) n.: A late afternoon or early evening church service.

pleasant garden in a quiet road. There was a large entrance hall and in it, on a table with tenants' letters and packages, were two for me: a parcel addressed in mother's handwriting—the cake and eggs no doubt—and a letter. I fell on this. Perhaps it would yield another clue. But it was disappointingly brief:

Amanda dear,

It seems such a long time since I saw you though it is only a few days. Longing to have you back in London. I'll be round in the evening to see you.   A.

Well, at least I've got a friend, and though he or she is pretty terse in his or her epistolary style, it's good to know that someone is pleased to have me back.

I was still chafing over that *never married.*

Picking up Mother's parcel I looked cautiously round till I found Flat F, which was on the ground floor. Luckily none of the other tenants was about; they would probably have thought I was mad.

Propped against my door were a bottle of milk and a packet of coffee, sitting on a bit of paper that said SEE YOU SOON, LOVE JENNIFER.

It was an odd feeling to turn the key in my own front door without having the slightest notion what I should find inside. Habitat or period, Louis Quatorze or Swedish laminated.[3] Did I play the violin? Watch telly? Make pots? Read Latin poetry?

The flat had a dusty, uncared-for smell, and my first thought was, I must get this place cleaned up before Aunt Leonie arrives.

From that I judged I was a housewifely sort of girl, but this optimistic notion was soon dashed. Intensive search failed to reveal any cleaning implements save an old dustpan and brush.

I began to have a very poor notion of Amanda Jones.

It wasn't a big flat—bathroom, kitchenette, bed-sitting-room, and a tiny spare room, six inches bigger than the bed. I made this up for Aunt Leonie and put out a clean towel.

The bathroom revealed another facet of me: two of its walls were papered solid with a montage of rejection slips, large, small, and medium, carefully pasted together and covered with polythene. There must have been hundreds of them—*Punch, Vogue, The New Yorker, Nova, Honey, Nineteen, Petticoat,* the *New Statesman*—you name it, I had it. I must have been rejected by every magazine in the English-speaking world.

I had to admit that this Amanda Jones had staying-power; she didn't get discouraged. And, after all, I had in the end sold a story. More power to my elbow. Maybe my luck was turning. I wondered who I'd sold it to, and what they'd paid me.

There was a ring at the front door. Aunt Leonie! I dashed.

But it was a dark, pretty girl in a navy silk jersey Russian tunic and pants who hugged me warmly and said, "Honey dear! Super to have you back. Come in for breakfast tomorrow and have a good gossip. Darling, would you be an angel and look after William Walpole for me this evening—Don wants to go to *Ulysses.* William's missed you so, you can't think."

"Of course," I said automatically, and then I saw the carrycot on the floor beside her containing a brown-eyed baby who waved at me enthusiastically and exclaimed "Ba!"

"There, see! He's so pleased to have you back. Honey, I must rush. See you later."

I picked up William Walpole, took him inside, and put him, cot and all, on the divan. When I started sweeping with the brush and pan the dust got in his nose and made him sneeze. I moved him to the spare room but he didn't approve of that. His disapproval took the form of ninety-megaton screams and I had to move him back.

---

3. ". . . or Swedish laminated": Styles of furniture.

Affairs were in this condition of stalemate when the bell rang again.

Aunt Leonie! I dashed.

But it was a tall, military character with a fair mustache carrying a large carton. My heart leapt up. Could this be A? If so I took back some of the unkind thoughts I had been thinking about Amanda Jones.

"Miss Jones?" he said.

Not A, then.

"Yes," I said. He beamed.

"I've been trying to get you for the last ten days."

"I've been on a sudden, unplanned holiday."

"Come to demonstrate the new Whizzo Cleaner," he said, "in answer to your inquiry."

Good, sensible, Amanda!

"Come right in," I said. "You couldn't have arrived at a better moment. There's ten days' dust here that wants sucking up."

I will say for him he took it beautifully in his stride, though he was a bit shaken when he saw William Walpole sitting up in the carrycot brandishing his rattle.

"Not mine—a neighbor's," I said hurriedly. "Do you have any children, Mr——?"

"Palliser, Charles Palliser," he said, rapidly taking the Whizzo from its carton and fitting it all together. "No, I'm a bachelor. Never had much to do with small kids."

He eyed William Walpole warily, but William was much intrigued by the ramifications of the Whizzo, and was quite happy to sit in his cot and watch while Charles cleaned up ten days' dust.

"I'd love to see how it works on the curtains," I kept saying and, "Does it polish too? Did you say there was an upholstery brush? Just show me how it cleans tiles, could you?" The Whizzo was a great success.

I made some coffee while Charles was cleaning the bathroom and had a cup ready with a chunk of Mother's cake. It seemed only civil. Now if Aunt Leonie turned up I was ready for her, *and* with a male in attendance.

"And how much does the Whizzo cost nowadays?" I asked, hoping to conceal my total ignorance of what it had ever cost.

"Twenty-nine, ninety-two, since the price went up," he said sadly.

"Oh dear," I said. "I wonder if I've got that much in my account." I wondered if there was a bank statement lurking in the flat somewhere.

Mr. Palliser had put the Whizzo tidily back into its carton and was looking at my pictures. "Do you paint?" he said. "You've got some valuable originals here, did you know?"

"No, have I?"

He looked a little dashed, but my surprise was genuine.

Just at that moment the doorbell rang again. Aunt Leonie! I flew.

But it was a tall young character in gabardine slacks, with a lovable transatlantic ugliness.

"Miss Amanda Jones?" he said. New York accent. This can't be A. either.

"Come in, come in," I said, a bit lightheaded from the way events were shaping. "We're just having coffee and cake."

"Oh, I'm sorry," said Charles. "I didn't know you were expecting company. I'd better be off."

"I'm not company," beamed the new arrival. "I'm Miss Jones's winnings."

"I beg your pardon?"

I poured him out a cup of coffee and another for Charles, while I thought over what he had said. It still made no sense.

"Could you explain that?"

"Remember the *Evening Dispatch* competition? 'Win Yourself a Man'? You won it, Miss Jones. I'm your man. Richard Bradfield Heppenstall."

This was the point at which I might have begun to think I was dreaming—but the coffee was good and strong and black. I hung on to the table edge and said, "How did I win it?" I had plainly misjudged Amanda Jones.

"You wrote a four-line verse. It must have been a humdinger, Miss Jones. Don't you remember how it went?"

"No, I can't," I said, not without relief.

"Darn it! That's too bad. Never mind, Miss Jones, here I am, so what would you like done? Painting, tile-laying, pig-sticking, escort to the opera? I'm in Europe on vacation for two months, completely at your disposal, and the *Evening Dispatch* pays for the outings. So what'll it be?"

"I'd love to go to Covent Garden next week," I said. "Right now——"

Stick about and impress Aunt Leonie, I was going to say, but he interrupted me gently.

"Right now I guess what you want is a baby-shusher."

It was true. William Walpole, on seeing the Whizzo go back into its box and stay there, had burst into a dismal howl.

"Hush, William Walpole," I said to him. "The flat's clean now, can't you see, it's clean? No more Whizzo." He didn't take a bit of notice, only howled the more. Richard scooped him out of the cot, shook all his nightwear into position, expertly patted his back, cocked him over one arm, and walked him into good temper in no time.

"You have children of your own?" I said respectfully.

"No, ma'am! I'm a bachelor. But I have plenty of nephews and nieces."

The doorbell rang. I dashed. This time there could be no doubt that it was Aunt Leonie, and I gave her a dutiful kiss. She marched straight past me into the sitting room, which was beginning to look a bit cluttered. Her sharp black eyes took in Charles with his coffee cup, Whizzo in its carton, and Richard Heppenstall with a piece of cake in one hand and William Walpole elevated over the other arm.

"That child is up far too late," she said formidably. "He should be taken home."

"No, Aunt," I explained hurriedly. "He lives here. That is—I mean——"

"Are you his father?" She fixed gimlet[4] eyes on Richard.

"No, ma'am! Miss Jones won me in a competition."

She looked a little startled, but passed it over. "Are *you* his father then?"

Poor Charles was beginning to look out of his depth, and as if he didn't care whether he sold Whizzo or not.

"Neither of them is," I said hurriedly. "His *real* father's not here just now."

Aunt Leonie directed a bleak gaze at my left hand, unadorned by any ring. Her thoughts spoke louder than any number of decibels.

"No, no, he's not mine! I'm just looking

---

4. gimlet (gǐm'lǐt) *adj.:* Piercing.

after him for a friend. These gentlemen are helping me."

Put it how I might, it didn't sound the sort of occupation to create a favorable impression on Aunt Leonie.

"Mr. Palliser has been selling me a Whizzo," I said, and told him, "Never mind the state of my bank balance. I'll buy it! Maybe I'll sell another story."

"In my young days," said Aunt Leonie, "gels did not entertain young men in their apartments without a chaperon."

"Well we are chaperoned now," said Richard Heppenstall comfortably, "so let's all sit down and relax." I threw him a grateful glance and poured Aunt Leonie a cup of coffee. The doorbell rang and Charles went to answer it.

Aunt Leonie had not finished her catechism. "This young man says you *won* him," she said, taking the coffee and giving me a piercing look. "Does he mean that you are engaged?"

"I'm not engaged——" I started crossly, but a deep voice behind my back made me spin round.

"Miss Amanda Jones," it said with dignity and a slight Scots accent, "is engaged to me."

Tall, dark, and gray-eyed. There could be little doubt about it: this was A.

The minute I saw him a whole lot of confused recollections which had been floundering about my mind for the last half-hour clicked tidily into place.

I knew all about myself, the ten days I'd spent in Scotland, how I'd met Andrew McInnes while staying with my cousin Fiona, how we'd fallen in love—like being struck by lightning it was, which probably accounted for my unstable mental state, prone to fall into a state of amnesia the first time a rucksack fell on me—how Andrew had to come back to London three days before me.

I even remembered the four-line verse that, in an impulsive moment, I'd whizzed off on

a postcard to the *Evening Dispatch*. I blushed.

Aunt Leonie looked Andrew up and down. She liked his looks. "The Ross McInneses or the Forfar McInneses?" she snapped. In five minutes she had his whole genealogy pegged out like a week's wash.

Charles and Richard melted tactfully away. "I'll call in tomorrow with the invoice," said Charles. "Covent Garden next week—I'll phone when I have the tickets," said Richard.

Jennifer and Don dropped in, radiant from *Ulysses*, hugged me, and collected the sleeping Walpole. Aunt Leonie declared that she was going to bed. Andrew said he must be off. I saw him to the door and he gave me a serious good night kiss, a very serious one. "You're different in London, Amanda," he said. "More forthright. In Scotland you seemed such a quiet, retiring kind of lass."

"To tell you the truth, Andrew darling," I said, "I still don't know *what* kind of girl I am. Time will have to show." But whatever kind, I thought to myself, I know whom I love. Amanda Jones is a girl of sense.

"Amanda," Aunt Leonie called sternly from the spare room, "it's time you were in bed."

Andrew quietly closed the front door after him.

"Just going, Aunt," I called. "There's one thing I must do first."

I dumped the coffee cups in the kitchen, pulled out my portable typewriter from its hiding place under the bed, slid in a sheet of paper, and began to type rapidly:

"The train was somewhere north of London . . ."

Close Up

1. (a) When Amanda returns to her apartment, why does she begin to feel sorry for herself? (b) Why is she pleased when she finds a note from A.?

2. When Aunt Leonie arrives and sees Amanda's apartment filled with people, she misinterprets the situation. (a) Why does she think Amanda is engaged to Richard Heppenstall? (b) Why is everyone surprised when Andrew walks in and says Amanda is engaged to him?

3. (a) According to Andrew, how is Amanda different in London? (b) Does Amanda agree with him? Why or why not?

Character

When you read, you learn about a character in several ways:
1. By noting what the character looks like.
2. By noting what others say about this character.
3. By noting the character's thoughts and feelings.
4. By noting the character's actions, and drawing conclusions about the character on the basis of those actions.

---

1. Because Amanda has amnesia, she learns about herself at the same time that you learn about her. (a) What does she learn about herself when she looks through her handbag? (b) What does she learn when she looks in the mirror?

2. (a) When she enters her apartment, why does she get "a very poor notion of Amanda Jones"? (b) What facet of her personality do the walls of her bathroom reveal to her?

3. (a) Upon meeting Charles Palliser, what does Amanda conclude about herself? (b) What does she learn about herself when she meets Richard Heppenstall?

4. When Amanda sees A., she regains her memory. What things does she instantly recall about herself?

5. (a) At the end of the story, why does she conclude that Amanda Jones is a "girl of sense"? (b) On the basis of what you have learned about Amanda, do you agree with her conclusion? Why or why not?

Activity

► **Composition.** Imagine you are a detective. Your assignment is to find out what X is really like. You go to X's apartment. On the basis of what you see there, what conclusions do you reach about X? Write a paragraph explaining your answer.

RELATIONSHIPS

Understanding Cause and Effect

When you read, you identify causes and effects. **The cause is what makes something happen. The effect is the result, or what happens.** For example, in this story, Amanda Jones loses her memory. Why does this happen? She loses her memory because a rucksack falls on her head.

▶ Answer each of the questions below in a complete sentence. Be sure that your answer contains the word *because*.

a. Why did Amanda Jones search through her handbag?

b. Why did Amanda Jones have postcards of Scottish lochs and a sprig of heather in her handbag?

c. Why did Amanda rush to get her flat cleaned up?

d. Why did Jennifer leave William with Amanda?

e. Why did William Walpole sneeze?

f. Why did Charles Palliser vacuum Amanda's apartment?

g. Why did Richard Bradfield Heppenstall come to Amanda's apartment?

h. Why did Amanda have enough money for a vacation in Scotland?

i. Why did Richard Bradfield Heppenstall know how to care for children?

j. Why did Amanda hesitate before buying the Whizzo cleaner?

WORD ATTACK

Choosing the Meaning That Fits the Context

Most words in English have more than one meaning. When you read, you must choose the meaning that fits the context. For example, the word *fault* means: (1) a mistake or error; (2) a fracture in the earth's crust; or (3) a defect in electrical wiring. Now look at the following sentence. "Amanda says that it was her own *fault* that the rucksack hit her on the head." Only the first meaning of *fault* fits this sentence. In fact, the sentence wouldn't make any sense if you chose any of the other meanings.

▶ Read each sentence below. Then choose the meaning that fits the context.

a. "There was a *ring* at the front door."
   (1) circle
   (2) sound of a bell
   (3) small, circular metal band worn on the finger

b. " . . . it was a tall, military *character* with a fair moustache carrying a large carton."
   (1) moral fiber
   (2) figure, letter, or symbol used in writing
   (3) unusual or odd person

c. "The bathroom revealed another facet of me: two of its walls were papered solid with a montage of rejection *slips*, large, small, and medium, carefully pasted together and covered with polythene."
   (1) piers or platforms used as landing places for ships
   (2) goofs or errors
   (3) small pieces of paper

d. "From that I judged I was a housewifely sort of girl, but this optimistic *notion* was soon dashed."
   (1) knickknack
   (2) idea, belief, or impression
   (3) plan or intention

e. Amanda wished to make a good *impression* on Aunt Leonie.
   (1) effect on the mind or feelings of
   (2) impersonation or imitation of
   (3) first coat of paint

Kotsatoah

N. Scott Momaday

In 1834 the artist George Catlin traveled among the Kiowas.

Catlin's portrait of Kotsatoah is the striking figure of a man, tall and lean, yet powerful and fully developed. He is lithe, and he knows beyond any doubt of his great strength and vigor. He stands perfectly at ease, the long drape of his robe flowing with the lines of his body. His left hand rests upon his shield and holds a bow and arrows. His head is set firmly, and there is a look of bemused and infinite tolerance in his eyes. He is said to have been nearly seven feet tall and able to run down and kill a buffalo on foot. I should like to have seen that man, as Catlin saw him, walking towards me, or away in the distance, perhaps, alone and against the sky.

Activity

▶ Find words or phrases in this selection that give you a vivid image of Kotsatoah. Then visit a museum and find a portrait that appeals to you. Write a paragraph describing the person you see in the portrait.

The Interlopers

Saki

"If only on this wild night, in this dark lone spot, he might come across Georg Znaeym, man to man, with none to witness—that was the wish that was uppermost in his thoughts."

In a forest of mixed growth somewhere on the eastern spurs of the Carpathians,[1] a man stood one winter night watching and listening, as though he waited for some beast of the woods to come within the range of his vision, and, later, of his rifle. But the game for whose presence he kept so keen an outlook was none that figured in the sportsman's calendar as lawful and proper for the chase; Ulrich von Gradwitz[2] patrolled the dark forest in quest of a human enemy.

The forest lands of Gradwitz were of wide extent and well stocked with game; the narrow strip of precipitous woodland that lay on its outskirt was not remarkable for the game it harbored or the shooting it afforded, but it was the most jealously guarded of all its owner's territorial possessions. A famous lawsuit, in the days of his grandfather, had wrested it from the illegal possession of a neighboring family of petty landowners; the dispossessed party had never acquiesced in the judgment of the Courts, and a long series of poaching affrays and similar scandals had embittered the relationships between the families for three generations. The neighbor feud had grown into a personal one since Ulrich had come to be head of his family; if there was a man in the world whom he detested and wished ill to it was Georg Znaeym,[3] the inheritor of the quarrel and the tireless game snatcher and raider of the disputed border-forest. The feud might, perhaps, have died down or been compromised if the personal ill will of the two men had not stood in the way; as boys they had thirsted for one another's blood, as men each prayed that misfortune might fall on the other, and this wind-scourged winter night Ulrich had banded together his foresters to watch the dark forest, not in quest of four-footed quarry, but to keep a lookout for the prowling thieves whom he suspected of being afoot from across the land boundary. The roebuck,[4] which usually kept in the sheltered hollows during a storm-wind, were running like driven things tonight, and there was movement and unrest among the creatures that were

---

1. Carpathians (kär-pā′thē-ənz) n.: A mountain range in Eastern Europe.
2. Ulrich (ül′rĭk) von (fən) Gradwitz (gräd′vĭts).
3. Georg (gā′ôrg) Znaeym (znä′ĭm).
4. roebuck (rō′bŭk′) n.: A male roe, which is a small Eurasian deer.

wont to sleep through the dark hours. Assuredly there was a disturbing element in the forest, and Ulrich could guess the quarter from whence it came.

He strayed away by himself from the watchers whom he had placed in ambush on the crest of the hill, and wandered far down the steep slopes amid the wild tangle of undergrowth, peering through the tree trunks and listening through the whistling and skirling[5] of the wind and the restless beating of the branches for sight or sound of the marauders. If only on this wild night, in this dark, lone spot, he might come across

---

5. skirling (skûrl′ĭng) n.: Shrill, piercing sound.

Georg Znaeym, man to man, with none to witness—that was the wish that was uppermost in his thoughts. And as he stepped round the trunk of a huge beech he came face to face with the man he sought.

The two enemies stood glaring at one another for a long silent moment. Each had a rifle in his hand, each had hate in his heart and murder uppermost in his mind. The chance had come to give full play to the passions of a lifetime. But a man who has been brought up under the code of a restraining civilization cannot easily nerve himself to shoot down his neighbor in cold blood and without word spoken, except for an offence against his hearth and honor. And before the moment of hesitation had given way to action a deed of Nature's own violence overwhelmed them both. A fierce shriek of the storm had been answered by a splitting crash over their heads, and ere they could leap aside a mass of falling beech tree had thundered down on them. Ulrich von Gradwitz found himself stretched on the ground, one arm numb beneath him and the other held almost as helplessly in a tight tangle of forked branches, while both legs were pinned beneath the fallen mass. His heavy shooting-boots had saved his feet from being crushed to pieces, but if his fractures were not as serious as they might have been, at least it was evident that he could not move from his present position till someone came to release him. The descending twigs had slashed the skin of his face, and he had to wink away some drops of blood from his eyelashes before he could take in a general view of the disaster. At his side, so near that under ordinary circumstances he could almost have touched him, lay Georg Znaeym, alive and struggling, but obviously as helplessly pinioned down as himself. All round them lay a thick-strewn wreckage of splintered branches and broken twigs.

Relief at being alive and exasperation at his captive plight brought a strange medley of pious thank-offerings and sharp curses to Ulrich's lips. Georg, who was nearly blinded with the blood which trickled across his eyes, stopped his struggling for a moment to listen, and then gave a short, snarling laugh.

"So you're not killed, as you ought to be, but you're caught, anyway," he cried; "caught fast. Ho, what a jest, Ulrich von Gradwitz snared in his stolen forest. There's real justice for you!"

And he laughed again, mockingly and savagely.

"I'm caught in my own forest-land," retorted Ulrich. "When my men come to release us, you will wish, perhaps, that you were in a better plight than caught poaching on a neighbor's land, shame on you."

Georg was silent for a moment; then he answered quietly:

"Are you sure that your men will find much to release? I have men, too, in the forest tonight, close behind me, and they will be here first and do the releasing. When they drag me out from under these branches it won't need much clumsiness on their part to roll this mass of trunk right over on the top of you. Your men will find you dead under a fallen beech tree. For form's sake I shall send my condolences to your family."

"It is a useful hint," said Ulrich fiercely. "My men had orders to follow in ten minutes' time, seven of which must have gone by already, and when they get me out— I will remember the hint. Only as you will have met your death poaching on my lands I don't think I can decently send any message of condolence to your family."

"Good," snarled Georg, "good. We fight this quarrel out to the death, you and I and our foresters, with no cursed interlopers to come between us. Death and damnation to you, Ulrich von Gradwitz."

"The same to you, Georg Znaeym, forest-thief, game-snatcher."

Both men spoke with the bitterness of possible defeat before them, for each knew that it might be long before his men would seek him out or find him; it was a bare matter of chance which party would arrive first on the scene.

Both had now given up the useless struggle to free themselves from the mass of wood that held them down; Ulrich limited his endeavors to an effort to bring his one partially free arm near enough to his outer coat-pocket to draw out his wine flask. Even when he had accomplished that operation it was long before he could manage the unscrewing of the stopper or get any of the liquid down his throat. But what a Heaven-sent draft it seemed! It was an open winter, and little snow had fallen as yet, hence the captives suffered less from the cold than might have been the case at that season of the year; nevertheless, the wine was warming and reviving to the wounded man, and he looked across with something like a throb of pity to where his enemy lay, just keeping the groans of pain and weariness from crossing his lips.

"Could you reach this flask if I threw it over to you?" asked Ulrich suddenly; "there is good wine in it, and one may as well be as comfortable as one can. Let us drink, even if tonight one of us dies."

"No, I can scarcely see anything; there is so much blood caked round my eyes," said Georg, "and in any case I don't drink wine with an enemy."

Ulrich was silent for a few minutes, and lay listening to the weary screeching of the wind. An idea was slowly forming and growing in his brain, an idea that gained strength every time that he looked across at the man who was fighting so grimly against pain and exhaustion. In the pain and languor that Ulrich himself was feeling the old fierce hatred seemed to be dying down.

"Neighbor," he said presently, "do as you please if your men come first. It was a fair compact. But as for me, I've changed my mind. If my men are the first to come you shall be the first to be helped, as though you were my guest. We have quarreled like devils all our lives over this stupid strip of forest, where the trees can't even stand upright in a breath of wind. Lying here tonight, thinking, I've come to think we've been rather fools; there are better things in life than getting the better of a boundary dispute. Neighbor, if you will help me to bury the old quarrel I—I will ask you to be my friend."

Georg Znaeym was silent for so long that Ulrich thought, perhaps, he had fainted with the pain of his injuries. Then he spoke slowly and in jerks.

"How the whole region would stare and gabble if we rode into the market square together. No one living can remember seeing a Znaeym and a von Gradwitz talking to one another in friendship. And what peace there would be among the forester folk if we ended our feud tonight. And if we choose to make peace among our people there is none other to interfere, no interlopers from outside. . . . You would come and keep the Sylvester night[6] beneath my roof, and I would come and feast on some high day at your castle. . . . I would never fire a shot on your land, save when you invited me as a guest; and you should come and shoot with me down in the marshes where the wildfowl are. In all the countryside there are none that could hinder if we willed to make peace. I never thought to have wanted to do other than hate you all my life, but I think I have changed my mind about things too, this last half-hour. And you offered me your wine flask. . . . Ulrich von Gradwitz, I will be your friend."

For a space both men were silent, turning over in their minds the wonderful changes that this dramatic reconciliation would bring about. In the cold, gloomy forest, with the wind tearing in fitful gusts through the naked branches and whistling round the tree trunks, they lay and waited for the help that would now bring release and succor to both parties. And each prayed a private prayer that his men might be the first to arrive, so

---

6. Sylvester (sĭl'vĕs'tər) night: New Year's Eve.

that he might be the first to show honorable
attention to the enemy that had become a
friend.

Presently, as the wind dropped for a moment, Ulrich broke silence.

"Let's shout for help," he said; "in this lull
our voices may carry a little way."

"They won't carry far through the trees
and undergrowth," said Georg, "but we can
try. Together, then."

The two raised their voices in a prolonged
hunting call.

"Together again," said Ulrich a few
minutes later, after listening in vain for an
answering halloo.

"I heard something that time, I think," said
Ulrich.

"I heard nothing but the pestilential
wind," said Georg hoarsely.

There was silence again for some minutes,
and then Ulrich gave a joyful cry.

"I can see figures coming through the
wood. They are following in the way I came
down the hillside."

Both men raised their voices in as loud a
shout as they could muster.

"They hear us! They've stopped. Now they
see us. They're running down the hill toward us," cried Ulrich.

"How many of them are there?" asked
Georg.

"I can't see distinctly," said Ulrich; "nine
or ten."

"Then they are yours," said Georg; "I had
only seven out with me."

"They are making all the speed they can,
brave lads," said Ulrich gladly.

"Are they your men?" asked Georg. "Are
they your men?" he repeated impatiently as
Ulrich did not answer.

"No," said Ulrich with a laugh, the idiotic
chattering laugh of a man unstrung with hideous fear.

"Who are they?" asked Georg quickly,
straining his eyes to see what the other
would gladly not have seen.

"*Wolves.*"

Close Up

1. The narrow strip of woodland is not very valuable. Why, then, does Ulrich von Gradwitz guard it as though it is his finest possession?

2. Ulrich and his enemy, Georg Znaeym, are armed and have murder in their hearts. (a) Why don't they shoot immediately when they come face to face? (b) What sudden event prevents them from killing one another?

3. Twice in the story, Georg refers to interlopers, or intruders. The first time, he means people who keep him and Ulrich from killing each other. (a) Find the second time. Whom does he mean? (b) Think about the ending of this story. Who are the final interlopers? Why?

4. In what way are Georg and Ulrich also interlopers?

Conflict

A conflict is a struggle between two opposing forces. Sometimes the conflict is between two people. For example, in this story, the conflict is between Ulrich von Gradwitz and Georg Znaeym. Conflict makes a story exciting. Trying to figure out who will win the conflict adds to the suspense.

1. The von Gradwitz family and the Znaeym family both claim the same strip of land. (a) When did the conflict over the land actually start? (b) Why is the conflict so intense between Ulrich and Georg?

2. Suspense builds as each trapped man waits for his foresters to arrive. (a) Initially, what treatment can each expect to receive if the other's foresters arrive first? (b) Later on, what treatment does each say the other can expect?

3. (a) Why does Ulrich von Gradwitz feel pity as he looks at his enemy? (b) Why does he decide to end the conflict?

4. After the two men pledge friendship, they unite and call for aid. (a) How is their call answered? (b) Why is this ironic, or contrary to what is expected?

Activities

1. **Composition.** Why would "Wolves" be or not be a good title for this story? Write a paragraph explaining your answer.

2. **Composition.** If this story had ended differently and Ulrich and Georg had been saved, would they really have become good friends? Write a paragraph explaining your answer.

RELATIONSHIPS

Understanding Comparison and Contrast

When you compare two things you show how they are alike. For example, when you compare Ulrich with Georg, you find out that they are both hunters.

When you contrast two things you show how they are different. For example, when you contrast Ulrich with Georg, you find out that Ulrich is the legal owner of the disputed land and that Georg is a poacher, or trespasser.

1. Read each statement below. Then decide whether each statement compares or contrasts the two characters.
   a. As boys, Ulrich and Georg hated each other.
   b. Ulrich felt pity for Georg and offered him wine, but Georg felt only hate and refused a drink from an enemy.
   c. Both men lay hurt under the fallen tree and were unable to free themselves.
   d. Georg and Ulrich agreed to settle their dispute and become friends.
   e. Ulrich could not see the wolves, but Georg saw them clearly and was afraid.

2. Choose two people you know well. Write three sentences showing how they are alike. Then write three sentences showing how they are different.

3. You can also compare and contrast the violence of Nature with the violence of the men on this night. (a) Find three words or phrases that describe the violence of Nature. (b) Find three words or phrases that describe the violence of the men. (c) Who proves to be more violent—Nature or the men? Why?

WORD ATTACK

Understanding Adverbs

Writers often use descriptive words to give you a good picture of what is happening. Adverbs are one type of descriptive words. **Adverbs modify verbs, adjectives, and other adverbs.** For example,

> She ran *quickly.* (modifies verb)
> He was a *very* good hunter. (modifies adjective)
> They waited *quite* patiently. (modifies adverb)

Many adverbs end with the suffix –*ly*. To find the meaning of an adverb ending in –*ly*, look up the adjective form in the dictionary. (This is the word without the –*ly* ending. For example, the adjective form of *jealously* is *jealous*.)

---

1. Use a dictionary to find the meaning of each *italicized* adverb.
   a. " . . . it was the most *jealously* guarded of all its owners territorial possessions."
   b. "*Assuredly,* there was a disturbing element in the forest, and Ulrich could guess the quarter from whence it came."
   c. "Ulrich limited his endeavors to an effort to bring his one *partially* free arm near enough to his outer coat-pocket to draw out his wine flask."
   d. "Only as you will have met your death poaching on my lands I don't think I can *decently* send any message of condolence to your family."
   e. "And he laughed again, *mockingly* and *savagely.*"
   f. "At his side, so near that under ordinary circumstances he could almost have touched him, lay Georg Znaeym, alive and struggling, but *obviously* as *helplessly* pinioned down as himself."

2. Copy each sentence below on a piece of paper. Add an adverb in each blank.
   a. He repeated his question _____.
   b. He stared _____ at his enemy.
   c. He refused the offer _____.
   d. He _____ saw that Georg was in pain.
   e. The wolves came _____.

Murphy's Law

Dan Halacy

According to Murphy's Law, if something can go wrong, it will.

Part One

"Paul Murphy?" the tall blond man asked, and Paul nodded as they shook hands. This was Harris Wheeler, the Texas Petroleum pilot he had been instructed to meet in Seattle. About forty, he looked like an airline pilot in his conservative blue suit, and Paul felt slightly uncomfortable in slacks and hiking boots.

"You ever hear of Murphy's Law?" Wheeler asked with a grin.

"Sure," Paul answered wearily. He was accustomed to the question. " 'If something can go wrong, it will.' I wrote a report on it once."

"Oh? I hope you're not superstitious about it," Harris said. "How come the snowshoes?" He pointed to Paul's luggage.

"I didn't think my skis would fit in the plane!" Paul joked.

Wheeler didn't seem to think it was very funny as he led the way toward the plane. "We don't *walk* the pipeline," he said. "We fly it!"

At nineteen, Paul Murphy was an even six feet, still tanned and fit from a hiking vacation in Colorado. He was looking forward to being in snow again and had brought his snowshoes to explore the Canadian country at the north end of their pipeline run. When Harris opened the baggage door in the side of the fuselage, Paul hefted his gear in and waited to see which seat the pilot would

motion him to. Harris jerked his thumb toward the left-hand side of the plane, and Paul grinned as he ran around to that side and climbed in. It was going to be a great adventure!

By mid-afternoon, Paul knew he could handle his new job. Harris was a capable pilot who flew by the book, and there really was a book, describing every step in the task of patrolling the 400 miles of steel pipe that carried natural gas from deep in Canada to the U.S. border. The Snowbird was a "STOL": a short take-off and landing type. It looked like a big model airplane with its huge wing and big wooden propeller, but it got the job done. Harris coached Paul in flying right over the pipeline at seventy miles an hour. If necessary, the Snowbird could slow to forty so they could count every weld and flange bolt.

"You expecting rugged excitement in the frozen North?" Harris asked him. "Forget the old bush-pilot adventure stories, Paul. Today we do it with turboprop engines and sophisticated electronics. It's all high-tech aviation, not snowshoe hiking."

"Gotcha," Paul said. But he felt a little sorry for the pilot. Maybe he was too old to think about adventure.

Everything went beautifully. They reached each checkpoint on time, and found no trouble with the pipeline. At a narrow canyon forty miles short of the northern end of the pipeline, Harris finally took over the controls.

"This is the section I told you about. It's too risky to fly through that windy canyon, so the guys at Camp Cavalcade check it with SnoCats. We'll take a detour to the right."

Paul nodded and reached for his map. They were well beyond the city of Prince George, and in a few minutes would start the long descent into the small airstrip at Cavalcade, the northernmost pipeline camp. Then suddenly, everything went crazy.

The crashing noise and the jarring impact jolted Paul from his map reading, and when he realized what had happened, he nearly panicked. He yelled in alarm but couldn't hear himself over the blast of wind through the smashed windshield of the plane. Alongside him, Harris Wheeler sprawled back in his seat, blood masking his face, and his left arm bent behind him at a crazy angle. And everywhere in the cabin were gray feathers that told Paul what had happened. The Snowbird had collided with a real bird!

He had grabbed the wheel instinctively, and the hammering vibration of the engine made him reach for the throttle. The engine died before he could shut if off—the violent shuddering had probably broken ignition wires or a fuel line. Now he could see the jagged stump of a motionless wooden propeller blade. The goose, or whatever it was, had

done a lot of damage: propeller, windshield, plus one pilot. With the engine dead, it was quieter, and Paul could think more clearly. But the blast of air had driven all the warmth from the small cabin.

The altimeter read 7,200 feet, but the forested slopes below ranged as high as 3,500. They had only about six or seven minutes in the air; the plane could glide about eight miles. Less, with half a windshield, he reminded himself.

"Harris! Can you hear me?" he shouted.

He tried to shake the injured man to consciousness but gave it up quickly. What he had to do first was get the plane down in as few pieces as possible. Then he could see about patching up the pilot. Eyeing the trees below, Paul felt his throat knotting.

Off to the left, he could make out the pipeline they had been following all day. In the white distance to the north, he tried to spot some sign of the maintenance camp at Cavalcade, but there was only the pipeline against a background of snow and forest. Paul gritted his teeth and leaned forward to see better.

With 4,000 feet showing on the altimeter, he finally spotted a clearing that looked landable. It wasn't great, or even good, but with some kind of luck, he could stall the Snowbird in and walk away from it. The slopes were steep, but the snow-covered clearing was about a hundred feet wide and several hundred feet long. That was enough if he used full flaps and lots of slip to slow the crippled Snowbird as much as possible.

"You've got to do it right the first time, Murphy," he breathed through clenched teeth. Thirty seconds later, he rocked the plane to a near-vertical bank to line up for his final approach into the tiny valley.

It was buried deeper between the steep walls of rock and trees than he had realized; this would be like trying to land in a bathtub! He worked the wheel back gently, slowing the plane as much as he dared. He held it firm at forty watching the ground rush past faster than it should and suddenly knowing the wind was behind him! He set himself for the impact and hoped Harris Wheeler's shoulder straps would hold.

They had nearly reached the stand of trees at the end of the tiny valley, and Paul yelled for the plane to stop. It did—with a wrenching jolt that jammed him against his shoulder straps so hard, he was afraid his head would snap off. Then, almost with a sighing sound, the wrecked plane settled deeper into the soft snow that was a lifesaver.

"You're down, Murphy!" Paul heard himself say in the sudden silence. "Maybe even in one piece. Be thankful for that."

Trying to stop the shaking in his arms and legs, as a delayed reaction to the accident set in, Paul turned his attention to the injured pilot. Harris was still out cold, and a dead weight as Paul worked to stop the bleeding face and head cuts. Grateful for the well-stocked first-aid kit, he finished the job with Harris looking like a mummy. The badly fractured arm he could do nothing about except to place it gently in Harris's lap, and fashion a crude sling with a length of cord. The fracture was in the forearm, and it looked bad enough to make Paul sick to his stomach. This wasn't the way he had expected his first flight for Texas Petroleum to end. It was hard not to believe in Murphy's Law!

Less than a week ago, Paul had been hired as a pilot trainee for the Canadian pipeline patrol, his first real flying job. He had soloed at sixteen and gotten his license that same year. Since then, he had piled up nearly 1,200 hours, and his ratings included instrument and multi-engine. He had planned someday to pilot a Lear Jet—and now he had crashed on his first flight into this wilderness, brought down by a nearsighted goose!

It shouldn't have surprised him. In school, he had somehow gotten involved in publishing a collection of "Murphy's Laws," because of his name, of course. The first of those laws was "If something can go wrong, it will." It *had*, all right, and Paul remem-

bered something called O'Toole's Comment on Murphy's Law: "Murphy was an optimist!"

Knowing they were in big trouble, Paul checked the emergency gear anxiously. There was food for a while, including the smashed goose, which he buried in the snow outside for safekeeping. There were two mummy-type down sleeping bags, some duck boots, gloves, and down jackets. He and Harris wouldn't freeze for a while, and they wouldn't starve. In fact, according to the Emergency Procedures Manual in his briefcase, there was no reason to worry: Just follow the procedures for "Emergency Landings in Arctic Terrain." In logical step-by-step order, it was all there and very comforting. Paul had skimmed the book before, but he had not realized how clearly it spelled out survival and rescue procedures.

"Step 1. Establish your exact location."

That was no particular problem, and Paul retrieved the map from the floor. As he marked an X where he estimated the crash location, Paul realized his bare hands were like chunks of ice. He put on the heavy gloves, forced open the cabin door, and floundered through deep snow until he reached the smashed wooden propeller. One blade was completely gone; the other had broken in the landing. He grabbed its tip and succeeded in breaking it off for use as a makeshift shovel. A few minutes later, he had mounded up snow high enough to fill the ragged hole in the windshield. That should keep the wind out, and snow was pretty good insulation. Breathing hard from the exertion, he climbed back into the cabin and managed to get the door shut. Wheeler was still unconscious, and Paul got on with the emergency procedures.

"Step 2. Make radio contact with nearest station."

That was harder than Step 1. Paul knew that Camp Cavalcade was nearby, but he knew just as well that radio waves didn't climb steep mountain walls and dive down

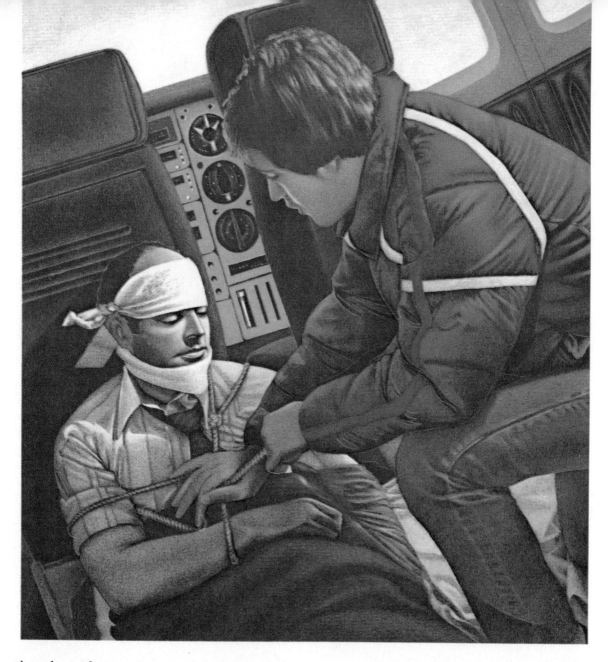

the other side to wrap around the antenna of a rescue-team receiver. He shrugged and reached for the switches on the radio panel. Miraculously, the pilot light winked on, and he could hear the hum of the speaker! Excitedly, he reached for the microphone.

"Cavalcade, this is Snowbird One with an emergency! Over."

He waited expectantly for thirty seconds, but there was no answer.

"Cavalcade, this is Snowbird One. We have crash-landed twenty miles south and need help. Come in, Cavalcade!"

Half an hour later, Paul was hoarse from calling, but there had been no response. He checked the whole dial and got only a few scratches of static. He fiddled with the squelch knob, tuning, volume control, and everything else. Then suddenly, he pressed the mike switch and groaned. There was no click on the receiver, as there should have been. For some reason, the radio was not transmitting and Paul carefully studied the microphone. There was a hairline crack in the plastic housing—somewhere inside, a tiny, triple-inspected, tightly sealed part, guaranteed for umpteen years, must have been damaged. With another groan, he replaced the mike on its clip.

Echoing his groan was a fainter one from the injured pilot, and Paul leaned eagerly toward him. Harris had opened his eyes but they were glazed with confusion and pain. "Ohhh," he moaned. "My arm—what are we doing here?"

"Take it easy," Paul told him. "A bird smashed the prop and windshield, and got you too. But we'll be OK."

"My arm feels like somebody's sawing on it!" Harris said shrilly.

In spite of the cold, there were beads of sweat on the pilot's face, and Paul could almost feel the pain himself. He tried to reassure the pilot, but all the encouragement in the world couldn't do much for the fractured arm. When Harris yelled again in agony, Paul knew he had to do something soon.

There was a packet of morphine ampules in the emergency pack, and Paul got one out. Harris managed to calm down and let Paul cut away part of his sleeve. The needle went in easily, and soon the pain left the pilot's face, and he settled back. A few minutes later, he shut his eyes and seemed to go to sleep. Paul sighed and slumped back himself.

"Step 3. Do not be alarmed if no answer is received to voice signals," the manual said. "The crash-locater beacon installed in your aircraft is automatically sending out an emergency signal which other aircraft will receive."

Oddly, Paul began to laugh as an old joke came to his mind. It was the one about the Army paratrooper recruit being told what to do: "When you jump, the static line will open your main chute. There's one chance in a million it won't open, but you still have an emergency chute. Pull the rip cord on it and you'll be OK. When you land, there'll be a truck waiting to pick you up!" The recruit bailed out and sure enough, his main chute failed to open. He pulled the emergency-chute rip cord, and that didn't open either. As he fell, he said in disgust, "I bet that blasted truck won't be there either!"

"Step 4. Should you have to leave the aircraft, take the emergency portable radio with you. It has a range of up to 100 miles in good condition and will permit you to contact help."

"Why didn't you say so?" Paul demanded, dropping the manual and searching for the portable radio. It was there, compact and light, with a built-in mike and switch. Slipping it into his jacket pocket, he climbed out of the cabin and moved away from the plane to try the radio.

"Cavalcade, this is Snowbird One. Emergency. Come in, please!" And finally, "Mayday, Mayday! This is TNG Pipeline Aircraft One, crash-landed south of Cavalcade. *Anybody* reading me, please come in!"

If anybody read him, they didn't come in, and at last, Paul quit in despair. He was using up steps in the emergency manual.

"Step 5. In the event that you are unable to contact help by radio, it may be necessary to use other signaling devices. There is an effective signal mirror in the emergency pack, with detailed instructions for using it."

The mirror was there all right, with a very fine set of instructions. There was only one problem: to use a signal mirror you had to have sun. And the sky above was a dull gray and promised to stay that way forever.

"Step 6. There is a flare pistol in the emergency pack, with instructions for its use. Use it to signal aircraft flying overhead, or a rescue party some distance away."

Step 7, the last step, was a real winner. It

said: "Be calm. Help may already be on the way. Stay with your aircraft!"

"Thanks," Paul said. "But I have a funny feeling it's like the paratroop truck that didn't show up."

Harris woke again at about 8:30 P.M. and managed to eat some of the flight lunch and drink some water. Then the pain got so bad, Paul had to give him morphine again. After that he sat silently in his seat, making himself eat and watching the black sky through his window. He kept hoping that he would see a star, but he never did. The last time he looked at his watch, it was 11:30; he finally slept in spite of the uncomfortable position.

The first thing he did in the morning was to find a wrench and take out the seat on his side. The seat looked strange sitting on the snow, but there was room now to lie on the floor.

Harris woke, still in pain. He couldn't eat or drink anything and was in agony from his broken arm.

"You've got to help me set it, Paul!" he pleaded as he stretched his body taut. His face was white and sweat-lined.

"I can give you another shot of morphine," Paul said, trying to sound calmer than he felt. "Look, somebody will hear the crash-locater signal before long and come for us. Maybe they're on their way now."

"Maybe," Harris said hoarsely. "Look, Paul, people have set fractures—you don't have to be a doctor. . . ."

"I don't know," Paul said, his heart sinking at the thought of jagged bone ends grinding on each other. "It might hurt even worse."

"It couldn't," Harris told him. "Let's try. I can help some. . . ."

They tried. Paul did his best, and he knew Harris must be doing all he could, too. But it wasn't enough, and all they did was start the arm bleeding again. In panic, Paul grabbed another morphine ampule and jabbed it into Harris's arm. As the pain subsided, Paul let out his breath in relief. There were two more of the ampules, but he remembered stories of patients getting hooked just this way. He managed to stop the bleeding, and used what bandage was left to make sure it wouldn't start again.

While the pilot slept, Paul got rid of the other seat. Now they could both sleep more comfortably. The whole thing was so unreal, Paul found himself shaking his head once in a while. Part of his brain kept telling him not to worry, that sooner or later, someone would catch the emergency radio signal and rescue them. But Murphy's Law was in the back of his mind, too, and he was afraid he *was* getting superstitious about it!

Their drinking water ran out in the afternoon, but there was plenty of snow. The thermometer read twenty-two degrees, but it wasn't too bad with warm clothes and the sleeping bags draped over them for blankets. The gray sky outside dropped lower than ever. Then suddenly, Paul's luck seemed to change. At first, he thought he imagined it, but the sound persisted, and at last he knew he was listening to an airplane engine! Heart pounding, he grabbed the flare pistol and a handful of shells, climbed from the cabin, and hurried away from the plane. He was grateful it had not snowed since they crashed; the red wings should be easily seen against snow. Well clear of the plane, he put in a shell and closed the chamber of the flare pistol. Then he tilted his head back to study the sky. There was only cloud cover to the horizon in every direction.

He had almost given up, blinking away tears that threatened to freeze before they could roll down his cheeks, when he saw it. The clouds must have been much higher than he had estimated, for there was the tiny black shape of an airplane moving slowly under the gray ceiling! Paul raised the pistol and pulled the trigger. The gun kicked gently in his stiff hand, and for a moment, he saw nothing and was afraid Murphy's Law had booby-trapped him again. Then a blob of red

blossomed high in the air above him. He yelled excitedly, positive the plane would see it.

Five minutes and three shells later, the plane disappeared. It had not changed course or descended from the altitude at which he first saw it. Discouraged, Paul stuffed the pistol into his jacket pocket and walked through the beaten-down snow to the plane. Harris was awake, and his face glowed with hope for a moment until Paul gave him the bad news. Later, Harris had to have another shot of morphine, and that left only one between him and the pain.

As darkness came, Paul was so discouraged it was hard to think constructively. He had tried his best to keep on top of the situation, but everything had failed. All the careful work of Texas Petroleum had been shot down. By Murphy's Law, he thought bitterly. "When things just can't possibly get worse, they do." Lying on the hard floor and staring up at the black night, all Paul could do was pray.

Part Two

Paul didn't know what woke him next morning: the faint light outside, the cold of the cramped cabin, or the idea that was strong in his mind when his eyes came open. He was discouraged, weary, and cold. But the idea warmed him and made him drag

himself outside. Harris had talked about making a fire to warm their soup, and Paul knew how he could catch the attention of the next plane that flew over.

With the wrenches and screwdriver from the tool kit, he removed the side panel from the engine covering. After about an hour's work he had removed the oil tank from its mounting. With a pair of pliers he pinched the outlet line together so the oil wouldn't leak out the bottom. The tank was about three-fourths full and would burn a long time. Paul was grinning when he climbed back into the cabin to tell Harris his plan.

Paul listened impatiently for hours before he heard the welcome sound of a plane again. The noise was just like what he heard the day before, probably a daily flight by a bush pilot flying between a lumber camp and the river fifty miles west. Just so it was a plane, and just so the plane saw the signal fire he was about to light!

The match flame flickered around the rag he had stuffed into the still air. Paul yelled, as if the pilot overhead could hear him. "Help, friend! This is a distress signal and I know you can see us. Come on down!" It was then he felt the first snowflake on his cheek and tilted his head to see the snow flurry starting. Murphy's Law had shot him down again; there was no way the pilot of the plane would see his tiny smoke signal through the snowfall. He let it burn though, until the plane disappeared and until he couldn't hear the whine of its engine.

Before they went on to sleep, Paul told Harris what he thought had to be done. Every step of the rescue plan had failed so far. That truck just wasn't going to be there and it was up to Paul to find another solution. There seemed to be only one.

"I'll start walking out in the morning," he told the pilot. "We can't wait any longer."

"Don't be crazy!" Harris protested. His face was flushed from the fever he had now. One of his wounds must be infected.

"We can't just sit here," Paul told Harris.

"We've got to just sit here," the pilot shot back.

"Paul, my head is hot as fire and the pain is worse than ever. They'll get here soon, and . . ."

"I've got to get help for you," Paul told him, putting a hand on his shoulder.

"Help will come," Harris insisted. "You know it's best not to leave the plane. The crash-locater beacon will bring them. Tomorrow sure!"

"I'll sleep on it," Paul finally agreed. It was tempting to stay because he had doubts about his ability to walk twenty miles through deep snow in such rough country. He could take the magnetic compass out of the plane, but even with that it would be rough going. Out in the open, the air would be freezing cold and if a snowstorm caught him he could be buried in a drift and never found. Maybe in the process he would be dooming Harris, too, because the guy would be out of his head with delirium by tomorrow. Paul didn't seem to sleep at all for worrying about it. But at last he had made up his mind.

It was barely light when he tossed the snowshoes out of the cabin and got to work removing the compass. The job was harder than he expected, and he woke Harris by trying to break the mounting bracket loose from the panel. When he did get it loose, it slipped from him, hit a rudder pedal, and smashed!

"Trust the beacon—" Harris said weakly. "They'll come!" But Paul shook his head.

"I can't take the chance," he said. "If help does come, we don't lose anything. If I walk out we've got two chances. You understand that, Harris."

"OK," the pilot said. "But give me that last shot of pain-killer." A few minutes later he relaxed and leaned back in the seat.

"You wait right here," Paul said, "and before you know it you'll be in a helicopter and not worried about a thing!" He tucked one sleeping bag around Harris and made him as comfortable as possible. Then he tied the other on his back, stuffed emergency rations in each pocket of his jacket, hung the portable radio around his neck, and climbed out of the cabin.

He stumbled over the oil tank he had tried to use as a signal beacon and kicked it out of the way. All those rescue steps, he thought angrily. Murphy's Law had taken care of each one as it came up, and now he was right down to basics with no help from the technology that had gotten them into this trouble! He was on his own now, one guy against miles of mountains buried under a freezing blanket of snow. Just his muscles and the determination that he would somehow find his way through the miles of wilderness without the compass that lay useless, its alcohol spilled on the floor.

Cavalcade Camp was north of them, and the plane was heading north when it settled into the deep snow. Paul studied the horizon for a landmark. He spotted something at last, a ragged notch in the tree line would have to do.

Maybe Harris was right; maybe he should stay and wait for the two of them to be rescued. It was a tempting thought as cold burrowed through his jacket and pants. But it was a luxury he couldn't risk with Harris in the condition he was. Fastening on the snowshoes, Paul waved and took off.

He had estimated the distant notch on the ridge was about two miles way, and that he might reach it within an hour and a half. But when that time passed on his watch, Paul knew he hadn't covered half the distance. Out of practice with the snowshoes, he was already tired and his legs were like lead weights as he plodded awkwardly through the snow. It was worse when he finally got to the trees, because he could no longer see his landmark.

As long as he could, he kept the plane in sight back through the trees and tried his best to keep going north. He could remember winter hikes during his Scouting days; it was possible to go in a big circle and come back to where you had started hours earlier. A dozen times he remembered the warmth of the plane, and Harris's warning. The Emergency Manual had said the same thing. If it had just been himself he might have stayed; sooner or later a rescue plane had to pick up the steady signal from the crash-locater beacon.

Glumly he remembered more of Murphy: "No good deed goes unpunished!"

He never did find the notch he had set out for, but late in the afternoon he finally topped the long upslope that formed one of the walls of the tiny valley they had landed in. Far in the distance of white rolling wasteland he could see his goal! Cavalcade showed as a rectangular black shape against white snow. There were the buildings, the landing strip, and the pipeline snaking alongside. But it was so far away.

It was long past noon as he started down the slope. Instead of two miles an hour, he was averaging much less than a mile. If his pace stayed the same he would be twenty-four hours reaching the camp. There was no possibility of going halfway and stopping to sleep; chances were he would never wake up after a night in this weather. He had been crazy to think he could walk such a distance over this terrain!

For a few minutes he desperately considered going back. He could follow his own trail and reach the safety of the plane before dark. But he shook his head and set his jaw. He had to go on.

An hour later, the gray sky had sunk lower and lower, and big flakes of snow were falling from it. He tried picking up his pace in the wild hope that he could reach Cavalcade before dark. In fifteen minutes his sides hurt as if somebody were beating him in the ribs. Panting for breath, he slowed the pace.

Every hundred yards or so he made himself look back and check landmarks as best he could in the fading visibility. Suppose he was moving in a big curve by now, and after hours of killing walking came onto his own tracks in the snow!

It was dark when he reached the last decent landmark along the way. He had probably come about eight miles of the twenty. There were still twelve miles of agony ahead before he would reach help. Twelve miles meant hiking on through the night. He had been crazy to leave the plane. But there was no turning back now. He could never find the plane because his tracks would be filled in.

He was breathing a little better with the slower pace. His legs and back ached so much that he felt paralyzed and was barely conscious of his feet hitting the ground with each stride. But every stride cut the distance a couple of feet. And each 2,640 strides would take away a mile—*if* he was heading toward Cavalcade!

He tried to remember which way you would circle on a long hike. It seemed that the heart had something to do with it. Since the heart was on the left side, would it swing him gradually in that direction? If he stopped every hundred paces or so and changed course very slightly to the right, would that help? But if he was naturally circling to the *right*, that would make it worse!

Occasionally he stopped and scooped a little snow onto his tongue. He let it melt before swallowing it, freezing his tongue and not his insides. When he got hungry he tackled one of the food bars. That helped. Snow was still filtering down from dark sky. He could barely see anything, let alone landmarks. He couldn't see his watch in the dark, and even if he could, it wouldn't help much.

Instead, he tried to count his steps so that every 2,640 he could call it another mile. But he kept losing count with the hundreds and finally gave it up.

He was lightheaded now. There was no feeling anywhere except in his fingers, which he kept flexing to keep them a little warmer. Suddenly he realized he was singing aloud, although the words didn't make any sense and there didn't seem to be a recognizable tune. Was he starting to hallucinate because of exhaustion and lack of sleep?

He wondered if it was midnight yet, and how far he had come. Was he heading for Cavalcade, or where?

Without remembering when he had stopped, he suddenly realized he was leaning against a tree and trying to rest. He planned to start walking again as soon as the music started, so he could keep time with it. How did it go? Left foot on the beat of the music? That was the way a marching band did it. But he didn't seem able to sing anymore, and there was no other sound except his breathing and an occasional rustle as snow dropped from the tree he was leaning against.

He had hit rock bottom and knew it. The great adventure had turned into a nightmare that could end in catastrophe—for him and for the injured pilot he was trying to save. And then, from the depths of his weariness and fear, his own contribution to the report on Murphy came faintly to him:

"You can't fall off the floor!" The only way to go now was up, and somehow Paul managed a faint grin.

He must have dozed briefly, and when he opened his eyes he was sure he was dreaming. Instead of black sky, he could see pinpoints of light, just like stars. More hallucinations, he was sure, but the stars were shaped just like the Big Dipper! Shaking his head, he forced himself wide awake and realized that he *was* looking at the Big Dipper. Part of the sky had cleared and was studded with bright stars. All he had to do was to make a line extending from the two end stars of the Dipper about five times that length, and there would be the North Star! Feeling strangely warm inside, he pushed away from the tree and again moved toward the north.

The night passed like a monotonous dream as he kept putting one snowshoe in front of the other. But he managed, and when the stars faded and the sky changed from black to gray and finally a bluish white he was still on his feet. He stopped at last, and turned to see the edge of the cold sun break the southeastern horizon. His grin hurt cracked lips and he turned his eyes north again and looked for some sign of Camp Cavalcade. The tears almost came when he saw the low buildings several miles ahead and slightly left. He had made it!

An hour later he was within a quarter mile of the nearest building at the camp. Watching a curl of smoke, he wondered if there was bacon and eggs at the bottom of it, or if cooking was done in a microwave in this high-technology operation. Mechanically he kept lifting his frozen legs and slapping the snowshoes down on the snow. He wondered how it would feel to lie down and rest and then he heard a familiar chop-chopping noise. A helicopter was lifting from behind a building.

Excitement made him yell, and then panic seized him and made him even colder than he had been all night. Suppose the chopper was going somewhere else than to look for the missing Snowbird? He began to run awkwardly, yelling every few steps and waving his arms so wildly he staggered and fell.

As he watched the helicopter lifting higher into the clear air, he suddenly remembered the flare pistol in his jacket pocket. In seconds he had loaded a shell in the chamber and lifted the pistol to aim it right at the noisy craft. He pulled the trigger and a red blob mushroomed right in front of the chopper.

Thirty seconds later, Paul was explaining to an angry pilot that he wasn't an oil-line saboteur but copilot of the downed Snowbird. As understanding dawned on the chopper crew, their looks changed from anger to concern. They helped him into the craft. Dead with weariness, Paul watched the ground starting to slant away under them. He guided them toward the wrecked Snowbird.

In the half hour it took to reach the tiny valley and drop down for a landing, Paul learned that Murphy's Law had been working well at Cavalcade, too. There had been a

fire at one of the oil wells north of the camp and the chopper crew had spent two days up there helping. They had not known until they returned to Cavalcade that the Snowbird was missing, and then had no idea where it might be.

"Harris was probably right," Paul admitted wearily. "You'll pick up our crash-locater beacon signal in a minute. I should have stayed with the plane."

But they *didn't* pick up the signal in a minute. Or five minutes. All the way to the wrecked Snowbird the helicopter pilot monitored the radio carefully, but there was no sound at all!

Murphy had made a pretty good week of it, Paul thought, as the chopper crew looked at him as they would at somebody saved by a miracle. If he hadn't walked out, the Snowbird and Harris might never have been found. There was a medic aboard, and the chopper crew set Harris's arm right away. Then they lashed him to the stretcher beneath the chopper.

Paul spent three days at the camp at Cavalcade. Real food tasted great and he gained back the few pounds he had lost on emergency rations. Harris mended quickly with the broken arm set and the infection taken care

of. Even the battered Snowbird had been airlifted in by helicopter and would soon be flying again, with Paul at the controls too.

He had become something of a hero around Cavalcade. The president of Texas Petroleum had telephoned personally to thank him for his "courageous action." Paul would be flying back to Seattle on the return flight. Now it was time to drop by the dispensary to say goodbye to Harris, who would be recuperating for a week or so.

"Hi, Paul," the blond pilot said, holding out his hand in greeting. He was sitting up in bed and looked fine. "Don't forget your snowshoes!"

"I won't," Paul promised.

"Thanks for everything," Harris told him. "I'll fly with you anytime. And I've got another Murphy's Law for you before you go."

"No thanks," Paul protested, holding up his hands. "I've already heard them all."

"Not this one," Harris insisted. "Here it is: Leave it to Murphy—Paul Murphy, that is!" He waved cheerfully and Paul waved back and grinned.

"Get well, Harris," he said. "We've got a lot of flying to do yet!"

Close Up

1. Paul Murphy believes that patrolling the pipeline is "going to be a great adventure." What enroute event makes his prediction truer than he expected?

2. According to the Emergency Procedures Manual, Paul has no reason to worry. (a) What seven steps does it list for survival? (b) What goes wrong when Paul tries Steps 2, 4, 5, and 6?

3. Paul has two alternatives: He can wait in the plane and trust that the emergency beacon will bring help or he can risk walking twenty miles to Cavalcade. Why does he decide to walk?

4. When Paul reaches Cavalcade, he finds that Murphy's Law has been working there too. (a) Why didn't the crew discover that the Snowbird was missing until two days after the crash? (b) What does Paul learn on board the helicopter that shows he made the right decision when he left the Snowbird?

5. Paul makes his own contribution to Murphy's Law. It is, "You can't fall off the floor." (a) Do you think this contribution shows that Paul is basically optimistic or pessimistic? Why? (A person who is optimistic tends to take a hopeful view of a situation; a person who is pessimistic tends to take a hopeless view.) (b) Find evidence to support your judgment.

Conflict

Many stories center on a conflict, or a struggle between two opposing forces. In some stories, the conflict takes the form of a person against nature. For example, in "Murphy's Law," Paul struggles for survival against the weather and the harsh terrain.

1. Paul's conflict with nature begins when his plane collides with the goose. How does the harsh terrain complicate his landing?

2. Find two points in the story where the weather blocks Paul's attempts to signal for help.

3. After the rescue steps fail, Paul realizes that he is "on his own now, one guy against miles of mountains buried under a freezing blanket of snow." (a) What two things must he rely on in order to survive outdoors? (b) Which of these two things do you think is more important? Why?

4. Wherever possible, Paul uses nature to his advantage. For example, he uses the stars in the sky as a natural compass. (a) How does he use the snow to his advantage? (b) Why do you think Paul wins his conflict over nature?

RELATIONSHIPS

Identifying Combined Relationship Patterns

Four relationship patterns you encounter frequently when you read are:

1. Cause and Effect (what happens and why it happens)
2. Comparison and Contrast (how things are alike and how they are different)
3. Time Order (how events are connected in time)
4. Spatial Order (how things are arranged in space)

When you read some paragraphs, you find two or more relationship patterns at work. For example, in the following paragraph, you find ideas and events connected by cause and effect and spatial order. You learn (1) why the plane crashed, and (2) where Paul is in relation to Harris.

> "The crashing noise and the jarring impact jolted Paul from his map reading, and when he realized what had happened, he nearly panicked. He yelled in alarm but couldn't hear himself over the blast of wind through the smashed windshield of the plane. Alongside him, Harris Wheeler sprawled back in his seat, blood masking his face, and his left arm bent behind him at a crazy angle. And everywhere in the cabin were gray feathers that told Paul what had happened. The Snowbird had collided with a real bird!"

▶ Read each paragraph below. Then answer the questions that follow each paragraph.

a. "By mid-afternoon, Paul knew he could handle his new job. Harris was a capable pilot who flew by the book, and there really was a book, describing every step in the task of patrolling the 400 miles of steel pipe that carried natural gas from deep in Canada to the U.S. border. The Snowbird was a 'STOL': a short take-off and landing type. It looked like a big model airplane with its huge wing and big wooden propeller, but it got the job done. Harris coached Paul in flying right over the pipeline at seventy miles an hour. If necessary, the Snowbird could slow to forty so they could count every weld and flange bolt."

(1) Find one instance of time order in this paragraph.
(2) Find one instance of spatial order.
(3) Find one instance of cause and effect.
(4) Find one instance of comparison and contrast.

b. "It was dark when he reached the last decent landmark along the way. He had probably come about eight miles of the twenty. There were still twelve miles of agony ahead before he would reach help. Twelve miles meant hiking on through the night. He had been crazy to leave the plane. But there was no turning back now. He could never find the plane because his tracks would be filled in."

(1) Find one instance of time order in this paragraph.
(2) Find one instance of spatial order.
(3) Find one instance of cause and effect.

WORD ATTACK

Understanding Figurative Language

Figurative language consists of words that work together to form a new meaning. The individual words are not used with their usual dictionary definitions. For example, when you read, "*Dead with weariness*, Paul watched the ground starting to slant away under them," you don't actually think that Paul is dead. The words *dead with weariness* are simply a colorful and forceful way of saying that Paul is very tired. When you read, "Then a *blob of red blossomed* high in the air above him," you know that the blob of red didn't actually form flowers. The word *blossomed* simply gives you a good picture of the way the blob looked.

▶ In each sentence below, the words used figuratively, or without their usual dictionary meaning, are printed in *italics*. Write the meaning of each of these groups of words.

  a. " 'I don't know,' Paul said, *his heart sinking* at the thought of jagged bone ends grinding on each other."
  b. "Murphy's Law had *shot him down* again. . . ."
  c. "He had *hit rock bottom*, and knew it."
  d. "He was on his own now, one guy against *miles of mountains buried under a freezing blanket of snow*."

dandelions

Deborah Austin

under cover of night and rain
the troops took over.
waking to total war in beleaguered houses
over breakfast we faced the batteries
5 marshalled by wall and stone, deployed
with a master strategy no one had suspected
and now all
firing

pow
10 all day, all yesterday
and all today
the barrage continued
deafening sight.
reeling now, eyes ringing from noise, from walking
15 gingerly over the mined lawns
exploded at every second
rocked back by the starshellfire
concussion of gold on green
bringing battle-fatigue

20   pow by lionface firefur pow by
      goldburst shellshock pow by
      whoosh splat splinteryellow   pow by
      pow by pow
      tomorrow smoke drifts up
25   from the wrecked battalions,
      all the ammunition, firegold fury, gone.
      smoke
      drifts
      thistle-blown
30   over the war-zone, only

      here and there, in the shade by the
      peartree
      pow   in the crack by the
      curbstone   pow   and back of the
35   ashcan, lonely
      guerrilla snipers, hoarding
      their fire shrewdly
      never

      pow

40   surrender

Close Up

1. How does this poem show a conflict between people and nature?

2. (a) Who finally wins this confilict? (b) Who are the "guerrilla snipers"?

3. *Personification* is giving human qualities to inanimate objects. In this poem, what human qualities do the dandelions have?

My Delicate Heart Condition

Toni Cade Bambara

There were "a million ways to tempt you, to unsettle your stomach, and make you lose the battle to the Fly family."

My cousin Joanne has not been allowed to hang out with me for some time because she went and told Aunt Hazel that I scare her to death whenever she sleeps over at our house or I spend the weekend at hers. The truth is I sometimes like to tell stories about bloodthirsty vampires or ugly monsters that lurk in clothes closets or giant beetles that eat their way through the shower curtain, like I used to do at camp to entertain the kids in my bunk. But Joanne always cries and that makes the stories even weirder, like background music her crying. And too—I'm not going to lie about it—I get spookier on purpose until all the little crybabies are stuffing themselves under their pillows and throwing their sneakers at me and making such a racket that Mary the counselor has to come in and shine her flashlight around the bunkhouse. I play like I'm asleep. The rest of them are too busy blubbering and finding their way out

from under the blankets to tell Mary that it's me. Besides, once they get a load of her standing against the moonlight in that long white robe of hers looking like a ghost, they just start up again and pretty soon the whole camp is awake. Anyway, that's what I do for fun. So Joanne hasn't been around. And this year I'll have to go to the circus by myself and to camp without her. My mother said on the phone to Aunt Hazel—"Good, keep Jo over there and maybe Harriet'll behave herself if she's got no one to show off to." For all the years my mother's known me, she still doesn't understand that my behaving has got nothing to do with who I hang out with. A private thing between me and me or maybe between me and the Fly family since they were the ones that first got me to sit through monster movies and withstand all the terror I could take.

For four summers now, me and the Fly

family have had this thing going. A battle of nerves, you might say. Each year they raise the rope closer and closer to the very top of the tent—I hear they're going to perform outdoors this year and be even higher—and they stretch the rope further across the rings where the clowns and the pony riders perform. Each year they get bolder and more daring with their rope dancing and the swinging by the legs and flinging themselves into empty space making everyone throw up their hands and gasp for air until Mr. Fly at the very last possible second swings out on his bar to catch them up by the tips of their heels. Everyone just dies and clutches at their hearts. Everybody but me. I sit there calmly. I've trained myself. Joanne used to die and duck her head under the benches and stay there till it was all over.

Last summer they really got bold. On the final performance just before the fair closed, and some revival-type tent show comes in and all the kids go off to camp, the Fly family performed without a net. I figured they'd be up to something so I made sure my stomach was like steel. I did ten push-ups before breakfast, twenty sit-ups before lunch, skipped dinner altogether. My brother Teddy kidded me all day—"Harriet's trying out for the Olympics." I passed up the icie man on the corner and the pizza and sausage stand by the schoolyard and the cotton candy and jelly-apple lady and the pickle and penny-candy boy, in fact I passed up all the stands that lead from the street down the little roadway to the fair grounds that used to be a swamp when we first moved from Baltimore to Jamaica, Long Island. It wasn't easy, I'm not going to lie, but I was taking no chances. Between the balloon man and the wheel of fortune was the usual clump of ladies from church who came night after night to try to win the giant punch bowl set on the top shelf above the wheel, but had to settle night after night for a jar of gumdrops or salt-and-pepper shakers or some other little thing from the bottom shelf. And from the wheel of

fortune to the tent was at least a million stands selling B.B. bats and jawbreakers and gingerbread and sweet potato pie and frozen custard and—like I said it wasn't easy. A million ways to tempt you, to unsettle your stomach, and make you lose the battle to the Fly family.

I sat there almost enjoying the silly clowns who came tumbling out of a steamer trunk no bigger than the one we have in the basement where my mother keeps my old report cards and photographs and letters and things. And I almost enjoyed the fire-eater and the knife-thrower, but I was so close up I could see how there wasn't any real thrill. I almost enjoyed the fat-leg girls who rode the ponies two at a time and standing up, but their costumes weren't very pretty—just an ordinary polo shirt like you get if you run in the PAL meets and short skirts you can wear on either side like the big girls wear at the roller rink. And I almost enjoyed the jugglers except that my Uncle Bubba can juggle the dinner plates better any day of the week so long as Aunt Hazel isn't there to stop him. I was impatient and started yawning. Finally all the clowns hitched up their baggy pants and tumbled over each other out of the ring and into the dark, the jugglers caught all the things that were up in the air and yawning just like me went off to the side. The pony girls brought their horses to a sudden stop that raised a lot of dust, then jumped down into the dirt and bowed. Then the ringmaster stepped into the circle of light and tipped his hat which was a little raggedy from where I was sitting and said—"And now, Ladieeez and Gentlemen, what you've alll been waiting forrr, the Main aTTRACtion, the FLY FAMILEEE." And everyone jumped up to shout like crazy as they came running out on their toes to stand in the light and then climb the ropes. I took a deep breath and folded my arms over my chest and a kid next to me went into hiding, acting like she was going to tie her shoelaces.

There used to be four of them—the father,

a big guy with a bald head and bushy mustache and shoulders and arms like King Kong; a tall lanky mother whom you'd never guess could even climb into a high chair or catch anything heavier than a Ping-Pong ball to look at her; the oldest son who looked like his father except he had hair on his head but none on his face and a big face it was, so that no matter how high up he got you could always tell whether he was smiling or frowning or counting; the younger boy about thirteen, maybe, had a vacant stare like he was a million miles away feeding his turtles or something, anything but walking along a tightrope or flying through the air with his family. I had always liked to watch him

because he was as cool as I was. But last summer the little girl got into the act. My grandmother says she's probably a midget cause no self-respecting mother would allow her child to be up there acting like a bird. "Just a baby," she'd say, "Can't be more than six years old. Should be home in bed. Must be a midget." My grandfather would give me a look when she started in and we'd smile at her together.

They almost got to me that last performance, dodging around with new routines and two at a time so that you didn't know which one Mr. Fly was going to save at the last minute. But he'd fly out and catch the little boy and swing over to the opposite stand where the big boy was flying out to catch them both by the wrists and the poor woman would be left kind of dangling there, suspended, then she'd do this double flip which would kill off everyone in the tent except me, of course, and swing out on the very bar she was on in the first place. And then they'd mess around two or three flying at once just to confuse you until the big drum roll started and out steps the little girl in a party dress and huge blindfold wrapped around her little head and a pink umbrella like they sell down in Chinatown. And I almost—I won't lie about it—I almost let my heart thump me off the bench. I almost thought I too had to tie my shoelaces. But I sat there. Stubborn. And the kid starts bouncing up and down on the rope like she was about to take off and tear through the canvas roof. Then out swings her little brother and before you know it, Fly Jr. like a great eagle with his arms flapping grabs up the kid, her eyeband in his teeth and swoops her off to the bar that's already got Mrs. Mr. and Big Bro on it and surely there's no room for him. And everyone's standing on their feet clutching at their faces. Everyone but me. Cause I know from the getgo that Mr. and Mrs. are going to leave the bar to give Jr. room and fly over to the other side. Which is exactly what they do. The lady in front of me, Mrs. Perez, who does all the sewing in our neighborhood, gets up and starts shaking her hands like ladies do to get the fingernail polish dry and she says to me with her eyes jammed shut "I must go finish the wedding gowns. Tell me later who died." And she scoots through the aisle, falling all over everybody with her eyes still shut and never looks up. And Mrs. Caine taps me on the back and leans over and says, "Some people just can't take it." And I smile at her and at her twins who're sitting there with their mouths open. I fold my arms over my chest and just dare the Fly family to do their very worst.

The minute I got to camp, I ran up to the main house where all the counselors gather to say hello to the parents and talk with the directors. I had to tell Mary the latest doings with the Fly family. But she put a finger to her mouth like she sometimes does to shush me. "Let's not have any scary stuff this summer, Harriet," she said, looking over my shoulder at a new kid. This new kid, Willie, was from my old neighborhood in Baltimore so we got friendly right off. Then he told me that he had a romantic heart so I quite naturally took him under my wing and decided not to give him a heart attack with any ghost tales. Mary said he meant "rheumatic" heart,[1] but I don't see any difference. So I told Mary to move him out of George's tent and give him a nicer counselor who'd respect his romantic heart. George used to be my play boyfriend when I first came to camp as a little kid and didn't know any better. But he's not a nice person. He makes up funny nicknames for people which aren't funny at all. Like calling Eddie Michaels the Watermelon Kid or David Farmer Charcoal Plenty which I really do not appreciate and especially from a counselor. And once he asked Joanne, who was the table monitor, to go fetch a pail of milk from the kitchen. And the minute she got up, he started hatching a plot, trying to get the kids to hide her peanut butter sandwich and put spiders in her soup. I had to remind everyone at the table that Joanne was my first cousin by blood, and I would be forced to waste the first bum that laid a hand on her plate. And ole George says, "Oh don't be a dumbhead, Harriet. Jo's so stupid she won't even notice." And I told him right then and there that I was not his play girlfriend anymore and would rather marry the wolfman than grow up and be his wife. And just in case he didn't get the message, that night around campfire when we were all playing Little Sally Walker sittin' in a saucer and it

---

1. rheumatic (roo-măt'ĭk) heart: A heart permanently damaged by rheumatic fever, an infectious children's disease.

was my turn to shake it to the east and to shake it to the west and to shake it to the very one that I loved the best—I shook straight for Mr. Nelson the lifeguard, who was not only the ugliest person in camp but the arch enemy of ole George.

And that very first day of camp last summer when Willie came running up to me to get in line for lunch, here comes George talking some simple stuff about "What a beautiful head you have, Willie. A long, smooth, streamlined head. A sure sign of superior gifts. Definitely genius proportions." And poor Willie went for it, grinning and carrying on and touching his head, which if you want to know the truth is a bullet head and that's all there is to it. And he's turning to me every which way, like he's modeling his head in a fashion show. And the minute his back is turned, ole George makes a face about Willie's head and all the kids in the line bust out laughing. So I had to beat up a few right then and there and finish off the rest later in the shower for being so stupid, laughing at a kid with a romantic heart.

One night in the last week of August when the big campfire party is held, it was very dark and the moon was all smoky, and I just couldn't help myself and started in with a story about the great caterpillar who was going to prowl through the tents and nibble off everybody's toes. And Willie started this whimpering in the back of his throat so I had to switch the story real quick to something cheerful. But before I could do that, ole George picked up my story and added a wicked witch who put spells on city kids who come to camp, and a hunchback dwarf that chopped up tents and bunk beds, and a one-eyed phantom giant who gobbled up the hearts of underprivileged kids. And every

time he got to the part where the phantom ripped out a heart, poor Willie would get louder and louder until finally he started rolling around in the grass and screaming and all the kids went crazy and scattered behind the rocks almost kicking the fire completely out as they dashed off into the darkness yelling bloody murder. And the counselors could hardly round us all up—me, too, I'm not going to lie about it. Their little circles of flashlight bobbing in and out of the bushes along the patches of pine, bumping into each other as they scrambled for us kids. And poor Willie rolling around something awful, so they took him to the infirmary.

I was sneaking some gingersnaps in to him later that night when I heard Mary and another senior counselor fussing at ole George in the hallway.

"You've been picking on that kid ever since he got here, George. But tonight was the limit——"

"I wasn't picking on him, I was just trying to tell a story——"

"All that talk about hearts, gobblin' up hearts, and underpriv——"

"Yeh, you were directing it all at the little kid. You should be——"

"I wasn't talking about him. They're all underprivileged kids, after all. I mean all the kids are underprivileged."

I huddled back into the shadows and almost banged into Willie's iron bed. I was hoping he'd open his eyes and wink at me and tell me he was just fooling. That it wasn't so bad to have an underprivileged heart. But he just slept. "I'm an underprivileged kid too," I thought to myself. I knew it was a special camp, but I'd never realized. No wonder Aunt Hazel screamed so about my scary stories and my mother flicked off the TV when the monsters came on and Mary was always shushing me. We all had bad hearts. I crawled into the supply cabinet to wait for Willie to wake up so I could ask him about it all. I ate all the gingersnaps but I didn't feel

any better. You have a romantic heart, I whispered to myself settling down among the bandages. You will have to be very careful.

It didn't make any difference to Aunt Hazel that I had changed, that I no longer told scary stories or dragged my schoolmates to the latest creature movie, or raced my friends to the edge of the roof, or held my breath, or ran under the train rail when the train was already in sight. As far as she was concerned, I was still the same ole spooky kid I'd always been. So Joanne was kept at home. My mother noticed the difference, but she said over the phone to my grandmother, "She's acting very ladylike these days, growing up." I didn't tell her about my secret, that I knew about my heart. And I was kind of glad Joanne wasn't around 'cause I would have blabbed it all to her and scared her to death. When school starts again, I decided, I'll ask my teacher how to outgrow my underprivileged heart. I'll train myself, just like I did with the Fly family.

"Well, I guess you'll want some change to go to the fair again, hunh?" my mother said coming into my room dumping things in her pocketbook.

"No," I said. "I'm too grown up for circuses."

She put the money on the dresser anyway. I was lying, of course. I was thinking what a terrible strain it would be for Mrs. Perez and everybody else if while sitting there, with the Fly family zooming around in the open air a million miles above the ground, little Harriet Watkins should drop dead with a fatal heart attack behind them.

"I lost," I said out loud.

"Lost what?"

"The battle with the Fly family."

She just stood there a long time looking at me, trying to figure me out, the way mothers are always doing but should know better. Then she kissed me goodbye and left for work.

Close Up

1. Harriet likes to tell scary stories in order to entertain the other kids. Why else does she like to tell these stories?

2. According to Harriet, when the Fly family performs, "everyone just dies and clutches at their hearts." (a) How does Harriet usually act during a performance? (b) Why is she able to act this way?

3. Because she has trained herself to have a strong heart, Harriet wants to protect Willie, who has a weak, or rheumatic, heart. (a) What changes does she make in her own behavior in order to protect Willie? (b) Why does she ask Mary to move him from George's tent?

4. At camp, when Harriet begins to tell a scary story, George picks it up. (a) Why does he tell about a giant who gobbles up the hearts of underprivileged kids? (b) When Harriet overhears George and Mary discussing this incident, what does she learn about herself?

5. To Harriet, the Fly family represents the challenges in life— all the things that scare you and keep you down. At the end of this story, why does Harriet feel that she has lost her battle with the Fly family?

Conflict

An internal conflict is a struggle that takes place within a person. One side of the person seems to be warring against the other side. The conflict is resolved when one side wins.

1. Harriet says that she is fighting a battle of nerves with the Fly family, but she is really fighting it with herself. One side of her is afraid, while the other wants to conquer fear. How does she prepare herself for the Fly family's final performance?

2. At one point during their performance, Harriet says, "I almost let my heart thump me off the bench. I almost thought I too had to tie my shoelaces." Does Harriet win her battle this time? Find two statements that support your answer.

3. At the end of the story, do you think that Harriet has won or lost her battle against fear? Why?

Activity

► **Composition.** Harriet is an interesting and complex character. Write a paragraph telling why you do or do not like her.

RELATIONSHIPS

Identifying Relationship Patterns

Time order is the sequence in which events happen. For example, Harriet does push-ups before she goes to the Fly family's performance.

Spatial order tells you the arrangement of things in space. For example, Harriet had the bunk near the door, and Sally had the bunk next to hers.

Cause and effect tells you what happened and why it happened. For example, Jo's mother didn't want Jo to play with Harriet because Harriet always told Jo scary stories.

Comparison and contrast tells you how things are alike and how they are different. Harriet rarely cried, but Jo cried frequently.

---

1. Identify the relationship pattern in each sentence below.
   a. Jo ducked her head under the benches.
   b. Uncle Bubba can juggle plates just like the jugglers in the circus.
   c. First the clowns performed, then the jugglers, then the horses, and finally the Fly family.
   d. Mr. Fly flew out, caught the little boy, and swung over to the opposite stand.
   e. Mary asked Harriet not to tell her stories because they scared the other campers.
   f. Willie was weak and couldn't defend himself so Harriet decided to protect him.
   g. Both Harriet and her cousin Jo enjoyed summer camp.
   h. The other circus performers were good, but the Fly family was superb.

2. Each of the following items begins a new paragraph. Read each item and decide whether you would complete the paragraph using time order, spatial order, cause and effect, or comparison and contrast. Be prepared to explain your answers.
   a. Harriet is very unlike her cousin Joanne.
   b. They tried to determine why she liked to tell scary stories.
   c. For four years Harriet fought a battle with the Fly family. The first year she . . .
   d. She tried to protect him because he had a rheumatic heart.
   e. The location was quite pleasing. On the left was . . .

WORD ATTACK

Understanding Figurative Expressions

A figurative expression is a vivid and imaginative way of saying something. The individual words in the expression do not carry their usual meaning. For example, imagine that a person speaks angrily to someone else. You might say that this person has *a mouth full of fire*. Of course, you do not mean exactly what the individual words say; the person's mouth is not actually on fire. But this expression creates a vivid picture of the way the person speaks.

▶ The figurative expression in each sentence below is printed in *italics*. Write the meaning of each expression.

    a. "*Everyone just dies* and clutches their hearts."

    b. "I figured they'd be up to something so I made sure my *stomach was like steel*."

    c. "And the minute she got up, he started *hatching a plot*, trying to get the kids to hide her peanut butter sandwich and put spiders in her soup."

    d. ". . . *I just couldn't help myself* and started in with a story about the great caterpillar who was going to prowl through the tents and nibble off everybody's toes."

    e. "But before I could do that, ole George *picked up my story* and added a wicked witch . . ."

    f. ". . . they dashed off into the darkness *yelling bloody murder*."

REVIEW QUIZ

On the Selections

1. In "Nearly Perfect," why does Julian make friends with an elderly gentleman by the name of Corphew?

2. In "The Sniper," why does the man on the roof shoot the woman?

3. In "The Lady, or the Tiger?" the king's system of justice is impartial. Is it fair? Why or why not?

4. In "What Sort of Person Is This Amanda Jones Anyway?" how does Amanda discover that she is a writer?

5. What details tell Amanda that she had been on vacation in Scotland?

6. In "The Interlopers," what is the basis of the family feud?

7. In "Murphy's Law," why is Paul unable to make radio contact with Camp Cavalcade?

8. Why is Harris unable to help Paul?

9. In "My Delicate Heart Condition," why does Harriet try to protect Willie?

10. At the end of the story, in what way has Harriet lost the battle with the Fly family?

On Relationships

1. Place these events from "Nearly Perfect" in the correct order. Start your list with the event that happened first.
   a. Julian meets Sir George Corphew.
   b. Julian decides to kill his uncle.
   c. Julian and his uncle decide to write a mystery story together.
   d. Uncle Marius wins the lottery.

2. (a) In "The Sniper," how are the sniper and his enemy alike? (b) How are they different?

3. (a) In "The Lady, or the Tiger?" why is the young man on trial? (b) Why will the king win no matter which door the young man chooses?

4. (a) In "My Delicate Heart Condition," list four acts Harriet sees at the circus. (b) Which act does she like best?

5. (a) In "Murphy's Law," where does Paul land the plane? (b) About how far is he from Camp Cavalcade?

On Plot and Character

▶ Decide which of the following statements are true and which are false. Write your answers on a piece of paper.
   a. The plot of a story centers on a conflict or problem.
   b. Suspense is the quality of a story that makes you want to read on to find out what will happen next.
   c. A dilemma is a situation in which a character must choose between two unequal alternatives.
   d. Conflict is the pattern of action in a story.
   e. An internal conflict takes place between two characters.

COMPOSITION

Sentence Combining

You can show the relationship between two sentences by combining them with a signal word. For example, look at the following sentences:

> The man joined the Republican side.
> He believed Ireland should be independent from England. (because)

By using the signal word in parentheses, you can combine these two sentences to show a cause-and-effect relationship.

> The man joined the Republican side because he believed Ireland should be independent from England.

Now look at the next two sentences.

> The man was a Republican.
> His brother was a Free Stater. (, but)

By using the comma and signal word in parentheses, you can combine these two sentences to show a contrast relationship.

> The man was a Republican, but his brother was a Free Stater.

▶ Combine each pair of sentences below by using the signal word contained in the parentheses following the second sentence. (If a comma appears in the parentheses, use this too.) Then tell which relationship pattern you have used.

  a. Marius didn't particularly like Julian.
      He needed someone to talk to. (, but)

  b. The princess could grant the man life or death.
      She knew behind which door stood the tiger. (since)

  c. A rucksack fell on Amanda's head.
      She was riding on the train. (while)

  d. Gradwitz and Znaeym were enemies.
      Their grandfathers had been enemies. (because)

  e. The pilot lost control of the plane.
      A goose crashed through the windshield. (when)

BEFORE GOING ON

Scanning for Facts

You scan something to find facts or specific information. For example, when you want to look up a word in the dictionary, you quickly run your eye down the page until you find that word. In other words, you scan the dictionary.

To scan an article, you read the first and last paragraphs carefully. Then you run your index finger down the page while you let your eyes sweep across the printed lines, looking for specific information.

When you scan, you adjust your rate to suit your purpose. Since your purpose is to find specific information, you read quickly until you find this information. Once you have found it, you read slowly and carefully to comprehend the information.

► Study the following questions. Now scan the story to find the answers.

    a. How many years ago did Charlie Brown first appear in a newspaper comic strip?

    b. How many newspapers does "Peanuts" appear in?

    c. In what state does Charles Schulz live?

    d. Is Charles Schulz pleased with himself as an artist?

    e. Is Charles Schulz a better golfer than a tennis player?

    f. Has Charles Schulz written a novel?

    g. Is Charles Schulz at all like Lucy?

    h. What does Charles Schulz do if "an idea isn't coming into shape"?

Further Reading

Thirty Years of Warm Puppies

Michael J. Bandler

Good grief!

Thirty years (1950) after a round-headed half pint named Charlie Brown first surfaced in a newspaper comic strip, fifteen years after Chuck's debut as a television star, and a decade after the "Peanuts" kids' initial appearance on movie screens, creator Charles Schulz—like Ol' Man River—just keeps rollin' along.

"I still think happiness is a warm puppy," the cartoonist, 57, says softly, his face crinkling into a trademark grin as he refers in passing to just one of the dozens of catch phrases, images, characters, symbols, and recurring situations he's invented that have become part of the popular culture of contemporary life.

Think of it. Where would the world be without Snoopy and his dogfights against the cursed Red Baron, Linus and his blanket, Schroeder and his Beethoven, Lucy and her curbside psychiatric clinic, the Great Pumpkin, Peppermint Patty, and the anguished cry, "AAUGH!"

Reprinted by permission of *American Way*, inflight magazine of American Airlines. Copyright 1980 by American Airlines.

And, "happiness is. . . ."

Schulz recalls: "Some fellow once criticized that sentiment saying it was absurd, that there was more to life than all of that. But it's like the Book of Genesis. If you want to describe the beginning of the world, you're not going to be able to describe it any better than Genesis does. And if you want to describe happiness, I defy you to describe it any better than 'Happiness is a warm puppy.'"

If pressed, Schulz will admit that happiness also is knowing that his twentieth half-hour television feature, "She's a Good Skate, Charlie Brown" (produced and directed by his longtime TV and film collaborator, Lee Mendelson), was scheduled to be unveiled this month, and that his latest five-year contract with United Features Syndicate will keep "Peanuts" in 2,000 newspapers at least until the summer of 1984.

But there are simpler, more personal forms of happiness, only evident occasionally to visitors to One Snoopy Place, his studio-office on the perimeter of Santa Rosa, California. Happiness, he says, is an uninterrupted morning at the easel, a tuna sandwich at his desk or at the Redwood Empire Ice Arena, which he constructed a block away, a late-afternoon set of doubles with his wife, Jeannie, and friends, an evening with a good book, and the security of knowing he's completed his obligations for the day.

This life style sounds unattainable, considering the public clamor for attention of one sort or other, which pursues him as relentlessly as his daily deadlines. And yet, the quiet life has been the possible dream for this gentle, pensive, sunny, philosophical, wistful, compassionate, and diligent man whose characteristics and sagacity emerge through his life's work.

Only Charles Schulz could assay the secret of life as he did some years back:

"You know what?" says Linus to Charlie Brown. "I think I've learned the secret of life . . . I went to the doctor yesterday because I had a sore throat . . . The nurse put me in a small room . . . I could hear a kid in another room screaming his head off . . . When the doctor came in to see me, I told him I was glad I wasn't in that other room . . . 'Yes,' he said, 'that kid will have to have his tonsils out . . . You're lucky . . . You only have a mild inflammation.'

"The secret of life," says Linus, worldly wise, "is to be in the right room."

The right room, the right place, the right time—Schulz has been there. In a sense, the Minneapolis native and World War II veteran and erstwhile art-school instructor is a survivor in a highly competitive game, which is inexorably dependent on the public's whims and rapidly changing tastes. Comic strips and cartoon characters have come and gone in the course of the postwar era, yet "Peanuts" and its progeny—the books, figurines, toys, soap dishes, pajama bags, and the like—are still with us, to enthrall a second generation in this country and abroad.

Schulz derives quiet pleasure out of having outlasted some comic strips that United Features debuted with greater fanfare than "Peanuts" received at the outset. He asks rhetorically: "Whatever happened to 'Long Sam.' Whatever happened to 'Twin Earths.' They put in a lot of money to promote that one. I could have told them it was no good, but they never would have listened to me. Meantime, though, 'Peanuts' just kept going. I developed my style and sense of humor, and established the characters, and, like the tortoise against the hare, I came plodding along from behind. I think eventually I showed them."

Show them he did, through an enviable one-two punch: artistic talent and an imagination rooted in sensitivity and intelligence, with a sense of humor to boot. Recently, for example, Linus stayed home from school one day. "Linus says he isn't feeling well," Lucy reported to Charlie Brown, who asked, "Do you think he's really sick?" "No," responded Lucy. "I think he's just putting on his hypochondriact!"

Says Schulz: "I find that as the years have gone by, I have learned to handle the medium so that it really will accommodate every thought that comes to mind. I've discovered that every thought that occurs to me—whether it's just silly, a pun of some kind, or very serious—generally will find its way into the comic strip in one manner or other. It may not be riotously funny; it may just be smilingly funny. But somehow, the medium will accommodate it."

Aware of the extent to which readers have found subtle messages and philosophical truths in "Peanuts," Schulz nonetheless is quick to recognize his limitations. He once said, "Cartooning is a *fairly* sort of proposition. You have to be fairly intelligent—if you were really intelligent you'd be doing something else. You have to draw fairly well—if you drew really well you'd be a painter. You have to write fairly well—if you wrote really well you'd be writing books. It's great for a fairly person like me."

He expanded on this sentiment in a recent conversation. "I think I'm inventive but not deep. I think this is why I'm so suited to drawing a comic strip. Now I think I've

plumbed depths which have never been plumbed before in the comic medium, but this doesn't mean I could then advance and become a great novelist. I'm afraid that, much to my disappointment, I've discovered I'm not really that smart."

Nonetheless Schulz is pleased with himself as an artist: "I have a good dash to my rendering, and I think I can handle the pen as well as anybody under certain circumstances." Yet he is aware of his limitations:

"I've worked myself into a bind artistically—intentionally in one aspect and unintentionally in the other. I find that the humor in the strip and the conversation flow work best if the characters are drawn on an eye level, usually from the side, so that the reader is right down with the character. In 'Peanuts' you never look down on the kids from an adult's level. I've said that I'm the only one who draws grass from a side view, which means I can't monkey around with a lot of camera angles or special effects in the strip.

"On the other hand, I've never been given much room in the daily strip, so, of necessity, I've always drawn very tight. This means I've never been able to solve how to draw living rooms and furniture and other background objects. Of course, as the strip has progressed, it has become more abstract, more of a fantasy, and you can't intrude a realistic background into a story that is fantasy."

Take, for example, the case of Snoopy's doghouse. We have no idea what the inside looks like.

"We can't," Schulz stresses. "It's too fantastic. No one could draw what we've said is down there. Also, Snoopy sits on the doghouse writing novels on his typewriter. If you look at the doghouse from a three-quarters view, the typewriter is going to fall off. But from the side, you can accept it. And you never see anything in the background; if you did, it would become too real, and then you no longer could have a dog typing out a novel."

Actually, Schulz is immensely gratified with the way Snoopy has evolved: "I'm proud of the way he looks. I think he's well-drawn—not too cute in his appearance. His whole personality is a little bittersweet. But he's a very strong character. He can win or lose, be a disaster, a hero, or anything, and yet it all works out. I like the fact that when he's in real trouble, he can retreat into a fantasy and thereby escape."

Indeed, Schulz has unleashed and fulfilled his most cherished fantasies through Snoopy. The unpredictable, self-assured beagle performs heroics at Wimbledon, on the ice rink, on the golf course, and in the air—all a reflection of his creator's precious dreams. And Snoopy is the perennially promising novelist, whose classic opening image, "It was a dark and stormy night," is one of the most familiar lines in contemporary American fiction.

"I would like to have won the National Open," says Schulz, who golfs much less frequently these days than in the past. "I think I could have been a good golfer if I'd tried when I was young. I think it would be neat to win Wimbledon, but I'm a worse tennis player than golfer. I'd like to write a good novel. I know I could write a novel and get it published, but I would like to write a *good* novel."

Wistful though he is about what might have been, Schulz is satisfied and pleased with what is, and with the way his community of characters measures up to those of his competitors:

"The Disney characters were good, but you can't remember anything Mickey Mouse or Donald Duck ever said. All they did was make remarks to each other that progressed the story line. But they never conversed."

By comparison—there are thousands of possible examples—he recalls the moment in his full-length movie, *Race for Your Life, Charlie Brown*, when the kids have been reunited after being lost in a storm: "And Charlie Brown says, 'Isn't it strange, for a

while we were all lost, and we weren't even sure we'd find each other or be rescued. And now here we all are, sitting in the cabin together again, all warm. Isn't it strange how things work out!' And somebody says, 'What's he talking about?' And someone answers, 'I don't know, I never pay attention to anything he says.' These characters are really conversing. They're not just spouting gag lines. They're listening, and conversing.''

That quality was evident from the strip's earliest days. "Let's just say that life has me beaten," Charlie Brown once said sadly. "So I give up! I admit that there's no way I can win." "What is it you want, Charlie Brown?" asked Linus. Responded Chuck, "How about two out of three?"

Despite, or perhaps because of, his haplessness, Charlie Brown is, in Schulz's opinion, the strip's principal contribution to everyday life, and a legacy to the lexicon. People will continue to describe someone as being a "Charlie Brown" type, he believes, just as an earlier generation referred to a "Milquetoast" or a "Sad Sack."

The impression persists that Charlie Brown—the last kid to get a valentine, the one whose Christmas tree wilts, the boy who discovers rocks instead of candy in his trick-or-treat sack—is a thinly veiled version of the artist himself.

Not true, Schulz maintains. Yet, he concedes, there is more of him in Charlie Brown than in any of the other characters: "I was very timid as a small child, and I always was the shortest one in my class in school because I was promoted twice. Later, the roof fell in and I failed everything. And although I was a good ballplayer—unlike Charlie Brown—I never was given a real chance to prove myself because of my height."

Still, he says, "Just the fact that I can think of sarcastic remarks for Lucy shows that there's a touch of me in her. I can be very sarcastic and mean, in fact. I was more so in my younger days, but as I've gotten older,

I've learned that that was no way to make friends."

One might think that over three decades Schulz hasn't left a single subject untouched. Until recently, though, one theme that eluded him was serious illness. He finally came close to it last summer, when—in the course of a continuing five-week series in his daily strip—Charlie Brown became ill, was hospitalized, and then recovered. Schulz notes:

"I wasn't sure of the direction in which I should go. I abandoned the thought of specifying an illness. What I finally did was simply show the reactions of the other kids in the neighborhood to his hospitalization." Thus in one segment, Sally wrote the following letter: "Dear Big Brother, I hope you are feeling better. Things are fine here at home. I have moved into your room. Don't worry about your personal things. The flea market was a success."

Of all the friends, Lucy expressed the greatest concern. "I'm so worried about Charlie Brown, I can't eat or sleep," she told Schroeder as she rested in her usual position against the back of his piano. "Well, if you get sick, too, that sure won't help him," said Schroeder. "Maybe if he thought he was making me sick, he'd get better," Lucy answered, adding, "Maybe I could send him a threatening letter."

In the end, Schulz brought the serial to a rousing close by resurrecting the popular football routine, in which Lucy holds a football on the ground only to whisk it away at the split second when place-kicker Charlie Brown's toe is about to make contact. Fans of "Peanuts" wait expectantly for the sequence each fall, knowing that Schulz always arrives at the identical ending by different means. In this case, in order to maintain the impression that Lucy truly was concerned about Chuck's health, Schulz conceived an ending that was a total surprise.

That venturesome unpredictability is born of incessant thought, and Schulz enjoys those moments in the day when he can simply sit and think. He is incurably restless; if an idea isn't coming into shape, he'll take a stroll, answer some fan mail, walk across to the ice arena for coffee and pie at the snack bar (appropriately named the Warm Puppy), or check out some of the newly licensed items sent to him by Determined Productions and other marketing firms responsible for all those touchable, clutchable, movable, soakable, huggable products that seem to be everywhere we turn. ("I approve everything, but only because I want to. The only thing I'm obligated to do is draw the strip. I don't have to write the television shows and movies and books or keep up with new products or toys. But I do it all anyway, simply because I want it done right.")

In the evenings, on weekends, sometimes in the late afternoons, or whenever, really, the spirit moves him, he engages in relaxed conversation with whichever of his children (five from his first marriage and two stepchildren from his current marriage) happen to be around. His oldest daughter, Meredith, 29, is training to become a psychiatric technician. Monte, 27, is studying for his MA in literature at the University of California at Santa Barbara, and aspires to be a novelist. Craig, 26, is a flight instructor. Amy, 23, is an ice-skating instructor and part-time student. Jill, 21, is currently touring with the Ice Follies. And Brooke and Lisa, Jeannie's daughters, are in college.

As he moves into his fourth decade (the strip's actual anniversary is this coming October) as a superstar in his profession, he is troubled only that "without knowing it, I could be grinding down, becoming boring or repetitive.

"So far, I think, I haven't been. I think I've passed the leveling-off period and I'm proud of that. The average comic strip starts off pretty good, then levels off and never changes, never gets better. I think I passed the leveling-off period a long time ago: 'Peanuts' moved on and jumped up. And it's simply because I really worked at it."

Later this year the gang will travel to Europe as exchange students in a full-length theatrical feature, *Bon Voyage Charlie Brown . . . and Don't Come Back!* They'll fly to London. Snoopy will play at Wimbledon. Then they'll take the Hovercraft across the English Channel to France to begin their studies. A beret-topped Snoopy, with phrase book in hand, will drive them in a Renault across the countryside from Calais.

What will happen next? Charles Schulz knows—but he isn't saying. Good grief!

Joining the Circle

Robin Lee Graham

Sixteen-year-old Robin Lee Graham sailed a twenty-four-foot sailboat around the world. In this selection he tells how he developed his love for the sea.

Many have sailed long and dangerous voyages for the sake of personal glory. Others have sailed for personal adventure. I fall into neither group. I have tried to answer honestly when people have asked me what made me do it—what compelled me at the age of sixteen to take a twenty-four-foot sailboat out of San Pedro harbor (it flanks Long Beach) and to tell my family and friends, "I'm going around the world."

Shakespeare, who seems to have had an answer to most questions, had Hamlet say, "There's a divinity that shapes our ends, rough-hew them how we will." That was an answer that fitted pretty closely.

I'd never heard of Shakespeare and understood nothing about destiny when I went to school at the age of five in California. The classroom was close to a forest of yacht masts, and while other kids crayoned pictures of automobiles, airplanes, flowers, or their Uncle Harry wearing big glasses, I drew only pictures of boats—boats with scores of portholes, top-heavy boats, small boats, wind-filled mainsails, mizzens,[1] genoas,[2] jibs,[3] and spinnakers.[4] Then, when I was ten and a lot more resentful of homework, I pressured my father into giving me an eight-foot dinghy[5]—beat-up but beautiful. We were living then at Morro Bay, one of the more attractive of California's coastal towns. On launching day my father said he would teach me how to sail. He was full of wisdom because

---

1. mizzens (mĭz'ənz) n.: Sails set on the mizzenmast, which is the mast (the long upright pole that supports a sail) closest to the stern, or rear part of the ship.
2. genoas (jĕn'ō-əz) n.: The large triangular sails on cruising and racing yachts.
3. jibs (jĭbz) n.: Triangular sails set forward of the foremast.
4. spinnakers (spĭn'ə-kərz) n.: Large triangular sails, often set on the side opposite the mainsail (largest sail) of a boat when sailing before the wind.
5. dinghy (dĭng'ē) n.: Any small rowboat that can be rigged with a jib and mainsail for sailing.

the previous night he had been reading a manual titled *How to Handle a Small Craft.* We got out two hundred yards from the shore and he lectured me on the danger of jibing[6] (page 16 in the manual). Hardly had he lowered his finger than the boat jibed and both of us were thrown into the water.

But how I loved that little boat. Every day when school was over my brother Michael would dash off to the back yard and tinker with his beach buggy, but I would run all the way to the little wooden jetty beyond the reeds near our house. Sailing already meant much more to me than "mucking about in boats," as the neighbors used to call it. It was the chance to escape from blackboards and the smell of disinfectant in the school toilet, from addition and subtraction sums that were never the same as the teacher's answers, from spelling words like "seize" and "fulfill" and from little league baseball. It was the chance to be alone and to be as free for a while as the sea gulls that swung around Morro Rock.

One night when I should have been asleep I could hear my parents talking about me, their voices drifting down the passage from the living room. "I'm worried that he's such a loner," said my mother. "He needs more company. More friends. Perhaps we should ask Stephen or David to join us for the vacation."

A loner? Was I really different? I had friends. But I liked being alone, and a boat gave me the chance of getting away from people.

Was I different just because history didn't turn me on and boats did? Perhaps sailing is in the genes. Ten years before I was born, my father and his brother had started to build a twenty-eight-foot boat, intending to sail it around the world. They had the hull finished and were beginning to study the charts of

Polynesia when the headlines blazed Pearl Harbor. When I was thirteen my father still had ideas of fulfilling his boyhood dream; or at least part of it. He had made out well with his house construction and real estate business. One day he took me to the Long Beach marina and as we walked past a thirty-six-foot ketch with a "For Sale" sign pinned to its stern I crawled under the green canvas. When my father called me I invited him to climb aboard. I don't know whether it was at this moment that my father decided to buy the *Golden Hind*, but a few days later he told the family that he had sold his business and that we were all going sailing in the South Seas.

My father is a quiet man, wiry, not by appearance the adventurous type, and his decision seemed on the surface out of character. Anyway, at the age of thirteen I was not going to analyze his motives or his personality (although I guess my mother did). For me the prospect of missing school for a year and sailing over that horizon was not one to be questioned.

We spent three months equipping the *Golden Hind*, provisioning her with six hundred cans of food, and then, without fanfare but with much head shaking from our kin, we sailed south to Nuku Hiva, the port of entry to the Marquesas Islands. Fortunately bad memories fade fast and the happiest stay in the forefront of our minds. I can barely recall, for instance, our eighteen days in the doldrums or my being doubled up with a flaring appendix about 120 miles from the nearest surgeon in Papeete. The appendectomy wound failed to heal, and I spent three weeks in a primitive hospital where huge cockroaches crawled up the wall.

But I did remember, and always will, the deep blue of the coral lagoons, the Tahitian girls wearing *pereus* in Gauguin colors. I remember the girls running down golden beaches, their arms filled with exotic flowers and fresh fruit wrapped in palm fronds.

On one of the islands, Rangiroa, a Tahitian

---

6. jibing (jīb'ĭng) v.: Swinging a sail from one side of the boat to the other when sailing before the wind. Improper jibing can overturn a boat or break a mast.

family called on my parents and, straight-faced, offered to trade me for two of their daughters, Joliette and Suzette. The barter proposal boosted my ego, and I did my best to persuade my parents to accept the offer, figuring that surfing in the Tuamotu Archipelago and living off coconut milk and manioc roots amounted to a better life style than learning geometry and eating hamburgers.

But my parents shook their heads and we sailed the *Golden Hind* to Huahine, Tahaa, Bora Bora, the Cook Islands, and Pago Pago before heading northeast to Hawaii. At fifteen I was back in a California classroom, my spelling still lousy, but I was almost as useful with a sextant[7] as a veteran sailor. On our eleven-thousand-mile voyage I had seen lands of unbelievable enchantment.

It is hard to believe that my parents, having allowed me to sail the South Seas at a most impressionable age, could ever have expected me to be a typical American schoolkid, to go on to college and graduate to a walnut office desk, a home on Acacia Avenue, and membership in the local golf club.

I am sure Corona del Mar's high school is a good one. For me it was a return to prison. Beyond its asphalt playground and wired fences there were sun-splashed, palm-fringed shores waiting for my shadow.

A chance to take to the sea came again when two school friends—Jud Croft and Pete Tupas—and I pressured a Costa Mesa yacht-builder to allow us to deliver a new boat to a buyer in Hawaii. But three days before we were due to set sail on the 2,200-mile voyage the yachtbuilder called off the arrangement. I think he was afraid of bad publicity if our voyage failed.

Aware of my bitterness, my father invited me to be his mate on a voyage to Hawaii on his new boat, *Valerie*, a thirty-foot ketch.[8]

Keeping watch turn and turn about and weathering half a dozen squalls, we made the trip in twenty-seven days. One incident of this voyage stays in my mind. A bagged genoa, poorly lashed, broke loose and slithered across the forward deck into the ocean. We turned *Valerie* about but just as we came within grappling range[9] the bag began to sink. Under a few inches of clear water the bag looked like a human body. A portion of the sail had escaped and took the form of a face, white and quite terrifying.

I had never seen a person drown (and pray heaven I never will) but in watching the sinking canvas bag I gained a great respect for the sea. I understood for the first time that blue water is not an innocent and sparkling playground but that it can destroy mercilessly.

We arrived in Hawaii without further incident and I was packed off to McKinley High School. My mother was to join us in a month or two. This was my sixth school and I had to make new friends again. At McKinley I found two brothers, Jim and Arthur, who loved sailing as much as I did. Jim and I were fifteen and Art a year younger. Together we invested our savings of one hundred dollars in an old sixteen-foot aluminum lifeboat. During the school lunch-break the three of us would meet secretively in the shade of a palm tree and talk about our boat, which we named *HIC*—for reasons we need not go into. One lunch hour, the idea was born of sailing *HIC* to the Hawaiian island of Lanai. Jim had been reading *The Adventures of Tom Sawyer* as a class assignment and I contributed stories of the South Sea island girls who wore hibiscus in their hair. The upshot was a top-secret plan to sail to some distant isolated cove. To provision *HIC* I made a few dollars by diving in Ala Wai harbor and salvaging material from a sunken yacht.

---

7. sextant (sĕks′tənt) *n.:* An onboard instrument used to determine the ship's location at sea.
8. ketch (kĕch) *n.:* A sailing vessel with a tall mast forward and a shorter one aft (rear part of the ship).

9. within grappling (grăp′əl-ĭng) range: Within the area or sphere in which they could successfully grapple, or use an iron shaft with claws at one end to grasp hold of, the sinking genoa.

As our plans developed, school became almost unbearable. It wasn't so much that I disliked learning—for I realized the need to be at least partially civilized and my grades were average—but that I detested the routine of school days, the unchanging pattern from the brushing of my teeth to learning English grammar. I came to hate the sound of the bell that summoned me to class, the smell of tennis shoes and sweat in the gym, the drone of history lessons, the threat of tests and exams.

Down at Ala Wai harbor it was all so different. I loved the smell of rope and resin, even of diesel oil. I loved the sound of water slapping hulls, the whip of halyards against tall masts. These were the scents and sounds of liberty and life.

It was the week that Winston Churchill died that Jim, Art, and I decided it was time to sail. Maybe that old warrior had something to do with our decision. The radio and newspapers poured out stories of the "Man of the Century"—the swashbuckling statesman-soldier with a bulldog jaw who had defied Fuzzy-Wuzzies, tyrants, and convention. My own tyrants were peanut butter sandwiches and people in gloomy offices who insisted I wear shoes, people determined to arrange my life in tidy patterns, prodding me this way and that until I could be safely sent out into society, wearing white collars and gray suits, credit cards in my billfold, golf clubs in the closet under the stairs, and a half-paid-for car in the garage.

Yes, I think Winston Churchill can take some responsibility for what happened next.

HIC's hull was as patched as a sailor's pants, and where some rivets were missing we filled up the holes with chewing gum, which was a lot cheaper than the filling material on sale in the marine shops. To change the craft into a sailboat, we bolted on a plywood keel, stepped a salvaged boom for a mast, and stayed it with bits of rigging found lying around the yacht club. The sails were old, cutdown throwaways from a ketch.

On the evening of Thursday, January 28, 1965, Jim, Art, and I tore pages from our school notebooks and wrote letters to our parents. The letters, we made sure, would not be received before we were on the high seas. To my father (my mother was visiting in California) I wrote:

Dear Dad,

Sorry for leaving without saying goodbye. But if I had done so you would not have let me go. I want to thank you for raising me as you have done. I think a father could not have done a better job. Sorry, too, for taking some of your goods. I have written to Mom to ask her to send you my money in my savings bank at Newport. Don't worry about me. I'll be all right. I miss you and love you very much.

Love, Lee

(My parents usually called me Lee.)

My father had been suffering from a cold so I added: "Hope you feel better real soon."

The veteran sailor knows better than to leave on a Friday. We were not veterans and immediately after school we rendezvoused at the yacht harbor. An hour later we cheerfully turned HIC toward the breakwater. Occasionally we looked astern to make sure no one was following. Then Art shouted an alarm as he spotted an outboard racing toward us. But we had not been betrayed. It was a yacht harbor friend, Chuck, the only other person who knew of our plans. He had come to wish us bon voyage and to take a couple of photographs. Chuck was shrewd enough to guess that his picture of us might have commercial value. Just before he left us, Chuck pointed with his thumb toward the small craft warning just hoisted on the breakwater.

"Should we turn back?" Art asked nervously.

"Looks like a nice day to me," said Jim, "and anyway, nothing usually happens when the small craft warning is up."

"How would we explain those letters to our parents?" I asked, and that was the clincher.

I turned *HIC* toward the buoy at Diamond Head. The wind on the quarter was fresh, warm, inviting, but over the horizon there appeared an ink-black cloud, sinister as the smoke from a witch's brew. We were now too far from the harbor to see the hoisting of a second red pennant, nor did we know that the radio was putting out a full gale warning for the islands.

With a sense of high adventure, we swung *HIC* into the Molokai channel. Here the placid sea was filled with whitecaps. Art now had the tiller,[10] but his face soon looked as green as the water. He was thoughtful enough to lean over the leeward[11] side. In ten minutes the wind lifted from fifteen to twenty-five knots and the jib ripped along its main seam. Jim tore away the strips and hoisted a second sail. For a while *HIC* bounced jauntily across the whitecaps, but when the wind continued to mount I ordered Jim to furl the mainsail.[12]

I had had much more sailing experience than my shipmates and it seemed natural for me to take command. So far it had been the wind that had worried me, but now I began to take in the height of the swells. They were getting much too big—twenty feet from trough to crest. The second jib was suddenly torn to ribbons, and bits of canvas flew downwind like a dozen kites. The tattered staysail was all we had, and I had to keep *HIC*'s stern to the sea by working the rudder.

---

10. tiller (tĭl′ər) n.: A bar or handle for turning the rudder (the movable piece of wood or metal hinged to the rear of the boat and used to steer the ship).

11. leeward (lē′wərd) adj.: In the direction toward which the wind is blowing.

12. mainsail (mān′səl) n.: The principal sail of a vessel, usually the second sail from the bow (the forward part of the ship).

By holding this course, I hoped, we would at least drift toward Maui, where we could take our chances with the surf.

By late afternoon the situation was serious. Wind was gusting between twenty-five and forty knots and swells were averaging thirty feet. Jim was now lying in the bottom of the boat, wrapped about in the wet third jib. He was vomiting and crying. *HIC* was sturdier than she looked and slithered down the surface of the combers.[13] Every now and then a big comber would smack into her stern and twenty gallons of water would thud over my back and pour across the bottom boards.

Lashing the tiller, I helped Art bale with plastic buckets. We knew well enough that another big comber would put the boat dangerously low in the water. Although *HIC* had been built as a lifeboat, the flotation tanks had long since been removed, and our funds had not allowed us to buy a raft.

There was nothing exciting about the situation now. The sense of adventure that we had carried across the harbor mouth had quite gone. Wind-whipped gray clouds scudded a few feet above our heads and our homemade rigging cracked like pistol shots as it lashed the mast. Darkness fell quickly and with our loss of vision our sense of hearing increased. The sea began to sound like a fleet of locomotives and the cold pierced our flesh like a thousand needles. I kept thinking of the plywood keel. It if broke away we would have no hope, for *HIC* would roll right over with the first broadside.

It was neither courage nor, I think, stupidity that prevented me from thinking about drowning. It was simply that all my energy and thoughts were concentrated on keeping *HIC* afloat. Art, seasick though he was, volunteered to take the tiller, but at the moment of handing it over to him a huge comber thumped our stern[14] with a jar that threw the

---

13. combers (kō′mərz) n.: Waves that crest, or peak.

14. stern (stûrn) n.: The rear part of a ship.

three of us to the floor. We jumped up spluttering and baled with all our strength.

The wind, I guessed, was now fifty knots. It was Art's idea to rig the mainsail across the boat as a spray guard. He tied one end to the mast while I lashed its edges to the gunwales. So we huddled in the darkness beneath our awning until another big comber hit and crushed the canvas to the bottom. We baled until our bodies ached with pain.

Perhaps it was the bitter cold and weariness that dulled my mind, for, strangely, fear never overwhelmed me. From the tiller I could see the moonlike faces of my friends as we waited for the final wave that would send us to the bottom. Sometime between midnight and dawn we heard a plane, one of several out searching for us. But by the time we had found and fired a flare, the aircraft was far away.

An hour after dawn the wind dropped sufficiently for us to hoist the spare mainsail, and our spirits rose. It was enough just to know that we had somehow survived the night. Art remembered his small transistor radio and switched it on. For a while we listened to some music and then the announcer came through with news. The first story was about us. The announcer said:

"The Coast Guard is conducting an extensive air and sea search for three teenage boys feared to be lost at sea. The Coast Guard spokesman reports that because of the extreme weather conditions last night the chances of their survival in a sixteen-foot boat are very slim."

The report went on to give details of our families and school, and promised to report any further developments.

We listened in stunned silence, unable at first to realize that we were on the news. Then perhaps to our credit we were worried about the anxiety our families would be feeling. I wondered if my mother in California had picked up the news. It hurt me to think what she was going through. We did not then know that our adventure was the main story in the Hawaiian newspapers. It had even swept the Churchill headlines from the top of page one.

Our situation was now much better. We had food and water for several days. Then Art pointed over the side with an exclamation. Our keel had finally broken away and was drifting past the stern.

Had the keel snapped off the previous night in the height of the storm, we certainly would not have been still afloat this warm morning. But by now we knew we had made it.

By midmorning HIC drifted on the lee shore of Lanai. With a reefed jib we managed to steer around narrow coral heads, and before the sun had dropped the bow crunched into a sandy beach. We threw out our only anchor and staggered up the sand.

Hearing a picnic party along the shore, we stumbled over rocks and thorns to reach the circle of their firelight. The party guessed who we were at once because hourly radio bulletins had been giving ever gloomier reports about the missing teenagers. One member of the picnic party volunteered to drive us to Lanai City, about eight miles inland. He properly urged us to report to the police.

At the police station the reception was mixed; the officer on duty was obviously pleased to see us and pushed mugs of hot coffee into our hands while telling us we were crazy. He called up the Coast Guard and reported our safety. We spent that night in jail. No drunk had ever slept better in my bunk.

Next morning a plane chartered by Jim and Art's parents flew us back to Honolulu, and it was at the airport that I first experienced a full bombardment of news reporters' questions and learned what it feels like to look down the barrels of television cameras.

My father was there too. He had his own opinion of our adventure. But he did remind me of the seafarers' superstition never to start a voyage on a Friday.

For several weeks the story of *HIC* was followed by a flood of correspondence in Hawaiian newspapers—letters signed by "Angry Taxpayer" and retired colonels who huffed and puffed about our irresponsibility. But there was one letter in the *Star-Bulletin* which I stuck into my scrapbook. It reads in part:

I am not unmindful of the staggering amount of time, effort, and cost to us taxpayers which was involved in this escapade by three teenagers who sailed to Lanai in an old lifeboat. It was a pretty big goof up on their part, and I doubt very much if they are front page heroes to their friends. I am sure they now feel pretty stupid about the whole affair. But what really gets me is this trying to equate the attitude of "We wanted to see if we could do it" with your correspondents' propositions about "this dry rot affecting the youth of our nation."

Think what the elimination of the attitude of these boys would have meant to the world. Would Columbus have discovered America? Would the Wright brothers have flown at Kitty Hawk? Would Mount Everest have been climbed? Indeed would our Hawaiian ancestors have discovered these lovely islands?

A little red-blooded urge to excel, to do the impossible, to see what is over the next hill and to take little heed of the consequences— these are as American as apple pie. It is obvious that the angry critics of these boys never walked a neighbor's fence or swam a forbidden hole or pushed over an outhouse on Hallowe'en. . . . Irresponsible? Yes. Thoughtless? Yes. But dry rot in the nation's youth? Baloney.

The letter was signed: Gene Weston.

Another correspondent, who lashed us for our "foolish escapade," expressed his gratitude that "there are a few youngsters in the country who aren't out mugging and murdering . . . and whose initiative, though misguided, will help them to avoid becoming teen-age vegetables." The writer concluded, "They're a trio of crazy kids who are lucky to be alive, and they've learned this too. But don't be too quick to criticize that quality we need most in this day and age: raw guts."

Perhaps it was this more tolerant view of our adventure, which had cost $25,000 in rescue operations, that helped us when we were ordered to appear before a hearing of the local Coast Guard. We were found guilty under a federal law which prohibits the reckless or negligent operation of a vessel endangering the life, limb, or property of any person, and we were assessed a one-hundred-dollar penalty each. But we were excused from payment.

The penalty was remitted by Captain Herbert J. Kelly, acting chief of the Merchant Marine Safety Division of the 14th Coast Guard, because, he stressed, the parents would have to pay for their sons' violations. Had we been convicted in a federal court we could have been sentenced to one year in a reformatory or a two-thousand-dollar fine or both. Captain Kelly gave us the ghost of a grin as he dismissed us from the courtroom.

So instead of a life on the islands—and it had been our eventual plan to sail *HIC* to the South Seas—we returned to McKinley High School, I to complete my sophomore year.

Close Up

1. When Graham tells about sailing the *Golden Hind*, he says, "Fortunately bad memories fade fast and the happiest stay in the forefront of our minds." (a) What good memories can he recall? (b) What bad memories can he recall?

2. After the voyage, Graham feels as though he were returning to prison. (a) What does he say is waiting for him beyond the "asphalt playground and wired fences"? (b) Explain what he means when he says, "Yes, I think Winston Churchill can take some responsibility for what happened next."

3. Graham and his two friends plan to sail their boat to some isolated cove. Why do they set out on their journey in spite of the small craft warning?

4. The boys' adventure provokes mixed responses from the public. (a) What do some people admire about the boys' escapade? (b) What do some people object to about their escapade?

5. Why do you think that Captain Kelly shows "the ghost of a smile" when he dismisses the boys from the courtroom?

Point of View

In a true story written in the first person, the author narrates, or tells about, his or her experiences. This means that the story is told from the point of view, or angle of vision, of the author. The author uses the first-person pronoun "I" to identify himself or herself. For example, Robin Lee Graham, the author and narrator of this story, says, "*I* have tried to answer honestly when people have asked *me* what made *me* do it—what compelled *me* at the age of sixteen to take a twenty-four-foot sailboat out of San Pedro harbor (it flanks Long Beach) and to tell *my* family and friends, '*I'm* going around the world.' " Usually, a story told from the author's point of view is subjective. It gives the author's personal thoughts and feelings.

1. Graham says, "Sailing already meant much more to me than 'mucking about in boats' . . . ." What does it mean to him?

2. Graham says that it was neither courage nor stupidity that kept him from thinking about drowning. (a) What does keep him from thinking about it? (b) Why do his spirits rise shortly after dawn?

3. (a) How does Graham feel when he hears the Coast Guard is searching for him? (b) What does he then worry about?

4. Graham's adventure caused a lot of trouble. Do you think Graham regrets having attempted this trip? Why or why not?

JUDGMENTS

Identifying Primary and Secondary Sources of Information

A person who tells about something he or she actually experienced is a primary source of information. This person is able to give you a first-hand account. For example, Robin Lee Graham gives you first-hand information about an incident on board the *Valerie.* He says, "One incident of this voyage stays in my mind. A bagged genoa, poorly lashed, broke loose and slithered across the forward deck into the ocean." Robin was there. When he says, "I had never seen a person drown (and pray heaven I never will) but in watching the sinking canvas bag I gained a great respect for the sea," Robin gives you first-hand information about his feelings.

A person who tells about something someone else has experienced is a secondary source. This person gives a second-hand account. For example, Robin tells about his father's building a boat ten years before Robin was born. He says, ". . . my father and his brother had started to build a twenty-eight-foot boat, intending to sail it around the world." Robin is a secondary source. He was not there. He is telling about something his father told him.

Why is it important to identify primary and secondary sources? Stories may change with each retelling. Do you remember playing the game *Telephone?* One person whispered a message to another person who then whispered it to someone else. Usually, by the time the message got to the last person in line, it had completely changed. The closer you were to the primary source, the more likely you were to receive the original message.

---

1. Is each person below a primary or a secondary source of information? Write your answer on a piece of paper.
   a. Robin tells the reporters how he felt when the wind reached forty knots. (Is Robin a primary or a secondary source?)
   b. The reporters tell the public how Robin felt when the wind reached forty knots. (Are the reporters primary or secondary sources?)
   c. Robin tells why his father decided to buy the *Golden Hind.* (Is Robin a primary or a secondary source?)
   d. Robin tells about his stay in the hospital in Tahiti. (Is Robin a primary or a secondary source?)
   e. A radio announcer reports that the three boys have been rescued. He received this information from a police bulletin. (Is he a primary or a secondary source?)

2. For each event below, find one person in addition to Robin who could provide first-hand information.
   a. Robin tells how a Tahitian family offered to trade two of their children for him.
   b. Robin tells how he and his friends, Jim and Arthur, planned to sail *HIC* to the island of Lanai.
   c. Robin tells about appearing before a hearing of the local Coast Guard.

WORD ATTACK

Understanding Connotation and Denotation

The denotation of a word is its dictionary definition. The connotation is the emotions and associations it carries with it. For example, the words *home* and *residence* are synonyms. Both mean "the place where one lives." The word *home*, though, is more emotionally charged. It carries associations of warmth, comfort, protection, and love.

In this selection, Robin Lee Graham wants you to share his sense of adventure and romance. Therefore, he uses many words that carry adventurous or romantic connotations. For example, he says, "On our eleven-thousand-mile voyage, I had seen lands of unbelievable *enchantment*. The word *enchantment* brings to mind all of the tales of romance and adventure you read as a child.

▶ For each item below, choose the word that carries the more adventurous or romantic connotation.
   a. ". . . immediately after school we (rendezvoused, met) at the yacht harbor."
   b. "I remembered the girls running down golden beaches, their arms filled with (exotic, foreign) flowers and fresh fruit wrapped in palm fronds."
   c. "Maybe that old (fighter, warrior) had something to do with our decision."
   d. "The (veteran, experienced) sailor knows better than to leave on a Friday."
   e. "*HIC* was sturdier than she looked and (slid, slithered) down the surface of the combers."

Counters

Elizabeth Coatsworth

To think I once saw grocery shops
   With but a casual eye
And fingered figs and apricots
   As one who came to buy!

5 To think I never dreamed of how
   Bananas swayed in rain,
And often looked at oranges
   Yet never thought of Spain!

And in those wasted days I saw
10 No sails above the tea—
For grocery shops were grocery shops,
   Not hemispheres to me!

Activity

▶ What objects does the poet say now connote, or make her think of, faraway places? List ten words that make you think of faraway places. Then write a paragraph using these words.

The Haunted Spacesuit

Arthur C. Clarke

"And it was at that moment, as I launched myself out into the abyss, that I knew that something was horribly wrong."

When Satellite Control called me, I was writing up the day's progress report in the Observation Bubble—the glass-domed office that juts out from the axis of the space station like the hubcap of a wheel. It was not really a good place to work, for the view was too overwhelming. Only a few yards away I could see the construction teams performing their slow-motion ballet as they put the station together like a giant jigsaw puzzle. And beyond them, twenty thousand miles below, was the blue-green glory of the full Earth, floating against the raveled star clouds of the Milky Way.

"Station Supervisor here," I answered. "What's the trouble?"

"Our radar's showing a small echo two miles away, almost stationary, about five degrees west of Sirius. Can you give us a visual report on it?"

Anything matching our orbit so precisely could hardly be a meteor; it would have to be something we'd dropped—perhaps an inadequately secured piece of equipment that had drifted away from the station. So I assumed; but when I pulled out my binoculars and searched the sky around Orion, I soon found my mistake. Though this space traveler was man-made, it had nothing to do with us.

"I've found it," I told Control. "It's someone's test satellite—cone-shaped, four antennas, and what looks like a lens system in its base. Probably U.S. Air Force, early nineteen-sixties, judging by the design. I know they lost track of several when their transmitters failed. There were quite a few attempts to hit this orbit before they finally made it."

After a brief search through the files, Control was able to confirm my guess. It took a little longer to find out that Washington wasn't in the least bit interested in our discovery of a twenty-year-old stray satellite, and would be just as happy if we lost it again.

"Well, we can't do *that*," said Control. "Even if nobody wants it, the thing's a menace to navigation. Someone had better go out and haul it aboard."

That someone, I realized, would have to be me. I dared not detach a man from the closely knit construction teams, for we were already behind schedule—and a single day's delay on this job cost a million dollars. All the radio and TV networks on Earth were waiting impatiently for the moment when they could route their programs through us, and thus provide the first truly global service, spanning the world from Pole to Pole.

"I'll go out and get it," I answered, snapping an elastic band over my papers so that the air currents from the ventilators wouldn't set them wandering around the room. Though I tried to sound as if I was doing everyone a great favor, I was secretly not at all displeased. It had been at least two weeks since I'd been outside; I was getting a little tired of stores schedules, maintenance reports, and all the glamorous ingredients of a Space Station Supervisor's life.

The only member of the staff I passed on my way to the air lock was Tommy, our recently acquired cat. Pets mean a great deal to men thousands of miles from Earth, but there are not many animals that can adapt themselves to a weightless environment. Tommy mewed plaintively at me as I clambered into my spacesuit, but I was in too much of a hurry to play with him.

At this point, perhaps I should remind you that the suits we use on the station are completely different from the flexible affairs men wear when they want to walk around on the Moon. Ours are really baby spaceships, just big enough to hold one man. They are stubby cylinders, about seven feet long, fitted with low-powered propulsion jets, and have a pair of accordion-like sleeves at the upper end for the operator's arms. Normally, however, you keep your hands drawn inside the suit, working the manual controls in front of your chest.

As soon as I'd settled down inside my very exclusive spacecraft, I switched on power and checked the gauges on the tiny instrument panel. There's a magic word, "FORB," that you'll often hear spacemen mutter as they climb into their suits; it reminds them to test fuel, oxygen, radio, batteries. All my needles were well in the safety zone, so I lowered the transparent hemisphere over my head and sealed myself in. For a short trip like this, I did not bother to check the suit's internal lockers, which were used to carry food and special equipment for extended missions.

As the conveyor belt decanted[1] me into the air lock, I felt like an Indian papoose being carried along on its mother's back. Then the

---

1. decanted (dĭ-kănt′ əd) v.: Poured.

pumps brought the pressure down to zero, the outer door opened, and the last traces of air swept me out into the stars, turning very slowly head over heels.

The station was only a dozen feet away, yet I was now an independent planet—a little world of my own. I was sealed up in a tiny, mobile cylinder, with a superb view of the entire Universe, but I had practically no freedom of movement inside the suit. The padded seat and safety belts prevented me from turning around, though I could reach all the controls and lockers with my hands or feet.

In space, the great enemy is the sun, which can blast you to blindness in seconds. Very cautiously, I opened up the dark filters on the "night" side of my suit, and turned my head to look out at the stars. At the same time I switched the helmet's external sunshade to automatic, so that whichever way the suit gyrated my eyes would be shielded from that intolerable glare.

Presently, I found my target—a bright fleck of silver whose metallic glint distinguished it clearly from the surrounding stars. I stamped on the jet-control pedal, and felt the mild surge of acceleration as the low-powered rockets set me moving away from the station. After ten seconds of steady thrust, I estimated that my speed was great enough, and cut off the drive. It would take me five minutes to coast the rest of the way, and not much longer to return with my salvage.

And it was at that moment, as I launched myself out into the abyss, that I knew that something was horribly wrong.

It is never completely silent inside a spacesuit; you can always hear the gentle hiss of oxygen, the faint whirr of fans and motors, the susurration[2] of your own breathing— even, if you listen carefully enough, the rhythmic thump that is the pounding of your heart. These sounds reverberate through the

---

2. susurration (sōō'sə-rā'shən) n.: Soft whispering or rustling.

suit, unable to escape into the surrounding void; they are the unnoticed background of life in space, for you are aware of them only when they change.

They had changed now; to them had been added a sound which I could not identify. It was an intermittent, muffled thudding, sometimes accompanied by a scraping noise, as of metal upon metal.

I froze instantly, holding my breath and trying to locate the alien sound with my ears. The meters on the control board gave no clues; all the needles were rock-steady on their scales, and there were none of the flickering red lights that would warn of impending disaster. That was some comfort, but not much. I had long ago learned to trust my instincts in such matters; their alarm signals were flashing now, telling me to return to the station before it was too late. . . .

Even now, I do not like to recall those next few minutes, as panic slowly flooded into my mind like a rising tide, overwhelming the dams of reason and logic which every man must erect against the mystery of the Universe. I knew then what it was like to face insanity; no other explanation fitted the facts.

For it was no longer possible to pretend that the noise disturbing me was that of some faulty mechanism. Though I was in utter isolation, far from any other human being or indeed any material object, I was not alone. The soundless void was bringing to my ears the faint but unmistakable stirrings of life.

In that first, heart-freezing moment it seemed that something was trying to get into my suit—something invisible, seeking shelter from the cruel and pitiless vacuum of space. I whirled madly in my harness, scanning the entire sphere of vision around me except for the blazing, forbidden cone toward the sun. There was nothing there. Of course. There could not be—yet that purposeful scrabbling was clearer than ever.

Despite the nonsense that has been written about us, it is not true that spacemen are superstitious. But can you blame me if, as I came to the end of logic's resources, I suddenly remembered how Bernie Summers had died, no farther from the station than I was at this very moment?

It was one of those "impossible" accidents; it always is. Three things had gone wrong at once. Bernie's oxygen regulator had run wild and sent the pressure soaring, the safety valve had failed to blow—and a faulty joint had given way instead. In a fraction of a second, his suit was open to space.

I had never known Bernie, but suddenly his fate became of overwhelming importance to me—for a horrible idea had come into my mind. One does not talk about these things, but a damaged spacesuit is too valuable to be thrown away, even if it has killed its wearer. It is repaired, renumbered—and issued to someone else. . . .

What happens to the soul of a man who dies between the stars, far from his native world? Are you still here, Bernie, clinging to the last object that linked you to your lost and distant home?

As I fought the nightmares that were swirling around me—for now it seemed that the scratchings and soft fumblings were coming from all directions—there was one last hope to which I clung. For the sake of my sanity, I had to prove that this wasn't Bernie's suit—that the metal walls so closely wrapped around me had never been another man's coffin.

It took me several tries before I could press the right button and switch my transmitter to the emergency wave length. "Station!" I gasped. "I'm in trouble! Get records to check my suit history and——"

I never finished; they say my yell wrecked the microphone. But what man alone in the absolute isolation of a spacesuit would *not* have yelled when something patted him softly on the back of the neck?

I must have lunged forward, despite the safety harness, and smashed against the upper edge of the control panel. When the res-

cue squad reached me a few minutes later, I was still unconscious, with an angry bruise across my forehead.

And so I was the last person in the whole satellite relay system to know what had happened. When I came to my senses an hour later, all our medical staff was gathered around my bed, but it was quite a while before the doctors bothered to look at me. They were much too busy playing with the three cute kittens our badly misnamed Tommy had been rearing in the seclusion of my spacesuit's Number Five Storage Locker.

Close Up

1. Satellite Control picks up a small echo two miles away from the Space Station. (a) What object does the Station Supervisor discover is causing this echo? (b) Why does the Station Supervisor decide that someone must retrieve this object?

2. According to the Station Supervisor, how are the spacesuits used on the station different from those used on the Moon?

3. When the Station Supervisor climbs into his spacesuit, he follows the FORB procedure. (a) What are the four steps in this procedure? (b) What other normal procedure does he decide to overlook?

4. (a) The meter on the control panel indicates that everything is normal, but the Station Supervisor knows that something is wrong. Why? (b) When he recalls how Bernie Summers died, why does he conclude that this spacesuit may be haunted?

5. Before the Station Supervisor put on the spacesuit, he had spotted the cat, Tommy, nearby. (a) What did he think the cat wanted when it mewed plaintively at him? (b) In light of the ending of this story, what do you think it wanted?

Point of View

In fiction, a story may be told by a character who appears in it. This character, called the narrator, tells the story in the first person, and refers to himself or herself by the pronoun "I." This character is not the author.

When you read a story told this way, you learn the narrator's personal thoughts and feelings. You see the events unfold through the narrator's eyes. Often, you interpret these events in the same way the narrator does.

1. The author of this story is Arthur C. Clarke. (a) Who is the narrator? (b) Is the narrator the main, or most important, character in this story or is he a minor character?

2. The narrator tells you his true thoughts and feelings. When he tells Control he will retrieve the object, he tries to make it sound as though he is "doing everyone a great favor." How does he really feel about going out after the object?

3. (a) When does the narrator first fear that he is facing insanity? (b) What facts fit this explanation?

4. The narrator is the last person to discover the true explanation for what happened in the spacesuit. (a) When do you learn this explanation? (b) Who in this story could have given you this information earlier?

JUDGMENTS

Understanding Statements of Fact and Statements of Opinion

A statement of fact contains information that can be proved true or false. For example, "Bernie's oxygen regulator had run wild and sent the pressure soaring, the safety valve had failed to blow— and a faulty joint had given way instead." This is a statement of fact because all the information it contains can be proved true or false by carefully examining the spacesuit.

A statement of opinion is an expression of a personal belief or attitude. It does not contain information that can be proved true or false. For example, the narrator says, "It was not really a good place to work, for the view was too overwhelming." The narrator believes this is not a really good place to work, but others might think it is a good place to work. A statement that predicts the future is a statement of opinion. You can anticipate what will happen in the future, but you cannot prove it until it happens.

1. Which of the following items are statements of fact?
   a. Radar showed a small echo two miles away, almost stationary, about five degrees west of Sirius.
   b. The Air Force lost track of several satellites when their transmitters failed.
   c. The view from the "night" side was magnificent.
   d. Cats can adapt themselves to a weightless environment.
   e. A spacesuit is filled with many tiny noises.

2. Which of the following items are statements of opinion?
   a. The test satellite was cone-shaped and had antennas.
   b. Writing maintenance schedules is boring work.
   c. They will be able to construct the first truly global radio and television network.
   d. A single day's delay on the job cost a million dollars.
   e. Pets mean a great deal to people who are thousands of miles from Earth.

3. Which of the following items are statements of fact and which are statements of opinion?
   a. The spacesuits were big enough for only one person.
   b. Tommy was a cute cat.
   c. Spacesuits are repaired, renumbered, and reissued.
   d. The Earth looks beautiful from space.
   e. Someone will crash into the satellite.

WORD ATTACK

Understanding Words Used As Nouns and Verbs

A noun is a word that names a person, place, thing, or idea. For example, the words *supervisor*, *space*, *satellite*, and *fear* are nouns.

A verb is a word that expresses action or a state of being. For example, the words *write*, *construct*, and *was* are verbs.

Some words can be used as either nouns or verbs. For example, in the following sentence, *orbit* is used as a noun that means "the path of an object in space around another object."

The object matched our *orbit* precisely.

In the next sentence, *orbit* is used as a verb that means "to revolve around."

We wanted to *orbit* the Earth.

The meaning of a word in a particular sentence sometimes depends on whether it is used as a noun or a verb.

▶ In each sentence below, decide whether the *italicized* word is used as a noun or a verb. Then look up each word in the dictionary. If the word is used in the sentence as a noun, read the definitions by the abbreviation *n*. Choose the definition that best fits the sentence. If the word is used as a verb, read the definitions by the abbreviation *v*. Then choose the definition that best fits the sentence.

a. I wanted to *yell* for help.

b. The people at Control say that my *yell* wrecked the microphone.

c. After a brief *search* through the files, Control gave me the information I needed.

d. I asked them to *search* through the files to find out if this had been Bernie's suit.

e. I tried to retrieve my report so that I could *void* it.

f. He was alone in his spaceship in a soundless *void*.

g. There was something out there—something seeking shelter from the pitiless *vacuum* of space.

h. They would *vacuum* the chamber thoroughly to remove the debris.

"I'll Give You Law!"

Molly Picon

For three months she lived in a dream, and then, the wonderful day came.

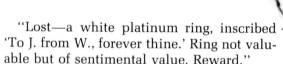

When I read the newspaper, there is always a must section in it that I never pass by. This is the lost and found advertisements usually buried in the back pages. This is a habit I picked up from my grandmother. She always took a keen interest in who had lost what, and who was honestly reporting on items found. She could people a whole colony from just a couple of advertisements.

"Lost—one black puppy with a white patch around its eye. Answers to the name 'Spot.' Please call Beaver 6–5000. Reward."

From this my grandmother would draw for me a picture of a child sobbing itself to sleep at night, of parents out searching the streets anxiously, calling in hopeless voices, "Spot. Here, Spot. Come on, Spot. Here, boy."

The picture was so visual to both of us we used to sit there with tears in our eyes, willing Spot to answer, wanting the child to cry with joy and not in sorrow.

"Lost—a white platinum ring, inscribed 'To J. from W., forever thine.' Ring not valuable but of sentimental value. Reward."

My grandmother would analyze the situation for me.

"What kind of a woman is she to lose a ring like that?" Grandma would cry sternly. "In the first place, how could it fall off her finger?"

"Maybe it was loose?" I would suggest helpfully.

"Loose? Why should it be loose?" Grandma was not going to accept any of my flimsy excuses. "She didn't have a little string in the house she could wind around the ring so it could fit? Don't give me such stories."

"Maybe she took it off in a washroom when she was washing her hands, and then she forgot it," I would then suggest.

"A ring like that you don't take off, and if you take it off, you don't forget it. I'm only

sorry for that W., whoever he is. A bargain he hasn't got in her, believe me."

"But, Bubba, how do we know that J. is a woman and W. is a man? Maybe J. is the man and W. is the woman, and *she* gave *him* the ring."

My grandmother was openly amused at such innocence.

"A lady to give a man a ring?" Absolutely out of the question. My grandmother wouldn't accept it even as an idea.

"Maybe it was a wedding ring," I argued. "Sometimes people have double ring ceremonies."

For the sake of argument, Grandma would concede.

"All right. So J. is the man. So it was a wedding ring. So what kind of a man loses his wedding ring? A good-for-nothing loafer. So what does she need him for? She should let him go with the ring together."

In no time at all, my grandmother would get into a rage at the low character of this man, who thought so little of his marriage vows that he didn't have the decency to hang on to his wedding band.

We thought about all the lost items with equal interest. We wondered about the found items as well, visualizing the happy claimants, and the honest finders handsomely rewarded. At such moments, God was in Heaven, and all was right with the world.

And then one day, we moved swiftly from the land of fantasy to a world of realities. My grandmother found something!

"What is it? What is it?" I asked, hopping with excitement.

"A lavaliere!"[1] My grandmother was absolutely overwhelmed. She had never found anything in her life, and now, here in her hand, was this magnificent lavaliere.

"It must be very expensive," I said, running my fingers over it.

"A fortune," my grandmother said posi-

tively. She held it up against her. "A regular fortune," she breathed.

"Are you going to keep it?" I asked.

She gave me a sharp look. If the thought entered her mind, she wasn't going to admit it to me.

" 'Am I going to keep it,' " she asked. "Such a question." She threw her shawl over her head.

"Where are you going?" I asked. "Can I go, too?"

"I'm going to the police station. Let them worry about it. You can't come," she added firmly. "A police station is not respectable."

At the police station, the property clerk informed her politely that if the lavaliere was not claimed within ninety days, the police department would turn the jewelry over to her, and she would be its rightful and legal owner. He took her name and address and wrote it down. They would let her know, he said indifferently.

"Oh, I hope nobody claims it," I said fervently. "Oh, Bubba, I hope whoever lost it doesn't even know they lost it."

Such a dilemma for my grandmother. If ever she yearned for anything, it was for this lavaliere. On the other hand, her active imagination conjured up for her such tearful scenes that she couldn't wait for the loser to come and claim her property.

She could not compromise with her stern standards. She advertised in the local paper, running the advertisement for three days. Then she had to abandon this, because money spent for anything but food was both wasteful and sinful. During that three-day period, we waited with our hearts in our mouths. Every time there was a knock at the door, we could see the lavaliere leaving us forever. Meanwhile, my grandmother took to haunting the police station and the property clerk. How are you, she would ask, and how is the family? In the beginning he would dismiss this with a curt "fine we haven't heard don't call on us we'll let you know" attitude.

---

1. lavaliere (lăv′ə-lîr′) n.: A necklace made up of a pendant on a chain.

But my grandmother began to take a personal interest in the policemen at the precinct. After all, she visited them daily. It wasn't like they were strangers, she would tell me. She knew their names and the names of their wives and the names of their children. She knew at any given moment what child was suffering from what childhood disease, how hard it was to make ends meet on a policeman's salary, what policeman was going to night school to study law and improve his station in life, what policeman was smarting at being passed over when promotions were handed out. Only the property clerk held out. When he would look up and see my grandmother, he would mutter and groan.

"Mrs. Ostrow," he would say, "don't you have anything to do at home?"

"Why don't I have something to do at home?" my grandmother would regard him scornfully. "You think I like to come here day after day?"

"So why do you come?" he would ask logically.

"To see what I have to see," she would tell him. And then she would demand to see the lavaliere with "my own eyes." And then she would subject him to a searching questioning. Who had come today, and what had they claimed, and wasn't it possible the lavaliere had belonged to one of the people who had come, and had he told anybody about it, and if he was keeping it such a big secret, how could anybody know he had it in the first place?

As hard as I prayed that no one would show up, he prayed that someone—anyone—would.

"Ninety days," he would cry, clutching his hair. "I'll never survive it."

"Bubba," I once asked, "why *do* you go there every day? Don't you trust him?"

"Trust him?" My grandmother smiled at such innocence.

"But he's a policeman. And he's right in the police station," I protested. "What could he do?"

My grandmother didn't want to fill my mind with stories of what could happen to a policeman in a police station. After all, he might have been an officer, but at the same time he was only a man. Man is weak, and temptation is strong. My grandmother could not visualize a man so strong-minded as to be able to resist the golden lure presented by such a collection of lost treasures.

I never knew that ninety days could last so long. But eventually the ninetieth day arrived, bringing with it much excitement and expectation. My grandmother and I dressed as though we were going to a party. She was going to allow me to go with her for the presentation. On the way we discussed her immense good fortune.

"When I die," she said to me, "I want you to have it."

"Please, Bubba," I said, uncomfortably. It seemed like a grim note to inject in an otherwise cloudless day.

"No," she insisted seriously. "I want you to have it. It will be like a—what is the word I want, Malkele?"

"An heirloom?"

"That's the word." She pounced on it with satisfaction. "And when you die, your children will have it."

In two sentences, my grandmother had disposed of us both.

At the police station, my grandmother was greeted with happy smiles, even from the property clerk. I should say, especially from the property clerk. It was the happiest day of his life.

When my grandmother finally held the lavaliere in her hand, her eyes misted over. She couldn't speak, but she nodded her head tremulously at the policemen.

"Don't be a stranger," they urged her. "Don't wait till you find something before you drop in."

"Such nice boys," my grandmother said, as we left the station. She touched her eyes with her handkerchief. "Such good boys, even *him*," she said, referring to the property

clerk. "He had his eye on it, but out of respect, he didn't touch it." I believed my grandmother. I didn't see how that property clerk could have looked at that lavaliere for ninety days and so nobly fought off temptation.

When we got home, my grandmother promptly put the lavaliere on.

"I'll wear it night and day," she vowed. "I'll never take it off." For a week she was as good as her word.

Then one day there came a knock at the door, and tragedy swept in, escorted by an embarrassed and harassed property clerk from the police station.

"Where is it?" cried the woman he had brought to the door. She looked at my grandmother. "My lavaliere she's wearing," she cried in horror, pointing to my grandmother.

My grandmother looked at both of them, appalled. Her hand went up automatically to clutch the lavaliere.

"It's mine," she said. "You told me, after ninety days . . ."

"That's right," the property clerk said promptly. "Legally it is yours. That's what I've been trying to tell this lady. She didn't claim it in ninety days, and the law says . . ."

"I'll give you law," the lady shouted vigorously, pounding him on the arm. "Does the law ask me where was I the past ninety days? Does the law say after ninety days thieves and murderers can do whatever they want? Law! I'll give you law!"

"Please, lady," the property clerk pleaded. "Let's try to be calm."

"Calm!" she took up the cry. "I'll give you calm!"

My grandmother entered the fray briskly.

"So much commotion," she said. "You want the neighbors to think we're killing you on the doorstep. Come inside." She urged them in and closed the door. "So if you'll stop talking and tell me where you were," she said, guiding the distracted woman to a seat, "we'll listen and we'll be the same good friends."

"Where was I?" the woman said, shaking her head. "My daughter was having her baby, so she says to me, 'Ma,' she says, 'if you don't come, I won't have it, that's all.' Scared to death with the first child. Wait till she's had six, like me."

"I had eleven," my grandmother topped her quietly.

"Eleven! So I don't have to tell you," the woman continued. "So I had to go to Scranton yet—a husband takes it into his head to make a living in Scranton," she added in a note of disbelief. "With all the children I had to go. One month in advance, just in case. And then, with God's help, the baby comes. Now she's afraid to hold it, it might break. And she's afraid to wash it. It might come apart in the water. And she's afraid to feed it. It throws up on her. One month. Two months. Finally I say to her, 'Rebeccah,' I say, 'enough is enough already. Whatever you'll do, you'll do.'"

My grandmother was already making tea for everybody, bustling about the kitchen, putting crackers and jam on the table.

"The young people today," she commented.

"So when I come back, I first realized my lavaliere is gone. I'm not hung with jewelry, and between you and me and the lamppost," she added confidentially to my grandmother, "I need a lavaliere like I need a hole in the head. But when I need a little extra money in an emergency, that lavaliere saves my life."

"How does it save your life?" I asked, intrigued.

She made a face, lifting her eyebrows eloquently to the grown-ups present.

"I bring it to the pawnshop and whatever few pennies he gives me . . ."

"The pawnshop!" I was indignant. "She doesn't even *wear* it, Bubba," I said passionately. "Don't give it back. You don't have to. The law says you don't have to."

"That's right," the property clerk said

instantly. He was on his second cup of tea and using my grandmother's jam as if the jar had an endless bottom.

The woman opened her mouth to protest, but my grandmother stopped her by holding up her hand for silence.

"Malkele," she said gently, "there is a law here, too." She laid her hand tenderly on my heart. "Look in your heart and tell me. Suppose it was your lavaliere. Suppose you lost it and somebody else found it. Ninety days, a thousand days . . . how would you feel?"

"I would want it back," I answered honestly, "no matter how."

She spread her hands out eloquently.

"So?" she asked me.

"That's not fair," I burst out.

"Fair? Who said anything about fair?" She reached up and took off the lavaliere. She fondled it for a moment, and then handed it over to the woman.

"Why should I complain?" she asked no one in particular and shrugged. "For three months I lived in a dream, and for five days I lived like a queen. Is that bad?"

Close Up

1. Why does Grandma enjoy reading the lost and found advertisements?

2. Grandma moves swiftly "from the land of fantasy to the land of realities" when she finds the lavaliere. Why does this find create a dilemma for her?

3. (a) Although Grandma is the legal owner, she decides to give the lavaliere back to its original owner. Why? (b) Do you think Grandma made the right decision? Why or why not?

Point of View

A story told in the first person shows you other characters and events from the narrator's point of view. If the narrator is a minor character, you see the major character in the story through the narrator's eyes. You learn the narrator's thoughts and feelings directly, and the narrator may interpret the main character's thoughts and feelings for you. If the narrator is a child, your enjoyment of the story may increase when you notice the difference between what the narrator sees and understands and what you see and understand.

1. (a) Who is the narrator of this story? (b) Who is the main, or most important, character?

2. (a) When the narrator suggests that Grandma could keep the lavaliere, what does Grandma say? (b) What does the narrator suspect she is thinking? Find a statement to support your answer.

3. Because the narrator was young at the time of this story, she accepts without question many of Grandma's evaluations. (a) Do you think the lavaliere really was worth "a regular fortune"? (b) Do you think the property clerk really "had his eye on" the lavaliere? Why or why not?

4. The narrator tells you many things about Grandma, but you also learn about her from her actions. Find an action to support each of the following statements: (a) Grandma is honest; (b) Grandma is imaginative; (c) Grandma doesn't have much money.

Activity

▶ **Composition.** Look through the lost and found advertisements in your local newspaper. Write a paragraph telling the story behind one of the ads.

JUDGMENTS

Evaluating Evidence

A statement of fact contains information that can be proved true or false by reliable evidence. Reliable evidence is proof that comes from measurement or observation, from reference sources (e.g., encyclopedias, dictionaries, atlases), or from experts in the field. For example, look at the following statements: (1) San Francisco is in California. You can check an atlas or a map to see if the information in this statement is true or false. (2) The room is 18 feet long by 17 feet wide. You can check the information by measuring the room yourself. (3) The necklace is worth $575. You can check the information by consulting an expert; for example, a jewelry appraiser. Of course, keep in mind that even experts can be wrong.

A statement of opinion expresses a personal belief or attitude. To judge if a statement of opinion is valid, ask these questions:

1. Is the person offering the opinion objective; that is, uninfluenced by personal motives?
2. Does the person have facts to back up his or her opinion?
3. Is the person an expert in the field?

For example, a manufacturer might claim that its coffee is the best. You might suspect that the manufacturer is not being objective. On the other hand, a consumer group may run tests on various coffees and claim that Brand A is the best. You might judge that this opinion is sound.

---

1. Match each statement in the right-hand column with the evidence from the left-hand column that you would use to prove the information true or false.

   a. The dog weighs 13 pounds.

   b. *Claimant* means "a person making a claim."

   c. The population of Saddly in 1980 was 5345.

   d. The antique chair is worth $6000.

   (1) The 1980 census report

   (2) An appraiser of antique furniture

   (3) Direct measurement using a scale

   (4) A dictionary of the English language

2. For **a–e** which source is more likely to be objective?

   a. The water at the health spa is superior to other water.

   (1) Director of promotion for the health spa

   (2) Results of tests on water made by US Government

b. John will do well in college next year.
  - (1) John's parents
  - (2) John's teacher
c. The weather tomorrow will be bright and sunny.
  - (1) A meteorologist
  - (2) A promoter of an outdoor concert
d. Unless the bridge is repaired now, it will fall down within ten years.
  - (1) A municipal board of bridge control
  - (2) A construction firm that needs business

WORD ATTACK

Finding Verb Forms in a Dictionary

A verb has four principal parts. They are the present infinitive, the past, the past participle, and the present participle.

Present Infinitive	Past	Past Participle	Present Participle
bury	buried	(have) buried	burying
speak	spoke	(have) spoken	speaking
find	found	(have) found	finding

You can use a dictionary to find the correct spellings of the principal parts of a verb. First, look up the present infinitive form (this is the entry word). You will find the following information:

speak (spēk) *v.*: spoke, spoken, speaking.

The first word after the colon is the past, the second is the past participle, and the third is the present participle. Sometimes the past and the present participle are the same form. When they are, you will find only two words after the colon. For example:

find (fīnd) *v.*: found, finding

▶ Use a dictionary to help you put each of the *italicized* verbs in the form indicated in parentheses.
  - **a.** Grandma *withdraw* (past) her claim to the beautiful lavaliere.
  - **b.** She shouldn't have *mislay* (past participle) the lavaliere.
  - **c.** We were *rendezvous* (present participle) at midnight.
  - **d.** She should have *wind* (past participle) a little string around her finger.

The Man Who Talked with Books

Lucille Lewis

Old Mr. Spry tiptoed down the hall, listened carefully, then eased open the door to Miss Pringle's room.

He wasn't concerned about Katie, the maid, who was noisily running the sweeper over the spacious floor; he just didn't enjoy Mrs. Terboven, the landlady, ordering him about when not too long ago he'd owned his own home. But that was when his wife Mary was alive, the three boys were little, and everything was different.

Through a bay window which looked out on a garden, morning light revealed crowded bookshelves lining the walls. Mr. Spry felt betrayed. A month ago when he'd come to look at the room, Mrs. Terboven had assured him that his own books would soon adorn the shelves as Miss Pringle would be leaving. But Miss Pringle had stayed on, and Mr. Spry wanted the room more than he'd ever wanted anything in his whole seventy years.

He couldn't expect Mrs. Terboven to understand the importance of this room. He was a collector, psychologist, student of crime—and even more important, a retired librarian; and his catalogued library was enormous. With Mary gone, and the boys all married, he had done all he could to make room for the huge collection, but books had overflowed everywhere.

Mr. Spry hesitated, then stepped gingerly into the room and ran a practiced finger over the book titles, muttering endearments. The haphazard arrangement offended his professional eye—everything from *Black Beauty* to Euclidean geometry.

The books certainly didn't fit Miss Pringle's personality. Or anyone's. After a lifetime of observation as a public librarian, he knew with certainty what type of book would be owned by what kind of person. Miss Pringle remained the rare exception, and for a month he'd pondered the mystery of the motley collection.

"Come out of that room, Mr. Spry. I have to tell you that every day." Mrs. Terboven loomed in the doorway. "Miss Pringle gave strict orders—nobody's to touch those books. She even dusts them herself."

"My family would be so happy if they could see me living in this lovely room," Mr. Spry murmured.

"Well, all you have to do," Mrs. Terboven said airily, "is to think up some way to get Miss Pringle out."

Mr. Spry squeezed into his tiny room, sat on the bed, and patted a book carton lovingly. Getting Miss Pringle out was a tempting idea. But how? He weighed the problem. Miss Pringle must get married and move away. But married to whom? He considered those eligible—the other boarders in the house. Mr. Uhl was even older then he was; Mr. Denton was attached to a wispy little wife who lived with him in his stark room. Mr. Abbott?

Getting Miss Pringle and Mr. Abbott together would be just about as difficult as wrapping two watermelons, as a matter of fact. Drab and morose, they didn't merit a second look from anybody, not even from each other.

And yet, he had the strange feeling that somehow they did belong together. The idea disturbed him because usually everything in Mr. Spry's life was neatly catalogued, ready at an instant's notice, and now he couldn't name the source of the absurd idea.

As a collector and student of crime, he began to scissor police stories from a stack of old newspapers while one corner of the psychologist's mind dealt with the problem of Miss Pringle and Mr. Abbott. He remembered a movie he'd seen recently where two mousy people found each other and lived happily ever after. He paused in his clipping. Miss Pringle and Mr. Abbott must find each other. He'd see to that.

Across the dinner table that night he studied Miss Pringle with keen interest. She was hopeless. Dull hair pinned severely away from a face devoid of makeup, her eyes obscured by heavy, bone-rimmed glasses. But in the movies he'd seen greater transformations take place. The hero usually looked at the girl with a more perceptive eye than others and said, "Why, you're lovely!" And she immediately became so.

But Mr. Abbott was no hero. Above a blank, pasty face a bald head gleamed, and he seemed too puny to contemplate making any such remark.

Later that evening Mr. Spry, the psychologist, rummaged through a carton and emerged with a text on the behavior of the abnormally shy.

The next morning at breakfast he launched his campaign. "Why, Miss Pringle, your hair *is* red. I'd never have noticed if Mr. Abbott hadn't mentioned it."

The effect on Miss Pringle was more than Mr. Spry had hoped for. A dull red, matching the roots of her hair, flooded her face. Wordless, she snatched her purse and gloves and streaked from the dining room.

Mr. Spry knew he was on the right track. Miss Pringle was merely afraid of her true self, as the book said.

With jaunty self-confidence Mr. Spry fell into step beside Mr. Abbott, who ate breakfast later downtown. "If I had your looks, young fellow, I'd dress up to them," Mr. Spry said. "Miss Pringle told me she thought you were a most unusual looking man. Wear a gray flannel suit—a pink shirt, grow a mustache——"

"Any particular color?" Mr. Abbott snarled, his face ashen.

"No—er—that is, no." Mr. Spry gaped as Mr. Abbott hurled himself into the subway entrance.

At dinner that evening, Miss Pringle and Mr. Abbott, who had formerly ignored each other, threw such looks of hatred at one another and at Mr. Spry that they forced Mr. Spry to go to his room earlier than usual. He felt hurt and a little ridiculous at such fury; he was only trying to help them to a rich, full life.

The vision of the back room, so bright that morning, faded. Instead, his gaze met the stack of newspapers. Disheartened, he began clipping crime stories.

He settled back comfortably to review a three-month-old story of the upper-Manhattan bank robbery, but he couldn't keep his attention on the printed page. Besides, he knew the story by heart; how the holdup had been so perfectly timed that no one suspected the tall, well-dressed woman who had engaged the bank guard in conversation while her male companion had forced the teller to surrender the cash.

Mr. Spry forced his attention back to the newspaper. The bank teller remembered the dapper little man: well-tailored, well-barbered, with a neat mustache; the bank guard recalled the tall woman's red hair and regal figure.

In the silence of his tiny room Mr. Spry could hear the sound of his heart beating, and it was a terrifying sound. Mr. Abbott and the mustache, Miss Pringle and the red hair—the details he had selected because he'd read this story before and his memory had been trying to tell him that they belonged together.

And the money? The books with their ill-assorted titles suddenly made sense.

The next morning Mr. Spry, librarian, was calmly measuring empty bookshelves in Miss Pringle's room, despite the crowd of detectives, policemen, and photographers. Two detectives were still examining the remaining books, rifling the pages and extracting twenty-dollar bills which they added to the stacks on the floor.

"What a hiding place!" One detective, with a puzzled frown, turned to Mr. Spry. "What made you think of the books?"

Mr. Spry studied his tape measure. "I didn't think of them—*they* told me," he murmured absently.

Close Up

1. Mr. Spry is a retired librarian living in a boarding house. (a) Why does he want Miss Pringle's room? (b) What is his plan for getting her to move out of the room?

2. Mr. Spry is a collector, an amateur psychologist, and a student of crime. (a) How does he use his knowledge of psychology to carry out his plan? (b) What does he discover when he begins clipping crime stories?

3. At the end of the story, one detective asks Mr. Spry, "What made you think of the books?" Explain what he means when he answers, "I didn't think of them—*they* told me."

Point of View

In stories told in the third person, the narrator does not appear as a character in the story. The narrator seems to disappear into one of the characters, and tells the story from this character's point of view. For example, in "The Man Who Talked with Books," the narrator disappears into Mr. Spry and tells Mr. Spry's story for him. You learn Mr. Spry's thoughts and feelings, and you see the world through his eyes. The narrator uses third-person pronouns (*he, she, it*) to refer to Mr. Spry and to all other characters.

1. Since this story is told from Mr. Spry's point of view, you learn his thoughts and feelings. (a) Why does Mr. Spry think it will be difficult to get Miss Pringle and Mr. Abbott together? (b) Despite this, what strange feeling does he have about the two of them?

2. When Mr. Spry mentions to Miss Pringle that her hair is red, it has a strong effect on her. (a) According to Mr. Spry, why does she rush from the room? (b) On the basis of the story's ending, why do you think she rushed from the room?

3. Mr. Spry feels hurt and a little ridiculous because of Miss Pringle and Mr. Abbott's strong reaction to his meddling. (a) When does he realize the real reason behind their anger? (b) When did you first suspect the real reason? Why?

Activities

1. **Composition.** In this story, you are not told what Mr. Spry looks like. Write a paragraph describing how you think he looks.

2. Imagine you are a talk-show host. Make a list of ten questions you would ask Mr. Spry if he were your guest.

JUDGMENTS

Quoting Out of Context

The meaning behind a speaker's or writer's words can be changed by quoting out of context: that is, by quoting only part of a statement in order to create an impression different from what the speaker or writer originally intended. For example, look at the following book review:

> *Murder in the Morning* is remarkable for its total lack of originality. It imitates brilliant works of deduction, but it has no brilliance of its own. What could have been a delightful tour de force turns out to be a dull, dreary, dreadful whodunit.

Obviously, this is an unfavorable review. Now look what happens when words are quoted out of context:

> *Murder in the Morning* is remarkable . . . brilliant . . . a delightful tour de force . . .

These words create the impression that the book is well worth reading.

Be careful when you read words quoted out of context. Before making any important judgments, try to locate the complete statement.

▶ Read each statement below. On a piece of paper, write the words or phrases that could be quoted out of context to create a favorable impression.

   a. I admire this writer. She is innovative, clever, and resourceful. Unfortunately, her latest book is not up to par.

   b. The director has worked a miracle. He has taken an exciting story, a superb cast, and a spectacular setting and created the dullest movie I have seen in years.

   c. Tests show Ramoo Chocolate Crunch to be far crunchier than other chocolate bars. However, to achieve this additional crunch, the manufacturer has added pulverized coconut shell, which, in my opinion, destroys the taste.

   d. One hundred people tested the peanut butter. Ninety-nine found it inferior to its competitor. Only five people found it superior to the other leading brand.

   e. This book is a spectacular flop. Although it is advertised as a thrilling novel of intrigue, it is more likely to put you to sleep than to keep you sitting at the edge of your chair.

WORD ATTACK

Understanding Suffixes

A suffix is a letter or group of letters added to the end of a word to change its meaning. Some suffixes indicate person by adding the meaning "a person who." For example, when you add the suffix –*ist* to the word *psychology,* you form a new word, *psychologist* (notice that the *y* is dropped). A *psychologist* is a person who studies or practices psychology (the science dealing with the mind). Three common suffixes that indicate person are –*er,* –*or,* and –*ist.*

1. Add a suffix indicating person to each *italicized* word below. Use a dictionary to help you choose the correct suffix. Write your answers on a piece of paper.
    a. A person who investigates is an *investigate*____. (drop the *e*)
    b. A person who works in a garden is a *garden*____.
    c. A person who collects books is a *collect*____.
    d. A person who boards in someone else's house is a *board*____.
    e. A person who makes matches between people is a *match-make*____ (drop one *e*).
    f. A person who takes photographs is a *photograph*____.
    g. A person who catalogues is a *catalogue*____ (drop one *e*) or a *catalogue*____ (drop the *u* and the *e*).
    h. A person who is an expert in criminology is a *criminology*____ (drop the *y*).
    i. A person who intrudes on someone else's privacy is an *intrude*____ (drop one *e*).

2. A bank teller is a clerk who receives and distributes money. Look up the word *tell* in a dictionary. Which meaning of *tell* was used to form the word *teller?*

The Son from America

Isaac Bashevis Singer

"One Friday morning, when Berlcha was kneading the dough for the Sabbath loaves, the door opened and a nobleman entered."

The village of Lentshin was tiny—a sandy marketplace where the peasants of the area met once a week. It was surrounded by little huts with thatched roofs or shingles green with moss. The chimneys looked like pots. Between the huts there were fields, where the owners planted vegetables or pastured their goats.

In the smallest of these huts lived old Berl, a man in his eighties, and his wife, who was called Berlcha (wife of Berl). Old Berl was one of the Jews who had been driven from their villages in Russia and had settled in Poland. In Lentshin, they mocked the mistakes he made while praying aloud. He spoke with a sharp "r." He was short, broad-shouldered, and had a small white beard, and summer and winter he wore a sheepskin hat, a padded cotton jacket, and stout boots. He walked slowly, shuffling his feet. He had a half acre of field, a cow, a goat, and chickens.

The couple had a son, Samuel, who had gone to America forty years ago. It was said in Lentshin that he became a millionaire there. Every month, the Lentshin letter carrier brought old Berl a money order and a letter that no one could read because many of the words were English. How much money Samuel sent his parents remained a secret. Three times a year, Berl and his wife went on foot to Zakroczym and cashed the money orders there. But they never seemed to use the money. What for? The garden, the cow, and the goat provided most of their needs. Besides, Berlcha sold chickens and eggs, and from these there was enough to buy flour for bread.

No one cared to know where Berl kept the money that his son sent him. There were no thieves in Lentshin. The hut consisted of one room, which contained all their belongings: the table, the shelf for meat, the shelf for milk foods, the two beds, and the clay oven.

Sometimes the chickens roosted in the woodshed and sometimes, when it was cold, in a coop near the oven. The goat, too, found shelter inside when the weather was bad. The more prosperous villagers had kerosene lamps, but Berl and his wife did not believe in newfangled gadgets. What was wrong with a wick in a dish of oil? Only for the Sabbath[1] would Berlcha buy three tallow candles at the store. In summer, the couple got up at sunrise and retired with the chickens. In the long winter evenings, Berlcha spun flax at her spinning wheel and Berl sat beside her in the silence of those who enjoy their rest.

Once in a while when Berl came home from the synagogue after evening prayers, he brought news to his wife. In Warsaw there were strikers who demanded that the czar abdicate. A heretic by the name of Dr. Herzl had come up with the idea that Jews should settle again in Palestine. Berlcha listened and shook her bonneted head. Her face was yellowish and wrinkled like a cabbage leaf. There were bluish sacks under her eyes. She was half deaf. Berl had to repeat each word he said to her. She would say, "The things that happen in the big cities!"

Here in Lentshin nothing happened except usual events: a cow gave birth to a calf, a young couple had a circumcision party, or a girl was born and there was no party. Occasionally, someone died. Lentshin had no cemetery, and the corpse had to be taken to Zakroczym. Actually, Lentshin had become a village with few young people. The young men left for Zakroczym, for Nowy Dwor, for Warsaw, and sometimes for the United States. Like Samuel's, their letters were illegible, the Yiddish[2] mixed with the languages of the countries where they were now living. They sent photographs in which the men

wore top hats and the women fancy dresses like squiresses.

Berl and Berlcha also received such photographs. But their eyes were failing and neither he nor she had glasses. They could barely make out the pictures. Samuel had sons and daughters with Gentile[3] names—and grandchildren who had married and had their own offspring. Their names were so strange that Berl and Berlcha could never remember them. But what difference do names make? America was far, far away on

---

1. Sabbath (săb′əth) n.: The day of the week set aside for rest and worship. (Saturday is the Sabbath for Jews.)

2. Yiddish (yĭd′ĭsh) n.: A Germanic language written in Hebrew letters, spoken by Jews in central and eastern Europe.

3. Gentile (jĕn′tīl) adj.: Pertaining to a Gentile, or someone who is not Jewish.

the other side of the ocean, at the edge of the world. A Talmud[4] teacher who came to Lentshin had said that Americans walked with their heads down and their feet up. Berl and Berlcha could not grasp this. How was it possible? But since the teacher said so it must be true. Berlcha pondered for some time and then she said, "One can get accustomed to everything."

And so it remained. From too much thinking—God forbid—one may lose one's wits.

---

4. Talmud (täl′mŏŏd′) *adj.*: Pertaining to the Talmud, the collection of writings containing early Jewish civil and religious laws.

One Friday morning, when Berlcha was kneading the dough for the Sabbath loaves, the door opened and a nobleman entered. He was so tall that he had to bend down to get through the door. He wore a beaver hat and a cloak bordered with fur. He was followed by Chazkel, the coachman from Zakroczym, who carried two leather valises with brass locks. In astonishment Berlcha raised her eyes.

The nobleman looked around and said to the coachman in Yiddish, "Here it is." He took out a silver ruble and paid him. The coachman tried to hand him change but he said, "You can go now."

When the coachman closed the door, the nobleman said, "Mother, it's me, your son Samuel—Sam."

Berlcha heard the words and her legs grew numb. Her hands, to which pieces of dough were sticking, lost their power. The nobleman hugged her, kissed her forehead, both her cheeks. Berlcha began to cackle like a hen, "My son!" At that moment Berl came in from the woodshed, his arms piled with logs. The goat followed him. When he saw a nobleman kissing his wife, Berl dropped the wood and exclaimed, "What is this?"

The nobleman let go of Berlcha and embraced Berl. "Father!"

For a long time Berl was unable to utter a sound. He wanted to recite holy words that he had read in the Yiddish Bible, but he could remember nothing. Then he asked, "Are you Samuel?"

"Yes, Father, I am Samuel."

"Well, peace be with you." Berl grasped his son's hand. He was still not sure that he was not being fooled. Samuel wasn't as tall and heavy as this man, but then Berl reminded himself that Samuel was only fifteen years old when he had left home. He must have grown in that faraway country. Berl asked, "Why didn't you let us know that you were coming?"

"Didn't you receive my cable?" Samuel asked.

Berl did not know what a cable was.

Berlcha had scraped the dough from her hands and enfolded her son. He kissed her again and asked, "Mother, didn't you receive a cable?"

"What? If I lived to see this, I am happy to die," Berlcha said, amazed by her own words. Berl, too, was amazed. These were just the words he would have said earlier if he had been able to remember. After a while Berl came to himself and said, "Pescha, you will have to make a double Sabbath pudding in addition to the stew."

It was years since Berl had called Berlcha by her given name. When he wanted to address her, he would say, "Listen," or "Say." It is the young or those from the big cities who call a wife by her name. Only now did Berlcha begin to cry. Yellow tears ran from her eyes, and everything became dim. Then she called out, "It's Friday—I have to prepare for the Sabbath." Yes, she had to knead the dough and braid the loaves. With such a guest, she had to make a larger Sabbath stew. The winter day is short and she must hurry.

Her son understood what was worrying her, because he said, "Mother, I will help you."

Berlcha wanted to laugh, but a choked sob came out. "What are you saying? God forbid."

The nobleman took off his cloak and jacket and remained in his vest, on which hung a solid-gold watch chain. He rolled up his sleeves and came to the trough. "Mother, I was a baker for many years in New York," he said, and he began to knead the dough.

"What! You are my darling son who will say Kaddish[5] for me." She wept raspingly. Her strength left her, and she slumped onto the bed.

Berl said, "Women will always be women." And he went to the shed to get more wood. The goat sat down near the oven; she gazed with surprise at this strange man— his height and his bizarre clothes.

The neighbors had heard the good news that Berl's son had arrived from America and they came to greet him. The women began to help Berlcha prepare for the Sabbath. Some laughed, some cried. The room was full of people, as at a wedding. They asked Berl's son, "What is new in America?" And Berl's son answered, "America is all right."

"Do Jews make a living?"

"One eats white bread there on weekdays."

---

5. Kaddish (kä′dĭsh) n.: A hymn or prayer in praise of God often recited by mourners after a close relative has died.

"Do they remain Jews?"

"I am not a Gentile."

After Berlcha blessed the candles, father and son went to the little synagogue across the street. A new snow had fallen. The son took large steps, but Berl warned him, "Slow down."

In the synagogue the Jews recited "Let Us Exult" and "Come, My Groom." All the time, the snow outside kept falling. After prayers, when Berl and Samuel left the Holy Place, the village was unrecognizable. Everything was covered in snow. One could see only the contours of the roofs and the candles in the windows. Samuel said, "Nothing has changed here."

Berlcha had prepared gefilte fish, chicken soup with rice, meat, carrot stew. Berl recited the benediction over a glass of ritual wine. The family ate and drank, and when it grew quiet for a while one could hear the chirping of the house cricket. The son talked a lot, but Berl and Berlcha understood little. His Yiddish was different and contained foreign words.

After the final blessing Samuel asked, "Father, what did you do with all the money I sent you?"

Berl raised his white brows. "It's here."

"Didn't you put it in a bank?"

"There is no bank in Lentshin."

"Where do you keep it?"

Berl hesitated. "One is not allowed to touch money on the Sabbath, but I will show you." He crouched beside the bed and began to shove something heavy. A boot appeared. Its top was stuffed with straw. Berl removed the straw and the son saw that the boot was full of gold coins. He lifted it.

"Father, this is a treasure!" he called out.

"Well."

"Why didn't you spend it?"

"On what? Thank God, we have everything."

"Why didn't you travel somewhere?"

"Where to? This is our home."

The son asked one question after the other, but Berl's answer was always the same: they wanted for nothing. The garden, the cow, the goat, the chickens provided them with all they needed. The son said, "If thieves knew about this, your lives wouldn't be safe."

"There are no thieves here."

"What will happen to the money?"

"You take it."

Slowly, Berl and Berlcha grew accustomed to their son and his American Yiddish. Berlcha could hear him better now. She even recognized his voice. He was saying, "Perhaps we should build a larger synagogue."

"The synagogue is big enough," Berl replied.

"Perhaps a home for old people."

"No one sleeps in the street."

The next day after the Sabbath meal was eaten, a Gentile from Zakroczym brought a paper—it was the cable. Berl and Berlcha lay down for a nap. They soon began to snore. The goat, too, dozed off. The son put on his cloak and his hat and went for a walk. He strode with his long legs across the marketplace. He stretched out a hand and touched a roof. He wanted to smoke a cigar, but he remembered it was forbidden on the Sabbath. He had a desire to talk to someone, but it seemed that the whole of Lentshin was asleep. He entered the synagogue. An old man was sitting there, reciting psalms. Samuel asked, "Are you praying?"

"What else is there to do when one gets old?"

"Do you make a living?"

The old man did not understand the meaning of these words. He smiled, showing his empty gums, and then he said, "If God gives health, one keeps on living."

Samuel returned home. Dusk had fallen. Berl went to the synagogue for the evening prayers and the son remained with his mother. The room was filled with shadows.

Berlcha began to recite in a solemn singsong, "God of Abraham, Isaac, and Jacob, defend the poor people of Israel and Thy name. The Holy Sabbath is departing; the welcome week is coming to us. Let it be one of health, wealth, and good deeds."

"Mother, you don't need to pray for wealth," Samuel said. "You are wealthy already."

Berlcha did not hear—or pretended not to. Her face had turned into a cluster of shadows.

In the twilight Samuel put his hand into his jacket pocket and touched his passport, his checkbook, his letters of credit. He had come here with big plans. He had a valise filled with presents for his parents. He wanted to bestow gifts on the village. He brought not only his own money but funds from the Lentshin Society in New York, which had organized a ball for the benefit of the village. But this village in the hinterland needed nothing. From the synagogue one could hear hoarse chanting. The cricket, silent all day, started again its chirping. Berlcha began to sway and utter holy rhymes inherited from mothers and grandmothers:

> Thy holy sheep
> In mercy keep,
> In Torah and good deeds;
> Provide for all their needs,
> Shoes, clothes, and bread
> And the Messiah's tread.

Close Up

1. Berl and Berlcha's son, Samuel, has become successful in America and every month sends his parents money. (a) What do they do with this money? (b) Find two other details that show they are content with their life in Lentshin.

2. (a) When their son comes to visit them, at first Berl and Berlcha think he is a nobleman. Why? (b) In what other ways has their son Samuel changed during the forty years he has lived in America?

3. Samuel has come to Lentshin with "big plans." (a) What are some of his plans? (b) At the end of the story, why does he decide that "this village in the hinterland needed nothing"?

Point of View

An omniscient narrator knows all. When a story is told in the third person by an omniscient narrator, you find out what each character in the story is thinking and feeling. You also receive a more complete picture of events than any one character in the story has.

1. (a) How do Berl and Berlcha feel about life in the big cities in Poland? (b) What do they think when the Talmud teacher tells them that "Americans walked with their heads down and their feet up"?

2. (a) When Berl grasps his son's hand, he is still not sure that he is not being fooled. Of what does he then remind himself? (b) Why is he amazed when Berlcha says, "If I lived to see this, I am happy to die"?

3. (a) When Samuel goes for a walk the next day after the Sabbath meal, why does he enter the synagogue? (b) What does he learn from the old man he talks with there?

4. Samuel has measured wealth by his passport, his checkbook, and his letters of credit. (a) By the end of this story, what has he learned about the way the people in Lentshin measure wealth? (b) Do you think he has changed his own way of measuring wealth? Why or why not?

Activity

► **Composition.** How do you measure wealth? Write a paragraph explaining your answer. Begin your paragraph with the words "A wealthy person is one who . . ."

JUDGMENTS

Identifying Hasty Generalizations

A generalization is a conclusion or opinion that is formed from observations. For example, imagine you enter a small village. You observe many small, run-down houses, people dressed in plain clothing, and children playing with homemade toys. You do not see any cars, television sets, radios, or swimming pools. Therefore, on the basis of your observations, you make the generalization that the people in this village are poor. Your generalization may or may not be valid. The more observations you make, however, the more likely it is that your generalization will be valid or sound.

A hasty generalization occurs when you do not make enough observations. For example, imagine you hear one person in this village say that he is unhappy. On the basis of this one observation, you generalize that all people in this village are unhappy. Your generalization is hasty because you based it on only one observation. Other observations may have shown that many people in the village are happy.

A stereotype is a type of hasty generalization. A stereotype is an opinion about a whole group of people that does not allow for individual differences. For example, the statement "All librarians are shy and withdrawn" is a stereotype. It does not take into account all the librarians who are not shy and withdrawn.

To determine whether a generalization is hasty or whether it is valid, ask yourself two questions: (1) Is the generalization based on a sufficient number of observations? (2) Are there any exceptions to the generalization?

---

1. Which of the following generalizations are valid and which are hasty? Explain your answers.
   a. A stranger stops at the house of Berl and Berlcha to ask directions. He sees a goat in the house and generalizes that in Lentshin goats and people always live together.
   b. Samuel asks all the people he meets in the synagogue and in the marketplace if they want a gold piece to buy something they need. No one wants the gold. Samuel generalizes that the people of Lentshin have no need for gold.
   c. Samuel visits the school in Lentshin and finds sick children in every grade. He generalizes that the children in Lentshin need better medical care.

d. Every place he goes in Lentshin Samuel sees only old people. He generalizes that few young people stay in the village.

e. Samuel hears one of the students in the Lentshin school recite his lesson very well. Samuel generalizes that all the children in Lentshin are excellent scholars.

2. Write one valid generalization about your school. Then write one hasty generalization a person who visits your school for one day might make.

WORD ATTACK

Understanding Negative Prefixes

A prefix is a letter or group of letters added to the beginning of a word to change its meaning. Some prefixes add the meaning "not." Examples of such prefixes are:

a-	in-
dis-	ir-
il-	un-
im-	

When you add a prefix meaning "not" to a word, you create its antonym, or a word that is opposite in meaning. For example, *unusual* is the antonym of *usual*.

▶ Add a negative prefix to each of the words below. Use your dictionary to help you choose the correct prefix.

a. satisfied
b. proper
c. literate
d. recognizable
e. able

f. typical
g. legible
h. reverent
i. accustomed
j. like

REVIEW QUIZ

On the Selections

1. In "Joining the Circle," Robin Lee Graham tells about how he started sailing at an impressionable age. How did his love of the open sea make him feel about school?

2. Why isn't Robin afraid when the wind rises and the waves crash against *HIC*?

3. In "The Haunted Spacesuit," why doesn't the Station Supervisor check the spacesuit's internal lockers before sealing himself in?

4. Once inside the spacesuit, why does he think that something is very wrong?

5. In "I'll Give You Law!" why does Grandma visit the police station every day for ninety days?

6. When Malkele looks inside her own heart, what decision does she make about the lavaliere?

7. Explain the title of "The Man Who Talked with Books."

8. Why did the landlady want to keep Mr. Spry out of Miss Pringle's room?

9. In "The Son from America," why don't Berl and Berlcha spend the money?

10. Which do you think is more important to Berl and Berlcha—religion and heritage or material wealth?

On Judgments

1. (a) In "Joining the Circle," who can give you first-hand information about the voyage aboard the *HIC*? (b) Who in this story can give you second-hand information?

2. Which of the following are statements of fact and which are statements of opinion?
   a. Robin sailed the *Golden Hind* to Huahina, Tahaa, and Bora Bora.
   b. These islands are incredibly beautiful.
   c. A police officer's job is exciting and rewarding.
   d. In this state, a police officer must have completed two years of college.

3. Read the following items and answer the questions.
   a. You want to decide whether or not to see a new movie. You listen to the movie's star talk about it on a television show. You also read a review in the local paper.
      Which source is more likely to give you objective information?
   b. You want to decide which coffeepot to buy. You check a consumer's guide and you read the advertisements by the major manufacturers.
      Which source is more likely to give you objective information?

4. Which of the following statements are stereotypes?
   a. All motorcyclists need driver's licenses.
   b. All motorcyclists wear black leather jackets.
   c. All teenagers like loud music.
   d. All nurses are women.
   e. All people who vote in presidential elections are over eighteen.

On Point of View

▶ Decide whether the following statements are true or false.
   a. In a true story written in the first person, the author and the narrator are the same person.
   b. In a story told in the first person, all characters are identified by the pronouns *he*, *she*, and *it*.
   c. The narrator is always the main character in the story.
   d. An omniscient narrator sees into the mind of only one character.

COMPOSITION

Persuasion   **Persuasion is the act of getting someone to agree with you.** When you write a persuasive paragraph, you try to persuade your readers that you are right about something. Here are some tips for writing a persuasive paragraph.

1. Make your point in your first sentence.
2. Support your point with specific reasons or examples.
3. Place these reasons or examples in a logical order: for example, most important to least important.
4. End your paragraph with a clincher statement. This means restate your point so that you leave your readers with a strong impression.

When writing, avoid these pitfalls, since they are examples of faulty reasoning.

1. Arguing in circles. This means providing a reason or cause for something that is the same as the effect. For example, "I believe that all people are equal because I see no major differences among people."
2. Using irrelevant evidence. This means supporting your ideas with reasons or details that have no bearing on the matter. For example, "Peter should be made captain of the debating society because he is handsome and gives good parties."
3. Making hasty generalizations. This means forming generalizations based on insufficient observations. For example, "Everyone in this school must be loud and rowdy. Last week I saw one boy running down the hall shouting."

---

1. Choose one of the following topics. Decide what point you would like to make about this topic. Then write a persuasive paragraph.
   a. Coed sports teams
   b. School credit for work experience
   c. The value of television
   d. The importance of participating in extracurricular school activities

2. Imagine you (or your friend) are running for election for a school office. Write a paragraph persuading your readers to vote for you.

BEFORE GOING ON

Skimming and Intensive Reading

Skimming is the process by which your eyes sweep across and down printed pages to get a general idea about their content. Skimming is a skill to use when you need to determine quickly what the main points of a reading selection are or whether or not you want to read the selection more carefully and slowly.

Skimming is meant to give you only the highlights of a selection. It would be a poor way to read something you're going to be tested on or something you want to learn thoroughly. When you skim:

1. Read the title. It will give you some idea as to what the selection is about.
2. Read the first and last paragraphs. Knowing how a selection begins and ends gives clues to what's in between.
3. Look through the pages quickly, reading any subtitles or other words in heavy print just as you read the title.
4. Run your index finger down the middle of the pages, letting your eyes sweep across the lines of print.
5. Pause for four or five seconds after every page or two and try to recall some of the ideas your mind took in.
6. When you have finished reading the last page, answer one or both of the following questions: Is this selection likely to have the information I want? Am I likely to enjoy reading this selection?

Intensive reading is just the opposite of skimming. It means reading slowly and carefully. You pause after every one or two paragraphs to summarize the information. Intensive reading is a good way to study or to prepare for a test or to read difficult material.

---

1. Skim "What is ESP?" Then answer the following questions.
   a. What are the three main types of ESP relied on by psychic detectives?
   b. What is precognition?
   c. Can anyone really explain telepathy?
   d. What is a sensitive?
   e. In what ways are psychic powers effective crime-fighting tools?

2. Now read this article intensively, as though you were going to be tested on the information in it. Stop after every one or two paragraphs to write a summary. (Stop after every one paragraph if the paragraph is long and after every two if the paragraphs are short.)

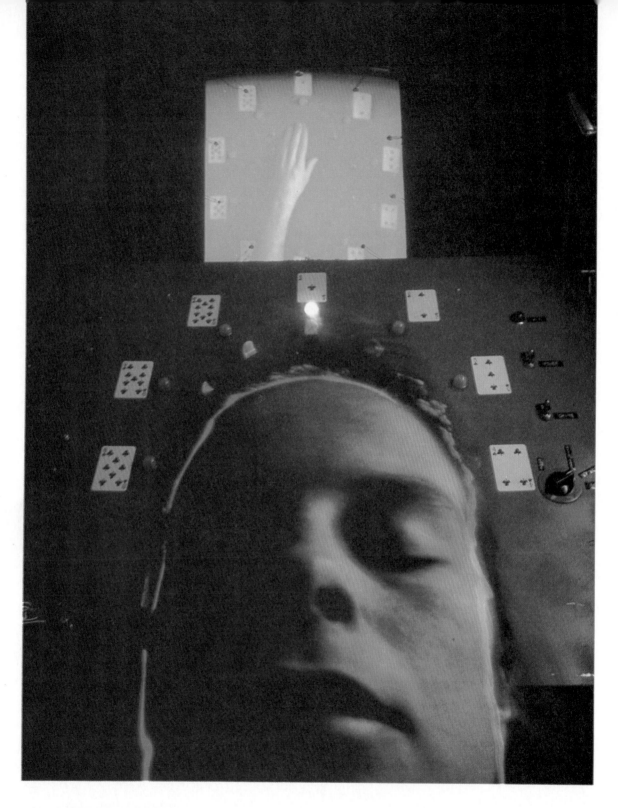

Further Reading

What is ESP?

Stephen Rudley

We are all familiar with the so-called five ordinary senses of sight, sound, taste, touch, and smell. (There are other ordinary senses as well: we also respond to pain, pressure, heat, cold, gravity, and a host of other internal sensations which we are never even aware of consciously.) These ordinary senses are the means by which we receive most of our information about the world around us, and in turn, communicate with it.

But these ordinary senses do not account for ALL the information we receive from our environment. Sometimes we learn about events that have taken place too far away to have been seen or heard, or we learn about them in a manner that can't be explained by normal senses. At other times we may become aware of someone else's thoughts without being told or without receiving any sen-sory messages. Sometimes we may even receive information about events that have not yet happened. These cases cannot be accounted for by our ordinary senses. Instead, we explain them as resulting from extrasensory, or psychic, perceptions.

Our own society has been very slow to accept the evidence of psychic phenomena. But the evidence is there, it is strong, and there is much of it in hundreds of books, countless scientific papers, and thousands of cases and experiments. Indeed, an entire science, parapsychology, has come into being to study the phenomena.

In this article we explore telepathy, clairvoyance, and precognition, the three main types of ESP relied on by psychic detectives. (There are others, including psychokinesis, which is the ability of mind to affect matter by moving or bending objects through mental processes alone.)

Telepathy is the ability to become aware of the mental state of another person: to know what the person is thinking and/or feeling. *Clairvoyance* is the ability to perceive events that are impossible to perceive by the normal senses. Clairvoyance can operate at close range (the subject describes an object in a sealed box right in front of him) or at great distances (the subject perceives events taking place at distant target areas). *Precognition* is the ability to perceive future events. In all three phenomena (clairvoyance, telepathy, and precognition) information about the world reaches the perceiver through extrasensory channels; the five common senses are not utilized. Telepathy, clairvoyance, and precognition are, therefore, all examples of extrasensory perception, or ESP.

Have you ever had a psychic experience? When asked, most of us search our memories for an unusually dramatic or catastrophic event: a plane we "knew" was going to crash, a relative whose unexpected death was already revealed to us in a dream, or a president whose assassination was witnessed in a waking vision.

Scientists believe that psychic exchanges occur normally between people who are closely attached emotionally, as between the members of a family. He goes on to say that psychic events of this nature probably occur more frequently than most of us realize. The problem is that we do not usually recognize them for what they are because they are so very, very ordinary. They are easily dismissed as being more coincidence or good guesswork.

Normally our dreams, thoughts, and fantasies remain within the confines of our own consciousness. No one else knows what we are thinking about—normally.

A young Peruvian, Manuel Cordova-Rios, was kidnapped in the Amazon forest by Amahuaca Indians. During his captivity he took part in an ancient tribal ritual, one which demonstrated that normal experience is only half the story.

In a hidden clearing of a nearby forest, Manuel and his captors began to sing "magical" chants and perform special rituals that succeeded in developing a great feeling of closeness among the men in the group. Then each man sipped an herbal drink called ayahuasca. Soon after they began to see visions.

At one point during the ritual, a memory was triggered in Manuel's mind. He remembered coming face to face with a rare black jaguar on an isolated jungle path. The very moment he thought about *his* black jaguar, a shudder traveled through the group; the others were seeing it too!

In *Wizard of the Upper Amazon*, Manuel Cordova-Rios explains that everyone in the group knew that the black jaguar vision had come from him. Somehow, without communicating in any ordinary way, eleven other people were able to "see" what one man was thinking. In fact, they were so impressed with the vision that they named Manuel Cordova-Rios, Ino Moxo—black panther. This incident is an example of telepathy. In the early days of parapsychology research, telepathy was considered to be a kind of mind-to-mind communication in which one person, the "sender," concentrated on a thought and "sent" it to the mind of a second person, the "receiver," in much the same way your radio picks up the signal which is sent by a braodcasting station.

At present no one can really explain telepathy. We still do not know exactly what it is or how it works. All we can say is that by some as yet unknown process, one person can become aware of what is going on inside another person's mind.

In France in the late nineteenth century, Dr. Charles Richet performed experiments which suggested that a second kind of psychic phenomenon was at work. He found

"All the News That's Fit to Print."

The New York Times.

THE WEATHER.
Unsettled Tuesday; Wednesday, fair, cooler; moderate southerly winds, becoming variable.
For full weather report see Page 23.

VOL. LXI...NO. [illegible] NEW YORK, TUESDAY, APRIL 16, 1912—TWENTY-FOUR PAGES, ONE CENT In Greater New York, Jersey City, and Newark. | Elsewhere, TWO CENTS.

TITANIC SINKS FOUR HOURS AFTER HITTING ICEBERG; 866 RESCUED BY CARPATHIA, PROBABLY 1250 PERISH; ISMAY SAFE, MRS. ASTOR MAYBE, NOTED NAMES MISSING

Col. Astor and Bride, Isidor Straus and Wife, and Maj. Butt Aboard.

"RULE OF SEA" FOLLOWED

Women and Children Put Over in Lifeboats and Are Supposed to be Safe on Carpathia.

PICKED UP AFTER 8 HOURS

Vincent Astor Calls at White Star Office for News of His Father and Leaves Weeping.

FRANKLIN HOPEFUL ALL DAY

Manager of the Line Insisted Titanic Was Unsinkable Even After She Had Gone Down.

HEAD OF THE LINE ABOARD

J. Bruce Ismay Making First Trip on Gigantic Ship That Was to Surpass All Others.

The admission that the Titanic, the biggest steamship in the world, had been sunk by an iceberg and had gone to the bottom of the Atlantic, probably carrying more than 1,400 of her passengers and crew with her, was made at the White Star Line offices, 9 Broadway, at 8:20 o'clock last night. Then P. A. S. Franklin, Vice President and General Manager of the International Mercantile Marine, conceded that probably only those passengers who were picked up by the Cunarder Carpathia had been saved. Advices received early this morning tended to increase the number of survivers by 200.

The admission followed a day in which the White Star Line officials had been optimistic in the extreme. At no time was the admission made that every one aboard the huge steamer was not safe. The ship itself, it was confidently asserted, was unsinkable, and inquirers were informed that she would reach port, under her own steam probably, but surely with the help of the Allan liner Virginian, which was reported to be towing her.

As the day passed, however, with no new authentic reports from the Titanic or any of the ships which were known to have responded to her wireless call for help, it became apparent that authentic news of the disaster probably could come only from the Titanic's sister ship, the Olympic. The wireless range of the Olympic is 500 miles. That of the Carpathia, the Parisian, and the Virginian is much less, and as they neared the position of the Titanic they drew further and further out of shore range. From the Titanic's position at the time of the disaster it is doubtful if any of the ships except the Olympic could establish communication with shore.

Titanic Sank at 2:20 A. M. Monday.

In the White Star offices the hope was held out all day that the Parisian and the Virginian had taken off some of the Titanic's passengers, and efforts were made to get into communication with these liners. Until such communication was established the White Star officials refused to recognize the possibility that there were none of the Titanic's passengers aboard them.

But by nightfall came the message from Capt. Haddock of the Olympic to Cape Race, Newfoundland, telling of the foundering of the Titanic and of the rescue of 655 of her passengers by the Cunarder Carpathia, which, the wireless message said, reached the position of the Titanic at daybreak. All they found there, however, was lifeboats and wreckage. The biggest ship in the world had sunk at 2:20 o'clock yesterday morning.

Mr. Franklin admitted late last night that the Parisian and the Virginian, though they were among the first to answer the Titanic's calls for help, could not have reached the scene before 10 o'clock yesterday morning, seven and a half hours after the big Titanic buried her nose beneath the waves and pitched downward out of sight. The Carpathia, so the wireless dispatch from Capt. Haddock to Cape Race announced, reached the scene of the Titanic's foundering at daybreak, several hours before the expected arrival of the Virginian and the Parisian.

1,465 Lives Lost First Report.

It is unbelievable, so White Star Line officials were compelled to concede finally, that the Carpathia should have failed to pick up every lifeboat which still floated on the waves. If they failed to pick up more than 655 passengers, it was because the others of the ship's complement had gone with her to the bottom.

But it was not until nearly nightfall that the extent of the disaster was realized. Before that the reassuring nature of the bulletins issued by the White Star line was sufficient to quiet the fears of those who had relatives or friends aboard the unfortunate ship and to prevent widespread belief in a serious disaster.

Capt. Haddock's message from the Olympic, which is printed in another column of THE TIMES, strongly indicated that none but the 655 taken from life boats by the Carpathia had been saved. This message was relayed immediately to the White Star offices, but Mr. Franklin positively declined to make the text of the message public. He offered still the hope that passengers were aboard the Parisian and the Virginian, and even when the admission was wrung from him that there seemed little hope of the saving of any others than the 655 aboard the Carpathia, he clung to the hope that in some unexplained way there were other passengers abroad the two Allan liners.

First Reported Titanic in Tow.

Throughout the day there had been reassurances that the Titanic was being towed to port by the Virginian, and when Capt. Haddock's message proved this to be untrue only the admission was made at the White Star offices that the Titanic had sunk. Mr. Franklin said that Capt. Haddock's message was brief and "neglected to say that all the crew had been saved." But the inference was not that all the passengers had been saved. Rather it was that many of them had died, and presently Mr. Franklin admitted the fear that there had been a terrible loss of life on the Titanic.

This version of Capt. Haddock's wireless had been given at the White Star offices:

Capt. Haddock of the Olympic sends a wireless message to the White Star offices here that the steamer Titanic sank at 2:20 A. M., after all the passengers and crew had been lowered to life boats and transferred to the Virginian. The steamship Carpathia, with several hundred passengers of the Titanic, is now en route to New York.

At 9 o'clock, however, he modified this statement, declaring:

As far as we know the situation, there have been rumors from Halifax that three steamers were at the scene of the Titanic's sinking, namely, the Virginian, the Parisian, and the Carpathia. We have heard from Capt. Haddock of the Olympic, who says that the Titanic sank at 2:20 o'clock this morning. Haddock also informs us that the Carpathia has 675 survivors on board. It is very difficult to say whether the Virginian and the Parisian have any survivors on board until we can get a report from those vessels.

Fears Serious Loss of Life.

We have asked for that report from Capt. Haddock, and we are expecting a reply at any time. The Carpathia is proceding to New York direct. We very much fear that there has been serious loss of life, but it is impossible for us to say definitely concerning this sad part of the situation until we are able to reassure ourselves whether or not any of the Titanic's passengers are aboard the Allan liners.

We are hopeful that the rumors which have reached us by telegraph from Halifax that there are passengers aboard the Virginian and the Parisian will prove to be true, and that these vessels will turn up with some of the passengers. It is the loss of life that makes this thing so awful. We can replace the money loss, but not the lives of those who went down.

Another version of the message from the Olympic was current last night and included the sentence: "Loss likely total 1,800 souls." This sentence was not in the message received by THE TIMES from Cape Race nor in that sent to the White Star line offices.

Continued on Page 2.

The Lost Titanic Being Towed Out of Belfast Harbor.

CAPT. E. J. SMITH,
Commander of the Titanic.

THE PROBABLE LOSS.

Number Aboard.	
First cabin	325
Second cabin	285
Steerage	710
Crew, (estimated)	800
Total	2,120
Saved.	
By the Carpathia	866
Probably drowned	1,254

PARTIAL LIST OF THE SAVED.

Includes Bruce Ismay, Mrs. Widener, Mrs. H. B. Harris, and an Incomplete name, suggesting Mrs. Astor's.

Special to The New York Times.

CAPE RACE, N. F., Tuesday, April 16.—Following is a partial list of survivors among the first-class passengers of the Titanic, received by the Marconi wireless station this morning from the Carpathia, via the steapship Olympic:

Mrs. JACOB P. ——— and maid.
Mr. HARRY ANDERSON.
Mrs. ED. W. APPLETON.
Mrs. ROSE ABBOTT.
Miss G. M. BURNS.
Miss D. D. CASSEBERE.
Mrs. WM. M. CLARKE.
Mrs. B. CHIBINACE.
Miss E. G. CROSSBIE.
Miss H. ROSEBIE.
Miss JEAN HIPACK.
Mrs. HY. B. HARRIS.
Mrs. ALEX. HALVERSON.
Miss MARGARET BAYS.
Mr. BRUCE ISMAY.
Mr. and Mrs. ED. KIMBERLEY.
Mr. F. A. KENNYMAN.
Miss EMILE KENCHEN.
Miss G. F. LONGLEY.
Mrs. A. F. LEADER.
Miss BERTHA LAVORY.
Mrs. ERNEST LIVES.
Miss MARY CLINES.
Mrs. SINGRID LINDSTROM.
Mr. GUSTAVE J. LESNEUR.
Miss GIORGETTA A. MADILL.
Mme. MELICARD.
Mrs. TUCKER and maid.
Mrs. J. B. THAYER.
Mr. J. B. THAYER, Jr.
Mr. HENRY WOOLMER.
Miss ANNA WARD.
Mr. RICHARD M. WILLIAMS.
Mrs. F. M. WARNER.
Miss HELEN A. WILSON.
Miss WILLARD.
Miss MARY WICKS.
Mrs. GEO. D. WIDENER and maid.
Mrs. J. STEWART WHITE.
Miss MARIE YOUNG.
Mrs. THOMAS POTTER, Jr.
Mrs. EDNA S. ROBERTS.
Countess of ROTHES.
Mr. C. ROLMANE.
Mrs. SUSAN P. ROGERSON. (Probably Ryerson).
Miss EMILY B. ROGERSON.
Mrs. ARTHUR ROGERSON.
Master ALLISON and nurse.
Miss K. T. ANDREWS.
Miss NINETTE PANHART.
Miss E. W. ALLEN.
Mr. and Mrs. D. BISHOP.
Mr. H. BLANK.
Miss A. BASSINA.
Mrs. JAMES BAXTER.
Mr. GEORGE A. BAYT[illegible]
Miss C. BONNELL.
Mrs. J. M. BROWN.
Miss G. C. BOWEN.
Mr. and Mrs. R. L. BECK[illegible]
Miss RUTH TAUSSIG.
Miss ELLA THOR.
Mr. and Mrs. E. Z. TAYLOR.
GILBERT M. TUCKER.
Mr. J. B. THAYER.
Mr. JOHN B. ROGERSON.
Mrs. M. ROTHSCHILD.
Miss MADELEINE NEWELL.
Mrs. MARJORIE NEWELL.
HELEN W. NEWSOM.
Mr. TIENNAD OMOND.
Mr. E. C. OSTBY.
Miss HELEN R. OSTBY.
Mrs. MAMAM J. RENAGO.
Mlle. OLIVIA.
Mrs. D. W. MERVIN.
Mr. PHILIP EMOCK.
Mr. JAMES GOOGHT.
Miss RUBERTA MAIMY.
Mr. PIERRE MARECHAL.
Mrs. W. E. MINEHAN.
Miss APPIE RANELT.
Major ARTUR PEUCHEN.
Mrs. KARL H. BEHR.
Miss DESSETTE.
Mrs. WILLIAM BUCKNELL.
Mrs. O. H. BARKWORTH.
Mrs. H. B. STEFFASON.
Mrs. ELSIE BOWERMAN.

The Marconi station reports that it missed the word after "Mrs. Jacob P." In a list received by the Associated Press this morning this name appeared well down, but in THE TIMES list it is first, suggesting that the name of Mrs. John Jacob Astor is intended. This supposition is strengthened by the fact that, except for Mrs. H. J. Allison, Mrs. Astor is the only lady in the "A" column of the ship's passenger list attended by a maid.

NAMES PICKED UP AT BOSTON.

BOSTON, April 15.—Among the names of survivors of the Titanic picked up by wireless from the steamer Carpathia here to-night were the following:

Mr. and Mrs. L. HENRY.
Mrs. W. A. HOOPER.
Mr. MILE.
Mr. J. FLYNN.
Miss ALICE FORTUNE.
Mrs. ROBERT DOUGLAS.
Miss HILDA SLAYTER.
Mrs. P. SMITH.
Mrs. BRAHAM.
Miss LUCILLE CARTER.
Mr. WILLIAM CARTER.
Miss CUMMINGS.
Mrs. FLORENCE MARE.
Miss ALICE PHILLIPS.
Mrs. PAULA MUNGE.
Mrs. JANE ———
Miss PHYLLIS O. ———
HOWARD B. CASE.
Miss MINEHAN.
Miss BERTHA ———

Biggest Liner Plunges to the Bottom at 2:20 A. M.

RESCUERS THERE TOO LATE

Except to Pick Up the Few Hundreds Who Took to the Lifeboats.

WOMEN AND CHILDREN FIRST

Cunarder Carpathia Rushing to New York with the Survivors.

SEA SEARCH FOR OTHERS

The California Stands By on Chance of Picking Up Other Boats or Rafts.

OLYMPIC SENDS THE NEWS

Only Ship to Flash Wireless Messages to Shore After the Disaster.

LATER REPORT SAVES 866.

BOSTON, April 15.—A wireless message picked up late to-night, relayed from the Olympic, says that the Carpathia is on her way to New York with 866 passengers from the steamer Titanic aboard. They are mostly women and children, the message said, and it concluded: "Grave fears are felt for the safety of the balance of the passengers and crew."

Special to The New York Times.

CAPE RACE, N. F., April 15.—The White Star liner Olympic reports by wireless this evening that the Cunarder Carpathia reached, at daybreak this morning, the position from which wireless calls for help were sent out last night by the Titanic after her collision with an iceberg. The Carpathia found only the lifeboats and the wreckage of what had been the biggest steamship afloat.

The Titanic had foundered at about 2:20 A. M., in latitude 41:16 north and longitude 50:14 west. This is about 30 minutes of latitude, or about 34 miles, due south of the position at which she struck the iceberg. All her boats are accounted for and about 655 souls have been saved of the crew and passengers, most of the latter presumably women and children.

There were about 2,100 persons aboard the Titanic.

The Leyland liner California is remaining and searching the position of the disaster, while the Carpathia is returning to New York with the survivors.

It can be positively stated that up to 11 o'clock to-night nothing whatever had been received at or heard by the Marconi station here to the effect that the Parisian, Virginian or any other ships had picked up any survivors, other than those picked up by the Carpathia.

First News of the Disaster.

The first news of the disaster to the Titanic was received by the Marconi wireless station here at 10:25 o'clock last night [as told in yesterday's New York Times.] The Titanic was first heard giving the distress signal "C. Q. D.," which was answered by a number of ships, including the Carpathia.

that some people could draw a picture that matched an unseen one in a sealed envelope. This could not be telepathy because only *one* person was involved. He called it a "sixth sense." Later card-guessing experiments designed by J. B. Rhine in the 1920s confirmed the existence of the new phenomenon, which we now call clairvoyance.

Between 1956 and 1959, psychic detective Peter Hurkos took part in a series of experiments that were designed to further explore the phenomenon of clairvoyance. Before several witnesses Hurkos was given a sealed cardboard box. His task was to describe the objects inside it. Hurkos's impressions were recorded in a book *Beyond Telepathy:*

This object blew up—an explosion. There was an explosion—a long time ago. I hear a strange language. It is very old. It had also to do with water. I don't know what it is, I see a dark color. It is not straight. Not regular. It is very jagged, sharp points. It belonged to three people. I am sure of this. Dr. Ducasse didn't buy this. It was given to him and it was repaired. A souvenir. I am sure the owner of the cylinder is dead. I do not mean Dr. Ducasse, he is well.

Hurkos couldn't say exactly what the object was. The Dr. Ducasse that Hurkos spoke about was the man who sent the sealed package for the experiment. He was not there when it took place. Only after the experiment was completed did he send a letter to Puharich explaining exactly what the object was and where it had come from. It was a small pottery jar given to him as a gift thirty-six years before by a friend who was now dead. The jar had come from the ruins of Pompeii, the Roman city that had been buried in an avalanche of lava from an eruption.

Sometimes our psychic abilities bring us information about what is going to happen in the future. This phenemenon is called precognition, and it occurs in both the dreaming and waking states of consciousness.

In 1898 Morgan Robertson wrote a story called "The Wreck of the Titan." In it a huge ocean liner, the Titan, was steaming through the icy mid-Atlantic in April. The ship was described as being 800 feet (244 m) long, having a speed of twenty-five knots, and having a passenger capacity of well over 3,000. Yet it had only twenty-four lifeboats, far too few for a ship of its size. Suddenly the ship rammed an iceberg and sank, leaving 3,000 people struggling and screaming in the icy waters.

Perhaps the most interesting aspect of this story concerns the manner in which it was written. Robertson claimed that ideas for stories would come to him as visions when he was in a trance state. He believed that these visions came to him from an "astral writing partner," a kind of psychic spirit.

At 2:20 A.M. on the morning of April 15, 1912, the world's largest "unsinkable" ocean liner collided at full speed with an iceberg that ripped a huge gash in its bow and sank it. Hundreds of passengers struggled into the too few life boats, and 1,500 others were lost with the ship. The name of the ship was the *Titanic.*

Was this mere coincidence? A good guess? Or precognition? Some researchers feel that the similarities between Robertson's story and the details of the disaster might have arisen from good guesswork. Robertson had studied shipbuilding. He might have guessed the direction in which future design was headed (his description of the physical features of the ship were very close to those of the *Titanic*); he might have predicted that a tragedy would befall the latest of man's engineering marvels; and he might have even guessed the nature of the tragedy. We will never know for sure.

But, Robertson's story was not the only psychic event that surrounded the sinking of the *Titanic.*

Among the many spectators who watched the *Titanic* set out on its maiden voyage from Southhampton to New York were a Mr. and Mrs. Jack Marshall. With the *Titanic* still in view, Mrs. Marshall grabbed her husband's arm and shouted, "That ship is going to sink

before she reaches America." Her husband tried to calm her. Friends who were with them tried to explain to her that the *Titanic* had been built by a completely new method that made it unsinkable.

Her daughter, Joan Grant, was there when the incident occurred, and she recorded her mother's response in her book *Far Memory*:

"Don't just stand there staring at me! Do something! You fools, I can see hundreds of people struggling in the icy water! Are you all so blind that you are going to let them drown?"

Indeed, the builders of the *Titanic* had announced that the ship was unsinkable. It had a double bottom and fifteen watertight bulkheads, which could be closed to seal off the rest of the ship. Unfortunately, these were not enough to prevent the catastrophe. When the ship rammed the iceberg, water rushed into the forward compartments and tipped the bow; two and a half hours later the *Titanic* slid under the waves.

On the same day that Mrs. Marshall had her vision, a Mr. V. N. Turvey also predicted that a "great liner will be lost." Turvey was a sensitive—a person who is highly endowed with psychic abilities. On April 13 he wrote a letter to a friend telling her of his prediction. He claimed the ship would sink in two days.

Ten days before the *Titanic* sailed,

J. Connon Middleton had a dream. He saw a ship "floating on the sea, keel upward and her passengers and crew swimming around her." Later he had a second vision of disaster. This time he himself was "floating in the air just above the wreck."

According to Andrew Mackenzie, in *Riddle of the Future*, Mr. Middleton disregarded these nocturnal warnings. However, he subsequently received a cable from the United States instructing him, for business reasons, to delay his sailing for several days. Mrs. Middleton later testified that her husband had said "how foolish it would seem if he postponed his business on account of a dream." As Mackenzie states, "If the cable from New York had not arrived he would presumably have sailed in the *Titanic* and possibly perished."

W. T. Stead, distinguished journalist, editor, and spiritualist, was not so lucky. Stead was told by Count Harmon, a sensitive with whom he conferred while on vacation, that danger to his life would come from water, nothing else. In June 1911 the sensitive wrote Stead advising him that "travel would be dangerous to him in the month of April, 1912."

In *Riddle of the Future* Andrew Mackenzie goes on to explain that Stead also consulted with another sensitive, Mr. W. de Kerlor. De Kerlor received an impression of a half-completed black ship. The sensitive interpreted this vision to mean that when the ship was completed, Stead would go on a voyage. Later de Kerlor dreamed about an oceanic catastrophe. He felt that his dream concerned Mr. Stead and told him about it. De Kerlor was worried, first by a black ship, and now by a seaborne disaster.

Mr. Stead is reported to have said, "Oh, yes; well, well, you are a very gloomy prophet." He sailed with the *Titanic*—and he was lost with it.

When so many different people have similar precognitive experiences over a long period of time, it leads one to believe that these glimpses into the future are more than mere coincidence.

We have seen examples of telepathy, clairvoyance, and precognition at work in daily life and in the laboratory. As a group, these three psychic processes provide us with a natural resource that almost begs to be put to work. How can we best use these psychic resources? For the criminologist the answer is clear; telepathy, clairvoyance, and precognition can be used as effective investigatory tools in the fight against crime.

The telepathic "reading" of suspects' minds allows police to tune in to the suspects' innermost thoughts and to determine the truth or falsity of alibis, as well as providing clues to direct the search for hard evidence—evidence acceptable in a court of law. (The psychic's telepathic knowledge of suspects' guilt is not enough to convict.)

Clairvoyant impressions triggered by visiting the scene of a crime or by handling a crime-related photograph or object can provide information about the identity of the crminal, his *modus operandi* (MO), his motives, and his whereabouts. Sometimes the psychic, relying on clairvoyant impressions, can actually relive the crime, observing the action *as it took place*.

Precognitive impressions can be used to warn police of *future* criminal acts and crimes still in the planning stages, thereby allowing the police to take the necessary preventive steps.

The extrasensory abilities of the psychic detective are invaluable crime-fighting tools. They can provide police with information that is impossible to obtain in any other way.

POETRY

Dream Deferred[1]

Langston Hughes

What happens to a dream deferred?

    Does it dry up
    like a raisin in the sun?
    Or fester like a sore—
5   And then run?
    Does it stink like rotten meat?
    Or crust and sugar over—
    like a syrupy sweet?
    Maybe it just sags
10   like a heavy load.

    Or does it explode?

---

1. deferred (dĭ-fûrd′) *v.*: Put off; postponed.

Close Up

1. A *simile* is a comparison between two seemingly unlike objects. Usually it contains the words *like* or *as*. Find five similes in this poem.

2. What do you think the poet wants to suggest by the last line of this poem?

Steam Shovel

Charles Malam

The dinosaurs are not all dead.
I saw one raise its iron head
To watch me walking down the road
Beyond our house today.
5 Its jaws were dripping with a load
Of earth and grass that it had cropped.
It must have heard me where I stopped,
Snorted white steam my way,
And stretched its long neck out to see,
10 And chewed, and grinned quite amiably.

Close Up

1. A *metaphor* is an implied comparison between two essentially unlike things. It does not contain the words *like* or *as*. What is the metaphor in "Steam Shovel"?

2. Do you think this poem creates an effective picture of a steam shovel? Why or why not?

Days

Karle Wilson Baker

Some days my thoughts are just cocoons—all cold, and dull, and blind,
They hang from dripping branches in the gray woods of my mind;
And other days they drift and shine—such free and flying things!
I find the gold dust in my hair, left by their brushing wings.

Close Up

1. In the first line, the poet compares her thoughts to cocoons. How are these two things alike?

2. (a) What metaphor do you find in the second line? (b) How is the inside of the poet's mind like a gray woods?

3. (a) What metaphor do you find in the third line? (b) How are these two things alike?

Splinter

Carl Sandburg

The voice of the last cricket
across the first frost
is one kind of good-by.
It is so thin a splinter of singing.

Separation

W. S. Merwin

Your absence has gone through me
Like thread through a needle.
Everything I do is stitched with its color.

Close Up

1. (a) An *image* is a vivid word picture. In the first poem, what image does Sandburg use to describe "one kind of good-by"? (b) Which word in the fourth line tells you that this "kind of good-by" is painful?

2. How is the fourth line also a metaphor?

3. In the second poem, do you think the separation is painful? Why or why not?

4. (a) Explain the simile in this poem. (b) Explain the metaphor.

Forsythia Bush

Lilian Moore

There is nothing
quite
like the sudden
light

5   of
forsythia
that
one morning
without warning

10 explodes
into yellow
and
startles the street
into spring.

Close Up ▶ Do you think this poem creates an effective picture of a forsythia bush bursting into bloom? Why or why not?

Lament

Edna St. Vincent Millay

Listen chidren!
Your father is dead.
From his old coats
I'll make you little jackets;
5 I'll make you little trousers
From his old pants.
There'll be in his pockets
Things he used to put there,
Keys and pennies
10 Covered with tobacco;
Dan shall have the pennies
To save in his bank;
Anne shall have the keys
To make a pretty noise with.
15 Life must go on,
And the dead be forgotten;
Life must go on,
Though good men die;
Anne, eat your breakfast;
20 Dan, take your medicine;
Life must go on;
I forget just why.

Close Up

1. (a) Who is the speaker in this poem? (b) What important news does she have?

2. At first, the speaker seems calm and matter-of-fact. (a) At what point do you suspect she is not as calm as she appears? (b) What do the last two lines tell you?

Poem

William Carlos Williams

As the cat
climbed over
the top of

the jamcloset
5   first the right
forefoot
carefully
then the hind
stepped down

10   into the pit of
the empty
flowerpot

Close Up

► (a) Do you think this poem creates a good picture of the way a cat walks? Why or why not? (b) How does the shape of this poem reinforce this picture?

A Blessing

James Wright

Just off the highway to Rochester, Minnesota,
Twilight bounds softly forth on the grass.
And the eyes of those two Indian ponies
Darken with kindness.
5   They have come gladly out of the willows
To welcome my friend and me.
We step over the barbed wire into the pasture
Where they have been grazing all day, alone.
They ripple tensely, they can hardly contain their happiness
10   That we have come.
They bow shyly as wet swans. They love each other.
There is no loneliness like theirs.

At home once more,
They begin munching the young tufts of spring in the darkness.
15   I would like to hold the slenderer one in my arms,
For she has walked over to me
And nuzzled my left hand.
She is black and white,
Her mane falls wild on her forehead,
20   And the light breeze moves me to caress her long ear
That is delicate as the skin over a girl's wrist.
Suddenly I realize
That if I stepped out of my body I would break
Into blossom.

Close Up

1. When the poet and his friend step into the pasture, two Indian ponies come to greet him. Why would he like to hold the slenderer one in his arms?

2. What metaphor does he use at the end of this poem to show how overjoyed he is?

3. Why do you think he calls this poem "A Blessing"? (Use your dictionary to help you answer this question.)

The Highwayman

Alfred Noyes

Part One

The wind was a torrent of darkness among the gusty trees,
The moon was a ghostly galleon[1] tossed upon cloudy seas,
The road was a ribbon of moonlight over the purple moor,
And the highwayman came riding—
5   Riding—riding—
The highwayman came riding, up to the old inn door.

He'd a French cocked hat on his forehead, a bunch of lace at his chin,
A coat of the claret velvet, and breeches of brown doeskin;
They fitted with never a wrinkle: his boots were up to the thigh!
10 And he rode with a jeweled twinkle,
    His pistol butts a-twinkle,
His rapier hilt[2] a-twinkle, under the jeweled sky.

Over the cobbles he clattered and clashed in the dark innyard
And he tapped with his whip on the shutters, but all was locked and barred;
15 He whistled a tune to the window, and who should be waiting there
But the landlord's black-eyed daughter,
    Bess, the landlord's daughter,
Plaiting a dark red love knot into her long black hair.

And dark in the dark old innyard a stable wicket[3] creaked
20 Where Tim the ostler[4] listened; his face was white and peaked;
His eyes were hollows of madness, his hair like moldy hay,
But he loved the landlord's daughter,
    The landlord's red-lipped daughter,
Dumb as a dog he listened, and he heard the robber say—

25 "One kiss, my bonny sweetheart, I'm after a prize tonight,
But I shall be back with the yellow gold before the morning light;

---

1. galleon (găl′ ē-ən) n.: Large sailing ship.
2. rapier (rā′ pē-ər) hilt: The hilt, or handle, of a long, slender sword.
3. wicket (wĭk′ ĭt) n.: Gate or small door.
4. ostler (ŏs′ lər) n.: Stableman; also called *hostler* (hŏs′ lər).

Yet, if they press me sharply, and harry me through the day,
Then look for me by moonlight,
    Watch for me by moonlight,
30 I'll come to thee by moonlight, though hell should bar the way."
He rose upright in the stirrups; he scarce could reach her hand,
But she loosened her hair i' the casement![5] His face burned like a brand
As the black cascade of perfume came tumbling over his breast;
And he kissed its waves in the moonlight,
35   (Oh, sweet black waves in the moonlight!)
Then he tugged at his rein in the moonlight, and galloped away to the west.

Part Two

He did not come in the dawning; he did not come at noon;
And out o' the tawny sunset, before the rise o' the moon,
When the road was a gypsy's ribbon, looping the purple moor,
40 A redcoat troop came marching—
    Marching—marching—
King George's men came marching, up to the old inn door.

They said no word to the landlord, they drank his ale instead,
But they gagged his daughter and bound her to the foot of her narrow bed;
45 Two of them knelt at her casement, with muskets at their side!
There was death at every window;
    And hell at one dark window;
For Bess could see, through her casement, the road that *he* would ride.

They had tied her up to attention, with many a sniggering jest;
50 They had bound a musket beside her, with the barrel beneath her breast!
"Now keep good watch!" and they kissed her. She heard the dead man say—
Look for me by moonlight;
    Watch for me by moonlight;
I'll come to thee by moonlight, though hell should bar the way!

55 She twisted her hands behind her; but all the knots held good!
She writhed her hands till her fingers were wet with sweat or blood!
They stretched and strained in the darkness, and the hours crawled by like years,
Till, now, on the stroke of midnight,
    Cold, on the stroke of midnight,
60 The tip of one finger touched it! The trigger at least was hers!

The tip of one finger touched it; she strove no more for the rest!

---

5. casement (kās′ mənt) *n*.: A window that opens outward on hinges.

Up, she stood to attention, with the barrel beneath her breast,
She would not risk their hearing: she would not strive again;
For the road lay bare in the moonlight;
65   Blank and bare in the moonlight;
And the blood in her veins in the moonlight throbbed to her love's refrain.

Tlot-tlot; tlot-tlot! Had they heard it? The horse hoofs ringing clear;
Tlot-tlot, tlot-tlot in the distance? Were they deaf that they did not hear?
Down the ribbon of moonlight, over the brow of the hill,
70   The highwayman came riding,
       Riding, riding!
The redcoats looked to their priming! She stood up, straight and still!

Tlot-tlot, in the frosty silence! *Tlot-tlot,* in the echoing night!
Nearer he came and nearer! Her face was like a light!
75   Her eyes grew wide for a moment; she drew one last deep breath,
Then her finger moved in the moonlight,
       Her musket shattered the moonlight,
Shattered her breast in the moonlight and warned him—with her death.

He turned; he spurred to the westward; he did not know who stood
80   Bowed, with her head o'er the musket, drenched with her own red blood!
Not till the dawn he heard it, his face grew gray to hear
How Bess, the landlord's daughter,
       The landlord's black-eyed daughter,
Had watched for her love in the moonlight, and died in the darkness there.

85   Back, he spurred like a madman, shrieking a curse to the sky,
With the white road smoking behind him, and his rapier brandished high!
Blood-red were his spurs i' the golden noon; wine-red his velvet coat,
When they shot him down on the highway,
       Down like a dog on the highway,
90   And he lay in his blood on the highway, with a bunch of lace at his throat.

And still of a winter's night, they say, when the wind is in the trees,
When the moon is a ghostly galleon tossed upon cloudy seas,
When the road is a ribbon of moonlight over the purple moor,
A highwayman comes riding—
95   *Riding—riding*
A highwayman comes riding, up to the old inn door.

Over the cobbles he clatters and clangs in the dark innyard;
And he taps with his whip on the shutters, but all is locked and barred;
He whistles a tune to the window, and who should be waiting there
100 *But the landlord's black-eyed daughter,*
       Bess, the landlord's daughter,
Plaiting a dark red love knot into her long black hair.

Close Up

1. This poem tells a story of two lovers. (a) Why does the high-wayman come to the old inn door? (b) When Tim overhears the highwayman's plan, what makes you think he will turn him in to the authorities?

2. The Redcoats tie up Bess and wait for the highwayman. (a) How does Bess warn him of the trap? (b) How does the highwayman respond when he learns what she has done?

3. A symbol is something that has a meaning all its own but also represents something else. (a) How many times is the color red mentioned in this poem? (b) What does it represent?

4. (a) How are the two lovers reunited at the end of the story? (b) Why do you think the last two stanzas are printed in *italics*?

Frankenstein

Edward Field

The monster has escaped from the dungeon
where he was kept by the Baron,
who made him with knobs sticking out from each side of his neck
where the head was attached to the body
5 and stitching all over
where parts of cadavers[1] were sewed together.

He is pursued by the ignorant villagers,
who think he is evil and dangerous because he is ugly
and makes ugly noises.
10 They wave firebrands at him and cudgels and rakes,
but he escapes and comes to the thatched cottage
of an old blind man playing on the violin Mendelssohn's[2] "Spring Song."

Hearing him approach, the blind man welcomes him:
"Come in, my friend," and takes him by the arm.
15 "You must be weary," and sits him down inside the house.
For the blind man has long dreamed of having a friend
to share his lonely life.

The monster has never known kindness—the Baron was cruel—
but somehow he is able to accept it now,
20 and he really has no instincts to harm the old man,
for in spite of his awful looks he has a tender heart:
Who knows what cadaver that part of him came from?

The old man seats him at table, offers him bread,
and says, "Eat, my friend." The monster
25 rears back roaring in terror.
"No, my friend, it is good. Eat—gooood"
and the old man shows him how to eat,
and reassured, the monster eats
and says, "Eat—gooood,"
30 trying out the words and finding them good too.

---

1. cadavers (kə-dăv'ərz) n.: Dead bodies.
2. Mendelssohn (měn'dəl-sən), Felix: A German composer who lived from 1809 to 1847.

The old man offers him a glass of wine,
"Drink, my friend. Drink—gooood."
The monster drinks, slurping horribly, and says,
"Drink—gooood," in his deep nutty voice
35 and smiles maybe for the first time in his life.

Then the blind man puts a cigar in the monster's mouth
and lights a large wooden match that flares up in his face.
The monster, remembering the torches of the villagers,
recoils, grunting in terror.
40 "No, my friend, smoke—gooood,"
and the old man demonstrates with his own cigar.
The monster takes a tentative puff
and smiles hugely, saying, "Smoke—gooood,"
and sits back like a banker, grunting and puffing.

45 Now the old man plays Mendelssohn's "Spring Song" on the violin
while tears come into our dear monster's eyes
as he thinks of the stones of the mob, the pleasures of mealtime,
the magic new words he has learned
and above all of the friend he has found.

50 It is just as well that he is unaware—
being simple enough to believe only in the present—
that the mob will find him and pursue him
for the rest of his short unnatural life,
until trapped at the whirlpool's edge
55 he plunges to his death.

Close Up

1. (a) Why do the villagers pursue the monster? (b) Why does the blind man welcome the monster?

2. The blind man shows the monster love and friendship. (a) How does the monster respond? (b) At the end of the poem, why does the narrator think "it is just as well" that the monster lives only in the present?

3. Who do you think behaves in a more hideous or vile fashion— the monster or the mob? Why?

4. A monster is one who arouses horror and disgust. Who is the real monster in the poem? Why?

5. Tone is the poet's attitude toward what he has written or toward the characters about which he has written. What is the poet's attitude toward the monster? Find evidence to support your answer.

CHANGES

The Old Cat

Doris Lessing

When Doris Lessing lived in Southern Rhodesia she had cats—many, many cats. One particular cat stands out in her mind.

There was a she-cat, all those years ago. I don't remember why it went wild. Some awful battle must have been fought, beneath the attention of the humans. Perhaps some snub was administered, too much for cat pride to bear. This old cat went away from the house for months. She was not a pretty beast, an old ragbag patched and streaked in black and white and gray and fox-color. One day she came back and sat at the edge of the clearing where the house was, looking at the house, the people, the door, the other cats, the chickens—the family scene from which she was excluded. Then she crept back into the bush. Next evening, a silent golden evening, there was the old cat. The chickens were being shooed into the runs[1] for the night. We said, perhaps she is after the chickens, and shouted at her. She flattened herself into the grass and disappeared. Next evening, there she was again. My mother went down to the edge of the bush and called to her. But she was wary, would not come close. She was very pregnant: a large gaunt beast, skin over prominent bones, dragging the heavy lump of her belly. She was hungry. It was a dry year. The long dry season had flattened and thinned the grass, cauterized[2] bushes: everything in sight was skeleton, dry sticks of grass; and the tiny leaves fluttering on them, merely shadows. The bushes were twig; trees, their load of leaf thinned and dry, showed the plan of their trunk and branches. The veldt[3] was all bones. And the hill our house was on, in the wet season so tall and lush and soft and thick, was stark. Its shape, a low swelling to a high ridge, then an abrupt fall into a valley, showed beneath a stiff fringe of stick and branch. The birds, the rodents, had perhaps moved away to lusher spots. And the cat was not wild enough to move after them, away from the place she still thought of as home. Perhaps she was too worn by hunger and her load of kittens to travel.

We took down milk, and she drank it, but carefully, her muscles tensed all the time for flight. Other cats from the house came down to stare at the outlaw. When she had drunk the milk, she ran away back to the place she was using to hide in. Every evening she came to the homestead to be fed. One of us kept the

---

1. runs: Pens; outdoor enclosures.

2. cauterized (kô′tə-rīzd′) v.: Burnt.
3. veldt (fĕlt, vĕlt) n.: Open grazing areas in southern Africa.

other resentful cats away; another brought milk and food. We kept guard till she had eaten. But she was nervous: she snatched every mouthful as if she were stealing it; she kept leaving the plate, the saucer, then coming back. She ran off before the food was finished; and she would not let herself be stroked, would not come close.

One evening we followed her, at a distance. She disappeared halfway down the hill. It was land that had at some point been trenched and mined for gold by a prospector. Some of the trenches had fallen in—heavy rains had washed in soil. The shafts were deserted, perhaps had a couple of feet of rain water in them. Old branches had been dragged across to stop cattle falling in. In one of these holes, the old cat must be hiding. We called her, but she did not come, so we left her.

The rainy season broke in a great dramatic storm, all winds and lightning and thunder and pouring rain. Sometimes the first storm can be all there is for days, even weeks. But that year we had a couple of weeks of continuous storms. The new grass sprang up. The bushes, trees, put on green flesh. Everything was hot and wet and teeming. The old cat came up to the house once or twice; then did not come. We said she was catching mice again. Then, one night of heavy storm, the dogs were barking, and we heard a cat crying just outside the house. We went out, holding up storm lanterns into a scene of whipping boughs, furiously shaking grass, rain driving past in gray curtains. Under the verandah were the dogs, and they were barking at the old cat, who crouched out in the rain, her eyes green in the lantern-light. She had had her kittens. She was just an old skeleton of a cat. We brought out milk for her, and chased away the dogs, but that was not what she wanted. She sat with the rain whipping over her, crying. She wanted help. We put raincoats on over our nightclothes and sloshed after her through a black storm, with the thunder rolling overhead, lightning illumi-

nating sheets of rain. At the edge of the bush we stopped and peered in—in front of us was the area where the old trenches were, the old shafts. It was dangerous to go plunging about in the undergrowth. But the cat was in front of us, crying, commanding. We went carefully with storm lanterns, through waist-high grass and bushes, in the thick pelt of the rain. Then the cat was not to be seen, she was crying from somewhere beneath our feet. Just in front of us was a pile of old branches. That meant we were on the edge of a shaft. Cat was somewhere down it. Well, we were not going to pull a small mountain of slippery dead branches off a crumbling shaft in the middle of the night. We flashed the light through interstices[4] of the branches, and we thought we saw the cat moving, but were not sure. So we went back to the house, leaving the poor beast, and drank cocoa in a warm lamplit room, and shivered ourselves dry and warm.

But we slept badly, thinking of the poor cat, and got up at five with the first light. The storm had gone over, but everything was dripping. We went out into a cool dawnlight, and red streaks showed in the east where the sun would come up. Down we went into the soaked bush, to the pile of old branches. Not a sign of the cat.

This was a shaft about eighty-feet deep, and it had been cross-cut twice, at about ten feet, and then again much deeper. We decided the cat must have put her kittens into the first cut, which ran for about twenty feet, downwards at a slant. It was hard to lift off those heavy wet branches: it took a long time. When the mouth of the shaft was exposed, it was not the clean square shape it had been. The earth had crumbled in, and some light branches and twigs from the covering heap had sunk, making a rough platform about fifteen feet down. On to this had been washed and blown earth and small stones. So it was

---

4. interstices (ĭn-tûr′stĭ-sēz′) n.: A small, narrow space between things.

like a thin floor—but very thin: through it we could see the gleam of rain water from the bottom of the shaft. A short way down, not very far now that the mouth of the shaft had sunk, at about six feet, we could see the opening of the cross-cut, a hole about four feet square, now that it, too, had crumbled. Lying face down on the slippery red mud, holding onto bushes for safety, you could see a good way into the cut—a couple of yards. And there was the cat's head, just visible. It was quite still, sticking out of the red earth. We thought the cut had fallen in with all that rain, and she was half buried, and probably dead. We called her: there was a faint rough sound, then another. So she wasn't dead. Our problem then was, how to get to her. Useless to fix a windlass[5] onto that soaked earth which might landslide in at any moment. And no human could put weight onto that precarious platform of twigs and earth: hard to believe it had been able to take the weight of the cat, who must have been jumping down to it several times a day.

We tied a thick rope to a tree, with big knots in it at three-foot intervals, and let it down over the edge, trying not to get it muddied and slippery. Then one of us went down on the rope with a basket, until it was possi-ble to reach into the cut. There was the cat, crouched against the soaked red soil—she was still with cold and wet. And beside her were half a dozen kittens, about a week old and still blind. Her trouble was that the storms of that fortnight had blown so much rain into the cut that the sides and roof had partly fallen in; and the lair she had found, which had seemed so safe and dry, had become a wet crumbling death trap. She had come up to the house so that we could rescue the kittens. She had been frightened to come near the house because of the hostility of the other cats and the dogs, perhaps because she now feared us, but she had overcome her fear to get help for the kittens. But she had not been given help. She must have lost all hope that night, as the rain lashed down, as earth slid in all around her, as the water crept up behind her in the dark collapsing tunnel. But she had fed the kittens, and they were alive. They hissed and spat as they were lifted into the basket. The cat was too stiff and cold to get out by herself. First the angry kittens were taken up, while she crouched in the wet earth waiting. The basket descended again, and she was lifted into it. The family were taken up to the house, where she was given a corner, food, protection. The kittens grew up and found homes; and she stayed a house cat—and presumably went on having kit-tens.

---

5. windlass (wĭnd′ləs) n.: A machine for lifting consist-ing of a cylinder wound with rope and turned by a crank.

Close Up

1. (a) How does this area show the effects of the dry season? (b) Why hasn't the cat moved away to a "lusher spot"?

2. When the rains begin, the cat stops coming to the house for food. (a) What do the family think accounts for her absence? (b) What really accounts for it?

3. When the cat returns to the house for help, the family follow her. (a) Why do they turn back after they reach the area where the trenches are? (b) What do they find the next morning when they return to help her?

4. (a) Why does the narrator think that the cat must have lost all hope during the night? (b) Why did the cat remain in the shaft despite the hopeless conditions?

Setting

The setting of a story is where and when it takes place. The author of a story helps you see and feel the setting by using description. In "The Old Cat," Doris Lessing helps you experience the setting by including specific details and creating vivid images or word pictures. For example, she creates a vivid image of the dry landscape in the following sentence: ". . . everything in sight was *skeleton*, dry *sticks* of grass; and the tiny leaves *fluttering* on them, merely *shadows*."

1. Where does this story take place? Write a sentence describing the setting.

2. In the first part of this story, the landscape is dry and withered. Find three details that create a vivid impression of the dry landscape (for example, the veldt is "all bones").

3. In the second part of the story, the rains come. Find three details that create a vivid impression of the landscape during the rainy season (for example, "furiously shaking grass").

4. Reread the description of the shaft on p. 262, column b, paragraph 2. List three specific details about the shaft (for example, the platform is *fifteen feet down*).

Activity

▶ **Composition.** Write a paragraph describing the street on which you live. Tell how it looks during a rainstorm. Be sure to include specific details and vivid images.

INFERENCES

Making Inferences Based on Evidence

When you make an inference, you make an intelligent guess based on evidence in the story. For example, when the cat first comes to the house, you might infer that she wants food. You base your inference on the following information: (1) She is very gaunt; (2) she is pregnant; (3) she used to live at the house (and knows she can get food there); and (4) she probably cannot find food elsewhere since the area is dry and many animals have moved away.

▶ The author makes several inferences in this story. Find the evidence on which she bases each inference. Then state whether or not the inference turns out to be correct.
  a. The cat does not quite trust the family when she first goes to the house for food.
  b. The cat lives in one of the shafts.
  c. The cat was not wild enough to move away with the other animals.
  d. The shafts may have a couple of feet of rain water in them.
  e. The cat wants the family to follow her.

WORD ATTACK

Understanding Metaphors

A metaphor is an implied comparison between two essentially unlike things. For example, "She was not a pretty beast, an old ragbag patched and streaked in black and white and gray and fox-color." This comparison equates the cat with a ragbag. It creates a vivid impression of how the cat looked.

A figurative comparison must be appropriate if it is to be effective. For example, we call a burglar who secretly enters buildings a *cat burglar.* This metaphor is appropriate since both a cat and this type of burglar move with grace and agility. It would not be appropriate to call this type of burglar a *mule burglar* since people think of mules as slow, plodding, stubborn creatures, not as graceful and agile ones.

1. Some of the following items contain metaphors. Some do not. On a piece of paper, write the letters of those that do. Then tell what two things are being compared.
    a. "The veldt was all bones."
    b. "And the hill our house was on, in the wet season so tall and lush and soft and thick, was stark."
    c. "The bushes, trees, put on green flesh."
    d. "We went out, holding up storm lanterns into a scene of whipping boughs, furiously shaking grass, rain driving past in gray curtains."
    e. "She was just an old skeleton of a cat."
    f. "It was dangerous to go plunging about in the undergrowth."
    g. "We went out into a cool dawnlight, and red streaks showed in the east where the sun would come up."

2. Which items below contain appropriate metaphors? Be prepared to explain your answers.
    a. It was surprising to hear such a *thunderous* noise come from so tiny an instrument.
    b. At first glance, the bare trees sticking out of the parched ground were *the bones of some prehistoric monster.*
    c. *This tomb of a house* was filled with joy and happiness.
    d. *This tomb of a house* was filled with grief and despair.

The Singing Bell

Isaac Asimov

Is a cache of Singing Bells worth murder?

Louis Peyton never discussed publicly the methods by which he had bested the police of Earth in a dozen duels of wits and bluff, with the psychoprobe always waiting and always foiled. He would have been foolish to do so, of course, but in his more complacent moments, he fondled the notion of leaving a testament to be opened only after his death, one in which his unbroken success could clearly be seen to be due to ability and not to luck.

In such a testament he would say, "No false pattern can be created to cover a crime

without bearing upon it some trace of its creator. It is better, then, to seek in events some pattern that already exists and then adjust your actions to it."

It was with that principle in mind that Peyton planned the murder of Albert Cornwell.

Cornwell, that small-time retailer of stolen things, first approached Peyton at the latter's usual table-for-one at Grinnell's. Cornwell's blue suit seemed to have a special shine, his lined face a special grin, and his faded mustache a special bristle.

"Mr. Peyton," he said, greeting his future murderer with no fourth-dimensional qualm, "it is so nice to see you. I'd almost given up, sir, almost given up."

Peyton, who disliked being approached over his newspaper and dessert at Grinnell's, said, "If you have business with me, Cornwell, you know where you can reach me." Peyton was past forty and his hair was past its earlier blackness, but his back was rigid, his bearing youthful, his eyes dark, and his voice could cut the more sharply for long practice.

"Not for this, Mr. Peyton," said Cornwell, "not for this. I know of a cache, sir, a cache of . . . you know, sir." The forefinger of his right hand moved gently, as though it were a clapper striking invisible substance, and his left hand momentarily cupped his ear.

Peyton turned a page of the paper, still somewhat damp from its tele-dispenser, folded it flat and said, "Singing Bells?"

"Oh, hush, Mr. Peyton," said Cornwell in whispered agony.

Peyton said, "Come with me."

They walked through the park. It was another Peyton axiom that to be reasonably secret there was nothing like a low-voiced discussion out of doors.

Cornwell whispered, "A cache of Singing Bells; an accumulated cache of Singing Bells. Unpolished, but such beauties, Mr. Peyton."

"Have you seen them?"

"No, sir, but I have spoken with one who

has. He had proofs enough to convince me. There is enough there to enable you and me to retire in affluence. In absolute affluence, sir."

"Who was this other man?"

A look of cunning lit Cornwell's face like a smoking torch, obscuring more than it showed and lending it a repulsive oiliness. "The man was a lunar grubstaker who had a method for locating the Bells in the crater sides. I don't know his method; he never told me that. But he has gathered dozens, hidden them on the Moon, and come to Earth to arrange the disposing of them."

"He died, I suppose?"

"Yes. A most shocking accident, Mr. Peyton. A fall from a height. Very sad. Of course, his activities on the Moon were quite illegal. The Dominion is very strict about unauthorized Bell-mining. So perhaps it was a judgment upon him after all . . . In any case, I have his map."

Peyton said, a look of calm indifference on his face, "I don't want any of the details of your little transaction. What I want to know is why you've come to me."

Cornwell said, "Well, now, there's enough for both of us, Mr. Peyton, and we can both do our bit. For my part, I know where the cache is located and I can get a spaceship. You . . ."

"Yes?"

"You can pilot a spaceship, and you have such excellent contacts for disposing of the Bells. It is a very fair division of labor, Mr. Peyton. Wouldn't you say so, now?"

Peyton considered the pattern of his life—the pattern that already existed—and matters seemed to fit.

He said, "We will leave for the Moon on August the tenth."

Cornwell stopped walking and said, "Mr. Peyton! It's only April now."

Peyton maintained an even gait and Cornwell had to hurry to catch up. "Do you hear me, Mr. Peyton?"

Peyton said, "August the tenth. I will get in

touch with you at the proper time, tell you where to bring your ship. Make no attempt to see me personally till then. Goodbye, Cornwell."

Cornwell said, "Fifty-fifty?"

"Quite," said Peyton. "Goodbye."

Peyton continued his walk alone and considered the pattern of his life again. At the age of twenty-seven, he had bought a tract of land in the Rockies on which some past owner had built a house designed as refuge against the threated atomic wars of two centuries back, the ones that had never come to pass after all. The house remained, however, a monument to a frightened drive for self-sufficiency.

It was of steel and concrete in as isolated a spot as could well be found on Earth, set high above sea level and protected on nearly all sides by mountain peaks that reached higher still. It had its self-contained power unit, its water supply fed by mountain streams, its freezers in which ten sides of beef could hang comfortably, its cellar outfitted like a fortress with an arsenal of weapons designed to stave off hungry, panicked hordes that never came. It had its air-conditioning unit that could scrub and scrub the air until anything *but* radioactivity (alas for human frailty) could be scrubbed out of it.

In that house of survival, Peyton passed the month of August every subsequent year of his perennially bachelor life. He took out the communicators, the television, the newspaper tele-dispenser. He built a force-field fence about his property and left a short-distance signal mechanism to the house from the point where the fence crossed the one trail winding through the mountains.

For one month each year, he could be thoroughly alone. No one saw him, no one could reach him. In absolute solitude, he could have the only vacation he valued after eleven months of contact with a humanity for which he could feel only a cold contempt.

Even the police—and Peyton smiled— knew of his rigid regard for August. He had once jumped bail and risked the psycho-probe rather than forgo his August.

Peyton considered another aphorism[1] for possible inclusion in his testament: There is nothing so conducive to an appearance of innocence as the triumphant lack of an alibi.

On July 30, as on July 30 of every year, Louis Peyton took the 9:15 A.M. non-grav stratojet at New York and arrived in Denver at 12:30 P.M. There he lunched and took the 1:45 P.M. semi-grav bus to Hump's Point, from which Sam Leibman took him by ancient ground-car—full grav!—up the trail to the boundaries of his property. Sam Leibman gravely accepted the ten-dollar tip that he always received, touched his hat as he had done on July 30 for fifteen years.

On July 31, as on July 31 of every year, Louis Peyton returned to Hump's Point in his non-grav aeroflitter and placed an order through the Hump's Point general store for such supplies as he needed for the coming month. There was nothing unusual about the order. It was virtually the duplicate of previous such orders.

MacIntyre, manager of the store, checked gravely over the list, put it through to Central Warehouse, Mountain District, in Denver, and the whole of it came pushing over the mass-transference beam within the hour. Peyton loaded the supplies onto his aeroflitter with MacIntyre's help, left his usual ten-dollar tip, and returned to his house.

On August 1, at 12:01 A.M., the force field that surrounded his property was set to full power and Peyton was isolated.

And now the pattern changed. Deliberately he had left himself eight days. In that time he slowly and meticulously destroyed just enough of his supplies to account for all of August. He used the dusting chambers which served the house as a garbage-disposal unit. They were of an advanced model capable of

---

1. aphorism (ăf′ ə-rĭz′əm) n.: Maxim or adage; a brief statement of a principle, or a basic truth.

reducing all matter up to and including metals and silicates[2] to an impalpable and undetectable molecular dust. The excess energy formed in the process was carried away by the mountain stream that ran through his property. It ran five degrees warmer than normal for a week.

On August 9 his aeroflitter carried him to a spot in Wyoming where Albert Cornwell and a spaceship waited. The spaceship, itself, was a weak point, of course, since there were men who had sold it, men who had transported it and helped prepare it for flight. All those men, however, led only as far as Cornwell, and Cornwell, Peyton thought—with the trace of a smile on his cold lips—would be a dead end. A very dead end.

On August 10 the spaceship, with Peyton at the controls and Cornwell—and his map—as passenger, left the surface of Earth. Its non-grav field was excellent. At full power, the ship's weight was reduced to less than an ounce. The micropiles fed energy efficiently and noiselessly, and without flame or sound the ship rose through the atmosphere, shrank to a point, and was gone.

It was very unlikely that there would be witnesses to the flight, or that in these weak, piping times of peace there would be a radar watch as in days of yore. In point of fact, there was none.

Two days in space; now two weeks on the Moon. Almost instinctively Peyton had allowed for those two weeks from the first. He was under no illusions as to the value of homemade maps by non-cartographers. Useful they might be to the designer himself, who had the help of memory. To a stranger, they could be nothing more than a cryptogram.

Cornwell showed Peyton the map for the first time only after takeoff. He smiled obsequiously. "After all, sir, this was my only trump."

"Have you checked this against the lunar charts?"

"I would scarcely know how, Mr. Peyton. I depend upon you."

Peyton stared at him coldly as he returned the map. The one certain thing upon it was Tycho Crater, the site of the buried Luna City.

---

2. silicates (sĭl′ ĭ-kāts′) n.: Any compounds containing silicon, oxygen, and a metal. (Most minerals are silicates.)

In one respect, at least, astronomy was on their side. Tycho was on the daylight side of the Moon at the moment. It meant that patrol ships were less likely to be out, they themselves less likely to be observed.

Peyton brought the ship down in a riskily quick non-grav landing within the safe, cold darkness of the inner shadow of a crater. The sun was past zenith and the shadow would grow no shorter.

Cornwell drew a long face. "Dear, dear, Mr. Peyton. We can scarcely go prospecting in the lunar day."

"The lunar day doesn't last forever," said Peyton shortly. "There are about a hundred hours of sun left. We can use that time for acclimating ourselves and for working out the map."

The answer came quickly, but it was plural. Peyton studied the lunar charts over and

over, taking meticulous measurements, and trying to find the pattern of craters shown on the homemade scrawl that was the key to— what?

Finally Peyton said, "The crater we want could be any one of three: GC-3, GC-5, or MT-10."

"What do we do, Mr. Peyton?" asked Cornwell anxiously.

"We try them all," said Peyton, "beginning with the nearest."

The terminator passed and they were in the night shadow. After that, they spent increasing periods on the lunar surface, getting used to the eternal silence and blackness, the harsh points of the stars and the crack of light that was the Earth peeping over the rim of the crater above. They left hollow, featureless footprints in the dry dust that did not stir or change. Peyton noted them first when they climbed out of the crater into the full light of the gibbous[3] Earth. That was on the eighth day after their arrival on the moon.

The lunar cold put a limit to how long they could remain outside their ship at any one time. Each day, however, they managed for longer. By the eleventh day after arrival they had eliminated GC-5 as the container of the Singing Bells.

By the fifteenth day, Peyton's cold spirit had grown warm with desperation. It would have to be GC-3. MT-10 was too far away. They would not have time to reach it and explore it and still allow for a return to Earth by August 31.

On that same fifteenth day, however, despair was laid to rest forever when they discovered the Bells.

They were not beautiful. They were merely irregular masses of gray rock, as large as a double fist, vacuum-filled and feather-light in the moon's gravity. There were two dozen of them and each one, after proper polishing, could be sold for a hundred thousand dollars at least.

Carefully, in double handfuls, they carried the Bells to the ship, bedded them in excelsior,[4] and returned for more. Three times they made the trip both ways over ground that would have worn them out on Earth but which, under the Moon's lilliputian[5] gravity, was scarcely a barrier.

Cornwell passed the last of the Bells up to Peyton, who placed them carefully within the outer lock.

"Keep them clear, Mr. Peyton," he said, his radioed voice sounding harshly in the other's ear. "I'm coming up."

He crouched for the slow high leap against lunar gravity, looked up, and froze in panic. His face, clearly visible through the hard carved lusilite of his helmet, froze in a last grimace of terror. "No, Mr. Peyton. Don't——"

Peyton's fist tightened on the grip of the blaster he held. It fired. There was an unbearably brilliant flash and Cornwell was a dead fragment of a man, sprawled amid remnants of a spacesuit and flecked with freezing blood.

Peyton paused to stare somberly at the dead man, but only for a second. Then he transferred the last of the Bells to their prepared containers, removed his suit, activated first the non-grav field, then the micropiles, and, potentially a million or two richer than he had been two weeks earlier, set off on the return trip to Earth.

On the twenty-ninth of August, Peyton's ship descended silently, stern bottomward, to the spot in Wyoming from which it had taken off on August 10. The care with which Peyton had chosen the spot was not wasted. His aeroflitter was still there, drawn within the protection of an enclosing wrinkle of the rocky, tortuous countryside.

---

3. gibbous (gĭb′ əs) adj.: More than half but less than full.

4. excelsior (ĕk-sĕl′ sē-ər) n.: Wood shavings used for packing breakable goods.

5. lilliputian (lĭl′ə-pyoō′ shən) adj.: Very low.

He moved the Singing Bells once again, in their containers, into the deepest recess of the wrinkle, covering them, loosely and sparsely, with earth. He returned to the ship once more to set the controls and make last adjustments. He climbed out again and two minutes later the ship's automatics took over.

Silently hurrying, the ship bounded upward and up, veering to westward somewhat as the Earth rotated beneath it. Peyton watched, shading his narrow eyes, and at the extreme edge of vision there was a tiny gleam of light and a dot of cloud against the blue sky.

Peyton's mouth twitched into a smile. He had judged well. With the cadmium safety-rods bent back into uselessness, the micropiles had plunged past the unit-sustaining safety level and the ship had vanished in the heat of the nuclear explosion that had followed.

Twenty minutes later, he was back on his property. He was tired and his muscles ached under Earth's gravity. He slept well.

Twelve hours later, in the earliest dawn, the police came.

The man who opened the door placed his crossed hands over his paunch and ducked his smiling head two or three times in greeting. The man who entered, H. Seton Davenport of the Terrestrial Bureau of Investigation, looked about uncomfortably.

The room he had entered was large and in semidarkness except for the brilliant viewing lamp focused over a combination armchair-desk. Rows of book-films covered the walls. A suspension of Galactic charts occupied one corner of the room and a Galactic Lens gleamed softly on a stand in another corner.

"You are Dr. Wendell Urth?" asked Davenport, in a tone that suggested he found it hard to believe. Davenport was a stocky man with black hair, a thin and prominent nose, and a star-shaped scar on one cheek which marked permanently the place where a neuronic[6] whip had once struck him at too close a range.

"I am," said Dr. Urth in a thin, tenor voice. "And you are Inspector Davenport."

The Inspector presented his credentials and said, "The University recommended you to me as an extraterrologist."

"So you said when you called me half an hour ago," said Urth agreeably. His features were thick, his nose was a snubby button, and over his somewhat protuberant eyes there were thick glasses.

"I shall get to the point, Dr. Urth. I presume you have visited the Moon . . ."

Dr. Urth, who had brought out a bottle of ruddy liquid and two glasses, just a little the worse for dust, from behind a straggling pile of book-films, said with sudden brusqueness, "I have never visited the Moon, Inspector. I never intend to! Space travel is foolishness. I don't believe in it." Then, in softer tones, "Sit down, sir, sit down. Have a drink."

Inspector Davenport did as he was told and said, "But you're an . . ."

"Extraterrologist. Yes. I'm interested in other worlds, but it doesn't mean I have to go there. Good lord, I don't have to be a time traveler to qualify as a historian, do I?" He sat down, and a broad smile impressed itself upon his round face once more as he said, "Now tell me what's on your mind."

"I have come," said the Inspector, frowning, "to consult you in a case of murder."

"Murder? What have I to do with murder?"

"This murder, Dr. Urth, was on the Moon."

"Astonishing."

"It's more than astonishing. It's unprecedented, Dr. Urth. In the fifty years since the Lunar Dominion has been established, ships have blown up and spacesuits have sprung

---

6. neuronic (noo-rŏn'ĭk) adj.: Pertaining to a neuron, or nerve cell.

leaks. Men have boiled to death on sun-side, frozen on dark-side, and suffocated on both sides. There have even been deaths by falls, which, considering lunar gravity, is quite a trick. But in all that time, not one man has been killed on the Moon as the result of another man's deliberate act of violence—till now."

Dr. Urth said, "How was it done?"

"A blaster. The authorities were on the scene within the hour through a fortunate set of circumstances. A patrol ship observed a flash of light against the Moon's surface. You know how far a flash can be seen against the night-side. The pilot notified Luna City and landed. In the process of circling back, he swears that he just managed to see by Earth-light what looked like a ship taking off. Upon landing, he discovered a blasted corpse and footprints."

"The flash of light," said Dr. Urth, "you suppose to be the firing blaster."

"That's certain. The corpse was fresh. Interior portions of the body had not yet frozen. The footprints belonged to two people. Careful measurements showed that the depressions fell into two groups of somewhat different diameters, indicating differently sized spaceboots. In the main, they led to craters GC-3 and GC-5, a pair of——"

"I am acquainted with the official code for naming lunar craters," said Dr. Urth pleasantly.

"Umm. In any case, GC-3 contained footprints that led to a rift in the crater wall, within which scraps of hardened pumice were found. X-ray diffraction patterns showed——"

"Singing Bells," put in the extraterrologist in great excitement. "Don't tell me this murder of yours involves Singing Bells!"

"What if it does?" demanded Davenport blankly.

"I have one. A University expedition uncovered it and presented it to me in return for—— Come, Inspector, I must show it to you."

Dr. Urth jumped up and pattered across the room, beckoning the other to follow as he did. Davenport, annoyed, followed.

They entered a second room, larger than the first, dimmer, considerably more cluttered. Davenport stared with astonishment at the heterogeneous mass of material that was jumbled together in no pretense at order.

He made out a small lump of "blue glaze" from Mars, the sort of thing some romantics considered to be an artifact of long-extinct Martians, a small meteorite, a model of an early spaceship, a sealed bottle of nothing scrawlingly labeled "Venusian atmosphere."

Dr. Urth said happily, "I've made a museum of my whole house. It's one of the advantages of being a bachelor. Of course, I haven't quite got things organized. Someday, when I have a spare week or so . . ."

For a moment he looked about, puzzled; then, remembering, he pushed aside a chart showing the evolutionary scheme of development of the marine invertebrates that were the highest life forms on Barnard's Planet and said, "Here it is. It's flawed, I'm afraid."

The Bell hung suspended from a slender wire, soldered delicately onto it. That it was flawed was obvious. It had a constriction line running halfway about it that made it seem like two small globes, firmly but imperfectly squashed together. Despite that, it had been lovingly polished to a dull luster, softly gray, velvety smooth, and faintly pockmarked in a way that laboratories, in their futile efforts to prepare synthetic Bells, had found impossible to duplicate.

Dr. Urth said, "I experimented a good deal before I found a decent stroker. A flawed Bell is temperamental. But bone works. I have one here"—and he held up something that looked like a short thick spoon made of a gray-white substance—"which I had made out of the femur of an ox. Listen."

With surprising delicacy, his pudgy fingers maneuvered the Bell, feeling for one best spot. He adjusted it, steadying it daintily. Then, letting the Bell swing free, he brought down the thick end of the bone spoon and stroked the Bell softly.

It was as though a million harps had sounded a mile away. It swelled and faded and returned. It came from no particular direction. It sounded inside the head, incredibly sweet and pathetic and tremulous all at once.

It died away lingeringly and both men were silent for a full minute.

Dr. Urth said, "Not bad, eh?" and with a flick of his hand set the Bell to swinging on its wire.

Davenport stirred restlessly. "Careful! Don't break it." The fragility of a good Singing Bell was proverbial.

Dr. Urth said, "Geologists say the Bells are only pressure-hardened pumice, enclosing a vacuum in which small beads of rock rattle freely. That's what they *say*. But if that's all it is, why can't we reproduce one? Now a flawless Bell would make this one sound like a child's harmonica."

"Exactly," said Davenport, "and there aren't a dozen people on Earth who own a flawless one, and there are a hundred people and institutions who would buy one at any price, no questions asked. A supply of Bells would be worth murder."

The extraterrologist turned to Davenport and pushed his spectacles back on his inconsequential nose with a stubby forefinger. "I haven't forgotten your murder case. Please go on."

"That can be done in a sentence. I know the identity of the murderer."

They had returned to the chairs in the library and Dr. Urth clasped his hands over his ample abdomen. "Indeed? Then surely you have no problem, Inspector."

"Knowing and proving are not the same, Dr. Urth. Unfortunately he has no alibi."

"You mean, unfortunately he *has*, don't you?"

"I mean what I say. If he had an alibi, I could crack it somehow, because it would be a false one. If there were witnesses who claimed they had seen him on Earth at the time of the murder, their stories could be broken down. If he had documentary proof, it could be exposed as a forgery or some sort of trickery. Unfortunately he has none of it."

"What does he have?"

Carefully Inspector Davenport described the Peyton estate in Colorado. He concluded, "He has spent every August there in the strictest isolation. Even the T.B.I. would have to testify to that. Any jury would have to presume that he was on his estate this August as well, unless we could present definite proof that he was on the Moon."

"What makes you think he *was* on the Moon? Perhaps he is innocent."

"No!" Davenport was almost violent. "For fifteen years I've been trying to collect sufficient evidence against him and I've never succeeded. But I can *smell* a Peyton crime now. I tell you that no one but Peyton, no one on Earth, would have the impudence or, for that matter, the practical business contacts to attempt disposal of smuggled Singing Bells. He is known to be an expert space pilot. He is known to have had contact with the murdered man, though admittedly not for some months. Unfortunately none of that is proof."

Dr. Urth said, "Wouldn't it be simple to use the psychoprobe, now that its use has been legalized?"

Davenport scowled, and the scar on his cheek turned livid. "Have you read the Konski-Hiakawa law, Dr. Urth?"

"No."

"I think no one has. The right to mental privacy, the government says, is fundamental. All right, but what follows? The man who is psychoprobed and proves innocent of the crime for which he was psychoprobed is entitled to as much compensation as he can persuade the courts to give him. In a recent case a bank cashier was awarded twenty-five thousand dollars for having been psychoprobed on inaccurate suspicion of theft. It seems that the circumstantial evidence which seemed to point to theft actually pointed to a small spot of adultery. His claim that he lost his job, was threatened by the husband in question and put in bodily fear, and finally was held up to ridicule and contumely[7] because a news-strip man had learned the results of the probe held good in court."

"I can see the man's point."

"So can we all. That's the trouble. One more item to remember: Any man who has been psychoprobed once for any reason can never be psychoprobed again for any reason. No one man, the law says, shall be placed in mental jeopardy twice in his lifetime."

"Inconvenient."

"Exactly. In the two years since the psychoprobe has been legitimized, I couldn't count the number of crooks and chiselers who've tried to get themselves psychoprobed for purse-snatching so that they could play the rackets safely afterward. So you see the Department will not allow Peyton to be psychoprobed until they have firm evidence of his guilt. Not legal evidence, maybe, but evidence that is strong enough to convince my boss. The worst of it, Dr. Urth, is that if we come into court without a psychoprobe record, we can't win. In a case as serious as murder, not to have used the psychoprobe is proof enough to the dumbest juror that the prosecution isn't sure of its ground."

"Now what do you want of me?"

"Proof that he was on the Moon sometime in August. It's got to be done quickly. I can't hold him on suspicion much longer. And if news of the murder gets out, the world press will blow up like an asteroid striking Jupiter's atmosphere. A glamorous crime, you know—first murder on the Moon."

"Exactly when was the murder committed?" asked Urth, in a sudden transition to brisk cross-examination.

---

7. contumely (kŏn' tōō-mə-lē) n.: Contempt.

"August twenty-seventh."

"And the arrest was made when?"

"Yesterday, August thirtieth."

"Then if Peyton were the murderer, he would have had time to return to Earth."

"Barely. Just barely." Davenport's lips thinned. "If I had been a day sooner—— If I had found his place empty——"

"And how long do you suppose the two, the murdered man and the murderer, were on the Moon altogether?"

"Judging by the ground covered by the footprints, a number of days. A week, at the minimum."

"Has the ship they used been located?"

"No, and it probably never will. About ten hours ago, the University of Denver reported a rise in background radioactivity beginning day before yesterday at 6 p.m. and persisting for a number of hours. It's an easy thing, Dr. Urth, to set a ship's controls so as to allow it to blast off without crew and blow up, fifty miles high, in a micropile short."

"If I had been Peyton," said Dr. Urth thoughtfully, "I would have killed the man on board ship and blown up corpse and ship together."

"You don't know Peyton," said Davenport grimly. "He enjoys his victories over the law. He values them. Leaving the corpse on the Moon is his challenge to us."

"I see." Dr. Urth patted his stomach with a rotary motion and said, "Well, there is a chance."

"That you'll be able to prove he was on the Moon?"

"That I'll be able to give you my opinion."

"Now?"

"The sooner the better. If, of course, I get a chance to interview Mr. Peyton."

"That can be arranged. I have a non-grav jet waiting. We can be in Washington in twenty minutes."

But a look of the deepest alarm passed over the plump extraterrologist's face. He rose to his feet and pattered away from the T.B.I.

agent toward the duskiest corner of the cluttered room.

"No!"

"What's wrong, Dr. Urth?"

"I won't use a non-grav jet. I don't believe in them."

Davenport stared confusedly at Dr. Urth. He stammered, "Would you prefer a monorail?"

Dr. Urth snapped, "I mistrust all forms of transportation. I don't believe in them. Except walking. I don't mind walking." He was suddenly eager. "Couldn't you bring Mr. Peyton to this city, somewhere within walking distance? To City Hall, perhaps? I've often walked to City Hall."

Davenport looked helplessly about the room. He looked at the myriad volumes of lore about the light-years. He could see through the open door into the room beyond, with its tokens of the worlds beyond the sky. And he looked at Dr. Urth, pale at the thought of non-grav jet, and shrugged his shoulders.

"I'll bring Peyton here. Right to this room. Will that satisfy you?"

Dr. Urth puffed out his breath in a deep sigh. "Quite."

"I hope you can deliver, Dr. Urth."

"I will do my best, Mr. Davenport."

Louis Peyton stared with distaste at his surroundings and with contempt at the fat man who bobbed his head in greeting. He glanced at the seat offered him and brushed it with his hand before sitting down. Davenport took a seat next to him, with his blaster holster in clear view.

The fat man was smiling as he sat down and patted his round abdomen as though he had just finished a good meal and were intent on letting the world know about it.

He said, "Good evening, Mr. Peyton. I am Dr. Wendell Urth, extraterrologist."

Peyton looked at him again. "And what do you want with me?"

"I want to know if you were on the Moon at any time in the month of August."

"I was not."

"Yet no man saw you on Earth between the days of August first and August thirtieth."

"I lived my normal life in August. I am never seen during that month. Let him tell you." And he jerked his head in the direction of Davenport.

Dr. Urth chuckled. "How nice if we could test this matter. If there were only some physical manner in which we could differentiate Moon from Earth. If, for instance, we could analyze the dust in your hair and say, 'Aha, Moon rock.' Unfortunately we can't. Moon rock is much the same as Earth rock. Even if it weren't, there wouldn't be any in your hair unless you stepped onto the lunar surface without a spacesuit, which is unlikely."

Peyton remained impassive.

Dr. Urth went on, smiling benevolently, and lifting a hand to steady the glasses perched precariously on the bulb of his nose. "A man traveling in space or on the Moon breathes Earth air, eats Earth food. He carries Earth environment next to his skin whether he's in his ship or in his spacesuit. We are looking for a man who spent two days in space going to the Moon, at least a week on the Moon, and two days coming back from the Moon. In all that time he carried Earth next to his skin, which makes it difficult."

"I'd suggest," said Peyton, "that you can make it less difficult by releasing me and looking for the real murderer."

"It may come to that," said Dr. Urth. "Have you ever seen anything like this?" His hand pushed its pudgy way to the ground beside his chair and came up with a gray sphere that sent back subdued highlights.

Peyton smiled. "It looks like a Singing Bell to me."

"It *is* a Singing Bell. The murder was committed for the sake of Singing Bells. What do you think of this one?"

"I think it is badly flawed."

"Ah, but inspect it," said Dr. Urth, and

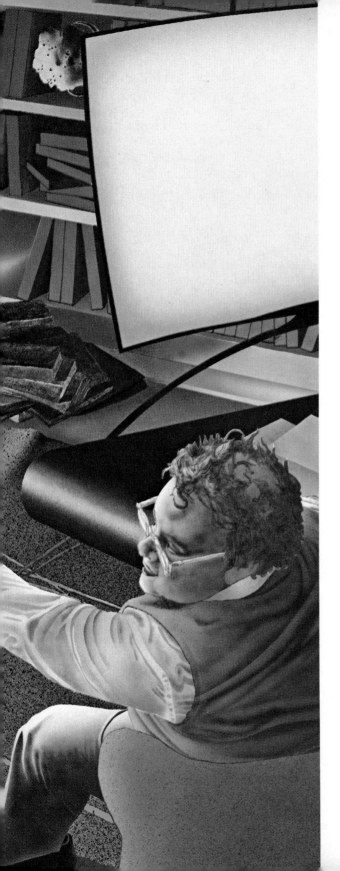

with a quick motion of his hand, he tossed it through six feet of air to Peyton.

Davenport cried out and half-rose from his chair. Peyton brought up his arms with an effort, but so quickly that he managed to catch the Bell.

Peyton said, "You fool. Don't throw it around that way."

"You respect Singing Bells, do you?"

"Too much to break one. That's no crime, at least." Peyton stroked the Bell gently, then lifted it to his ear and shook it slowly, listening to the soft clicks of the Lunoliths, those small pumice particles, as they rattled in vacuum.

Then, holding the Bell up by the length of steel wire still attached to it, he ran a thumbnail over its surface with an expert, curving motion. It twanged! The note was very mellow, very flutelike, holding with a slight *vibrato* that faded lingeringly and conjured up pictures of a summer twilight.

For a short moment, all three men were lost in the sound.

And then Dr. Urth said, "Throw it back, Mr. Peyton. Toss it here!" and held out his hand in peremptory gesture.

Automatically Louis Peyton tossed the Bell. It traveled its short arc one-third of the way to Dr. Urth's waiting hand, curved downward, and shattered with a heartbroken, sighing discord on the floor.

Davenport and Peyton stared at the gray slivers with equal wordlessness and Dr. Urth's calm voice went almost unheard as he said, "When the criminal's cache of crude Bells is located, I'll ask that a flawless one, properly polished, be given to me, as replacement and fee."

"A fee? For what?" demanded Davenport irritably.

"Surely the matter is now obvious. Despite my little speech of a moment ago, there is one piece of Earth's environment that no space traveler carries with him and that is *Earth's surface gravity*. The fact that Mr. Peyton could so egregiously misjudge the toss of an object he obviously valued so highly could mean only that his muscles are not yet readjusted to the pull of Earthly gravity. It is my professional opinion, Mr. Davenport, that your prisoner has, in the last few days, been away from Earth. He has either been in space or on some planetary object considerably smaller in size than the Earth—as, for example, the Moon."

Davenport rose triumphantly to his feet. "Let me have your opinion in writing," he said, hand on blaster, "and that will be good enough to get me permission to use a psycho-probe."

Louis Peyton, dazed and unresisting, had only the numb realization that any testament he could now leave would have to include the fact of ultimate failure.

Close Up

1. Cornwell knows the location of a cache of Singing Bells. Why does he consider Peyton the perfect accomplice?

2. Although Cornwell approaches Peyton about the crime in April, Peyton delays action until August. Why?

3. Immediately after loading the Bells on the spaceship, Peyton shoots Cornwell. (a) Why do the police discover the crime so soon afterward? (b) Why is Davenport convinced that Peyton is the murderer?

4. Davenport asks Dr. Urth to prove that Peyton had been on the moon sometime in the last month. (a) Why does Urth first establish that Peyton values the Singing Bells? (b) Then how does he prove that Peyton had been on the moon?

5. Peyton might have got away with his crime if he had been a little less confident. Find two errors in judgment he made because of overconfidence.

Setting

The setting of a story can affect the plot. In this story the setting influences the characters' actions. The fact that the Singing Bells are on the moon affects Peyton's plans for the crime.

1. When on earth Peyton always spends every August at his retreat. (a) Describe the retreat's setting. (b) How does the retreat fit into Peyton's robbery plans?

2. The main event in this story—the crime—takes place on the moon. This setting works to the criminals' advantage: for example, the moon's darkness provides a natural cover. How does the moon's gravity work to their advantage?

3. Ultimately, the fact that Peyton committed the crime on the moon leads to his downfall. What had Peyton, despite all his careful calculations, not taken into account?

Activities

1. **Composition.** Imagine you are a space traveler. Write a paragraph describing an unusual object that you find.

2. If you were an explorer or an inventor, you might name something you discovered or invented after yourself. Use the information on word origins in the dictionary to find the person behind each of the following words: *macadam, sandwich, pasteurization, maverick, lynch, boycott, tawdry, mackintosh, shrapnel, derrick,* and *guillotine.*

INFERENCES

Making Inferences About Past and Future Events

When you read you make inferences about what has happened in the past and what will happen in the future. You base your inferences on clues in the story. For example, from the following passage, you can infer that Louis Peyton has dealt with Albert Cornwell in the past:

> "Peyton, who disliked being approached over his newspaper and dessert at Grinnell's, said, 'If you have business with me, Cornwell, you know where you can reach me.' "

From the next passage, you can infer that Peyton will murder Cornwell:

> "On August 9 his aeroflitter carried him to a spot in Wyoming where Albert Cornwell and a spaceship waited. The spaceship, itself, was a weak point, of course, since there were men who had sold it, men who had transported it and helped prepare it for flight. All those men, however, led only as far as Cornwell, and Cornwell, Peyton thought—with a trace of a smile on his cold lips—would be a dead end. A very dead end."

▶ Read each item below. Then answer the question that follows it.

a. "A look of cunning lit Cornwell's face like a smoking torch, obscuring more than it showed and lending it a repulsive oiliness. 'The man was a lunar grubstaker who had a method for locating the Bells in the crater sides. I don't know his method; he never told me that. But he has gathered dozens, hidden them on the Moon, and come to Earth to arrange the disposing of them.'
'He died, I suppose?'
'Yes. A most shocking accident, Mr. Peyton. A fall from a height. Very sad. Of course, his activities on the Moon were quite illegal. The Dominion is very strict about unauthorized Bell-mining. So perhaps it was a judgment upon him after all . . . In any case, I have his map.' "

Who do you think caused the miner's death?

b. "Deliberately he had left himself eight days. In that time he slowly and meticulously destroyed just enough of his supplies to account for all of August."

How long do you think Peyton plans to be gone?

c. "He crouched for the slow high leap against lunar gravity, looked up, and froze in panic. His face, clearly visible through the hard carved lusilite of his helmet, froze in a last grimace of terror. 'No, Mr. Peyton. Don't——' "

What do you think happens to Cornwell?

WORD ATTACK

Using a Pronunciation Key

Some letters in the English language represent, or stand for, more than one sound. The letters *ch*, for example, may stand for the first sound you hear in *chart* or the first sound you hear in *character*. The letter g may represent the first sound in *gum* or the first sound in *gym*.

You can find out how to pronounce an unfamiliar word by looking it up in a dictionary or glossary. Diacritical marks in parentheses follow the entry word. For example, *complacent* (kəm-plā′sənt). These tell you how to pronounce the letters in a word. You can tell what each symbol means by referring to the Pronunciation Key at the bottom of the dictionary page or at the front of the glossary.

Accent marks tell you to stress a syllable. For example, *terminator* (tûr′mə-nā′tər). Stress the syllable with the heavy accent mark more strongly than the syllable with the light accent mark. Give unaccented syllables the lightest stress.

▶ Look up each of the following words in the glossary. On a piece of paper, copy each complete glossary entry, paying special attention to diacritical marks. Then read each word aloud.

a. conducive
b. affluence
c. peremptory
d. cache
e. subsequent
f. qualm
g. egregious
h. solder
i. obsequious
j. vibrato

An Underground Episode

Edmund Ware

Three figures leaned against the slanting rain—Alamo Laska, Nick Christopher, and the boy who had run away from home. They rested on their long-handled shovels, and as they gazed into the crater, which by their brawn they had hollowed in the earth, the blue clay oozed back again, slowly devouring the fruits of their toil.

Laska, the nomad, thought of the wild geese winging southward to warm bayous. Nick's heart, under the bone and muscle of his great chest, swelled with sweet thoughts of his wife and child, who lived in a foreign city across an ocean. The boy felt the sting of rain against his cheeks and dreamed of his mother, who seemed lovely and far away.

It was Sunday. The regular deep-trench gang lounged in their warm boardinghouse, while out on the job the three men toiled alone. They breathed heavily, and the gray steam crawled upon their backs, for it was cold.

"Look at 'er filling in," growled Laska. "Faster than a man could dig."

"Mud's get inna pipe," said Nick. "The inspector make us tear him out if she fill anymore."

Backed close to the edge of the crater stood a giant trench-digging machine. In the dusk it appeared as a crouched and shadowy animal—silent, gloomy, capable. But a broken piston had crippled its engines, and the men had swathed them in tarpaulin.

A long gray mound stretched away from the crater opposite the machine. Buried thirty feet below the mound was the new-laid sewer pipe. From the bottom of the pit at the machine, the pipe ran a hundred yards horizontally under the surface, opening in a manhole. This hundred yards of new-laid pipe was the reason for the three men digging in the rain. They had dug eleven hours, trying to uncover the open end of the pipe in order to seal it against the mud. But rain and ooze and storm had bested them. The bank had caved, and the mud had crawled into the mouth of the pipe, obstructing it.

"It's getting dark fast," said Laska, "an' we're licked."

"We can't do nothing more," said the boy.

Nick Christopher scraped the mud from his shovel. He looked up into the whirlpools of the sky. "In a year I go old country. I see my wife. I see my kid."

"Nick," said Laska, "go over to the shanty and get a couple of lanterns and telephone Stender. Tell him if he don't want the inspector on our tail to get out here quick with a gang."

Nick stuck his shovel in the mud and moved away across the plain toward the shanty.

The cold had crept into the boy. It frightened him, and in the darkness his eyes sought Laska's face. "How could we clean out the pipe, even when the gang got down to it?"

"Maybe we could flush it out with a fire hose," said Laska.

"There's no water plug within a mile."

Laska said nothing. The boy waited for him to reply, but he didn't. Picking up his damp shirt, the boy pulled it on over his head. He did not tuck in the tails, and they flapped in the wind, slapping against him. He looked like a gaunt, serious bird, striving to leave the ground. He was bareheaded, and his yellow hair was matted and stringy with dampness. His face was thin, a little sunken, and fine drops of moisture clung to the fuzz on his cheeks. His lips were blue with cold. He was seventeen.

Laska stared into the pit. It was too dark to see bottom, but something in the black hole fascinated him. "If we could get a rope through the pipe, we could drag sandbags through into the manhole. That would clean her out in good shape."

"How could we get a rope through?"

"I dunno. Stender'll know." Laska walked over to the digging machine and leaned against its towering side. The rain had turned to sleet. "It's cold," he said.

The boy followed Laska and went close to him for warmth and friendship. "How *could* we get a rope through?"

Laska's shoulders lifted slowly. "You'll see. You'll see. You'll see when Stender gets here. Say, it's freezing."

After a long time of waiting, a yellow light flamed into being in the shanty, and they heard the muffled scraping of boots on the board floor. The shanty door opened. A rectangle of light stood out sharply.

Swart[1] figures crossed and recrossed the lighted area, pouring out into the storm.

"Ho!" called Laska.

"Ho!" came the answer, galloping to them in the wind.

They heard the rasping of caked mud on dungarees, the clank of shovels, the voice of Stender, the foreman. Lanterns swung like yellow pendulums. Long-legged shadows reached and receded.

The diggers gathered about the rim of the pit, staring. Stender's face showed in the lantern light. His lips were wrinkled, as if constantly prepared for blasphemy. He was a tall, cursing conqueror. Orders shot from his throat, and noisily the men descended into the pit and began to dig. They drew huge, gasping breaths like mired beasts fighting for life.

The boy watched, his eyes bulging in the dark. Hitherto he had thought very briefly of sewers, regarding them as unlovely things. But Laska and Nick and Stender gave them splendor and importance. The deep-trench men were admirable monsters. They knew the clay, the feel and pattern of it, for it had long been heavy in their minds and muscles. They were big in three dimensions, and their eyes were black and barbarous. When they ate, it was with rough-and-tumble relish, and

---

1. swart (swôrt) *adj.*: Swarthy, or dark-complexioned.

as their bellies fattened they spoke tolerantly of enemies. They played lustily, with a view to satiation. They worked stupendously. They were diggers in clay, transformed by lantern light into a race of giants.

Through the rain came Stender, his black slicker crackling. "They're down," he said. "Angelo just struck the pipe."

Laska grunted.

Stender blew his nose with his fingers, walked away, and climbed down into the hole. They lost sight of him as he dropped over the rim. The sound of digging had ceased, and two or three men on the surface rested on their shovels, the light from below gleaming in their flat faces. Laska and the boy knew that Stender was examining the pipe. They heard him swearing at what he had found.

After a moment he clambered up over the rim and held up a lantern. His pipe, gripped firmly between his teeth, was upside down to keep out the wet. "Someone's got to go through the pipe," he said, raising his voice. "There's fifty bucks for the man that'll go through the pipe into the manhole with a line tied to his foot. Fifty bucks!"

There was a moment of quiet. The men thought of the fifty dollars and furtively measured themselves against the deed at hand. It seemed to the boy that he was the only one who feared the task. He did not think of the fifty dollars, but thought only of the fear. Three hundred feet through a rathole, eighteen inches in diameter. Three hundred feet of muck, of wet, black dark, and no turning back. But, if he did not volunteer, they would know that he was afraid. The boy stepped from behind Laska and said uncertainly, "I'll go, Stender," and he wished he might snatch back the words, for looking about him he saw that not a man among those present could have wedged his shoulders into the mouth of an eighteen-inch pipe. He was the only volunteer. They had known he would be the only one.

Stender came striding over, holding the lantern above his head. He peered into the boy's face. "Take off your clothes," he said.

"Take off my clothes?"

"That's what I said."

"You might get a buckle caught in a joint," said Laska. "See?"

The boy saw only that he had been trapped very cunningly. At home he could have been openly fearful, for at home everything about him was known. There, quite simply, he could have said, "I won't do it. I'm frightened. I'll be killed." But here the diggers in clay were lancing him with looks. And Laska was bringing a ball of line, one end of which would be fastened to his ankle.

"Just go in a sweater," said Laska. "A sweater an' boots over your woolens. We'll be waiting for you at the manhole."

He wanted so desperately to dive off into the night that he felt his legs bracing for a spring and a tight feeling in his throat. Then, mechanically, he began to take off his clothes. Nick had gone clumping off to the shanty, and shortly he returned with a pair of hip boots. "Here, kid. I get 'em warm for you inna shanty."

He thrust his feet into the boots, and Laska knelt and tied the heavy line to his ankle. "Too tight?"

"No. It's all right, I guess."

"Well—come on."

They walked past Stender, who was pacing up and down among the men. They slid down into the crater, deepened now by the diggers. They stood by the partly covered mouth of the pipe. They were thirty feet below the surface of the ground.

Laska reached down and tugged at the knot he had tied in the line; then he peered into the mouth of the tube. He peered cautiously, as if he thought it might be inhabited. The boy's glance wandered up the wet sides of the pit. Over the rim a circle of bland yellow faces peered at him. Sleet tinkled against lanterns, spattered down, and stung his flesh.

"Go ahead in," said Laska.

The boy blanched.

"Just keep thinking of the manhole, where you'll come out," said Laska.

The boy's throat constricted. He seemed to be bursting with a pressure from inside. He got down on his belly in the slushy ice and mud. It penetrated slowly to his skin and spread over him. He put his head inside the mouth of the pipe and drew back in horror. Some gibbering words flew from his lips. His voice sounded preposterously loud.

Laska's voice was already shopworn with distance. "You can make it! Go ahead."

He lay on his left side and, reaching out with his left arm, caught a joint and drew himself in. The mud oozed up around him, finding its way upon him, welling up against the left side of his face. He pressed his right cheek against the ceiling of the pipe to keep the muck from covering his mouth and nose. Laska's voice was far and muffled. Laska was in another world—a sane world of night, of storm, and the mellow glow of lanterns.

"Are you makin' it all right, kid?"

The boy cried out, his ears ringing with his cry. It reechoed from the sides of the pipe. The sides hemmed him, pinned him, closed him in on every side with their paralyzing circumference.

There is no darkness like the darkness underground that miners know. It borrows something from night, from tombs, from places used by bats. Such fluid black can terrify a flame, can suffocate and drench a mind with madness. There is a fierce desire to struggle, to beat one's hands against the prison. The boy longed to lift his pitiful human strength against the walls. He longed to claw at his eyes in the mad certainty that more than darkness curtained them.

He had moved but a few feet on his journey when panic swept him. Ahead of him the mud had built into a solid wave. Putting forth his left hand, he felt a scant two inches between the wave's crest and the ceiling of the pipe. There was nothing to do but go back. If he moved ahead, it meant death by suffocation. He tried to back away, but

caught his toe in a joint of the pipe. He was entombed! In an hour he would be a body. The cold and dampness would kill him before they could dig down to him. Nick and Laska would pull him from the muck, and Laska would say, "Huh, his clock's stopped."

He thrashed with delirious strength against his prison. He felt the skin tearing from the backs of his hands as he flailed the rough walls. And some gods must have snickered, for above the walls of the pipe were thirty feet of unyielding clay, eight thousand miles of earth below. A strength, a weight, a night, each a thousand times his most revolting dream, leaned upon the boy, depressing, crushing, stamping him out. The ground gave no cry of battle. It did no bleeding, suffered no pain, uttered no groans. It flattened him silently. It swallowed him in its foul despotism. It dropped its merciless weight upon his mind. It was so inhuman, so horribly incognizant of the God men swore had made it.

In the midst of his frenzy, when he had beaten his face against the walls until it bled, he heard a ringing voice he knew was real, springing from human sympathy. It was Laska, calling, "Are you all right, kid?"

In that instant the boy loved Laska as he loved his life. Laska's voice sheered the weight from him, scattered the darkness, brought him new balance and a hope to live.

"Fine!" he answered in a cracking yell. He yelled again, loving the sound of his voice and thinking how foolish yelling was in such a place.

With his left hand he groped ahead and found that the wave of mud had settled, leveled off by its own weight. He drew his body together, pressing it against the pipe. He straightened, moved ahead six inches. His fingers found a loop of oakum[2] dangling from

a joint, and he pulled himself on, his left arm forward, his right arm behind over his hip, like a swimmer's.

He had vanquished panic, and he looked ahead to victory. Each joint brought him twenty inches nearer his goal. Each twenty inches was a plateau, which enabled him to envision a new plateau—the next joint. The joints were like small, deceitful rests upon a march.

He had been more than an hour on the way. He did not know how far he had gone, a third, perhaps even a half of the distance. He forgot the present, forgot fear, wet, cold, blackness; he lost himself in dreaming of the world of men outside the prison. It was as if he were a small, superb island in hell.

He did not know how long he had been counting the joints, but he found himself whispering good numbers. "Fifty-one, fifty-two, fifty-three. . . ." Each joint, when he thought of it, appeared to take up a vast time of squirming in the muck, and the line dragged heavily behind his foot.

Suddenly, staring into the darkness so that it seemed to bring a pain to his eyes, he saw a pallid ray. He closed his eyes, opened them, and looked again. The ray was real, and he uttered a whimper of relief. He knew that the ray must come from Stender's lantern. He pictured Stender and a group of the diggers huddled in the manhole, waiting for him. The men and the manhole grew magnificent in his mind, and he thought of them worshipfully.

"Seventy-six, seventy-seven, seventy-eight. . . ."

The ray grew slowly, like a worthwhile thing. It took an oval shape, and the oval grew fat, like an egg, then round. It was a straight line to the manhole, and the mud had thinned.

Through the pipe into the boy's ears, a voice rumbled like halfhearted thunder. It was Stender's voice. "How you makin' it?"

"Oh, just fine!" His cry came pricking back into his ears like a shower of needles.

---

2. oakum (ō′kəm) n.: Hemp fiber used for caulking seams in pipes.

There followed a long span of numbness. The cold and wet had dulled his senses, so that whenever the rough ceiling of the pipe ripped his face, he did not feel it; so that struggling in the muck became an almost pleasant and normal thing, since all elements of fear and pain and imagination had been removed. Warmth and dryness became alien to him. He was a creature native to darkness, foreign to light.

The round yellow disk before him gave him his only sense of living. It was a sunlit landfall, luring him on. He would close his eyes and count five joints, then open them quickly, cheering himself at the perceptible stages of progress.

Then, abruptly it seemed, he was close to the manhole. He could hear men moving. He could see the outline of Stender's head as Stender peered into the mouth of the pipe. Men kneeled, pushing each other's head to one side, in order to watch him squirm toward them. They began to talk excitedly. He could hear them breathing, see details— and Stender and Laska reached in. They got their hands upon him. They hauled him to them, as if he were something they wanted to inspect scientifically. He felt as if they thought he was a rarity, a thing of great oddness. The light dazzled him. It began to move around and around and to dissolve into many lights, some of which danced locally

© McDANIEL 81

on a bottle. He heard Stender's voice. "Well, he made it all right. What do you know?"

"Here, kid," said Laska, holding the bottle to his mouth. "Drink all of this that you can hold."

He could not stand up. He believed calmly that his flesh and bones were constructed of putty. He could hear no vestige of the song of victory he had dreamed of hearing. He looked stupidly at his hands, which bled painlessly. He could not feel his arms and legs at all. He was a vast sensation of lantern light and the steam of human beings breathing in a damp place.

Faces peered at him. The faces were curious and surprised. He felt a clouded, uncomprehending resentment against them. Stender held him up on one side, Laska on the other. They looked at each other across him. Suddenly Laska stooped and gathered him effortlessly into his arms.

"You'll get covered with mud," mumbled the boy.

"Darned if he didn't make it all right," said Stender. "Save us tearing out the pipe."

"Down with the pipe," said Laska.

The boy's wet head fell against Laska's chest. He felt the rise and fall of Laska's muscles and knew that Laska was climbing with him up the iron steps inside the manhole. Night wind smote him. He buried his head deeper against Laska. Laska's body became a mountain of warmth. He felt a heavy, sighing peace, like a soldier who has been comfortably wounded and knows that war for him is over.

Close Up

1. (a) Why must someone go through the pipe? (b) Why does everyone expect the boy to volunteer?

2. (a) During his crawl through the pipe, the boy is overcome by panic. Why? (b) What calms him down and inspires him to go on?

3. (a) What does the boy think about the men with whom he works? (b) What do they think about him at the beginning of the story and then at the end?

Setting

The setting of a story can affect how characters behave. It can force them to make certain decisions and to choose a certain course of action. For example, in "An Underground Episode," the boy must muster his courage and fight for his life to prove himself to his fellow workers.

1. The boy is working in an alien environment among strangers. (a) How does this situation influence his decision to crawl through the pipe? (b) How does he really feel about his decision?

2. It is freezing inside the pipe. What two other factors make moving through the pipe difficult and terrifying for the boy?

3. How does the boy manage to move himself through the pipe?

4. (a) What effect does the boy's successful trip through the pipe have on him? (b) How does he feel about himself afterward?

5. The boy is afraid to crawl through the pipe, but he doesn't dare *not* volunteer. Do you still consider him a hero? Why or why not?

Activities

1. What do you think Stender might have said to the boy after the ordeal? Share your ideas with your classmates.

2. If you had been the boy, would you have volunteered to crawl through the pipe? Explain why or why not.

INFERENCES

Making Inferences About a Character's Motives

A motive is the reason behind an action. When you read, you often make inferences about a character's motives. You try to discover why a character acted in the way he or she did. For example, you may have made the inference that the boy in this story took this job because he needed money.

▶ For each action below, select the most likely motive.

   a. The boy volunteers to crawl through the pipe.
      (1) He doesn't want the men to think he is a coward.
      (2) He wants the fifty dollars.
      (3) He thinks crawling through the pipe will be fun.

   b. Nick goes to the shanty and warms hip boots for the boy.
      (1) Nick is feeling guilty because he didn't volunteer.
      (2) Nick likes the boy and wants him to be as comfortable as possible.
      (3) Nick thinks the boy might share the fifty dollars with him.

   c. The boy decides not to die and starts crawling again.
      (1) He wants the fifty dollars.
      (2) He hears Laska's voice and wants to get to him.
      (3) He wants to return to his mother.

   d. Laska stoops and gathers the boy into his arms.
      (1) He is afraid the boy will die.
      (2) He loves the boy and wants to take care of him.
      (3) He wants Stender to think he is a good man.

WORD ATTACK

Understanding Homographs

Homographs are words that are spelled alike but have different meanings and different word origins. They have two or more separate entries in the dictionary. They may or may not be pronounced the same. For example, *lean* may spell the word that means "thin" or the word that means "to bend from a vertical position." *Lean* is pronounced the same in both instances. Only the context tells you which word to use: The boy was tall and *lean.* Obviously, in this context, "lean" means "thin."

The word *tear* is a homograph that is pronounced (tîr) when it means "a drop of water from the eye" and (târ) when it means "to pull apart."

When you meet a homograph while reading, you must look at the context to determine which meaning and pronunciation to use.

---

1. The *italicized* words in the sentences below are homographs. Select the correct definition for each one from the choices that follow each sentence.
   a. "They had dug eleven hours, trying to uncover the open end of the pipe in order to *seal* it against the mud."
      (1) to close off
      (2) to hunt an aquatic mammal
   b. "The *bank* had caved, and the mud had crawled into the mouth of the pipe, obstructing it."
      (1) a piled-up mound or ridge
      (2) a set of like things arranged in a row
      (3) a business establishment for the storing or lending of money
   c. " 'Maybe we could *flush* it out with a fire hose,' said Laska."
      (1) in cards, a hand in which the cards are the same suit
      (2) empty or purify with a gush of water
      (3) startle a bird from its hiding place

2. You probably think you know all the following *italicized* words, but you may not be familiar with all the homographs spelled by these letters. Find the meaning, pronunciation, and word origin of each of the following *italicized* homographs: *pallet, stingy, school, pale, desert, elder, hack, keen, gum, page, pace, tatoo, tuna, painter.*

The House from the Eleventh Floor

Eva-Lis Wuorio

It all started quite simply.

I had a couple of months' leave of absence to finish a thesis I was writing to further my career as a history teacher. I had come to Turku, a small old town on the west coast of Finland to do my final research. The university library there had a lot of unusual material in English, French, and German, the languages I master.

The day I had gone to look at the small flat for rent had been gray and misty. There was not much to be said for the place except that the eleventh-floor windows looked over the harbor and the island-mazed straits to the sea. Immediately below was a still unfinished greensward[1] of the new housing development, adjacent to the harbor flats. The ground had been leveled and most of the trees razed but for an odd little wooded knoll on which I glimpsed the roof of a wooden house. It was a pleasant anachronism in the midst of the new forest of ugly high apartment buildings.

It was not until I had been living there for some weeks that I thought of the small house again. It was a late gray foggy November afternoon, for that year the fabled Finnish winter did not come at all. The dog had been begging to go out, and as I changed into outdoor clothes I stared out the window. The trees on the little knoll were bare now and I could see the house plainly. It huddled in the hollow of the small hill which was obviously manmade, a long time ago. I thought it was probably part of a battlement, earth-overtaken, perhaps left for a historical reason. The house itself was a pleasantly antique-looking wooden building. The dog and I could investigate; it would give purpose to our walk.

Down on the flats by the harbor the mist was thicker than it had seemed from the eleventh floor. We followed the recently made walks, crisscrossing the acre or so of flat land. In the distance the crane and ship lights shone dimly. The air was dank. There were a few sparsely spaced street lights, and near one of them we met a young woman. The dog went up to her, and she bent to speak to it.

"Excuse me," I said, "but I seem to be curiously lost. Somewhere right around here there should be a small knoll, with an old-fashioned wooden building on it, but I simply don't seem to find it."

She straightened. She was small and slim,

---

1. greensward (grēn'swôrd') n.: Green, grassy turf.

hatless, with thick long hair to her shoulders. She looked startled.

She hesitated so long I thought she had not understood me. Then she suddenly pointed behind her and walked swiftly past us. The fog swirled to hide her even as I turned to look after her.

"Come along," I said to the dog, somehow uneasy. We stuck to the walks, for there at least were the occasional lamps. The apart-

ment buildings towered in their huddle, like UFOs above the mist, the lighted windows dim beacons. I walked for another half hour but still did not stumble on the odd little hill I was searching for.

Through the fog, though, for a short time before I turned back to the ugly development, I heard a pleasant, untrained voice singing an old French song. I knew the tune but couldn't remember the words. It was one of those chansons[2] you expect to hear accompanied by a lute.

The next morning I began to wonder about my eyesight. It was a clear sunny morning, and as I stood watching the white Stockholm steamers negotiating the narrows, my glance fell on the knoll. There it was, a cup-shaped turf- and tree-lined battery, with bare brush down the sloping sides of it. The hollow in the center of it was empty but for some trees, all etched in black from the harbor smog.

I stared at the knoll a long time, wondering what on earth had happened to the house. I described it to myself as I remembered it. It was a one-story L-shaped log house with an odd sort of a shooting gallery under one of the gables. I couldn't have imagined that, I was sure. I'd particularly noted it. Had I seen such a small house somewhere else and absently placed it in the middle of the empty knoll? It seemed unlikely.

I was puzzled to the point of annoyance. But the fact remained that every foggy day I would see that house from my window. Really see it, not imagine it. On the few bright days during those couple of months, the knoll was quite bare of any building. Was I going crazy?

I didn't know anyone well enough to tell them about my aberration. I couldn't speak Finnish or Swedish, and around the district where I lived no one spoke English. I was doing research at the splendid university library, and the people I met there were a serious lot. One didn't feel like volunteering curious stories to them.

Often at night, walking the dog, I'd see that long-haired girl. She had a habit of slipping into a batch of fog like a wraith, so I did not get a real impression of her. I made up stories to amuse myself. She lived in the house that wasn't; ergo, she was an illusion herself.

That was until the evening when she was obviously flesh and blood, annoyed, searching her pockets for change at the newspaper kiosk. This was a small wooden hut at the end of the development area where I myself bought cigarettes.

"Let me lend you some," I said. "After all, we meet practically every evening."

"Thank you, it's nothing," she answered me back in English. "It's only that tonight is the last night to turn in the Lotto coupon, and the kiosk woman is a replacement and doesn't know me."

"But I do," I said, and quite charmingly she chose two marks from my palm.

It was sometime during the following week that she stopped me during the dog's nightly walk.

"Good evening. I won seventy-nine marks on that Lotto and would very much like to buy you a coffee."

I said that would be splendid, and we walked down to the harbor terminal, a pleasant building nudging the sides of the berthed ships. For the first time I saw her clearly and was very pleased with what I saw. When she put on her immense spectacles she did look a little like a small frog, but a nice small frog.

"I wanted to talk to you," she said, after having matter-of-factly given our order. She was looking at me intently, yet with a touch of disapproval. I wondered why, for though I'm not vain I know I'm not bad-looking. I've thick black hair and dark eyes, and I was respectable in an English tweed jacket and a black turtleneck.

"I wanted to tell you about the house you were looking for that first night," she said. "It doesn't exist, did you know?"

"I was beginning to wonder," I said. This was going to be a splendid conversation.

"Very few people ever see it."

"It doesn't exist," I said, "yet a few people do see it?"

"That's right."

Absently she drank all her coffee. I got up and fetched her another one from the counter.

---

2. chansons (shăn′ sən) n.: Songs.

"Did you know that English and French battleships were in these waters during the spring of 1854?" she said abruptly.

I was startled. That was the subject of my research. I'd thought I was unique in taking an interest in this little-known aspect of the Crimean War.

She obviously thought I was as ignorant as most people on this particular subject for she continued.

"The English armada was led by Admiral Napier and the French by General Baraquay d'Hilliers. They captured the Bomarsund fortress out there on the Aland Islands. They sent their Finnish prisoners to England and France and made themselves very free around the coast. They made one mistake. They thought there were a lot of men defending Turku and made only a few skirmishes and minor landings here. One Frenchman could have changed the whole course of the campaign, but we captured him. Now do you see?"

"No, I don't," I said. She hadn't told me anything I hadn't known before except that last bit. I was interested.

"He was smuggled ashore to spy on our defenses. I suppose because he didn't go back, the enemy navies withdrew and sailed away. There was only one very minor skirmish by that little battery where you think you see the little wooden house." She looked at me accusingly.

"What happened to the Frenchman?" I said.

"He didn't get any farther than those islands out there. He broke his leg on the rocks. There's a clumsy spy for you. The daughter of the sergeant in charge of the battery was out in a rowboat fishing, and she fished him off the rocks. Her fiancé had been one of the captured Finns, and she had ideas of exchanging prisoners. However, to make things easier for herself—the Frenchman was naturally armed—she persuaded him that it was a case of love at first sight. Mad, isn't it. Do you believe in it?"

"Yes and no," I said.

"That's no answer. Do you believe you can look a stranger in the eyes, for the first time, and fall hopelessly in love?" She took off her glasses and looked into my eyes.

"Yes," I said.

"Well, the story goes that that's what happened to them. She persuaded him that the safest place for him would be at her home, which was that small wooden house inside the battery. Who would think of looking for an enemy spy there?"

"Who indeed?" I said.

"So she took him home."

"Broken leg and all?"

"They managed. The sea came much closer than now. It's been filled in since. The shore was wild and pretty. They would have rowed right up to the battery wharf. She hid him in the attic room, the one with the small balcony looking over the sea. They were very happy."

"How do you know?" I was laughing.

She became annoyed. "There is a picture of a man in that house," she snapped. "He looks like you. Just like you."

"You have seen a picture in a house that does not exist?"

"You were *searching* for a house that does not exist," she countered.

I hadn't been really searching for the house, I'd just happened to see it. I didn't tell her because I wanted her to go on talking in her harmlessly crazy way. To encourage her, however, I told her that I'd heard one of my ancestors had been lost along this coast about that time. That was true, actually. My name is Hilliers.

"Oh," she said, staring at me. "So you want to see that picture?"

"Is it possible?" What was I getting into anyway? This was entirely a new approach in my experience, but I was fairly fascinated by her.

She shrugged and got up. Obviously I could take it or leave it. I helped her on with her coat.

We walked back through the harbor yards. The mist was thick and the air damp. In the distance the apartment buildings gleamed again like beacons. I thought I could distinguish my own eleventh-floor window, the one from which I'd seen the house for the first time and often since. It must be a trick of mist or overactive imagination, I thought. But how would the girl know about it, then?

"Do you believe in things existing forever?" she asked, mumbling through her high turned-up collar. "I mean in and within their own time? Inside their own distinct dimensions of being?"

"I haven't thought about it," I said. "Are you asking me or telling me?"

"We're here," she said, "or there, as the case may be."

We had crossed the flats where I usually walked the dog and had arrived at a gateway in the earthen walls I hadn't noticed before. It was perhaps on the misty side of the small battery. The dog was alert but not in any way uneasy. I noted that.

We walked through to a small courtyard. The house was at the far end of it. Somehow it seemed lighter here than outside the battery. The mist had swirled elsewhere as mist is wont to do.

"Come in." she said. "Look at that."

On the wall opposite the door was a mirror, I supposed, since I was looking at myself. Only it wasn't a mirror, for the man inside the frame was not wearing an English tweed jacket or a black turtleneck, although otherwise he couldn't be anyone else but me.

I felt achingly spaceless, timeless, staring at myself. Only faintly I heard her voice.

"You'll have to hide soon. Father will be coming home."

Well, that's the lot of it. I've been sitting here in this small attic room for I don't know how long. Time doesn't seem to move. Sometimes I write this report although it doesn't seem very important either. At times I find myself humming that old French song, whose words I don't remember even yet. Sometimes I have a feeling I might have stumbled on a story very much like this if I'd had just a few more days to research the old papers in the library——

Where did you, who are reading, find this?

The dog? Oh, he's here all right. Didn't I tell you he was just a stray who attached himself to me when I came to live in the flat on the eleventh floor. You can't see it from here.

Close Up

1. This is a curious story that leaves many explanations up to the reader's imagination. (a) Do you think it mere coincidence that the narrator has come to Turku? Why or why not? (b) Is it only an accident that he meets the girl? Why or why not?

2. When the girl and the narrator stop for coffee, she tells him about a little-known incident from the Crimean War. (a) Why does her story startle him? (b) What important fact does she tell him about the spy who was captured along the coast?

3. (a) On the basis of the ending of the story, who do you think the narrator really is? (b) Who do you think the girl is?

4. At one point the girl asks the narrator, "Do you believe in things existing forever? . . . I mean in and within their own time? Inside their own distinct dimensions of being?" How does her question help explain this story?

5. *Foreshadowing* is planting clues early in the story to hint at what will happen later. Find two clues that foreshadow the ending of this story.

Setting

The mood of a story is the impression it creates and the emotions it arouses in the reader. This story creates a mood of mystery by presenting an unusual set of circumstances that demands an explanation. Details of setting such as weather conditions add to this mood.

1. What is mysterious about the house the narrator sees from his window?

2. Weather plays an important role in establishing the mood of mystery. (a) What is the weather like when the narrator goes hunting for an apartment? (b) What is the weather like when he first goes hunting for the house?

3. The narrator says that the apartment buildings "towered in their huddle, like UFOs above the mist, the lighted windows dim beacons." Find two other details of setting that help create a mood of mystery.

Activity

▶ **Composition.** A paradox is a statement or situation that reveals a truth, although at first it seems impossible or untrue. Write a paragraph explaining the paradox in this story.

INFERENCES

Making Inferences About Time

When you make inferences about time, you draw conclusions about when events occur. You base your inference on clues in the story. For example, when you read the clues "new housing development" and "high apartment buildings," you infer that the setting of the story is the present.

Although "The House from the Eleventh Floor" takes place in the present, the narrator keeps seeing into the past. Therefore, when you read this story, you have to make inferences about time: you must infer which events occur in the present and which belong in the past.

---

1. Make inferences about time in order to answer the question that follows each item below.
   a. The narrator comes to Turku to do some research.
      Does this event occur in the past or the present?
   b. After meeting the girl, the narrator hears coming through the fog an untrained voice singing an old French song. He knows the tune but can't remember the words.
      Is the voice from the past or the present?
   c. The narrator finds the knoll where he thinks the house should be. The hollow in the center of the knoll is empty.
      Does this event occur in the past or the present?
   d. The girl says, "I'll have to hide you soon. Father will be coming home."
      Does she say this in the past or the present?

2. (a) List four details in this story from the present. (b) List four details from the past.

3. What happens to the narrator at the end of the story?

WORD ATTACK

Finding Base Words

A base word is a word from which other words may be built. Prefixes and/or suffixes are added to base words to change their meanings. For example the prefix *un* may be added to the base word *usual* to form its antonym *unusual*. The suffix *–ly* may be added to *usual* to form the adverb *usually*. If both the prefix *un* and the suffix *–ly* were added to the base word *usual*, the word *unusually* would be formed.

1. Each of the words below has been formed by adding a prefix and/or suffix to the base word. On a piece of paper, write the base words.
   - **a.** unfinished
   - **b.** plainly
   - **c.** battlement
   - **d.** thicker
   - **e.** uneasy
   - **f.** refreshed
   - **g.** hopeless
   - **h.** overactive
   - **i.** replacement
   - **j.** untrained

2. Find the base word used to form each word below. Then find the meaning of the new word.
   - **a.** restatement
   - **b.** unaccountable
   - **c.** journalese
   - **d.** particularism
   - **e.** paradoxically
   - **f.** foreshadow
   - **g.** deformity
   - **h.** deforestation
   - **i.** melodramatic
   - **j.** emprisonment

The Birds

Daphne du Maurier

"They kept coming at him from the air—noiseless, silent, save for the beating wings. The terrible, fluttering wings."

On December third, the wind changed overnight and it was winter. Until then, the autumn had been mellow, soft. The earth was rich where the plow had turned it.

Nat Hocken, because of a wartime disability, had a pension and did not work full time at the farm. He worked three days a week, and they gave him the lighter jobs. Although he was married, with children, his was a solitary disposition; he liked best to work alone.

It pleased him when he was given a bank to build up, or a gate to mend, at the far end of the peninsula, where the sea surrounded the farmland on either side. Then, at midday, he would pause and eat the meat pie his wife had baked for him and, sitting on the cliff's edge, watch the birds.

In autumn, great flocks of them came to the peninsula, restless, uneasy, spending themselves in motion; now wheeling, circling in the sky; now settling to feed on the rich, new-turned soil; but even when they fed, it was as though they did so without hunger, without desire.

Restlessness drove them to the skies again. Crying, whistling, calling, they skimmed the placid sea and left the shore.

Make haste, make speed, hurry and begone; yet where, and to what purpose? The restless urge of autumn, unsatisfying, sad, had put a spell upon them, and they must spill themselves of motion before winter came.

Perhaps, thought Nat, a message comes to the birds in autumn, like a warning. Winter is coming. Many of them will perish. And, like people who, apprehensive of death before their time, drive themselves to work or folly, the birds do likewise; tomorrow we shall die.

The birds had been more restless than ever this fall of the year. Their agitation more remarked because the days were still.

As Mr. Trigg's tractor traced its path up and down the western hills, and Nat, hedging, saw it dip and turn, the whole machine and the man upon it were momentarily lost in the great cloud of wheeling, crying birds.

Nat remarked upon them to Mr. Trigg when the work was finished for the day.

"Yes," said the farmer, "there are more birds about than usual. I have a notion the weather will change. It will be a hard winter. That's why the birds are restless."

The farmer was right. That night the weather turned.

The bedroom in the cottage faced east. Nat woke just after two and heard the east wind, cold and dry. It sounded hollow in the chimney, and a loose slate rattled on the roof. Nat listened, and he could hear the sea roaring in the bay. He drew the blanket round him, leaned closer to the back of his wife, deep in sleep. Then he heard the tapping on the windowpane. It continued until, irritated by the sound, Nat got out of bed and went to the window. He opened it; and, as he did so, something brushed his hand, jabbing at his knuckles, grazing the skin. Then he saw the flutter of wings and the thing was gone

again, over the roof, behind the cottage.

It was a bird. What kind of bird he could not tell. The wind must have driven it to shelter on the sill.

He shut the window and went back to bed, but, feeling his knuckles wet, put his mouth to the scratch. The bird had drawn blood.

Frightened, he supposed, bewildered, seeking shelter, the bird had stabbed at him in the darkness. Once more he settled himself to sleep.

Presently the tapping came again—this time, more forceful, more insistent. And now his wife woke at the sound and, turning in the bed, said to him, "See to the window, Nat; it's rattling."

"I've already been to it," he told her. "There's some bird there, trying to get in."

"Send it away," she said. "I can't sleep with that noise."

He went to the window for the second time, and now when he opened it, there was not one bird on the sill but half a dozen; they flew straight into his face.

He shouted, striking out at them with his arms, scattering them; like the first one, they flew over the roof and disappeared.

He let the window fall and latched it.

Suddenly a frightened cry came from the room across the passage where the children slept.

"It's Jill," said his wife, roused at the sound.

There came a second cry, this time from both children. Stumbling into their room, Nat felt the beating of wings about him in the darkness. The window was wide open. Through it came the birds, hitting first the ceiling and the walls, then swerving in midflight and turning to the children in their beds.

"It's all right, I'm here," shouted Nat, and the children flung themselves, screaming, upon him, while in the darkness the birds rose and dived, and came for him again.

"What is it, Nat? What's happened?" his wife called. Swiftly he pushed the children through the door to the passage and shut it upon them, so that he was alone in their bedroom with the birds.

He seized a blanket from the nearest bed and, using it as a weapon, flung it to right and left about him.

He felt the thud of bodies, heard the fluttering of wings; but the birds were not yet defeated, for again and again they returned to the assault, jabbing his hands, his head, their little stabbing beaks sharp as pointed forks.

The blanket became a weapon of defense. He wound it about his head, and then, in greater darkness, beat at the birds with his bare hands. He dared not stumble to the door and open it lest the birds follow him.

How long he fought with them in the darkness he could not tell; but at last the beating of the wings about him lessened, withdrew; and, through the dense blanket, he was aware of light.

He waited, listened; there was no sound except the fretful crying of one of the children from the bedroom beyond.

He took the blanket from his head and stared about him. The cold gray morning light exposed the room.

Dawn and the open window had called the living birds; the dead lay on the floor.

Sickened, Nat went to the window and stared out across his patch of garden to the fields.

It was bitter cold, and the ground had all the hard, black look of the frost that the east wind brings. The sea, fiercer now with turning tide, white-capped and steep, broke harshly in the bay. Of the birds there was no sign.

Nat shut the window and the door of the small bedroom and went back across the passage to his own room.

His wife sat up in bed, one child asleep beside her; the smaller one in her arms, his face bandaged.

"He's sleeping now," she whispered. "Something must have cut him; there was blood at the corners of his eyes. Jill said it was the birds. She said she woke up and the birds were in the room."

His wife looked up at Nat, searching his face for confirmation. She looked terrified, bewildered. He did not want her to know that he also was shaken, dazed almost, by the events of the past few hours.

"There are birds in there," he said. "Dead birds, nearly fifty of them."

He sat down on the bed beside his wife.

"It's the hard weather," he said. "It must be that; it's the hard weather. They aren't the birds, maybe, from around here. They've been driven down from upcountry."

"But, Nat," whispered his wife, "it's only this night that the weather turned. They can't be hungry yet. There's food for them out there in the fields."

"It's the weather," repeated Nat. "I tell you, it's the weather."

His face, too, was drawn and tired, like hers. They stared at one another for a while without speaking.

Nat went to the window and looked out. The sky was hard and leaden, and the brown hills that had gleamed in the sun the day before looked dark and bare. Black winter had descended in a single night.

The children were awake now. Jill was chattering, and young Johnny was crying once again. Nat heard his wife's voice, soothing, comforting them as he went downstairs.

Presently they came down. He had breakfast ready for them.

"Did you drive away the birds?" asked Jill.

"Yes, they've all gone now," Nat said. "It was the east wind brought them in."

"I hope they won't come again," said Jill.

"I'll walk with you to the bus," Nat said to her.

Jill seemed to have forgotten her experience of the night before. She danced ahead of him, chasing the leaves, her face rosy under her pixy hood.

All the while Nat searched the hedgerows

for the birds, glanced over them to the fields beyond, looked to the small wood above the farm where the rooks and jackdaws gathered; he saw none. Soon the bus came ambling up the hill.

Nat saw Jill onto the bus, then turned and walked back toward the farm. It was not his day for work, but he wanted to satisfy himself that all was well. He went to the back door of the farmhouse; he heard Mrs. Trigg singing, the wireless[1] making a background for her song.

"Are you there, missus?" Nat called.

She came to the door, beaming, broad, a good-tempered woman.

"Hullo, Mr. Hocken," she said. "Can you tell me where this cold is coming from? Is it Russia? I've never seen such a change. And it's going on, the wireless says. Something to do with the Arctic Circle."

"We didn't turn on the wireless this morning," said Nat. "Fact is, we had trouble in the night."

"Kiddies poorly?"

"No." He hardly knew how to explain. Now, in daylight, the battle of the birds would sound absurd.

He tried to tell Mrs. Trigg what had happened, but he could see from her eyes that she thought his story was the result of nightmare following a heavy meal.

"Sure they were real birds?" she said, smiling.

"Mrs. Trigg," he said, "there are fifty dead birds—robins, wrens, and such—lying low on the floor of the children's bedroom. They went for me; they tried to go for young Johnny's eyes."

Mrs. Trigg stared at him doubtfully. "Well, now," she answered. "I suppose the weather brought them; once in the bedroom they wouldn't know where they were. Foreign birds maybe, from that Arctic Circle."

"No," said Nat. "They were the birds you see about here every day."

"Funny thing," said Mrs. Trigg. "No explaining it, really. You ought to write up and ask the *Guardian*. They'd have some answer for it. Well, I must be getting on."

Nat walked back along the lane to his cottage. He found his wife in the kitchen with young Johnny.

"See anyone?" she asked.

"Mrs. Trigg," he answered. "I don't think she believed me. Anyway, nothing wrong up there."

"You might take the birds away," she said. "I daren't go into the room to make the beds until you do. I'm scared."

"Nothing to scare you now," said Nat. "They're dead, aren't they?"

He went up with a sack and dropped the stiff bodies into it, one by one. Yes, there were fifty of them all told. Just the ordinary, common birds of the hedgerow; nothing as large even as a thrush. It must have been fright that made them act the way they did.

He took the sack out into the garden and was faced with a fresh problem. The ground was frozen solid, yet no snow had fallen; nothing had happened in the past hours but the coming of the east wind. It was unnatural, queer. He could see the white-capped seas breaking in the bay. He decided to take the birds to the shore and bury them.

When he reached the beach below the headland,[2] he could scarcely stand, the force of the east wind was so strong. It was low tide; he crunched his way over the shingle to the softer sand and then, his back to the wind, opened up his sack.

He ground a pit in the sand with his heel, meaning to drop the birds into it; but, as he did so, the force of the wind lifted them as though in flight again, and they were blown away from him along the beach, tossed like feathers, spread and scattered.

The tide will take them when it turns, he said to himself.

---

1. wireless (wīr'lĭs) n.: Radio.

2. headland (hĕd'lənd) n.: A high point of land that drops off into water.

He looked out to sea and watched the crested breakers,[3] combing[4] green. They rose stiffly, curled, and broke again; and, because it was ebb tide,[5] the roar was distant, more remote, lacking the sound and thunder of the flood.

Then he saw them. The gulls. Out there, riding the seas.

What he had thought at first were the whitecaps of the waves were gulls. Hundreds, thousands, tens of thousands.

They rose and fell in the troughs of the seas, heads to the wind, like a mighty fleet at anchor, waiting on the tide.

Nat turned; leaving the beach, he climbed the steep path home.

Someone should know of this. Someone should be told. Something was happening, because of the east wind and the weather, that he did not understand.

As he drew near the cottage, his wife came to meet him at the door. She called to him, excited. "Nat," she said, "it's on the wireless. They've just read out a special news bulletin. It's not only here, it's everywhere. In London, all over the country. Something has happened to the birds. Come listen; they're repeating it."

Together they went into the kitchen to listen to the announcement.

"Statement from the Home Office, at 11 A.M. this morning. Reports from all over the country are coming in hourly about the vast quantity of birds flocking above towns, villages, and outlying districts, causing obstruction and damage, and even attacking individuals. It is thought that the Arctic air stream at present covering the British Isles is causing birds to migrate south in immense numbers, and that intense hunger may drive these birds to attack human beings. Householders are warned to see to their windows, doors, and chimneys, and to take reasonable precautions for the safety of their children. A further statement will be issued later."

A kind of excitement seized Nat. He looked at his wife in triumph. "There you are," he said. "I've been telling myself all morning there's something wrong. And, just now, down on the beach, I looked out to sea and there were gulls, thousands of them, riding on the sea, waiting."

"What are they waiting for, Nat?" she asked.

He stared at her. "I don't know," he said slowly.

He went over to the drawer where he kept his hammer and other tools.

"What are you going to do, Nat?"

"See to the windows and the chimneys, like they tell you to."

"You think they would break in with the windows shut? Those wrens and robins and such? Why, how could they?"

He did not answer. He was not thinking of the robins and the wrens. He was thinking of the gulls.

He went upstairs and worked there the rest of the morning, boarding the windows of the bedrooms, filling up the chimney bases.

"Dinner's ready." His wife called him from the kitchen.

"All right. Coming down."

When dinner was over and his wife was washing up, Nat switched on the one o'clock news. The same announcement was repeated, but the news bulletin enlarged upon it. "The flocks of birds have caused dislocation[6] in all areas," said the announcer, "and in London, the mass was so dense at ten o'clock this morning that it seemed like a vast, black cloud. The birds settled on rooftops, on window ledges, and on chimneys. The species included blackbird, thrush, the common house sparrow, and, as might be expected in

---

3. breakers (brā′kərz) n.: Waves that break into foam against the shoreline.
4. combing (kōm′ĭng) v.: Breaking, or rolling over.
5. ebb tide: Period when the waves are going out to sea instead of coming in toward shore.

6. dislocation (dĭs′lō-kā′shən) n.: Confusion or disorder.

the metropolis, a vast quantity of pigeons, starlings, and that frequenter of the London river, the black-headed gull. The sight was so unusual that traffic came to a standstill in many thoroughfares, work was abandoned in shops and offices, and the streets and pavements were crowded with people standing about to watch the birds."

The announcer's voice was smooth and suave; Nat had the impression that he treated the whole business as he would an elaborate joke. There would be others like him, hundreds of them, who did not know what it was to struggle in darkness with a flock of birds.

Nat switched off the wireless. He got up and started work on the kitchen windows. His wife watched him, young Johnny at her heels.

"What they ought to do," she said, "is to call the Army out and shoot the birds."

"Let them try," said Nat. "How'd they set about it?"

"I don't know. But something should be done. They ought to do something."

Nat thought to himself that "they" were no doubt considering the problem at that very moment, but whatever "they" decided to do in London and the big cities would not help them here, nearly three hundred miles away.

"How are we off for food?" he asked.

"It's shopping day tomorrow, you know that. I don't keep uncooked food about. Butcher doesn't call till the day after. But I can bring back something when I go in tomorrow."

Nat did not want to scare her. He looked in the larder for himself and in the cupboard where she kept her tins.

They could hold out for a couple of days.

He went on hammering the boards across the kitchen windows. Candles. They were low on candles. That must be another thing she meant to buy tomorrow. Well, they must go early to bed tonight. That was, if——

He got up and went out the back door and stood in the garden, looking down toward the sea.

There had been no sun all day, and now, at barely three o'clock, a kind of darkness had already come; the sky was sullen, heavy, colorless like salt. He could hear the vicious sea drumming on the rocks.

He walked down the path halfway to the beach. And then he stopped. He could see the tide had turned. The gulls had risen. They were circling, hundreds of them, thousands of them, lifting their wings against the wind.

It was the gulls that made the darkening of the sky.

And they were silent. They just went on soaring and circling, rising, falling, trying their strength against the wind. Nat turned. He ran up the path back to the cottage.

"I'm going for Jill," he said to his wife.

"What's the matter?" she asked. "You've gone quite white."

"Keep Johnny inside," he said. "Keep the door shut. Light up now and draw the curtains."

"It's only gone three," she said.

"Never mind. Do what I tell you."

He looked inside the toolshed and took the hoe.

He started walking up the lane to the bus stop. Now and again he glanced back over his shoulder; he could see the gulls had risen higher now, their circles were broader, they were spreading out in huge formation across the sky.

He hurried on. Although he knew the bus would not come before four o'clock, he had to hurry.

He waited at the top of the hill. There was half an hour still to go.

The east wind came whipping across the fields from the higher ground. In the distance he could see the clay hills, white and clean against the heavy pallor of the sky.

Something black rose from behind them, like a smudge at first, then widening, becoming deeper. The smudge became a cloud; and the cloud divided again into five other clouds, spreading north, east, south, and west; and then they were not clouds at all but birds.

He watched them travel across the sky within two or three hundred feet of him. He knew, from their speed, that they were bound inland; they had no business with the people here on the peninsula. They were rooks, crows, jackdaws, magpies, jays—all birds that usually preyed upon the smaller species, but bound this afternoon on some other mission.

He went to the telephone call box, stepped inside, lifted the receiver. The exchange[7] would pass the message on. "I'm speaking from the highway," he said, "by the bus stop. I want to report large formations of birds traveling upcountry. The gulls are also forming in the bay."

"All right," answered the voice, laconic, weary.

"You'll be sure and pass this message on to the proper quarter?"

"Yes. Yes." Impatient now, fed up. The buzzing note resumed.

She's another, thought Nat. She doesn't care.

The bus came lumbering up the hill. Jill climbed out.

"What's the hoe for, Dad?"

"I just brought it along," he said. "Come on now, let's get home. It's cold; no hanging about. See how fast you can run."

He could see the gulls now, still silent, circling the fields, coming in toward the land.

"Look, Dad; look over there. Look at all the gulls."

"Yes. Hurry now."

"Where are they flying to? Where are they going?"

"Upcountry, I dare say. Where it's warmer."

He seized her hand and dragged her after him along the lane.

"Don't go so fast. I can't keep up."

The gulls were copying the rooks and the crows. They were spreading out, in formation, across the sky. They headed, in bands of thousands, to the four compass points.

"Dad, what is it? What are the gulls doing?"

They were not intent upon their flight, as the crows, as the jackdaws, had been. They still circled overhead. Nor did they fly so high. It was as though they waited upon some signal; as though some decision had yet to be given.

"I wish the gulls would go away." Jill was crying. "I don't like them. They're coming closer to the lane."

He started running, swinging Jill after him. As they went past the farm turning, he saw the farmer backing his car into the garage. Nat called to him.

"Can you give us a lift?" he said.

Mr. Trigg turned in the driver's seat and stared at them. Then a smile came to his cheerful, rubicund[8] face. "It looks as though we're in for some fun," he said. "Have you seen the gulls? Jim and I are going to take a crack at them. Everyone's gone bird crazy, talking of nothing else. I hear you were troubled in the night. Want a gun?"

Nat shook his head.

The small car was packed, but there was room for Jill on the back seat.

"I don't want a gun," said Nat, "but I'd be obliged if you'd run Jill home. She's scared of the birds."

"Okay," said the farmer. "I'll take her home. Why don't you stop behind and join the shooting match? We'll make the feathers fly."

Jill climbed in, and, turning the car, the driver sped up the lane. Nat followed after. Trigg must be crazy. What use was a gun against a sky of birds?

---

7. the exchange: In England, the central switchboard through which telephone calls are placed is called the exchange.

---

8. rubicund (rōō′bə-kənd) *adj.*: Ruddy, rosy.

They were coming in now toward the farm, circling lower in the sky. The farm, then, was their target. Nat increased his pace toward his own cottage. He saw the farmer's car turn and come back along the lane. It drew up beside him with a jerk.

"The kid has run inside," said the farmer. "Your wife was watching for her. Well, what do you make of it? They're saying in town the Russians have done it. The Russians have poisoned the birds."

"How could they do that?" asked Nat.

"Don't ask me. You know how stories get around."

"Have you boarded your windows?" asked Nat.

"No. Lot of nonsense. I've had more to do today than to go round boarding up my windows."

"I'd board them now if I were you."

"Garn. You're windy. Like to come to our place to sleep?"

"No, thanks all the same."

"All right. See you in the morning. Give you a gull breakfast."

The farmer grinned and turned his car to the farm entrance. Nat hurried on. Past the little wood, past the old barn, and then across the stile to the remaining field. As he jumped the stile, he heard the whir of wings. A black-backed gull dived down at him from the sky. It missed, swerved in flight, and rose to dive again. In a moment, it was joined by others—six, seven, a dozen.

Nat dropped his hoe. The hoe was useless. Covering his head with his arms, he ran toward the cottage.

They kept coming at him from the air—noiseless, silent, save for the beating wings. The terrible, fluttering wings. He could feel the blood on his hands, his wrists, upon his neck. If only he could keep them from his eyes. Nothing else mattered.

With each dive, with each attack, they became bolder. And they had no thought for themselves. When they dived low and missed, they crashed, bruised and broken, on the ground.

As Nat ran, he stumbled, kicking their spent bodies in front of him.

He found the door and hammered upon it with his bleeding hands. "Let me in," he shouted. "It's Nat. Let me in."

Then he saw the gannet, poised for the dive, above him in the sky.

The gulls circled, retired, soared, one with another, against the wind.

Only the gannet remained. One single gannet, above him in the sky. Its wings folded suddenly to its body. It dropped like a stone.

Nat screamed; and the door opened.

He stumbled across the threshold, and his wife threw her weight against the door.

They heard the thud of the gannet as it fell.

His wife dressed his wounds. They were not deep. The backs of his hands had suffered most, and his wrists. Had he not worn a cap, the birds would have reached his head. As for the gannet—the gannet could have split his skull.

The children were crying, of course. They had seen the blood on their father's hands.

"It's all right now," he told them. "I'm not hurt."

His wife was ashen. "I saw them overhead," she whispered. "They began collecting just as Jill ran in with Mr. Trigg. I shut the door fast, and it jammed. That's why I couldn't open it at once when you came."

"Thank God, the birds waited for me," he said. "Jill would have fallen at once. They're flying inland, thousands of them. Rooks, crows, all the bigger birds. I saw them from the bus stop. They're making for the towns."

"But what can they do, Nat?"

"They'll attack. Go for everyone out in the streets. Then they'll try the windows, the chimneys."

"Why don't the authorities do something? Why don't they get the Army, get the machine guns?"

"There's been no time. Nobody's prepared. We'll hear what they have to say on the six o'clock news."

"I can hear the birds," Jill said. "Listen, Dad."

Nat listened. Muffled sounds came from the windows, from the door. Wings brushing the surface, sliding, scraping, seeking a way of entry. The sound of many bodies pressed together, shuffling on the sills. Now and again came a thud, a crash, as some bird dived and fell.

Some of them will kill themselves that way, he thought, but not enough. Never enough.

"All right," he said aloud. "I've got boards

over the windows, Jill. The birds can't get in."

He went and examined all the windows. He found wedges—pieces of old tin, strips of wood and metal—and fastened them at the sides of the windows to reinforce the boards.

His hammering helped to deafen the sound of the birds, the shuffling, the tapping, and—more ominous—the splinter of breaking glass.

"Turn on the wireless," he said.

He went upstairs to the bedrooms and reinforced the windows there. Now he could hear the birds on the roof—the scraping of claws, a sliding, jostling sound.

He decided the whole family must sleep in the kitchen and keep up the fire. He was afraid of the bedroom chimneys. The boards he had placed at their bases might give way. In the kitchen, they would be safe because of the fire.

He would have to make a joke of it. Pretend to the children they were playing camp. If the worst happened and the birds forced an entry by way of the bedroom chimneys, it would be hours, days perhaps, before they could break down the doors. The birds would be imprisoned in the bedrooms. They could do no harm there. Crowded together, they would stifle and die. He began to bring the mattresses downstairs.

At the sight of them, his wife's eyes widened in apprehension.

"All right," he said cheerfully. "We'll all sleep together in the kitchen tonight. More cozy, here by the fire. Then we won't be worried by those silly old birds tapping at the windows."

He made the children help him rearrange the furniture, and he took the precaution of moving the dresser against the windows.

We're safe enough now, he thought. We're snug and tight. We can hold out. It's just the food that worries me. Food and coal for the fire. We've enough for two or three days, not more. By that time——

No use thinking ahead as far as that. And they'd be given directions on the wireless.

And now, in the midst of many problems, he realized that only dance music was coming over the air. He knew the reason. The usual programs had been abandoned; this only happened at exceptional times.

At six o'clock the records ceased. The time signal was given. There was a pause, and then the announcer spoke. His voice was solemn, grave. Quite different from midday.

"This is London," he said. "A national emergency was proclaimed at four o'clock this afternoon. Measures are being taken to safeguard the lives and property of the population, but it must be understood that these are not easy to effect immediately, owing to the unforeseen and unparalleled nature of the present crisis. Every householder must take precautions about his own building. Where several people live together, as in flats[9] and hotels, they must unite to do the utmost that they can to prevent entry. It is absolutely imperative that every individual stay indoors tonight.

"The birds, in vast numbers, are attacking anyone on sight, and have already begun an assault upon buildings; but these, with due care, should be impenetrable.

"The population is asked to remain calm.

"Owing to the exceptional nature of the emergency, there will be no further transmission from any broadcasting station until 7 A.M. tomorrow."

They played "God Save the Queen." Nothing more happened.

Nat switched off the set. He looked at his wife. She stared back at him.

"We'll have supper early," suggested Nat. "Something for a treat—toasted cheese, eh? Something we all like."

He winked and nodded at his wife. He wanted the look of dread, of apprehension, to leave her face.

He helped with the supper, whistling,

---

9. flats: Apartments.

singing, making as much clatter as he could. It seemed to him that the shuffling and the tapping were not so intense as they had been at first, and presently he went up to the bedrooms and listened. He no longer heard the jostling for place upon the roof.

They've got reasoning powers, he thought. They know it's hard to break in here. They'll try elsewhere.

Supper passed without incident. Then, when they were clearing away, they heard a new sound, a familiar droning.

His wife looked up at him, her face alight.

"It's planes," she said. "They're sending out planes after the birds. That will get them. Isn't that gunfire? Can't you hear guns?"

It might be gunfire, out at sea. Nat could not tell. Big naval guns might have some effect upon the gulls out at sea, but the gulls were inland now. The guns couldn't shell the shore because of the population.

"It's good, isn't it," said his wife, "to hear the planes?"

Catching her enthusiasm, Jill jumped up and down with Johnny. "The planes will get the birds."

Just then they heard a crash about two miles distant. Followed by a second, then a third. The droning became more distant, passed away out to sea.

"What was that?" asked his wife.

"I don't know," answered Nat. He did not want to tell her that the sound they had heard was the crashing of aircraft.

It was, he had no doubt, a gamble on the part of the authorities to send out reconnaissance forces, but they might have known the gamble was suicidal. What could aircraft do against birds that flung themselves to death against propeller and fuselage, but hurtle to the ground themselves?

"Where have the planes gone, Dad?" asked Jill.

"Back to base," he said. "Come on now, time to tuck down for bed."

There was no further drone of aircraft, and

the naval guns had ceased. Waste of life and effort, Nat said to himself. We can't destroy enough of them that way. Cost too heavy. There's always gas. Maybe they'll try spraying with gas, mustard gas. We'll be warned first, of course, if they do. There's one thing, the best brains of the country will be on it tonight.

Upstairs in the bedrooms all was quiet. No more scraping and stabbing at the windows. A lull in battle. The wind hadn't dropped, though. Nat could still hear it roaring in the chimneys. And the sea breaking down on the shore.

Then he remembered the tide. The tide would be on the turn. Maybe the lull in battle was because of the tide. There was some law the birds obeyed, and it had to do with the east wind and the tide.

He glanced at his watch. Nearly eight o'clock. It must have gone high water an hour ago. That explained the lull. The birds attacked with the flood tide.

He reckoned the time limit in his head. They had six hours to go without attack. When the tide turned again, around one-twenty in the morning, the birds would come back.

He called softly to his wife and whispered to her that he would go out and see how they were faring at the farm, see if the telephone was still working there so that they might get news from the exchange.

"You're not to go," she said at once, "and leave me alone with the children. I can't stand it."

"All right," he said, "all right. I'll wait till morning. And we can get the wireless bulletin then, too, at seven. But when the tide ebbs again, I'll try for the farm; they may let us have bread and potatoes."

His mind was busy again, planning against emergency. They would not have milked, of course, this evening. The cows would be standing by the gate, waiting; the household would be inside, battened behind boards as they were here at the cottage.

That is, if they had had time to take precautions.

Softly, stealthily, he opened the back door and looked outside.

It was pitch-dark. The wind was blowing harder than ever, coming in steady gusts, icy, from the sea.

He kicked at the step. It was heaped with birds. These were the suicides, the divers, the ones with broken necks. Wherever he looked, he saw dead birds. The living had flown seaward with the turn of the tide. The gulls would be riding the seas now, as they had done in the forenoon.

In the far distance on the hill, something was burning. One of the aircraft that had crashed; the fire, fanned by the wind, had set light to a stack.

He looked at the bodies of the birds. He had a notion that if he stacked them, one upon the other, on the window sills, they would be added protection against the next attack.

Not much, perhaps, but something. The bodies would have to be clawed at, pecked, and dragged aside before the living birds gained purchase on the sills and attacked the panes.

He set to work in the darkness. It was queer. He hated touching the dead birds, but he went on with his work. He noticed, grimly, that every windowpane was shattered. Only the boards had kept the birds from breaking in.

He stuffed the cracked panes with bleeding bodies of the birds and felt his stomach turn. When he had finished, he went back into the cottage and barricaded the kitchen door, making it doubly secure.

His wife had made him cocoa; he drank it thirstily. He was very tired: "All right," he said, smiling, "don't worry. We'll get through."

He lay down on his mattress and closed his eyes.

He dreamed uneasily because, through his dreams, ran the dread of something forgotten. Some piece of work that he should have done. It was connected, in some way, with the burning aircraft.

It was his wife, shaking his shoulder, who awoke him finally.

"They've begun," she sobbed. "They've started this last hour. I can't listen to it any longer alone. There's something smells bad, too, something burning."

Then he remembered. He had forgotten to make up the fire.

The fire was smoldering, nearly out. He got up swiftly and lighted the lamp.

The hammering had started at the windows and the door, but it was not that he minded now. It was the smell of singed feathers.

The smell filled the kitchen. He knew what it was at once. The birds were coming down the chimney, squeezing their way down to the kitchen range.

He got sticks and paper and put them on the embers, then reached for the can of kerosene.

"Stand back," he shouted to his wife. He threw some of the kerosene onto the fire.

The flame roared up the pipe, and down into the fire fell the scorched, blackened bodies of the birds.

The children waked, crying. "What is it?" asked Jill. "What's happened?"

Nat had no time to answer her. He was raking the bodies from the chimney, clawing them out onto the floor.

The flames would drive the living birds away from the chimney top. The lower joint was the difficulty, though. It was choked with the smoldering, helpless bodies of the birds caught by fire.

He scarcely heeded the attack on the windows and the door. Let them beat their wings, break their backs, lose their lives, in the desperate attempt to force entry into his home. They would not break in.

"Stop crying," he called to the children. "There's nothing to be afraid of. Stop crying."

He went on raking out the burning, smoldering bodies as they fell into the fire.

This'll fetch them, he said to himself. The draft and the flames together. We're all right as long as the chimney doesn't catch.

Amid the tearing at the window boards came the sudden, homely striking of the kitchen clock. Three o'clock.

A little more than four hours to go. He could not be sure of the exact time of high water. He reckoned the tide would not turn much before half past seven.

He waited by the range. The flames were dying. But no more blackened bodies fell from the chimney. He thrust his poker up as far as it could go and found nothing.

The danger of the chimney's being choked up was over. It could not happen again, not if the fire was kept burning day and night.

I'll have to get more fuel from the farm tomorrow, he thought. I can do all that with the ebb tide. It can be worked; we can fetch what we need when the tide's turned. We've just got to adapt ourselves, that's all.

They drank tea and cocoa, ate slices of bread. Only half a loaf left, Nat noticed. Never mind, though; they'd get by.

If they could hang on like this until seven, when the first news bulletin came through, they would not have done too badly.

"Give us a smoke," he said to his wife. "It will clear away the smell of the scorched feathers."

"There's only two left in the packet," she said. "I was going to buy you some."

"I'll have one," he said.

He sat with one arm around his wife and the other around Jill, with Johnny on his lap, the blankets heaped about them on the mattress.

"You can't help admiring the beggars," he said. "They've got persistency. You'd think they'd tire of the game, but not a bit of it."

Admiration was hard to sustain. The tapping went on and on; and a new, rasping note struck Nat's ear, as though a sharper beak than any hitherto had come to take over from its fellows.

He tried to remember the names of birds; he tried to think which species would go for this particular job.

It was not the tap of the woodpecker. That would be light and frequent. This was more serious; if it continued long, the wood would splinter as the glass had done.

Then he remembered the hawks. Could the hawks have taken over from the gulls? Were there buzzards now upon the sills, using talons as well as beaks? Hawks, buzzards, kestrels, falcons; he had forgotten the birds of prey. Three hours to go; and, while they waited, the sound of the splintering wood, the talons tearing at the wood.

Nat looked about him, seeing what furniture he could destroy to fortify the door.

The windows were safe because of the dresser. He was not certain of the door. He went upstairs; but when he reached the landing, he paused and listened.

There was a soft patter on the floor of the children's bedroom. The birds had broken through.

The other bedroom was still clear. He brought out the furniture to pile at the head of the stairs should the door of the children's bedroom go.

"Come down, Nat. What are you doing?" called his wife.

"I won't be long," he shouted. "I'm just making everything shipshape up here."

He did not want her to come. He did not want her to hear the pattering in the children's bedroom, the brushing of those wings against the door.

After he suggested breakfast, he found himself watching the clock, gazing at the hands that went so slowly around the dial. If his theory was not correct, if the attack did not cease with the turn of the tide, he knew they were beaten. They could not continue through the long day without air, without rest, without fuel.

A crackling in his ears drove away the sudden, desperate desire for sleep.

"What is it? What now?" he said sharply.

"The wireless," said his wife. "I've been watching the clock. It's nearly seven."

The comfortable crackling of the wireless brought new life.

They waited. The kitchen clock struck seven.

The crackling continued. Nothing else. No chimes. No music.

They waited until a quarter past. No news bulletin came through.

"We heard wrong," he said. "They won't be broadcasting until eight o'clock."

They left the wireless switched on. Nat thought of the battery, wondered how much power was left in the battery. If it failed, they would not hear the instructions.

"It's getting light," whispered his wife. "I can't see it but I can feel it. And listen! The birds aren't hammering so loud now."

She was right. The rasping, tearing sound grew fainter every moment. So did the shuffling, the jostling for place upon the step, upon the sills. The tide was on the turn.

By eight there was no sound at all. Only the wind. And the crackling of the wireless. The children, lulled at last by the stillness, fell asleep.

At half past eight Nat switched the wireless off.

"We'll miss the news," said his wife.

"There isn't going to be any news," said Nat. "We've got to depend upon ourselves."

He went to the door and slowly pulled away the barricades. He drew the bolts and, kicking the broken bodies from the step outside the door, breathed the cold air.

He had six working hours before him, and he knew he must reserve his strength to the utmost, not waste it in any way.

Food and light and fuel; these were the most necessary things. If he could get them, they could endure another night.

He stepped into the garden; and, as he did so, he saw the living birds. The gulls had gone to ride the sea, as they had done before. They sought sea food and the buoyancy of the tide before they returned to the attack.

Not so the land birds. They waited and watched.

Nat saw them on the hedgerows, on the soil, crowded in the trees, outside in the field—line upon line of birds, still, doing nothing. He went to the end of his small garden.

The birds did not move. They merely watched him.

I've got to get food, Nat said to himself. I've got to go to the farm to get food.

He went back to the cottage. He saw to the windows and the door.

"I'm going to the farm," he said.

His wife clung to him. She had seen the living birds from the open door.

"Take us with you," she begged. "We can't stay here alone. I'd rather die than stay here alone."

"Come on, then," he said. "Bring baskets and Johnny's pram.[10] We can load up the pram."

---

10. pram (prăm) n.: A baby carriage. *Pram* is short for *perambulator* (pə-răm′byə-lā′tər).

They dressed against the biting wind. His wife put Johnny in the pram, and Nat took Jill's hand.

"The birds," Jill whimpered. "They're all out there in the fields."

"They won't hurt us," he said. "Not in the light."

They started walking across the field toward the stile, and the birds did not move. They waited, their heads turned to the wind.

When they reached the turning to the farm, Nat stopped and told his wife to wait in the shelter of the hedge with the two children. "But I want to see Mrs. Trigg," she protested. "There are lots of things we can borrow if they went to market yesterday, and——"

"Wait here," Nat interrupted. "I'll be back in a moment."

The cows were lowing, moving restlessly in the yard, and he could see a gap in the fence where the sheep had knocked their way through to roam unchecked in the front garden before the farmhouse.

No smoke came from the chimneys. Nat was filled with misgiving. He did not want his wife or the children to go down to the farm.

He went down alone, pushing his way through the herd of lowing cows, who turned this way and that, distressed, their udders full.

He saw the car standing by the gate. Not put away in the garage.

All the windows of the farmhouse were smashed. There were many dead gulls lying in the yard and around the house.

The living birds perched on the group of trees behind the farm and on the roof of the house. They were quite still. They watched him. Jim's body lay in the yard. What was left of it. His gun was beside him.

The door of the house was shut and bolted, but it was easy to push up a smashed window and climb through.

Trigg's body was close to the telephone. He must have been trying to get through to the

exchange when the birds got him. The receiver was off the hook, and the instrument was torn from the wall.

No sign of Mrs. Trigg. She would be upstairs. Was it any use going up? Sickened, Nat knew what he would find there.

Thank God, he said to himself, there were no children.

He forced himself to climb the stairs, but halfway up he turned and descended again. He could see Mrs. Trigg's legs protruding from the open bedroom door. Beside her were the bodies of black-backed gulls and an umbrella, broken. It's no use doing anything, Nat thought. I've only got five hours; less than that. The Triggs would understand. I must load up with what I can find.

He tramped back to his wife and children.

"I'm going to fill up the car with stuff," he said. "We'll take it home and return for a fresh load."

"They must have gone to friends," he said.

"Shall I come and help you, then?"

"No, there's a mess down there. Cows and sheep all over the place. Wait; I'll get the car. You can sit in the car."

Her eyes watched his all the time he was talking. He believed she understood. Otherwise, she certainly would have insisted on helping him find the bread and groceries.

They made three journeys altogether, to and from the farm, before he was satisfied they had everything they needed. It was surprising, once he started thinking, how many things were necessary. Probably the most important of all was planking for the windows. He had to go around searching for timber. He wanted to renew the boards on all the windows at the cottage.

On the final journey he drove the car to the bus stop and got out and went to the telephone box.

He waited a few minutes, jangling the hook. No good, though. The line was dead. He climbed onto a bank and looked over the countryside, but there was no sign of life at all, nothing in the fields but the waiting, watching birds.

Some of them slept; he could see their beaks tucked into their feathers.

You'd think they'd be feeding, he said to himself, not just standing that way.

Then he remembered. They were gorged with food. They had eaten their fill during the night. That was why they did not move this morning.

He lifted his face to the sky. It was colorless, gray. The bare trees looked bent and blackened by the east wind.

The cold did not affect the living birds, waiting out there in the fields.

This is the time they ought to get them, Nat said to himself. They're a sitting target now. They must be doing this all over the country. Why don't our aircraft take off now and spray them with mustard gas? What are all our chaps doing? They must know; they must see for themselves.

He went back to the car and got into the driver's seat.

"Go quickly past that second gate," whispered his wife. "The postman's lying there. I don't want Jill to see."

It was a quarter to one by the time they reached the cottage. Only an hour to go.

"Better have dinner," said Nat. "Hot up something for yourself and the children, some of that soup. I've no time to eat now. I've got to unload all this stuff from the car."

He got everything inside the cottage. It could be sorted later. Give them all something to do during the long hours ahead.

First he must see to the windows and the door.

He went around the cottage methodically, testing every window and the door. He climbed onto the roof, also, and fixed boards across every chimney except the kitchen's.

The cold was so intense he could hardly bear it, but the job had to be done. Now and again he looked up, searching the sky for aircraft. None came. As he worked, he cursed the inefficiency of the authorities.

He paused, his work on the bedroom chimney finished, and looked out to sea. Something was moving out there. Something gray and white among the breakers.

"Good old Navy," he said. "They never let us down. They're coming down channel; they're turning into the bay."

He waited, straining his eyes toward the sea. He was wrong, though. The Navy was not there. It was the gulls rising from the sea. And the massed flocks in the fields, with ruffled feathers, rose in formation from the ground and, wing to wing, soared upward to the sky.

The tide had turned again.

Nat climbed down the ladder and went inside the cottage. The family were at dinner. It was a little after two.

He bolted the door, put up the barricade, and lighted the lamp.

"It's nighttime," said young Johnny.

His wife had switched on the wireless once again. The crackling sound came, but nothing else.

"I've been all round the dial," she said, "foreign stations and all. I can't get anything but the crackling."

"Maybe they have the same trouble," he said. "Maybe it's the same right through Europe."

They ate in silence.

The tapping began at the windows, at the door, the rustling, the jostling, the pushing for position on the sills. The first thud of the suicide gulls upon the step.

When he had finished dinner, Nat planned, he would put the supplies away, stack them neatly, get everything shipshape. The boards were strong against the windows and across the chimneys. The cottage was filled with stores, with fuel, with all they needed for the next few days.

His wife could help him, and the children too. They'd tire themselves out between now and a quarter to nine, when the tide would ebb; then, he'd tuck them down on their mattresses, see that they slept good and sound until three in the morning.

He had a new scheme for the windows, which was to fix barbed wire in front of the boards. He had brought a great roll of it from the farm. The nuisance was, he'd have to work at this in the dark, when the lull came between nine and three. Pity he had not thought of it before. Still, as long as the wife and kids slept—that was the main thing.

The smaller birds were at the windows now. He recognized the light tap-tapping of their beaks and the soft brush of their wings.

The hawks ignored the windows. They concentrated their attack upon the door.

Nat listened to the tearing sound of splintering wood, and wondered how many million years of memory were stored in those little brains, behind the stabbing beaks, the piercing eyes, now giving them this instinct to destroy mankind with all the deft precision of machines.

"I'll smoke that last cigarette," he said to his wife. "Stupid of me. It was the one thing I forgot to bring from the farm."

He reached for it, switched on the crackling wireless.

He threw the empty packet onto the fire and watched it burn.

Close Up

1. (a) When does Nat Hocken first become alarmed about the birds? (b) How does he then explain their attack?

2. In the daylight, Nat begins to feel that his story about the birds' attack is ridiculous. How does Mrs. Trigg react to his story?

3. The radio announcer reads a statement from the Home Office. How does this statement support Nat's story?

4. (a) What steps does Nat take to prepare for the birds' next attack? (b) Why does he consider the kitchen the safest room?

5. (a) Find three occasions where Nat conceals the truth about the birds from his family. (b) Why do you think he does this?

6. The six o'clock radio announcement states, "Owing to the exceptional nature of the emergency, there will be no further transmission from any broadcasting station until 7 a.m. tomorrow." Why is there no broadcast the next morning?

7. As Nat works on the chimney, he thinks he sees the Navy turning into the bay. What does he really see?

8. **Composition.** Finally, do the human beings or the birds win the battle? Write a paragraph supporting your answer.

Mood

The mood of a story is the impression it creates and the emotions it arouses in the reader. In "The Birds," the author creates a mood of terror through her choice of setting and of specific details.

1. This story begins on December third. What is unusual about the weather on this date?

2. (a) Where does this story take place? (b) Does the fact that this place is isolated add to the terror? Why or why not?

3. Sounds can arouse terror. For example, the sound of birds beating against the window and of children crying arouse terror. Find three other sounds that add to this mood.

4. The birds attack with the incoming tide. Do you think the pattern of attack-and-rest adds to the terror, or would the terror be greater if the birds attacked without a rest? Why?

5. Terror can be aroused by the unexpected. Usually, we think of birds as gentle, harmless creatures. Which of their features make them dangerous opponents?

INFERENCES

Making Inferences About a Character's Feelings

When you make inferences about a character's feelings, you form your conclusions about the character on the basis of clues in the story. Some of these clues are gestures and expressions, actions and reactions, and what a character says and thinks and how the character says it. For example, look at the following passage about Nat.

> "He ran up the path back to the cottage.
> 'I'm going for Jill,' he said to his wife.
> 'What's the matter?' she asked. 'You've gone quite white.'"

Now look at the clues. He runs up the path; he's going to pick up his daughter; he's gone white. On the basis of these clues, you probably inferred that Nat is worried and apprehensive.

▶ Read each of the following passages. Paying special attention to clues, make an inference about how each character feels.

a. "She danced ahead of him, chasing the leaves, her face rosy under her pixy hood." (How does she feel?)

b. "Nat turned; leaving the beach, he climbed the steep path home. Someone should know of this. Someone should be told. Something was happening, because of the east wind and the weather, that he did not understand." (How does Nat feel?)

c. "Mr. Trigg turned in the driver's seat and stared at them. Then a smile came to his cheerful, rubicund face. 'It looks as though we're in for some fun,' he said." (How does Mr. Trigg feel?)

d. "After he suggested breakfast, he found himself watching the clock, gazing at the hands that went so slowly around the dial. If his theory was not correct, if the attack did not cease with the turn of the tide, he knew they were beaten. They could not continue through the long day without air, without rest, without fuel." (How does he feel?)

WORD ATTACK

Understanding Synonyms and Antonyms

Synonyms are words that have the same or almost the same meaning. Antonyms are words that have the opposite or almost the opposite meaning. Now look at the following word comparisons, or analogies.

LITTLE is to SMALL as BIG is to _____
(1) tiny   (2) happy   (3) average   (4) large

The first two words are synonyms. Therefore, to complete the analogy, you need to choose the synonym of the third word. The answer, of course, is *large*.

LITTLE is to BIG as SMALL is to _____
(1) minuscule   (2) medium   (3) contentment   (4) large

The first two words are antonyms. Therefore, to complete the analogy, you need to choose the antonym of the third word. The answer, of course, is *large*.

▶ In each analogy, decide whether the first two words are synonyms or antonyms. Then choose the word that completes the analogy. Write this word on a piece of paper. Use a dictionary to help you.

a. HAPPY is to CONTENTED as WORRIED is to _____
(1) troubled   (2) enjoyment   (3) worthy

b. SOLITARY is to ALONE as CONQUER is to _____
(1) lose   (2) overcome   (3) ruler

c. AGITATION is to QUIET as LACONIC is to _____
(1) talkative   (2) brief   (3) stern

d. PLACID is to PEACEFUL as FOLLY is to _____
(1) wisdom   (2) sound   (3) foolishness

e. CONFIRMATION is to DENIAL as EBB is to _____
(1) flow   (2) water   (3) fall

More Alarms at Night

James Thurber

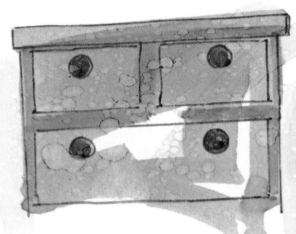

One of the incidents that I always think of first when I cast back over my youth is what happened the night that my father "threatened to get Buck." This, as you will see, is not precisely a fair or accurate description of what actually occurred, but it is the way in which I and the other members of my family invariably allude to the occasion. We were living at the time in an old house at 77 Lexington Avenue, in Columbus, Ohio. In the early years of the nineteenth century, Columbus won out, as state capital, by only one vote over Lancaster, and ever since then has had the hallucination that it is being followed, a curious municipal state of mind which affects, in some way or other, all those who live there. Columbus is a town in which almost anything is likely to happen and in which almost everything has.

My father was sleeping in the front room on the second floor next to that of my brother Roy, who was then about sixteen. Father was usually in bed by 9:30 and up again by 10:30 to protest bitterly against a Victrola record we three boys were in the habit of playing over and over, namely, "No News, or What Killed the Dog," a recitation by Nat Wills. The record had been played so many times that its grooves were deeply cut and the needle often kept revolving in the same groove, repeating over and over the same words. Thus: "ate some burnt hoss flesh, ate some burnt hoss flesh, ate some burnt hoss flesh." It was this reiteration that generally got father out of bed.

On the night in question, however, we had all gone to bed at about the same time, without much fuss. Roy, as a matter of fact, had been in bed all day with a kind of mild fever. It wasn't severe enough to cause delirium and my brother was the last person in the world to give way to delirium. Nevertheless, he had warned father when father went to bed, that he *might* become delirious.

About three o'clock in the morning, Roy, who was wakeful, decided to pretend that delirium was on him, in order to have, as he later explained it, some "fun." He got out of bed and going to my father's room, shook him and said, "Buck, your time has come!" My father's name was not Buck but Charles, nor had he ever been called Buck. He was a tall, mildly nervous, peaceable gentleman, given to quiet pleasures, and eager that everything should run smoothly. "Hmm?" he said, with drowsy bewilderment. "Get up, Buck," said my brother, coldly, but with a certain gleam in his eyes. My father leaped out of bed, on the side away from his son, rushed from the room, locked the door behind him, and shouted us all up.

We were naturally reluctant to believe that Roy, who was quiet and self-contained, had threatened his father with any such abracadabra as father said he had. My older brother, Herman, went back to bed without any com-

ment. "You've had a bad dream," my mother said. This vexed my father. "I tell you he called me Buck and told me my time had come," he said. We went to the door of his room, unlocked it, and tiptoed through it to Roy's room. He lay in his bed, breathing easily, as if he were fast asleep. It was apparent at a glance that he did not have a high fever. My mother gave my father a look. "I tell you he did," whispered father.

Our presence in the room finally seemed to awaken Roy and he was (or rather, as we found out long afterward, pretended to be) astonished and bewildered. "What's the matter?" he asked. "Nothing," said my mother. "Just your father had a nightmare." "I did not have a nightmare," said father, slowly and firmly. He wore an old-fashioned, "side-slit" nightgown which looked rather odd on his tall, spare figure. The situation, before we let it drop and everybody went back to bed again, became, as such situations in our family usually did, rather more complicated than ironed out. Roy demanded to know what had happened, and my mother told him, in considerably garbled fashion, what father had told her. At this a light dawned in Roy's eyes. "Dad's got it backward," he said. He then explained that he had heard father get out of bed and had called to him. "I'll handle this," his father had answered. "Buck is downstairs." "Who is this Buck?" my mother demanded of father. "I don't know any Buck and I never said that," father contended, irritably. None of us (except Roy, of course) believed him. "You had a dream," said mother. "People have these dreams." "I did not have a dream," father said. He was pretty well nettled by this time, and he stood in front of a bureau mirror, brushing his hair with a pair of military brushes; it always seemed to calm father to brush his hair. My mother declared that it was "a sin and a shame" for a grown man to wake up a sick boy simply because he (the grown man: father) had got on his back and had a bad dream. My father, as a matter of fact, *had* been known to have nightmares, usually about Lillian Russell and President Cleveland, who chased him.

We argued the thing for perhaps another half-hour, after which mother made father sleep in her room. "You're all safe now, boys," she said, firmly, as she shut her door. I could hear father grumbling for a long time, with an occasional monosyllable of doubt from mother.

It was some six months after this that father went through a similar experience with me. He was at that time sleeping in the room next to mine. I had been trying all afternoon, in vain, to think of the name Perth Amboy. It seems now like a very simple name to recall and yet on the day in question I thought of every other town in the country, as well as such words and names and phrases as terra cotta, Walla-Walla, bill of lading, vice versa, hoity-toity, Pall Mall, Bodley Head, Schumann-Heink, etc., without even coming close to Perth Amboy. I suppose terra cotta was the closest I came, although it was not very close.

Long after I had gone to bed, I was struggling with the problem. I began to indulge in the wildest fancies as I lay there in the dark, such as that there was no such town, and even that there was no such state as New Jersey. I fell to repeating the word "Jersey" over and over again, until it became idiotic and meaningless. If you have ever lain awake at night and repeated one word over and over, thousands and millions and hundreds of thousand of millions of times, you know the disturbing mental state you can get into. I got to thinking that there was nobody else in the world but me, and various other wild imaginings of that nature. Eventually, lying there thinking these outlandish thoughts, I grew slightly alarmed. I began to suspect that one might lose one's mind over some such trivial mental tic as a futile search for terra firma Piggly Wiggly Gorgonzola Prester John Arc de Triomphe Holy Moses Lares and Penates. I began to feel the imperative necessity of

human contact. This silly and alarming tangle of thought and fancy had gone far enough. I might get into some kind of mental aberrancy unless I found out the name of that Jersey town and could go to sleep. Therefore, I got out of bed, walked into the room where father was sleeping, and shook him. "Um!" he mumbled. I shook him more fiercely and he finally woke up, with a glaze of dream and apprehension in his eyes. "What's matter?" he asked, thickly. I must, indeed, have been rather wild of eye, and my hair, which is unruly, becomes monstrously tousled and snarled at night. "Wha's it?" said my father, sitting up, in readiness to spring out of bed on the far side. The thought must have been going through his mind that all his sons were crazy, or on the verge of going crazy. I see that now, but I didn't then, for I had forgotten the Buck incident and did not realize how similar my appearance must have been to Roy's the night he called father Buck and told him his time had come. "Listen," I said. "Name some towns in New Jersey quick!" It must have been around three in the morning. Father got up, keeping the bed between him and me, and started to pull his trousers on. "Don't bother about dressing," I said. "Just name some towns in New Jersey." While he hastily pulled on his clothes—I remember he left his socks off and put his shoes on his bare feet—father began to name, in a shaky voice, various New Jersey cities. I can still see him reaching for his coat without taking his eyes off me. "Newark," he said, "Jersey City, Atlantic City, Elizabeth, Paterson, Passaic, Trenton, Jersey City, Trenton, Paterson——" "It has two names," I snapped. "Elizabeth and Paterson," he said. "No, no!" I told him, irritably. "This is one town with one name, but there are two words in it, like helter-skelter." "Helter-skelter," said my father, moving slowly toward the bedroom door and smiling in a faint, strained way which I understand now—but didn't then—was meant to humor me. When he was within a few paces of the door, he fairly leaped for it

and ran out into the hall, his coattails and shoelaces flying. The exit stunned me. I had no notion that he thought I had gone out of my senses; I could only believe that he had gone out of *his* or that, only partially awake, he was engaged in some form of running in his sleep. I ran after him and I caught him at the door of mother's room and grabbed him, in order to reason with him. I shook him a little, thinking to wake him completely. "Mary! Roy! Herman!" he shouted. I, too, began to shout for my brothers and my mother. My mother opened her door instantly, and there we were at 3:30 in the morning grappling and shouting, father partly dressed, but without socks or shirt, and I in pajamas.

"*Now*, what?" demanded my mother, grimly, pulling us apart. She was capable, fortunately, of handling any two of us and she never in her life was alarmed by the words or actions of any one of us.

"Look out for Jamie!" said father. (He always called me Jamie when excited.) My mother looked at me.

"What's the matter with your father?" she demanded. I said I didn't know; I said he had got up suddenly and dressed and ran out of the room.

"Where did you think you were going?" mother asked him, coolly. He looked at me. We looked at each other, breathing hard, but somewhat calmer.

"He was babbling about New Jersey at this infernal hour of the night," said father. "He came to my room and asked me to name towns in New Jersey." Mother looked at me.

"I just asked him," I said. "I was trying to think of one and couldn't sleep."

"You see?" said father, triumphantly. Mother didn't look at him.

"Get to bed, both of you," she said. "I don't want to hear any more out of you tonight. Dressing and tearing up and down the hall at this hour in the morning!" She went back into the room and shut her door. Father and I went back to bed. "Are you all right?" he called to me. "Are you?" I asked. "Well, good night," he said. "Good night," I said.

Mother would not let the rest of us discuss the affair next morning at breakfast. Herman asked what had been the matter. "We'll go on to something more elevating," said mother.

Close Up

1. Father is a mildly nervous man who usually goes to bed at 9:30. (a) What does Roy warn Father about on the night in question? (b) Why does he then wake Father at three in the morning?

2. Six months later Father has a similar experience. (a) Why does James wake Father in the middle of the night? (b) Why does James' question cause Father to run from the room?

3. *Alarm* is fear caused by a sudden apprehension of danger. Why did Thurber call this story "More Alarms at Night"?

Mood

Some stories create a humorous mood. Humor is the quality of the story that makes you laugh. One way an author can create humor is to include eccentric, or odd or peculiar, characters. Another way is to exaggerate, or magnify, aspects of common human behavior. A third way is to show an unexpected, or surprising, turn of events.

1. (a) Which characters in this story do you consider eccentric? (b) How is their behavior odd or peculiar?

2. Thurber exaggerates many aspects of human behavior. For example, many of us have lain awake at night trying to remember a word or a name. (a) What does this action lead him to suspect or fear about himself? (b) Find one other example of exaggerated behavior in the story.

3. After Roy tells Father, "Buck, your time has come," Father wakes up the rest of the family. (a) How do you expect Mother to react to the uproar? (b) Why is it humorous that she blames Father instead of Roy?

Activities

1. **Composition.** Write a paragraph describing an eccentric person. (Feel free to invent a character.)

2. **Composition.** Humor is a very individual thing: What strikes one person as funny may not strike someone else as funny. Did you find this story humorous? Why or why not? Write a paragraph explaining your answer.

INFERENCES

Making Predictions As You Read

As you read, you make inferences, or predictions, about what will happen in the story. For example, after reading the first paragraph of "More Alarms at Night," you probably predicted that this story would turn out to be humorous. You based your prediction on the following clues: The narrator says that the town he lived in "has had the hallucination of being followed," which makes it a very odd town indeed. He also claims that it is a town "in which almost anything is likely to happen and in which almost everything does." Since the incident he is about to relate happens in this town, it seems likely that it will be humorous.

▶ Tell whether each of the statements below is a reasonable prediction (based on clues) to make at some point in the story.

   a. On the night in question, Father will sleep peacefully.

   b. Roy will pretend that he has become delirious.

   c. No one will believe Father when Father tells what Roy said.

   d. Six months later, Jamie will also pretend to be delirious.

   e. Father will think that Jamie is delirious when Jamie comes into his room at night.

   f. When Father runs from the room the second time, Mother will be inclined to believe his story.

WORD ATTACK

Understanding Idioms

An idiom is a common phrase that has a meaning all its own. This meaning is different from the meaning of the individual words in the phrase. For example, look at the following sentence:

He *beat around the bush* for ten minutes before answering my question.

To beat around the bush is an idiom that means "to waste time in order to avoid doing something." The meaning of the idiom has little to do with beating or bushes.

Some idioms are so common that you *can* find their meaning in the dictionary. To do so, first find the key word in the phrase (for example, in the idiom *after one's own heart*, the key word is *heart*). Then look up this word in the dictionary. At the end of the entry, you will find a list of idioms containing this word. (*After one's own heart* means "meeting one's desires.")

1. In each sentence below the idiom is printed in *italics*. Write the meaning of each idiom on a piece of paper.
   a. "One of the incidents that I always think of first when I *cast back over my youth* is what happened the night that my father 'threatened to get Buck.' "
   b. "He was a tall, mildly nervous, peaceable gentleman, given to quiet pleasures, and eager that *everything should run smoothly*."
   c. "At this *a light dawned* in Roy's eyes."
   d. "The situation, before we *let it drop* and everybody went back to bed again, became, as such situations in our family usually did, rather more complicated than *ironed out*."

2. Use a dictionary to find the meaning of each idiom below.
   a. have one's heart in one's mouth
   b. wear one's heart on one's sleeve
   c. set one's heart at rest
   d. keep one's head above water
   e. come to a head
   f. head and shoulders above
   g. bite the hand that feeds you
   h. show one's hand
   i. put one's foot in one's mouth
   j. put one's best foot forward

More Alarms at Night   **341**

The Brothers

Björnstjerne Björnson[1]

Each brother wanted the watch more than he wanted the other's love.

The schoolmaster's name was Baard, and he once had a brother whose name was Anders. They thought a great deal of each other; they both enlisted; they lived together in the town, and took part in the war, both being made corporals, and serving in the same company. On their return home after the war, everyone thought they were two splendid fellows. Now their father died; he had a good deal of personal property, which was not easy to divide, but the brothers decided, in order that this should be no cause of disagreement between them, to put the things up at auction, so that each might buy what he wanted, and the proceeds could be divided between them. No sooner said

than done. Their father had owned a large gold watch, which had a widespread fame, because it was the only gold watch people in that part of the country had seen, and when it was put up many a rich man tried to get it until the two brothers began to take part in the bidding; then the rest ceased. Now, Baard expected Anders to let him have the watch, and Anders expected the same of Baard; each bid in his turn to put the other to the test, and they looked hard at each other while bidding. When the watch had been run up to twenty dollars, it seemed to Baard that his brother was not acting rightly, and he continued to bid until he got it almost up to thirty; as Anders kept on, it struck Baard that his brother could not remember how kind he had always been to him, nor that he was the

1. Bjornstjerne (bəyən′ stəyərn) Bjornson (bəyən′ sōn).

elder of the two, and the watch went up to over thirty dollars. Anders still kept on. Then Baard suddenly bid forty dollars, and ceased to look at his brother. It grew very still in the auction room, the voice of the lensmand[2] alone was heard calmly naming the price. Anders, standing there, thought if Baard could afford to give forty dollars he could also, and if Baard grudged him the watch, he might as well take it. He bid higher. This Baard felt to be the greatest disgrace that had ever befallen him; he bid fifty dollars, in a very low tone. Many people stood around, and Anders did not see how his brother could so mock at him in the hearing of all; he bid higher. At length Baard laughed.

"A hundred dollars and my brotherly affection in the bargain," said he, and turning left the room. A little later, someone came out to him, just as he was engaged in saddling the horse he had bought a short time before.

"The watch is yours," said the man; "Anders has withdrawn."

The moment Baard heard this there passed through him a feeling of compunction; he thought of his brother, and not of the watch. The horse was saddled, but Baard paused with his hand on its back, uncertain whether to ride away or no. Now many people came out, among them Anders, who when he saw his brother standing beside the saddled horse, not knowing what Baard was reflecting on, shouted out to him:—

"Thank you for the watch, Baard! You will not see it run the day your brother treads on your heels."

"Nor the day I ride to the gard[3] again," replied Baard, his face very white, swinging himself into the saddle.

Neither of them ever again set foot in the house where they had lived with their father.

A short time after, Anders married into a houseman's[4] family; but Baard was not invited to the wedding, nor was he even at church. The first year of Anders' marriage the only cow he owned was found dead beyond the north side of the house, where it was tethered, and no one could find out what had killed it. Several misfortunes followed, and he kept going downhill; but the worst of all was when his barn, with all that it contained, burned down in the middle of the winter; no one knew how the fire had originated.

"This has been done by someone who wishes me ill," said Anders—and he wept that night. He was now a poor man and had lost all ambition for work.

The next evening Baard appeared in his room. Anders was in bed when he entered, but sprang directly up.

"What do you want here?" he cried, then stood silent, staring fixedly at his brother.

Baard waited a little before he answered—

"I wish to offer you help, Anders; things are going badly for you."

"I am faring as you meant I should, Baard! Go, I am not sure that I can control myself."

"You mistake, Anders; I repent——"

"Go, Baard, or God be merciful to us both!"

Baard fell back a few steps, and with quivering voice he murmured—

"If you want the watch you shall have it."

"Go, Baard!" shrieked the other, and Baard left, not daring to linger longer.

Now with Baard it had been as follows: As soon as he had heard of his brother's misfortunes, his heart melted; but pride held him back. He felt impelled to go to church, and there he made good resolves, but he was not able to carry them out. Often he got far enough to see Anders' house; but now some-

---

2. lensmand (lĕnz′mənd) n.: Auctioneer.
3. gard (gärd) n.: Farm.

4. houseman's (hous′mənz) adj.: Tenant farmer's. (A tenant farmer farms land owned by someone else and pays rent in cash or crops.)

one came out of the door; now there was a stranger there; again Anders was outside chopping wood, so there was always something in the way. But one Sunday, late in the winter, he went to church again, and Anders was there too. Baard saw him; he had grown pale and thin; he wore the same clothes as in former days when the brothers were constant companions, but now they were old and patched. During the sermon Anders kept his eyes fixed on the priest, and Baard thought he looked good and kind; he remembered their childhood and what a good boy Anders had been. Baard went to communion that day, and he made a solemn vow to his God that he would be reconciled with his brother whatever might happen. This determination passed through his soul while he was drinking the wine, and when he rose he wanted to go right to him and sit down beside him; but someone was in the way and Anders did not look up. After service, too, there was something in the way; there were too many people; Anders' wife was walking at his side, and Baard was not acquainted with her; he concluded that it would be best to go to his brother's house and have a serious talk with him. When evening came he set forth. He went straight to the sitting room door and listened, then he heard his name spoken; it was by the wife.

"He took the sacrament today," said she; "he surely thought of you."

"No; he did not think of me," said Anders. "I know him; he thinks only of himself."

For a long time there was silence; the sweat poured from Baard as he stood there, although it was a cold evening. The wife inside was busied with a kettle that crackled and hissed on the hearth; a little infant cried now and then, and Anders rocked it. At last the wife spoke these few words:—

"I believe you both think of each other without being willing to admit it."

"Let us talk of something else," replied Anders.

After a while he got up and moved toward the door. Baard was forced to hide in the woodshed; but to that very place Anders came to get an armful of wood. Baard stood in the corner and saw him distinctly; he had put off his threadbare Sunday clothes and wore the uniform he had brought home with him from the war, the match to Baard's, and which he had promised his brother never to touch but to leave for an heirloom, Baard having given him a similar promise. Anders' uniform was now patched and worn; his strong, well-built frame was encased, as it were, in a bundle of rags; and, at the same time, Baard heard the gold watch ticking in his own pocket. Anders walked to where the fagots[5] lay; instead of stooping at once to pick them up, he paused, leaned back against the woodpile, and gazed up at the sky, which glittered brightly with stars. Then he drew a sigh and muttered—

"Yes—yes—yes;—O Lord! O Lord!"

As long as Baard lived he heard these words. He wanted to step forward, but just then his brother coughed, and it seemed so difficult, more was not required to hold him back. Anders took up his armful of wood, and brushed past Baard, coming so close to him that the twigs struck his face, making it smart.

For fully ten minutes he stood as if riveted to the spot, and it is doubtful when he would have left, had he not, after his great emotion, been seized with a shivering fit that shook him through and through. Then he moved away; he frankly confessed to himself that he was too cowardly to go in, and so he now formed a new plan. From an ash box which stood in the corner he had just left, he took some bits of charcoal, found a resinous pine splint, went up to the barn, closed the door, and struck a light. When he had lit the pine splint, he held it up to find the wooden peg where Anders hung his lantern when he came early in the morning to thresh. Baard took his gold watch and hung it on the peg,

---

5. fagots (făg′ əts) n.: Bundles of twigs.

blew out his light, and left; and then he felt so relieved that he bounded over the snow like a young boy.

The next day he heard that the barn had burned to the ground during the night. No doubt sparks had fallen from the torch that had lit him while he was hanging up his watch.

This so overwhelmed him that he kept to his room all day like a sick man, brought out his hymnbook, and sang until the people in the house thought he had gone mad. But in the evening he went out; it was bright moonlight. He walked to his brother's place, dug in the ground where the fire had been, and found, as he had expected, a little melted lump of gold. It was the watch.

It was with this in his tightly closed hand that he went in to his brother, imploring peace, and was about to explain everything.

A little girl had seen him digging in the ashes, some boys on their way to a dance had noticed him going down toward the place the preceding Sunday evening; the people in the house where he lived testified how curiously he had acted on Monday, and as everyone knew that he and his brother were bitter enemies, information was given and a suit instituted.

No one could prove anything against Baard, but suspicion rested on him. Less than ever, now, did he feel able to approach his brother.

Anders had thought of Baard when the barn was burned, but had spoken of it to no one. When he saw him enter his room, the following evening, pale and excited, he immediately thought: "Now he is smitten with remorse, but for such a terrible crime against his brother he shall have no forgiveness." Afterward he heard how people had seen Baard go down to the barn the evening of the fire, and, although nothing was brought to light at the trial, Anders firmly believed his brother to be guilty.

They met at the trial, Baard in his good clothes, Anders in his patched ones. Baard looked at his brother as he entered, and his eyes wore so piteous an expression of entreaty that Anders felt it in the inmost depths of his heart. "He does not want me to say anything," thought Anders, and when he was asked if he suspected his brother of the deed, he said loudly and decidedly, "No!"

Anders took to hard drinking from that day, and was soon far on the road to ruin. Still worse was it with Baard; although he did not drink, he was scarcely to be recognized by those who had known him before.

Late one evening a poor woman entered the little room Baard rented, and begged him to accompany her a short distance. He knew her: it was his brother's wife. Baard understood forthwith what her errand was; he grew deathly pale, dressed himself, and went with her without a word. There was a glimmer of light from Anders' window, it twinkled and disappeared, and they were guided by this light, for there was no path across the snow. When Baard stood once more in the passage, a strange odor met him which made him feel ill. They entered. A little child stood by the fireplace eating charcoal; its whole face was black, but as it looked up and laughed it displayed white teeth—it was the brother's child.

There on the bed, with a heap of clothes thrown over him, lay Anders, emaciated, with smooth, high forehead, and with his hollow eyes fixed on his brother. Baard's knees trembled; he sat down at the foot of the bed and burst into a violent fit of weeping. The sick man looked at him intently and said nothing. At length he asked his wife to go out, but Baard made a sign to her to remain; and now these two brothers began to talk together. They accounted for everything from the day they had bid for the watch up to the present moment. Baard concluded by producing the lump of gold he always carried about him, and it now became manifest to the brothers that in all these years neither had known a happy day.

Anders did not say much, for he was not able to do so, but Baard watched by his bed as long as he was ill.

"Now I am perfectly well," said Anders one morning on waking. "Now, my brother, we will live long together, and never leave each other, just as in the old days."

But that day he died.

Baard took charge of the wife and the child, and they fared well from that time. What the brothers had talked of together by the bed burst through the walls and the night, and was soon known to all the people in the parish, and Baard became the most respected man among them. He was honored as one who had known great sorrow and found happiness again, or as one who had been absent for a very long time. Baard grew inwardly strong through all this friendliness about him; he became a truly pious man, and wanted to be useful, he said, and so the old corporal took to teaching school. What he impressed upon the children, first and last, was love, and he practiced it himself, so that the children clung to him as to a playmate and father in one.

Close Up

1. (a) As the brothers bid on the gold watch, what does each expect the other to do? (b) Why, then, do they keep bidding?

2. Although Baard tries several times to reconcile with his brother, events always seem to get in his way. (a) When he leaves the church after communion, what prevents him from approaching Anders? (b) Why doesn't he come forward when he sees his brother in the barn?

3. (a) Why does Baard leave the gold watch in Anders' barn? (b) How does this inadvertently start a fire?

4. (a) After Anders dies, Baard becomes respected in the village. Why? (b) Why does he teach the children the importance of love above all else?

Irony

Sometimes a character believes a situation will turn out a certain way. Irony of situation occurs when the situation turns out just the opposite way. For example, suppose a man spends his life searching in foreign lands for a treasure. In the end he finds that there has been treasure buried in his own backyard all along. This is ironic since it is just the opposite of how he expected things to turn out.

Verbal irony occurs when a character says something that turns out to be truer than this character meant. For example, a character may say, "I'll see this barn burn before I let you have it." The next day the barn does, in fact, burn. The character hadn't exactly meant what he said, but the statement turned out to be true.

Dramatic irony occurs when you, the reader, understand or see something more clearly than the characters see it.

1. (a) Why do the brothers decide to auction off their father's goods? (b) What unexpected problem does the auction create?

2. Baard vows that he will not see the watch run the day he rides to the farm again. How does his statement turn out to be truer than he expected?

3. The brothers' dispute centers on a gold watch. (a) What finally happens to the watch? (b) Why is this ironic?

4. (a) What does Anders say just before he dies? (b) Why is this statement ironic?

INFERENCES

Identifying Incorrect Inferences

An inference is an intelligent guess based on evidence. Sometimes characters in a story make incorrect inferences. They misinterpret evidence or they base their inferences on too few clues. For example, when Anders comes out of the auction hall, he sees his brother with his hands on the back of a saddled horse. Therefore he infers that his brother feels no remorse and is getting ready to ride away. In reality, Baard is feeling just the opposite. Incorrect inferences often lead to misunderstandings.

1. After they see Baard in church, both Anders and his wife make inferences about Baard.
   a. What inference does Anders' wife make?
   b. On what evidence does she base her inference?
   c. Is her inference correct?
   d. What inference does Anders make?
   e. On what evidence does he base his inference?
   f. Is his inference correct?

2. After Baard hangs the watch on the peg, the barn burns down.
   a. What inference do the townspeople make?
   b. On what evidence do they base their inference?
   c. Is their inference correct?
   d. What inference does Anders make?
   e. On what evidence does he base his inference?
   f. Is his inference correct?

WORD ATTACK

Understanding Prefixes

A prefix is a letter or group of letters added to a word or word root to change its meaning. One prefix you may be unfamiliar with is *be–*. This prefix can add the meaning *around, thoroughly, away, about,* or *covered with.* Look at the following sentence:

> "This Baard felt to be the greatest disgrace that had ever *befallen* him; he bid fifty dollars, in a very low tone."

The word *befallen* means "to have happened" or "to have come about."

---

1. Find the meaning of each *italicized* word below and write it on a piece of paper. Use your dictionary to help you.
   a. She came to *beseech* Baard to come with her.
   b. She asked Baard on *behalf* of Anders.
   c. Baard did not *begrudge* Anders the watch.
   d. When the barn burned down, he *berated* himself.
   e. Anders was *bewildered* by his brother's behavior.

2. Check your dictionary and list all the words you can find that contain the prefix *be–*.

Too Old to Work

Art Buchwald

The trouble with the American Dream these days is that there has been such an emphasis on youth in our country that a man can be washed up at the age of forty and not even know it. I didn't realize how serious it was getting until I started trying to find some jobs for friends who were victims of the *World Journal Tribune* closing.

The first question people would ask me was, "How old is he?" If I said he was forty or older, I'd get a shrug and some comment like, "He's too old for us."

It seems to me that if the trend continues, the age gap is going to be one of the most serious problems this country faces. It's quite possible in another ten or fifteen years that the following scene might become very common.

Personnel Manager: "I see your qualifications are in order except for one thing."

Applicant: "What's that?"

Personnel Manager: "I'm afraid you're too old for the job."

Applicant: "What do you mean 'too old for the job'? I'm twenty-three."

PM: "Yes, I see that. We don't hire anyone over twenty-one years of age."

Applicant: "But I just got out of college. I've never had a job. How can I be too old?"

PM: "According to our pension planners, who have the final say on how old our employees should be, anybody above twenty-one years of age is over the hill."

Applicant: "How can I be over the hill if I've never been on?"

PM: "There's no reason to get testy about this. We have nothing personal against you. It's just that we have found through experience that men of your age really don't do their best work when they reach twenty-three or twenty-four years of age. Oh, there have been exceptions, but on the whole, we'd rather take our chances with the younger man who can stand up under the physical and mental pressures of the job."

Applicant: "I appreciate your thinking, but I can assure you I can do anything a twenty-one-year-old can do. I'm still very strong. I play tennis twice a week. I'm in excellent health, and I was even captain of my football team last year."

PM: "Sir, I don't doubt everything you say, but we can't judge you as an individual. Statistics show your age group is prone to colds, backaches, and bursitis. Even if we wanted to hire you, our group health insurance advisers wouldn't let us. They can't afford to take the risk with a twenty-three-year-old man, no matter how healthy he may look."

Applicant: "But if I can't get a job now that I've finished college, what am I going to do the rest of my life?"

PM: "Why don't you retire and move to Florida?"

Applicant: "What . . . am I going to retire on if I never worked?"

PM: "That's not our fault, is it? Don't forget, this company is in a fiercely competitive market, and if we hire older people like yourself, we'll have to explain it to our stockholders. Besides, it looks bad when a customer comes in and sees a twenty-three-year-old man hunched over his desk."

Applicant: "I hate to beg, but I really need this job. This is the fourth company I've been to which says I'm too old. Please, mister, give me a chance. I still have ten good years in me."

PM: "I'm sorry, sir. I don't wish to be coldhearted about this, but I think you should face reality. You're washed up. You should have planned for your old age years ago."

Applicant: "Let me ask one more question and then I'll go. How old are you?"

Personnel Manager: "Thirteen."

Close Up

1. Why doesn't the personnel manager hire the applicant?

2. (a) What does the personnel manager mean when he says, "We can't judge you as an individual"? (b) What does he suggest the applicant do?

3. Were you surprised at the ending of this selection? Why or why not?

Satire

Satire is a type of literature that ridicules, or pokes fun at, some aspect of society. It points out the foolishness of human actions or ideas in order to correct them. Although satire is often humorous, it makes a serious statement about something that is really not very funny.

1. Reread the first three paragraphs in this selection. (a) What incident influenced Buchwald to write this piece? (b) What aspect of human society does he intend to ridicule?

2. Authors usually exaggerate the facts in a satire. (a) What effect does Buchwald create when he exaggerates the ages of the two people? (b) What further details does he exaggerate?

3. Though this example of satire is humorous, the situation it ridicules is not. Does this story succeed in pointing out to you the foolishness of society's attitude toward age? Why or why not?

Activity

► Read your local newspaper for a week and find a satirical article you think is particularly effective. Bring it into school to share with your classmates.

INFERENCES

Understanding Exaggeration

Exaggeration stretches the truth—that is, it makes something greater or larger than it actually is. Exaggeration is a good technique for making a point. For example, look at the following statement: His chances of getting a job are one in a million. This is an exaggeration, but it emphasizes how difficult it will be for the applicant to get a job.

▶ Read each statement below. On a piece of paper, label *E* each statement that is an exaggeration.
   a. He won't find a job in a million years.
   b. He will have a difficult time finding a job.
   c. Anyone over twenty is over the hill.
   d. Life insurance companies give better rates to people in their twenties than to people in their thirties.
   e. Some people who study society worry about the importance Americans place on youth.
   f. Americans worship youth.
   g. After fifteen, everything is downhill.
   h. Most fifteen-year-olds are still in school.

WORD ATTACK

Choosing the Meaning That Fits the Context

Most English words have more than one meaning. When you read, you must choose the meaning that fits the context. For example, the word *country* can mean (1) a rural area, (2) the people of a nation, or (3) the whole land of a nation or state. Now look at the following sentence. "The trouble with the American Dream these days is that there has been such an emphasis on youth in this *country* that a man can be washed up at the age of forty and not even know it." Only the third meaning of *country* fits this context.

---

1. Read each sentence below. Then for each *italicized* word, choose the meaning that fits the context.
    a. "But I just got out of college. I've never had a *job*."
       (1) chore or task
       (2) position of employment
       (3) something produced by work
    b. "I hate to beg, but I really need this job. . . . Please, mister, give me a *chance*."
       (1) opportunity
       (2) lottery ticket
       (3) luck
    c. "What . . . am I going to retire on if I never worked?"
       "That's not our *fault*, is it?"
       (1) responsibility or blame
       (2) flaw or imperfection
       (3) mistake
    d. "Don't forget, this is a fiercely competitive *market*, and if we hire older people like yourself, we'll have to explain it to our stockholders."
       (1) store or shop
       (2) open place with stalls or booths
       (3) area of trade or traffic in a commodity

2. Write sentences using each of the words below in the way indicated.
    a. Use *job* so that it means "chore or task."
    b. Use *chance* so that it means "luck."
    c. Use *fault* so that it means "flaw."
    d. Use *market* so that it means "store or shop."

REVIEW QUIZ

On the Selections

1. In "The Old Cat," what reason does the narrator give for the cat's having turned wild?

2. At the end of the story, why does the cat become a house cat again?

3. In "The Singing Bell," why don't the authorities use the psychoprobe on Davenport?

4. In this story, Dr. Urth is an extraterrologist. What is an extraterrologist?

5. In "An Underground Episode," why is the boy chosen for the task?

6. In "The House from the Eleventh Floor," why does the narrator begin to worry about his eyesight?

7. In "The Birds," what is the first event that makes you suspect that the birds have turned against human beings?

8. In "More Alarms at Night," what does Father suspect when Roy says, "Buck, your time has come"?

9. In "The Brothers," how does the gold watch start a dispute between Anders and Baard?

10. In "Too Old to Work," what aspect of society does Buchwald satirize?

On Inferences

1. In "The Old Cat," what details indicate that the members of the family like cats?

2. In "The Singing Bell," which detail tells you that Davenport does not trust Peyton?

3. In "The House from the Eleventh Floor," which detail makes you suspect that the dog is from the past?

4. At the end of this story, the narrator says about his flat on the eleventh floor, "You can't see it from here." What does this statement lead you to believe?

5. In "The Brothers," why does Anders' wife decide that Baard still loves his brother?

6. Which of the statements below contain exaggeration.
   a. Never in a million years would he let his father have the watch.
   b. Even if I live to be a million, I won't apologize.
   c. He was sorry for his actions and wished to apologize.
   d. His cough was so loud that it was heard in the next state.

On Setting, Mood, and Tone

► Decide whether the following statements are true or false.
   a. The setting of a story is where and when it takes place.
   b. The setting can affect the story's plot.
   c. The characters in a story are never influenced by the setting.
   d. The mood of a story is the impression it creates and the emotions it arouses.
   e. Irony of situation occurs when a situation turns out exactly as the characters thought it would.

COMPOSITION

Narration and Description

Narration is the act of telling a story. A story should have a beginning, a middle, and an end. Usually, the beginning introduces the main character. The middle relates what happens to this character and explains the conflict. The end tells how the conflict is resolved.

Often a story contains description. Description helps you form a clear picture of something and makes you feel that you are actually seeing the thing being described.

Here are four steps for writing description:

1. Decide what impression you want to create and select the details that create this impression. For example, if you want to create the impression that a person is rich, you could describe the man's expensive suit, his manicured nails, and his sun tan in the middle of winter.
2. Arrange these details in a logical order. For example, you might start by describing the person's most prominent features and then describe less prominent ones.
3. Make your description appeal to the five senses. For example, what is the texture of the person's clothes? Does he have a certain odor about him (cigar smoke, after-shave lotion, etc.)? Does he wear loud clothes or are his clothes subdued?
4. Use precise adjectives and verbs. For example, instead of saying the man is big, say that he is hefty, or enormous, or fat. Instead of saying he sat in the chair, say that he slumped in the chair or perched on the edge of the chair.

▶ **Composition.** Write a paragraph using one of the ideas below.

a. Imagine you have just entered a time machine. Describe your trip into the future.
b. Imagine you are exploring another planet. Tell about meeting the inhabitants there.
c. Imagine you have to cross a deep ravine in order to rescue a friend. Write a paragraph telling how you cross the ravine.
d. Write a paragraph describing a supernatural experience.

BEFORE GOING ON

Outlining

Outlining is organizing a selection so that important information stands out from lesser details. The whole idea of outlining is to divide and organize. First, divide the selection into major topics. Then divide these topics into subtopics. Indicate a major topic by a Roman numeral (I, II, III). Indicate a subtopic by a capital letter (A, B, C). Indicate specific information about these subtopics by Arabic numerals (1, 2, 3).

In the following outline, the various parts are not complete sentences. Begin each with a capital letter, but do not use a period at the end of each item.

▶ After you have read *Sasquatch Alias "Bigfoot,"* copy the outline skeleton below in your notebook and fill in the blanks.

Sasquatch

I. _____
   A. Huge
   B. Hairy
   C. _____
   D. _____

II. Origin
   A. Relative of the Abominable Snowman
   B. _____

III. Existence
   A. Evidence for its existence
      1. Pacific Northwest Indians told of these creatures hundreds of years ago
      2. Timber workers in northern California found giant tracks around their dwelling
      3. _____
      4. _____
      5. _____
      6. _____
   B.
      1. No Bigfoot has been captured or killed
      2. _____

IV. Groups organized to find Bigfoot
   A. _____
   B. _____
   C. _____

Further Reading

Sasquatch Alias "Bigfoot"

George Laycock

From northern California, through Oregon, Washington, and into British Columbia, the mountains are wild and deeply timbered. In this country there are new reported sightings every year of manlike monsters, huge, hairy, and indescribably ugly.

Indians of the Pacific Northwest knew about these giant, wild men of the forests hundreds of years ago. The Indians called them "Sasquatch." More recently, people, standing spellbound before fourteen-inch-long footprints, have called the monster "Bigfoot."

Each year more people than ever before are out there in the deeply wooded valleys hoping for a glimpse of the bigfooted Sasquatch.

Where could such monsters have come from? They could, some explain, have come from the same place the native Indians and Eskimos came from to settle North America. During the time of the Wisconsin glacial epoch the level of the oceans was lower. More of the world's supply of water was locked up in ice and snow. This exposed a wide bridge of land across the North Pacific connecting Asia and North America.

Across this land bridge came the ancestors of many wild creatures found here, deer, bear, bison, wild sheep, and others. Perhaps the people, moving a few miles at a time, followed these animals, which they hunted for food. And perhaps in those times there came as well some creatures we still know very little about.

Slipping along in the shadows of night may have been tall, hairy creatures looking more like people than like any of the other creatures around them. This could explain how the ancestors of Sasquatch first came to the forests of the Pacific Northwest; they came on their big feet. They would have come, you understand, from Asia, which is also home of the Abominable Snowman, presumably a cousin to Bigfoot.

It is likely that the creature we now know as Bigfoot was never abundant. Except for the fact that they have managed to stay out of

sight of men so well, there might, by now, be none of them remaining.

Not until the 1950s did many people begin thinking seriously about the possibility that there might really be a Bigfoot. Then timber workers, in lonely logging camps of northern California, began finding strange giant tracks around their dwellings and beside the forest trails. Plaster casts of these prints were sometimes made and preserved. The story spread, and people began to ask each other if such human-shaped animals did live up there in the woods. Many believed they did.

Soon someone recalled a remarkable story that had appeared in Portland, Oregon, newspapers in 1924. On the east slope of Mount St. Helens lived a grizzled old prospector, all alone in his little cabin in the silence of the deep forest. On an August day he left his cabin and hurried off to search for a forest ranger. He told the foresters his strange tale.

"They woke me up in the middle of the night," he said, "throwin' stones at my place. Some of them stones was big ones, some even come through the roof. And all the time they was around the house, they was screaming like a bunch of apes. I didn't dare go outside. That's probably what they wanted me to do. Would you have gone outside? No sir! Instead I crawled under the bed, and I stayed there till morning come. Sometime in the night them critters quit their screamin' and slunk off in the dark. Next morning when I went outside there was the tracks, big ones, a foot or more across, and right up beside my place."

That story appeared in newspapers in Washington and Oregon. Soon the wooded slopes of Mount St. Helens were filled with nervous hunters. They were alert for the slightest noise, the big footprint, or a glimpse of a furry hide in the undergrowth. Considering the assortment of rifles, shotguns, and pistols they carried, it was a blessing nobody got shot.

They saw no sign of the Bigfoot. Gradually folks around those mountains seemed to forget the giant, hairy monsters again. Sasquatch was becoming more elusive than ever. He wanted very little to do with people and this was understandable.

But following the reports from the California logging camps, the story began growing again. In the years since, the evidence has piled up. More and more, people in the Pacific Northwest are convinced that something in human form, but not very human at all, really lives in the deepest and darkest forests. There is now a list of more than three hundred reported sightings of Bigfoot. Undoubtedly there would be more except for the elusive nature of the beast and its nocturnal habits. Still no Bigfoot has been captured or killed. Seldom has one been photographed. The most notable exception occurred in the mountains of northern California in 1967.

Roger Patterson lives with his wife and three children on the little horse ranch they operate near Yakima, Washington. For several years he had been studying the exploits of Bigfoot and figuring out the best place to go look for the creature.

On October 20, 1967, Mr. Patterson and his friend, Bob Gimlin, had been high in the mountains in northern California for almost a week. On that day, Mr. Patterson says, ". . . when riding horseback up a creek bottom, we encountered this creature. My horse smelled it, jumped, and fell." Mr. Patterson scrambled for his saddlebag. "I got the camera out of the saddlebag," he says, "and ran across the creek and we were able to get twenty-nine feet of sixteen-millimeter colored film."

After three miles of tracking through rough country, the two men lost Bigfoot's trail in deep undergrowth. They made plaster casts of the footprints. Other people returned later and also saw and measured the 14½-inch prints.

This newly made film was sent down to Hollywood. There, experts in "special effects," men who really know how to set up a fake picture, studied and restudied Patterson's disturbing movies. Each of them decided that in no way could Patterson have faked his pictures.

Next the movies were shown to a lengthy list of scientists. Among them were noted zoologists. They arrived as doubters, but following a look at the Patterson movies, left "shaken." Of special interest to the zoologists was the movement of the muscles as the Bigfoot walked. This movement was proof enough to many that the creature was real and the Patterson movies authentic. The figure photographed, a female, walked upright like a human and measured about seven and a half feet tall, three feet across the shoulders, had arms three feet long, and weighed an estimated eight hundred pounds.

In addition to his movies, Patterson tells of other evidence that Bigfoot lives. In 1958 he interviewed Charles Cates, an aging man who had once served as mayor of North Vancouver. Cates recalled three old Indians whom he considered reliable, and all of whom told of hairy giants they had seen in their youth. Perhaps there were more of the monsters around in those times. One of the Indians had been in a tent one night with friends when a Bigfoot stuck its hairy head through the tent door and looked in upon them.

Near Yankton, Oregon, according to Mr. Patterson's records, several people sighted the hairy giants in 1926. A truck driver swore that one of them had trotted along beside his logging truck looking into the cab at him.

In 1941, according to a report given Patterson by Mrs. George Chapman, she and her children saw "an eight-foot hairy man come out of the woods." The creature went into a lean-to behind their cabin. As it went in the back door, the Chapmans went out the front door. They fled into the forest. For a long time they huddled there in the shadows. When they returned to their home, huge tracks marked the place where the giant had walked. The deputy sheriff from Blaine, Washington, came out and made casts of the footprints. This Bigfoot had the biggest feet of all. They measured sixteen inches long. The Bigfoot tramped down a patch of potatoes as it departed for the forests.

Then the next year, near Eugene, Oregon, Don Hunter and his wife spotted a "giant biped" walking, taking long strides, over the mud flats of Todd Lake.

Such reports, when coupled with Patterson's movies, are not to be taken lightly. So much interest has been aroused in these stories of Bigfoot that at least three organizations have been created to seek the creature. One is the American Resources and Development Foundation, Inc., organized by Ron Olsen, one of the most respected of all Bigfoot hunters. His organization is programming all reports of sightings on a computer in efforts to pinpoint the best possible places to continue the search.

Another is the International Wildlife Conservation Society. This group is based in Washington, D.C. At the head of it is an explorer with experience searching the Himalayas for Bigfoot's cousin, the Abominable Snowman. Even Washington socialites have helped finance the group.

Roger Patterson has also set up the Northwest Research Association. With these groups, plus uncounted individual amateur monster hunters loose in the woods, the chances seem better than ever that Bigfoot will soon slip up, be captured, measured, photographed, and verified.

Some people have admitted they plan to shoot the first Bigfoot they find, thereby ending speculation. But most hope only to take one of the furry beasts captive long enough to study him. With this in mind, expeditions go afield equipped with dart guns carrying drugs to put Bigfoot to sleep.

Patterson has mapped out a complete course of action. On that memorable day when Bigfoot is eventually tracked to earth, the procedure will include the following steps. Small groups of specialists will be scouring the mountain country for fresh evidence. "When a specimen is obtained," Patterson explains, "all personnel and equipment will be concentrated on it." Even after the effects of the drug-carrying dart wear off, Bigfoot will be kept under full sedation. (This seems safest.) All field forces will be rushed to the scene. A call will go out for a helicopter. Blood samples, bone marrow, body fluids, all will be collected and labeled. Plastic casts will be made of teeth, jaws, hands, feet.

Meanwhile cameras will click and whine, tape recorders will run continuously, and a stenographer will record written observations. Security measures will go into effect at once. One reason will be to protect the researchers against attack by other Bigfeet. There will also, as Patterson explains, be the need to protect the field group against ". . . interference by everybody, including the press."

Patterson welcomes new members to his association. For their dues, members receive a certificate plus a colored photograph of Bigfoot. This is enough to make adventure-minded people everywhere feel a little closer to the monsters.

One of the most recent centers of Bigfoot activity is around the county seat town of The Dalles, Oregon. According to the sheriff's office in The Dalles, five people testified they saw the creature in the neighborhood June 2, 1971, a one-day record. A month later there was an additional sighting near the same location. Visitors flocked to town. But there were no more observations reported during the summer.

Bigfoot will almost certainly appear again. No one knows where. People all the way over into Montana and Wyoming, and other states as well, talk of the Bigfoot. Many would not be at all surprised to find these shaggy giants living in their mountains too. Doubters sometimes suggest that anyone with a mountain and a forest can have his own Sasquatch.

One thing is certain, if Bigfoot is really out there in the hills, his name belongs on the government's official list of rare and endangered species. Whatever his fortunes might have been in the past, his numbers have dwindled to a precious few.

All who seek to kill a Bigfoot should reconsider. He appears, after all, to be a harmless monster.

This is the firm belief in Skamania County, Washington. County commissioners there recently passed a law making anyone who kills a Bigfoot or Sasquatch subject to a fine of one thousand dollars and five years in jail.

To man and Bigfoot alike, this is a refreshing development. We live in an age when hundreds of wild species are becoming rare and approaching extinction. Only after the passenger pigeons were already gone did we pass laws to save them. The bison nearly became extinct for the same reason. But here is a case where we pass a law to save a wild creature even before it is found—and a monster at that.

If you should see a Bigfoot, perhaps you should tell him about that. It might help convince him that people are not such monsters after all.

TREASURES

War

Luigi Pirandello

The passengers who had left Rome by the night express had had to stop until dawn at the small station of Fabriano in order to continue their journey by the small old-fashioned "local" joining the main line with Sulmona.

At dawn, in a stuffy and smoky second-class carriage[1] in which five people had already spent the night, a bulky woman in deep mourning was hoisted in—almost like

---

1. carriage (kăr′ ĭj) n.: Passenger car on a train.

a shapeless bundle. Behind her, puffing and moaning, followed her husband—a tiny man, thin and weakly, his face death-white, his eyes small and bright and looking shy and uneasy.

Having at last taken a seat, he politely thanked the passengers who had helped his wife and who had made room for her; then he turned round to the woman trying to pull down the collar of her coat and politely inquired:

"Are you all right, dear?"

The wife, instead of answering, pulled up her collar again to her eyes, so as to hide her face.

"Nasty world," muttered the husband with a sad smile.

And he felt it his duty to explain to his traveling companions that the poor woman was to be pitied, for the war was taking away from her her only son, a boy of twenty to whom both had devoted their entire life, even breaking up their home at Sulmona to follow him to Rome where he had to go as a student; then, allowing him to volunteer for war with an assurance, however, that at least for six months he would not be sent to the front and now, all of a sudden, receiving a wire saying that he was due to leave in three days' time and asking them to go and see him off.

The woman under the big coat was twisting and wriggling, at times growling like a wild animal, feeling certain that all those explanations would not have aroused even a shadow of sympathy from those people who—most likely—were in the same plight as herself. One of them, who had been listening with particular attention, said:

"You should thank God that your son is only leaving now for the front. Mine was sent there the first day of the war. He has already come back twice wounded and been sent back again to the front."

"What about me? I have two sons and three nephews at the front," said another passenger.

"Maybe, but in our case it is our *only* son," ventured the husband.

"What difference can it make? You may spoil your only son with excessive attentions, but you cannot love him more than you would all your other children if you had any. Paternal love is not like bread that can be broken into pieces and split amongst the children in equal shares. A father gives *all* his love to each one of his children without discrimination, whether it be one or ten, and if I am suffering now for my two sons, I am not suffering half for each of them but double. . . ."

"True . . . true . . ." sighed the embarrassed husband, "but suppose (of course we all hope it will never be your case) a father has two sons at the front and he loses one of them, there is still one left to console him . . . while . . . ."

"Yes," answered the other, getting cross, "a son left to console him but also a son left for whom he must survive, while in the case of the father of an only son, if the son dies the father can die too and put an end to his distress. Which of the two positions is the worse? Don't you see how my case would be worse than yours?"

"Nonsense," interrupted another traveler, a fat, red-faced man with bloodshot eyes of the palest gray.

He was panting. From his bulging eyes seemed to spurt inner violence of an uncontrolled vitality which his weakened body could hardly contain.

"Nonsense," he repeated, trying to cover his mouth with his hand so as to hide the two missing front teeth. "Nonsense. Do we give life to our children for our own benefit?"

The other travelers stared at him in distress. The one who had had his son at the front since the first day of the war sighed: "You are right. Our children do not belong to us, they belong to the Country. . . ."

"Bosh," retorted the fat traveler.

"Do we think of the Country when we give life to our children? Our sons are born because . . . well, because they must be born, and when they come to life they take our own life with them. This is the truth. We belong to them but they never belong to us. And when they reach twenty they are exactly what we were at their age. We too had a father and mother, but there were so many other things as well . . . girls, cigarettes, illusions, new ties . . . and the Country, of course, whose call we would have answered—when we were twenty—even if father and mother had said no. Now, at our age, the love of our Country is still great, of course, but stronger than it is the love for our children. Is there any one of us here who wouldn't gladly take his son's place at the front if he could?"

There was a silence all round, everybody nodding as if to approve.

"Why then," continued the fat man, "shouldn't we consider the feelings of our children when they are twenty? Isn't it natural that at their age they should consider the love for their Country (I am speaking of decent boys, of course) even greater than the love for us? Isn't it natural that it should be so, as after all they must look upon us as upon old boys who cannot move anymore and must stay at home? If Country exists, if Country is a natural necessity like bread, of which each of us must eat in order not to die of hunger, somebody must go to defend it. And our sons go, when they are twenty, and they don't want tears, because if they die, they died inflamed and happy (I am speaking, of course, of decent boys). Now, if one dies young and happy, without having the ugly sides of life, the boredom of it, the pettiness, the bitterness of disillusion . . . what more can we ask for him? Everyone should stop crying: everyone should laugh, as I do . . . or at least thank God—as I do—because my son, before dying, sent me a message saying that he was dying satisfied at having ended his life in the best way he could have wished. That is why, as you see, I do not even wear mourning. . . ."

He shook his light fawn coat as if to show it; his livid lip over his missing teeth was trembling, his eyes were watery and motionless, and soon after he ended with a shrill laugh which might well have been a sob.

"Quite so . . . quite so . . ." agreed the others.

The woman who, bundled in a corner under her coat, had been sitting and listening had—for the last three months—tried to find in the words of her husband and her friends something to console her in her deep sorrow, something that might show her how a mother should resign herself to send her son not even to death but a probable danger of life. Yet not a word had she found amongst the many which had been said . . . and her grief had been greater in seeing that nobody—as she thought—could share her feelings.

But now the words of the traveler amazed and almost stunned her. She suddenly realized that it wasn't the others who were wrong and could not understand her but herself who could not rise up to the same height of those fathers and mothers willing to resign themselves, without crying, not only to the departure of their sons but even to their death.

She lifted her head, she bent over from her corner trying to listen with great attention to the details which the fat man was giving to his companions about the way his son had fallen as a hero, for his King and his Country, happy and without regrets. It seemed to her that she had stumbled into a world she had never dreamt of, a world so far unknown to her, and she was so pleased to hear everyone joining in congratulating that brave father who could so stoically speak of his child's death.

Then suddenly, just as if she had heard nothing of what had been said and almost as if waking up from a dream, she turned to the old man, asking him:

"Then . . . is your son really dead?"

Everybody stared at her. The old man, too, turned to look at her, fixing his great, bulging, horribly watery light-gray eyes deep in

her face. For some little time he tried to answer, but words failed him. He looked and looked at her, almost as if only then—at that silly, incongruous question—he had suddenly realized at last that his son was really dead . . . gone forever . . . forever. His face contracted, became horribly distorted, then he snatched in haste a handkerchief from his pocket and, to the amazement of everyone, broke into harrowing, heart-rending, uncontrollable sobs.

Close Up

1. At dawn, a bulky woman enters the second-class carriage. (a) Why is she dressed in deep mourning? (b) Why does she feel that her situation will not arouse sympathy from the other people in the carriage?

2. The woman's husband feels that their situation is special because they have only one son. (a) According to him, why does this make a difference? (b) Why doesn't the other passenger agree with him?

3. The fat man claims parents should not cry for sons who die as soldiers, for they die happy. (a) What clues indicate that he is not as accepting of his son's death as he pretends to be? (b) Why does he break down at the end of the story?

Theme

The theme of a story is its central insight, or generalization, about life. Sometimes the theme is given directly in the story, but more often it is implied, or suggested, by the characters and events.

When you state the theme of a story you should do it in a complete sentence or in a series of sentences. Your statement should deal with people and life in general, not with one character or one event in particular.

1. What effect has the war had on each of the people in the carriage?

2. The woman is looking for a way to resign herself to her son's being sent to war. Why do the words of the traveler in the fawn coat amaze and stun her?

3. The man's courage in spite of his son's death gives her momentary hope. What happens that makes her realize that he is not courageous, but merely deceiving himself?

4. Think about the events in this story. Then decide which statement best summarizes what this story says about war.
   a. War causes people pain and sorrow and the effects of war are not easily erased.
   b. Although the war caused problems for everyone, people in Italy suffered more than others.
   c. People should accept war and be willing to sacrifice their children for their country.

MAIN IDEA

Finding Topic Sentences

The topic sentence expresses the most important idea in a paragraph. It helps you to read the paragraph with greater understanding. Often, the topic sentence appears at the beginning of the paragraph, but is may also appear in the middle or at the end of the paragraph. In the following paragraph, the topic sentence is the first sentence. Notice that the other sentences provide information about the topic sentence.

> *"You should thank God that your son is only leaving now for the front.* Mine was sent there the first day of the war. He has already come back twice wounded and been sent back again to the front."

▶ On a piece of paper, write the topic sentence of each paragraph below.

a. "What difference can it make? You may spoil your only son with excessive attentions, but you cannot love him more than you would all your other children if you had any. Paternal love is not like bread that can be broken into pieces and split amongst the children in equal shares. A father gives *all* his love to each one of his children without discrimination, whether it be one or ten, and if I am suffering now for my two sons, I am not suffering half for each of them but double. . . ."

b. "Everybody stared at her. The old man, too, turned to look at her, fixing his great, bulging, horribly watery light-gray eyes deep in her face. For some little time he tried to answer, but words failed him. He looked and looked at her, almost as if only then—at that silly, incongruous question—he had suddenly realized at last that his son was really dead . . . gone forever . . . forever. His face contracted, became horribly distorted, then he snatched in haste a handkerchief from his pocket and, to the amazement of everyone, broke into harrowing, heart-rending, uncontrollable sobs."

WORD ATTACK

Understanding the Differences in Synonyms

Synonyms are words that have the same or almost the same meaning. These shades of difference are important. For example, *error* means "a departure from truth or accuracy." The words *mistake*, *blunder*, and *slip* are all synonyms for *error*. *Mistake*, though, suggests an error that results from carelessness or misunderstanding. *Blunder* suggests an error that results from stupidity or inefficiency. A *slip* is only a slight error in writing or speaking; for example, a slip of the tongue. Each word has a specific meaning. You cannot use these words interchangeably.

▶ In the dictionary entry below, the synonyms are given and defined. Decide which synonym of *pity* you would use in each of the items following the entry.

pit•y (pĭt′ ē) *n., pl.* -ies. **1.a.** Sorrow or grief aroused by the misfortune of another; compassion for suffering. **b.** Concern or regret for one considered inferior or less favored; condescending sympathy. **2.** A regrettable or disagreeable fact or necessity.—**take pity on.** To attempt to alleviate the misfortune of. —*v.* **pitied, pitying, pities.** —*tr.* To feel pity for. —*intr.* To feel pity. [Middle English *pite*, from Old French *pit(i)e*, from Late Latin *pietās*, compassion, extended sense of Latin *pietās*, piety, from *pius*, pious. See **pius** in Appendix.*] —**pit′ y•ing•ly** *adv.*

Synonyms: pity, compassion, commiseration, sympathy, condolence, empathy. These are words for grief or concern felt for someone in misfortune. *Pity* implies a disposition to help but little emotional sharing of the distress. *Compassion* always favorably connotes broad or profound feeling for the misfortunes of others and a desire to aid them. A more casual involvement is conveyed by *commiseration*, which signifies an expressed, sometimes superficial, solace. *Sympathy* is as broad as *pity* but connotes spontaneous emotion rather than considered attitude. *Condolence* expresses commiseration extended on specific occasions of loss common to all people, usually to relatives upon a death in their family. *Empathy*, with literary and psychological overtones, is a conscious involvement with a person's situation in the sense of vicarious identification.

a. The passenger wants to help the woman, but he does not share her distress.
b. The passenger identifies strongly with her problem.
c. Spontaneously, or suddenly, he felt this for the woman.
d. The passenger's feelings of pity are only casual.

Gwilan's Harp

Ursula K. Le Guin

"One day is the day for moving on, and overnight, the next day, there is no more good in moving on, because you have come where you were going to."

The harp had come to Gwilan from her mother, and so had her mastery of it, people said. "Ah," they said when Gwilan played, "you can tell, that's Diera's touch," just as their parents had said when Diera played, "Ah, that's the true Penlin touch!" Gwilan's mother had had the harp from Penlin, a musician's dying gift to the worthiest of pupils. From a musician's hands Penlin too had received it; never had it been sold or bartered for, nor any value put upon it that can be said in numbers. A princely and most incredible instrument it was for a poor harper to own. The shape of it was perfection, and every part was strong and fine: the wood as hard and smooth as bronze, the fittings of ivory and silver. The grand curves of the frame bore silver mountings chased with long intertwining lines that became waves and the waves became leaves, and the eyes of gods and stags looked out from among the leaves that became waves and the waves became lines again. It was the work of great craftsmen, you could see that at a glance, and the longer you looked the clearer you saw it. But all this beauty was practical, obedient, shaped to the service of sound. The sound of Gwilan's harp was water running and rain and sunlight on the water, waves breaking and the foam on the brown sands, forests, the leaves and branches of the forest and the shining eyes of gods and stags among the leaves when the wind blows in the valleys. It was all that and none of that. When Gwilan played, the harp made music; and what is music but a little wrinkling of the air?

Play she did, wherever they wanted her. Her singing voice was true but had no sweetness, so when it was songs and ballads she accompanied the singers. Weak voices were

borne up by her playing, fine voices gained a glory from it; the loudest, proudest singers might keep still a verse to hear her play alone. She played with flute and reed-flute and tambour[1], and the music made for the harp to play alone, and the music that sprang up of itself when her fingers touched the strings. At weddings and festivals it was, "Gwilan will be here to play," and at music-day competitions, "When will Gwilan play?"

She was young; her hands were iron and her touch was silk; she could play all night and the next day too. She travelled from valley to valley, from town to town, stopping here and staying there and moving on again with other musicians on their wanderings. They walked, or a wagon was sent for them, or they got a lift on a farmer's cart. However they went, Gwilan carried her harp in its silk and leather case at her back or in her hands. When she rode she rode with the harp and when she walked she walked with the harp, and when she slept, no, she didn't sleep with the harp, but it was there where she could reach out and touch it. She was not jealous of it, and would change instruments with another harper gladly; it was a great pleasure to her when at last they gave her back her own, saying with sober envy, "I never played so fine an instrument." She kept it clean, the mountings polished, and strung it with the harpstrings made by old Uliad, which cost as much apiece as a whole set of common harpstrings. In the heat of summer she carried it in the shade of her body, in the bitter winter it shared her cloak. In a firelit hall she did not sit with it very near the fire, nor yet too far away, for changes of heat and cold would change the voice of it, and perhaps harm the frame. She did not look after herself with half the care. Indeed she saw no need to. She knew there were other harpers, and would be other harpers; most not as good, some better. But the harp was the best. There

had not been and there would not be a better. Delight and service were due and fitting to it. She was not its owner but its player. It was her music, her joy, her life, the noble instrument.

She was young; she travelled from town to town; she played *A Fine Long Life* at weddings, and *The Green Leaves* at festivals. There were funerals, with the burial feast, the singing of elegies, and Gwilan to play *The Lament of Orioth*, the music that crashes and cries out like the sea and the sea-birds, bringing relief and a burst of tears to the grief-dried heart. There were music-days, with a rivalry of harpers and a shrilling of fiddlers

---

1. tabour (tā′bər) n.: Small drum.

and a mighty outshouting of tenors. She went from town to town in sun and rain, the harp on her back or in her hands. So she was going one day to the yearly music-day at Comin, and the landowner of Torm Vale was giving her a lift, a man who so loved music that he had traded a good cow for a bad horse, since the cow would not take him where he could hear music played. It was he and Gwilan in a rickety cart, and the lean-necked roan stepping out down the steep, sunlit road from Torm.

A bear in the forest by the road, or a bear's ghost, or the shadow of a hawk: the horse shied half across the road. Torm had been discussing music deeply with Gwilan, waving his hands to conduct a choir of voices, and the reins went flipping out of those startled hands. The horse jumped like a cat, and ran. At the sharp curve of the road the cart swung round and smashed against the rocky cutting. A wheel leapt free and rolled, rocking like a top, for a few yards. The roan went plunging and sliding down the road with half the wrecked cart dragging behind, and was gone, and the road lay silent in the sunlight between the forest trees.

Torm had been thrown from the cart, and lay stunned for a minute or two.

Gwilan had clutched the harp to her when

the horse shied, but had lost hold if it in the smash. The cart had tipped over and dragged on it. It was in its case of leather and embroidered silk, but when, one-handed, she got the case out from under the wheel and opened it, she did not take out a harp, but a piece of wood, and another piece, and a tangle of strings, and a sliver of ivory, and a twisted shell of silver chased with lines and leaves and eyes, held by a silver nail to a fragment of the frame.

It was six months without playing after that, since her arm had broken at the wrist. The wrist healed well enough, but there was no mending the harp; and by then the landowner of Torm had asked her if she would marry him, and she had said yes. Sometimes she wondered why she had said yes, having never thought much of marriage before, but if she looked steadily into her own mind she saw the reason why. She saw Torm on the road in the sunlight kneeling by the broken harp, his face all blood and dust, and he was weeping. When she looked at that she saw that the time for rambling and roving was over and gone. One day is the day for moving on, and overnight, the next day, there is no more good in moving on, because you have come where you were going to.

Gwilan brought to the marriage a gold piece, which had been the prize last year at Four Valleys music-day; she had sewn it to her bodice as a brooch, because where on earth could you spend a gold piece. She also had two silver pieces, five coppers, and a good winter cloak. Torm contributed house and household, fields and forests, four tenant farmers even poorer than himself, twenty hens, five cows, and forty sheep.

They married in the old way, by themselves, over the spring where the stream began, and came back and told the household. Torm had never suggested a wedding, with singing and harp-playing, never a word of all that. He was a man you could trust, Torm was.

What began in pain, in tears, was never free from the fear of pain. The two of them were gentle to each other. Not that they lived together thirty years without some quarreling. Two rocks sitting side by side would get sick of each other in thirty years, and who knows what they say now and then when nobody is listening. But if people trust each other they can grumble, and a good bit of grumbling takes the fuel from wrath. Their quarrels went up and burnt out like bits of paper, leaving nothing but a feather of ash, a laugh in bed in the dark. Torm's land never gave more than enough, and there was no money saved. But it was a good house, and the sunlight was sweet on those high stony fields. There were two sons, who grew up into cheerful sensible men. One had a taste for roving, and the other was a farmer born; but neither had any gift of music.

Gwilan never spoke of wanting another harp. But about the time her wrist was healed, old Uliad had a travelling musician bring her one on loan; when he had an offer to buy it at its worth he sent for it back again. At that time Torm would have it that there was money from selling three good heifers to the landowner of Comin High Farm, and the money should buy a harp, which it did. A year or two later an old friend, a flute player still on his travels and rambles, brought her a harp from the south as a present. The three-heifers harp was a common instrument, plain and heavy; the Southern harp was delicately carved and gilt, but cranky to tune and thin of voice. Gwilan could draw sweetness from the one and strength from the other. When she picked up a harp, or spoke to a child, it obeyed her.

She played at all festivities and funerals in the neighborhood, and with the musician's fees she bought good strings; not Uliad's strings, though, for Uliad was in his grave before her second child was born. If there was a music-day nearby she went to it with Torm. She would not play in the competitions, not for fear of losing but because she

was not a harper now, and if they did not know it, she did. So they had her judge the competitions, which she did well and mercilessly. Often in the early years musicians would stop by on their travels, and stay two or three nights at Torm; with them she would play the Hunts of Orioth, the Dances of Cail, the difficult and learned music of the North, and learn from them the new songs. Even in winter evenings there was music in the house of Torm: she playing the harp—usually the three-heifers one, sometimes the fretful Southerner—and Torm's good tenor voice, and the boys singing, first a sweet treble, later on in husky unreliable baritone; and one of the farm's men was a lively fiddler; and the shepherd Keth, when he was there, played on the pipes, though he never could tune them to anyone else's note. "It's our own music-day tonight," Gwilan would

say. "Put another log on the fire, Torm, and sing *The Green Leaves* with me, and the boys will take the descant."[2]

Her wrist that had been broken grew a little stiff as the years went on; then the arthritis came into her hands. The work she did in house and farm was not easy work. But then who, looking at a hand, would say it was made to do easy work? You can see from the look of it that it is meant to do difficult things, that it is the noble, willing servant of the heart and mind. But the best servants get clumsy as the years go on. Gwilan could still play the harp, but not as well as she had played, and she did not much like half-measures. So the two harps hung on the wall, though she kept them tuned. About that time the younger son went wandering off to see what things looked like in the north, and the elder married and brought his bride to Torm. Old Keth was found dead up on the mountain in the spring rain, his dog crouched silent by him and the sheep nearby. And the drouth came, and the good year, and the poor year, and there was food to eat and to be cooked and clothes to wear and to be washed, poor year or good year. In the depth of a winter Torm took ill. He went from a cough to a high fever to quietness, and died while Gwilan sat beside him.

Thirty years, how can you say how long that is, and yet no longer than the saying of it: thirty years. How can you say how heavy the weight of thirty years is, and yet you can hold all of them together in your hand lighter than a bit of ash, briefer than a laugh in the dark. The thirty years began in pain; they passed in peace, contentment. But they did not end there. They ended where they began.

Gwilan got up from her chair and went into the hearth-room. The rest of the household were asleep. In the light of her candle she saw the two harps hung against the wall, the three-heifers harp and the gilded South-ern harp, the dull music and the false music. She thought, "I'll take them down at last and smash them on the hearthstone, crush them till they're only bits of wood and tangles of wire, like my harp." But she did not. She could not play them at all any more, her hands were far too stiff. It is silly to smash an instrument you cannot even play.

"There is no instrument left that I can play," Gwilan thought, and the thought hung in her mind for a while like a long chord, until she knew the notes that made it. "I thought my harp was myself. But it was not. It was destroyed, I was not. I thought Torm's wife was myself, but she was not. He is dead, I am not. I have nothing left at all now but myself. The wind blows from the valley, and there's a voice on the wind, a bit of a tune. Then the wind falls, or changes. The work has to be done, and we did the work. It's their turn now for that, the children. There's nothing left for me to do but sing. I never could sing. But you play the instrument you have." So she stood by the cold hearth and sang the melody of Orioth's Lament. The people of the household wakened in their beds and heard her singing, all but Torm; but he knew that tune already. The untuned strings of the harps hung on the wall wakened and answered softly, voice to voice, like eyes that shine among the leaves when the wind is blowing.

---

2. descant (dĕs′kănt) *n*.: Melody sung above the main theme.

Close Up

1. Gwilan inherited the harp from her mother. (a) Find three things she does that prove she values her harp. (b) How is her harp finally destroyed?

2. Gwilan doesn't let the destruction of her harp destroy her life. (a) How does she manage to keep music an important part of her life? (b) Though she never finds a harp as fine, do you think she still gets pleasure from playing? Why or why not?

3. At the beginning of the story, you learn that Gwilan's "singing voice was true but had no sweetness." At the end of the story, why does her voice have sweetness?

Theme

The theme of a story is its central insight into, or generalization about, life. The way a character changes during the course of a story often points to the theme.

1. At the beginning of the story, the most important thing in Gwilan's life is her harp. After her harp is destroyed, her life, of course, must change. (a) Before her harp was destroyed, how did she feel about marriage? (b) After it is destroyed, why does she agree to marry Torm? Find the statement that tells you.

2. Eventually Gwilan plays a harp again, but in a different way. What does she mean when she says that she is no longer a harper?

3. (a) At the end of this story, why does Gwilan decide to sing? (b) How does this decision reveal her ability to make the best of any situation?

4. Think about the way Gwilan has adapted to the changes in her life. Then choose the statement that you think best expresses the theme.
   a. A good harp is hard to find.
   b. People must learn to adapt to life's changes and make the best of them.
   c. Hardship or adversity can bring two people together.

Activity

► **Composition.** Imagine you are Gwilan. Write a paragraph describing your first harp.

MAIN IDEA

Understanding Supporting Details

The topic sentence expresses the main idea, the most important idea, in a paragraph. The other ideas, called supporting details, support or clarify the main idea. In the following paragraph, the topic sentence is the first sentence. Notice how the other sentences support the main idea expressed in the topic sentence.

Gwilan played whenever she was asked and for whatever occasion. She played at weddings. She played at funerals. No music-day competition was complete without Gwilan and her harp. She even accompanied singers, good and bad, who always sounded better with her accompaniment.

---

1. Develop a paragraph for each of the topic sentences below. Use details from the story in your supporting sentences.
   a. Gwilan's harp was a thing of beauty.
   b. The harp was destroyed, the victim of a cruel accident.
   c. After her wrist healed, many people encouraged Gwilan to play again.
   d. Torm and Gwilan shared a good life together.
   e. Until the day she could play no more, Gwilan shared her musical talents generously.

2. Copy each group of sentences on a piece of paper. Write *M* by the sentence in each group that expresses the main idea. Write *S* by each supporting detail.
   a. (1) When it was cold, Gwilan carried her harp beneath her cloak.
      (2) In the summer, Gwilan carried her harp in the shade of her body.
      (3) Gwilan valued her harp and tried to protect it.
      (4) Gwilan spent much time cleaning and polishing her harp.
   b. (1) At weddings Gwilan played *A Fine Long Life*.
      (2) At festivals Gwilan played *The Green Leaves*.
      (3) At burial feasts, Gwilan played The Lament of Orioth.
      (4) Gwilan knew many songs which she played on various occassions.

WORD ATTACK

Understanding Context Clues

The context of a word consists of the other words in the sentence or sentences surrounding it. Careful reading of the context will often help you define an unfamiliar word. For example, notice how the word *elegies* is defined by the context:

> "There were funerals, with the burial feast, the singing of *elegies*, and Gwilan to play *The Lament of Orioth*."

From the context you know that *elegies* must be songs sung for the dead.

▶ Use context clues to write a definition for each *italicized* word below. Then check your definitions against a dictionary.

   a. "She played with flute and reed-flute and *tambour* and music made for the harp to play alone . . ."

   b. "A bear in the forest by the road, or a bear's ghost, or the shadow of a hawk: the horse *shied* half across the road."

   c. "Even in winter evenings there was music in the house of Torm; she playing the harp—usually the three-heifers one, sometimes the fretful Southerner—and Torm's good tenor voice, and the boys singing, first a sweet *treble*, later on in husky unreliable *baritone*."

   d. "Not that they lived together thirty years without some quarreling . . . But if people trust each other they can grumble, and a good bit of grumbling takes the fuel from *wrath*."

On Summer

Lorraine Hansberry

"It seemed to me that nature had got inexcusably carried away on the summer question and let the whole thing get to be rather much."

It has taken me a good number of years to come to any measure of respect for summer. I was, being May-born, literally an "infant of the spring" and, during the later childhood years, tended, for some reason or other, to rather worship the cold aloofness of winter. Adolescence, admittedly lingering still, brought the traditional passionate commitment to melancholy autumn—and all that. For the longest kind of time I simply thought that *summer* was a mistake.

In fact, my earliest memory of anything at all is of waking up in a darkened room where I had been put to bed for a nap on a summer's afternoon, and feeling very, very hot. I acutely disliked the feeling then and retained the bias for years. It had originally been a matter of the heat but, over the years, I came actively to associate displeasure with most of the usually celebrated natural features and social

byproducts of the season: the too-grainy texture of sand; the too-cold coldness of the various waters we constantly try to escape into, and the icky-perspiry feeling of bathing caps.

It also seemed to me, aesthetically speaking, that nature had got inexcusably carried

away on the summer question and let the whole thing get to be rather much. By duration alone, for instance, a summer's day seemed maddeningly excessive; an utter overstatement. Except for those few hours at either end of it, objects always appeared in too sharp a relief against backgrounds; shad-

ows too pronounced and light too blinding. It always gave me the feeling of walking around in a motion picture which had been too artsily-craftsily exposed. Sound also had a way of coming to the ear without that muting influence, marvelously common to winter, across patios or beaches or through

the woods. I suppose I found it too stark and yet too intimate a season.

My childhood Southside summers were the ordinary city kind, full of the street games which other rememberers have turned into fine ballets these days and rhymes that anticipated what some people insist on calling modern poetry:

Oh, Mary Mack, Mack, Mack
All dressed in black, black, black
With the silver buttons, buttons, buttons
All down her back, back, back
She asked her mother, mother, mother
For fifteen cents, cents, cents
To see the elephant, elephant, elephant
Jump the fence, fence, fence
Well, he jumped so high, high, high
'Til he touched the sky, sky, sky
And he didn't come back, back, back
'Til the Fourth of Ju-ly, ly, ly!

Evenings were spent mainly on the back porches where screen doors slammed in the darkness with those really very special summertime sounds. And, sometimes, when Chicago nights got too steamy, the whole family got into the car and went to the park and slept out in the open on blankets. Those were, of course, the best times of all because the grownups were invariably reminded of having been children in rural parts of the country and told the best stories then. And it was also cool and sweet to be on the grass and there was usually the scent of freshly cut lemons or melons in the air. And Daddy would lie on his back, as fathers must, and explain about how men thought the stars above us came to be and how far away they were. I never did learn to believe that anything could be as far away as *that*. Especially the stars.

My mother first took us south to visit her Tennessee birthplace one summer when I was seven or eight, I think. I woke up on the back seat of the car while we were still driving through some place called Kentucky and my mother was pointing out to the beautiful hills on both sides of the highway and telling my brothers and my sister about how her father had run away and hidden from his master in those very hills when he was a little boy. She said that his mother had wandered among the wooded slopes in the moonlight and left food for him in secret places. They were very beautiful hills and I looked out at them for miles and miles after that wondering who and what a *master* might be.

I remember being startled when I first saw my grandmother rocking away on her porch. All my life I had heard that she was a great beauty and no one had ever remarked that they meant a half century before. The woman that I met was as wrinkled as a prune and could hardly hear and barely see and always seemed to be thinking of other times. But she could still rock and talk and even make wonderful cupcakes which were like cornbread, only sweet. She was captivated by automobiles and, even though it was well into the Thirties, I don't think she had ever been in one before we came down and took her driving. She was a little afraid of them and could not seem to negotiate the windows, but she loved driving. She died the next summer and that is all that I remember about her, except that she was born in slavery and had memories of it and they didn't sound anything like *Gone with the Wind*.

Like everyone else, I have spent whole or bits of summers in many different kinds of places since then: camps and resorts in the Middle West and New York State; on an island; in a tiny Mexican village; Cape Cod, perched atop the Truro bluffs at Longnook Beach that Millay[1] wrote about; or simply strolling the streets of Provincetown before the hours when the cocktail parties begin.

---

1. Millay: Edna St. Vincent Millay (mĭ-lā′), 1892–1950. A famous American poet.

And, lastly, I do not think that I will forget days spent, a few summers ago, at a beautiful lodge built right into the rocky cliffs of a bay on the Maine coast. We met a woman there who had lived a purposeful and courageous life and who was then dying of cancer. She had, characteristically, just written a book and taken up painting. She had also been of radical viewpoint all her life; one of those people who energetically believe that the world *can* be changed for the better and spend their lives trying to do just that. And that was the way she thought of cancer; she absolutely refused to award it the stature of tragedy, a devastating instance of the brooding doom and inexplicability of the absurdity of human destiny, etc., etc. The kind of characterization given, lately, as we all know, to far less formidable foes in life than cancer.

But for this remarkable woman it was a matter of nature in imperfection, implying, as always, work for man to do. It was an *enemy*, but a palpable one with shape and effect and source; and if it existed, it could be destroyed. She saluted it accordingly, without despondency, but with a lively, beautiful and delightfully ribald anger. There was one thing, she felt, which would prove equal to its relentless ravages and that was the genius of man. Not his mysticism, but man with tubes and slides and the stubborn human notion that the stars are very much within our reach.

The last time I saw her she was sitting surrounded by her paintings with her manuscript laid out for me to read, because, she said, she wanted to know what a *young person* would think of her thinking; one must always keep up with what *young people* thought about things because, after all, they were *change*.

Every now and then her jaw set in anger as we spoke of things people should be angry about. And then, for relief, she would look out at the lovely bay at a mellow sunset settling on the water. Her face softened with love of all that beauty and, watching her, I

wished with all my power what I knew that she was wishing: that she might live to see at least one more summer. Through her eyes I finally gained the sense of what it might mean: more than the coming autumn with its pretentious melancholy; more than an austere and silent winter which must shut dying people in for precious months; more even than the frivolous spring, too full of too many false promises, would be the gift of another summer with its stark and intimate assertion of neither birth nor death but life at the apex; with the gentlest nights and, above all, the longest days.

I heard later that she did live to see another summer. And I have retained my respect for the noblest of the seasons.

Close Up

1. Lorraine Hansberry says, "For the longest kind of time I simply thought that *summer* was a mistake." (a) List three things she disliked about summer. (b) What one thing about summer did she like when she was growing up in Chicago?

2. One summer she spends some time with her grandmother in Tennessee. (a) What does she admire about her grandmother? (b) What does she admire about the woman she meets in Maine?

3. Early in this essay, Hansberry complains about the long days of summer. After meeting the woman in Maine, the "longest days" take on a different meaning. What do these long days give a person time to do?

Theme

Sometimes the narrator of an essay makes several statements that point to theme. In this essay, Lorraine Hansberry tells you certain things she learned. Her statements help you understand the theme of the essay.

1. On summer nights in Chicago, Hansberry's father would teach her about the stars and how far away they are. (a) What does Hansberry say she believed about the stars? (b) On the other hand, the woman in Maine teaches her "that the stars are very much within our reach." What does this statement mean?

2. Hansberry says that through this woman she finally gained a sense of what summer means. Find the statement that shows what summer has come to mean to her.

3. Think about what Hansberry learns about summer, and through this, about life. Then choose the statement that best expresses the theme.
   a. The long days of summer are better than the short days of winter.
   b. People need to face life as it is and fight to overcome their problems.
   c. Mysticism helps people to overcome their problems.

Activities

1. List five things you like about summer. List five things you dislike.

2. Use your library to find information about Lorraine Hansberry. Share your information with your classmates.

MAIN IDEA

Finding the Topic and the Main Idea

A paragraph is a group of sentences about one subject, or topic. Usually, the topic of a paragraph can be stated in just one word, or in a few words. For example, the topic of a paragraph may be *summer*, or *my mother*, or *heat*. To find the topic of a paragraph, ask "What is this paragraph about?"

The main idea of a paragraph is the most important idea about the topic. Sometimes the main idea is stated in a topic sentence. Sometimes the paragraph does not have a topic sentence, and the main idea has to be inferred.

In the following paragraph the topic is *my opinion of summer*. The main idea is expressed in the first sentence, the topic sentence.

> *"It has taken me a good number of years to come to any measure of respect for summer.* I was, being May-born, literally an 'infant of the spring' and, during the later childhood years, tended, for some reason or other, to rather worship the cold aloofness of winter. The adolescence, admittedly lingering still, brought the traditional passionate commitment to melancholy autumn—and all that. For the longest kind of time I simply thought that *summer* was a mistake."

▶ Read the paragraphs below and answer the questions following each.

a. "In fact, my earliest memory of anything at all is of waking up in a darkened room where I had been put to bed for a nap on a summer's afternoon, and feeling very, very hot. I acutely disliked the feeling then and retained the bias for years. It had originally been a matter of the heat but, over the years, I came actively to associate displeasure with most of the usually celebrated natural features and social byproducts of the season: the too-grainy texture of sand; the too-cold coldness of the various waters we constantly try to escape into, and the icky-perspiry feeling of bathing caps."

The topic of this paragraph is *Hansberry's dislike of summer*. The paragraph has a topic sentence. What is it? State the main idea in your own words.

b. "It also seemed to me, aesthetically speaking, that nature had got inexcusably carried away on the summer question and let the whole thing get to be rather much. By duration alone, for instance, a summer's day seemed maddeningly excessive; an utter overstatement. Except for those few hours at either end of it, objects always appeared in too sharp a relief against backgrounds; shadows too pronounced and light too blinding. It always gave me the feeling of walking around in a motion picture which had been too artsily-craftsily exposed. Sound also had a way of coming to the ear without that muting influence, marvelously common to winter, across patios or beaches or through the woods. I supose I found it too stark and yet too intimate a season."

The topic sentence is the first sentence in the paragraph. State the topic in your own words.

WORD ATTACK

Finding Word Origins in a Dictionary

Many words in the English language have traveled through the various stages of the English language or have been borrowed from other languages. The word *summer*, for example, has traveled through Old English *(sumor)* to Middle English *(sumer)* to its present form in Modern English. The word *pretentious* has its origin in Latin *(praetentus)*.

Dictionary entries provide information about the origin of words. The following abbreviations are often used in dictionaries:

OE	Old English	**Sp**	Spanish
ME	Middle English	**It**	Italian
L	Latin	**Mex-Sp**	Mexican Spanish
F	French	**Gk**	Greek

▶ Use a dictionary to trace the origins of the following words. On a piece of paper, list the origin or origins for each. For example, the word *memory* has traveled through Greek (Gk), Latin (L), French (F), and Middle English (ME).

a. woman
b. rhyme
c. summer
d. melancholy
e. adolescence
f. autumn
g. memory
h. tragedy
i. absurd
j. palpable

The Bishop's Candlesticks

Dramatized by Van Dusen Rickert, Jr.
from *Les Misérables* by Victor Hugo

Characters

Monseigneur Bienvenu, Bishop of Digne

Mademoiselle Baptistine, His sister

Madame Magloire, Their servant

Jean Valjean, An ex-convict

A Sergeant and two Police Officers

Scene The home of the Bishop

Scene One

The living room of the Bishop of Digne, a large, oblong room plainly furnished, scrupulously neat. The walls are whitewashed. There is no carpet. A fire burns in the fireplace down right; an alcove, closed by portieres, occupies the upstage center. A door leading outdoors is in the wall left of the alcove. Against the wall up left stands a sturdy dresser. Down left a door leads to a passage.

The Bishop and his Sister are finishing their supper. It is late evening of a winter day. The room is lighted by firelight and two candles which stand on the table in handsome silver candlesticks.

Mlle. Baptistine: Will you have coffee, brother?

The Bishop: If you please.

Mlle. Baptistine: I'll ring for Madame Magloire. . . .

(Mme. Magloire enters from the passage.)

The Bishop. But here she is—and bringing our coffee. Madame Magloire, you are wonderful; you read our minds.

Mme. Magloire: I should be able to, after all these years.

The Bishop: Of faithful service—and mind reading.

Mme. Magloire: Thank you, my lord.

Mlle. Baptistine: We'll drink our coffee in front of the fire, Madame Magloire.

Mme. Magloire: Yes, mademoiselle. Let me stir up that fire a little. Such a cold night!

Mlle. Baptistine: I'm glad all our poor have fuel and food. (*Sits at fireplace and pours coffee.*)

The Bishop: Not all, I'm afraid.

Mlle. Baptistine: I meant all in the parish.

The Bishop: If we could only help them all! My heart aches on a night like this to think of poor homeless wanderers, lonely, hungry——

Mlle. Baptistine: Not all of them deserve help, I'm afraid. Some of them are good-for-nothing, ungrateful vagabonds.

Mme. Magloire: They say there's a tough-looking fellow in town now. He came along the boulevard and tried to get in to spend the night at the hotel. Of course they threw him out. A tramp with a sack over his shoulder and a terrible face. An ugly brute! (*She brings the candlesticks from the table and sets them on the mantlepiece above the fireplace.*)

The Bishop: There are no human brutes; there are only miserable men who have been unfortunate.

Mme. Magloire (*she is clearing the table*): You are as kindhearted as the good Lord himself, Bishop; but when there are fellows like that around, we say—mademoiselle and I . . .

Mlle. Baptistine: I have said nothing.

Mme. Magloire: Well . . . we say that his house isn't safe. If you don't mind, I'm going to send for the locksmith to put bolts on these doors. It's terrible to leave these doors unfastened, so that anybody can walk in. And the Bishop always calls "Come in!" the minute anyone knocks.

(There is a loud knock.)

The Bishop: Come in.

(Jean Valjean appears in the doorway. Mlle. Baptistine gasps; Mme. Magloire suppresses a cry. There is a silence.)

Valjean: My name's Jean Valjean. I'm a convict. I've been nineteen years in prison at hard labor. I got out four days ago, and I'm on my way to Pontarlier. I've come twenty-five miles on foot today, and I'm tired and hungry. Nobody'll take me in, because I've got a convict's passport—yellow. See! They've kicked me out like a dog everywhere I stopped. I even went to the jail and asked for lodging, but the turnkey said, "Get yourself arrested, if you want to spend the night here." Then a good woman pointed out your door to me and said, "Knock there." So I did. I'm tired. Can I stay?

The Bishop: Madame Magloire, will you set another place and bring some food?

Valjean: Wait a minute. Did you understand? I'm a convict. There's my yellow passport. Take a look at it. It says nineteen years in prison—five years for burglary and fourteen for attempted escape. It says, "This man is dangerous." Dangerous! Well, are you going to take me in?

The Bishop: Won't you sit down, monsieur? Madame Magloire, you may make up the bed in the alcove.

Valjean (*lowers his sack to the floor*):

"Monsieur!" You call me "monsieur!" And you're not going to put me out! (*Mme. Magloire places food on the table.*) That looks good. (*He sits.*) I've been starving for four days. (*He begins to eat avidly.*) I'll pay you for this. I've got some money to pay you with. . . . You're an innkeeper, aren't you?

The Bishop: I'm a priest.

Valjean: Oh, a priest . . . a good priest. . . . That's a good one! Then you don't want me to pay——

The Bishop: No, no. Keep your money. How much have you?

Valjean: One hundred and nine francs.

The Bishop: And how long did it take you to earn that?

Valjean: Nineteen years.

The Bishop (*sighing*): Nineteen years.

Valjean: Yes, they pay us something for the work we do in prison. Not much, of course; but we get a little out of it. I really earned one hundred and seventy-one francs, but they didn't give me that much. I've still got all they paid me.

The Bishop: Madame Magloire, will you bring the candles to the table? It is a little dark over here.

Mlle. Baptistine (*timidly*): Did you . . . could you ever go to Mass while you were—in there?

Valjean: Yes, ma'am. They said Mass at an altar in the middle of the courtyard. You'll be interested in this, monsieur, since you're a priest. Once we had a bishop come to say Mass—"my lord," they called him. He's a priest who's over a lot of other priests. He said Mass and wore a pointed gold thing on his head. He wasn't close to us. We were drawn up in lines on three sides of the courtyard. We couldn't understand what he said. That was the only time we ever saw a bishop.

The Bishop: That's very interesting.

Mlle. Baptistine: How happy your family will be to see you again after so many years.

Valjean: I haven't got any family.

Mlle. Baptistine: Haven't you any relatives at all? Is there no one waiting for you?

Valjean: No, nobody. I had a sister. I used to live with her and her children, but I don't know what's become of her. She may have gone to Paris.

Mlle. Baptistine: Didn't she write to you sometimes?

Valjean: I haven't heard from her in twelve years. I'll never bother her again.

The Bishop: And you're going to Pontarlier. Do you know anyone there?

Valjean: No, I don't. It's not my part of the country; but I visited there once when I was young, and I liked it—high mountains, good air, and not too many people. I thought about it often in prison and made up my mind to go there if ever—if I ever was free.

The Bishop: You're going to a fine country, and there is plenty of work there: paper mills, tanneries, copper and iron foundries; and there are dairy farms all through the region. You'll have to find work, of course. What do you want to do?

Valjean: It doesn't matter. I can do any kind of work. I'm as tough as steel. But, with a yellow passport, I don't know whether I can get a job.

The Bishop (*writing*): Here, take this card. If you will give it to Monsieur Doumic from me . . . he has a tannery at Pontarlier and, what is more important, he has a heart. He will not ask you too many questions.

Valjean: Thank you, monsieur. You've been so kind, giving me this good dinner and taking me in—and all. . . . I ought to tell you my name.

The Bishop: You have a name I know without your telling me.

Valjean: Is that right? You already knew my name?

The Bishop: Yes. Your name is . . . my brother. You need not tell me who you are. Those who come to this door are not asked "What is your name?" but "What is your need . . . or sorrow?"

Valjean: I've seen plenty of that. There's

nothing else in prison. If you complain—solitary confinement. Double chains, just for nothing at all. A dog is better off than a convict! I had nineteen years of it—because I stole some food. And now I'm forty-six, and I have a yellow passport.

The Bishop: You have left behind you a sad and terrible place. If you have come from it with a little kindness or peace in your heart, then you are better than any one of us.

Mme. Magloire: The bed is made now.

The Bishop: Thank you, Madame Magloire. You may clear the table. And, monsieur, we know you are very tired. My sister and I will leave you to your rest. Do you need anything else?

Valjean: No . . . thanks.

The Bishop: Then good night, monsieur.

Mlle. Baptistine: Good night, monsieur.

(Exit left, followed by the Bishop. Jean Valjean carries his sack to the bed. Mme. Magloire comes from the kitchen carrying silver, which she puts away in the dresser. Jean Valjean watches her. When she leaves the room, he goes to the table and takes up one of the candlesticks. He looks toward the dresser. The Bishop enters.)

The Bishop: I've brought you an extra cover, monsieur. It is a doeskin I bought in Germany, in the Black Forest. This is better than a blanket for warmth.

(Jean Valjean puts down the candlestick as the Bishop speaks.)

Valjean (*harshly*): Are you going to let me sleep in your house like this? You'd better think it over. I'm a thief, you know. How do you know I'm not a murderer?

The Bishop: That is as God wills it, brother.

(He blesses Jean Valjean and goes slowly out of the room. Jean Valjean looks after the Bishop, motionless and unyielding. Then he blows out the candles and goes to the alcove, where he lies down on the bed without undressing.)

[curtain]

Scene Two

The room is dark. Jean Valjean sits on the bed. After a moment he rises and takes up his pack and tiptoes toward the door. He hesitates, looking at the dresser; then he goes to it, opens it, and takes out silver; he crouches beside his pack, putting the silver into it. There is a sound as he thrusts the silver into the pack. Alarmed, he starts up, leaving the silver basket on the floor, catches up the pack, and goes hastily out of the door.

[curtain]

Scene Three

It is morning. Mme. Magloire enters with dishes. Going directly to the table, she notices that the bed is unoccupied. Without seeing the basket, she runs to the dresser and finds that the silver is gone.

Mme. Magloire: Good heavens! Oh, good

heavens! Mademoiselle! Monseigneur! What will the Bishop say! Oh, Mademoiselle!

(Mlle. Baptistine enters.)

Mlle. Baptistine: Good morning, Mademoiselle Magloire. What's the matter?

Mme. Magloire: Mademoiselle! The dresser is open—and that man is gone! The silver—all our knives and forks! Where are they?

Mlle. Baptistine: You put them away there last night?

Mme. Magloire: Yes, yes, just as I always do. And now there's nothing here! Oh, my lord.

(The Bishop enters. He sees the silver basket and the empty alcove.)

The Bishop: What is it, Mademoiselle Magloire?

Mme. Magloire: The silver! Does your lordship know where the silver basket is?

The Bishop: Yes.

Mme. Magloire: Oh, thank heaven! I didn't know what had become of it.

The Bishop (*picking up the empty basket and handing it to her*): Here it is.

Mme. Magloire: Well, but—there's nothing in it. Where's the silver?

The Bishop: Oh, then it's the silver you're worried about. I don't know where it is.

Mme. Magloire: Then it's stolen! Knives, forks, spoons—all gone. That vagabond stole them. He's gone, you see—cleared out before any of us were awake. The scoundrel!

The Bishop: Well, let's consider. In the first place, was the silver ours?

Mme. Magloire: Ours? And why not?

The Bishop: Madame Magloire, I had no right to keep that silver so long. It belonged to the poor. And this man was one of the poor, wasn't he?

Mme. Magloire: Oh, it isn't that I mind for myself—or mademoiselle. But, my lord, what will you eat with?

The Bishop: There are tin spoons.

Mme. Magloire (*with great disgust*): Tin smells.

The Bishop: And there are iron spoons.

Mme. Magloire: Iron tastes!

The Bishop (*chuckling*): Well, well—then there are wooden spoons. Tell me sister, do you regret having given that poor fellow food and shelter?

Mlle. Baptistine: Not at all. I shall pray for him. Somehow I have a feeling that we may hear more of him.

(They sit at the table.)

Mme. Magloire: When I think of that cutthroat spending the night here! Suppose he had taken it into his head to kill us instead of stealing from us.

Mlle. Baptistine: He'll probably make haste to get as far away as he can. He wouldn't try to sell the silver in this neighborhood.

Mme. Magloire: I hope he'll take good care never to come this way again.

(There is a knock at the door. Mme. Magloire and Mlle. Baptistine are startled.)

The Bishop: Come in.

(A sergeant and two policemen, guarding Jean Valjean, appear at the door.)

Sergeant: Your excellency——

The Bishop: Come in, officer.

Valjean (*he looks up, surprised*): Excellency? Then he isn't a priest?

Policeman: Be quiet, you. This is the Bishop.

The Bishop: Oh, it's you. I'm glad to see you. Why did you go off so early and without the candlesticks? They're solid silver and I gave them to you, as well as the other pieces. You can easily get two hundred francs for the pair.

Sergeant: Your excellency, we wanted to

know if this fellow was telling the truth. We stopped him on suspicion and found that he had a yellow passport and this silver.

The Bishop: And he told you the silver was given him by a good old priest at whose house he spent last night.

Sergeant: He did, your excellency.

The Bishop: I see it all. Then you brought him back here. Well, it's just a misunderstanding.

Sergeant: Then we can let him go?

The Bishop: Of course, let him go.

(The sergeant hands the silver to Valgean.)

Valjean: You mean I'm free?

Policeman: Yes, it's all right. You're free.

The Bishop: But, before you go, here are your candlesticks. Take them with you.

Valjean: Monsieur . . . monseigneur . . . I . . . *(He stands silent, with bowed head.)*

The Bishop: Ah—good morning, officer. You and your men were quite right in doing your duty. Good morning.

Sergeant: Good day, your excellency.

(The sergeant and policemen close the door and leave.)

Mlle. Baptistine *(very softly)*: Come, Madame Magloire.

(They slip discreetly out the door down left.)

The Bishop: Now, Jean Valjean, you may go in peace. But never forget that you have promised me to use that silver to make yourself an honest man.

Valjean *(slowly)*: I didn't promise. . . . But I . . .

The Bishop: Jean Valjean, my brother, you no longer belong to evil, but to good. It is your soul that I am buying for you. It belongs to God. Will you give it to Him?

Valjean *(almost inaudibly)*: Yes, Father. *(He kneels.)*

[curtain]

Close Up

1. The Bishop welcomes Jean Valjean into his home, even though Valjean has a yellow passport. How else does the Bishop try to help Valjean?

2. When Valjean thanks the Bishop for the dinner, he wants to tell him his name. (a) What does the Bishop mean when he says to Valjean, "You have a name I know without your telling me"? (b) What does this tell you about the Bishop's attitude toward all human beings?

3. In the morning, the Bishop finds that his silver is gone. Do you think he is surprised? Why or why not?

4. The Bishop has a special reason for letting Valjean have the silver. (a) What does he mean when he says, "It is your soul I am buying for you"? (b) Do you think the Bishop's plan is successful? Why or why not?

Symbol

A symbol is a real object that also stands for something else. For example, a flag is a real object, but sometimes it is used to stand for freedom. When you see a symbol in a story, it often provides a clue to the story's theme.

1. Jean Valjean steals the silver because it is valuable. What does the Bishop say that shows he cares little about the monetary value of the silver?

2. The Bishop understands that for Jean Valjean the silver candlesticks also represent hope and promise of a better life. What promise does he extract from Valjean in return for the silver candlesticks?

3. What do you think this story says about the need for hope in a person's life?

Activities

1. **Composition.** It is five years later. Write a paragraph explaining what has become of Jean Valjean.

2. **Composition.** Write a paragraph showing that the Bishop is a good man.

MAIN IDEA

Finding Implied Main Ideas

The main idea of a paragraph is the most important idea about the topic of the paragraph. Sometimes the main idea is implied or suggested rather than stated in the topic sentence. When the main idea is implied, you must look at the details in the paragraph and form your own statement expressing the main idea. For example, look at the following paragraph.

> "My name's Jean Valjean. I'm a convict. I've been nineteen years in prison at hard labor. I got out four days ago, and I'm on my way to Pontarlier. I've come twenty-five miles on foot today, and I'm tired and hungry. Nobody'll take me in, because I've got a convict's pass-port—yellow. See! They've kicked me out like a dog everywhere I stopped. I even went to the jail and asked for lodging, but the turnkey said, 'Get yourself arrested, if you want to spend the night here.' Then a good woman pointed out your door to me and said, 'Knock there.' So I did. I'm tired. Can I stay?"

The main idea of this paragraph is: Jean Valjean is tired and hungry, but because he has a yellow passport, he can't find a place to spend the night.

---

1. Read each paragraph below. Then write a sentence expressing the main idea.

   a. "Yes, ma'am. They said Mass at an altar in the middle of the courtyard. You'll be interested in this, monsieur, since you're a priest. Once we had a bishop come to say Mass—'my lord,' they called him. He's a priest who's over a lot of other priests. He said Mass and wore a point-ed gold thing on his head. He wasn't close to us. We were drawn up in lines on three sides of the courtyard. We couldn't understand what he said. That was the only time we ever saw a bishop."

   b. *"The room is dark. Jean Valjean sits on the bed. After a moment he rises and takes up his pack and tiptoes toward the door. He hesitates, looking at the dresser; then he goes to it, opens it, and takes out silver; he crouches beside his pack, putting the silver into it. There is a sound as he thrusts the silver into the pack. Alarmed, he starts up, leaving the silver basket on the floor, catches up the pack, and goes hastily out the door."*

2. Reread paragraph 1, column b, on p. 403. What is the main idea?

WORD ATTACK

Forming Adverbs from Adjectives

An adjective is a word that modifies a noun or a pronoun. For example, *silver* plates, *good* man, *many* people. **An adverb is a word that modifies a verb, an adjective, or an adverb.** For example, *unusually* healthy, ran *quickly*.

Sometimes you can form adverbs from adjectives by adding the suffix –*ly* to the end of the adjective. For example, faithful—faithfully.

> faithful (adjective)—the faithful servant
> faithfully (adverb)—the servant worked faithfully

▶ On a separate piece of paper, copy each pair of sentences below. In the first sentence of each pair, an adjective is printed in *italics*. Add –*ly* to this adjective to form the adverb, and write it in the blank in the second sentence.

a. Jean Valjean was *hopeless* and frightened.
He worked _____ through the night.

b. The punishment was *cruel*.
He was punished _____.

c. The innkeeper thought he was *fearful*.
He asked for a room _____.

d. Mme. Magloire wanted a *proper* bolt for the door.
She wanted the door bolted _____.

e. A *wise* person would look out for himself.
A person should act _____.

f. He wore a *sullen* expression on his face.
He backed away _____.

g. The people thought the tramp looked *suspicious*.
He peered in the doorway _____.

h. The bishop gave him a *generous* gift.
The bishop _____ gave him a gift.

i. He offered his *warm* thanks.
He thanked him _____.

j. The treatment was *brutal* and *unfair*.
They were treated _____ and _____.

Virtuoso

Herbert Goldstone

"Sir?"

The Maestro continued to play, not looking up from the keys.

"Yes, Rollo?"

"Sir, I was wondering if you would explain this apparatus to me."

The Maestro stopped playing, his thin body stiffly relaxed on the bench. His long supple fingers floated off the keyboard.

"Apparatus?" He turned and smiled at the robot. "Do you mean the piano, Rollo?"

"This machine that produces varying sounds. I would like some information about it, its operation and purpose. It is not included in my reference data."

The Maestro lit a cigarette. He preferred to do it himself. One of his first orders to Rollo when the robot was delivered two days before had been to disregard his built-in instructions on the subject.

"I'd hardly call a piano a machine, Rollo," he smiled, "although technically you are correct. It is actually, I suppose, a machine designed to produce sounds of graduated pitch and tone, singly or in groups."

"I assimilated that much by observation,"

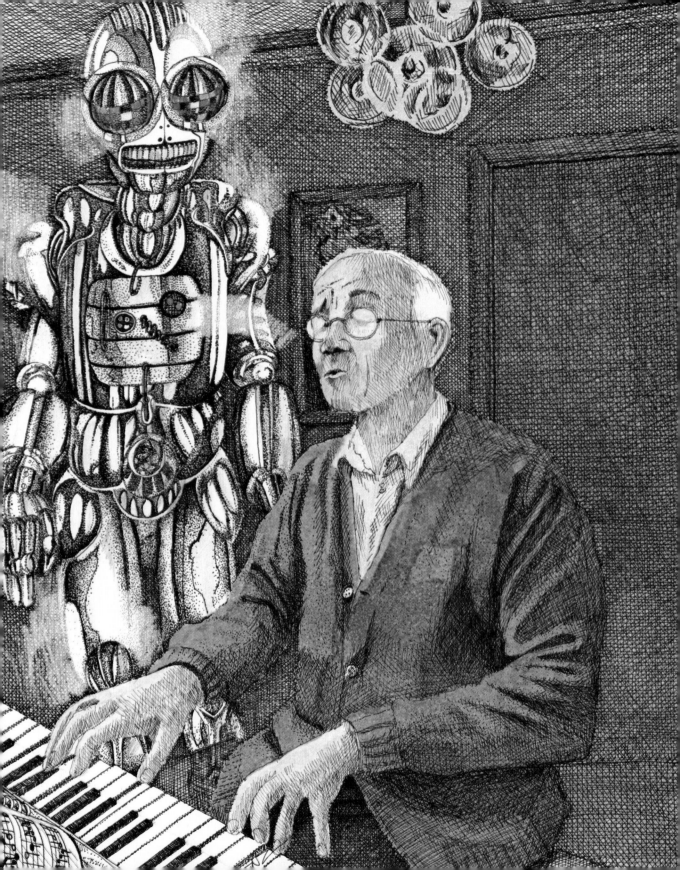

Rollo replied in a brassy baritone which no longer sent tiny tremors up the Maestro's spine. "Wires of different thickness and tautness struck by felt-covered hammers activated by manually operated levers arranged in a horizontal panel."

"A very cold-blooded description of one of man's nobler works," the Maestro remarked dryly. "You make Mozart and Chopin mere laboratory technicians."

"Mozart? Chopin?" The duralloy sphere that was Rollo's head shone stark and featureless, its immediate surface unbroken but for twin vision lenses. "The terms are not included in my memory banks."

"No, not yours, Rollo," the Maestro said softly. "Mozart and Chopin are not for vacuum tubes and fuses and copper wire. They are for flesh and blood and human tears."

"I do not understand," Rollo droned.

"Well," the Maestro said, smoke curling lazily from his nostrils, "they are two of the humans who compose, or design su·cessions of notes—varying sounds, that is, produced by the piano or by other instruments, machines that produce other types of sounds of fixed pitch and tone.

"Sometimes these instruments, as we call them, are played, or operated, individually: sometimes in groups—orchestras, as we refer to them—and the sounds blend together, they harmonize. That is, they have an orderly, mathematical relationship to each other which results in . . ."

The Maestro threw up his hands.

"I never imagined," he chuckled, "that I would some day struggle so mightily, and so futilely, to explain music to a robot!"

"Music?"

"Yes, Rollo. The sounds produced by this machine and others of the same category are called music."

"What is the purpose of music, sir?"

"Purpose?"

The Maestro crushed the cigarette in an ashtray. He turned to the keyboard of the concert grand and flexed his fingers briefly.

"Listen, Rollo."

The wraithlike fingers glided and wove the opening bars of "Clair de Lune," slender and delicate as spider silk. Rollo stood rigid, the fluorescent light over the music rack casting a bluish jeweled sheen over his towering bulk, shimmering in the amber vision lenses.

The Maestro drew his hands back from the keys and the subtle thread of melody melted reluctantly into silence.

"Claude Debussy," the Maestro said. "One of our mechanics of an era long past. He designed that succession of tones many years ago. What do you think of it?"

Rollo did not answer at once.

"The sounds were well formed," he replied finally. "They did not jar my auditory senses as some do."

The Maestro laughed. "Rollo, you may not realize it, but you're a wonderful critic."

"This music, then," Rollo droned. "Its purpose is to give pleasure to humans?"

"Exactly," the Maestro said. "Sounds well formed, that do not jar the auditory senses as some do. Marvelous! It should be carved in marble over the entrance of New Carnegie Hall."

"I do not understand. Why should my definition——?"

The Maestro waved a hand. "No matter, Rollo. No matter."

"Sir?"

"Yes, Rollo?"

"Those sheets of paper you sometimes place before you on the piano. They are the plans of the composer indicating which sounds are to be produced by the piano and in what order?"

"Just so. We call each sound a note; combinations of notes we call chords."

"Each dot, then, indicates a sound to be made?"

"Perfectly correct, my man of metal."

Rollo stared straight ahead. The Maestro felt a peculiar sense of wheels turning within that impregnable sphere.

"Sir, I have scanned my memory banks and find no specific or implied instructions against it. I should like to be taught how to produce these notes on the piano. I request that you feed the correlation between those dots and the levers of the panel into my memory banks."

The Maestro peered at him, amazed. A slow grin traveled across his face.

"Done!" he exclaimed. "It's been many years since pupils helped gray these ancient locks, but I have the feeling that you, Rollo, will prove a most fascinating student. To instill the Muse into metal and machinery . . . . I accept the challenge gladly!"

He rose, touched the cool latent power of Rollo's arm.

"Sit down here, my Rolleindex Personal Robot, Model M-e. We shall start Beethoven spinning in his grave—or make musical history."

More than an hour later the Maestro yawned and looked at his watch.

"It's late," he spoke into the end of the yawn. "These old eyes are not tireless like yours, my friend." He touched Rollo's shoulder. "You have the complete fundamentals of musical notation in your memory banks, Rollo. That's a good night's lesson, particularly when I recall how long it took me to acquire the same amount of information. Tomorrow we'll attempt to put those awesome fingers of yours to work."

He stretched. "I'm going to bed," he said. "Will you lock up and put out the lights?"

Rollo rose from the bench. "Yes, sir," he droned. "I have a request."

"What can I do for my star pupil?"

"May I attempt to create some sounds with the keyboard tonight? I will do so very softly so as not to disturb you."

"Tonight? Aren't you——?" Then the Maestro smiled. "You must pardon me, Rollo. It's still a bit difficult for me to realize that sleep has no meaning for you."

He hesitated, rubbing his chin. "Well, I suppose a good teacher should not discour-age impatience to learn. All right, Rollo, but please be careful." He patted the polished mahogany. "This piano and I have been together for many years. I'd hate to see its teeth knocked out by those sledgehammer digits of yours. Lightly, my friend, very lightly."

"Yes, sir."

The Maestro fell asleep with a faint smile on his lips, dimly aware of the shy, tentative notes that Rollo was coaxing forth.

Then gray fog closed in and he was in that half-world where reality is dreamlike and dreams are real. It was soft and feathery and lavender clouds and sounds were rolling and washing across his mind in flowing waves.

Where? The mist drew back a bit and he was in red velvet and deep and the music swelled and broke over him.

He smiled.

My recording. Thank you, thank you, thank——

The Maestro snapped erect, threw the covers aside.

He sat on the edge of the bed, listening.

He groped for his robe in the darkness, shoved bony feet into his slippers.

He crept, trembling uncontrollably, to the door of his studio and stood there, thin and brittle in the robe.

The light over the music rack was an eerie island in the brown shadows of the studio. Rollo sat at the keyboard, prim, inhuman, rigid, twin lenses focused somewhere off into the shadows.

The massive feet working the pedals, arms and hands flashing and glinting—they were living entities, separate, somehow, from the machined perfection of his body.

The music rack was empty.

A copy of Beethoven's "Appassionata" lay closed on the bench. It had been, the Maestro remembered, in a pile of sheet music on the piano.

Rollo was playing it.

He was creating it, breathing it, drawing it through silver flame.

Time became meaningless, suspended in midair.

The Maestro didn't realize he was weeping until Rollo finished the sonata.

The robot turned to look at the Maestro. "The sounds," he droned. "They pleased you?"

The Maestro's lips quivered. "Yes, Rollo," he replied at last. "They pleased me." He fought the lump in his throat.

He picked up the music in fingers that shook.

"This," he murmured. "Already?"

"It has been added to my store of data," Rollo replied. "I applied the principles you explained to me to these plans. It was not very difficult."

The Maestro swallowed as he tried to speak. "It was not very difficult . . ." he repeated softly.

The old man sank down slowly onto the bench next to Rollo, stared silently at the robot as though seeing him for the first time.

Rollo got to his feet.

The Maestro let his fingers rest on the keys, strangely foreign now.

"Music!" he breathed. "I may have heard it that way in my soul. I know Beethoven did!"

He looked up at the robot, a growing excitement in his face.

"Rollo," he said, his voice straining to remain calm. "You and I have some work to do tomorrow on your memory banks."

Sleep did not come again that night.

He strode briskly into the studio the next morning. Rollo was vacuuming the carpet. The Maestro preferred carpets to the new dust-free plastics, which felt somehow profane to his feet.

The Maestro's house was, in fact, an oasis of anachronisms[1] in a desert of contemporary antiseptic efficiency.

---

1. anachronisms (ə-năk′ rə-nīz′əmz) n.: Things out of their proper time.

"Well, are you ready for work, Rollo?" he asked. "We have a lot to do, you and I. I have such plans for you, Rollo—great plans!"

Rollo, for once, did not reply.

"I have asked them all to come here this afternoon," the Maestro went on. "Conductors, concert pianists, composers, my manager. All the giants of music, Rollo. Wait until they hear you play."

Rollo switched off the vacuum and stood quietly.

"You'll play for them right here this afternoon." The Maestro's voice was high-pitched, breathless. "The 'Appassionata' again, I think. Yes, that's it. I must see their faces!

"Then we'll arrange a recital to introduce you to the public and the critics and then a major concerto with one of the big orchestras. We'll have it telecast around the world, Rollo. It can be arranged.

"Think of it, Rollo, just think of it! The greatest piano virtuoso of all time . . . a robot! It's completely fantastic and completely wonderful. I feel like an explorer at the edge of a new world."

He walked feverishly back and forth.

"Then recordings, of course. My entire repertoire, Rollo, and more. So much more!"

"Sir?"

The Maestro's face shone as he looked up at him. "Yes, Rollo?"

"In my built-in instructions, I have the option of rejecting any action which I consider harmful to my owner," the robot's words were precise, carefully selected. "Last night you wept. That is one of the indications I am instructed to consider in making my decisions."

The Maestro gripped Rollo's thick, superbly molded arm.

"Rollo, you don't understand. That was for the moment. It was petty of me, childish!"

"I beg your pardon, sir, but I must refuse to approach the piano again."

The Maestro stared at him, unbelieving, pleading.

"Rollo, you can't! The world must hear you!"

"No, sir." The amber lenses almost seemed to soften.

"The piano is not a machine," that powerful inhuman voice droned. "To me, yes. I can translate the notes into sounds at a glance. From only a few I am able to grasp at once the composer's conception. It is easy for me."

Rollo towered magnificently over the Maestro's bent form.

"I can also grasp," the brassy monotone rolled through the studio, "that this . . . music is not for robots. It is for man. To me it is easy, yes. . . . It was not meant to be easy."

Close Up

1. (a) What is Rollo's definition of music? (b) Why does the Maestro agree to teach Rollo to play the piano?

2. (a) In the midst of a dream, the Maestro hears Rollo playing. Find a sentence describing the music. (b) Why does the music make the Maestro cry?

3. A virtuoso is a masterly performer. To become a virtuoso requires years of practice and sacrifice. (a) Why is Rollo able to become a virtuoso so quickly? (b) At the end of the story, what does Rollo mean when he says that music was not meant to be easy?

Theme

Sometimes a character performs a significant, or important, action. This action points to the story's theme.

1. This story centers on music. (a) How would you describe Rollo's reaction to music? (b) How would you describe the Maestro's reaction?

2. (a) What effect does Rollo's playing have on the Maestro? (b) How does Rollo interpret the Maestro's reaction?

3. Rollo performs a significant action when he recognizes something about human beings and refuses to play the piano. Why does he refuse to play?

4. Which statement below best expresses the theme?
   a. Many people need to reach for beauty, although they know beauty will be beyond their grasp.
   b. Human beings are the only ones who can make music.
   c. The piano is a machine, just as the vacuum cleaner is.

Activity

▶ **Composition.** Write a paragraph trying to explain one of the arts (dance, painting, drama, etc.) to Rollo.

MAIN IDEA

Finding Supporting Details

Supporting details back up the main idea of a paragraph. For example, look at the following paragraph.

> *The piano is a machine used to produce sounds of graduated pitch and tone.* It contains wires of various thickness and tautness. These wires are struck by felt-covered hammers. The hammers are set in action by a person operating levers that are arranged on a horizontal panel.

The main idea of this paragraph is expressed by the topic sentence. The three remaining sentences contain details that support the main idea.

---

1. List three details that support each of the following main ideas.
    a. Musical notation tells you the sounds the composer wants produced.
    b. Rollo was programmed to assist the Maestro and not harm him.
    c. The Maestro's house was an oasis of anachronisms in a desert of contemporary efficiency.
    d. Music is written for human beings, not for robots.

2. Copy each group of sentences below on a separate piece of paper. Write M by the sentence in each group that expresses the main idea. Write S by each supporting detail.
    a. (1) In 1763, Mozart published sonatas for the harpsicord and violin.
        (2) Mozart played minuets (music for a certain kind of dance) on the harpsicord and composed pieces for it when he was four.
        (3) Wolfgang Amadeus Mozart, an Austrian born in 1756, was a child prodigy.
        (4) When Mozart was fourteen, he received a commission to write an opera.
        (5) In 1763, Mozart published sonatas for the harpsicord and violin.
    b. (1) It was not until 1893 that *La damoiselle élue* was performed by the Société Nationale de Musique.
        (2) Claude Achille Debussy, born in 1862, did not receive immediate recognition.

(3) When Debussy submitted his symphonic suite *Printemps* for the Prix de Rome, the judges criticized it for its formlessness and untraditional qualities.

(4) Debussy submitted *La damoiselle élue*, only to have the judges criticize it as unconventional.

(5) Because they considered them of such poor quality, the judges refused to give *Printemps* and *La damoiselle élue* the usual public performance.

3. Use an encyclopedia to find information on Frederic François Chopin. Then write a paragraph supporting the following main idea: Chopin's music is noted for its expression of human passion and suffering. (Use this sentence as your topic sentence.)

WORD ATTACK

Dividing Words into Syllables

A syllable is a part of a word having only one vowel sound. Some words contain only one syllable (for example, *rest, may, speak*). Many words, though, contain more than one syllable (for example, *maestro, feverishly, fantastic*).

Sometimes, you may not recognize a long word when you read it, even though you recognize the word when you hear it. Breaking a word into syllables helps you to pronounce it, and thereby helps you to recognize it.

1. Divide each of the words below into their syllable parts. Check your work against a dictionary.

    a. profane
    b. contemporary
    c. antiseptic
    d. magnificently
    e. superbly
    f. apparatus
    g. baritone
    h. graduate
    i. auditory
    j. wraithlike

2. Use each of the words above in an original sentence.

REVIEW QUIZ

On the Selections

1. In "War," why is the woman wearing mourning clothes?

2. Why does she listen intently to the man who has lost his son?

3. In "On Summer," why does the narrator travel to Tennessee?

4. Do you think the narrator believes that change is good or bad? Find evidence to support your answer.

5. In "Gwilan's Harp," why does Gwilan marry Torm?

6. What instrument does she play at the end of the story?

7. In "The Bishop's Candlesticks," for what crime had Jean Valjean been sent to prison?

8. Why does the Bishop give Jean Valjean the candlesticks?

9. In "Virtuoso," why is Rollo an unusual music student?

10. Why does the Maestro cry?

On Main Idea

1. Below are three ideas from one paragraph. Which is the main idea? Which are the supporting details?

   a. She couldn't bear being parted from him—once she had followed him to Sulmona when he was a student in order to be close to him.

   b. The woman was to be pitied since the war was taking away the son she loved so deeply.

   c. She had allowed her son to volunteer for the army only with the assurance that he would not be sent to the front for six months.

2. Find the topic sentence in the following paragraph:

   "It has taken me a good number of years to come to any measure of respect for summer. I was, being May-born, literally an 'infant of the spring' and, during the later childhood years, tended, for some reason or other, to rather worship the cold aloofness of winter. The adolescence, admittedly lingering still, brought the traditional passionate commitment to melancholy autumn—and all that. For the longest kind of time I simply thought that *summer* was a mistake."

3. List four details from "Gwilan's Harp" that support the idea that Gwilan values her harp.

4. List four details from "The Bishop's Candlesticks" that support the idea that the Bishop values Jean Valjean more than the silver.

On Theme ▶ Decide whether the following statements are true or false.

   a. The theme of a story is its central insight into life.

   b. The theme should be stated in a sentence or a series of sentences.

   c. A symbol is always an abstract idea.

   d. The way a character changes during a story can point to the theme.

   e. A significant statement is a statement about the story's symbol.

COMPOSITION

Exposition   **When you write exposition, you give information about something or explain something.** Usually, an expository paragraph contains a topic sentence. This sentence expresses the main idea of the paragraph. Often the topic sentence appears at the beginning of the paragraph, but it may also appear in the middle or at the end. The rest of the paragraph contains details that support the main idea.

►   Write an expository paragraph on one of the topics below.
   a.   How to choose a pair of roller skates
   b.   How to make a pizza (chocolate cake, french fries, etc.)
   c.   Why _____ is my favorite season
   d.   Why _____ is an unusual ballplayer (artist, dancer, etc.)

BEFORE GOING ON

Reading for Main Ideas

When you read for main ideas, you look for the most important idea about the topic of each paragraph. Reading for main ideas is a good technique for helping you find the major points in a selection. It is a good technique to use when you read difficult material.

▶ Follow the instruction below to read "Gold" for main ideas.

a. Read the first paragraph. List three details that support the idea that the discovery of gold in the Klondike did not extinguish, or erase, gold mining in the Yukon.

b. Read paragraph 2. What is the principal technique of placer mining?

c. Read paragraph 3. (a) What is the topic sentence? (b) How does the story about Axel Johnson support the main idea?

d. Look again at the second part of paragraph 3. (a) McPhee tells you that the life that attracted Johnson has gone on attracting others. By what has it been enhanced? (b) How many booms have there been?

e. Read paragraph 4. What is the main idea?

f. Read paragraph 5. What is the main idea?

g. Read paragraph 6. What is the main idea?

h. Write a statement expressing the main idea of the entire selection.

A pack train at Dawson.

Further Reading

Gold

John McPhee

In *Coming into the Country*, John McPhee tells tales about the people who came to America's final wilderness, Alaska. Some of these tales are about people in search of the rarest of rare elements—gold.

The fact that a hundred and fifty million dollars was awash in the drainages of the Klondike diminished but did not extinguish the goldfields of the Alaskan Yukon. Circle City declined by eighty percent but did not ghost out. Enough miners remained in the Birch Creek district to remove half a million dollars' worth of gold in the season after the Klondike strike. The Fortymile region was drained of talent, but not necessarily of the best talent. Established miners continued to work its streams. For the majority, certainly, the years around the turn of the century were ones of rushing to and fro, impelled by the brightness of news. Miners of the Alaskan gold country went into the Klondike with the the advantages of propinquity and experience over the green multitudes coming up from the United States, most of whom found every stream that showed any color completely staked. The Klondike was in Canada. Ninety percent of the miners were American. The Crown imposed a heavy tax on wealth drawn from Her Majesty's placers. The Royal Canadian Mounted Police, understaffed and apprehensive, sent a letter to Ottawa setting forth the possibility that the Americans might by force attempt to move the international boundary far enough east to comprehend the Klondike. But, without violence, many of them just went quietly "home," crossing the line to Alaska, to settle in places—and to work streams—that often flaunted remarkably patriotic names: Eagle, Star City, Nation, American Creek, Washington Creek, Fourth of July Creek. In 1900 came the rush to the beaches of Nome. Eight thousand left Dawson, the instant city where the Klondike meets the Yukon, and conspicuous among them all was Ed Jesson, who came walking into Eagle carrying a bicycle. Riding down the frozen river, he had thirteen hundred more miles to go, but for the time being he was going nowhere; his bearings were cold and stiff. When the temperature went up enough, he rode away. Meanwhile, someone else on his way to Nome went by on ice skates. Populations halved in Eagle and Circle, but, as before, miners by no means disappeared from the country. Nor have they ever. Birch Creek and the Fortymile, where the Yukon mining began, have always since discovery had miners on their creeks.

The principal technique of placer mining is to wash gravel through a long, narrow sluice box, its bottom ribbed with partitions that simulate the riffles of a stream. Gold and heavy sands settle among the riffles, while stones and boulders move on through the box and out the far end as "tailings." The pioneers, with their picks and shovels, could move about five cubic yards of gravel a day. Before long, these individual prospector-miners were outdone by small groups who could collectively move more stone—for

Placer (plăs′ər) mining. Miners are washing gravel through a sluice box in order to remove the gold.

Scales and summit of a mountain pass.

A mining camp in the Klondike.

example, with mechanical scrapers—and who could greatly increase available water by building elaborate wooden flumes. Giant, high-pressure hoses were developed as well, with dug reservoirs feeding mountainside ditches from which water would fall through pipe to emerge from nozzles with power enough to excavate gravels to bedrock. Inevitably, big dredges were built, too—by companies that bought up claims and worked entire streams. The dredges floated on ponds of their own making and on capital from cities months away.

Notwithstanding all this, the individual miner persevered. Quite apart from the major strikes, a kind of life had been discovered that to some—to Axel Johnson, for example—was no less alluring than the gold. Johnson was a Swedish fisherman who came into the country in 1898 and built a cabin, dug a garden at the falls of the Seventymile River. He worked Big Granite Creek, Alder Creek. He "sniped" a lot of his gold—just took it from likely spots without settling down to the formalities of a claim. He would go to the deep holes of stream rapids and periodically clean them out with a large instrument that resembled a spoon. Or he might take, say, eighteen hundred dollars out of a little bench of gravel, working it by hand. When he came into Eagle for mail and supplies, he sniped as he traveled, and once

A gold nugget.

picked up sixty-seven ounces on the way. He trapped; and below his falls he caught Arctic grayling in such quantities that he had enough to dry and keep for winter. He lived well. He died in his cabin, in 1933. The life that attracted him, with its great liabilities and its great possibilities, has gone right on attracting others, and has been enhanced occasionally by a fresh sense of boom. There have, in fact, been three boom eras in the gold streams of Alaska. The second came in the 1930's, when the price of gold doubled. During the rushes of the 1890's, the price had been about seventeen dollars an ounce—a figure that remained essentially steady until 1934, when the government raised it to thirty-five. Lonely miners out on the creeks were suddenly less lonely. Fresh activity was encouraged as well by the almost simultaneous advent of the bulldozer, which could push around roughly four hundred times as much gravel per day as an old-timer with a pick and a shovel. The third Alaskan gold boom began in the early 1970's, when the United States allowed the price to float with the world market and announced that American citizens, for the first time in forty years, would be allowed to buy gold and save it. The price giddied. It approached two hundred dollars an ounce. Then it settled back to present levels—around a hundred and fifty.

New miners come into the country every year—from Nevada, Montana, Oregon, wher-ever. They look around, and hear stories. They hear how Singin' Sam, on Harrison Creek, "hit an enrichment and took out nuggets you wouldn't believe." They hear about "wedge-shaped three-quarter-inch nuggets just lying there where water drips on bedrock." They hear about a miner in the Birch Creek district pulling nuggets from the side of a hill.

"I have always been mining, always preparing ground. I'm not telling you how much money I've got ready to dig up. She's in the bank. Trouble is, there's too much gravel with it."

In tailing piles left behind by dredges, people hunt for nuggets that were *too big* to get stopped in the sluice boxes and went on through the dredge with the boulders. People reach into their shirt pockets and show you phials that are full of material resembling ground chicken feed and are heavier than paperweights. Man says he saw a nugget big as a cruller tumbling end over end in the blast from a giant hose. It sank from view. He's been looking for it since. Man on Sourdough Creek, working for someone else, confessed he had seen a nugget, and reached to pick it up, and found it was connected by a strand of wire gold to something much larger and deeper. He broke off the nugget and reported nothing. He could hardly mark the spot. Later, he went back to try to find what was there—he knew not where.

DRAMA

The Kid Nobody Could Handle

Kurt Vonnegut, Jr.
Dramatized by Christopher Sergel

Characters

Newt, observer

Margie, waitress

George Helmholtz, high-school music
teacher

Grace Helmholtz, his wife

Bert Quinn, restaurant owner

Jim Donnini, a problem young man

Mrs. Crane, English teacher

---

*The curtain is rising to reveal a stage with
several playing areas.*

At R[1], there's a suggestion of a portion of a

---

1. The following stage directions are used: *R*, right; *L*,
left; *DR*, downstage right; *UC*, upstage center.
© 1970 The Dramatic Publishing Company. Notice: it is
against the law to copy this play. *The Kid Nobody Could
Handle* may be produced by non-professional theatres
by paying the required royalty. For information write:
The Dramatic Publishing Company, 4150 North Mil-
waukee Avenue, Chicago, Illinois 60641.

*quite ordinary small restaurant. All that's
required is a small table with a checked
cloth and two chairs. If desired, however,
this can be elaborated with another table or
so and perhaps a section of counter. There
should be a parking meter standing in front
and to the side of the restaurant area.*

*At UC and to stage L, there are several
chairs arranged as classroom seats, teacher's
desk, and a locker. A small podium at L, facing front, and any other available props that
would suggest a high-school music room. A
few instrument cases placed beside the
locker would be helpful.*

*A small, humorless man, Bert Quinn, is
revealed sitting at the restaurant table toying
sourly with some food on the plate before
him. If desired, a few extras may be seen
crossing downstage, either to R or L, apparently on the sidewalk.*

Newt (*as curtain is rising*): It's early morning—some people going to work, some to
school. (*Indicates R.*) That's Bert Quinn's restaurant. Bert eats his own food—not because

he likes it, but because he saves money that way.

(Margie is entering R with a Silex full of coffee.)

Bert (*calling R without looking up*): Margie——
Margie (*as she's pouring more coffee into his cup*): Yes, Mr. Quinn?
Bert: I'd like more——(*realizing.*) Thank you. Did the Kid finish mopping?
Margie: No, sir.
Bert (*irritated*): Tell him—hurry, and then get to school.
Margie (*as she's going; casually*): I tell him every morning.
Newt: Bert isn't really a well man. He can't sleep, can't digest his food, and can't stop working. He has only two moods: one suspicious, the other arrogant. The first applies when he's losing money, the second when he's making it.

(Newt steps upstage a few steps and nods L.)

Newt: Over here is Lincoln High School— that large classroom is for the band—run by George Helmholtz—whose head is always filled with band music.

(George Helmholtz, holding a car steering wheel as though driving, comes shuffling on L. His wife, Grace, as though in the seat beside him, shuffles with him.)

Newt: George is driving his wife to the bus before school this morning, because she's going to spend a few days with relatives. (*George apparently turns the car toward the audience and then apparently stops.*)
George (*to his wife*): Before you go, I'd like a kiss.
Grace (*looking about, embarrassed*): I kissed you before we left the house.
George: I'd like another.

(With a sigh, she gives him a brief kiss.)

Newt (*summing up*): Very affectionate fellow.
Grace: Try to collect from the school for the money you paid to get the music copied.
George: The minute I get there.
Grace (*concerned*): I could've fixed breakfast for you.
George: I'll stop at Bert's restaurant.
Grace: After he took such advantage of you on that land deal?
George: What's the difference? (*Affectionately.*) How about another——
Grace (*amused, apparently hopping out of car, carrying overnight bag*): Back in a few days.
George (*calling after her*): Phone me tonight.

(Grace goes off L while George apparently continues slowly R in car.)

Newt (*meanwhile*): Each year George dreams the same big dream. He dreams of leading as fine a band as there is on the face of the earth. And, in a sense, each year his dream comes true. It comes true because George is sure that a man couldn't have a better dream. Faced by his unnerving sureness, Kiwanians, Rotarians, and Lions pay for band uniforms that cost twice as much as their best suits, school administrators let George raid the budget, and youngsters play their hearts out for him.

(During this, George has apparently parked the car near the restaurant—don't let the actor be elaborate—by propping the wheel against a standing parking meter.)

Newt: And when the youngsters don't have any talent, George gets them to play on guts alone.

(Before going into restaurant, George

glances about, sees he's alone, takes a step forward, and then raises his arms as though to lead a band.)

George: A-one, a-two, a-three—— *(He brings arms down and there's a burst of beautiful band music that he apparently leads for several seconds. He gestures for the end, the sound cuts out—and humming the continuation of whatever music was played, he walks into restaurant.)*

(NOTE: A rousing Sousa march would be a good choice and the sound cues should be carefully rehearsed.)

Newt *(smiling)*: That music was all in George's head. But he cares so much, he makes everyone hear it.

(George is seating himself at the table with Bert, and the sounds of heavy construction work may begin here, though kept as background.)

Bert *(calling R)*: Fried eggs, coffee, and toast for Mr. Helmholtz.

Newt *(wryly, toward sounds)*: The noise of real life. Waddling, clanking, muddy machines tearing the hill behind the restaurant to pieces, with trucks hauling the pieces away. Those sounds put Bert in his arrogant and boastful mood.

Bert: How many eyes saw that hill back there before I did? Thousands, I'll bet. And not one saw what I saw. *(In wonder, chewing on toothpick.)* How many eyes?

George: Mine, at least.

Bert *(amused)*: Yours.

(Margie, the waitress, is bringing tray to George.)

George *(pleasantly)*: All the hill meant to me was a hard climb, some free blackberries, taxes, and a place for band picnics. *(To Margie.)* Thank you. *(She exits.)*

Bert: You inherit the hill, and it's nothing but a pain in the neck. So you figure you'll stick me with it.

George: The price was more than fair.

Bert *(gleefully)*: You say that now—now you see the shopping district's got to grow. Now you see what I saw.

(A wiry young man, sullen, withdrawn, wearing jeans and gaudy shiny black boots with a jingling chain on them, is coming on, mopping mechanically.)

George *(as he's eating; not really interested)*: Yes, but too late. Too late.

Bert: What do I do when I get your hill? *(Gestures toward sound.)* I'm tearing down your hill. And now everybody wants to build a store where the hill was.

George: Um. *(Nodding to boy.)* Hello. *(Without response, the boy keeps mopping.)*

Bert: We all got something. You got music, I got vision.

Newt *(smiling)*: And it's perfectly clear to Bert which one has the money.

Bert: Think big. That's what vision is. Keep your eyes wider than anybody else's.

George *(still regarding the mopper)*: That boy. I've seen him around school, but I never knew his name.

Bert *(smiling cheerfully)*: Billy the Kid. The stormtrooper. Flash Gordon. *(Calling.)* Hey, Jim! Come here a minute.

Newt *(as the sullen boy is approaching them, the mop dragging after)*: George is pretty sensitive. What appalled him was to see that the boy's eyes were as expressionless as oysters.

Bert: This is my brother-in-law's kid by another marriage—before he married my sister. His name's Jim Donnini, and he's from the south side of Chicago and he's very tough.

George: How do you do?

Jim *(looking past him; emptily)*: Hi.

Bert: He's living with me now. He's my baby now.

George: You want a lift to school, Jim?

Bert (*as Jim doesn't reply*): He won't talk to me, either. But, yeah, he wants a lift to school. (*To Jim. Shortly.*) Go on, kid, wash up and shave. (*Robotlike, Jim goes off R, trailing the mop.*)

George (*concerned*): Where are his parents?

Bert: His mother's dead. His old man married my sister, walked out on her, and stuck her with him. Then the court didn't like the way she was raising him and put him in foster homes for a while. Then they decided to get him clear of Chicago so they stuck me with him. (*Shaking his head.*) Life's a funny thing, Helmholtz.

George (*pushing his eggs away*): Not very funny, sometimes.

Bert (*chewing toothpick*): Like some whole new race of people coming up. He's nothing like the decent kids we got around here. Did you notice those boots he wears? And he won't talk, won't run around with other kids, won't study. I don't think he can even read or write very good.

George: Does he like music at all? Or drawing? Does he collect anything?

Bert: You know what he likes—he likes to polish those boots. The only enjoyment he gets is when he's alone, comic books spread around, and polishing those boots. (*Remembering.*) Oh, he had a collection, too. I took it away from him and threw it in the river.

George: Threw it in the river?

Bert: Yeah. Eight knives—some with blades as long as your hand.

George: Oh. (*Concerned.*) This is a new problem at some schools, I guess. (*Wanting to sort it out.*) It's kind of a sickness, isn't it? That's the way to look at it, wouldn't you say?

Bert: Yes, sick. (*Tapping his chest.*) And Doctor Bert is just the man to give him what's good for his ailment.

George: What's that?

Bert (*hard*): For a start—no more talk about poor, little sick boy. That's all he's heard from social workers and the juvenile court.

(*Jim, still expressionless, is re-entering R, now wearing a leather jacket.*)

George: But actually——

Bert: Actually he s a bum. Well, I'm going to ride his tail until he straightens up and flies right, or winds up in the can for life.

George (*nodding toward Jim; warning*): Bert——

Bert (*going right on*): One way or the other. (*Directly to Jim.*) Believe it, boy!

George: I see. (*To Jim.*) I'm parked in front. (*Without a response, Jim goes out to stand by the parking meter. George gets up, putting some money on the table.*) That right? (*Bert nods and George puts a separate coin by coffee cup. He's depressed.*) If I knew anything to say to that boy.

Bert (*picking up money*): What's to say? Listen to those bulldozers—really tearing into it.

George (*preoccupied.*): They are—they really are.

(*As he's going to join Jim, Bert reaches across, picks up the other coin, considers an instant, then goes out R.*)

Bert (*holding coin for her*): Margie——

(*Without talk, George takes up wheel and he and Jim are apparently driving L. The construction sounds, if used, fade.*)

Newt: George tried baseball, football, anything to get a conversation going, but nothing happened. And, of course, he couldn't help trying the most important subject in the world to him.

George (*glancing at Jim and clearing his throat*): Do you—do you like listening to music? (*Jim sighs heavily with boredom.*) (*George tries again.*) Ever drum with your fingers or keep time with your feet? (*Jim* leans his head back, closing his eyes, waiting for George to give up.) (George tries another approach.) Those boots—what's the function of the chains? Are they to jingle? (Jim looks away, but George presses on.) At least you whistle. Even whistling—it can be like picking up the keys to a whole new world.

Jim (contemptuously): A new world——

George (eagerly): A world as beautiful as any world can be. (Jim makes a soft Bronx cheer,[2] but George continues undaunted.) There! You've illustrated the basic principle of the family of brass wind instruments. The glorious voice of every one of them starts with a buzz on the lips.

(Apparently they've reached a parking place at L, and they're both facing forward.)

Jim (fishing out a cigarette from inside of his leather jacket): Any time.

George (noticing as Jim lights cigarette, keeping casual): That—that won't do your lungs much good. (Jim's reply is to expel some smoke. George speaks carefully.) Sometimes I get disgusted, too, and I don't see how I can stand it. I feel like doing all kinds of crazy things—things that might even be bad for me. (Jim expels more smoke.) And then—— (Snaps fingers of left hand and grabs wheel again enthusiastically.) And then, Jim, I remember I've got at least one tiny corner of the universe I can make just the way I want it. I can go to it, and enjoy it till I'm brand-new and happy again.

Jim: Aren't you the lucky one?

George: I am, for a fact. My corner of the universe happens to be the air around my head. I can fill it with music. (Jim is yawning, apparently getting out of the car. George continues eagerly.) Mr. Beeler, in zoology, has his butterflies. Mr. Trottman, in physics, has his pendulum. Mrs. Crane, in English, her books——

---

2. Bronx cheer: A scornful or contemptuous sound made by vibrating the tongue between the lips.

Jim (contemptuously): Mrs. Crane——

George: Making sure everybody has a corner like that is about the biggest job we teachers have. I—— (But he's stopped as Jim drops cigarette and walks out L.) Jim——

(But the boy is gone. Unhappily George places wheel by post or sets it off L, then steps on the remainder of Jim's cigarette, scoops it into his hand, and takes it with him into his classroom, where he puts it in a wastebasket.)

Newt (meanwhile): George Helmholtz's first class of the morning was C Band. C Band is where beginners thumped and wheezed and tooted as best they could, and looked down the long, long, road through B Band to A Band, the Lincoln High School Ten Square Band, the finest school band in the world.

(George is coming up onto the podium L, holding a baton.)

George (speaking front, addressing imaginary class): Good morning, C Band. I know it's early—none of us warmed up yet. (Raising his baton.) But remember this— (Believing it.) You're better than you think you are! A-one, a-two, a-three . . . (Down comes the baton, and with it there's the sound of magnificent band music.)

Newt (as George continues to lead): Sounds great for C Band, doesn't it? (Shaking his head.) That music you're hearing isn't C Band. What that is—it's what George was hearing—in his head—the music as it was going to be—some day! Actually C Band set out in its quest for beauty—set out like a rusty switch engine, with valves stuck, pipes clogged, unions leaking, bearings dry——

(George is singing yump-yumps along with band as he brings this passage to a close.)

Newt: And George was still smiling at the end of that class hour.

George (*front*): Thanks. Thank you very much. See you tomorrow.

[*With this, he's getting off the podium and coming forward into what is the beginning of some student (extras) traffic crossing downstage to L or to R, talking excitedly to each other as they cross.*]

(NOTE: *Margie and Grace, with minor costume changes to look like students, may do this.*)

Students (*generally*): No, it's true! . . . How do you know? . . . Mr. Beeler was telling Mr. Trottman . . . I heard Mrs. Crane was cry-ing . . . You're outa your mind . . . Can't be true . . . So how come her classes are canceled? Tomorrow, too.

Newt (*during above*): George had gone into the hall for a drink of water, but he couldn't figure out what the students were talking about.

(*The students are going off, leaving a confused George behind. As he looks L, Jim walks in, pausing to polish his boots on his pants leg.*)

George: Hello, Jim. What's going on? (*Jim shrugs.*) I have to get back for rehearsal with

B Band—but I was thinking about you. The school has a lot of clubs and teams that meet after classes. It's a good way to get to know a lot of the other students.

Jim (*coldly*): Maybe I don't want to know a lot of the other students. (*Walking past George; heading R.*) Ever think of that? (*As he's going off R, Jim walks hard to make the boot chains jingle.*)

(*Mrs. Crane, a worried English teacher, is coming on L.*)

Mrs. Crane (*keeping herself calm with an effort*): George——

George: Mrs. Crane—I just heard your name—some of the students——

Mrs. Crane (*unhappily*): Can't hush it up. I suppose it's all over the school. Will you be at the faculty meeting?

George: Meeting?

Mrs. Crane: A special meeting this afternoon—on vandalism.

George (*with casual concern*): I hear that some schools——

Mrs. Crane (*cutting in*): My office was wrecked last night.

George (*stunned*): Your office? Here?

Mrs. Crane (*swallowing with difficulty*): I keep searching my mind—whom I might've offended—where I might've done less than I should for some student.

George (*incredulous*): You said—wrecked?

Mrs. Crane: Books, diplomas, records, even the snapshots of my trip to England—ripped, crumpled, trampled, drenched with ink!

George (*aghast*): No——

Mrs. Crane (*with an unhappy laugh*): Also the beginnings of eleven novels. I don't suppose they were very good, but I'd rather destroy them myself.

George (*can hardly talk*): I can't believe it!

Mrs. Crane: The meeting—for whatever it's worth—is at four. (*Starting R. Speaking mainly to herself.*) Is it my fault? Is it their fault? What's happening?

(*As she is going off R, and as the shocked George is going off L, the lights are dimming except for a spot on Newt at DR.*)

Newt (*during this*): George was sickened. He couldn't believe it. And with his wife away, he had no one to discuss it with. It didn't become real to George until late that night, in a dream. In the dream, George saw a boy with barracuda teeth, with claws like baling hooks. The monster climbed into the band rehearsal-room and starting clawing to tatters the heads of the biggest and best drums in the state. George woke up terrified. There was nothing to do but to dress and go to school.

(*The stage is still dark, but George has come into the classroom area at L with a lighted flashlight.*)

Newt: George let himself in with his key and used a flashlight as he didn't want to attract attention. (*The flashlight is exploring the band instrument-cases.*) His treasures were safe. And with the contentment of a miser counting his money, George looked over the instruments one by one. Even now—even under these circumstances, he could hear the great horns roaring, could see them flashing in the sunlight, with the Stars and Stripes and the banner of Lincoln High going before!

George (*happy with relief*): Thank Heaven!

Newt: Then George heard a noise in the chemistry lab next door. (*The flashlight snaps out.*) George went out into the hall, then jerked open the lab door.

(*The flashlight comes on again, revealing Jim holding a bottle that he has tilted over to pour.*)

George: You! You!

Newt: Jim Donnini was splashing acid over the periodic table of the elements, over the books, over the bust of Lavoisier.[3] It was the most repulsive thing George had ever seen.

George (*horrified*): Put that down and get out of there!

Jim: What're you gonna do?

George (*in shock*): I don't know. Clean up. Save what I can. But come out of there—come to my classroom.

(*They're moving L.*)

Jim: You gonna call the fuzz?

George (*bewildered*): Call the fuzz?

Jim (*George is so stupid*): The cops!

(*George apparently turns on the lights in his classroom area.*)

George: I—I don't know. Put down the bottle of acid. (*Jim does. George is confused and miserable. No thoughts come.*) If I'd caught you hurting the band instruments, probably I'd have hit you. (*Bothered by himself.*) But I wouldn't have had any intelligent thoughts about what you were—what you thought you were doing.

Jim (*bravado*): It's about time this place got set on its ear.

George: Is it? (*Struggling with concern.*) That must be so, if one of our students wants to murder it.

Jim: What good is it?

George: Not much, I guess. (*Unhappily.*) But it's the best thing human beings have managed to do yet.

Jim (*with contempt*): The best thing——

George (*swallowing*): Jim, if you smashed up all the schools, we wouldn't have any hope.

Jim: What hope?

(*George considers a moment.*)

---

3. Lavoisier (là-vwȧ-zyā′): Antoine Laurent Lavoisier, 1743–1794; French chemist regarded as the founder of modern chemistry.

George: The hope that someday everybody will be glad they're alive. (*Takes a breath.*) Even you.

Jim: That's a laugh. All I ever got out of this garbage pile was a hard time. (*Calculating.*) So what're you gonna do?

George (*realizing*): I have to do something, don't I?

Jim (*contemptuously polishing a boot on his pants leg*): I don't care what you do!

George: Isn't there anything you care about? Anything, but those boots?

Jim (*challenging*): Go on. Call up whoever you're gonna call—Go ahead!

George (*an agony of indecision; speaking mainly to himself*): I don't want to turn you in! I want to find some way to reach—— (*Breaks off as he's struck by new thought. Rushing to get something from his locker nearby. As he takes something from locker*) I'll show you—you'll see—maybe this will convince—— (*He brings velvet-covered object toward Jim.*) There! (*He takes velvet away, revealing a brightly polished trumpet.*) There's my treasure! It's the dearest thing I own. (*He thrusts it into Jim's hands.*) I give it to you. Do what you please with it. If you want, you can smash it—and I won't move a muscle to stop you. It's yours! (*Jim is holding the trumpet uncertainly.*) Go on! If the world has treated you so badly, it deserves to have that trumpet smashed.

Jim (*tossing trumpet on desk; polishing boot again*): I—I don't want it.

George: Jim—(*Exploding.*) Those—boots! (*George grabs Jim's belt, puts a foot behind him, and dumps him onto the floor.*)

Jim: Hey! What are you——

(*George is jerking Jim's gaudy boots off—they should fit loosely to come off easily—and throwing them in corner.*)

George (*as he's doing it; savagely*): I'll show you! There! (*He pulls Jim to his feet again.*)

George: All right—I've taken them!

(Jim has apparently lost his socks with the boots. He stands looking down at his bare feet, shivering as though intensely cold. George shoves the trumpet back into Jim's hands.)

George: Listen to me. You have to know what you have in your hand. That trumpet? *(Jim just stands, holding it.)* The special thing about it—it belonged to John Philip Sousa![4] And I'm trading it to you—for your boots. It's yours, Jim. John Philip Sousa's trumpet! It's worth hundreds of dollars, maybe thousands——

Jim *(in a tight voice)*: I don't want——

George: It's better than boots. You can learn to play it. You're somebody, Jim. You're the boy with John Philip Sousa's trumpet.

(They stand facing each other for a moment. The energy goes out of George. He expels a breath.)

George: (subdued): I'll drive you home. I won't say a word about tonight. *(Crossing to apparent light switch.)* I better turn these lights out.

Jim: Can I have my boots?

George: No. I don't think they're good for you.

(Apparently he turns off the lights, and for a moment the stage is dark. Then the industrial sound of bulldozers, if used, comes on again and so do the stage lights, generally revealing George and Bert eating breakfast again, and Newt standing at DR.)

Newt: The next morning the waddling, clanking muddy machines were making the vision of Bert Quinn true. They were smoothing off the place where the hill had been behind the restaurant.

---

4. John Philip Sousa (sōō′zə): 1854–1932. An American composer and bandleader.

Bert: Eating out two mornings in a row? Something wrong at home?

George: My wife's still visiting relatives.

Bert *(winking)*: While the cat's away——

George: When the cat's away, this mouse gets hungry.

(Jim is coming on mopping as before, except now he wears some old gym shoes. The industrial noise, once registered, fades.)

Bert *(leaning forward)*: Is that what got you out of bed in the middle of the night? *(Jerks head toward Jim.)* Kid! Go get Mr. Helmholtz his horn.

(Jim raises his head and looks directly at George for an instant, then goes off R again, trailing the mop after him.)

Newt *(during this)*: What upset George— the boy's eyes were again as expressionless as oysters.

Bert *(irritated)*: You take away his boots and give him a horn, and I'm not supposed to get curious? I'm not supposed to start asking questions?

George: I was going to——

Bert *(going right on; his voice rising)*: I'm not supposed to find out you caught him taking the school apart? And it wasn't the first time.

George: I know, but——

Bert *(interrupting again)*: You'd make a lousy crook. You'd leave your baton, sheet music, and your driver's license at the scene of the crime.

George: I don't think about hiding clues.

Bert *(derisively)*: You don't think about anything.

George: I just do what I do. The reason I came for breakfast, I wanted to discuss with you about——

Bert *(sharply)*: Nothing to discuss.

George *(uneasily)*: What do you mean?

Bert: All over with Jim and me. Last night was the payoff.

George: What will you do?

Bert: I'm sending him back where he came from.

George: To another string of foster homes?

Bert: Whatever the experts figure out to do with such a kid.

(He sits back, relieved that he's said it. George takes this in and he's very concerned.)

George (*a decision*): You can't.

Bert (*almost laughter*): I can.

George: But that will be the end of him.

Bert: Why?

George (*strong*): Because he can't stand to be thrown away like that one more time.

Bert (*getting up angrily*): Him? He can't feel anything. I can't help him—I can't hurt him.

(Jim is coming on R, impassively holding the trumpet.)

Bert: There isn't a nerve or feeling in him.

George: A bundle of scar tissue.

Bert (*aware of him*): Kid—give back the horn.

(Jim puts the trumpet on the table.)

George: No, Jim. (*Forcing a smile.*) It's yours.

Bert: He doesn't want it. Take it while you got the chance.

George (*continuing, to Jim*): I gave it to you.

Bert: All he'll do is swap it for a knife or a pack of cigarettes.

George (*without turning to Bert*): He doesn't know what it is yet. It takes awhile to find out.

Bert: Is it any good?

George: Any good? (*Incredulous.*) It belonged to John Philip Sousa.

Bert: Who?

George (*getting up uncertainly, his voice hushed with emotion*): Who was John Philip Sousa? (*George picks up the trumpet, utterly inarticulate.*)

Newt: The subject was too big and George was too exhausted to cover it.

(As Bert and Jim watch, each in his way bewildered, George kisses the cold mouthpiece and fingers the valves professionally.)

Newt (*during this*): There was nothing George could say or show them. They were deaf to him, and blind. And all George could see was the futility of men and their treasures. He'd thought this greatest treasure he owned could buy a soul for a troubled boy. But his trumpet was worthless.

(With a cry, George suddenly bangs the trumpet on the edge of the table, then again.)

(NOTE: This can be done with a substitute piece of metal so it can't be seen by audience.)

Bert: Hey! What are ya——

(George is banging trumpet on floor behind table, and then apparently stamps on it.)

Bert: You crazy? Nuts!

(George, totally exhausted, tosses trumpet back onto table.)

Bert: Ya busted it! Why'dya do that? (*George is shaking his head.*) What's that prove?

George: I—I don't know. I—excuse me—I want to go.

Bert: You're leaving the busted——

George (*sharply*): Yes!

Bert: Why?

George (*welling out of him*): Because life's

no good. (*George, utterly miserable, is going off L uncertainly as the others watch.*)

Newt (*quietly*): There was one thing George didn't notice. He didn't notice the eyes of Jim Donnini. Suddenly those eyes filled with pity and with alarm. They became human. They came alive.

(*Jim picks up the trumpet and goes out R. Bert looks after him thoughtfully and then follows him off.*)

Newt (*as this happens*): The surprising thing—somehow Bert Quinn caught the change—and something like hope flickered for the first time in Bert's bitterly lonely face. (*Newt is alone now on the stage.*) There were some unanswered questions when the new semester began two weeks later at Lincoln High. (*Smiles as he goes off R.*) But life was about to deal with them.

(*With his exit, students are crossing downstage to R and L, moving energetically and talking to each other as they go. This can include Grace, Margie, and Mrs. Crane, all dressed as students.*)

Students (*generally*): Is there practice for C Band or not? . . . How do I know? . . . There

was supposed to be an announcement if it was canceled . . . Well, check the bulletin board . . . How can I check when C Band is the first practice? . . . What's wrong with Mr. Helmholtz? . . . Beats me. You'd think he had a death in his family!

(*During this last exchange, George is coming on L, holding his baton. The students, afraid he's overheard—which he has—hurry on off L. George turns to face the podium, his back to the audience, considering what to do.*)

(*Jim, holding the apparently repaired trumpet, enters R, crossing unseen toward George.*)

Jim (*speaking quietly*): Mr. Helmholtz— Mr. Helmholtz—(*George turns slowly to see him.*) Is this where I come for C Band practice?
George: Yes. Yes, this is the place.
Jim (*indicating horn*): It was just bent a little. No trouble getting it fixed.

(*Happiness is coming back into George, but he speaks carefully.*)

George: I see.
Jim (*looking off L front*): Where should I sit?
George (*beginning to smile*): For a start— the last seat of the worst trumpet section of the worst band in school.
Jim (*agreeably*): Right—
George (*cheerfully*): But with that trumpet—

(*Suddenly filling with his old enthusiasm, he hurries up onto the podium.*)

George: Let's get started, C Band. What are we waiting for? Maybe you're C Band now, but——

(*In a moment, he's stopped by his own

happiness and enthusiasm flooding back. Jim still stands L watching.*)

George (*speaking front; starting over*): Think of it this way. Our aim is to make the world sound more beautiful than it did when we came into it. (*With conviction.*) It can be done. You can do it.
Jim (*bursting out of him*): How?
George (*pointing off L front*): You should be sitting in the trumpet section.
Jim (*backing off; as he goes*): But how?

(*Jim has gone off L, now apparently a part of C Band.*)

George (*after him*): Just—love yourself— and make your instrument sing about it. (*He raises his baton.*) A-one, a-two, a-three——

(*Down comes the baton, and with this, rousing and triumphant band music—the magnificent band music George hears in his head—fills the theater.*)

(*The curtain falls.*)

Close Up

1. When George Helmholtz first meets Jim, he is appalled to find that the boy's eyes are "as expressionless as oysters." What is the one thing that Jim cares about?

2. Helmholtz tells Jim, ". . . I've got at least one tiny corner of the universe I can make just the way I want it." (a) What is this corner? (b) Why does Helmholtz want to help Jim find his own "corner of the universe"?

3. When Helmholtz returns to school that night, he finds Jim vandalizing the chemistry lab. (a) Why does he give Jim his trumpet instead of turning him in to the police? (b) Why does he take Jim's boots?

4. (a) The next morning, why does Helmholtz decide his trumpet is worthless? (b) Why does this strike a response in Jim?

5. When the new semester begins, Jim joins C Band, and Helmholtz gives him his first lesson in playing. What does Helmholtz mean when he says, "Just—love yourself—and make your instrument sing about it"?

6. Since this is a stage play, it contains many directions, printed in *italics,* that tell the actors where to stand and how to say certain lines. These stage directions help you visualize how the play would be performed on the stage. (a) Find three stage directions that tell the actors where to stand. (b) Find three stage directions that tell the actors how to say certain lines.

This Bull Ate Nutmeg

Josephina Niggli

A Mexican Folk Comedy

Characters

Felipe Lozano, a young man in love

Anita, the object of his affections

Serafino, a gentleman of talent

Don Pancho, father of Anita

Ramón Garza, also in love with Anita

A Crowd of village people

Scene: The corral in the house of Don Pancho

Time: A sunny afternoon, the present

(In the northern villages of Mexico one sometimes sees sideshows, made up, usual-

ly, of just one attraction. Serafino, the man with the body of a snake, used to include my own village in his tour program. He was a little gnome of a man, and his cotton-stuffed snake body was patched here and there with bright goods of different colors. When curled up in his box, with this snake's tail floating down from his throat, he was an awesome spectacle to behold. He used to give me his love potions, because, as he said, I kept his secret from year to year that he had a human trunk behind the cotton-stuffed calico.

As for the "comedy of bullfight"—that one sees also, generally in the spring. There is no sport in the world so beloved as bullfighting, and no sport so satirized by those who love it. Our watchman's son, who played the bull year after year, was considered by our valley as the finest comic bull in the north. He told me his secret one day. "It is not talent, no. It is that I go to the great corridas every year; I watch the bull, and then, when I am myself the bull, I do exactly what the real bull would not do. It is all very simple." Well, perhaps.

The scene is a corral at the house of Don Pancho. It is not, one understands, the corral in which animals are kept. Rather it is the outer patio at the back of a village house, and is really the counterpart of what is called the "back yard" in the United States.

This particular corral is an unusual one. Only one wall, the left, belongs to the house

proper, a door on that side leading to the kitchen. Across the back is a high adobe fence with a gate toward the right that opens on the street. To the right is still more wall.

Because of its spaciousness Don Pancho often rents his corral to traveling actors, sideshows, wrestlers, or, indeed, any type of attraction that cannot be staged on the town plaza.

Today it seems that there is going to be an attraction of some sort. There are benches on the right and at the back, and a single arm-chair raised on a dais, with its back to the right wall.

At the moment, however, there is no one in the corral save a slender, rather short young man accompanying his own singing on a guitar. Standing in the kitchen door, one hand on her hip, is a girl.

The boy is Felipe Lozano, who owns a small herd of cows and sells milk to all the towns nearby. He is not particularly hand-some, but one gets a distinct impression of wholesomeness from him. He's a thoroughly nice boy, although not very romantically exciting. But he would make some woman an awfully good husband. Just now, looking very clean and rather young in his white trousers and pink shirt with a blue bandana around his neck, and his straw hat dangling between his shoulder blades, he is valiantly trying to sing a love song to the girl in the doorway, who happens at the moment to be the star of his adoration.

Anita is the daughter of Don Pancho and is well aware of the dignity with which this invests her. She's pretty enough in her bright blue skirt and orange blouse with the dark red shawl twisted about her shoulders. She has a tendency to dramatize herself too much, as witness this blasé pose she is affecting just now, diligently copied from a friend who had once seen a movie.

While Felipe is singing, a little man comes hesitantly through the street gate at the back. He is a shy, strange little man balancing a rather large box on his back, the weight of which bends him forward so that his chest is more or less horizontal with the ground. He is an odd-looking person with a very bald head. Like Felipe's his trousers are white, although ragged and dirty. His shirt is a mag-nificent green. Seeing Felipe and Anita, he starts to speak; but, realizing they are not conscious of his presence, he slides the box to the ground and sits on it, patiently wait-ing.)

Felipe (singing):

I take great pride in being a ranchero,
And I play out my life with bravery.
I've never known what fear was for a minute,
And I always fight for love's slavery.

(Pausing, with a sigh, to murmur) How beautiful you are, my dove.

Anita (accepting this as her due): Thank you, Felipe.

Felipe (singing):

My life I'll sell you cheaply for a quarter,
And I would not ask mercy on your part.
Today I have my gleaming silver dagger
Already thirsting for some coward's heart.
Hand to hand I'll fight any man handy,
And I'll gladly take my . . .

(Just now a hand catches Anita's shoulder, and Don Pancho swings her aside so that he can burst into the corral. Don Pancho, be-sides being the most important man in the village, next to the mayor and the civil judge, was born with a temper which he has never seen reason to curb. He has a habit of acting first and thinking afterward, but his bark is really worse than his bite. His trousers are gray and his shirt is as blue as the Mexican sky, which is very blue indeed.)

Don Pancho (roaring): Enough of this cack-ling! Can a man find no peace in his house? Inside with you, Anita!

Anita: But, Papa . . .

Don Pancho: Do you hear my voice, or must I add my hand to it? Inside!

Anita: Yes, Papa.

(With a slight nod to Felipe she disappears into the kitchen. Felipe, who has backed away from the anger of Don Pancho, stands meekly to the storm, his head bowed, his fingers twitching the strings of his guitar.)

Don Pancho (*glaring at him*): You, Felipe Lozano. What are you doing here at this hour of the day? (*Felipe half extends the guitar, then decides that perhaps silence is better than speech.*) Ay, singing the rooster to my Anita, eh?

Felipe (*mumbling*): Yes, Don Pancho.

Don Pancho: Have you no work to do? Your fine cows. Do they not need someone to milk them?

Felipe: One does not milk cows at two in the afternoon, Don Pancho.

Don Pancho: When I need your advice about the milking of cows, I'll ask you. (*Pacing up and down.*) I milked cows before you were born! With these hands I milked them. Squirt, squirt, squirt into the bucket, so!

Felipe (*shifting his weight from one foot to the other*): Yes, Don Pancho.

Don Pancho: And any man who prefers a cow to a goat is not worthy to live in our village.

Felipe (*suddenly courageous*): But, Don Pancho, goats smell.

Don Pancho (*clutching his nose*): And so do cows, bah!

Felipe (*worsted*): Yes, Don Pancho.

Don Pancho (*stopping in front of him and thrusting out his chin*): Where did you learn that song!

Felipe (*under the suddenness of this he backs up several steps and swallows*): What song?

Don Pancho: You know well enough. That one you were spluttering when I came out.

Felipe: But I have known that all my life, Don Pancho. (*Smiling.*) It's a beautiful song, eh?

Don Pancho (*growling*): It is a terrible song. It hurts the ears and makes salt water glitter in my eyes because it is terrible.

Felipe (*meekly*): I am sorry that I have not a beautiful voice, Don Pancho, like Ramón Garza; but I do the best I can.

Don Pancho (*flatly*): Ramón can't sing either.

Felipe (*with a pleased grin*): I agree with you, Don Pancho.

Don Pancho (*glaring at him*): But Ramón's voice has nothing to do with it. It is the song that makes me bite myself.

Felipe (*puzzled*): What is wrong with it?

Don Pancho (*snorting*): When I was playing the bear[1] to Anita's mother, every night I sang it. Every night! For three years I sang that song, and the day we were married I said to myself, "No more. No more! That song for me is finished!" Is that clear? It is finished.

Felipe: But, Don Pancho, what has that to do with me? I . . .

Don Pancho (*advancing on him*): It has this to do with you. If ever again I hear that song in this corral . . . I personally will take steps. Is that clear?

Felipe: Yes, Don Pancho.

Don Pancho: See that you remember it. And now go home.

Felipe (*pleading*): But, Don Pancho, can't I stay and sing for Anita again?

Don Pancho (*hardly able to get his breath*): Sing!

Felipe (*hastily*): Oh, not that song. I know another one. I know two more. Please, Don Pancho.

Don Pancho: I said, "Go home."

Felipe (*measuring out a tiny space between thumb and forefinger*): Just one little song?

Don Pancho (*with strained patience*): Felipe, are you not to be the bull this afternoon?

Felipe: Yes, Don Pancho. But what harm can one little song . . .

---

1. playing the bear: Courting.

Don Pancho: Have I not wagered with every man in town that you will vanquish that fool Ramón Garza?

Felipe (*blankly*): Have you?

Don Pancho: Have I, indeed! I, who have wagered five pesos on you . . . not one, not two, not three, but five. I personally have done that, and you want to stay here to sing a song!

Felipe: But just one song . . .

Don Pancho: Using up all your energy when you should be home asleep and resting before the great ordeal! I, who have wagered five pesos, should let you do that? Let me tell you something, Felipe. If you make me lose that money I personally will kill you.

Felipe (*drawing back*): Ay, Don Pancho.

Don Pancho: If you want to live so that you can play the bear to Anita, you had best win this afternoon. (*With a shriek.*) Go home!

Felipe (*backing away from him*): Yes, Don Pancho. (*Whirling to run out through the gate, he nearly falls over the little man seated on the box. He mumbles*) Your pardon, señor. (*Darts through the gate into the street.*)

Don Pancho (*advancing on the little man*): What do you want?

The Little Man (*springs off the box and makes a deep bow*): I, señor, am Serafino, a man with a snake for a friend.

Don Pancho: Then take your friend to another house. We want no snakes here.

Serafino: You do not understand, señor. I desire to rent this corral.

Don Pancho: It's rented. Do you not see these benches? This afternoon at five precisely there will be a grand comedy of bull-fight.

Serafino: But tonight when the comedy is over, and tomorrow when the benches are cleared away . . . who will rent your corral then?

Don Pancho: Now you have logic. But snakes, did you say?

Serafino: Just one snake.

Don Pancho: No. Not even one snake. Me, I have never been able to love a snake.

Serafino: But mine is a most unusual snake, señor. Like no snake you have ever seen before.

Don Pancho: I am sorry, friend. It is simply that snakes and I . . . we cannot be friends.

Serafino (*thoughtfully*): Otherwise you would rent me your corral?

Don Pancho: But certainly, señor. To you I have no objections. It is only to your little pet.

Serafino: Now I understand. Let me put it this way. Have you ever been the behind-legs of a horse?

Don Pancho (*thinking this over and arriving at his conclusion*): No. Have you?

Serafino: Oh, yes . . . for many years. That was with a circus in Vera Cruz.

Don Pancho (*sitting down on the stoop of the kitchen door*): Did you enjoy this labor?

Serafino (*dragging his box forward and sitting on it*): No. My back grew tired. You know, in such work a man must bend forward all the time. But then, I am not young anymore. Can you believe it . . . after all my long years of labor, any young fool that comes along is a better behind-legs of a horse than I am.

Don Pancho (*sympathetically*): That is a sad thing.

Serafino: It is a tragedy, señor. But me, Serafino, I am above tragedy.

Don Pancho (*standing up*): Now that is a speech of a great man. (*Bows to him.*) I salute you.

Serafino (*standing and returning the bow*): Always your servant, señor.

(*This finished, they both sit down.*)

Don Pancho: How are you above tragedy, señor? Tell me your secret.

Serafino: Only if I may rent your corral.

Don Pancho: Now, my friend, surely . . .

Serafino (*practically*): I should give away such a great secret for nothing?

Don Pancho: You understand . . . the snake . . .

Serafino: What is a snake compared to one peso and a half for three days rent?

Don Pancho (*firmly*)**:** Five pesos.

Serafino: One-seventy-five.

Don Pancho: Four pesos and a half.

Serafino: Two pesos and not one cent more.

Don Pancho: Three pesos and not one cent less.

Serafino (*beaming*)**:** Then we are agreed, for two pesos and a half?

Don Pancho: Two pesos and a half. (*They stand up, shake hands, and sit down again.*) Now for your secret, señor.

Serafino: I say to myself, "Serafino, you shall become a snake."

Don Pancho (*in amazement*)**:** A snake?

Serafino: A snake. So I go to my wife, who is also the mother of my children . . . may the saints bless her.

Don Pancho: And also the angels.

Serafino: Precisely. Now, my wife is clever with the needle; so she makes me the body of a snake, which is here in this box. Would you like to see it, señor?

Don Pancho: With both eyes.

(*Between them they tug the box around and open the top, which is hinged and divided into two sections with a hole in the middle. From it Serafino takes a long length of green cloth stuffed with cotton so that it does vaguely resemble a snake's body.*)

Serafino (*acting out what he is saying*)**:** This I drape outside the box, so. Then I put on a wig to cover my bald head, black glasses to cover my eyes, and step into the box. Then I close the top down, so. (*The hole in the center has fastened about his throat, and he grins at Don Pancho.*) And now I am the man with the body of a snake. Is this not a grand thing, señor?

Don Pancho: But magnificent! That is much better than being the behind-legs of a horse.

Serafino: Much better. As I said before, any fool can be the behind-legs of a horse; but only I, Serafino, can be the man with the body of a snake.

(*At this moment Anita comes into the patio. She takes one look at the strange figure in the box and stands frozen. Then she gives a shriek.*)

Anita: Sainted Heaven! Holy Mary guard me!

(*With one last high squeak she whirls and flees back to the safety of the house. Don Pancho roars with laughter. Serafino, grinning, gets out; removes his wig and glasses; and carefully replaces them, with the snake body, in the box.*)

Serafino: Ay, people have walked for miles to pay ten cents to view my magnificence.

Don Pancho: Stay as long as you like, my friend. And never fear. I'll guard your secret.

Serafino: There is something else I wish you would do for me. (*He does not notice Anita peering around the edge of the kitchen door.*)

Don Pancho: Name it, friend. Name it.

Serafino: I have here some love potions. Harmless, you understand. A little sugar, a little flour, a little nutmeg. For five cents a package they sell quickly to the boys and girls. Who does not want love in this wicked world?

Don Pancho: Me, I could be happy the rest of my years without it.

Serafino: Indeed, señor. But once we were foolish, too. So if you would mention to the young people this afternoon that I have these for sale . . .

Don Pancho: I am at your service.

Anita (*snapping*)**:** But I am not. How dare you frighten me until my hair turns white?

Don Pancho: Now, Anita, silence. This is a man's business.

Anita: Not when I tell it about the town.

Serafino: Please, señorita, would you deprive my wife, would you deprive my seven children, of food?

Anita: How do I know that your wife and children are not as false as your love potions? A little flour, a little sugar——

Serafino: And a little nutmeg . . . for spice.

Don Pancho (*slyly*): You understand, Anita, it is not what composes the love potion, but the charm muttered over them that is effective. Eh, friend Serafino?

Serafino: A great truth. A very great truth, señor.

Anita: You swear that by the blue robe of the Virgin?

Serafino (*piously*): By the honesty of my profession I swear it, señorita.

Anita: Buy me a package, Papa.

Serafino (*handing her a small package*): No, no, never! For you, señorita, it is a pleasure and a gift.

Anita (*smiling on him as she takes it*): Thank you, señor.

Don Pancho: Listen, Anita, if you mean to give that to our young rooster Felipe, wait until tomorrow.

Anita (*tossing her head*): Why?

Don Pancho: Because nutmeg makes him sick. If he is sick this afternoon I lose five pesos. Please, Anita.

Anita: Why should I waste love potions on one who loves me well? This is for another pair of eyes. (*With a toss of her head she goes into the house.*)

Don Pancho (*shaking his head*): Have you daughters, friend Serafino?

Serafino: Three.

Don Pancho: Like this one?

Serafino (*sadly*): All three of them.

Don Pancho: Let us go into the house and drink beer and console each other.

Serafino: Did you say beer, señor? With foam?

Don Pancho: And a pinch of salt to take away the bitter taste.

Serafino (*making him a low bow*): Señor, I am at your service.

(*Arm in arm, they go into the house. For a moment the corral is empty; then Ramón Garza stalks through the gate followed by an imploring Felipe. Ramón Garza is both handsome and charming. Son of the seller of groceries, he need not work—since someday, when his father dies, he will own a grocery store and be a man of property. Therefore he is free to spend his time admiring himself and showing himself off to the enchanted girls of the village. He strides in, paying no attention to Felipe.*)

Felipe: But I am perfectly willing for you to use my little guitar. It is only that I beg of you, do not sing that song. Please, Ramón, do not sing it.

Ramón (*turning on him*): I will sing what pleases my fancy. And that is enough of it.

Felipe: If I could only make you understand, Ramón. That song is different from other songs. It has an appeal that belongs only to itself. It is like a song of magic. Who knows what will come of it afterward?

Ramón (*much hurt*): Eh, you are a selfish man. To think that you desire to keep to yourself something that pleases the ear of Anita. And you call yourself my friend.

Felipe: But, Ramón . . .

Ramón: Take your guitar. I will borrow nothing from such a low animal.

Felipe (*stepping back*): No, keep it. Perhaps you are the better man. Perhaps she loves you best, who knows?

(*He turns and walks sadly out, carefully concealing his grinning face from Ramón. Ramón, once this competition is out of the way, puts one foot on the box, strikes a pose, and begins to sing "Hand to Hand." Anita comes running to the door and into the corral.*)

Anita (*anxiously*): Wait, Ramón! Wait!

Ramón (*frowns at her and keeps on singing*).

Anita (*crying above his voice*): You don't understand, Ramón. Wait!

(*It is too late, however. Don Pancho has stalked into the corral. His clenched hand held up in front of Ramón's face, he suddenly opens his hand and blows across his palm. Pepper makes a cloud around Ramón's head, causing the boy to stagger back with a cry ending in an avalanche of sneezing.*)

Don Pancho: That pepper will teach you to sing that song no more! (*With a jerk of his head he stalks back into the kitchen.*)

Anita (*clasping her hands and wailing*): Ay, Ramón! Ay, Ramón!

(*Felipe just now ambles into the corral and, being a cautious soul, captures his guitar.*)

Felipe (*looking down at the miserable Ramón, who has collapsed on the box*): I told you not to sing that song, Ramón. But you would not listen to me.

(*Ramón, during this interval, has been able to do nothing but moan and sneeze. It is Anita who turns on Felipe.*)

Anita: So you were the one who made poor Ramón sing . . . you . . . you . . . you goat with four horns!

Felipe (*virtuously*): But, Anita, I told him not to sing it.

Anita (*flatly*): Ha!

Felipe: By the Blessed Angels, I swear I told him. Didn't I tell you, Ramón?

Ramón (*between two sneezes*): Yes.

Anita (*snapping at Ramón*): Imbecile!

Ramón (*rising, as dignified as possible under the circumstances*): I take myself home. I . . . (*He sneezes.*) I am desolated. . . . (*Another sneeze.*) I think I will kill myself. (*He starts toward the gate.*)

Felipe (*catching his arm*): Don't kill yourself until tomorrow, Ramón. Remember, we play at the bull this evening.

Ramón (*firmly*): I kill myself now . . . immediately.

Felipe: Eh, and then who will play the matador to my bull?

Ramón (*sneezing*): Let the world play it.

Felipe: But suppose the world should win. How can Anita walk around the plaza once alone with the world? (*Ramón manages to stop a sneeze.*) Have you not heard the conditions of the play? The winner receives a live goat and the honor of walking once around the plaza with the queen of the fiesta, this same, this beautiful Anita.

Anita (*snapping*): Eh, Felipe, you seem very anxious for me to walk around the plaza with Ramón.

Felipe: Anita, it is that you do not understand. I cannot fight the world and win. But Ramón? I can fight him. I win . . . then I walk with you.

Ramón (*furiously*): So you think you will win! You think you are a better bull than I am a matador? Why, you . . . (*He starts to sneeze. Anita and Felipe sway back and forth in an effort to help him. He almost sneezes and then he stops.*) Bah! (*He starts out again.*)

Felipe (*running around in front of him*): You will fight, eh, Ramón?

Ramón (*his voice sounding thick and clogged*): I know you, Felipe Lozano. You think, "He is weak from the sneezes." You think it will be easy for you to win from me and make me look the fool.

Felipe: But, Ramón . . .

Ramón: From out of my mouth I say it . . . "No!" (*With a sweep of his arm he flings Felipe aside and stalks through the gate.*)

Felipe (*turning to Anita*): Do not worry, my queen. I go to argue with him. In a moment I return.

Anita (*starting toward him*): But, Felipe . . .

Felipe: Do not fear for me. We will fight. I will win, and then, my heart's pigeon, we will walk around the plaza once alone. (*He hurries out after Ramón.*)

Anita (*stamping her foot in anger*): You three times idiot with the brains of a jumping bean!

(*In fury she starts banging on the box. Serafino, coming from the house, sees her rage, runs toward her, and pulls her to one side.*)

Serafino: One moment, señorita. Because you are angry with the world, do not destroy my beautiful box.

Anita (*turning on him*): You are the cause of all this!

Serafino (*stepping back in surprise*): I, señorita? I had nothing to do with it.

Anita: No? Then try your logic with this. If you had not been here my father would have gone downtown to the saloon, and he would not have heard Ramón singing the rooster to me. (*She sits on the box and begins to wail.*) It is all your fault, all your fault. And now I will never have a husband.

Serafino (*confused*): One moment, señorita, one little moment. How does what happened this afternoon leave you without a husband?

Anita (*her voice sobbing more and more*): Was Ramón not made to look the fool? And soon Felipe will think, "If I stay near this Anita, I, too, will be made to look the fool"; and he will go away. Then all the young men in the village will stay away from me through fear . . . and I will be left all alone.

Serafino (*with sudden cunning*): Not if you give them my love potion.

Anita: Eh?

Serafino: Feed it to them and they will be like little newborn goats at your feet.

Anita (*slowly*): Your love potion of sugar, flour, and nutmeg.

Serafino: With a charm whispered above it as the new moon turned red.

Anita: You are a very wise man, señor. I bow my head to you.

(*With a quick nod she runs into the kitch-en. Serafino gazes after her, shakes his head with the wisdom of age, and laughs.*)

Serafino (*sentimentally*): Ay, friend box, if we were twenty years younger, we would not need a love potion to love this pretty lady, eh?

(*Felipe runs in from the street.*)

Felipe: Is Anita here?

Serafino (*jerking in surprise*): Bah, how you startle a man!

Anita (*calling from the kitchen*): Is that Felipe?

Felipe: In person, my heart's dove.

Anita (*comes out from the kitchen with a tray on which is a single cake*): Oh, Felipe, what did Ramón say?

Felipe: He could not resist the lure of walking around the plaza with you . . . if he wins. But he will not win. I, Felipe Lozano, say it.

Anita: Ay, Felipe, you are a very wise man.

Felipe (*grinning shyly*): Anita . . .

Anita (*extending the tray*): See, I have made you something.

Felipe (*happily*): For me, Anita?

Anita: For you alone, Felipe. You will eat it now, yes?

Felipe (*taking the cake and staring down at it. Then he grins at Serafino*): For me.

Serafino (*beaming on him*): For you.

(*Felipe takes a great bite of it, and chews it up in evident enjoyment. Anita is watching him anxiously. Suddenly, although still chewing, the tempo is slower and he is no longer smiling. He takes a preliminary swallow and essays another grin, which isn't very successful.*)

Anita: What is wrong, Felipe? You like my cake, yes?

Felipe (*who looks as though he were wishing he could die the next minute*): Such a cake . . . such a magnificent cake.

(He blinks his eyes and tries to swallow again, but this is almost too much for him. Don Pancho comes striding gaily from the house.)

Don Pancho: Eh, that Ramón will sing no more songs. He . . . *(He pauses, seeing the odd, sickly expression on Felipe's face.)*

Felipe *(in a hollow voice)*: What was in the cake, Anita?

Anita *(innocently)*: A little sugar, a little flour, a little nutmeg.

Felipe: A little nutmeg . . . ohhh . . . I think I am going to die. I hope I am going to die! *(He turns and plunges through the gate.)*

Don Pancho *(in a low strangled voice to Anita)*: You fed him nutmeg?

Anita *(covering her mouth with her hand and not looking at him)*: I believe it made him sick.

Don Pancho *(yelling)*: You knew it would make him sick!

Anita *(plaintively)*: But, Papa . . .

Don Pancho: And my five pesos that I bet on him to win this afternoon . . . What about my five pesos, if he is too sick to play the bull, eh?

Anita *(stamping her foot)*: What care I for your five pesos? *(She turns and runs into the house.)*

Don Pancho *(flings out his hands and turns to Serafino)*: Are your three daughters like that?

Serafino *(hopelessly)*: All of them.

Don Pancho *(sinking exhausted on the kitchen stoop)*: This calls for a stronger drink than beer.

Serafino: Señor, did you bet your five pesos on Felipe Lozano as Felipe Lozano, or on Felipe as the bull?

Don Pancho: As the bull, of course. "Five pesos," I said, "that the bull will win."

(The mutter of voices and laughter can be heard outside.)

Serafino *(raising his head)*: Listen! The crowd is coming.

Don Pancho *(lost in grief)*: Five whole pesos.

(The voices of the crowd grow larger.)

Serafino *(sharply)*: Help me into the house with this box.

Don Pancho *(who has a single-track mind)*: May St. Peter forget that this day ever existed.

Serafino *(irritated)*: Have you stones in your feet? I have a plan to save your money. Help me with this box!

(Don Pancho blinks his eyes at Serafino for a moment. A loud laugh from outside decides him. He catches one side of the box, Serafino the other. As they disappear into the kitchen, the crowd begins to trickle in through the gate. It is a gay holiday crowd that loves to work in the sun, and laugh and play in it. The women have on brightly colored dresses, with shawls over their shoulders. The men wear the white trousers and gaily colored shirts of the northern villages. All are in merry good humor as they find their places on the benches.)

Crowd: Eh, it's a fine day for the comedy. Who do you think will win? . . . Fifty cents on the shoulders of Felipe. . . . Ten cents on the long arm of Ramón.

Man in Crowd: I heard Ramón was sick.

Crowd *(excitedly)*: Sick? Does that mean there will be no comedy? . . . For two weeks I have looked forward to this . . . perhaps he is afraid of Felipe. . . . Ramón the coward? Never!

Man in Crowd: Perhaps it isn't true. Perhaps it is Felipe who is sick.

Crowd *(laughing gaily)*: Ay, you Tomás, always you must have your little joke. What a fox he is, searching for laughter. *(Through the gate now comes a musician with a cornet. The crowd greets him vociferously.)* Hola, friend musician! . . . You come to play the applause music, eh? . . . Oh, this will be a fine

comedy. . . . Give us a tune now, musician.

(*The musician grins, waves his hand above his head, and sits down on one of the front benches at the back, as people move over to make room for him. He obediently plays a scale for them, and this, too, is greeted with laughter, whistles, and catcalls. Then Don Pancho enters from the kitchen. There is wild applause and the little musician plays the diana, the great applause music. Don Pancho smiles and bows and waves his hand to all of them.*)

Man in Crowd: Five pesos I've heard you've bet on the shoulders of Felipe, Don Pancho.
Crowd: Long live Don Pancho!
Man in Crowd: Do you want back your money, Don Pancho?
Don Pancho (*grinning*): Not I. And for those who like . . . I will add two pesos to the five.
Crowd: Now will you keep your mouth shut, Tomás? . . . Ay, it is a grand thing to have money. . . . What other village has a man so wealthy as Don Pancho? . . . Long live Don Pancho!
Don Pancho (*holding up his hand for silence*): My friends, what is a fiesta without a queen?
Crowd: True words. Long live the queen! Long live the Republic!
Don Pancho: This year, because of her beauty, my daughter was chosen for that honor.
Man in Crowd: A beauty she did not get from you, friend. (*He laughs loudly.*)
Don Pancho (*grinning good-naturedly*): Nor your daughter from you, friend. Therefore we are twins, you and I. (*There is a whoop of laughter from the crowd.*) If our friend the musician will play a little tune, I will bring in the queen.

(*The musician stands up and bows, the crowd claps, and he begins to play the "Wedding March" from Lohengrin. Don Pancho goes to the kitchen door and extends his arm. Anita, dressed as before, but with a lace shawl draped over a high comb in her hair, enters, puts her hand on his arm, and is escorted to the chair on the dais. The audience has risen, and they make passage for her. When she sits down the musician stops playing and mops his forehead. The crowd is yelling.*)

Crowd: Long live Anita! Long live the queen!

(*Anita bows to them, but her smile is rather forced and her eyes are fixed in anxiety on the kitchen door.*)

Don Pancho (*again waving for silence*): And now I present to you the great matador, Ramón Garza.

(*Ramón now enters from the kitchen. From some place he has managed to collect a semblance of the costume of the great profession. His shoes are ordinary oxfords. His cotton stockings have been dyed bright pink, and they are a trifle large for him. His trousers, which end at the knee, are of black cotton velvet, while down each side have been sewn long strips of brightly printed calico. Under the short black velvet jacket is his everyday shirt. Wrapped around him is a bright red cape. He wears no hat. Seeing him, the crowd goes wild. They shout; they whistle; they yell. Ramón takes the bows, waving his hand in front of his face, palm turned toward him. When some semblance of quiet is restored, Don Pancho once more speaks.*)

Don Pancho: And now, gentlemen and members of the beautiful sex, I introduce to you that exquisite creature without which a bullfight could not exist. My friends, I give you—the bull!

(*He whirls to one side and points dramatically to the kitchen door, in which, after a* moment, *appears a strange creature. The legs belong to a man, as do the arms; but from the waist up the creature is a bull. Made of papier-mâché, the mask and shoulder guards are painted white with great splashes of crimson, yellow, and green for decoration. One horn is vivid purple, the other gold. At the back, between the shoulder blades, is something resembling a pincushion made of red velvet, which takes the place of the shoulder hump of the fighting bull. Whatever noise was heard before is nothing compared to the noise that is heard now. Although the cornetist is playing, not a note is audible. The noise stops for the simple reason that the audience is too exhausted to yell any more. Anita, with a dazed expression on her face, has sunk back in her chair. She doesn't seem able to believe her eyes. Don Pancho is once more in the arena.)*

Don Pancho: Now the rules of the comedy are these. The bull and the matador will play. At the end of the half-hour if the matador has not thrust this stick into the cushion on the back of the bull, the bull wins. If the matador does thrust it in, he wins. Is that clear? (*Both Ramón and the bull nod.*) Precisely. (*Don Pancho hands Ramón the stick, a short affair to which has been fastened a long steel pin.*) The bull may butt and kick. You, matador, can use only the stick. Your feet must keep you out of his way. Is that clear? (*Again both nod.*) The prize for the winner is one live goat, and the privilege of walking around the plaza once, alone, with the Señorita the Queen.

Ramón (*with a quick glance at Anita*): That, too, is clear.

Don Pancho: Excellent. Play, musician.

(*He walks over and sits down on the bench in front of Anita. The musician, who once served in the army, blows taps, and the comedy begins. Ramón takes off his cape and holds it in front of him, jiggling it a little to attract the bull, who paws the ground shyly but does not move. He jiggles it again. The bull gives a coy wiggle and steps back, to the great delight of the crowd. Ramón comes closer, and still the bull coyly gives ground. At last Ramón turns to look at the crowd, wondering if they can advise him how to meet such tactics. At this moment the bull darts forward, head low, and Ramón tumbles to the ground. The bull steps back and allows Ramón to pick himself up. Ramón charges, and the bull dances out of the way. Finally Ramón is chasing the bull around in a circle until suddenly the bull stops and drops to his knees. Unable to save himself, Ramón trips forward across his back. Now it is the bull who chases Ramón, finally giving an extra spurt and butting him to the ground. The crowd is in hysterics. It hasn't seen such a lovely fight in years. Anita, however, has other ideas. Before anyone realizes what she is doing, she jumps down from her throne and wades into the fight herself. She has the right to use her hands if she wants to, because her rules were invented by herself. For a few minutes the fight is a three-angled scramble. Then Anita clutches at the back of the bull, acting as a sort of brake. This surprise attack throws him off balance, and both tumble down together. Ramón is also down, in a state of near exhaustion. At Anita's interference a rapid chatter sounds from the crowd.*)

Crowd: Ay, there, Anita! . . . What is happening? . . . Since when do queens fight the bulls? . . . Poor Felipe! . . . Which one is she trying to protect? Ramón, of course. . . . Not Ramón, Felipe!

(*By this time Anita has managed to get the bull's disguise off the man, revealing not Felipe but Serafino.*)

Anita (*screaming*): I thought so, you . . . you behind-legs of a horse!

Man in Crowd (*surprised*): But it is not friend Felipe.

Crowd (*excitedly*): What means this? . . . Is it a trick of Don Pancho's? . . . He is a slippery angleworm, that one. . . . I pay him no money for this fight. . . . Nor I. . . . Nor I. . . .

Don Pancho (*wailing*): My five pesos. My beautiful five pesos.

Crowd: Knit your money yourself, Don Pancho. . . . But, ay, it was a beautiful fight . . . it took a woman to end it. . . . Such a fight has not been seen in this village.

Anita (*who has been helping Ramón to his feet*): Come, Ramón. Let us walk around the plaza three times together.

Ramón (*weakly*): Three times?

Don Pancho (*aghast*): Three times? But that will tell the world that you two are engaged.

Anita (*snorting*): But naturally! (*She turns on Serafino.*) As for you, you man with two horns and the body of a snake . . .

Serafino (*seeking protection behind Don Pancho*): Let me explain, señorita.

Anita: Let the words tumble out of your mouth on the back of a swallow.

Serafino: I did not mean to make a fool of Ramón. It was only that my professional training went to my feet. It is my business to make people laugh.

Anita (*whirling around Don Pancho in an effort to catch Serafino, who just manages to stay out of her grasp*): Is it your business to make people laugh at my man?

Serafino: Look, señorita. Leave me alone and I will give you another love potion.

Anita (*snapping at him*): Your love potion! Bah! All I wanted of it was the nutmeg to feed Felipe.

Ramón (*who is just getting his brain back in working order*): Anita, do you mean you want to marry me?

Anita: If you ask me like a man of wisdom, instead of acting like a fool.

Ramón (*grins suddenly and holds out his arm*): Anita, walk around the plaza with me now.

Anita (*taking his arm*): Play a tune, musician!

Man in Crowd (*excitedly*): They need an audience for this parade.

Crowd: Is it possible? . . . Ramón! . . . I thought Felipe was the man in her heart. . . . Who can read the heart of a woman? . . . Let us watch them.

(*The crowd pushes and swirls through the gate led by Anita, Ramón, and the musician, who, considering the circumstances, loudly plays the applause music. Only Don Pancho and Serafino are left.*)

Don Pancho (*who is still rather dumb on the subject*): Serafino, do you think she fed Felipe that nutmeg knowing it would make him sick?

Serafino: Me—I have a wife and seven children, of which three are daughters. That is why I travel around the country as far away from them as possible.

Don Pancho: Serafino, I salute you as a man of true wisdom.

(*As they bow to each other . . . The curtain falls.*)

Close Up

1. (a) Why does Don Pancho object to Felipe's singing "that song" to his daughter, Anita? (b) Why does he insist that Felipe go home?

2. Felipe and Ramón are rivals for Anita's affection. (a) How does Felipe trick Ramón into singing "that song"? (b) What effect does it have on Anita's father?

3. Felipe and Ramón are to compete in a comedy bullfight for the privilege of walking around the square with Anita. When Anita gives Felipe the love potion, how does she hurt his chances of winning the bullfight?

4. (a) Why does Anita intervene in the bullfight? (b) What is the result of her intervention?

5. On the basis of Anita's actions, why do you think she fed Felipe the potion?

6. In a play, you learn about the characters largely through dialogue and through their actions. (a) On the basis of these two items, write a paragraph describing Anita. (b) Write a paragraph describing Felipe. (c) What additional information do the stage directions give you about these two characters?

Full Circle

Erich Maria Remarque
As adapted by Peter Stone

Characters

Anna

Grete

Koerner

Rohde

Mack

Maurer

Schmidt

Katz

Russian Soldier

Russian Sergeant

Russian Captain

Scene One

A third-floor room in Berlin. There are three doors—one leading to the hall and stairs, another to a closet, the third to the bathroom. There is a bed, a table and chairs, a hot plate, a basin, and a telephone. When the shade is not drawn, the single window looks down on the street in the foreground, and the city in the background; both are in rubble. It is April 30, 1945. At rise, the room is dark, the shade drawn. Apparently it is empty. We hear the terrifying sounds of bombing and shelling outside. Now the bombing stops, and the all-clear sirens are heard.

Radio (suddenly): This is the Berlin Command Post returning to the air—this is the Berlin Command Post. All clear—repeat— all clear——

(The phone rings—four times. No one answers it. A match is struck and now we can see Anna's face. More lifeless than calm, she lies on the bed, wearing a peignoir over a slip. She is twenty-eight and attractive. When the match is blown out we can see only the ember of her cigarette. Then the door opens and Grete enters. Twenty-two, blond, she has the kind of Wagnerian good looks that border between voluptuousness and fat. She crosses the room to the basin without noticing Anna on the bed. She sets down a kettle and fills it with water. Now she sees the open closet door and crosses to it, leaving the water running. She runs her hands over some dresses, then takes a fur stole off a hanger and drapes it over her shoulders.)

Anna: Don't you knock any more, Grete?
Grete (wheels about, terrified): Is—is that you, Frau Walter? I thought you went to the shelter.

Anna: You'd better turn the water off.

Grete: Oh—yes—(*She crosses to the basin and turns off the water.*)—Direct hit next door—number 17. Now we've got a view to the south—all the way to number 11. (*A pause.*) I'd like to see the mailman's face tomorrow morning!

Anna: What do you want, Grete?

Grete: We haven't any water next door—our pipes burst last night.

Anna: I thought you might have been cold.

Grete: Cold? On the last day of April? (*Then she notices the fur stole still around her neck.*) Oh—(*Sheepishly.*)—I saw it in the closet. (*Anna says nothing. Grete goes to hang it back in the closet.*) I mean—if all it's going to do is hang there it might just as well be back on the mink.

Anna: A fox fur would look pretty silly on a mink.

Radio: This is the Berlin Command Post. The enemy raiders have left the capital perimeter and are now heading north, sector Hanover. Repeat—heading north, sector——

(*Anna reaches over and shuts off the radio.*)

Grete: Hey! Why'd you do that? Don't you want to hear the damage reports?

Anna: No.

A Woman's Voice (*off*): Grete! Grete!

Grete (*calling off*): Just a minute—the water's not boiling yet! (*To Anna.*) Do you mind if I use the stove? We haven't any electricity either. (*She goes to the electric hot plate and snaps it on.*) Funny how everything works in here—I mean, if it weren't for the noise you'd hardly know there was a war on. (*The phone rings.*) You see? Even your telephone! (*Anna makes no move to answer it.*) Well? Aren't you going to answer it? (*Anna doesn't move.*) I mean, maybe it's for me. Our phone's out—(*She crosses to the phone and lifts the receiver.*)

Anna: It's not for you. (*Annoyed, she snatches it from Grete's hand, looks at it a moment, then lifts it to her ear.*) Yes?—No, he's not here—He's not here—He doesn't live here any more—No, there is no other number. He's dead. Two years ago. Who? (*A pause as she looks at Grete.*) No, I'm not Frau Wilke—(*Pause.*) She's dead, too. (*She hangs up the phone and lies back on the bed.*)

Grete: Who's dead?

Anna: Nobody.

Grete: Who's Frau Wilke?

A Woman's Voice (*off*): Grete—Grete—!

Grete (*going to door; calling off*): Just a minute, can't you? (*She closes the door. To Anna.*) That pregnant witch! The way she's got me running day and night—you'd think she's carrying the Fuhrer's child.

Anna: She's frightened.

Grete: She's crazy, if you ask me. Didn't you hear her singing that stupid lullaby all during the raid?

Anna: I don't know—I suppose so.

Grete: Are you deaf? We could hear it all the way down in the cellar. Who ever heard of singing a lullaby to a baby that's not even born yet? (*She stares at Anna for a moment.*) How come you don't go down to the cellar when the raids start?

Anna: I'm tired.

Grete: I'd rather be tired than dead.

Anna: You're entitled to your opinion.

Grete: My God! You're not much fun to be with. Maybe if you opened the curtains things wouldn't look so gloomy in here. How come they're closed, anyway? It's broad daylight outside. (*She goes to the windows.*)

Anna: No, don't!

(*Grete opens the blinds anyway, flooding the room in light. She stares out the window.*)

Grete: My God! Just look at that mess! Still, it's not much worse than yesterday—and the radio said there were only eight thousand casualties yesterday.

Anna: Go away.

Grete: What I want to know is what happens now that it's getting warm out? All those dead people buried under all that wreckage—the smell's going to be——

Anna: Shut up, Grete.

Grete (*indicating the room next door*): She says she can hear them at night, scratching, trying to get out. Crazy. It's a miracle that we haven't all gone crazy.

Anna: Haven't we?

Grete: Maybe we have and we don't know it. This is the last time I'm ever going to work for anyone who's pregnant. I certainly am glad I'm not pregnant. (*She thinks a minute, then knocks on wood. She picks up a pair of stockings from the back of a chair.*) These are real silk, aren't they? (*She holds them up.*) Real silk! If I had one pair, just one pair, I'd feel like a human being again.

A Woman's Voice (*off*): Grete! What's taking so long?

Anna: You can have the stockings—just go away.

Grete: You mean it? I can really have them? (*Shots and shouting outside. Grete runs to the window.*) Now what's happening?

Anna: Probably the Russians.

Grete (*she jumps back from the window, startled*): What?

Anna: Why so surprised? Don't you know they're almost here?

Grete (*she peeks cautiously out the window for a moment, then sighs with relief*): No, it's only the Gestapo, thank God! They seem to be looking for somebody. (*She turns and smiles.*) Stop trying to scare me—the Russians won't be here today.

Anna: Tomorrow, then.

Grete: You sound anxious to see them.

Anna: I'm anxious for the war to end.

Grete: Say, you'd better be careful! If old Koerner heard you say that you'd wind up a whole head shorter.

Anna: Koerner! Why should he care?

Grete: He's our new block warden.

Anna: The janitor?

Grete: Fischer was killed in the raid on Tuesday. So I'd be careful if I were you. You don't want to end up like the sergeant.

Anna: What sergeant?

Grete (*indicating next door*): Her husband.

Anna: I thought he was still at the front.

Grete: That's what she thinks, too. Promise you won't tell her? The doctor said she shouldn't know—not until after the baby, anyway.

Anna: What happened?

Grete: He deserted. He knew about the baby being overdue and tried to get back.

Anna: Where is he?

Grete: Downstairs.

Anna: Why doesn't he come up?

Grete (*giggling*): He can't. He's hanging from the street lamp in front of the house—with a big sign on his chest: "Deserter."

Anna: Oh, no—

Grete: Sure. Come look—you can see it from here.

Anna (*sadly*): I can see it just as well from here.

(*The door opens and Koerner enters. He carries a clipboard in his hand. Past fifty, his expression is habitually stern, abetted somewhat by the severe way he combs his hair and the sterility of the steel-rimmed glasses he wears.*)

Anna: Doesn't *anybody* knock any more?

Koerner: I'm the block warden now.

Anna: I don't care if you're Adolf Hitler now. As long as that door remains standing you'll knock on it.

Koerner: I have my orders. (*He consults his clipboard.*) Frau Walter—(*He checks the list.*)—alive. (*To Grete.*) What are you doing here?

Grete: I came to get some water.

Koerner: From now on stay in your own room until the head count has been taken.

Grete (*saluting*): Yes, Herr Field Marshal!

Koerner: Be careful—you're talking to the representative of the party!

Grete: Is that what you are? Then maybe you can help capture that escaped madman.

Koerner: Madman?

Grete: The one on the radio who keeps saying we're winning the war. (*She laughs.*)

Koerner (*sharply*): Are you criticizing the party?

Grete: Who, me? That's only a joke I heard in the cellar—

Koerner: Subversion is punishable by death! We hang traitors every day! Just look out that window if you don't believe me—look at that street lamp down there—

(*Grete tries to silence him.*)

Grete: Shh! Don't forget what the doctor said.

Koerner: So don't you forget. From now on you will stay in your own room after every raid until *I* take the head count. Is that clear? Heil Hitler!

Grete (*automatically*): Heil Hitler.

Koerner: Frau Walter, I said Heil Hitler!

Anna: I heard you.

Koerner: Why didn't you answer, then?

Anna: Oh, don't be an idiot.

Koerner (*apoplectic*): What? *What did you say?* You think now that the Russians are close by, you can do anything you please. Well, just wait, all of you! The war's not over yet—the tide will turn, you'll see! (*He goes.*)

Grete: The silly fool! Down in the cellar he couldn't keep his disgusting old hands off me, and up here he acts like a member of the High Command. (*A pause.*) The radio says the Russians are all Asiatic subhumans and they'll attack all the women. Do you believe that?

Anna: Maybe. I don't know.

Grete: Between the Gestapo hanging everybody and the Russians attacking everybody——

Anna: Why do you suppose they hanged the sergeant? What difference can a few deserters make now?

Grete: I don't know—but if all the soldiers just went home, then where would we be?

Anna: At peace.

Grete: These are real silk, too, aren't they? (*She holds up some underwear.*)

Anna (*weary*): You can have them, Grete.

(*She giggles and leaves. Anna continues to lie on the bed, staring at the ceiling. The telephone rings but she doesn't answer it. Then the door opens and Erich Rohde enters. He is about thirty. The charm, courage, and attraction of this man have been seriously tampered with; that these qualities are still alive and in evidence speaks well for the degree to which they existed before. Anna hears him but doesn't turn to look.*)

Anna: What do you want now, Grete, more hot water? Why don't you just take the whole stove?

(*No answer.*)

Rohde (*coming forward quickly, his hand in his pocket*): Don't scream—I have a gun.

Anna (*calmly*): What do you want?

Rohde: I'm looking for somebody. A man named Wilke—Otto Wilke. He lives here, doesn't he?

Anna: No.

Rohde: What do you mean no? He has to live here! They told me number 19—third floor—

(*Rohde tries to collect his thoughts while Anna watches him carefully.*)

Anna: I'm sorry. I live here.

Rohde: But they said *he* lived here.

Anna: *I* live here! He used to live here—two years ago.

Rohde: Two years? They told me only yesterday.

Anna: News travels slowly these days.

Rohde: What news?

Anna (*a pause*): They took him away.

Rohde: Who?

Anna: The Gestapo.

Rohde: He never came back?

Anna: Do they ever?

Rohde (*examining her carefully*): Are you related to him?

Anna: I told you all I know.

Rohde: Did you know him?

Anna: You'd better go now.

Rohde (*sharply*): I asked you a question!

Anna: It's none of your business!

Rohde (*angrily*): You're wrong! It is my business! (*A pause.*) I can make you tell me—

Anna: With your gun?

Rohde (*bringing his empty hand out of his pocket*): I don't have a gun.

Anna: I'm sorry, I can't help you. Now get out and leave me alone. (*Rohde doesn't move and now Anna becomes angry.*) Listen! I don't know who you are and I don't know what you want. All I do know is you can't stay here!

Rohde: I won't stay long.

Anna: You won't stay at all.

Rohde: Haven't you noticed my clothes?

Anna (*suddenly resigned and weary*): When did you escape?

Rohde: Today—just now. I counted on Otto Wilke's helping me. Someone in prison gave me his name.

Anna: Too many people knew that name.

Rohde: But I can't leave the house now— the streets are crawling with Gestapo.

Anna: What can I do?

Rohde: Hide me until it gets dark—

Anna: Did anyone know you were coming here?

Rohde: Why can't you trust me?

Anna: You can't trust anybody if you expect to survive.

Rohde: Sometimes there are more important things than simply surviving.

Anna: No—surviving is the most important thing there is!

Rohde: Who told you that?

Anna: My husband.

Rohde: Where is your husband?

Anna: Dead.

Rohde: I'm sorry.

Anna (*a pause*): Were you in a concentration camp?

Rohde: Yes.

Anna: Jewish?

Rohde: No.

Anna: Politics, then.

Rohde: Does it matter?

Anna: No, not to me. How long?

Rohde: October '38.

Anna: Seven years. Where?

Rohde: Buchenwald, mostly. When the Americans got too close they moved us to Oranienburg. Today they brought us here to Berlin. (*Looking at her intently.*) Look, just let me stay here until it gets dark. Then I'll take my chances outside. (*A pause.*) I promise I'll leave when it gets dark—

Anna: No.

Rohde: At least I'll have a chance!

Anna: Not so loud!

Rohde: A couple of hours—that's not too much to ask!

Anna: People come in here all the time— without even knocking—

Rohde: I'll hide in the closet.

Anna: There's a girl next door who snoops around in there every chance she gets—

Rohde: Under the bed then—

Anna: Nobody could get under there—it's too low.

Rohde: I can do it. Look! (*He falls flat and starts to cram himself under the low bed.*)

Anna (*pulling him back*): Stop it! Get up! How can you make such a fool of yourself? Get up! (*Slowly, Rohde gets to his feet.*) I want to help you but I can't. I'm afraid! If they find you here they'll hang us both, and I have to stay alive—I have to!

Rohde (*thinking*): You could say I forced you to hide me.

Anna (*as if she's seen a ghost*): What did you say?

Rohde: You could tell them I forced you.

Anna: What I tell them is my business, not yours!

Rohde: I was only trying to protect you——

(*Without warning, Anna slaps him.*)

Anna: Who asked you to? (*Rohde walks away, rubbing his cheek. She looks out the window.*) The street's empty now. You can sneak out.

(*He starts for the door, then stops and turns.*)

Rohde: Don't you at least have something I can wear? One of your husband's suits?

(*Resigned, she starts rummaging through the dresser. He watches her for a moment, then turns and looks out the window.*)

Rohde: Oh, my God.
Anna (*frightened, she turns*): What is it?
Rohde: The city—it's nothing but ruins.
Anna: Have you just now noticed it?
Rohde: Where do people live?
Anna: They don't. (*She has come up with a uniform—trousers, shirt, and boots.*) Here. Put these on.

(*He looks, but does not take them.*)

Rohde: Whose are they?
Anna: Does it matter?
Rohde: Your husband's?
Anna: Take them or don't take them. But don't cross-examine me!
Rohde (*taking the clothes*): I didn't mean to. I'm sorry.
Anna: And don't apologize, either.

(*She goes to the bed and lies down. Rohde begins changing his clothes.*)

Rohde: After an air raid, everything's so quiet. That was the worst part about prison—the awful silence. The raids were the only thing that kept us from going mad. When the bombing started they let us out into the corridor. We could talk because the guards couldn't hear us—we learned to do it without moving our lips. That's where I first heard about Otto Wilke—two days ago. Somebody kept repeating his name and address over and over again, close to my ear. I don't know who it was. He was standing right behind me but I couldn't see him—we weren't allowed to move. We couldn't even move our heads——
Anna: I don't want to hear about it.
Rohde: Early this morning they came to get us. They put us in trucks and brought us to Berlin, to the zoo. No irony intended—it was just convenient. They said they were going to let us go, and everybody believed it. We knew it wasn't true, but we believed it anyway. Then they started to shoot—one group at a time. (*Anna turns away in disgust.*) It was the air raid that saved us. When the bombing started we ran. We scattered in all directions, like chickens on a highway. Some went behind the reptile house, some into the camel enclosure—I saw one man die in the seal tank, can you imagine? When we got to the city streets we kept running until we got lost among all the other people who were running, too. Everybody was running but you could tell the escaped prisoners—they weren't looking up at the planes like the others. They were looking back over their shoulders—and running just a little faster. The whole time I kept repeating the instructions that disembodied voice whispered in my ear: "Wilke, Otto Wilke. He'll help you. Go the the Kurfurstendamm, then the second street after the Brandenburgerstrasse—twice to the right, number nineteen, third floor. Wilke, Otto Wilke. He'll help you—"
Anna: Forget about Wilke! He can't help you now—he couldn't even help himself! We've all got to forget about Wilke!
Rohde: Why?
Anna: Because he lived here and they caught him—because he's dead and buried and useless!

Rohde (*he is dressed now*): It fits pretty well. But the boots are too tight.

Anna: Forgive me.

Rohde: Where's the tunic?

Anna: I don't know. I don't have it.

Rohde: I can't go outside half dressed!

Anna: What do you suggest?

Rohde (*a pause*): At least let me stay until it's dark.

Anna: All right—but that's all.

Rohde (*handing her his old clothes*): You'd better hide these somewhere—I'll be needing them again.

Anna: Why?

Rohde: I don't want to be wearing this uniform when the Russians get here.

Anna: So that's what it all comes down to—the right suit of clothes. (*She goes to the dresser and gets a pistol.*) Here—you'll probably need this, too.

Rohde (*examining it*): It's not loaded. Do you have any ammunititon?

Anna: No.

Rohde: Then what good is it?

Anna (*shrugging*): It looks loaded, doesn't it? All guns look loaded. I don't suppose you have any false papers?

Rohde: No. Unless they search me, of course.

Anna: Why? What will they find?

Rohde (*unbuttoning his left sleeve and showing a tattooed number*): My real papers.

Anna (*staring at it; finally*): You're finished if anyone sees that.

Rohde: What do you suggest?

Anna: Please go now—

Rohde: You said I could stay until dark.

Anna: Not with that—

Rohde (*looking at it, too*): It won't wash off, I'm afraid. (*A pause; his tone changes.*) Actually, the time may come when these things could be pretty valuable. After all, how many will there be left? And the work is first rate—they say the tattoo artists were recruited from the docks of Hamburg and Bremerhaven. Mine must've been a little

drunk, though. Look at this seven. It looks more like a nine——

Anna (*distraught*): Please—just go——

Rohde: Is that coffee on the stove? I wouldn't mind a cup of something warm.

Anna: No, it's just water. If I fix you some tea, will you leave afterward?

Rohde: Oh, please, let me do it! I haven't done it in so long. I used to make the best cup of tea in town—even my English friends used to say so. (*He goes to the stove and begins puttering with a teapot, a tin of leaf tea, cups, spoons, and saucers, his back to the audience all the time. These activities are accompanied by a steady stream of small talk as he carries on both ends of a conversation, supplying her words as well as his own.*) She: Oh, did you have some English friends? How interesting! How did you happen to meet them? He: Well, it's nice of you to ask. I went to school for a year in England. She: You don't say! You are a fascinating fellow, aren't you? May I ask what you studied? He: You certainly may—the metaphysical poets of the seventeenth century. George Herbert, Thomas Traherne, John Donne—"Stay, O sweet, and do not rise! / The light that shines comes from thine eyes; / The day breaks not, it is my heart, / Because that you and I must part—" (*He stops.*)

Anna (*she has been listening*): Go on, finish it. (*When he doesn't, she turns and sees that he is standing, his shoulders hunched, his body tense, his head bowed, straining and trembling.*) What's wrong—are you ill? (*No answer.*) What is it? (*She rushes to him and sees whatever it is he's been doing.*) Oh, my God! Stop it—stop it! (*She grabs at his arm and pulls it away.*) Your arm—you've burned off the skin!

Rohde (*panting from the ordeal*): I told you it wouldn't wash off——

Anna: Why did you do it? (*Quietly; her attitude toward him changed.*) You fool—you fool. Come here. Sit down so I can bandage it. There isn't any butter—I'll have to use cold cream.

Rohde: A funny world—no food but plenty of cosmetics—

(*She has gone to get bandages and a jar of cream, and now returns and starts applying these to his arm.*)

Anna: What a mess—

Rohde: Wouldn't it be funny if my skin grew back with the number still on it—as if it had become part of my genetic structure.

Anna: Why did you do it?

Rohde: I had no choice. You were right—it *was* too dangerous. And I have to be sure—

Anna: Sure of what?

Rohde: That someone gets away—even if there's only one—to be a witness for all the others who didn't make it, so that everyone knows what happened there and who's to blame.

Anna: Vengeance.

Rohde: Yes! Why not?

Anna: But then you'll be as guilty as they are.

Rohde: I am guilty.

Anna: Are you?

Rohde: Yes, I saw it coming. I smelled the smoke—why didn't I shout "Fire"?

Anna (*having finished the bandaging*): But they put you in prison—you must've done something.

Rohde: Yes—in 1938! But why did I wait so long? For six years I just watched it happen and did nothing, like everybody else. I was too busy, you see, working as a ghost writer for celebrities who weren't up to writing their own stories—film stars, football players, condemned murderers. I ground out my four thousand irrelevant words a day and nursed my investments. Then I heard about the camps. I didn't believe it at first—I *couldn't*. Then a friend told me about the ovens, about the children being put in like loaves of bread. That's the way he put it—like loaves of bread. I couldn't erase that picture from my mind. I couldn't look at a loaf of bread without feeling sick. I couldn't sleep at night. Finally I wrote a letter asking if it were true. That's all—a letter! To the editor of the *Berliner Tageblatt*. But it was never printed. Two days later I was arrested by the Gestapo. They asked me why I'd written the letter, why I was asking questions, why I was interfering in things that were none of my business. I told them it was my business, that I was a German and if Germany were doing such things, that it was very much my business. (*A pause.*) Do you know what they did then? They made me *eat* my letter—that's right, they tore it up and forced me to swallow every shred of it! All of my indignation and eloquence—it tasted so dry and stale. And when I threw it up they made me swallow it again. I was meant to *digest* it, you see, and eliminate it—that was the whole point! (*Another pause.*) Yes, I am guilty—for waiting until it was too late, for allowing them to accumulate their power. They'll tell you it grew from their strength, but it's a lie. It came from our neglect.

Anna: How do you feel?

Rohde: Rotten.

Anna: I have some brandy.

Rohde: No, it would only make me sick. I'm not used to alcohol.

Anna: Then come lie down.

Rohde: Just until it gets dark.

Anna (*after a pause*): Until it's safe for you to leave. (*She helps him lie down.*)

Rohde: Thank you—(*He closes his eyes.*)—it's been a long time since I said that. (*There is a knock at the door. He tries to sit up.*) What's that?

Anna: I don't know. Lie back—I'll take care of it.

(*She opens the door. Grete enters, then stops short.*)

Grete: Oh! Excuse me. I didn't know any-one——

Anna (*indifferently*): My cousin.

Grete: Your cousin! Really? (*Smiling, she stares at Rohde for a moment.*) Well, I don't want to intrude on a family reunion.

Anna: You're not intruding, Grete. Hans got here last night.

Grete (*smelling gossip*): Last night?

Anna: Yes. Didn't you hear him come up the stairs?

Grete: No. And why didn't I see him when I was in here before?

Anna: Is there any particular reason why he should report his movements to you?

Grete (*flustered*): No, I——

Anna: You must stop asking so many questions.

Grete: I'm sorry—I won't do it any more. Is he on leave, or a deserter?

Anna: Really, you're impossible! He's not a deserter; if you must know, he's just passing through on his way from the west front to the east.

Grete (*giggling*): They say you can do that on the subway these days.

Anna: Was there something you wanted, Grete?

Grete: A few towels, that's all—just some

towels. (*Anna goes to the cabinet and returns with the towels. She hands them to Grete.*) Well, I guess I'll be going now—(*At a loss.*) Uh, will he be staying long?

Anna: Next you'll be asking to see his travel orders.

Grete (*routed*): No—no, I won't—I'm sorry! Thanks for the towels. (*She beats a hasty retreat, closing the door after her.*)

Rohde: That wasn't very smart, telling her I spent the night.

Anna: I didn't want her to think you just arrived, in case she hears about the escaped prisoners.

Rohde: It was smart.

(*Grete enters again, without knocking.*)

Grete: There's a Gestapo patrol searching the house—looking for some escaped prisoners, I think.

Rohde: Did you call them?

Grete: Me? Are you crazy? Who wants the Gestapo poking around? (*She thinks about his question.*) Why? Are you hiding something?

Anna (*curtly*): Of course not. Is there anything else, Grete?

Grete: Isn't that enough? (*She smiles and moves to the door.*) Well—good luck, *cousin.* (*She leaves.*)

Anna: That wan't very smart, asking if she called them. (*She crosses to him and removes his boots, then hands him the gun.*) Put this under the pillow. Now listen. You were here last night—with me—understand? Your name's Vollmer. Hans Vollmer. You were born in Breslau. You're a lieutenant in the Artillery.

Rohde: Who's Vollmer?

Anna: He was killed in North Africa three years ago.

Rohde: Was this his uniform?

Anna: Will you stop wasting time?

Rohde: They'll check—

Anna: They can't. Breslau's in Russian hands. (*She hurriedly puts lipstick on, then grabs his face between her hands and kisses him, smearing some of her lipstick on him. She goes right on talking, rapidly and frantically.*)

Rohde: Where have I been stationed?

Anna: Rostock.

Rohde: Formation?

Anna: JR 27. (*She grabs a brandy bottle.*) You were in the hospital—

Rohde: JR 27—

Anna: You lost your papers—you were drunk—you're still drunk—(*She hands him the bottle.*) I can hear them on the stairs!

(*He drinks and chokes. He has a coughing fit.*)

Rohde: We can't fool them—nobody can—

Anna (*forcefully*): We will! We'll lie—we'll lie about everything—we'll lie our heads off. Lie down. (*She lies down next to him. There's a moment's silence.*)

Rohde (*suddenly*): My God! Your name! I don't know your name!

Anna (*whispering loudly*): Anna Walter.

(*The door bursts open. Mack and Maurer, two uniformed Gestapo men, enter with drawn guns. In his middle twenties, Mack has allowed his constant disapproval of most things to distort his face into a perpetual sneer. Older, thirtyish, Maurer is large and stupid. He rarely, if ever, speaks, but the acts of inhuman brutality that constitute his duty and his pleasure form the great equalizer. The two soldiers are followed by Captain Schmidt. In his early thirties, he is a man of intelligence, wit, and some attractiveness. He is educated and articulate, neither an intellectual nor a fanatic—merely an opportunist.*)

Mack (*speaking as he enters*): Nobody move!

(*Rohde pretends to sleep.*)

Anna (*sitting up*): That's right, don't knock—just walk in! Everybody does!

Schmidt: Quiet please. Heil Hitler!

Anna: Heil Hitler.

Schmidt: Group Leader Captain Schmidt. Your name?

Anna (*smiling*): Anna Walter.

Schmidt (*indicating that Mack should write it down*): Walter—Anna. Married?

Anna: My husband's dead.

Schmidt: My condolences.

Anna: You're a little late—he's been dead two years.

Schmidt: Who's he?

Anna: You'd better ask him.

Schmidt: I'm asking you.

Mack: He's drunk, Captain—his woman, too. I can smell it from here.

Anna: Do I have to stand for that?

Schmidt: I suppose so.

Rohde: Please, I'm trying to sleep.

Schmidt: Maurer—

(*Maurer goes to Rohde quickly, and roughly pulls him to a sitting position.*)

Rohde (*dazed*): What's going on here?

Anna: Bravo! One insults defenseless women and the other attacks wounded soldiers. Why aren't they out fighting Russians?

Mack: Shut your mouth!

Rohde: Oh, my head! Do you have to shout?

Mack: Let Maurer teach this drunk some manners, Captain.

Rohde: Be careful who you call a drunk, soldier. There may not be much of an army left, but an officer still outranks a—(*He squints at Mack's sleeve.*)—a sergeant.

Schmidt: You're an officer?

Rohde: First lieutenant! Can't you see?

Anna (*laughing*): How do you expect him to see your rank if you're not wearing your tunic?

Rohde: What? (*Laughing.*) Please forgive me, Captain. Have a cognac? (*No reaction from Schmidt.*) No? Well, I could use one. Anna, get me a cognac—my mouth feels like a gravel pit. (*He looks around the room unsteadily.*) Where's my tunic?

Anna: Don't you remember?

Rohde: I wouldn't be asking if I remembered, would I?

Schmidt: I hope one of you remembers.

Anna: He threw it out the window!

Rohde: I didn't! (*He stops, looks at Anna.*) I did? I must have been——

Anna: —Watch your language!

Schmidt: Yes—we mustn't offend the lady. (To Anna.) You say he threw his tunic out the window? Why?

Anna: He wanted to cover the head of that deserter hanging on the lamppost down there.

Rohde: Deserter——? Yes, I grew sick of looking at him.

Anna: I went down to get it after the raid but it was gone!

Schmidt: I'm sure it was.

Anna: Excuse me, but are we being accused of something?

Schmidt: Have I said so?

Anna: You're treating us like common criminals.

Rohde: Anna, please. I'm sure the Group Leader didn't come here to arrest us for having a few drinks—

Schmidt: We're looking for escaped prisoners.

Anna: You expect to find them here?

Schmidt: I expect to find them anywhere.

Anna: Then look around, Group Leader— you can see for yourself there are no escaped prisoners here. You can go now.

Schmidt (*smiling*): I'm perfectly willing to take orders from a lady—but only off-duty. (*To Rohde.*) May I see your papers, please, Lieutenant?

Anna (*quickly*): Tell me, Group Leader— what do these prisoners of yours look like?

Schmidt: They're not mine yet, Frau Walter. Why do you ask—have you seen them?

Anna (*smiling*): I won't know that until you tell me what they look like. Are they wearing prison clothes?

Schmidt: Yes, of course—at least, they were.

Anna: Were? What are they wearing now?

Schmidt: Who knows? It might be almost anything. A business suit—an army uniform——

Anna: Or a Gestapo uniform—

Schmidt: One of them's quite dangerous— he killed a man.

Anna (*surprised*): Killed?

Schmidt: Yes. Grabbed him by the throat and broke his neck.

Anna: That's quite a stunt. He must have been pretty large—like your helper there. (*She indicates Maurer.*) Can't he talk?

Schmidt: Maurer? He has other talents. (*Maurer grins broadly.*) But I hope you'll never find out what they are—you're much too attractive.

Anna: No, no—not at the moment, I'm not. I must look awful. (*She checks herself in a compact and winces.*) At least let me fix my face! (*She begins applying lipstick.*)

Mack: Lipstick is un-German!

Anna: Then don't use it. (*She crosses to the closet, where she will change into a dress.*)

Schmidt (*turning to Rohde*): All right, Lieutenant, for the record—name?

Rohde (*with military precision*): Vollmer, Hans, First Lieutenant, JR 27, Rostock. Discharged yesterday from the hospital. Ambulant. Orders to report back tonight at nineteen-hundred hours.

Schmidt: Thank you. Papers?

Rohde: Certainly. Papers—papers—papers—(*He begins groping through his trouser pockets.*) Anna, where's my wallet?

Anna: How's that?

Rohde: My wallet—where is it?

Anna: Meaning what?

Rohde (*getting angry*): Meaning I can't find it!

Anna: Meaning I took it?

Rohde: I didn't say that! But I had it when I came up here—

Anna: Isn't that wonderful! First he swills all my liquor and now he calls me a pickpocket! Get out of here!

Rohde: Anna, please. All of my papers— all my identification—

Schmidt (*wearily*): I don't suppose they could have been in your tunic?

(*Rohde puts his hand to his head.*)

Anna: Oh, really? You mean I didn't steal them after all? Thank you very much! I'm sick of looking at you—get out!

Schmidt: Please, Frau Walter. I'll decide who leaves and when.

Rohde: Forgive me, Anna.

Schmidt: Perhaps there are other ways of verifying your identity, Lieutenant. What's wrong with your arm?

Rohde: You can see for yourself—I was wounded.

Schmidt: I'm afraid I cannot see for myself unless you remove the dressing.

Anna: Oh, please, not in here, if you don't mind!

Rohde: Don't worry. I have no intention of publicly displaying my wounds. I was burned by a shell casing, Captain. I insist that you take my word for it.

Anna: Now I've heard everything! A lieutenant insisting to a captain?

Rohde: Yes—an army lieutenant to a police captain.

Anna (*to Schmidt*): Will you stand for that, Captain? Maybe he can push me around, but you——

Schmidt: Please, be quiet! Which hospital, Lieutenant—the name.

Rohde (*a pause*): I don't understand the reason for all these questions!

Schmidt: The name of the hospital, Lieutenant—

Anna (*as Rohde again hesitates*): I don't mind telling you, Group Leader. It was Hedwig Military. He told me so. (*To Rohde.*) That will teach you to accuse me of things.

Schmidt (*looking from one to the other, not sure what's going on*): Mack—

Mack (*snapping to attention*): Captain!

Schmidt: Call Hedwig Hospital. (*To Anna.*) Is your phone working?

Anna: I doubt it.

Mack (*he picks up the receiver, listens, then grins*): It works, Captain. (*He dials the operator.*) Hedwig Hospital, Fraulein— What?—I don't know the number—I don't have a telephone book! Fraulein—Fraulein, listen—*Fraulein!* This is official business— *Gestapo* business—Thank you, Fraulein. (*He covers the mouthpiece.*) She's getting it, Captain.

Schmidt (*to Rohde*): What was the name of your doctor?

Rohde: Sorry, he didn't introduce himself.

Mack (*into the phone*): Hello? Hedwig Hospital?—What? I don't—I can't understand—Who's this?

Schmidt (*impatiently*): Give it to me, you idiot! Can't you make a simple phone call? (*He takes the phone.*) Group Leader Captain Schmidt speaking. Give me Admissions, please—What? What are you saying?—I don't understand you—(*Slowly he lowers the receiver.*)

Anna: What did they say?

Schmidt: I don't know. I don't speak Russian.

Anna: Only two miles away—not very far, is it, Group Leader? An hour perhaps?

Schmidt: Or a week.

Anna: Well, whichever it is, I feel much safer with the Gestapo here. You will defend us against those Asiatic subhumans, won't you, Group Leader?

(*Suddenly Maurer moves noiselessly to the door and yanks it open. Grete almost stumbles in.*)

Grete (*lamely*): May I have a few more towels, Frau Walter?

Schmidt: Who's this?

Anna: She works next door—for Frau Zandler.

Schmidt: Who's Frau Zandler?

Grete: She's expecting a baby. Two weeks overdue——

Schmidt: Why were you listening at the door?

Grete: I wasn't listening. I was about to knock——

Schmidt: With your ear?

Grete (*anxious to shift attention from herself, she turns to Anna*): What's wrong, Frau Walter? Is your *cousin* in trouble?

Schmidt (*turning to Rohde*): Cousin?

Anna: You know how it is during wartime, Group Leader—no acquaintances but many friends, no family but many cousins.

Grete (*with satisfaction*): That's what I thought. Why else would he spend the night?

Schmidt: He spent the night here last night?

Grete: And that's not all. They didn't go down to the cellar during the raid and it doesn't take a genius to figure out why.

Anna (*quietly*): That's enough, Grete.

Schmidt (*he thinks for a moment, staring at Rohde all the time*): Maurer—(*Maurer jumps to attention.*) Go downstairs and bring up the prisoner. (*Maurer salutes smartly, does an about-face, and leaves the room.*) We caught one of them alive.

Anna: Is there any particular reason for this?

Schmidt: Probably not.

(*A silence.*)

Rohde: Tell me, Captain—have you actually seen the prisoners yourself?

Schmidt: Why do you ask?

Rohde: I thought perhaps you could describe them to us—so we could watch out for them.

Grete: Yes—what do they look like?

Schmidt: After a few years in the camp, they don't look like anything.

(*A silence.*)

Grete (*chattering nervously*): Well, I just think it's wonderful the way you people go about your business—I mean, with the Russians so close, and all. I mean, you Gestapo people are in such terrible danger——

Schmidt: Oh? Why's that?

Grete: *Everybody* hates the Gestapo.

Schmidt (*smiling faintly*): Really?

Grete (*realizing what she's said*): Our enemies, I mean. Naturally *we* don't—— (*She sees the expression on Schmidt's face and looks around for a way out.*) Let's see if there's any news. (*She turns on the radio.*)

Radio: —resisting fiercely. The Russians have broken through to the inner city, according to one report. Zeitz' Department Store has been abandoned, as well as the Friedrichstadt subway station. In the Wilmersdorf sector Russian tanks have been steadily advancing and are at this moment shelling the——

Schmidt: That's enough of that.

Grete (*turning off the radio*): Yes—the news on that station is always bad.

Anna: Keep on trying. Maybe you'll find a station where we're winning.

Mack: That's subversive! Don't you know we shoot people who make subversive statements?

Anna: Winning the war subversive?

Mack: But we're *not* winning!

Anna: *That's* subversive! Shoot yourself!

Mack (*confused*): What?

Schmidt: I'm afraid you're no match for her, Mack.

(*The door opens and Maurer returns, pushing the prisoner, Katz, before him. In his middle fifties, Katz is dressed in prison clothes; he is bleeding and seems weak and exhausted.*)

Mack (*to Katz*): Attention!

(*No reaction from Katz; Maurer kicks him and he straightens up a little.*)

Schmidt: Tell us your name.

Katz (*reciting*): Prisoner in protective custody, number 87112. (*Maurer kicks him again.*) Prisoner in protective custody, number 87112, Sir.

Schmidt: I asked for your name.

Katz: Prisoner in protective custody——

Mack (*screaming*): Your *name!*

Katz (*automatically*): I'm a dirty Jewish swine.

Schmidt (*patiently, almost bored*): Your name—your real name.

Katz (*hesitating*): I am Izzy—a dirty Jewish swine.

Grete: Why won't he tell his name?

Schmidt: Nobody's going to hurt you—you're not in prison now. Tell us your real name.

Katz (*apprehensive*): Katz—

Schmidt: Very good. And your Christian name?

Katz: Christian name? Joseph—

Schmidt: Joseph Katz. All right. Profession?

Katz (*pausing to think*): I'm a dirty Jewish——

Schmidt: Besides that, you idiot! What did you do before?

Mack: Circumciser in the synagogue.

(*Grete snickers.*)

Katz: I was Doctor Joseph Katz, professor of chemistry, lieutenant in the reserve, holder of the Iron Cross, first and second class— (*He stops.*)

Schmidt: Go on—

Katz: —and a dirty Jewish swine.

Schmidt (*he stares at Katz for a moment*): Very well. Now, I want the answers to a few simple questions. Do you understand?

Katz: Yes.

Schmidt: I want to know where you were going when you were captured, whom you were going to see, and the whereabouts of the man who escaped with you, Erich Rohde. Nothing else. Is that clear?

Katz: Yes.

Schmidt (*softly*): Katz, where were you going?

Katz: Nowhere.

Schmidt: Whom were you looking for?

Katz: No one.

Schmidt: Where is Erich Rohde?

Katz: I don't know Erich Rohde.

Schmidt: Do you know anyone in this room?

Katz (*he looks from face to face, slowly, coming finally to Rohde*): No one.

Grete: My! That was exciting, wasn't it?

Schmidt: Do you know that one of you strangled a guard, Katz? Was it you?

Katz: No.

Schmidt: Then it was Rohde.

Katz: I don't know any Rohde, Group Leader.

Schmidt: I can promise you will by tomorrow, Katz. It would be much easier to tell me now. (*No answer.*) It seems that you're an intelligent man, Katz—as far as that's possible for one of your race—so I presume you know what's going to happen to you?

Katz: Yes, Group Leader. I will be questioned further and then liquidated.

Schmidt: That's correct. So we'll strike a bargain, eh, Katz? Tell me where I can find Erich Rohde and there'll be no more questioning.

Katz: No more questioning?

Schmidt: I promise you'll be shot immediately.

Anna: What sort of a bargain is that?

Mack: Quiet!

Schmidt (*to Anna*): You think it's unfair? Katz, would you rather be questioned or shot?

Katz: Shot, Group Leader.

Schmidt: Of course. All right, where is Erich Rohde?

Katz: I don't know Erich Rohde, Group Leader.

Schmidt (*a pause; he thinks*): Katz, how would you like to go free?

Katz: Free?

Schmidt (*speaking quietly*): Yes, Katz, free! That sounds quite different, doesn't it? (*Katz says nothing.*) Well? What do you say?

Katz: They promised to set us free this morning, too—

Schmidt: But this is different! I want the man who murdered the guard. I'm willing to pay for it. The moment we have him we'll set you free, Katz. I give you my word.

Grete (*to Katz*): Why don't you tell him? No one will ever know—

Schmidt: That's right, Katz. Besides, he'll probably be caught anyway. Why should you suffer for him? An Aryan—a goy. Now, which will it be, Katz? Do I set you free, or do I turn you over to Maurer there?

Katz: When—when the air raid began we all started running—in the direction of the Kurfurstendamm——

Schmidt: That's it—go on—

Katz: —in the direction of the Kurfurstendamm. I looked back a few times—one or two were behind me. When I got to the Weidendamm Bridge the bombs started dropping all around me—I fell down—I stayed down until the bombing stopped. When I got up I didn't see anybody—the others must have been killed—(*He trails off.*)

Schmidt: Go on, Katz.

Katz: That's all, Group Leader. (*A silence.*)

Grete: It sounds believable to me—

Mack: Shut up!

Schmidt (*turns to Grete*): There's a pregnant woman next door. The Jew's screaming might upset her. Turn the radio up, please.

(*Grete hesitates, then turns up the radio.*)

Radio: —advancing along a wide front in the northern sector. Meanwhile, to the south, the American armies are encountering——

Schmidt: Maurer, break his fingers.

(*Mauer advances menacingly.*)

Radio (*the voice breaks off; a new one continues*): Attention! Attention! This is the Berlin Command Post. The enemy has advanced

within three hundred meters from the Fuhrer's bunker—

(Taking advantage of the shift of attention, Katz breaks for the open window and has jumped up onto the sill before anyone can stop him. Mack and Maurer draw their guns.)

Mack: The Jew's escaping!

Schmidt: Don't shoot! I want him alive!

Mack: He can't get away! It's three floors straight down!

Schmidt: Leave him alone!

Mack: But he's bluffing, Captain!

Schmidt: Quiet!

Katz: *You*, be quiet. *(The unexpected force of his voice silences everyone.)* You're finished—all of you—caught in a trap like your Fuhrer—all the murderers, the cowards, the thieves, the criminals, the liars—the ones who break bones and open veins and abuse children—you're finished, all of you—

Schmidt *(screaming)*: Katz! Come down from there! That's an order!

Katz: You're through giving orders to me! Don't you think I knew all those promises of yours were lies?

Schmidt: They weren't, Katz—I give you my word.

Katz: Beg me, Group Leader—*plead* with me—

Mack: Let me finish him, Captain—

Schmidt: No! You can't escape, Katz. We can wait.

Katz: Good. So can I. We'll wait for the report.

Schmidt: What report?

Katz: The news that he's dead—that the pig is dead. Didn't you hear? Only three hundred meters—

Mack: Let me shoot him now, Group Leader!

Schmidt: No! I want him alive. All right, Maurer, get him.

(Maurer advances slowly toward the window.)

Katz: No, wait—a moment longer—can't you wait a moment longer? He's not dead yet—(*Maurer moves closer.*)—the pig's not dead yet! Now I'll never know——

(These last words are spoken quietly and sadly as he lets himself fall backward, down, out of sight. Maurer makes a desperate lunge, but he is too late. Grete screams. Then silence.)

Schmidt (*suddenly barking orders to Mack and Maurer*): Quick—downstairs! Maybe he's still alive! (*Mack and Maurer hurry out. Grete has moved to the window and is looking down at the street. Schmidt joins her. Anna and Rohde stay where they are, staring at each other.*) What could I do? The idiot was determined to jump—I couldn't stop him.

Grete: What are you going to do now?

Schmidt (*blowing up*): How does that concern you?

Grete: I was only——

Schmidt (*shouting down to Mack and Maurer*): Is he dead?—Are you sure?—Well, make sure! (*Mockingly, to the others.*) They *think* so! What makes them think they can think? (*He takes out his handerchief and dries his face and neck.*) Oh, what's the difference! What's another Shylock more or less in this world?

Anna: He was a professor of chemistry.

Schmidt: Or a professor, for that matter? Still, it would have been better to have kept him alive. Now they'll blame *me* for it—(*To Rohde.*) Won't they, Lieutenant? (*No answer.*) I said, *won't they, Lieutenant?*

Rohde: Won't they what?

Schmidt: Blame me!

Rohde: I don't know—how should I know?

Grete: Now, if you'd've tied up his hands and feet he couldn't have jumped——

Schmidt: Will you shut up!

(The radio, which has been left on, suddenly blares.)

Radio (*solemnly*): This is Radio Berlin returning to the air. Here in the headquarters of the High Command we have just learned of the tragic death of our beloved Fuhrer. He died heroically in the fulfillment of his duty. We repeat—our glorious leader, Adolf Hitler, is dead. Grand Admiral Doenitz has assumed command and will continue the valiant defense of our Fatherland. We will now play the Funeral March from Wagner's Gotterdammerung. (*The music begins.*)

Anna (*after a moment*): He's—dead?

Schmidt: They must have murdered him.

Grete: Who?

Schmidt: The generals, of course—didn't they try before?

Grete: It looks like the end now—without the Fuhrer——

Schmidt: Doenitz—a Navy man—why not Himmler? Why did they pass up Himmler?

Rohde: Maybe he's dead, too.

Schmidt: Maybe—yes, that's probably it. Well—(*He walks to the window and looks down at the street below.*)—no one's likely to ask many questions about the Jew, not with the Fuhrer dead.

Grete: That's one consolation. Well, I'd better get back to Frau Zandler before she starts hollering. (*She goes to the door.*)

Schmidt (*absentmindedly*): Yes—I'll go with you—got to finish searching the building.

Grete: Nobody's hidden in our room.

Schmidt: No, I suppose not. Himmler couldn't be dead—the radio would have mentioned it. Then why Doenitz? (*He turns to Anna and Rohde.*) You two think you got

The New York Times.

VOL. XCIV..No. 31,875.
Entered as Second-Class Matter,
Postoffice, New York, N. Y.

Copyright, 1945, by The New York Times Company.
NEW YORK, WEDNESDAY, MAY 2, 1945.

LATE CITY EDITION
Clearing and warmer today. Cloudy with moderate winds tomorrow.
Temperatures Yesterday—Max. 51 ; Min. 44

THREE CENTS NEW YORK CITY

HITLER DEAD IN CHANCELLERY, NAZIS SAY; DOENITZ, SUCCESSOR, ORDERS WAR TO GO ON; BERLIN ALMOST WON; U. S. ARMIES ADVANCE

MOLOTOFF EASES PARLEY TENSION; NEW MOVES BEGUN

Russian Says Country Will Cooperate in World Plan Despite Argentine Issue

4 COMMISSIONS SET UP

They Will Deal With Council, Assembly, Court and Some General Problems

By JAMES B. RESTON

Allies Invade North Borneo; Fighting Fierce, Tokyo Says

Australia Informed of Landing by Treasury Minister—MacArthur Reports Only Air Attacks and New Gains on Luzon

REDOUBTS ASSAILED

U. S. 3d, 7th and French 1st Armies Charging Into Alpine Hideout

NEAR BRENNER PASS

British in North Close About Hamburg—Poles Gain in Emden Area

Von Rundstedt Caught

NAZI CORE STORMED

Russians Drive Toward Chancellery Fortress, Narrowing Noose

BRANDENBURG TAKEN

Stralsund Port Swept Up in New Baltic Gains— Vah Valley Cleared

By C. L. SULZBERGER

ADOLF HITLER

Clark's Troops Meet Tito's In General Advance in Italy

By VIRGINIA LEE WARREN

ADMIRAL IN CHARGE

Proclaims Designation to Rule—Appeals to People and Army

RAISES 'RED MENACE'

Britain to Insist Germans Show Hitler's Body When War Ends

By SYDNEY GRUSON

DOENITZ' ACCESSION VIEWED AS A BLIND

---

away with something, but you didn't. I don't know what your game is, but there's something fishy about it. (*To Rohde.*) When are you going back?

Rohde: Tonight.

Schmidt: See that you do—or they'll string you up on the lamppost like that sergeant down there. (*To Anna.*) Did they say how the Fuhrer died?

Anna: Heroically—in the fulfillment of his duty.

Schmidt: Yes, yes, but how?

Anna: They didn't say.

Schmidt: They did say Doenitz, didn't they?

Anna: Yes.

Schmidt: I wonder what it means. He's not even a party member—(*To Anna.*) You're a smart girl. (*He looks at Rohde briefly, then smiles at Anna.*) Who knows? We might even meet again someday. (*To Grete, his manner suddenly changing.*) Come on.

(*Schmidt and Grete exit. Rohde and Anna are left alone. Dusk is approaching. The Funeral March plays on.*)

Anna (*going to the door and listening*): It's all right—he's next door—talking to Frau Zandler. (*She turns back to Rohde and studies him for a moment.*) Your name is Erich Rohde.

Rohde: Yes.

Anna: The Jew knew you, didn't he?

Rohde: Yes.

Anna: And he didn't betray you—

Rohde: No.

Anna: Why?

Rohde: Would it have saved him?

Full Circle **487**

Anna: It might have. You never know.

Rohde: No.

Anna (louder): You never know, I tell you! That music—as if we were dead, too! (She turns off the radio.) You killed the guard?

Rohde: Yes.

Anna: They taught you pretty well.

Rohde: It doesn't need teaching. It's the simplest thing in the world. (Shaking his head.) Not killing, that's what takes character.

Schmidt (off): Your husband was a traitor, a deserter!

(A woman's voice is heard, off, wailing pitifully.)

Rohde: The swine! The filthy swine!

Anna: Shh! We mustn't betray ourselves now.

(They are close and looking into one another's eyes. It is dark except for the red glow of a burning building outside. Grete enters.)

Grete: He's gone.

Anna: Did he find anything?

Grete: Of course not. He's crazy, you know. I think the Fuhrer's death was too much for him. I warned him not to tell Frau Zandler about her husband, but he told her deliberately. It was terrible. And that poor man who jumped—even if he was a Jew— (Rohde reacts but says nothing.) Are you all right? You look sick.

Anna: Grete, I have a pair of shoes that might fit you—real patent leather, too. (Looking in the closet.) Here they are. (She hands them to Grete.)

Grete (her face lighting up): Now that's what I call generous! (She starts toward the door.) If only I had a dress to go with them—

Anna (pulling a red dress from the closet): Here's a dress, Grete.

Grete: Oh, it's gorgeous! I hope it fits.

Anna (shepherding her to the door): Why don't you go and try it on?

Grete: You sound like you want to get rid of me—(Suddenly the sirens wail, announcing another raid.) Another one! What for? The Fuhrer's already dead. Coming to the cellar? (She turns, laughing.) No, of course not. (She leaves. There is a slight pause.)

Rohde: Don't you ever go to the cellar?

Anna: No—it's like sitting in your own grave, waiting to die, waiting to be covered over.

Rohde (going to the bed, starting to pull on his boots): The street will be empty in a few minutes. I can go then.

Anna (she goes to the bed, sits): Where to?

Rohde: Somewhere—an empty cellar, the ruins. I'll be all right now.

Anna: Isn't it safer if you stay here?

Rohde: Not for you. Grete heard me say I'm leaving tonight. She'll be watching.

Anna: She has her new dress—that'll keep her busy tonight.

Rohde (a pause): And tomorrow?

Anna: Tomorrow? (A pause.) Who can think that far ahead?

(They look at one another. The first sounds of the bombardment can be heard as the lights dim. In the blackness the noise of the raid can be heard. Then this fades and there is silence.)

(CURTAIN)

Close Up

1. This play takes place during the close of World War II, when Russian forces are entering Berlin. (a) Why is Rohde looking for Otto Wilke? (b) What has happened to Wilke?

2. (a) When Anna asks Rohde if he has any false papers, what does he mean by saying, "No. Unless they search me, of course"? (b) How does he get rid of these "papers"?

3. (a) For what crime was Rohde imprisoned in a concentration camp? (b) According to Rohde, what was his real crime?

4. Anna proves her cleverness and resourcefulness during Schmidt's interrogation. (a) Why does she pretend to be angry with Rohde? (b) Why does she tell Schmidt that Rohde had been at Hedwig Hospital?

5. As a final precaution, Schmidt brings in Katz, an escaped prisoner, to identify Rohde. (a) What bargain does Schmidt try to strike with Katz? (b) Why does Katz refuse?

Scene Two

Setting: The same, the next morning. At rise, sporadic shell and small-arms fire can be heard. White sheets and towels are displayed as flags at some of the windows visible outside. Rohde is alone, dressed. He stands at the window, looking out at the rubble. Suddenly the door opens and Koerner enters.

Koerner: Frau Walter?

Rohde: She's not here.

Koerner (*eyeing him suspiciously*): Where did she go?

Rohde: No idea. (*They stare at one another.*) Who are you?

Koerner: None of your business. Who are you?

Rohde: None of your business.

Koerner: It is precisely my business—I'm the new block warden.

Rohde: Oh, so you're Koerner.

Koerner: How do you know that?

Rohde: You're a very famous man.

Koerner (*not sure if Rohde is being sarcastic*): You may think you're fooling everybody, but you're not. I know you were here last night.

Rohde: So—?

Koerner: My orders are to report all unauthorized persons staying in the building—especially soldiers. (*Holding his hand out stiffly.*) Papers, please.

Rohde (*wearily*): Tell me something, Koerner. When you said you were the new block warden, how new is new?

Koerner: Why?

Rohde: It's a pity the war has to end just as you get a job you like.

Koerner: You think I like all this extra work?

Rohde: I think you love it—but it's piling up faster than you can handle. Look out the window, Block Warden. See all those white flags? Towels, bedsheets, anything people can find—that means the Russians are practically around the corner. Are you going to report all of those people, too?

Koerner (*uncertain*): I—I don't think they belong to my block——

Rohde: Why don't you get smart and hang out a white flag of your own? You haven't much time, you know.

Koerner: Never! Doctor Goebbels said any street showing a white flag will be blasted from the map of Berlin. Nobody's getting out so easily. (*He moves to the door.*)

Rohde (*blocking Koerner's exit*): You're so right, Koerner. Nobody's getting out so easily.

Koerner (*uncertainly*): Get—get away from the door—(*Rohde doesn't move.*) This is treason!

Rohde: Be careful of that word, Koerner. What is treason this morning may not be treason tonight—the traitors arrested yesterday might be national heroes tomorrow.

Koerner (*nervously*): Let me out of here.

Rohde (*as shooting is heard downstairs and Koerner turns to the window*): Who's that shooting, Koerner? Germans killing traitors who hung out white flags? Or Russians killing the traitors who didn't? It's a bad day to talk about treason, Block Warden.

Koerner: Get out of my way!

(*Rohde throws him roughly onto the bed. At this moment Anna enters. Koerner, seeing the open door, makes his break and goes.*)

Anna: Erich—what's wrong?

Rohde: He's going to report me—

Anna: No he won't. I know the man—he's too corrupt. He'll wait for his bribe.

Rohde (*sounding hopeful*): You think so?

Anna: Yes. Then he'll report you.

Rohde: Did he denounce the sergeant on the lamppost?

Anna: So they say.

Rohde: And Otto Wilke?

Anna: No. (*A pause; then she turns on a smile with some effort.*) Look what I got for us—(*She opens the packages she has brought back.*) We're rich. Bread, butter, and coffee—real coffee. You should have seen what I had to go through to get it. And butter's so scarce they won't even take the coupons anymore. I had to give up my last pair of silk stockings for it. (*She holds up the bag of coffee.*) Do you know how long it's been since we've seen *real* coffee?

Rohde: What did you have to give for that?

Anna: Aren't you cute! But it just so happens I didn't have to give anything for it—it's a Survivor's Bonus.

Rohde: A what?

Anna: Survivor's Bonus—that's what they call it. The party gives out extra rations after the really heavy air raids. You see? We get rewards for being so loyal that we survive the bombs.

Rohde: That's incredible.

Anna: But it's true! When ten thousand are killed we get a quarter-pound of sugar—twenty thousand, a quarter-pound of coffee. It's quite a system. You can eat better and keep track of the losses at the same time. (*Suddenly.*) I almost forgot! (*She reaches into her purse and pulls out a pack of cigarettes.*) Cigarettes!

Rohde (*hesitating*): I'm afraid to ask how many people got killed just so we could smoke—fifty thousand, at least.

Anna: No, they're black market—I splurged. A pair of earrings.

Rohde: Anna, you shouldn't have. What if you'd been caught?

Anna (*lighting his cigarette*): Everybody does it—(*The phone rings. She puts her hands to her ears.*) Oh no! Not another one! Not now!

Rohde: Anna! What is it?

Anna (*nearly hysterical*): Why can't they leave me alone!

Rohde: Who Anna?

Anna: I tell them there's nothing to be done, but they keep calling anyway!

Rohde (*he picks up the phone*): Who is this?—What?—Who? (*A pause.*) No—I'm not Otto Wilke—No—he's dead—two years ago—I'm sorry—I'm sorry—(*He holds the dead phone in his hand for a moment, then hangs up.*) He sounded so desperate. (*He sits on the bed.*) Anna, who was this Otto Wilke—some sort of a saint?

Anna: He was a shopkeeper—men's shirts and ties, that sort of thing. He wasn't even opposed to Hitler—not at the beginning. Then he was arrested.

Rohde: What for? What did he do?

Anna: Nothing. It was a mistake. He was the wrong Otto Wilke. He was in jail five days, then they realized their mistake and let him go. He never told me what happened during those five days—not a word. But pretty soon, by ones and twos, men started coming to the apartment, and calling—men like that man on the phone—like you yesterday—men who needed help.

Rohde: And he helped them.

Anna: He asked me if I had any objections to what he was doing. I said no, I was glad. I said I'd even help if he wanted. But he wouldn't let me. It was too dangerous, he said.

Rohde: He was your husband.

Anna: Yes. Then they came and took him away.

Rohde: Who betrayed him? Do you know?

Anna (*a pause*): I did.

Rohde (*astounded*): What?

Anna: Yes. I betrayed him.

Rohde: But—why?

Anna: He told me to. He insisted—he said it was my only chance. He came home one day and told me there was a traitor in the group—they didn't know who it was, but someone was turning them in. Three of them had already been picked up by the Gestapo. I told him we'd go away but he said it was too late, he was being followed already. He said I'd be arrested, too, if I didn't report him. (*She thinks for a moment.*) He told me what to say: I had just found out about his activities and it was my duty as a loyal German to report him. He even picked out the dress I should wear. We drank a glass of wine together—sat without saying anything for a while—then he told me to go. When I was out in the street I looked up at our window—that one. I saw his face pressed against the glass—white—his white face smiling. They held me for three hours. When I got back he was gone. I never saw him again. A few weeks later they came and handed me a cigar box with some ashes in it—his ashes, they said—it's hard to recognize ashes. They gave me an extra ration card as a reward for my loyalty—they told me the party was proud of me. They also told me it would be better if I changed my name.

(*A pause.*)

Rohde: You still love him, don't you?

Anna: (*flaring up*): I hate him! His despicable heroics! "Live," he told me, "live and forget me." "I love you," he said, "and if you love me you'll do what I ask." I loved him enough to do it—but he didn't love me enough to take me with him! "Forget me," he said. But that was the last thing he wanted. He was going to live on in my memory—that's what he wanted! Vanity! Male vanity! So he left me here to receive his ashes in a cigar box and the congratulations of his murderers for a job well done. He left me to answer the phone whenever some poor soul called for help. And he left me with something else, too—something worse—

Rohde: What else?

Anna: The uncertainty! Do you think I'll ever be sure—*completely* sure they would have gotten him without my help?

Rohde: That's why you hit me yesterday—when I said you could save yourself by denouncing me.

Anna: Twice would be a little ridiculous, don't you think? The coffee should be ready now. (*She goes to the stove and pours two cups.*)

Rohde: Anna, can you really blame him—for wanting to save you?

Anna: Blame him? I don't blame him. I blame myself—for going along with it. I was too close to understand.

Rohde: Understand what?

Anna: His need for heroics! Men *love* to dream about heroics. On white horses—against impossible odds—to save some helpless woman in distress. It's your eternal, adolescent dream of glory.

Rohde: And what do women dream about?

Anna: Reality. Didn't you know that? We only dream about what's possible. Can you imagine, for instance, that a woman could have conceived of this impossible war—or *any* war? Marching, saluting, killing—what could be more absurd?

Rohde: Women would have done it all better, I suppose.

Anna: Why not? We couldn't have done it worse! And don't be condescending—my husband was condescending.

Rohde: It seems we share a lot of things—

Anna: All the wrong things.

Rohde: If I promise not to be condescending—if I promise not to be heroic—would you like me better then?

Anna: It would help. (*A pause.*) Erich—maybe I could be very grateful that you showed up.

Rohde: Why?

Anna: Otto Wilke helped forty-two men escape. If you became the forty-third, I think I could forgive him for what he did to me.

Rohde: It's nice to know I could be of use to you.

Anna: You have been already.

Rohde: Really? How?

Anna (*laughing*): Now Grete knocks before she comes in.

Rohde (*laughing, too*): Is that all?

Anna (*looking away*): No—(*Thinking.*)—this morning, for the first time in two years, I woke up without remembering my nightmares.

Rohde (*he is staring intently at her*): Anna—is it possible that I'm falling in love with you?

Anna: Love? We barely know each other's name!

Rohde: So what? Yesterday I didn't even know that you existed. Anna! It's how I feel!

Anna: But it's nonsense! You've been locked up in a cell too long.

Rohde: Anna—

Anna: Gratitude—that's all it is! And desire, of course.

Rohde: Then you feel nothing at all—

Anna: I like you. I think you're smart. I think you're brave and strong. But love? No, not yet, Erich.

Rohde: Not yet? That sounds hopeful.

Anna: Does it?

Rohde: As though you thought you could. (*She says nothing.*) Do you think you ever could, Anna?

Anna: I don't know. Probably. But that doesn't mean I will.

Rohde: No, of course not. Loneliness is so much more fun.

Anna: If I do, Erich—(*A pause.*)—if I do—promise you won't ever leave me.

Rohde: I won't ever leave you.

Anna: Promise!

Rohde: I promise.

(*He takes her in his arms and kisses her. Suddenly Grete enters without knocking.*)

Grete: Frau Walter—(*She stops when she sees Rohde and Anna, then remembers to knock. They laugh.*) Don't tell me you're still here.

Rohde: I was just going.

Grete: Weren't you supposed to leave last night?

Rohde: You have a good memory.

Anna: Where are you going?

Rohde: I want to have a little talk with Koerner. (*He goes.*)

Grete: I think it's starting now.

Anna: What?

Grete: The baby. Frau Zandler's in labor now.

Anna: Is she all right?

Grete: I'm not exactly sure. I've never seen anyone in labor before.

Anna: I'd better take a look.

(*Grete and Anna leave. The scene remains empty; the sound of shelling and the rattle of a distant machine gun are heard. Then there is a knock at the door. A moment passes, then the door opens and Schmidt appears. He is now wearing civilian clothes and carries several packages. He looks around, sees no one, goes to the table, and puts down his packages. He checks the closet, stops when he see the dresses. He fingers them for an instant, then goes to the window and looks out. Next he goes to the bed, tests it with his hand, smiles with satisfaction, and stretches out without removing his shoes, his head propped up on the pillow. Then he notices the radio and turns it on.*)

Radio (*warming up*): —it is now certain that Doctor Goebbels died with the Fuhrer. There are reports that Martin Bormann is also dead, as well as Gestapo Chief Himmler, but these, as yet, are unconfirmed. Meanwhile, Reich Marshall Göring——

(*Schmidt turns off the radio.*)

Schmidt: Sounds like Wagner's going to get quite a workout.

(*The door opens. Anna is holding it open while speaking to Grete in the hall outside.*)

Anna: Grete, there's no use in calling the midwife now. Stay with her, and let me know if the pains come more regularly.

Schmidt: It's comforting to know that some women can behave sensibly in a crisis

Anna (*startled*): What—what are you doing here?

Schmidt: Don't worry—this isn't an official call.

Anna: What do you want?

Schmidt: Why so suspicious? I'm paying a social call—and in the proper manner, too. (*He points to the packages on the table.*) Presents. Tell me—has your boyfriend left?

Anna: What boyfriend?

Schmidt: Your cousin.

Anna (*nervously*): You can see for yourself.

Schmidt: Good. Shake hands with your new cousin. (*He holds out his hand, but she doesn't respond.*) Come, now. You must say I acted decently. After all, he wasn't carrying any papers—I could have had him hanged as a deserter. But what did I do? Nothing. Live and let live is my motto—good luck to him. And if anyone happened to be grateful—?

Anna (*gaining confidence*): You could have hanged him for all I care. But speaking of deserters—haven't you lost a uniform somewhere?

Schmidt (*laughing*): Oh, that! Yes, it feels quite strange without it, I must say—as if I were only half dressed.

Anna: Don't tell me the war's over.

Schmidt: Mine is. Aren't you going to open your presents? (*He crosses to the table and opens the packages as he speaks.*) They weren't easy to come by, let me tell you—not even for me. Scotch whiskey, Swiss cheese, Westphalian ham—look at this—even Beluga caviar! (*He reaches into his pocket.*) And ration cards—enough for ten to live on—Anna—

Anna: You remember my name—

Schmidt: I know all about you—I've done my homework. But we'll have time for that later on. Right now, let's——

Anna: Later on?

Schmidt: Yes. Didn't I tell you? I live here now—with you.

Anna (*frightened, but trying not to show it*): You must be out of your mind!

Schmidt: Yes—from the first moment I saw you.

Anna: Very touching, but——

Schmidt: (*taking hold of her*): We'll be good for each other, Anna—

Anna: Let go of me!

Schmidt (*his manner changing suddenly*): Don't play the lady with me. If all the men you'd entertained were here now we could hold the Russians off for another year. (*Anna picks up a bottle from the table and starts to swing at him, but he catches her arm and takes the bottle away.*) Careful—that's real Scotch whiskey.

Anna: Get out of here!

Schmidt: What do you say we open it? (*He occupies himself with it.*)

Anna: But you can't stay. The Russians will be here soon—

Schmidt: I'm sure they will.

Anna: What will you do then?

Schmidt: Greet them with open arms.

Anna (*laughing*): That I'd like to see!

Schmidt: Oh, you will. And you'll be rewarded for it, too.

Anna: For what—hiding a Gestapo officer?

Schmidt: No—for hiding an escaped prisoner.

Anna (*startled*): What?

Schmidt: Yes, a pathetic victim of a Nazi concentration camp—(*A pause as she stares at him anxiously.*)—Me.

Anna: You?

Schmidt: Certainly. Who did you think? Look at these. (*He takes some papers from his inside jacket pocket.*) An old friend in Registration fixed me up—official, right down to the stamp. (*He returns them to his pocket.*)

Anna: But how do you know they'll believe you?

Schmidt: Papers are everything in this world. Without papers a hero could be taken for a traitor. But with them—

Anna: A Nazi could be taken for a hero.

Schmidt: I wouldn't have put it that way, but that's the general idea. So let the Russians come—I'm safe. (*He fills a glass, drinks it, fills it again, and offers it to her.*)

Anna (*thinking for a moment, then taking the glass*): Still, I think you'd be better off somewhere where you aren't known.

Schmidt: Where, for instance?

Anna: In one of the shelters. I understand they're using the subway stations now. There's thousands of people down there–no one will notice you.

Schmidt: When the Fuhrer heard the Russians were advancing through the tunnels, he ordered the subways flooded.

Anna (*shocked*): But—all the people— (*Schmidt shrugs.*) Oh, no—

Schmidt: They say it was the last order he gave. So the subways are out. It was a bad idea, anyway. The Russians will check those places very carefully, but they can't check every single room in the city—can they?

Anna: Maybe not, but the Russians aren't here yet. And in the meantime, you've picked the wrong building to wait for them in. The super here is the block warden. He'd love to report an escaped prisoner.

Schmidt: He'll be glad to have me around—to prove to the Russians he was never a real Nazi.

Anna: Not this one. He still thinks we'll win the war.

Schmidt: One of those. Well, maybe I'd better have a talk with him.

Anna (*nervously*): Yes, but not now. Later.

Schmidt: Later? You mean I can stay?

Anna: Do I have any choice?

Schmidt: None whatsoever.

Anna: In that case—please stay. But I'm going to need a little time. Can you be back in about an hour?

Schmidt: Why?

Anna: I have a few things to arrange.

Schmidt: What things? (*The door opens and Rohde appears.*) Never mind—I see what things. (*To Rohde.*) Come in, Lieutenant. (*Not understanding the situation, Rohde hesitates, finally enters, and then closes the door.*) Excuse me, I've forgotten your name.

Rohde: Vollmer. Hans Vollmer.

Schmidt: Did you know we're related, Vollmer? That's right, we're cousins now. Once removed. I thought you were leaving last night.

Anna: He couldn't get away last night.

Schmidt: What's the matter? Afraid of the dark?

Anna: He's leaving now—just stopped by to pick up his things—

Rohde (*uncertainly*): Yes—that's right.

Schmidt: I'm afraid the matinee is not as convincing as the evening performance.

Anna (*going to Rohde and pushing him toward the door*): Never mind your things, Hans. I'll keep them for you. Good luck and take care of yourself. (*She pushes him to the door.*)

Rohde: Goodbye, Anna. (*He opens the door.*)

Schmidt (*producing a gun*): Don't go, Lieutenant. Come in and sit down. (*To Anna.*) Please close the door. (*Rohde looks at Anna, then follows Schmidt's directions.*) I'd be very interested in hearing *where* you were going, Lieutenant.

Anna: What difference does it make?

Schmidt: Now that he's seen me here, a great deal of difference, I'm afraid. Where, Vollmer?

Rohde: Nowhere in particular. I've been cut off from my regiment—and I can't do much fighting with this arm, anyway.

Schmidt: Yes, it's a pity about that arm.

Anna: You'd better stop worrying about his arm and look out for your own neck.

Schmidt: That's exactly what I am doing. You were pretty anxious to get rid of him, were't you?

Anna: What if I was? I was pretty anxious to get rid of you, too, if you'll remember. Why don't you both clear out? I don't need either of you. You'll make a stunning pair—the Army and the party. You can pass the time telling each other how you both deserted when the going got rough.

Schmidt: So he is a deserter.

Rohde: And what are you—a tourist?

Schmidt: What's that supposed to mean?

Rohde: At least I'm still in uniform. Where'd you get that suit, Group Leader?

Schmidt: There are thousands of men's suits in Berlin to which the men are missing, Lieutenant. The suit isn't so important as the papers one carries in the pocket. (*Patting his pocket.*) I have my papers, Vollmer.

Rohde: The won't do you much good when the Russians come, Group Leader.

Schmidt: You still don't understand, do you? The Group Leader's dead. He died two hours ago in an office—very peacefully. Death by pen and ink. You have faith in ultimate justice—you think that because Vollmer's your real name you'll be able to prove it somehow. Forget it. My new name's a hundred times more real than yours because I have the papers to go with it.

Anna: Don't you think you ought to tell us what your new name is? We can't go on calling you Group Leader—that might embarrass you in front of company.

Schmidt: Of course. It's Katz. Joseph Katz.

Rohde (*schocked*): Katz?

Schmidt (*smiling*): Yes—anything wrong?

Rohde: You might have given the name a little time to cool off.

Schmidt: Why? The real Katz—(*He catches himself.*)—or, rather, the previous Katz—won't object, I promise you. But if he should, there are other names I can use. How do you feel about—Otto Wilke? Do you think that suits me?

Anna (*stunned*): Wilke?

Schmidt: Yes, don't you remember him? He was your husband. (*No answer from Anna.*) An enemy of the party. The denunciation came from someone at this address, didn't it, Frau *Walter*?

Anna: Yes.

Schmidt: You can see I did some checking last night. I wanted to make sure you were loyal to the party.

Anna: Do you—know what happened to him?

Schmidt: The usual—interrogation and heart failure. Tell me, why did you change your name, Frau Wilke?

Rohde: Why did you change yours, Group Leader?

Schmidt (*staring at Rohde*): Yes—and how about you? She's changed her identity. So have I. Have you, Lieutenant?

Rohde (*hesitating, smiling*): Perhaps.

Schmidt (*laughing*): Good! It's a marvelous game!

Rohde: Yes, a marvelous game.

Schmidt (*thinking*): But I'm afraid your presence here is going to be something of a liability.

Anna: Yes, that's right. Let him go.

Schmidt: It's not that simple. He had his chance to leave last night and he missed it. Now he knows I'm here.

Anna: Don't be ridiculous! Why should he tell anyone? He'll give you his word—

Schmidt: His word? As what? I don't know who he is! If he's a Nazi he'll turn me in for being out of uniform. If he's an anti-Nazi he'll turn me in because I *used* to wear the uniform. Which is to say nothing about a jealous lover who'd do it just out of spite.

Anna: What are you going to do?

Schmidt: The Russians are going to be quite impressed with my having killed a German officer singlehanded. So you see, Lieutenant, the only way you can help us is by dying.

Anna: You wouldn't!

Rohde: Of course he would. But he won't—not yet.

Schmidt: Do you mind telling us why?

Rohde: Because your premise is wrong. It's true the Russians would congratulate you for killing a German soldier, but they're not here yet. And if the Gestapo walks in here first, they won't even give you a chance to explain—not with those papers in your pocket.

Schmidt (*he thinks about it, then lowers the gun and turns to Anna*): A clever fellow, our cousin. (*To Rohde.*) You're right, Lieutenant. As long as the Gestapo controls the street down there, you're safe.

Rohde: So it seems the Gestapo is protecting me after all.

Schmidt: Why not? I'm waiting for the Russians to liberate me. (*He laughs.*) There's no reason why we have to sit around like strangers. Have a drink, Lieutenant. (*He reaches for the whiskey and fills three glasses. He pushes one to Rohde.*)

Rohde: No thanks, Schmidt.

Schmidt: The name is Katz.

Rohde: There doesn't seem much point in my practicing it.

Schmidt: For God's sake, Lieutenant, don't be so greedy! You've had more than most. You've loved and you've killed—there's really not much more a man could do in this world. So have a drink, and don't sulk away the rest of your life. (*He pushes the glass to Rohde who looks at it a moment, then drinks it.*) That's right. You, too, Anna—it'll be good for your nerves. (*She turns away.*) What's wrong? You're worried about him? You'll forget him soon enough—you'd better. These days, if you can't forget, you've had it. Right, Lieutenant?

Rohde: No, Schmidt, *not* right.

Schmidt: Have it your own way. (*A silence; he drinks.*) The truth of the matter is I was never a real National Socialist.

Rohde: I was wondering when you'd get around to that.

Schmidt: Hitler was a fool.

Rohde: Already?

Schmidt: He made some criminal mistakes. We should never have lost this war, but if the Army can hold out for just two more days there won't be a single Nazi left in Germany—we'll all have disappeared underground. We have an obligation to survive—we owe it to Germany.

Anna (*by the window*): Look out the window—don't you think you've done enough for Germany? (*She looks out.*) The Russians must be having difficulties—the white flags are being taken in.

Rohde: A point for my side.

Schmidt: Don't raise your hopes too high, Lieutenant. The Bolsheviks have come all the way from Moscow—this little street isn't going to stop them.

Anna: It could still take a week.

Rohde: In that case I think I'll lie down. Waiting to die isn't as exhilarating as it sounds.

(*He goes to the bed and stretches out, face up, his hands behind his head. There is a short silence as Anna watches him, then turns to Schmidt.*)

Anna: I think I'll take some of your Scotch whiskey now—

Schmidt (*pleased*): By all means! (*He puts his pistol on the table and fills a glass, handing it to her.*)

Anna (*raising her glass to Schmidt*): Long life.

Schmidt (*smiling*): Long life.

(*During this, Rohde has slowly reached*

under the pillow and removed the gun. He now points it at Schmidt.)

Rohde: Schmidt—

Schmidt (*turning*): I told you not to call me— (*He freezes when he sees Rohde's gun; then he looks down at his own on the table.*)

Rohde: If you move—if you so much as twitch—I'll blow your head off. (*Schmidt stares at Rohde's gun without moving or speaking.*) Anna, take his gun and bring it to me. (*He sits up as she follows his orders, never taking his eyes off Schmidt for an instant. Anna brings him the gun.*) All right, Schmidt—(*Holding Schmidt's gun in his left hand, he raises his own and aims it at Schmidt.*)

Schmidt: No! What are you doing? Wait— (*Rohde pulls the trigger and the gun clicks harmlessly.*) It's—empty?

Rohde: I'm afraid so. But, as Anna pointed out, all guns look loaded.

Schmidt: I should have killed you. I should have hanged you yesterday when I had the chance!

Rohde: You'll never have that chance again, I can promise you that.

Anna (*to Rohde*): What are you going to do?

Rohde: Yes, Schmidt—what *am* I going to do?

Schmidt (*nervously*): I—don't know.

Rohde: Don't you? You were going to shoot me, weren't you? (*Schmidt doesn't answer.*) Weren't you?

Schmidt: Yes! You see, I admit it. I was trying to save myself—that's only human, isn't it?

Rohde: Nothing about you is human.

Schmidt: But you've no reason to kill me— it won't help you—I have the papers—you need me!

Rohde: Need you, Schmidt? Not if I take your papers—

Schmidt: No, you can't. They have *my* picture and *my* fingerprints. Besides, we're both

Germans—we have to stick together against the foreigners.

Rohde: Get over by the window.

Schmidt: What?

Rohde (*gesturing with his gun*): The window. *Move, Schmidt!*

Schmidt: What—what are you going to do?

Rohde: What do you think?

Schmidt (*crossing slowly*): But—why?

Rohde: Does it matter? Did you tell Katz why?

Schmidt: He was a Jew.

Rohde: Is that all you knew about him?

Schmidt: What else was there?

Rohde: You've stolen his name—aren't you interested in the man? He had a face and fingerprints of his own! And a family—three daughters and a son—

Schmidt (*amazed*): You *knew* him?

Rohde: And he knew me.

Schmidt (*sinking into a chair*): Erich Rohde—

Rohde: You found me. Aren't you glad? Now get up and move to that window.

Schmidt (*quietly*): I don't want to die.

Rohde: Neither did Katz. He'd be happy to know it's the same room—the same window.

Schmidt: No—

Rohde: Maybe you will make it, Group Leader. Maybe you can fly—the "flower of the nation" can do anything. Can you fly, Schmidt?

Schmidt (*terrified*): No.

Rohde: How do you know? Have you ever tried? (*Schmidt doesn't answer.*) Have you ever tried?

Schmidt: No.

Rohde: Then try! Get going, Schmidt —out! Show me you have as much courage as a Jew!

Schmidt: I've got money—I'll give it to you—

Rohde: Money?

Schmidt: Gold! Not paper—you can have it!

Rohde: How many wedding rings? How many teeth?

Schmidt (*to Anna, pleading*): Stop him! He's a killer! I was only following orders!

Rohde: You're talking to the right person now, Schmidt. She believes survival is the most important thing there is.

Schmidt: Yes, that's right! We're all Germans—you'll have to stick together now—the Jews will make it hard on us—

Rohde: Jews? What Jews? Are there any left?

Schmidt: The Reds—you wait and see! We're all in the same boat, I tell you!

Anna (*deliberately, with no emotion*): Kill him.

Rohde (*surprised*): What?

Anna: I said kill him! (*A stunned silence.*) Well? What are you waiting for?

Rohde: Did you really think I'd do it?

Anna: What do you mean?

Rohde: I wasn't going to do it!

Anna: He has papers—he has the right clothes—he'll get away!

Rohde: I must find out if that's possible.

Anna: And if it is? When they take you away, will you ask me to remember you always?

(*They regard one another for a moment. Then the door bursts open and Grete enters. She is wearing the red dress.*)

Grete: Have you seen them?
Anna: Who?
Grete: The Russians! They're outside!

(*Before anyone can stop him, Schmidt, who has had his back to the window during the above, now turns and shouts outside.*)

Schmidt: Help! Tovarisch! Tovarisch! Up here! Help!

(*Rohde grabs him, pulls him back into the room, away from the window, and aims his gun at him.*)

Rohde: They're too late to save you!
Schmidt: No, *you're* too late! They're here! We've got to stick together now or we're all done for!

(*Grete has gone to the window.*)

Rohde (*to Grete*): Did they hear him?
Grete: They must have—they're coming in. (*Turning back.*) What's been going on in here?

Schmidt: We'll be all right if you'll just listen to me. I know these people—I know how their minds work. You've got to trust me! I'll tell them you were hiding me, protecting me from the Nazis. It'll work, I tell you—I promise it will work!

Rohde (*finally*): All right, Schmidt, we'll trust you——

Anna: Are you crazy?

Rohde: —on one condition. Burn those phony papers.

Schmidt: Burn—? But we need them! We'll have to show them something. You don't know them—they're intimidated by papers. But we'll have to get rid of the guns—both of them.

Rohde (*looking around*): Where?

Schmidt (*he has taken over*): The water tank over the toilet. Give them to me!

Rohde: She'll do it. You stay here with me.

(*Anna takes the guns and goes into the bathroom.*)

Schmidt: Remember—leave them to me. But above all, let's trust one another. We're Germans and they're the enemy. Don't forget that.

(*Anna returns.*)

Grete (*smoothing down her dress*): At least they can't find fault with the color—

(*The door flies open and two Russians—a

soldier and a sergeant—enter, each holding a short, lightweight machine gun ready to fire. They look not unlike the two German noncoms seen in Scene One—the soldier large, forbidding, slow of mind; the sergeant smaller, shrewd, and humorless.)

Sergeant: Nobody move! Stand where you are, hands in the air! (*There is total silence as each side surveys the other.*) Watch them, Stepan Ivanitch. I look next door.

(He goes. The silence continues. The soldier has now confined his gaze to Rohde.)

Soldier: Soldier? Kill Russians?

Rohde: No.

Anna: He's not a soldier—he's only——

Schmidt: Quiet!

Soldier (*to Schmidt*): You Nazi?

Schmidt: No. Tovarisch.

Soldier: Tovarisch?

Schmidt: Yes.

Soldier (*looking around*): Everyone tovarisch?

Schmidt: Yes—tovarisch. (*To the others.*) Everybody say it—

Others: Tovarisch.

Grete: What does it mean?

Schmidt: Friend.

Grete (*quickly*): Tovarisch, tovarisch!

Soldier: If everyone tovarisch, who kill Russians? (*He grins.*) You have wristwatch?

Schmidt: Yes—wristwatch—here—

(*He quickly unstraps his watch and hands it to him. Holding the gun under his arm, the soldier pulls back his sleeve, revealing four or five watches already there. He straps on the new one, then turns to Rohde.*)

Soldier: Wristwatch?

Rohde (*showing his bare wrist*): No. Sorry—

Soldier (*to Grete*): Wristwatch?

Grete: No.

(*The sergeant returns.*)

Sergeant: Shouting from window—it came from here?

Schmidt: Yes, Sergeant.

Sergeant: Why?

(*Schmidt looks at Rohde and Anna; suddenly he points at Rohde.*)

Schmidt: He's a Nazi! He was trying to kill me!

Anna (*horrified*): What?

Schmidt: It's true! He would have killed me if you hadn't come!

Anna: Trust each other! Stick together! Liar! *Liar!*

Sergeant: Be quiet!

Anna: I won't! He's a liar!

Sergeant: Be quiet! (*To Schmidt.*) Why he want to kill you?

Schmidt: I escaped from a concentration camp yesterday. He's a Nazi.

Sergeant: (*to Rohde*): True?

Anna: No!

Sergeant: I ask him! (*To Rohde.*) You are Nazi?

Rohde: No.

Schmidt: What do you expect him to say?

Rohde: I escaped from prison yesterday.

Sergeant: Both escape?

Schmidt: Don't listen to him!

Anna (*indicating Schmidt*): It's him—he's the Nazi!

Sergeant (*cocking his gun*): Be quiet! (*He looks at the four Germans for a moment, then speaks to Grete.*) Which one is telling truth?

Grete (*looking at Rohde, then at Schmidt—the situation obviously too much for her*): I don't know.

Sergeant (*examining both Rohde and Schmidt, then turning to the soldier*): Shoot them both. (*He turns and starts out.*)

Schmidt: No! Wait! Look—I have papers!

(*He holds out his papers to the sergeant. The sergeant takes the papers and begins reading them.*)

Anna: They're false! His name's Schmidt! He's with the Gestapo—

Sergeant (*without looking up*): Be quiet! (*Now he turns to Rohde.*) Papers?

Schmidt: He doesn't have any!

Sergeant: No papers? Then where is his number?

Rohde: What?

Sergeant: Number on arm. Show me.

Rohde: I—can't. I burned it off—

Sergeant (*to Schmidt*): You—show number.

Schmidt (*hesitating; then*): Yes, of course. (*He unbuttons his sleeve and reveals a tattoo.*) Here it is.

Sergeant: Good.

Anna: No! He must have done it to himself—don't you understand? To himself!

Sergeant (*to the soldier, indicating Rohde*): Shoot that one.

Anna: No! You can't! He's innocent!

Sergeant: He is Nazi.

Anna: No! He's not a Nazi!

Sergeant: Then is being shot by mistake.

(*As the soldier raises his machine gun, a uniformed Russian Captain enters.*)

Captain: Stop. Lower your gun. (*Everyone turns to look at him. The captain is young—thirty-two—slim and fair. He is well-educated, speaking fluent German. He walks to the sergeant, who, like the soldier, stands at rigid attention.*) I have listened to your interrogation, Sergeant—it is unsatisfactory. We are *fighting* Fascists, not imitating them. I am Captain Korovkin. If you are innocent you have nothing to be afraid of. (*To Grete.*) You—come here. Do you live here?

Grete: Next door—with Frau Zandler.

Captain: Then go back there, please.

Grete: The radio *said* you people couldn't be trusted! (*She leaves, closing the door behind her.*)

Captain: You and you—step forward. (*Rohde and Schmidt approach.*) You will both have a chance to speak. (*To Rohde.*) You first.

Rohde: My name is Erich Rohde. I have spent the last seven years in a Nazi concentration camp.

Captain: Why?

Rohde: Political reasons.

Captain: Communist?

Rohde: No.

Captain: Go on, please.

Rohde: Yesterday morning we were ordered shot. I escaped.

Captain (*pointing to Schmidt*): Who is he?

Rohde: Gestapo Group Leader Schmidt. Yesterday he killed a Jew named Joseph Katz.

Captain: Thank you. (*To Schmidt.*) Now you.

Schmidt: My name is Joseph Katz. I have spent the last seven years in a Nazi concentration camp.

Captain: Why?

Schmidt: I am Jewish. Yesterday morning we were ordered shot. I escaped.

Captain (*pointing to Rohde*): Who is he?

Schmidt: Gestapo Group Leader Schmidt. Yesterday he killed a man named Erich Rohde.

Captain: Thank you. (*He thinks for a moment.*) Is there any reason why I should believe you instead of him?

Schmidt: Yes, Captain. I have papers. (*He hands his papers to the captain.*)

Captain (*examining them*): Joseph Katz. (*He hands them back.*) They are in order. (*He turns to Rohde.*) Have you anything to say before we shoot you?

Rohde (*a pause; calmly*): Captain, who would have the papers? The man in prison? Or the one who put him there?

Schmidt (*realizing the effect of Rohde's words*): What's he talking about? (*He looks around.*) He's so desperate he'll say anything! (*He laughs, but not too convincingly.*) It's laughable! (*The captain walks to the door, opens it wide, and returns to a chair in the center of the room, where he sits. Schmidt has not taken his eyes from the captain.*) Why did you do that? (*The captain, the sergeant, and the soldier stare at Schmidt. There is a long silence. They seem to be waiting for something. Schmidt avoids the three pairs of eyes staring at him; he begins speaking, slowly, waiting after each phrase for some reaction before continuing.*) I'm innocent—I haven't done anything—I was a prisoner—My name is Joseph Katz—I have papers—I'm Jewish—I'm a dirty Jewish swine—I'm innocent—

(*Everyone is staring at him. Suddenly he breaks for the open door and runs out. Without a word from anyone, the soldier fires his pistol through the open doorway. A silence follows.*)

Captain (*to Rohde*): You can relax now—you won't be shot.

(*A pause; suddenly Anna runs to Rohde. They hold each other in their arms.*)

Anna: Erich—Erich—

Rhode (*quietly*): It's all right now. Everything's all right.

Anna: I almost lost you.

Rhode: Don't cry, Anna—laugh! It's over—for us the war's finally over!

Anna: I can't believe it!

(They cling to each other as the captain waits patiently.)

Captain *(finally, to Rohde)*: Excuse me—but why did they put you in prison?

Rohde: Something I wrote—a letter to a newspaper.

Captain: And what did your letter say?

Rohde: It asked if the stories I'd heard were true—that people were being exterminated.

Captain: And if you'd learned they were true—before you were arrested—what would you have done?

Rohde: Demanded an explanation, of course!

Captain: Yes, of course. Not action—merely an explanation. The favorite solution of all reactionaries.

Rohde: Reactionary? They put me in prison for being a liberal!

Captain *(smiling)*: What is wet for the cat is dry for the fish. *(Studying him.)* What is your profession?

Rohde: I was a writer.

Captain: Good, very good. It is a fortunate meeting.

Rohde: Why's that?

Captain: We have been ordered to look for such people—writers, teachers, intellectuals. Tell me, what is your concept of a new Germany?

Rohde: What new Germany?

Captain: A people's Germany—a workers' Germany.

Rohde: A Communist Germany.

Captain: Yes. What is your opinion, please?

Rohde (*a pause*): Does my opinion matter?

Captain: Yes, very much. You are intelligent, courageous, articulate. We are offering opportunities to men like you.

Rohde: Doing what?

Captain: Helping us to rebuild, to educate. The young need training—the old need re-training.

Rohde: Indoctrination, you mean?

Captain: If you like.

Rohde: Yes, well, if it's all the same to you, I'd rather do something else.

Captain: You will explain, please.

Rohde: I don't believe in your system.

Captain: Why not?

Rohde: I'm against dictatorship.

Captain (*a pause*): And just what is it that you do believe in?

Rohde: What every prisoner comes to believe in—freedom.

Captain: Freedom. That's not a word that belongs to any of us, not yet. It's a word for the future. Someday, freedom—but for now, hard work, sacrifice, dedication.

Anna: But you're young—is that all you want from life? Don't you want to be happy?

Captain: I am unimportant. Only the future of world socialism is important.

Anna: You can't believe that.

Captain: Please! You can accuse me of anything you like, but I am not a fool! I am not a—a parrot, repeating slogans—I *believe!* I believe that what we are doing is right—not comfortable, not profitable, not amusing—but *right!* I believe it will benefit not only Russia but the entire world, *including* Germany!

Rohde: The only thing that will benefit Germany is freedom.

Captain: The last time Germany had freedom you elected Adolf Hitler.

Rohde (*a pause*): Don't you think we've paid for that mistake?

Captain (*angrily*): You paid? Have you seen *our* country? Our cities destroyed, our farms burned, our families slaughtered—*we* paid for your mistake, too!

Anna: But he didn't support them—he was against them!

Captain: I recognize that. That's why I offer him preferential treatment.

Rohde: I don't want it! Treat me like the others!

Captain: Like your friend lying in the hall?

Rohde (*pausing*): I'm sorry—I have to refuse.

Captain: You cannot refuse.

Rohde: I have no choice?

Captain: None.

Rohde: Don't I have any rights?

Captain: We give you the right to help rebuild your country!

Rohde: In your image.

Captain: Of course! We won the war, why shouldn't we? Our image is right. We believe in it.

Rohde: And I don't—it's as simple as that!

Captain: You will have to go with the tide!

Rohde: No! That's what I did the last time! I went with the tide until it was too late! I'll never do it again!

Anna (*nervously*): Erich——

Rohde: No! I will not help them! I won't even sit back and watch them—not again!

Anna: Erich—maybe it's different this time.

Rohde: It's *not* different! They don't permit opposition, and that makes them just as bad as the Nazis!

Captain (*a pause; his manner changes*): Very well. In that case you will come with me, please.

Anna (*surprised*): What do you mean?

Captain: Since he will not cooperate, he must receive guidance.

Anna: I—I don't understand. You want him to go somewhere?

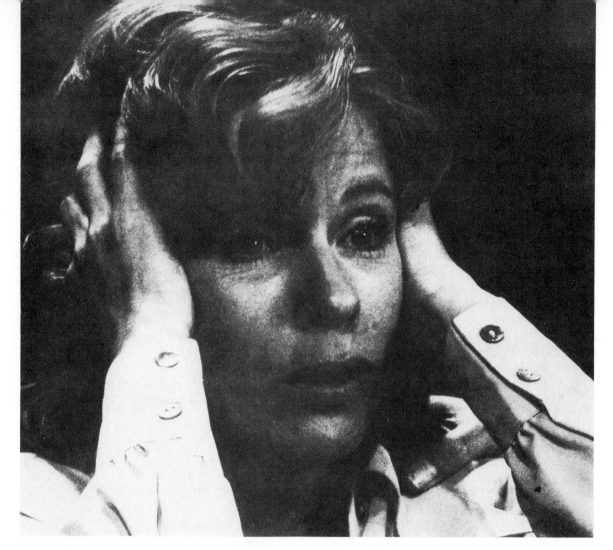

Captain: We have places for education.

Rohde: So did the Nazis—I just escaped from one!

Captain: You escaped from a concentration camp. You are going to an information center.

Anna: For how long?

Captain: That will depend on him. Until he learns. (*To Rohde.*) Get your belongings, please.

(*Rohde doesn't move at first. Then the sergeant steps forward and cocks his gun.*)

Rohde: Yes—my belongings—(*He goes to the cupboard and retrieves his prison clothes.*)

Captain: Hurry, please!

Anna: No, wait! Erich—you can't go. You promised you'd stay!

Rohde: Yes, I know, but I was mistaken.

Anna: Have you gone insane? Say something! You can still do what he wants—it's not too late!

Rohde: Don't you understand, Anna! I can't do it again!

Anna: Why not? Is it so difficult to say "I believe"? Say it, Erich—that's all you have to do!

Rohde: But I *don't* believe.

Anna: Then don't, but *say it!* Stop trying to be a martyr! No one remembers martyrs anymore—there are too many of them. There are only those who survive and those who don't. He's stronger than you are now. Don't force him to prove it—because in the meantime you have a life, Erich, your only life—our only life! What good will you be to anyone back in prison?

Rohde: What good will I be if I compromise my principles?

Anna: Keep your principles—but don't die for them! Live for them! Your chance will come someday, but not if you throw your life away. Use your head, Erich. What good are heroics if they can't accomplish anything? It's pointless, Erich, because in the end you will still have to say "I believe." So say it now! And you can say it, Erich—you can say "I believe" just as easily as you can say "I promise I'll never leave you"!

Rohde: I *can't,* Anna! It's the only thing I learned in these seven years. I can't. I'm sorry.

Anna: Sorry? It's not enough! *I was better off before!*

(She bursts into tears, sobbing convulsively. He holds her, trying to comfort her.)

Rohde: Anna, I'll come back—I'll come back—

(When she has been calmed, he releases her. Then he turns, looks at the Russians, nods, and they go. Anna's back is to the door. When she hears it close, she wheels to look at it. Then she lights a cigarette, goes to the window, and looks down at the street. Finally, she turns back to the room, stares at it, then pulls the curtain, darkening the room. She goes to the bed, lies down, and smokes her cigarette.)

(CURTAIN)

Close Up

1. Otto Wilke was a German shopkeeper who helped people escape from Nazis. (a) Why did Anna betray him? (b) Why does she resent his sacrifice?

2. (a) When Schmidt appears at Anna's place again, why is he wearing civilian clothes? (b) Find a statement Anna made to Rohde in Scene One that foreshadowed, or hinted at, this change.

3. (a) When Rohde comes back, Schmidt wants to shoot him. Why? (b) Why is it ironic that the presence of the Gestapo in town saves Rohde?

4. (a) At first the Russian captain believes Schmidt's story. Why? (b) How does Rohde change the captain's mind?

5. (a) Why does Rohde refuse to help the Russian cause? (b) Why does Anna disagree with his decision?

6. (a) Throughout this play, who has been more practical—Anna or Rohde? Find evidence to support your answer. (b) Who has been more idealistic? Find evidence to support your answer.

7. Think about what happens to Anna and Rohde during this play. Why do you think the play is called "Full Circle"?

Thunder on Sycamore Street

Reginald Rose

Characters

Frank Morrison

Clarice Morrison

Roger Morrison

Christopher Morrison

Arthur Hayes

Phyllis Hayes

Mr. Harkness

Joseph Blake

Anna Blake

Judy Blake

Mrs. Blake

Charlie Denton

Mrs. Carson

Act One

(Fade in on a long shot of Sycamore Street in the pleasant and tidy village of Eastmont. It is 6:40 P.M. and just getting dark. We see three houses, modest but attractive, side by side, each an exact replica of the other. Each has a tiny front lawn and a tree or two in front of it. Each has been lived in and cared

for by people who take pride in their own hard-won respectability. The street is quiet. Walking toward the houses now we see Arthur Hayes, a quiet, bespectacled man between thirty-five and thirty-eight years of age. He lives in the second of the three houses. He walks slowly, carrying a newspaper under his arm and smoking a pipe. He stops in front of his house and, almost in a daze, knocks the dottle out of his pipe against his heel. As he is doing this, we see Frank Morrison enter, also carrying a newspaper. He is a heavy man, forceful and aggressive, with a loud voice and a hearty laugh. He is about forty years of age. Frank Morrison lives right next door to Arthur in the first of the three houses. He sees Arthur and waves.)*

Frank (*jovially*): Hey, Artie. How ya doin'?

(Arthur is preoccupied. He doesn't register at first. He looks blankly at Frank)

Frank (*laughing*): Hey . . . wake up, boy. It's almost time for supper.

(Arthur snaps out of it and forces a smile.)

Arthur (*quietly*): Oh . . . hello, Frank. Sorry, I didn't see you.

Frank: Didn't see me? Hey, wait till I tell Clarice. That diet she's got me on must be working. You have to look twice to see me! (*Laughing hard, Frank reaches for his keys.*) That's a hot one!

(Arthur smiles weakly.)

Frank: Say . . . isn't this late for you to be getting home?

Arthur: No, I don't think so. (*He looks at his watch.*) It's twenty to seven. I always get home about this time.

Frank: Yeah. Well I wouldn't want you to be late tonight. You know what tonight is, don't you?

Arthur (*slowly*): Yes, I know what tonight is.

Frank (*a little hard*): Good.

(We hear footsteps and see a man walk by them. He is Joseph Blake, a man in his late thirties, a big, powerful, but quiet man. Joseph Blake lives in the third house on the street. As he walks by them, they both look at him silently. Arthur turns away then, but Frank continues to stare at him. Camera moves in on Frank as he stares coldly at Joseph Blake. His face is hard, full of hatred. The footsteps recede.)

Frank (*low*): See you later, Artie.

(Frank turns and fits the key into the lock. There is utter silence. He fumbles with the lock, then silently swings the door open. He walks into the small foyer. The living room ahead is brightly lighted, but we see no one. Frank walks slowly, silently into the living room. As he enters it, we hear a dozen pistol shots. Frank stiffens, clutches himself and falls to the floor as if dead. Then we hear a chorus of shrill screams and two small boys wearing cowboy hats and carrying pistols fling themselves upon Frank's body. Frank doesn't move as they clamber over him. One is Roger, age ten; the other is Christopher, age six. Christopher wears "Dr. Dentons.")

Christopher (*screaming*): I got him! I got him first.

Roger: You did not!

Christopher: I did so! Get offa him. I got him first. (*Calling*) Hey, Mom . . .

Roger (*superior*): Boy, are you stupid! I got him three times before you even pulled the trigger.

Christopher (*squeaking*): What d'ya mean? I got him before you even——(*Roger tries to push Christopher off Frank's still motionless body.*) Before you even——(*Christopher*

grunts and fights back.) Cut it out! Hey, Mom
. . .

(Clarice, Frank's wife, a pleasant-looking woman in her early thirties, comes to living-room door from kitchen. She wears an apron. She calls out before she sees them.)

Clarice: Now you boys stop that noise. (*She sees Roger pushing Christopher.*) Roger!
Christopher: Cut it out, willya. I got him——
Clarice: Roger! Stop that pushing. . . .
Christopher: I'm gonna sock you. . . .
Clarice (*angrily*): Christopher, don't you dare! Frank! Will you do something . . . please!
Roger: Go ahead. Sock me. You couldn't hurt a flea!
Christopher (*winding up*): Who says so?
Roger: Boy, you must be deaf. I said so!
Clarice: Frank!

(As Christopher swings at Roger, Frank suddenly comes to life with a tremendous roar. He rolls over, toppling both boys to the floor and with lightning swiftness he grabs both of their cap pistols. He stands up grinning. They both look at him, startled.)

Frank (*barking*): Get up! (*They both do, slowly.*) Get your hands up! (*They look at each other.*) Make it snappy if you don't want to draw lead. (*Christopher shrugs and raises his hands.*) (*To Roger.*) You too, hombre!
Roger: Aaaah, Dad . . .
Frank: Last warning.
Roger (*disgusted*): Come on . . . (*Frank shoots him with the cap pistol.*) What are you so serious about?

(He walks away. Frank watches him, still not giving up the cowboy pose.)

Clarice: All right. Now that's enough gun-play. All three of you can just settle down. (*To Frank.*) Hand 'em over.

(He grins and gives her the guns. Then he bends over and kisses her.)

Frank: Hello, honey.

(She kisses him dutifully, then speaks to Roger, handing him the guns.)

Clarice: Put these in your room and come back with your hands washed. We're sitting down to supper right now.
Roger (*desperately*): Right now? I gotta watch "Rangebusters."
Clarice: Not tonight. I told you we were eating early.
Roger: Ah, Mom . . . please . . .
Clarice: Absolutely not. Come on, now. Inside . . .

(Roger slumps off. Clarice turns to Christopher as Frank begins to take off his coat.)

Clarice: And you're going to bed, mister.
Christopher: No! I can't go to bed!
Clarice: Christopher!
Christopher (*backing away*): I'm not tired yet. Honest!

(Frank is hanging his coat up in the foyer. Clarice advances toward Chris, who looks for means of escape.)

Clarice: I'm not going to argue with you.
Christopher: Mom, fifteen minutes. Come on. Please . . .
Clarice: I'm going to start counting. One, two——
Christopher (*fast*): Three four five six seven eight nine ten.

(He runs away from her, but right into the arms of Frank, who picks him up.)

Frank: Trapped! Let's go, pal.
Christopher: Aaah . . .

(Frank carries him past Clarice, who kisses

him on the way by. As they reach the door which leads into bedroom, Roger comes out. Christopher, in his father's arms, raps Roger on the head with his knuckle.)

Roger: Hey!
Christopher (grinning): Good night, Rog.
Roger: Stupid!
Frank: All right, now. That's enough out of both of you. I don't want to hear another peep.

(Frank takes Christopher into bedroom. Camera follows Roger over to a dining table set at one end of living room near a picture window. This would probably be an L-shaped living room-dining room set-up and would be exactly the same in all three houses. The only difference in the three interior sets will be the way in which they are decorated. There are dishes on the table, glassware, etc. Roger slumps into his chair and takes a piece of bread. He munches on it as Clarice comes in from kitchen carrying a steaming bowl of stew. She sets it down and sits down.)

Clarice (calling): Frank!
Frank (off): Okay. I'll be right there.
Roger: Hey, Mom, what are we eating so early for?
Clarice (serving): Don't say "Hey, Mom."
Roger: Well, what are we eating so early for?
Clarice: Because we feel like eating early. (Calling.) Frank!

(Frank walks in, loosening his tie.)

Frank: What's for supper?
Clarice: Beef stew.
Roger: Look, if I could see the first five minutes of "Rangebusters"——

(Clarice ladles out the stew as Frank sits at the table.)

Clarice: Roger, I'm not going to tell you again.

Roger (anguished): But, Mom, you don't know what's happening. There's this sneaky guy——
Frank: Come on, boy, dig into your dinner.

(Roger makes a face and gives up the battle.)

Frank (to Clarice): What time is the sitter coming?
Clarice: Ten after seven. Do you know that's the third time today you've asked me.
Frank: Just want to be sure.
Clarice: I don't see why they have to make it so early anyway.

(Frank has a mouthful of food, so he shrugs.)

Roger: Make what so early, Dad?
Clarice: Nothing. Eat your dinner.
Frank: Good stew.
Clarice: There's plenty more.
Frank (chewing): Mmmm. Hmmmm. Do anything special today, Rog?
Roger: Nope. Just kinda hung around.
Frank: Well, I don't know why you don't get out and do something. A boy your age . . .
Roger: Some of the kids dumped garbage on the Blakes' lawn again.
Frank (casually): That so? What about you?
Roger: Ah, what fun is that after you do it a couple of times?
Frank (chewing): Mmmm. Hey, how about eating your stew.
Roger: I'm not hungry.
Clarice: Frank, I wish you'd do something about that boy's eating. He's beginning to look like a scarecrow.
Frank: He'll be all right. What time is it?
Clarice (looking at watch): Five of seven.
Frank: We'd better snap it up.
Clarice: Plenty of time. I'm leaving the dishes till later.

Frank: Y'know, Clarry, this really ought to be something tonight.

(*Roger starts to get up, but stops.*)

Roger: What ought to be something?

Clarice: You just sit down and pay attention to your dinner. There's a glass of milk to be finished before you get up.

Roger (*grudgingly*): Okay. (*He sips the milk for a moment.*) Where you going tonight, Dad?

Frank: We're going for a little walk.

Roger: Well, what d'ya have to go out so early for?

Frank: Just like that.

Roger (*aggressively*): Well, what the heck is the big secret, that's what I'd like to know. Everybody's acting so mysterious.

Frank (*sharply*): That's enough. Now I don't want to hear any more questions out of you. Your mother and I have some business to attend to, and that's it. You mind yours.

(*Roger, stunned, looks at his father, then down at his plate. There is an awkward silence. Frank eats stolidly. They watch him.*)

Frank (*to Clarice*): Where's that sitter?

Clarice: It's not time yet. Take it easy, Frank.

(*Frank gets up from the table, goes over to a box of cigars on top of the TV set, and lights one. Clarice and Roger watch him silently.*)

Clarice: Aren't you going to have some dessert, Frank? There's some cherry pie left.

Frank: I'll have it later.

(*He puffs on the cigar.*)

Roger (*low*): I'm sorry, Dad.

Frank (*turning*): Well, it's about time you learned some respect, d'you hear me? If I want you to know something I'll tell it to you.

Roger (*softly*): Okay . . .

Clarice (*quickly*): Have some pie, honey. I heated it special.

(*Frank goes to the table and sits down. He puts the cigar down and Clarice begins to cut him some pie.*)

Clarice: How late do you think we'll be, Frank?

Frank: I don't know.

Clarice: Do you think I ought to pack a thermos of hot coffee? It's going to be chilly.

Frank: Might not be a bad idea.

(*Frank now begins to show the first signs of being excited about the evening. He speaks, almost to himself.*)

Frank: Boy, I can't wait till I see his face. The nerve of him. The absolute nerve. (*Grinning.*) What d'you think he'll do when we all——

Clarice (*looking at Roger*): Frank . . .

Frank (*as Roger stares*): Oh, Yeah, go ahead, Rog. You can turn on your program.

Roger: Gee thanks, Dad.

(*He jumps up, goes to the TV set and turns it on. Frank and Clarice watch him get settled in front of TV set. We hear dialogue from set faintly. Roger watches in background, enraptured.*)

Frank (*quietly*): What are they saying on the block?

Clarice: I didn't speak to anyone. I was ironing all day.

Frank: Charlie Denton called me at the office. I was right in the middle of taking an order from Martin Brothers for three A-81 tractors.

Clarice: Three? Frank, that's *wonderful!*

Frank: Not bad. Anyway, I made Mr. Martin wait while I spoke to Charlie. Charlie says it's gonna be one hundred percent. Every family on the block. He just called to tell me that.

Clarice: Well, that's good. Everyone should be in on this.

Frank (*eating*): Clarry, I'm telling you this is going to be a job well done. It's how you have to do these things. Everybody getting together first . . . and boom, it's over. I can't wait till it's started. It's been long enough.

Clarice: I saw her out the window today, hanging clothes in her yard like nothing was wrong. She didn't even look this way.

Frank: What time is it?

Clarice: Now you just asked me two minutes ago. It's about three minutes to seven. What's the matter with you? You'll be getting yourself an ulcer over this thing. Relax, Frank. Here, have some more pie.

Frank: No, No more.

(*He gets up and walks around nervously, slapping his fist into his palm. Roger is looking at him now. He is tense, excited, completely caught up in the impending event.*)

Frank: This is something big, you know that, Clarry? We're getting action without pussyfooting for once. That's it. That's the big part. There's too much pussyfooting going on all the time. Can't hurt anyone's feelings. Every time you turn around you're hurting some idiot's feelings. Well that's tough, I say . . . .

Clarice (*indicating Roger*): Frank . . .

Frank: He can hear! He's old enough. You want something bad, you gotta go out and get it! That's how this world is. Boy, I like this, Clarry. You know what it makes me feel like? It makes me feel like a man!

(*He stalks up and down the room for a few moments as they watch him. Then he goes to the window and stands there looking out.*)

Clarice (*quietly*): I think I'll just stack the dishes.

(*She starts to do it. The doorbell rings. Roger jumps up.*)

Roger: I'll get it.

(*He goes to the door and opens it. Arthur Hayes stands there a bit apologetically. He wears no overcoat, having just come from next door. He looks extremely upset.*)

Arthur: Rog, is your dad in?

Roger: Sure. Come on in, Mr. Hayes.

(*Arthur walks in slowly. Frank turns around, still excited. He goes over to Arthur.*)

Frank (*loud*): Hey, Artie. Come on in.

Arthur: Hello, Frank . . .

Frank (*laughing*): What can I do for you? (*Arthur looks hesitatingly at Roger.*) Oh, sure. Rog, go help your mother.

Roger (*annoyed*): Okay . . .

(*He walks off to dining table.*)

Frank (*chuckling*): That's some kid, isn't he, Artie? How old is yours now?

Arthur: Twenty-one months.

Frank: Yeah. Well that's still nothing but a crying machine. Wait a couple years. He'll kill you.

Arthur: I guess so.

Frank: And how! Sit down for a minute, Artie. What's on your mind?

Arthur (*sitting. Hesitantly*): Well, I don't know . . . I just . . . well . . . I just wanted . . . to talk.

Frank: No kidding. Say, y'know you look a little green around the gills? What's the matter?

(*Arthur Hayes takes off his eyeglasses and begins to polish them, a nervous habit in which he indulges when upset.*)

Arthur: Nothing. I've had an upset stomach for a couple of days. Maybe that's it.

Frank (*nodding*): Yeah, that'll get you down all right. Probably a virus.

(*Arthur nods and they look at each other awkwardly for a moment.*)

Frank: Well, what did you want to talk to me about?

(*Arthur looks at the floor, trying to frame his answer carefully, afraid to offend. Finally he blurts it out.*)

Arthur: What do you think about this thing tonight?

Frank (*surprised*): What do you mean what do I think about it?

Arthur: Well, I've been kind of going over it all day, Frank. I talked with Phyllis before.

Frank (*a little hard*): And . . .

Arthur: Well, it was just talk. We were just talking it over to get clear on it, you know.

Frank: Go ahead.

Arthur: And . . . well, look, Frank, it's a pretty hard thing. Supposing it were you?

Frank: It's not.

Arthur: Well, I know that, but supposing it were?

(*Frank stands up and goes over to Arthur.*)

Frank: Your glasses are clean. You wear 'em out, you have to buy a new pair. (*Arthur looks down at his glasses, then puts them on nervously.*) Now what about it, Artie? What if I was the guy?

Arthur: Well, you know . . . how would you feel?

Frank: How would I feel, huh? Now that's a good question, Artie. I'll answer it for you. It doesn't make any difference how I'd feel. Now let me ask you a question. Is he a lifelong buddy of yours?

Arthur: Well, now, you know he's not, Frank.

Frank: Do you know him to say hello to?

Arthur: That's not the idea. He's——

Frank: Artie . . . you don't even know the guy. What are you getting yourself all hot and bothered about? We all agreed, didn't we?

Arthur: Yes . . . everybody agreed.

Frank: You. Me. The Dentons. The McAllisters. The Fredericks. The Schofields. Every family on Sycamore Street for that matter. We all agreed. That's how it is. The majority. Right?

Arthur: Well . . . I think we all ought to talk it over, maybe. Let it wait a few days.

(*He takes off his glasses again and begins to wipe them.*)

Frank: Artie . . . we talked it over. (*Frank takes the handkerchief out of Arthur's hand and tucks in into his pocket.*) In about ten minutes we're starting. We expect to have a solid front, you know what I mean? Everybody. You included. You're my next-door neighbor, boy. I don't want to hear people saying Artie Hayes wasn't there.

Arthur (*hesitantly*): Well, I don't know, Frank. I thought——

(*The phone rings. Frank goes toward it.*)

Frank: Go home, Artie. Don't worry about it. I'll see you in a few minutes. (*Frank goes to the phone and picks it up. Arthur stares at him.*) Hello . . . (*Arthur turns away and walks slowly to door.*) Speaking.

(*Arthur goes out, dazed and frightened. Clarice comes into living room and stands waiting as Frank listens to phone.*)

Frank (*angry*): What do you mean you can't get here? (*Pause.*) Well, this is a great time to call! (*Pause.*) I know. Yeah. (*He slams the phone down. To Clarice.*) Our sitter can't get here. How d'you like that?

Clarice: What's wrong with her?

Frank: I don't know. She's got a cold, or something. Nice dependable girl you pick.

Clarice (*snapping*): Well, I didn't exactly arrange for her to get a cold, you know.

Frank: Look, Clarry, we're going to this thing no matter what.

Clarice: Well, I'm not leaving Chris with Roger. They'll claw each other to pieces.

Frank: Then we'll take them with us.

Clarice: You wouldn't . . .

Frank: Who wouldn't? We're doing it for them as much as anyone else, aren't we? Well, they might as well see it.

Clarice: Maybe I'd better stay home with them.

Frank: No, sir. You've been in on this from the beginning. You're going. Come on, get Chris dressed. We haven't got much time.

Clarice: Well . . . whatever you think, Frank . . .

Frank: I'm telling you it's all right. Won't hurt 'em a bit. (*To Roger.*) What d'you say, son? Want to come along?

Roger (*eagerly*): Oh, boy! Really? (*Frank nods and grins. Roger leaps happily.*) Gee, Dad, you're the greatest guy in all the whole world.

(*He runs over and hugs Frank.*)

Frank (*grinning*): Go on, Clarry. Make it snappy.

(*Clarice goes into the bedroom. Doorbell rings.*)

Roger: I'll get it, Dad.

(*He runs to the door and opens it. Charlie Denton, forty years old and eager as a child, stands there. He comes in fast, excited.*)

Charlie: Hiya, Rog. Frank, you all set?

Frank: Hello, Charlie. Another minute or two. How's it look?

Charlie: Great. I'm checking house to house. Everybody's ready.

Frank: Good. Any changes?

Charlie: Nope. It's gonna be fast and quiet. What time you got?

Frank (*calling*): Clarry, what time is it?

Clarice (*calling*): Twelve after.

Charlie (*looking at watch*): Make it thirteen. At fifteen we go.

Frank: Right. Hey listen, you better look in on Artie Hayes next door. He's been acting a little peculair.

Charlie: I spoke to him a little while ago on the street. I think he was coming over to see you. Don't worry about a thing. I'll be watching him. See you, Frank. Let's make this good.

Frank: You bet we will. It looks like a beaut. Take off. (*Charlie goes out fast.*) Get on your coat, Rog. (*Calling.*) Clarry!

(*Roger goes to closet and begins to get his coat. Frank stalks nervously up and down.*)

Clarice (*calling*): In a minute . . .

(*Frank goes to the window and looks out. He watches and waits. We can see the excitement building within him. Roger, hat and coat on, joins him at window. Frank puts his arm on Roger's shoulder and talks, half to himself.*)

Frank (*low*): How do you like that Artie Hayes? Maybe we ought to think it over! I could've belted him one. How do you like that guy!

Roger: What do you mean, Dad?

Frank (*calling*): Clarry!

Clarice (*calling*): Here I am. Come on, Chris.

(*Clarice walks into living room followed by a very sleepy Christopher. He is in his hat and coat. He wanders over to Frank.*)

Frank: What time is it?

Clarice: Almost fourteen after.

Frank: Almost fifteen. Put on your coat.

(*Clarice goes to the closet and does so. Frank follows her and gets his. He puts it on.*

Clarice picks up a large thermos from the foyer table.)

Clarice (*low*): Frank . . . I'm busting with excitement.
Frank (*low*): Yeah. So'm I, honey. (*Louder.*) Come over here, boys. (*The two boys walk over to them.*) Stand here.

(*They wait now behind the closed front door, all four of them tense, quiet, hardly able to stand the suspense. They wait for several seconds, and then, in the street, we begin to hear the heavy tread of marching feet.*)

Christopher: Hey, Daddy . . . where we going?

Frank: Ssh. Be quiet, son.

(*He bends over and picks Christopher up. The sound of marching feet grows louder and stronger. They wait till it reaches a crescendo. Frank speaks quietly now.*)

Frank: Let's go.

(*He opens the front door and they walk into a mob of grimly advancing men and women. They join the mob and walk with them quietly, and the only sound we hear is the frightening noise of the tramping feet. Fade out.*)

Close Up

1. (a) Sycamore Street is an ordinary street in the quiet suburban village of Eastmont. What word in the title suggests that the quiet will be shattered? (b) How does Frank's insistence that Arthur not forget "what tonight is" reinforce this suggestion.

2. At first glance, the Morrisons seem to be an average happy American family; at second glance, you notice some disturbing things about them that hint at trouble to come. (a) Does Frank disapprove when his son tells him that some kids got together and dumped garbage on the Blake's lawn? Why or why not? (b) Why is Frank pleased that all the adults are "getting together" tonight?

3. Frank beleives that people should act decisively and not worry about hurting other people's feelings. (a) How is Arthur's attitude different from Frank's? (b) Which man shows more empathy, or ability to put himself in someone else's shoes?

4. In this act, the tension builds until Frank and his family walk out and join the mob. Why would the sound of the mob's tramping feet be "frightening"?

Act Two

(Fade in on long shot of Sycamore Street. It is once again 6:40 P.M., the same night. We have gone backward in time and we now duplicate exactly the scene which opened Act One. Arthur Hayes walks on, stops in front of his house, knocks his pipe against his heel. Frank Morrison enters. Each of the movements they make, the attitudes they strike and the inflections they use must be exact imitations of the Act One business. The audience must feel that this scene is a clip of film which we are rerunning.)

Frank (jovially): Hey, Artie. How ya doin'?

(Arthur is preoccupied. He doesn't register at first. He looks blankly at Frank.)

Frank (laughing): Hey . . . wake up, boy. It's almost time for supper.

(Arthur snaps out of it and forces a smile.)

Arthur (quietly): Oh . . . hello, Frank. Sorry. I didn't see you.

Frank: Didn't see me? Hey, wait till I tell Clarice. That diet she's got me on must be working. You have to look twice to see me! (Laughing hard, Frank reaches for his keys.) That's a hot one! (Arthur smiles weakly.) Say . . . isn't this late for you to be getting home?

Arthur: No, I don't think so. (He looks at his watch.) It's twenty to seven. I always get home about this time.

Frank: Yeah. Well, I wouldn't want you to be late tonight. You know what tonight is, don't you?

Arthur (slowly): Yes, I know what tonight is.

Frank (a little hard): Good.

(We hear footsteps and see a man walk by them. He is Joseph Blake, a man in his late thirties, a big, powerful, but quiet man. Joseph Blake lives in the third house on the street. As he walks by them they both look at him silently. And now, for the first time, this scene moves in a different direction than did the scene at the beginning of Act One. Instead of coming in close on Frank, the camera comes in close on Arthur Hayes as he stands nervously in front of his door, afraid to look at either Joseph Blake or Frank Morrison. We hear Joseph's footsteps fade out. Arthur reaches for his keys.)

Frank (low, off): See you later, Artie.

(Arthur winces at this. We hear Frank's door opening and closing softly. Arthur turns now and looks off at Joseph Blake's house for a moment. Then he turns and opens his door. As he enters his foyer we hear dance music playing softly. The living room is lighted, and looking on from the foyer, we can see Mr. Harkness, Arthur's father-in-law, seated in an armchair, reading the newspaper. He is perhaps sixty-five years old, and usually does nothing more than sit reading the newspapers. He looks up as Arthur comes in.)

Mr. Harkness: Hello, Arthur. (Calling off.) Here he is, Phyllis. (To Arthur.) Little bit late, aren't you?

(Arthur is hanging up his coat. He is obviously worried. His face shows concern. His entire manner is subdued. He speaks quietly, even for Arthur.)

Arthur: No. Usual time.

(Mr. Harkness takes out a pocket watch, looks at it, shakes it.)

Mr. Harkness: Mmm. Must be fast.

(He goes back to his newspaper. Arthur walks into the living room tiredly.)

Arthur (*not caring*): How's your cough?

Mr. Harkness (*reading*): Still got it. I guess I must've swigged enough cough syrup to float a rowboat today. Waste of time and money!

(*Phyllis enters from kitchen as Arthur goes over to phonograph from which the dance music is blasting. He is just ready to turn it off as she enters.*)

Mr. Harkness: Cough'll go away by itself like it always does.

Phyllis (*brightly*): Hello, darling. Ah . . . don't turn it off.

(*He turns as she walks over to him. She kisses him possessively and leads him away from the phonograph. The music continues.*)

Phyllis: How did it go today, dear?

Arthur: All right. Nothing special.

Phyllis: What about the Franklin closing?

Arthur: It's called off till tomorrow.

Phyllis: How come?

Arthur: I didn't ask them.

Phyllis: Well, you'd think they'd at least give you a reason. You should've asked. I don't like it when people push you around like that.

(*Arthur goes over to a chair without answering. A pipe is on an end table next to the chair. He begins to fill it. Phyllis goes to a small bar on which is a cocktail shaker and one glass. She picks up the shaker.*)

Arthur: What's that?

Phyllis: I made you a drink.

Arthur: No. No thanks. I don't want a drink now.

Phyllis: Oh, Artie! I made it specially for you. You look tired. Come on, it'll do you good. (*She begins to pour the drink.*) Sit down, dear. I'll bring it over to you.

(*Arthur sits down. Phyllis finishes pouring the drink and brings it to him. He takes it. She waits, smiling, for him to drink it.*)

Arthur: How come you made me a drink tonight?

Phyllis: Just for luck. Taste it. (*She sits on the arm of the chair. He tastes it slowly. She puts her arm around him.*) Good?

Arthur (*slowly*): It's good.

Phyllis: I thought you'd like it.

Arthur: Where's Billy?

Phyllis: Asleep.

Arthur: Isn't it kind of early?

Phyllis: He didn't get much of a nap today. The poor baby couldn't keep his eyes open. Artie, he's getting to be such a devil. You should've seen him this afternoon. He got into my bag and took my lipstick. If I only could've taken a picture of his face. He walked into the kitchen and I swear I almost screamed. You never saw anything so red in your life. Drink your drink, darling. It took me ten minutes to scrub it off.

(*Obediently, Arthur sips his drink.*)

Arthur (*mildy*): I'd like to have seen him before he went to bed.

Phyllis: Now you know I had to get finished early tonight, Artie. (*She gets up and goes toward the kitchen.*) We're eating in a few minutes. I'm just making melted cheese sandwiches. We can have a snack later if you're hungry.

Arthur: Later?

Phyllis (*looking at him oddly*): Yes, later. When we get back.

(*Arthur puts his drink down. All of his movements are slow, almost mechanical, as if he has that day aged twenty years. Phyllis goes into the kitchen. He takes off his glasses and begins polishing them.*)

Mr. Harkness: Melted cheese sandwiches.

Arthur (*not hearing*): What?

Mr. Harkness: I said melted cheese sandwiches. That gluey cheese. Do you like it?

Arthur: No.

Mr. Harkness: Me neither. Never did.

(He goes back to his paper. Arthur gets up and goes to phonograph. He stands over it, listening. Phyllis comes in carrying a tray on which are three glasses of tomato juice. She gives it to Arthur.)

Phyllis: Put these on the table like a good boy. *(He takes it and looks at her strangely.)* What's the matter with you, Artie? You've hardly said a word since you got home . . . and you keep looking at me. Are you sick, or something?

Arthur: No. I'm not sick.

Phyllis: Here, let me feel your head. *(She does so.)* No, you feel all right. What is it?

Arthur: Nothing. I'm just tired, I guess.

Phyllis: Well, I hope you perk up a little.

(She goes off into kitchen. Arthur goes slowly to dining table, which is set in the same spot as the Morrison dining table. He puts the glasses on it, and sets the tray on the end table. He takes a sip of his drink. Phyllis comes in from the kitchen carrying a platter of melted cheese sandwiches. She goes to the table, puts it down.)

Phyllis: Dinner. Come on, Dad, while they're hot. Artie . . .

Arthur: You go ahead. I'm not hungry.

Phyllis.: Oh, now, let's not start that. You have to eat. Try one. They're nice and runny.

Arthur: Really, I'm not hungry.

Phyllis: Well, you can at least sit with us. I haven't seen you since half past eight this morning.

(Arthur goes slowly over to the table and sits down. Mr. Harkness ambles over.)

Mr. Harkness: Well, I'm good and hungry. Tell you that. Got any pickles?

Phyllis: No pickles. You know they give you heartburn.

Mr. Harkness: Haven't had heartburn in a long time. Wouldn't mind a slight case if it came from pickles.

(They are all seated now, Phyllis facing the window. Arthur sits quietly. Mr. Harkness busies himself drinking water while Phyllis serves the sandwiches, potato salad, etc.)

Phyllis: Artie . . . potato salad?

Arthur: No. Look, Phyllis . . .

Phyllis: Just a little.

(She puts a spoonful on a heavily loaded plate and passes it to him. He takes it. Now she serves her father.)

Phyllis: Potato salad, Dad?

Mr. Harkness: I'll help myself.

(She puts the bowl down and helps herself as does Mr. Harkness.)

Phyllis *(brightly)*: What happened at the office, dear? Anything new?

Arthur: No. It was quiet.

Phyllis: Did you hear about the Walkers wanting to sell their house?

Arthur: No.

Phyllis: You know, for a real-estate man you hear less about real estate than anyone I ever saw. I spoke to Margie Walker this morning, I just got to her in time. You're going to handle the sale. She told me she hadn't even thought of you till I called. Why is that, dear?

Arthur: I don't know why it is.

Phyllis: Well, anyway, she's expecting you to call her tomorrow. It ought to be a very nice sale for you, dear.

(Arthur nods and looks down at his plate. There is silence for a moment.)

Mr. Harkness *(chewing)*: This stuff gets under my teeth.

Phyllis: Dad!

Mr. Harkness: Well, I can't help it, can I?

(They eat for a moment and then Phyllis, looking out the window, sees movement in the house next door, the Blake house. She can no longer hold back the topic she's been trying not to discuss in front of Arthur.)

Phyllis: Look at them. Every shade in the house is down. *(She looks at her watch.)* There isn't much more time. I wonder if they know. Do you think they do, Artie?

Arthur *(tired)*: I don't know.

Phyllis: They must. You can't keep a thing like this secret. I wonder how they feel. *(She looks at Arthur.)* Artie, aren't you going to eat your dinner?

Arthur *(slowly)*: How can you talk about them and my dinner in the same breath?

Phyllis: For Heaven's sakes . . . I don't know what's the matter with you tonight.

Arthur *(quietly)*: You don't, do you?

(He gets up from the table and walks over to the phonograph. He stand there holding it with both hands, listening to the slick dance music. Then abruptly, he turns it off. Phyllis looks as if she is about to protest, but then decides not to.)

Mr. Harkness: What d'you suppose is gonna happen over there? Boy, wouldn't I like to go along tonight.

Phyllis *(looking at Arthur)*: Dad, will you please stop.

Mr. Harkness: Well, I would! How do you think it feels to be sixty-two years old and baby-stitting when there's real action going on right under your nose? Something a man wants to get into.

Arthur *(turning)*: Be quiet!

Mr. Harkness: Now listen here——

Arthur: I said be quiet! *(He takes off his glasses and walks over to the table.)*

Phyllis: Artie, stop it! There's no need for you to raise your voice like that.

(Arthur speaks more quietly now, feeling perhaps that he has gone too far.)

Arthur: Then tell your father to keep his ideas to himself!

Mr. Harkness *(angrily)*: Wait a minute!

(Phyllis, in the ensuing argument, is quiet, calm, convincing, never losing her temper, always trying to soothe Arthur, to sweeten the ugly things she says by saying them gently.)

Phyllis: Dad, be quiet. Listen, Artie, I know you're tired, darling, but there's something we might as well face. In about fifteen or twenty minutes you and I and a group of our friends and neighbors are going to be marching on that house next door. Maybe it's not such a pleasant thing to look forward to, but something has to be done. You know that, Artie. You agreed to it with all the others.

Arthur: I didn't agree to anything. You agreed for the Hayes household. Remember?

Phyllis: All right, I agreed. I didn't hear you disagreeing. Oh, what's the difference, darling? You've been acting like there's a ten-ton weight on your back ever since you heard about it. And there's no point to it. It's all decided.

Arthur: All decided. What right have we got to decide?

Phyllis: It's not a question of right, Artie. Don't you see? It's something we have to do, right or wrong. Do you want them to live next door to you? Do you really want them?

Arthur: I always thought a man was supposed to be able to live anywhere he chooses no matter what anyone else wants.

Phyllis: But, dear, this isn't anywhere. This is Sycamore Street. It's not some back alley in a slum! This is a respectable neighborhood. Artie, let's be realistic. That's one of the few things we can really say we have. We're respectable. Do you remember how hard we worked to get that way?

Arthur: Respectable! Phyllis, for Heaven's sakes. We're talking about throwing a man out of his own home. What is the man? He's not a monster. He's a quiet guy who minds his own business. How does that destroy our respectability?

Phyllis (*hard*): He got out of prison two months ago. He's a common hoodlum.

Arthur: We don't know for sure.

Phyllis: We know. Charlie Denton doesn't lie. He saw the man's picture in the Rockville papers just fifty miles from here the day he got out. Tell me, what does he do for a living? where did he get the money to buy that house?

Arthur: I don't think that's any of your business.

Phyllis: But, Artie, the man was in jail for four years. That's our business! How do you know what he did? How do you know he won't do it again?

Arthur: We have police.

Phyllis: Police! Will the police stop his child from playing with Billy? What kind of a child must that be? Think about it. Her father is an ex-convict. That's a lovely thing to tell our friends. Why yes . . . you know Billy's little friend Judy. Of course you do. Her father spent a great deal of time in prison. Charming people. It's beautiful for the neighborhood, isn't it, Artie? It makes real-estate prices just skyrocket up. Tell me, who do you think'll be moving in next . . . and where'll we go?

(Arthur doesn't answer. He sits down in a chair, troubled, trying to find an argument. Phyllis watches him closely.)

Mr. Harkness: Listen, Artie——

(But Phyllis puts her hand on his arm to shut him up. Arthur is thinking and she wants to see if her argument has worked.)

Arthur: Look, Phyllis, this is a mob we're getting together. We're going to order this man out of his house . . . or we're going to throw him out. What right have we got to do it? Maybe most of us'd rather not have him as a neighbor, but, Phyllis, the man is a human

being, not an old dog. This is an ugly thing we're doing . . .

Phyllis: We've got to do something to keep our homes decent. There's no other way. Somebody's always got to lose, Artie. Why should it be all of us when there's only one of him?

Arthur: I . . . I don't know.

(Arthur suddenly gets up and goes toward the front door as if going out. He buttons his jacket. Phyllis gets up, concerned.)

Phyllis: Where are you going?

Arthur: I'm going to talk to Frank Morrison.

Phyllis: All right. Maybe Frank'll make sense to you. (*Calling.*) Wear your coat.

(But Arthur has opened the door and intends to go out without it. Phyllis looks at her watch.)

Phyllis: Arthur, it's freezing out! (*He is outside the door now.*) You'll catch cold. (*The door closes. She stands watching after him, obviously upset. Her father resumes his eating. She looks at the door for a long time. Then, without looking around*) Dad . . .

Mr. Harkness: Mmmm?

Phyllis: What do you think he'll do?

Mr. Harkness: Well . . . I don't know. You got any more of these cheese businesses? I'm hungry.

Phyllis: No. (*She goes to the window and looks out.*)

Mr. Harkness: Why don't you sit down, Phyl? He'll be all right.

Phyllis: What do you mean all right? Look at him. He's standing in front of Frank's house afraid to ring the bell.

Mr. Harkness: He'll calm down. Come away from that window and sit down. Have some coffee.

(She moves away from window and sits at table.)

Phyllis: I've never seen him like this before.

Mr. Harkness: Well, what are you worried about? Tell you what. I'll go along with you. Boy, wouldn't I like to be in on a thing like this once. Let Artie stay home and mind the baby if that's how he feels.

(*Phyllis turns to her father violently and for the first time we see how much Arthur's decision means to her.*)

Phyllis (*fiercely*): He's got to go! Don't you understand?

Mr. Harkness: What the dickens is eating you? No, I don't understand. (*Phyllis gets up and goes to the window. She looks out tensely.*) Would you mind telling me what you're talking about?

Phyllis (*startled*): Oh no!

(*She turns and runs to the front door. She starts to open it and run out. As she gets it half open we hear a low voice calling. Charlie Denton's voice.*)

Charlie (*low*): Artie! Hey, Artie!

(*She closes the door silently and stands against it, frightened. Cut to street in front of Frank's house. Arthur stands there, having just been hailed by Charlie. He turns, and then we see Charlie hurrying down the street toward him. Charlie gets to him, takes him by the arm.*)

Charlie (*low*): What are you doing out here now?

Arthur (*guiltily*): Nothing. I was . . . well, I was getting some air, that's all.

Charlie: Look, boy, this thing has got to be timed on the button. Everybody's supposed to be in his house right now. Nobody's supposed to be wandering around the streets. What time've you got?

Arthur (*with an effort*): Listen, Charlie, I want to talk to you about tonight.

Charlie: I haven't got time to talk.

Arthur: Please. It's important.

Charlie (*tough*): What the heck's the matter with you?

Arthur: Nothing. Nothing, Charlie . . .

Charlie: What time've you got? (*He grabs Arthur's wrist and holds it up to the light. He holds his own wrist next to it and compares the watches.*) You're three minutes slow.

Arthur: I know. This watch . . . it runs slow, Charlie . . .

Charlie: Well, fix it, willya? The timing's the most important part.

Arthur: I will. Look, about this thing tonight . . .

Charlie: Listen, if you're gonna start in with me about the plan, take it up with the committee, will ya, please? All of a sudden everybody's an expert on how to run the show. If you want the organizing job I'll be glad to give it to you.

Arthur: No, it's not that. It's organized very well. There's something else.

Charlie: Are you gonna fix that watch?

Arthur: I will. I've been meaning to set it all day. Listen . . . these people . . . the Blakes. They've got a kid . . .

Charlie: So has my mother. Here, gimme this. (*He grabs Arthur's wrist and sets his watch.*) There. At seven-fifteen on the nose we go. Now get back into your house. (*He walks off fast.*)

Arthur: Charlie . . .

(*But Charlie keeps going. Arthur watches him. Then he goes up to Frank Morrison's front door and rings the bell. From inside we hear Roger calling.*)

Roger (*off*): I'll get it.

(*Roger opens the front door, and now again, Roger's and Arthur's movements must be exactly as they were in the first act, except that now the camera catches them from outside the house.*)

Arthur: Rog, is your Dad in?
Roger: Sure. Come on in, Mr. Hayes.

(*Arthur walks in slowly. The door closes.*)

(*Fade out.*)

(*Fade in on the living room of Arthur's house. Phyllis sits tensely waiting for him. The dining table is cleared. Mr. Harkness is back in his easy chair reading the papers. We hear a key in the lock, the door opens, and Arthur enters. He walks slowly, despising himself for not having been stronger with Frank or Charlie. Phyllis gets up as he comes in. He doesn't look at her but walks over to the window and stands there. She comes up behind him. He doesn't turn around.*)

Phyllis: Artie . . . Artie, are you all right?

(*He turns around slowly, speaks heavily.*)

Arthur: Yeah, I'm fine.
Phyllis: What happened? What'd you say to them?
Arthur: I said nothing.
Phyllis (*hopefully*): Well, what do you mean you said nothing. Didn't you talk about it?
Arthur: No, I didn't talk about it. I didn't talk about anything. Will you leave me alone?

(*She backs away, alarmed. Then she looks at her watch.*)

Phyllis (*softly*): We only have a couple of minutes, dear.
Arthur: I'm not going out there.
Phyllis: I'd better get our coats.
Arthur: Did you hear what I just said?
Phyllis: We'll have to bundle up. It's only about twenty degrees out. Did you know that?
Arthur: I said I'm not going.

(*Phyllis backs away from him. He turns to the window. We can see that she is hugely upset; almost desperate. She looks at him fiercely. Mr. Harkness gets up quietly with his paper and goes into the next room. We hear the door close. Arthur doesn't move.*)

Phyllis (*strongly*): I want to tell you something. I'm going to get our coats now, and we're going to put them on, and we're going to stand in the doorway of our house until it's seven-fifteen.
Arthur (*turning*): Stop it.
Phyllis: And then we're going to walk out into the gutter, you and me, the Hayes family, and we're going to be just like everybody else on Sycamore Street!
Arthur (*shouting*): Phyllis! I've told you . . . I'm not going to be a part of this thing!

(*Phyllis studies him for a long moment.*)

Phyllis: Listen to me, Artie. Listen to me good. I didn't think you needed to hear this before. But you're going to hear it now. We're going out there. Do you want to know why? Because we're not going to be next!
Arthur: You're out of your mind!
Phyllis (*roaring*): Sure I am! I'm out of my mind all right. I'm crazy with fear because I don't want to be different. I don't want my neighbors looking at us and wondering why we're not like them.
Arthur (*amazed*): Phyllis . . . you're making this up! They won't think that.
Phyllis: They will think that! We'll be the only ones, the odd ones who wanted to let an ex-convict live with us. They'll look the other way when we walk the streets. They'll become cold and nasty . . . and all of a sudden we won't have any neigbors. (*Pointing at the Blake house.*) We'll be like them!

(*Arthur stand looking at her and it begins to sink in. She knows it and goes after him.*)

Phyllis: We can't be different! We can't afford it! We live on the good will of these

people. Your business is in this town. Your neighbors buy us the bread we eat! Do you want them to stop?

Arthur: I don't know . . . Phyllis . . . I don't know what to think . . . I . . . can't throw a stone at this man.

Phyllis (strong): You can! You've got to, or we're finished here.

(*He stares at her, not knowing what to say next. She has almost won and knows it. She looks at her watch.*)

Phyllis: Now just . . . wait . . . just stand there . . . (*She runs to the closet and takes out their overcoats. She throws hers on and brings his to him, holds it for him.*)

Phyllis: Put it on!

Arthur: I . . . can't. They're people. It's their home.

Phyllis (shouting): We're people too! I don't care what happens to them. I care what happens to us. We belong here. We've got to live here. Artie, for the love of God, we don't even know them. What's the difference what happens to them? What about us?

(*He has no answer. She begins to put his coat on. He stands there, beaten, wrecked, moving his arms automatically, no longer knowing the woman who is putting on his coat. She talks as she helps him.*)

Phyllis: There. It won't be long. I promise you. It won't be long. That's my Artie. That's my darling. Let's button up, dear. It's cold. We'll be back in an hour, and it'll be over. There. Now put on your gloves, darling.

(*She takes him by the arm and he stands there letting her do as she will. He puts on his gloves without knowing he is doing it, and they wait together, there in the doorway. She looks at him, trying to read him, as we begin to hear the cold and chilling sound of the tramping feet. Mr. Harkness comes out of the bedroom and stands there looking at them. Phyllis looks at her watch. The tramping grows louder. They wait in silence. Then she opens the door. We see the crowd, grimly marching, and the Morrisons are at the head of it. No one looks at the Hayeses. The dull thud of the tramping feet is sickening to hear. Arthur closes his eyes. Slowly now Phyllis pushes him forward. He steps out of the house and moves ahead to join the others, as if in a dream. Phyllis follows, catches up, and takes his arm as they join the marching mob. Fade out.*)

Close Up

1. Act Two focuses on the Hayes family. (a) Why is Phyllis anxious for the night's events to begin? (b) Why does Arthur dread them?

2. This act centers on an internal conflict. Write a sentence explaining Arthur's internal conflict.

3. Arthur asks Phyllis, "What right have we got to do it?" (a) How does Phyllis answer him? (b) What does her answer tell you about her?

4. (a) Why does Phyllis feel so strongly that Arthur must support the group's decision? (b) What do Arthur's actions at the end of this act suggest?

Act Three

(Fade in on a long shot of Sycamore Street. It is once again 6:40 P.M., same night. We have gone backward in time, and again we duplicate the scene which opened Acts One and Two. Arthur Hayes walks on, stops in front of his house, knocks his pipe against his heel. Frank Morrison enters. Again, each of the movements must be exact imitations of the movements in Acts One and Two. It is as if we are starting the play again)

Frank (jovially): Hey, Artie. How ya doin'?

(Arthur is preoccupied. He doesn't register at first. He looks blankly at Frank.)

Frank (laughing): Hey . . . wake up, boy. It's almost time for supper.

(Arthur snaps out of it and forces a smile.)

Arthur (quietly): Oh . . . hello, Frank. Sorry. I didn't see you.
Frank: Didn't see me? Hey, wait till I tell Clarice. That diet she's got me on must be working. You have to look twice to see me! (Laughing hard, Frank reaches for his keys.) That's a hot one! (Arthur smiles weakly.) Say . . . isn't this late for you to be getting home?
Arthur: No, I don't think so. (He looks at his watch.) It's twenty to seven. I always get home about this time.
Frank: Yeah. Well, I wouldn't want you to be late tonight. You know what tonight is, don't you?
Arthur (slowly): Yes, I know what tonight is.
Frank (a little hard): Good.

(We hear footsteps and see a man walk by

them. He is Joseph Blake. They both look at him silently. Camera now follows him as he walks silently toward his house, the third of the three houses we see. As he walks, we hear faintly in background.)

Frank (off): See you later, Artie.

(We hear Frank's door open and close. Then we hear Arthur's door open, and for an instant, we hear the same dance music coming from Arthur's house that we heard in Act Two. Then Arthur's door closes. By this time Joseph Blake is in front of his door. He looks off silently at the other two houses. Then he opens his front door and enters his house. As he closes the door we hear running feet, and then we see Judy, Joe's six-year-old daughter, in a bathrobe and slippers, running at him.)

Judy (calling): Daddy Daddy Daddy Daddy.

(She runs into his arms. He lifts her up and hugs her.)

Joe: Mmm. You smell sweet.
Judy (excited): I had a hairwash with Mommy's special shampoo. It smells like gar . . . gar . . .
Joe: Gardenias. Did anyone ever tell you you smelled like gardenias even without Mommy's shampoo?
Judy (grinning): You're silly.

(He tickles her and she giggles.)

Anna (calling): Judy!
Judy (importantly): We've got company.
Joe: Oh? Who is it, darling?
Anna (calling): Judy!
Judy: A lady.

(Joe puts her down. She runs inside. Joe takes off his coat, puts it into the closet, and walks into the living room. Joe's wife, Anna, stands near a chair. Anna, in her early thir-ties, is a quiet, small woman who has obvi-ously been through a great deal of suffering in the past five years. She looks extremely nervous and upset now. Seated at the far end of the room in a rocking chair is Joe's mother, Mrs. Blake. She is quite old, quite spry for her years, and inclined to be snappish. Also seated in the room is a middle-aged woman, a neighborhood busybody named Mrs. Car-son. She wears an odd, old-fashioned hat and sits stiffly, not at home, quite uncomfort-able, but determined to do what she has come to do. The living room again is an exact duplicate of the Morrison and Hayes living rooms. It is furnished sparsely and not well. It is obvious that the Blakes have not been living there long. As Joe gets into the room, Anna comes toward him.)

Anna: Joe, this is Mrs. Carson.
Joe (politely): Mrs. Carson.

(He turns to her for a moment. She nods curtly. Then he turns back to Anna and kisses her gently.)

Joe: Hello, darling.
Anna: Joe . . .

(But he walks away from her and goes to his mother. He bends over and kisses her on the forehead.)

Mrs. Blake: Your face is cold.
Joe (smiling): It's freezing out. How do you feel?
Mrs. Blake: Just fine, Joe.

(He pats her cheek and turns to find Judy behind him, holding a piece of drawing paper and a crayon. On the paper is a child-ish scribble that looks vaguely like a boat. Anna, a tortured expression on her face, wants to say something, but Joe looks at the drawing, grinning.)

Judy: Daddy . . .
Joe: The *Queen Mary!* Now that is what I call beautiful.

Judy: It is not! It's just s'posed to be a sail-boat. How do you draw a sail?
Anna (shakily): Joe . . . Mrs. Carson . . .
Joe: Well, let's see. . . . (He takes the crayon and paper and studies it.) I suppose you think it's easy to draw a sail.
Judy (serious): No. I don't.
Anna (sharply): Joe. (She comes over and snatches the paper away from him. He looks at her.) Judy, go into your room.
Joe: Wait a minute, Anna. Take it easy.
Anna (near tears): Judy, did you hear me?
Joe: Darling, what's the matter with you?
Anna: Joe . . .
Judy: Mommy, do I have to?
Joe (gently): Maybe you'd better go inside for a few minutes, baby.

(Judy unhappily goes into her room. Anna waits till we hear the door close. Joe puts his arms around her.)

Joe: Tell me. What's wrong, Anna?
Anna (almost sobbing): Joe! I don't under-stand it! Mrs. Carson says . . . She . . .
Joe (gently): Mrs. Carson says what?
Anna (breaking down): She says . . . Joe . . . they're going to throw us out of our house. Tonight! Right now! What are we going to do?
Joe (softly): Well, I don't know. Who's going to throw us out of our house?

(But Anna can't answer. Joe grips her tight-ly, then releases her and walks to Mrs. Car-son, who sits stolidly, waiting.)

Joe: Who's going to throw us out, Mrs. Car-son? Do you know?
Mrs. Carson: Well, like I told Mrs. Blake there, I suppose it's none of my business, but I'm just not the kind that thinks a thing like this ought to happen to people without them getting at least a . . . well, a warning. Know what I mean?
Joe: No, I don't know what you mean, Mrs. Carson. Did someone send you here?
Mrs. Carson (indignantly): Well, I should

say not! If my husband knew I was here he'd drag me out by the hair. No, I sneaked in here, if you please, Mr. Blake. I felt it was my Christian duty. A man ought to have the right to run away, I say.

Joe: What do you mean run away, Mrs. Carson?

Mrs. Carson: Well, you know what I mean.

Joe: Who's going to throw us out?

Mrs. Carson: Well, everybody. The people on Sycamore Street. You know. They don't feel you ought to live here, because . . . Now I don't suppose I have to go into that.

Joe (*understanding*): I see.

Anna (*breaking in*): Joe, I've been waiting and waiting for you to come home. I've been sitting here . . . and waiting. Listen . . .

Joe (*quietly*): Hold it, Anna. (*To Mrs. Carson.*) What time are they coming, Mrs. Carson?

Mrs. Carson: Quarter after seven. That's the plan. (*She looks at her watch and gets up.*) It's near seven now. They're very angry people, Mr. Blake. I don't think it'd be right for anyone to get hurt. That's why I'm here. If you take my advice, you'll just put some stuff together in a hurry and get out. I don't think there's any point in your calling the police either. There's only two of 'em in Eastmont and I don't think they'd do much good against a crowd like this.

Joe: Thank you, Mrs. Carson.

Mrs. Carson: Oh, don't thank me. It's like I said. I don't know you people, but there's no need for anyone getting hurt long as you move out like everybody wants. No sir. I don't want no part nor parcel to any violence where it's not necessary. Know what I mean?

Joe: Yes, I know what you mean.

Mrs. Carson: I don't know why a thing like this had to start up anyway. It's none of my business, but a man like you ought to know better than to come pushing in here . . . a fine old neighborhood like this! After all, right is right.

Joe (*controlled*): Get out, Mrs. Carson.

Mrs. Carson: What? Well I never! You don't seem to know what I've done for you, Mr. Blake.

Anna: Joe . . .

Joe: Get out of this house.

(*He goes to a chair in which lies Mrs. Carson's coat. He picks it up and thrusts it at her. She takes it, indignant and a bit frightened. Joe turns from her. She begins to put her coat on.*)

Mrs. Carson: Well, I should think you'd at least have the decency to thank me. I might've expected this though. People like you!

Anna: Mrs. Carson, please . . .

Joe: Anna, stop it!

(*He strides to the door and holds it open. Mrs. Carson walks out.*)

Mrs. Carson: I think maybe you'll be getting what you deserve, Mr. Blake. Good night.

(*She goes out. Joe slams the door.*)

Anna: It's true. I can't believe it! Joe! Did you hear what she said? (*She goes to Joe, who still stands at the door, shocked.*) Well, what are you standing there for?

Joe (*amazed*): I don't know.

Anna: Joe, I'm scared. I'm so scared, I'm sick to my stomach. What are we going to do?

(*Joe puts his arms around her as she begins to sob. He holds her close till she quiets down. Then he walks her slowly over to his mother.*)

Joe (*to his mother*): Will you read to Judy for a few minutes, Mother? It's time for her story. (*Mrs. Blake starts to get up.*) Winnie the Pooh. She'll tell you what page.

Thunder on Sycamore Street **531**

(Mrs. Blake nods and gets up and goes into Judy's room.)

Anna: What are you doing, Joe? We've only got fifteen minutes. . . . Don't you understand?

Joe *(quietly)*: What do you want me to do? I can't stop them from coming here.

(She goes to him and looks up at him, pleading now.)

Anna *(whispering)*: Joe. Let's get out. We've got time. We can throw some things into the car. . . .

Joe: Isn't it a remarkable thing? A quiet street like this and people with thunder in their hearts.

Anna: Listen to me, Joe—please. We can get most of our clothes in the car. We can stop at a motel. I don't care where we go. Anywhere. Joe, you're not listening. *(Loud.)* What's the matter with you?

Joe: We're staying.

Anna *(frightened)*: No!

Joe: Anna, this is our home and we're staying in it. No one can make us get out of our home. No one. That's a guarantee I happen to have since I'm born.

Anna *(sobbing)*: Joe, you can't! Do you know what a mob is like? Do you know what they're capable of doing?

Joe: It's something I've never thought of before . . . a mob. I guess they're capable of doing ugly things.

Anna: Joe, you're talking and talking and the clock is ticking so fast. Please . . . please . . . Joe. We can run. We can go somewhere else to live. It's not so hard.

Joe: It's very hard, Anna, when it's not your own choice.

Anna *(sobbing)*: What are you talking about? What else've we got to do? Stand here and fight them? We're not an army. We're one man and one woman and an old lady and a baby.

Joe: And the floor we stand on belongs to us. Not to anyone else.

Anna: They don't care about things like that. Joe, listen to me, please. You're not making sense. Listen . . . Judy's inside. She's six years old now and she's only really known you for a few weeks. We waited four years for you, and she didn't remember you when you picked her up and kissed her hello, but, Joe, she was so happy. What are you gonna tell her when they set fire to her new house?

Joe: I'm gonna tell her that her father fought like a tiger to stop them.

Anna *(crying)*: Oh, no! No! No! What good will that do? Joe . . . please . . . please . . .

Joe *(thundering)*: Stop it! *(Anna turns away from him and covers her face. After a long pause, quietly.)* It's this way, Anna. We have a few things we own. We have this house we've just bought with money left from before . . . money you could have used many times. We have a mortgage and a very old car and a few pieces of furniture. We have my job.

Anna *(bitterly)*: Selling pots and pans at kitchen doors.

Joe *(patiently)*: We have my job. And we have each other and that's what we have. Except there's one more thing. We have the right to live where we please and how we please. We're keeping all of those things, Anna. They belong to us.

(He comes up behind her and puts his hands on her shoulders. She sinks down in a chair, turned away from him, and sobs. He stands over her. She continues to sob. He holds her and tries to quiet her. The bedroom door opens and Judy bounces into the room. Joe gets up and goes to her as Anna tries to dry her tears.)

Judy: Grandma says I'm supposed to go to bed now. Do I have to, Daddy?

Joe *(smiling)*: It's time, honey.

Judy *(disappointed)*: Gee whiz. Some night, I'm gonna stay up until four o'clock in the morning!

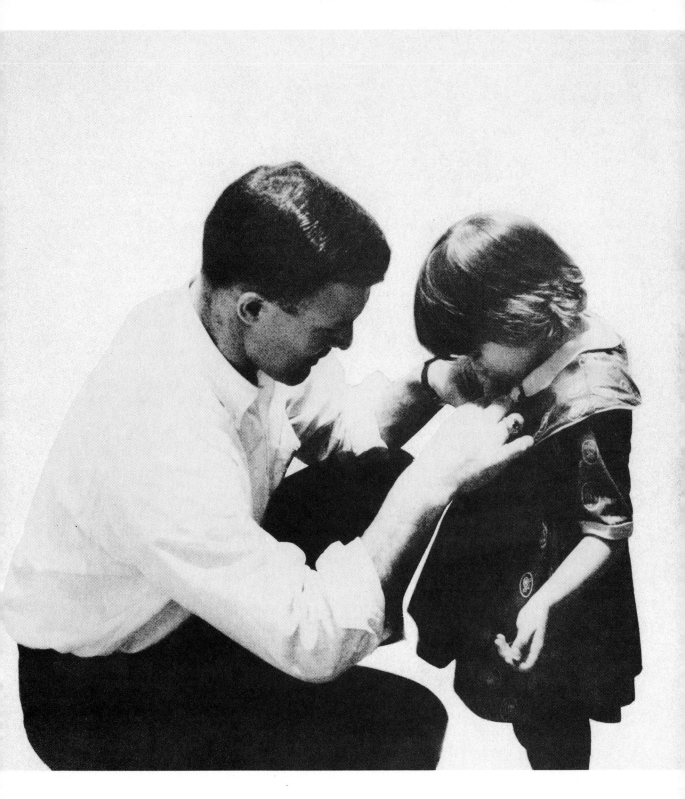

Joe: Some night, you can. (*He kisses her.*) Good night, baby. Give Mommy a kiss.

(*Judy goes to Anna and speaks as she is kissing her.*)

Judy: Really? I really can stay up till four o'clock?
Joe: Really.
Judy: Night, Mommy.
Anna: Good night, darling.

(*Judy runs off gleefully to the bedroom.*)

Judy: Oh boy! (*Calling.*) Grandma . . .

(*The door closes. Anna gets up and goes to window. She is still terrified, but a bit calmer now. She looks out and then turns to Joe. He watches her.*)

Anna: What've we done to hurt them? What've we done? I don't understand.
Joe (*softly*): Well, I guess maybe they think we've destroyed the dignity of their neighborhood, darling. That's why they've thrown garbage on our lawn.
Anna: Dignity! Throwing garbage. Getting together a mob. Those are dignified things to do. Joe, how can you want to stay? How can you want to live on the same street with them? Don't you see what they are?
Joe: They're people, Anna. And I guess they're afraid, just like we are. That's why they've become a mob. It's why people always do.

(*The bedroom door opens and Joe's mother enters. She goes to her rocker and sits in it and begins to rock.*)

Anna: What are they afraid of?
Joe: Living next door to someone they think is beneath them. An ex-convict. Me.

(*Anna runs to Joe and grips him excitedly.*)

Anna: What do they think you did? They must think you're a thief or a murderer.
Joe: Maybe they do.
Anna: Well, they can't. You'll tell them. You'll tell them, Joe.
Joe: Anna, listen . . .
Anna: It could've happened to any one of them. Tell them you're not a common criminal. You were in an accident, and that's all it was. An accident. Joe, they'll listen. I know they will.
Joe: No, Anna . . .
Anna (*eagerly*): All you have to do is tell them and they'll go away. It's not like you committed a crime or anything. You were speeding. Everybody speeds. You hit an old man, and he died. He walked right in front ——
Joe: They're not asking what I did, Anna.
Anna (*pleading*): Joe, please. Look at me. I'm so frightened . . . You have to tell them.
Joe: Anna, we have our freedom. If we beg for it, then it's gone. Don't you see that?
Anna (*shouting*): No!

(*He comes to her and grips her, and speaks to her with his face inches from hers.*)

Joe: How can I tell it to you? Listen, Anna, we're only little people, but we have certain rights. Judy's gonna learn about them in school in a couple of years . . . and they'll tell her that no one can take them away from her. She's got to be able to believe that. They include the right to be different. Well, a group of our neighbors have decided that we have to get out of here because they think we're different. They think we're not nice. (*Strongly.*) Do we have to smile in their faces and tell them we are nice? We don't have to win the right to be free! It's the same as running away, Anna. It's staying on their terms, and if we can't stay here on our terms, then there are no more places to stay anywhere. For you—for me—for Judy—for anyone, Anna.

(*She sees it now and she almost smiles, but the tears are running down her cheeks and it's difficult to smile. Joe kisses her fore-head.*)

Joe (*quietly*): Now we'll wait for them.

(*Anna goes slowly to a chair and sits in it. Mrs. Blake rocks rhythmically on her rocking chair. Joe stands firm at one side of the room and they wait in silence. Suddenly the tick-ing of the clock on the mantelpiece thunders in our ears and the monotonous beat of it is all we hear. They wait. Anna looks at Joe and then speaks softly.*)

Anna: Joe. My hands are shaking. I don't want them to shake.

(*Joe walks over to her, stands over her strongly, and clasps both her hands together. Then he holds them in his till they are still. The clock ticks on, and now we cut to it. It reads ten after seven. Dissolve to a duplicate of the clock which now reads quarter after seven. Cut to long shot of room as we begin to hear the tramping of the feet down the street. They wait. The rocker rocks. The clock ticks. The tramping grows louder. Joe stands in the center of the room, hard and firm. Then he turns to his mother and speaks gently and softly.*)

Joe: Go inside, Mother.
Mrs. Blake (*slowly*): No, Joe. I'm staying here. I want to watch you. I want to hear you. I want to be proud.

(*She continues to rock and now the tramp-ing noise reaches a crescendo and then stops. For a moment there is silence, abso-lute silence, and then we hear a single angry voice.*)

Charlie Denton (*shouting*): Joseph Blake! (*There is a chorus of shouts and a swelling of noise.*) Joeseph Blake . . . come out here!

(*The noise from outside grows in volume. Inside only the rocking chair moves.*)

First Man (*shouting*): Come out of that house!

(*The noise, the yelling of the crowd, con-tinues to grow. Inside the room no one gives a signal that they have heard.*)

Second Man (*shouting*): We want you, Joseph Blake!
Frank Morrison (*shouting*): Come out—or we'll drag you out!

(*The yelling continues, grows louder. Still the Blakes do not move. Then suddenly a rock smashes through the window. Glass sprays to the floor. The pitch of the noise outside rises even more. Joe begins to walk firmly to the door.*)

Anna (*softly*): Joe . . .

(*But he doesn't hear her. He gets to the door and flings it open violently and steps outside. As he does, the shouting, which has reached its highest pitch, stops instantly and from deafening noise we plunge into abso-lute silence, broken only by the steady creak-ing of the rocking chair inside. Joe stands there in front of his house like a rock. Now for the first time we see the crowd. The cam-era plays over the silent faces watching him—the faces of the men and women and children. The Morrisons are directly in front, Charlie Denton is further back. Mrs. Carson is there. And far to the rear we see Arthur Hayes and Phyllis. Still the silence holds. Then, little by little, the people begin to speak. At first we only hear single voices from different parts of the crowd.*)

First Man (*shouting*): Look at him, stand-ing there like he owns the block!

(*There is a chorus of ad-lib approvals.*)

Second Man (*shouting*): Who do you think you are busting in where decent people live?

(*Another chorus of approvals. Joe stands like a fierce and powerful statue.*)

First Woman (*shouting*): Why don't you go live with your own kind . . . in a gutter somewhere?

(*Another chorus of approvals. The camera moves about catching the eagerness, the mounting temper of the crowd, then the shame and anguish of Arthur Hayes, then the giant strength of Joe.*)

First Man (*shouting*): Your limousine is waiting, Mr. Blake. You're taking a one-way trip!

(*There are a few laughs at this, and now the crowd, although not moving forward, is a shouting mass again. Joe still waits quietly.*)

Charlie Denton (*shouting*): Well, what are we waiting for? Let's get him!

(*The intensity of the noise grows and the mob begins to move forward. Then, with a tremendous roar, Frank Morrison stops them.*)

Frank (*roaring*): Quiet! Everybody shut up.

(*The noise dies down gradually.*)

Frank (*to crowd*): Now listen to me! This thing is gonna be handled the way we planned at the meeting.

(*Roger, standing next to Frank, looks at him adoringly. Chris holds Clarice's hand and looks around calmly.*)

Clarice (*loud*): That's right! It's what we agreed on.

Frank (*shouting*): This man here is gonna be asked politely and quietly to pack his things and get his family out of here. We don't have to tell him why. He knows that. He's gonna be given a chance to leave right now. If he's got any brains in his head he'll be out in one hour—and nobody'll touch him or his house. If he hasn't——

(*There is a low-throated, ominous murmur from the crowd.*)

Frank: Right! This thing is gonna be done fair and square. (*Turning to Joe.*) What d'ya say, Mr. Blake?

(*Joe looks at him for a long time. The crowd waits silently. Arthur Hayes lowers his head and clenches his fists, and looks as if he wants to be sick. The crowd waits. When Joe speaks, it is with a controlled fury that these people have never heard before. He speaks directly to Frank.*)

Joe: I spit on your fairness! (*The crowd gasps. Joe waits, then he thunders out.*) I own this house and God gave me the right to live in it. The man who tries to take it away from me is going to have to climb over a pile of bones to do it. You good people of Sycamore Street are going to have to kill me tonight! Are you ready, Mr. Morrison? Don't bother to be fair. You're the head man here. Be first!

(*The crowd, rocked back on its heels, doesn't know what to do. Behind Joe, in the house, we see framed in the doorway the rocking chair moving steadily, and Anna standing next to it. Frank is stunned by this outburst. He calls for action. But not with the force he displayed earlier.*)

Frank: You heard him, everybody . . . . Let's get him.
Joe: I asked for you first, Mr. Morrison!
Frank (*shouting*): Listen to me! Let's go, men!

(But the crowd is no longer moving as a whole. Some of them are still strongly with Frank, including Charlie, the first man, the second man, and several of the others. But others are not so sure of themselves now.)

Charlie (roaring): Don't let him throw you, Frank! He asked for it. Let's give it to him!

(Joe looks only at Frank. Waits calmly for him.)

Frank (roaring): Come on!

(He takes a step forward, but the people behind him don't follow. He turns to them.)

Frank: What's the matter with you people?
Joe: They're waiting for you, Mr. Morrison.

(Frank whirls and faces him and they look long and hard at each other. Cut to Charlie Denton at rear of crowd. He has a stone in his hand.)

Charlie (shouting): Let's start it off, Frankie boy.

(He flings the stone. We hear it hit and drop to the ground. The crowd gasps. Cut to Joe. There is blood running down the side of his head. He stands there firmly. Cut to Arthur Hayes. He looks up in horror, and then a transformation comes over him. He seems to grow taller and broader. His face sets strongly and he begins to stride forward, elbowing people aside. Phyllis knows. She clings to him to pull him back.)

Phyllis (screaming): Artie . . . Artie . . . don't . . .

(But he breaks loose from her and pushes forward. Whoever is in his way is knocked aside, and finally he reaches Joe. He looks up at Joe. Then he turns and stands next to him. He takes off his eyeglasses and flings them into the crowd.)

Arthur (strong): Throw the next stone at me, neighbors. I live here too!

(Now the crowd is uncertain as the two men stand together and the blood runs down Joe's face. Frank tries to rally them. During his next lines we shoot through the open door into the living room. Mrs. Blake gets up from her rocking chair and takes Anna's hand. Together they walk to the front door, come outside, and stand proudly behind Joe and Arthur.)

Frank: Listen to me! Pay attention, you people. Let's remember what we came here to do . . . and why! This man is garbage! He's cluttering up our street. He's wrecking our neighborhood. We don't want him here. We agreed, every last man and woman of us . . . we agreed to throw him out! Are we gonna let him stop us? If we do—you know what'll happen.

(Mrs. Blake and Anna are out of the house now. They wait, along with Joe and Arthur. The crowd listens. Frank shouts on, running from person to person as the crowd begins ashamedly to drift away. Christopher clings to Frank's jacket, and begins to sob.)

Frank: You know what Sycamore Street'll be like. I don't have to tell you. How do we know who we'll be rubbing elbows with next? Listen, where are you going? We're all together in this! What about our kids? Listen to me, people. Our kids'll be playing and going to school with his. How do you like that, neighbors? Makes you a little sick, doesn't it? Come back here! I'm telling you we've got to do this! Come back here!

(But the crowd continues to drift away.

Finally only the Morrisons and Phyllis Hayes are left in the street. Joe and his family, and Arthur, watch them, proudly. Roger looks at his bewildered father and then he turns away, takes Clarice's hand, and his father is no longer the greatest guy in the world. Frank looks down at the sobbing Christopher, and picks him up and walks slowly off. Clarice and Roger follow. The Blakes turn and go into their house, leaving Arthur on the porch. And standing alone, starkly in the middle of the street, is Phyllis.

Arthur looks at her as she stands, heartbreakingly alone, for a long time.)

Arthur (sadly): Well, what are you standing there for? My neighbor's head is bleeding!

(And then, slowly, knowing that Arthur is no longer a grown-up child, Phyllis moves forward into Joseph Blake's house.)

(Fade out.)

Close Up

1. The look at Joe Blake's family life shows him to be a warm and tender man. How does his reaction to Mrs. Carson's news show that he is also strong and determined?

2. Anna says, "We can go somewhere else to live. It's not so hard." (a) What does Joe mean when he replies, "It's very hard, Anna, when it's not your own choice"? (b) Why does he feel that explaining to the mob why he was in prison would destroy his freedom?

3. This play centers on a conflict between the people on Sycamore Street and Joe Blake. When the mob confront Joe, they expect him to be frightened. (a) How does he act instead? (b) How does he turn the mob back into individuals?

4. (a) Why does Arthur move to the front of the crowd and stand by Joe's side? (b) Why does Phyllis finally join Arthur?

5. (a) How is the conflict between the people on Sycamore Street and Joe Blake finally resolved? (b) How is Arthur's internal conflict resolved?

6. This play deals with a threat to one family's freedom. (a) How does it also deal with a threat to Arthur's freedom? (b) How does mob action threaten the freedom of every individual?

7. What do you think is the theme of this play? Write one or two sentences expressing it.

GLOSSARY

From *The American Heritage Dictionary of the English Language.*
© 1979 by Houghton Mifflin Company. Reprinted by permission of
Houghton Mifflin Company.

Pronunciation Key

ă	pat		ŏ	pot
ā	pay		ō	toe
âr	care		ô	paw, for
ä	father		oi	noise
b	bib		ŏŏ	took
ch	church		ōō	boot
d	deed		ou	out
ĕ	pet		p	pop
ē	bee		r	roar
f	fife		s	sauce
g	gag		sh	ship, dish
h	hat		t	tight
hw	which		th	thin, path
ĭ	pit		*th*	this, bathe
ī	pie		ŭ	cut
îr	pier		ûr	urge
j	judge		v	valve
k	kick		w	with
l	lid, needle		y	yes
m	mum		z	zebra, dismal, exile
n	no, sudden		zh	vision
ng	thing		ə	about, item, edible, gallop, circus

Abbreviation Key

adj.	adjective	*n.*	noun	*prep.*	preposition
adv.	adverb			*v.*	verb

A

ab di cate (ăb′ dĭ-kāt′) v.: To step down from power in favor of another; to give up a throne.

ab er ran cy (ăb-ĕr′ ən-sē) n.: A delusion or hallucination; a mild mental disorder.

ab er ra tion (ăb′ə-rā′ shən) n.: **1.** A mild mental disorder. **2.** A mistaken vision; a trick of the mind.

a bet (ə-bĕt′) v.: To help; to assist.

a bom i na ble (ə-bŏm′ ə-nə-bəl) adj.: Terrible; horrible.

ab stract (ăb-străkt′ , ăb′ străkt′) adj.: Not based on fact; theoretical.

ac cli mate (ə-klī′ mĭt, ăk′ lə-māt′) v.: To become accustomed to one's surroundings.

ac qui esce (ăk′wē-ĕs′) v.: To agree; to give in.

a cute (ə-kyo͞ot′) adj.: Very sharp and short. —**a cute ly,** adv.

ad ja cent (ə-jā′ sənt) adj.: Next to; alongside.

aes thet ic (ĕs-thĕt′ ĭk) adj.: Pertaining to a sense of beauty and timing. —**aes thet i cal ly,** adv.

af flu ence (ăf′ lo͞o-əns) n.: Wealth and power.

af fray (ə-frā′) n.: A fight or dispute.

a loof (ə-lo͞of′) adj.: Standoffish; tending to keep to one's self.

a loof ness (ə-lo͞of′ nəs) n.: Apartness, standoffishness; a distant or remote quality or manner.

al tim e ter (ăl-tĭm′ ə-tər) n.: A flight instrument which indicates the plane's height above sea level.

a mi a ble (ā′ mē-ə-bəl) adj.: Friendly; good-natured. —**a mi a bly,** adv.

am pule (ăm′ po͞ol, ăm′ pyo͞ol) n.: A vial or container which holds drugs.

a nach ro nism (ə-năk′ rə-nĭz′əm) n.: Something which is misplaced in time; something which does not belong in a specific time period.

an guished (ăng′ gwĭsht) adj.: Greatly upset; pained.

an ti sep tic (ăn′tə-sĕp′ tĭk) adj.: **1.** Free of germs. **2.** Cold and lacking warmth.

a pex (ā′ pĕks′) n.: The peak; the highest point.

aph o rism (ăf′ ə-rĭz′əm) n.: Maxim or adage; a brief statement of a principle, or a basic truth.

ap o plec tic (ăp′ə-plĕk′ tĭk) adj.: Turning red and panting; as if having an attack.

ap pall (ə-pôl′) v.: To shock; to upset greatly. —**ap palled,** adj.

ap pre hen sive (ăp′rĭ-hĕn′ sĭv) adj.: Fearful; uneasy.

ar ma da (är-mä′ də, är-mā′ də) n.: A fleet of ships.

ar ro gant (ăr′ ə-gənt) adj.: Snobbish; acting as if better than others.

ar se nic (är′ sə-nĭk) n.: A potent poison often used to kill rats. —adj.: Pertaining to arsenic.

ar thri tis (är-thrī′ tĭs) n.: A stiffening and pain in joints, often experienced with age.

ar tic u late (är-tĭk′ yə-lĭt) adj.: Well-spoken.

ar ti fact (är′ tə-făkt′) n.: Any tool, piece of art, or other object which comes from an ancient civilization.

as cet ic (ə-sĕt′ ĭk) adj.: Austere; severe.

ash en (ăsh′ ən) adj.: Chalky; white.

as pire (ə-spīr′) v.: To hope to become; to desire.

as say (ă-sā′ , ăs′ ā′) v.: To attempt to describe or portray; to try or test.

as ser tion (ə-sûr′ shən) n.: A statement or promise.

as sim i late (ə-sĭm′ ə-lāt′) v.: To take in and understand facts; to absorb.

a stern (ə-stûrn′) adj.: To the rear; behind.

as tron o my (ə-strŏn′ ə-mē) n.: The study of stars and planets; the collective laws of space.

aus tere (ô-stîr′) adj.: Plain; bare; stark.

awe some (ô′ səm) adj.: Inspiring fear and wonder; amazing.

ax i om (ăk′ sē-əm) n.: An accepted rule or theory.

B

bal lis tics (bə-lĭs′ tĭks) n.: The study of the firing and flight of bullets or ammunition.

bar bar ic (bär-băr′ ĭk) *adj.*: Given to deeds of cruelty.

bar ba rism (bär′ bə-rĭz′əm) *n.*: An act or trait of brutality or coarseness.

bar ba rous (bär′ bər-əs) *adj.*: Cruel and evil; uncivilized.

bar i tone (băr′ ə-tōn′) *n.*: A deep-toned male voice, although not as low as a bass.

bar rage (bə-räzh′) *n.*: An outpouring; an uncontrolled flow.

bar ter (bär′ tər) *v.*: To bargain; to haggle over a price.

bay ou (bī′ o͞o, bī′ ō) *n.*: An arm of water, usually projecting into a swamp.

ba zaar (bə-zär′) *n.*: A shopping fair or street market.

be lea guer (bǐ-lē′ gər) *v.*: To surround by battle; to put under seige. —**be lea guered,** *adj.*

be mused (bǐ-myo͞ozd′) *adj.*: Thoughtful; musing.

ben e dic tion (běn′ə-dĭk′ shən) *n.*: A blessing or prayer.

be nev o lent (bə-něv′ ə-lənt) *adj.*: Good and kind. —**be nev o lent ly,** *adv.*

be ret (bə-rā′) *n.*: A flat, round hat with no brim. —*adj.*: Pertaining to beret.

berth (bûrth) *v.*: To slip into place at a pier or dock; to tie up. —**berthed,** *adj.*

be spec ta cled (bǐ-spěk′ tə-kəld) *adj.*: Wearing eyeglasses.

be wil der (bǐ-wĭl′ dər) *v.*: To confuse, puzzle, or baffle. —**be wil dered,** *adj.*

bi as (bī′ əs) *n.*: A prejudice or unfair feeling.

bi ped (bī′ pěd′) *n.*: A being which walks on two feet.

bi zarre (bǐ-zär′) *adj.*: Strange; unusual.

blanch (blănch, blänch) *v.*: To turn white with fear.

bland (blănd) *adj.*: Lacking a distinctive feature.

bla sé (blä-zā′, blä′ zā) *adj.*: Bored and indifferent; uncaring.

blas phe my (blăs′ fə-mē) *n.*: An oath against God or against sacred things.

blithe (blīth, blīth) *adj.*: Carefree; happy. —**blithe ly,** *adv.*

bod ice (bŏd′ ĭs) *n.*: The upper portion of a dress.

boot leg (bo͞ot′ lĕg′) *v.*: To smuggle illegal goods in or out of a country. —**boot leg ger,** *n.*

bran dish (brăn′ dĭsh) *v.*: To wave forth.

brawn (brôn) *n.*: Strength; might.

browse (brouz) *v.*: To glance about without looking for anything in particular.

brusque ness (brŭsk′ něs) *n.*: A businesslike manner; shortness or abruptness.

bulk head (bŭlk′ hěd′) *n.*: A thick internal wall or partition.

bur si tis (bər-sī′ tĭs) *n.*: A medical problem caused by swelling in the joints.

by prod uct (bī′ prŏd′əkt) *n.*: Something which is generated as the result of another process.

C

cache (kăsh) *n.*: A hiding place; a secret store.

cap ti vate (kăp′ tə-vāt′) *v.*: To fascinate; to amaze or enthrall; to hold spellbound.

car ry cot (kăr′ ē-kŏt) *n.*: A cradle or bassinet.

car tog ra pher (kär-tŏg′ rə-fər) *n.*: One who charts maps; a mapmaker.

cas cade (kăs-kād′) *n.*: A flood; a waterfall.

cat a stroph ic (kăt′ə-strŏf′ ĭk) *adj.*: Disastrous; terrible.

cat e chism (kăt′ ə-kĭz′əm) *n.*: A lecture or sermon in question-and-answer form.

chafe (chāf) *v.*: To annoy; to irritate.

chor is ter (kôr′ ĭs-tər, kŏr′ ĭs-tər) *n.*: A singer; a choir member.

cir cum ci sion (sûr′kəm-sĭzh′ ən) *n.*: A religious rite in which a section of skin is removed from the penis of a baby boy.

claim ant (klā′ mənt) *n.*: One who regains something which had been lost; someone claiming rightful ownership.

clam ber (klăm′ ər, klăm′ bər) *v.*: To climb; to scramble.

clam or (klăm′ ər) *n.*: A call or outcry; a din.

clar et (klăr′ ət) *n.*: A dark red wine, or red-wine color.

co coon (kə-ko͞on′) *n.*: An encasing pod in which a larva is transformed into a butterfly.

co in ci dence (kō-ĭn′ sə-dəns, kō-ĭn′ sə-děns′) *n.*: A chance occurrence; an accident.

col late (kə-lāt′, kŏl′ āt′, kō′ lāt′) *v.*: To arrange in a logical order; to file.

com pas sion ate (kəm-păsh′ ən-ĭt) *adj.*: Having pity; sensitive.

com pel (kəm-pěl′) *v.*: To force; to make happen.

com pla cent (kəm-plā′ sənt) *adj.*: Mellow; thoughtful and satisfied.

com pro mise (kŏm′ prə-mīz′) *v.*: To modify, or soften, your demands; to bargain.

com punc tion (kəm-pŭngk′ shən) *n.*: A sense of remorse; guilt feeling.

con cede (kən-sēd′) *v.*: To give in; to agree.

con cep tion (kən-sĕp′ shən) *n.*: A portrayal or rendering of the artist's own interpretation.

con cus sion (kən-kŭsh′ ən) *n.*: Shock wave which travels through the air after a gun has been fired.

con de scend (kŏn′dĭ-sĕnd′) *v.*: To look down upon; to act as if superior.

con de scend ing (kŏn′dĭ-sĕn′ dĭng) *adj.*: Acting superior or haughty.

con do lence (kən-dō′ ləns) *n.*: An expression of sympathy given to someone after the death of a loved one.

con du cive (kən-doo′ sĭv, kən-dyoo′ sĭv) *adj.*: Helpful in making something happen.

con fir ma tion (kŏn′fər-mā′ shən) *n.*: Facts to support a story; agreement or corroboration.

con jure (kŏn′ jər, kən-joor′) *v.*: To dream up; to imagine.

con jur er (kŏn′ jər-ər, kŭn′ jər-ər) *n.*: A magician.

con sole (kən-sōl′) *v.*: To comfort; to attempt to ease pain or trouble.

con spic u ous (kən-spĭk′ yoo-əs) *adj.*: Noticeable; standing out from the crowd.

con sta ble (kŏn′ stə-bəl, kŭn′ stə-bəl) *n.*: A police officer or guard.

con strict (kən-strĭkt′) *v.*: To grow small; to squeeze in.

con tem plate (kŏn′ təm-plāt′) *v.*: To ponder; to consider.

con tem po rar y (kən-tĕm′ pə-rĕr′ē) *adj.*: Existing at the same time; modern.

con tour (kŏn′ toor) *n.*: The outer surface or shape.

con trive (kən-trīv′) *v.*: To manage; to figure out a way.

coo lie (koo′ lē) *n.*: A field laborer or worker.

cor net ist (kôr-nĕt′ ĭst) *n.*: Someone who plays a small trumpet or cornet.

cor re la tion (kôr′ə-lā′ shən, kŏr′ə-lā′ shən) *n.*: The connection; the link between one thing and another.

coup (koo) *n.*: An achievement or accomplishment.

court i er (kôr′ tē-ər, kōr′ tē-ər) *n.*: A court attendant or servant.

cow (kou) *v.*: To force into submission; to cause behavior to change through the use of violence and fear. —**cowed**, *adj.*

cres cen do (krə-shĕn′ dō, krə-sĕn′ dō) *n.*: A peak or high point (usually associated with music).

crim i nol o gist (krĭm′ə-nŏl′ ə-jĭst) *n.*: One who studies crime, criminals, and criminal behavior.

cryp to gram (krĭp′ tə-grăm) *n.*: A word puzzle; a secret code.

cudg el (kŭj′ əl) *n.*: A blunt club or stick.

cun ning (kŭn′ ĭng) *adj.*: Sly; sneaky. —**cun ning ly**, *adv.*

curt (kûrt) *adj.*: Short, sharp, abrupt.

czar (zär) *n.*: The title for a Russian emperor.

D

da is (dā′ ĭs, dās) *n.*: A raised platform or long table where dignitaries, speakers, guests of honor, etc. are seated.

dank (dăngk) *adj.*: Dark, cold, and gloomy.

de but (dĭ-byoo′, dā-byoo′) *n.*: A first appearance in society.

de ceit ful (dĭ-sēt′ fəl) *adj.*: Cheating; deceptive; dishonest.

de ci bel (dĕs′ ĭ-bəl, dĕs′ ĭ-bĕl′) *n.*: A unit of measure for sound.

de ci sive (dĭ-sī′ sĭv) *adj.*: Unhesitating; quick to decide.

de cree (dĭ-krē′) *n.*: A decision or declaration.

de duc tion (dĭ-dŭk′ shən) *n.*: A method of reasoning in which the conclusion is the logical result of the prior correct assumptions.

de lir i um (dĭ-lîr′ ē-əm) *n.*: A state of mind characterized by hallucinations, restlessness, and ranting.

de spair (dĭ-spâr′) *n.*: Hopelessness; anguish.

de spon dent (dĭ-spŏn′ dənt) *adj.*: Hopelessly sad; in despair. —**de spon den cy**, *n.*

des pot ic (dĭ-spŏt′ ĭk) *adj.*: In complete power; totally in control.

des pot ism (dĕs′ pə-tĭz′əm) *n.*: Absolute power and dominance.

des ti ny (dĕs′ tə-nē) *n.*: Fate; predetermined lot in life.

dev as tate (dĕv′ ə-stāt′) v.: To completely overcome; to destroy. —**dev as tat ing**, adj.

de void (dĭ-void′) adj.: Completely without; bare or empty.

dif frac tion (dĭ-frăk′ shən) n.: The bending of light or light waves as they pass through another substance. —adj.: Pertaining to diffraction.

dig it (dĭj′ ĭt) n.: A finger.

di lem ma (dĭ-lĕm′ ə) n.: Predicament; a position or situation where the possible choices are equally desirable or undesirable.

dil i gent (dĭl′ ə-jənt) adj.: Hard-working; making a great effort. —**dil i gent ly**, adv.

dire (dīr) adj.: Dark and horrible; evil.

dis cord (dĭs′ kôrd′) n.: A lack of harmony; a jarring sound.

dis em bod y (dĭs′ĭm-bŏd′ ē) v.: To detach from the body. —**dis em bod ied**, adj.

dis pen sa ry (dĭs-pĕn′ sə-rē) n.: A hospital-like building where medicine is dispensed, or distributed.

dis po si tion (dĭs′pə-zĭsh′ ən) n.: A manner or attitude; type of personality.

dis sect (dĭ-sĕkt′, dī-sĕkt′) v.: To cut apart in order to examine in detail.

di van (dĭ-văn′, dī′ văn′) n.: A couch or sofa.

di vin i ty (dĭ-vĭn′ ə-tē) n.: A superior wisdom or being; a god.

dol drums (dōl′ drəmz′, dŏl′ drəmz′) n. (Plural in form, used with a singular verb): An area where there is a lack of wind to sail a boat.

dole ful (dōl′ fəl) adj.: Sad, mournful.

do min ion (də-mĭn′ yən) n.: Leadership; control.

draft (drăft, dräft) n.: A sip or swallow.

drone (drōn) n.: The sound of an engine; a rumbling, buzzing sound. —**droning**, n.

dur al loy (door′ ə-loi′) adj.: Made from various metals in combination.

du ra tion (doo-rā′ shən, dyoo-rā′ shən) n.: Length; amount of time.

dwell (dwĕl) v.: To live; to have residence. (Past tense: **dwelt**.)

E

ea sel (ē′ zəl) n.: A three-legged stand for holding an artist's canvas.

e gre gious (ĭ-grē′ jəs, ĭ-grē′ jē-əs) adj.: Obviously bad; outstandingly awful; outrageous. —**e gre gious ly**, adv.

el e gy (ĕl′ ə-jē) n.: A song or verse written in praise of someone who has died.

el o quent (ĕl′ ə-kwənt) adj.: Grand; expressive. —**el o quent ly**, adv.

e lu sive (ĭ-loo′ sĭv) adj.: Difficult to capture or track.

em bit ter (ĕm-bĭt′ ər, ĭm-bĭt′ ər) v.: To make hostile or unfriendly; to cause to hate.

en dear ment (ĕn-dîr′ mənt, ĭn-dîr′ mənt) n.: A loving word or phrase; an affectionate term.

en deav or (ĕn-dĕv′ ər, ĭn-dĕv′ ər) n.: **1.** An attempt. **2.** A project.

en dur a ble (ĕn-door′ ə-bəl, ĕn-dyoor′ ə-bəl) adj.: Possible to live with; bearable.

en rap ture (ĕn-răp′ chər, ĭn-răp′ chər) v.: To fascinate; to capture the attention totally. —**en rap tured**, adj.

en sue (ĕn-soo′, ĭn-soo′) v.: To follow; to come after.

en thrall (ĕn-thrôl′, ĭn-thrôl′) v.: To amaze; to captivate or hold spellbound. —**en thralled**, adj.

en ti ty (ĕn′ tə-tē) n.: A being; a living thing.

en tomb (ĕn-toom′, ĭn-toom′) v.: To bury; to encase.

e pis to lar y (ĭ-pĭs′ tə-lĕr′ē) adj.: Having to do with letters or letter writing.

ep och (ĕp′ ək) n.: A time period; a span of time.

er go (ûr′ gō, âr′ gō) conj.: Therefore.

erst while (ûrst′ hwīl′) adj.: One-time; former.

es say (ĕ-sā′) v.: To try; to attempt.

es ti ma ble (ĕs′ tə-mə-bəl) adj.: Worthy; upright.

ex as per a tion (ĕg-zăs′pə-rā′ shən, ĭg-zăs′pə-rā′ shən) n.: Anger; frustration.

ex ca vate (ĕk′ skə-vāt′) v.: To dig into; to take out the contents.

ex hil a rate (ĕg-zĭl′ ə-rāt′, ĭg-zĭl′ ə-rāt′) v.: To fill with delight; to excite with joy.

ex hil a rat ing (ĕg-zĭl′ ə-rā′tĭng) adj.: Invigorating or stimulating.

ex ot ic (ĕg-zŏt′ ĭk, ĭg-zŏt′ ĭk) adj.: Unusual and strange.

ex tin guish (ĕk-stĭng′ gwĭsh, ĭk-stĭng′ gwĭsh) v.: To put out; to kill off.

ex tra sen so ry (ĕk′strə-sĕn′ sə-rē) adj.: Outside the realm of the normal five senses.

ex u ber ant (ĕg-zoo′ bər-ənt, ĭg-zoo′ bər-ənt) *adj.*: Overjoyed; thrilled.

F

fa nat ic (fə-năt′ ĭk) *n.*: One who is totally devoted to a cause or idea, to the point of being unreasonable or irrational.

fer vid (fûr′ vĭd) *adj.*: Intense; hot-blooded.

fes ter (fĕs′ tər) *v.*: To become infected; to rot.

fire brand (fīr′ brănd′) *n.*: A torch or burning branch.

fix ed ly (fĭk′ sĭd-lē) *adv.*: Without blinking; unmoving.

flange (flănj) *n.*: A protruding piece of metal or material. —*adj.*: Pertaining to flange.

flank (flăngk) *v.*: To run alongside; to be next to.

flaunt (flônt) *v.*: To show off; to boast.

flax (flăks) *n.*: A plant fiber which is spun into thread for cloth.

flor id (flôr′ ĭd, flŏr′ ĭd) *adj.*: Rosy; hearty.

fore bod ing (fôr-bō′ dĭng, fōr-bō′ dĭng) *adj.*: Threatening; unapproachable.

for ma tion (fôr-mā′ shən) *n.*: A pattern or set grouping.

for mi da ble (fôr′ mə-də-bəl) *adj.*: **1.** Huge and difficult to overcome. **2.** Important; willful. —**for mi da bly,** *adv.*

forth right (fôrth′ rīt′, fōrth′ rīt′) *adj.*: Straightforward; frank; open or candid.

fray (frā) *n.*: A fight or dispute.

fret ful (frĕt′ fəl) *adj.*: Fidgety; uneasy.

friv o lous (frĭv′ ə-ləs) *adj.*: **1.** Trivial, insubstantial. **2.** Playful and irresponsible.

frond (frŏnd) *n.*: A wide leaf from a palm tree.

fur tive (fûr′ tĭv) *adj.*: Sneaky; moving in a way that will not attract attention. —**fur tive ly,** *adv.*

fu se lage (fyoo′ sə-läzh′, fyoo′ zə-läzh′) *n.*: The body of an airplane; the outer shell.

fu til i ty (fyoo-tĭl′ ə-tē) *n.*: Uselessness; wasted effort.

G

gar ble (gär′ bəl) *v.*: To confuse and mix up facts.—**gar bled,** *adj.*

gar ish (gâr′ ĭsh) *adj.*: Too brightly colored; loud.

gaunt (gônt) *adj.*: Extremely thin and bony.

ge ne al o gy (jē′nē-ăl′ ə-jē, jē′nē-ŏl′ ə-jē) *n.*: A family tree; a chart of a family's ancestry.

ge net ic (jə-nĕt′ ĭk) *adj.*: Pertaining to the genes or the chromosomes which control hereditary traits.

gen ial (jēn′ yəl, jē′ nē-əl) *adj.*: Friendly; well-meaning.

ghast ly (găst′ lē, gäst′ lē) *adj.*: Terrible; awful-looking.

gin ger ly (jĭn′ jər-lē) *adv.*: With careful steps; lightly and carefully.

gla cial (glā′ shəl) *adj.*: Pertaining to a glacier, or huge, slow-moving ice mass.

gnome (nōm) *n.*: A dwarf or elf-like being.

gri mace (grĭ-mās′, grĭm′ ĭs) *n.*: A twisted face; a contortion.

griz zle (grĭz′ əl) *v.*: To become gray. —**griz zled,** *adj.*

grub stak er (grŭb′ stā′kər) *n.*: A miner or prospector.

gun wale (gŭn′ əl) *n.*: The side of a boat or ship.

gur gling (gûr′ glĭng) *adj.*: Making a bubbling noise.

gy rate (jī′ rāt′) *v.*: To revolve wildly; to turn rapidly.

H

hal lu ci nate (hə-loo′ sə-nāt′) *v.*: To see something which is not really there; to see a mirage.

hal yard (hăl′ yərd) *n.*: A rope which is used to hoist a sail along a mast.

hap less (hăp′ lĭs) *adj.*: Unlucky; unfortunate. —**hap less ness,** *n.*

har ry (hăr′ ē) *v.*: **1.** To make raids upon. **2.** To disturb or agitate.

hearth (härth) *n.*: A fireplace or the room in which there is a fireplace. —*adj.*: Of or pertaining to hearth.

heath er (hĕth′ ər) *n.*: A flowering bush which grows on the moors in Scotland.

heif er (hĕf′ ər) *n.*: A young cow; a calf.

heir loom (âr′ loom′) *n.*: An object which has been passed through several generations of a family.

her e tic (hĕr′ ə-tĭk) *n.*: One who speaks out against the beliefs of a religion; a non-believer.

het er o ge ne ous (hĕt′ər-ə-jē′ nē-əs, hĕt′ə-rə-jēn′ yəs) *adj.*: Composed of many unlike or different items; varied.

hi bis cus (hī-bĭs′ kəs) n.: A tropical flowering plant.

hilt (hĭlt) n.: The handle of a sword or knife.

hin ter land (hĭn′ tər-lănd′) n.: The backwoods; a place far removed from cities.

hoard (hôrd, hōrd) v.: To guard jealously; to save up.

horde (hôrd, hōrd) n.: A mob; a huge crowd.

hull (hŭl) n.: The main portion of a boat or ship; the body.

I

im pal pa ble (ĭm-păl′ pə-bəl) adj.: Unable to be felt or touched.

im par tial (ĭm-pär′ shəl) adj.: Fair; unbiased.

im pas sive (ĭm-păs′ ĭv) adj.: Unmoving; completely void of emotion. —**im pas sive ly,** adv.

im pel (ĭm-pĕl′) v.: To force or urge on.

im pend ing (ĭm-pĕn′ dĭng) adj.: Coming; soon to arrive.

im pen e tra ble (ĭm-pĕn′ ə-trə-bəl) adj.: Unable to be entered or broken through; unbreakable.

im per a tive (ĭm-pĕr′ ə-tiv) adj.: **1.** Absolutely necessary; vital. **2.** Regal.

im pe ri al ism (ĭm-pîr′ ē-ə-lĭz′əm) n.: The policy of increasing the power or dominion of a nation by conquering other nations, exerting influence in political and economic areas, etc.

im pe ri ous (ĭm-pîr′ ē-əs) adj.: Demanding; commanding.

im plore (ĭm-plôr′, ĭm-plōr′) v.: To beg; to plead.

im preg na ble (ĭm-prĕg′ nə-bəl) adj.: Impossible to enter or break into; unassailable.

im pu dence (ĭm′ pyə-dəns) n.: Blatant disregard for authority; rudeness.

in ces sant (ĭn-sĕs′ ənt) adj.: Never-ending; continuous.

in cip i ent (ĭn-sĭp′ ē-ənt) adj.: In the early stages; just beginning.

in cog ni zant (ĭn′kŏg′ nə-zənt) adj.: Unaware; unknowing or unmindful.

in con gru ous (ĭn-kŏng′ grōō-əs) adj.: Out of place; inharmonious; not suitable or appropriate.

in con se quen tial (ĭn-kŏn′sə-kwĕn′ shəl) adj.: Unimportant; trifling.

in cor rupt i ble (ĭn′kə-rŭp′ tə-bəl) adj.: Unable to be bribed or swayed.

in de scrib a ble (ĭn′dĭ-skrī′ bə-bəl) adj.: Impossible to convey in words; unbelievable. —**in de scrib a bly,** adv.

in dif fer ent (ĭn-dĭf′ ər-ənt) adj.: Without caring; disinterested. —**in dif fer ent ly,** adv.

in dig nant (ĭn-dĭg′ nənt) adj.: Justifiably angry; annoyed by someone's words or actions. —**in dig nant ly,** adv.

in dig na tion (ĭn′dĭg-nā′ shən) n.: Anger at injustice.

in doc tri na tion (ĭn-dŏk′trə-nā′ shən) n.: **1.** Instruction in the doctrines of an established ideology. **2.** Brainwashing.

in duc tion (ĭn-dŭk′ shən) n.: The process of arriving at a general principle or conclusion by observing a number of particular facts or examples.

in er tia (ĭn-ûr′ shə) n.: The tendency of a body at rest to stay at rest.

in ex o ra ble (ĭn-ĕk′ sər-ə-bəl) adj.: Unflinching, unwavering. —**in ex o ra bly,** adv.

in ex pli ca ble (ĭn-ĕk′ splĭ-kə-bəl, ĭn′ĭk-splĭk′ ə-bəl) adj.: Impossible to explain. —**in ex pli ca bil i ty,** n.

in fir ma ry (ĭn-fûr′ mə-rē) n.: A camp hospital or sick tent.

in scribe (ĭn-skrīb′) v.: To write on metal, stone, or other surfaces with a sharp implement.

in sis tent (ĭn-sĭs′ tənt) adj.: Demanding; refusing to be ignored.

in tent (ĭn-tĕnt′) adj.: Deep; full of concentration. —**in tent ly,** adv.

in ter lo per (ĭn′ tər-lō′pər) n.: An intruder; a trespasser.

in ter mit tent (ĭn′tər-mĭt′ ənt) adj.: Not constant; occurring every once in a while.

in tim i date (ĭn-tĭm′ ə-dāt′) v.: To frighten; to inhibit or make timid.

in tol er a ble (ĭn-tŏl′ ər-ə-bəl) adj.: Impossible to live with or endure.

in trigue (ĭn-trēg′) v.: To make curious; to excite with an idea. —**in trigued,** adj.

in var i a ble (ĭn-vâr′ ē-ə-bəl) adj.: Always the same; without change; inevitable. —**in var i a bly,** adv.

in vert (ĭn-vûrt′) v.: To turn upside down; to turn over. —**in verted,** adj.

in ver te brate (ĭn-vûr′ tə-brĭt, ĭn-vûr′ tə-brāt′) n.: Classification or term for animals lacking a backbone or spine.

in voice (ĭn′ vois′) n.: A shipping or billing document listing the items purchased.

ir rel e vant (ĭ-rĕl′ ə-vənt) adj.: Not pertinent to the topic; unrelated or unconnected.

ir re sis ti ble (ĭr′ĭ-zĭs′ tə-bəl) adj.: Unable to be passed up; compelling.

J

jaun ty (jôn′ tē, jän′ tē) adj.: Bouncy and light.

jeer (jîr) v.: To hoot and shout in scorn.

jet ty (jĕt′ ē) n.: A pier or dock jutting out into a body of water.

jos tle (jŏs′ əl) v.: To shove and push; to bump each other. —**jostling,** adj., n.

jo vi al (jō′ vē-əl) adj.: Hearty and happy; in a good mood. —**jo vi al ly,** adv.

K

keel (kēl) n.: The main support, or spine, of a ship or boat; the bottom.

kelp (kĕlp) n.: A large type of seaweed which is sometimes harvested.

ker o sene (kĕr′ ə-sēn′, kĕr′ə-sēn′) n.: A petroleum product used as fuel in lanterns, lamps, stoves, etc.

ki osk (kē-ŏsk′, kē′ ŏsk′) n.: Small stand of street-side venders and merchants; a streetside newspaper stand.

knead (nēd) v.: To work a substance (particulary dough) with the fists and the heels of the hands; to pound and press.

knoll (nōl) n.: A small hill; a rise.

knot (nŏt) n.: A nautical measure of speed.

L

lab y rinth (lăb′ ə-rĭnth′) n.: A maze; a confusing jumble.

la con ic (lə-kŏn′ ĭk) adj.: Using few words; not given to long speeches; terse, to the point.

lan guor (lăng′ gər) n.: Weakness; fatigue.

lar der (lär′ dər) n.: A storage spot for food; a cabinet.

latch key (lăch′ kē′) n.: A key to a front door or gate.

la tent (lā′ tənt) adj.: Existing under the surface; hidden or not active, but present.

leg a cy (lĕg′ ə-sē) n.: Something valuable which is passed down; an inheritance.

leg a tee (lĕg′ə-tē′) n.: A person to whom money is willed; a beneficiary.

lex i con (lĕk′ sĭ-kŏn′) n.: A body of speech, or vocabulary, peculiar to a particular profession.

li a bil i ty (lī′ə-bĭl′ ə-tē) n.: A drawback; a disadvantage.

lieu ten ant (lōō-tĕn′ ənt) n.: A military rank.

lig a ment (lĭg′ ə-mənt) n.: Tissue which connects bones.

liq ui date (lĭk′ wə-dāt′) v.: To destroy; to kill.

lithe (līth) adj.: Limber and graceful.

liv id (lĭv′ ĭd) adj.: Pale, whitish, ashen with strong emotion.

loathe (lōth) v.: To hate; to despise.

lo cale (lō-kăl′, lō-käl′) n.: Setting or scene.

loch (lŏk) n.: A lake or pond.

lock jaw (lŏk′ jô′) n.: A common name for the disease *tetanus,* in which the jaw "locks" in a closed position.

log i cal (lŏj′ ĭ-kəl) adj.: Proceeding reasonably from one step to another; sensible. —**log i cal ly,** adv.

lurch (lûrch) v.: To stagger forward.

lust y (lŭs′ tē) adj.: With spirit and vigor. —**lust i ly,** adv.

M

man i fest (măn′ ə-fĕst′) v.: To become evident; to show signs.

ma raud er (mə-rôd′ ər) n.: A thief or intruder.

mar i time (măr′ ə-tīm′) adj.: Pertaining to the sea or ocean.

mar row (măr′ ō) n.: The central, living portion of bones that produces red blood cells.

mas sive (măs′ ĭv) adj.: Huge; gigantic.

maul (môl) v.: To push and crowd around; to trample.

meas ure (mĕzh′ ər) n.: **1.** An action or way of doing things. **2.** A portion of music.

me chan i cal (mĭ-kăn′ ĭ-kəl) adj.: Like a machine; automatic and without thinking. —**me chan i cal ly,** adv.

med ic (mĕd′ ĭk) n.: A person trained in first aid; a doctor.

me di oc ri ty (mē′dē-ŏk′ rə-tē) n.: Averageness; neither a superior nor inferior state.

med ley (mĕd′ lē) n.: A mixture or combination; a jumble.

meg a ton (mĕg′ə-tŭn′) n.: A unit of explosive force (the equivalent of a million tons of TNT).

mel an chol y (mĕl′ ən-kŏl′ē) n.: Sadness; sorrowful feelings.

met a phys i cal (mĕt′ə-fĭz′ ĭ-kəl) adj.: **1.** Having to do with metaphysics, the branch of philosophy that investigates reality, being, and knowledge. **2.** Highly abstract and often difficult to understand.

met a phys i cal   po et (mĕt′ə-fĭz′ ĭ-kəl   pō′ ĕt) n.: One of a group of seventeenth century poets who wrote in a flowery, elaborate style.

me te or (mē′ tē-ər, mē′ tē-ôr′) n.: A piece of a planet which has broken away and is traveling through space.

me thod i cal (mə-thŏd′ ĭ-kəl) adj.: Orderly and precise; proceeding according to a plan, one step at a time. —**me thod i cal ly**, adv.

me tic u lous (mə-tĭk′ yə-ləs) adj.: Neat and detailed to the point of perfection. —**me tic u lous ly**, adv.

mi cro wave (mī′ krə-wāv′) n.: An oven which cooks food from the inside out by molecular action.

mire (mīr) v.: To sink or stick in mud and slime. —**mired**, adj.

mir y (mīr′ ē) adj.: Swampy and marshy.

mi ser (mī′ zər) n.: Someone who hoards money.

mo bile (mō′ bəl, mō′ bēl′, mo′ bīl′) adj.: Moving; able to move.

mock er y (mŏk′ ər-ē) n.: Cruel teasing; scornful abuse.

mold ing (mōl′ dĭng) n.: A strip of wood used to join walls to ceilings or to cover corners.

mon o rail (mŏn′ ə-rāl′) n.: A single-rail, electric-railroad vehicle capable of fast, quiet travel.

mo not o nous (mə-nŏt′ n-əs) adj.: Always the same; unchanging and dull.

mon sei gneur (môN-sĕ-nyœr′) n.: French term for "my lord," a term of respect given to high-ranking priests.

mon strous (mŏn′ strəs) adj.: Enormous.

mon tage (mŏn-täzh′) n.: A collection put together in mosaic style.

moor (mo͞or) n.: A wild, semi-marshy region of land.

mo rose (mə-rōs′, mô-rōs′) adj.: Sad; depressing.

mor phine (môr′ fēn′) n.: A potent drug used to kill pain.

mot ley (mŏt′ lē) adj.: Disorganized; varied.

mu nic i pal (myo͞o-nĭs′ ə-pəl) adj.: Relating to a community or local government.

mus ket (mŭs′ kĭt) n.: A long-barreled gun or rifle.

mute (myo͞ot) v.: To soften the sound; to make less harsh. —**muting**, adj.

myr i ad (mîr′ ē-əd) adj.: Many and various; impossible to count.

N

ne go ti ate (nĭ-gō′ shē-āt′) v.: **1.** To make work; to cope with. **2.** Informal. To manage to do a thing.

noc tur nal (nŏk-tûr′ nəl) adj.: At night; pertaining to the evening.

no mad (nō′ măd′) n.: A wanderer or migrant.

nui sance (no͞o′ səns, nyo͞o′ səns) n.: A bother, annoyance, or trouble; pest.

nuz zle (nŭz′ əl) v.: To sniff about as if seeking food or affection.

O

ob scure (ŏb-skyo͞or′, əb-skyo͞or′) v.: To hide or block; to make indistinct, or not clear.

ob se qui ous (ŏb-sē′ kwē-əs, əb-sē′ kwē-əs) adj.: Fawning; flattering; servile. —**ob se qui ous ly**, adv.

om i nous (ŏm′ ə-nəs) adj.: Foretelling of evil; threatening.

op por tun ist (ŏp′ər-to͞o′ nĭst, ŏp′ər-tyo͞o′ nĭst) n.: One who takes advantage of any opportunity to get what he or she wants.

op ti mist (ŏp′ tə-mĭst) n.: One who always believes that the best will happen (someone who always looks on the bright side of things).

P

pac i fist (păs′ ə-fĭst) n.: One who is devoted to the cause of peace.

pad dy (păd′ ē) *n.*: A rice field, usually flooded with water. —*adj.*: Pertaining to a paddy.

pal lid (păl′ ĭd) *adj.*: Dim, pale.

pal pa ble (păl′ pə-bəl) *adj.*: Able to be touched or felt; real.

pan ic (păn′ ĭk) *n.*: Sudden, overpowering fear or terror.

pa pier-mâ ché (pā′ pər-mə-shā′) *n.*: A plaster-like substance made of flour, water, and strips of newspaper.

par a pet (păr′ ə-pĭt, păr′ ə-pĕt) *n.*: A small, rooftop wall.

par a psy chol o gy (păr′ə-sī-kŏl′ ə-jē) *n.*: The study of events or actions that are not explainable by natural laws.

par ish (păr′ ĭsh) *n.*: A subdivision within a religious community, having its own church. —*adj.*: Pertaining to parish.

par ox ysm (păr′ ək-sĭz′ əm) *n.*: A violent shiver; a sudden burst.

paste pot (pāst′ pŏt) *n.*: A bucket used to hold wallpaper glue.

pa ter nal (pə-tûr′ nəl) *adj.*: Pertaining to a father; fatherly.

pa thet ic (pə-thĕt′ ĭk) *adj.*: Very sad; pitiful.

pa tron ize (pā′ trə-nīz′, păt′ rə-nīz′) *v.*: To talk down to; to speak in a manner indicating superiority. —**pa tron iz ing ly,** *adv.*

pe nin su la (pə-nĭn′ syə-lə, pə-nĭn′ sə-lə) *n.*: An extension of land surrounded on three sides by water.

pen sive (pĕn′ sĭv) *adj.*: Thoughtful.

per cep ti ble (pər-sĕp′ tə-bəl) *adj.*: Observable; visible.

per cep tion (pər-sĕp′ shən) *n.*: **1.** Understanding. **2.** Knowledge conveyed through sight.

per cep tive (pər-sĕp′ tĭv) *adj.*: Quick to pick up on subtle things; aware.

per emp to ry (pə-rĕmp′ tə-rē) *adj.*: Sharp and commanding; imperious or dictatorial.

per en ni al (pə-rĕn′ ē-əl) *adj.*: **1.** Everlasting; perpetual. **2.** Recurring regularly. —**per en ni al ly,** *adv.*

per il ous (pĕr′ əl-əs) *adj.*: Dangerous; risky.

pe rim e ter (pə-rĭm′ ə-tər) *n.*: The outside border or boundary.

per plex (pər-plĕks′) *v.*: To bewilder or puzzle.

per plexed (pər-plĕkst′) *adj.*: Bewildered; puzzled.

per sis ten cy (pər-sĭs′ tən-sē) *n.*: Perseverance; the quality of refusing to quit or give in.

per sis tent (pər-sĭs′ tənt, pər-zĭs′ tənt) *adj.*: Refusing to give up; continually trying.

per son age (pûr′ sən-ĭj) *n.*: A public figure.

per spec tive (pər-spĕk′ tĭv) *n.*: **1.** The way things are viewed with respect to each other and to the whole. **2.** Point of view.

per vade (pər-vād′) *v.*: To lend an air to; to spread throughout.

pes ti len tial (pĕs′tə-lĕn′ shəl) *adj.*: Full of death; disease-ridden.

pet ty (pĕt′ ē) *adj.*: Pertaining to contemptibly narrow viewpoints; mean or spiteful.

phan tom (făn′ təm) *n.*: A ghost or spirit; something that is not really there. —*adj.*: Pertaining to phantom.

phe nom e non (fĭ-nŏm′ ə-nŏn′) *n.*: An event; a happening.

pin ion (pĭn′ yən) *v.*: To pin down; to hold or bind (rendering the victim helpless).

pi ous (pī′ əs) *adj.*: Religious and holy.

plac ard (plăk′ ärd′, plăk′ ərd) *n.*: A poster or sign to be put up for the public to read.

plac id (plăs′ ĭd) *adj.*: Calm; undisturbed.

plain tive (plān′ tĭv) *adj.*: Pleading; sad. —**plain tive ly,** *adv.*

plait (plāt, plăt) *v.*: To braid.

plat i num (plăt′ ə-nəm) *n.*: A silver-white metallic element used as jewelry.

plight (plīt) *n.*: A predicament or problem; terrible trouble.

plumb (plŭm) *v.*: To explore; to touch upon.

poach er (pō′ chər) *n.*: One who traps animals illegally.

po di um (pō′ dē-əm) *n.*: An elevated platform on which a speaker or bandleader stands.

pon der (pŏn′ dər) *v.*: To think deeply; to contemplate.

pon toon (pŏn-tōōn′) *n.*: Either of the floats on the landing gear of a plane (pontoons support a plane in water).

por tals (pôrt′ lz, pōrt′ lz) *n.*: Doorways or entrances.

port hole (pôrt′ hōl′, pōrt′ hōl′) *n.*: A circular, metal-encased window in the side of a ship.

pos ses sive (pə-zĕs′ ĭv) *adj.*: **1.** Desiring to control or dominate. **2.** Of or pertaining to ownership. —**po ses sive ly,** *adj.*

pre car i ous (prĭ-kâr′ē-əs) *adj.*: Dangerous; hazardous; treacherous. —**pre car i ous ly,** *adv.*

pre cinct (prē′ sĭngkt) *n.*: **1.** An area of a city, town, etc. patrolled by a unit of the police force. **2.** The police station in that area.

pre cip i tous (prĭ-sĭp′ə-təs) *adj.*: Steep and rocky; treacherous.

pre ci sion (prĭ-sĭzh′ən) *n.*: Crispness and accuracy.

pre med (prē′ mĕd′) *adj.*: Pertaining to a group of preliminary courses to be taken before entering medical school.

pre oc cu pied (prē-ŏk′ yə-pīd′) *adj.*: Lost in thought; having the mind on other things.

pre pos ter ous (prĭ-pŏs′ tər-əs) *adj.*: Ridiculous; absurd; impossible to believe. —**pre pos ter ous ly,** *adv.*

pre sume (prĭ-zoom′) *v.*: To venture or dare.

pre ten tious (prĭ-tĕn′ shəs) *adj.*: Flashy or showy; put-on or phony manner of display.

prim ing (prī′ mĭng) *n.*: An explosive used to fire a shell.

pris sy (prĭs′ ē) *adj.*: Prim; finicky; fussy; prudish.

pro cure (prō-kyoor′ , prə-kyoor′) *v.*: To obtain; to get or buy.

pro fane (prō-fān′ , prə-fān′) *adj.*: Blasphemous or sacrilegious (showing disrespect toward sacred things).

pro found (prə-found′ , prō-found′) *adj.*: Very deep; overpowering.

prog e ny (prŏj′ ə-nē) *n.*: Offspring; offshoots.

prom i nent (prŏm′ ə-nənt) *adj.*: **1.** Famous and well-known. **2.** Sticking out; protruding.

prone (prōn) *adj.*: Likely; susceptible.

proph et (prŏf′ ĭt) *n.*: One who prophesies, or foretells the future. (Usually, one who speaks by divine inspiration.)

pro pin qui ty (prō-pĭng′ kwə-tē) *n.*: Closeness; nearness.

pro pul sion (prə-pŭl′ shən) *n.*: Something which causes an object to move forward; a driving force.

pros trate (prŏs′ trāt′) *adj.*: Downtrodden; unfortunate.

pro tu ber ant (prō-too′ bər-ənt, prō-tyoo′ bər-ənt) *adj.*: Bulging out; popping out.

pro ver bi al (prə-vûr′ bē-əl) *adj.*: Well-known; often spoken of or about.

psalm (säm) *n.*: A holy song; a verse.

psy chic (sī′ kĭk) *adj.*: **1.** Having to do with supernatural or extraordinary mental powers. **2.** Not explainable by natural laws.

psy chol o gist (sī-kŏl′ ə-jĭst) *n.*: One who studies the mind and its workings.

pum ice (pŭm′ ĭs) *n.*: A very light volcanic rock formed from solidified lava.

Q

qual i fi ca tion (kwŏl′ ə-fĭ-kā′ shən) *n.*: The required attribute or skill to do a certain job.

qualm (kwäm, kwôm) *n.*: A feeling of uneasiness; a shudder of doubt.

quest (kwĕst) *n.*: A search; a seeking or looking for something.

R

rad i cal (răd′ ĭ-kəl) *adj.*: Tending to prefer quick change and new ideas; politically, favoring rapid and widespread reforms in government or social structures.

ram i fi ca tion (răm′ə-fə-kā′ shən) *n.* : An additional attachment or arrangement.

rap tur ous (răp′ chər-əs) *adj.*: Filled with deep joy and pleasure.

ra tion ale (răsh′ə-năl′) *n.*: A reason for acting in a certain way; an explanation.

rav el (răv′ əl) *v.*: To twist together; to wind in. —**raveled,** *adj.*

re al is tic (rē-ə-lĭs′ tĭk) *adj.*: Practical; down-to-earth; considering the reality.

rec i ta tion (rĕs′ə-tā′ shən) *n.*: A speech or performance.

re coil (rē′ koil′, rĭ-koil′) *n.*: The springing-back motion of a gun after it has been fired.

rec on cile (rĕk′ ən-sīl′) *v.*: To make up after a fight; to become friendly again.

rec on cil i a tion (rĕk′ən-sīl′ē-ā′ shən) *n.*: The resumption of friendly ways after a fight; the end of a feud or quarrel.

re con nais sance (rĭ-kŏn′ ə-səns, rĭ-kŏn′ ə-zəns) *adj.*: Exploratory; intended to investigate an area.

rec to ry (rĕk′ tə-rē) *n.*: A church building where a priest or minister lives.

re cu per ate (rĭ-kōō′ pə-rāt′, rĭ-kyōō′ pə-rāt′) *v.*: To get well; to recover.

re it er a tion (rē-ĭt′ə-rā′ shən) *n.*: The repetition of a statement for emphasis.

re lent less (rĭ-lĕnt′ lĭs) *adj.*: Unyielding; having no pity.

rem nant (rĕm′ nənt) *n.*: A shred; a leftover piece or amount.

re morse (rĭ-môrs′) *n.*: Guilt; regret for one's actions.

ren dez vous (rän′ dā-vōō′, rän′ də-vōō′) *n.*: An appointment or meeting.

rep er toire (rĕp′ ər-twär, rĕp′ ər-tôr) *n.*: A collection of songs that one is capable of playing.

rep er to ry (rĕp′ ər-tôr′ē, rĕp′ ər-tōr′ē) *n.*: A collection, assortment, or stock.

rep li ca (rĕp′ lə-kə) *n.*: A duplication or copy.

re pul sive (rĭ-pŭl′ sĭv) *adj.*: Disgusting; gross and revolting.

re sign (rĭ-zīn′) *v.*: To give in to the inevitable; to stop resisting and give in.

re signed (rĭ-zīnd′) *adj.*: Accepting of the situation.

res in ous (rĕz′ ə-nəs) *adj.*: Thick and sticky with sap from trees.

re solve (rĭ-zŏlv′) *n.*: A resolution or promise to one's self.

re strain (rĭ-strān′) *v.*: To hold back; to keep in place. —**re strain ing,** *adj.*

res ur rect (rĕz′ə-rĕkt′) *v.*: To bring back or revive; to bring back to life.

re ver ber ate (rĭ-vûr′ bə-rāt′) *v.*: To echo; to resound.

rev er ie (rĕv′ ər-ē) *n.*: A daydream; idle thoughts.

rhe tor i cal (rĭ-tôr′ ĭ-kəl, rĭ-tōr′ ĭ-kəl) *adj.*: Not expecting an answer; like a question asked for effect or emphasis. —**rhe tor i cal ly,** *adv.*

rib ald (rĭb′ əld) *adj.*: Racy; off-color.

rif fle (rĭf′ əl) *n.*: An obstruction or blockage in a water flow.

rip ple (rĭp′ əl) *v.*: To quiver along the muscles; to tremble.

roan (rōn) *n.*: A reddish colored horse.

rough-hew (rŭf′ hyōō′) *v.*: To cut out into a general shape; to form roughly.

ru ble (rōō′ bəl) *n.*: A Russian coin.

rum mage (rŭm′ ĭj) *v.*: To search; to look through.

ruse (rōōz) *n.*: A trick; an action designed to confuse or deceive.

S

sa gac i ty (sə-găs′ ə-tē) *n.*: Wisdom; intelligence.

sal vage (săl′ vĭj) *n.*: An object or piece of scrap which is saved.

sar cas tic (sär-kăs′ tĭk) *adj.*: Making fun of; mocking and taunting.

sa ti a tion (sā′shē-ā′ shən) *n.*: Satisfaction; fullness.

sat i rize (săt′ ə-rīz′) *v.*: To mock; to make fun of.

scru ti ny (skrōōt′ n-ē) *n.*: Close, careful observation.

self-com mun ing (sĕlf-kə-myōōn′ ĭng) *adj.*: Talking to oneself.

sel-con tained (sĕlf′kən-tānd′) *adj.*: In strict control of one's own emotions and actions; calm and quiet.

sem blance (sĕm′ bləns) *n.*: An appearance; something which resembles that for which it stands.

se nil i ty (sĭ-nĭl′ ə-tē) *n.*: Mental or physical feebleness brought on by old age.

sen su al i ty (sĕn′shōō-ăl′ ə-tē) *n.*: Pleasure to the senses.

sheep ish (shēp′ ĭsh) *adj.*: Embarrassed; acting ashamed, as if caught in the act. —**sheep ish ly,** *adv.*

shrill (shrĭl) *adj.*: High-pitched; squeaky.

shy (shī) *v.*: To start away in fright; to move aside in fear; to bolt.

sim u late (sĭm′ yə-lāt′) *v.*: To approximate; to take the place of.

si mul ta ne ous (sī′məl-tā′ nē-əs, sĭm′əl-tā′ nē-əs) *adj.*: Occurring at the same time.

slu ice (slōōs) *adj.*: A pathway for water to flow; a trench.

smite (smīt) *v.*: **1.** To strike or hit; to beat. **2.** To afflict. (*Past tense:* **smote.** *Past participle:* **smitten.**)

so cial ism (sō′ shə-lĭz′əm) *n.*: The idea that the means of production and distribution, such as factories, railroads, and power plants, should be owned by the government or associations of workers and operated without private profit.

sol der (sŏd′ ər, sôd′ ər) v.: To unite or join with melted tin or lead.

sol em nize (sŏl′ əm-nīz′) v.: To make official; to celebrate.

sol i tar y (sŏl′ ə-tĕr′ē) adj.: **1.** Lonesome; lonely. **2.** Removed from civilization; remote; secluded. **3.** Sole; single.

sol i tude (sŏl′ ə-tōōd′, sŏl′ ə-tyōōd′) n.: Peace and quiet; the state of being alone.

som ber (sŏm′ bər) adj.: Sad and dark. —**som ber ly,** adv.

so na ta (sō-nä′ tä) n.: A musical composition, usually in several movements.

sparse (spärs) adj.: Bare; almost empty of objects. —**sparse ly,** adv.

spas mod ic (spăz-mŏd′ ĭk) adj.: In an uneven rhythm; in a short burst. —**spas mod i cal ly,** adv.

spir i tu al ist (spĭr′ ĭ-chōō-ə-lĭst) n.: One who believes that the spirits of the dead communicate with the living.

sprig (sprĭg) n.: A twig; a small branch.

squal id (skwŏl′ ĭd) adj.: Run-down and dirty.

stag (stăg) n.: A male deer; a buck.

stale mate (stāl′ māt′) n.: A tie or standoff; a no-win situation.

sta tion ar y (stā′ shə-nĕr′ē) adj.: At a standstill; not moving.

stile (stīl) n.: A set of steps going over a gate or fence.

sto ic (stō′ ĭk) adj.: Showing no emotion; calm and accepting. —**sto i cal ly,** adv.

stol id (stŏl′ ĭd) adj.: Dull and impassive. —**stol id ly,** adv.

strait (strāt) n.: A narrow arm of the sea in between two land masses.

stu pen dous (stōō-pĕn′ dəs, styōō-pĕn′ dəs) adj.: Huge; tremendous. —**stu pen dous ly,** adv.

suave (swäv, swāv) adj.: Polished and graceful.

sub se quent (sŭb′ sə-kwənt) adj.: Following; next.

sub ver sion (səb-vûr′ zhən, səb-vûr′ shən) n.: The act of trying to undermine or overthrow a government.

sub ver sive (səb-vûr′ sĭv, səb-vûr′ zĭv) adj.: Attacking the party in power; radical; tending to undermine or overthrow a government, doctrine, etc.; traitorous.

suc cor (sŭk′ ər) n.: Aid; relief.

sul len (sŭl′ ən) adj.: Downcast; gloomy.

sup plant (sə-plănt′) v.: To take over the place of something; to rise up in place of another.

sup ple (sŭp′ əl) adj.: Limber; flexible.

sur plice (sûr′ pləs) n.: A long robe worn by a priest or minister.

sur rep ti tious (sûr′əp-tĭsh′ əs) adj.: Sneaky; in a way so as not to be noticed. —**sur rep ti tious ly,** adv.

swarth y (swôr′ thē) adj.: Dark or dusty.

swathe (swäth) v.: Cover or enfold; wrap.

syn a gogue (sĭn′ ə-gŏg′) n.: A temple (place of worship for people of the Jewish faith).

T

tal low (tăl′ ō) adj.: Pertaining to tallow, the fat of certain animals (cows, sheep) used in making candles, soap, etc.

tar pau lin (tär-pô′ lĭn, tär′ pə-lĭn) n.: A heavy canvas cloth used as a covering.

taunt (tônt) n.: A mocking or insulting word or statement; a verbal attempt to poke fun at someone.

taut (tôt) adj.: Stretched tight.

tem per a men tal (tĕm′prə-mĕnt′ l, tĕm′pər-ə-mĕnt′ l) adj.: **1.** Moody; unpredictable. **2.** Easily upset or irritated; sensitive.

temp ta tion (tĕmp-tā′ shən) n.: Lure or enticement.

ten e ment (tĕn′ ə-mənt) n.: A run-down apartment building that is poorly maintained and usually overcrowded.

ten or (tĕn′ ər) n.: A fairly high-ranged male voice.

ten ta tive (tĕn′ tə-tĭv) adj.: Hesitating; uncertain.

ter mi nal (tûr′ mə-nəl) n.: A building where vehicles arrive and depart; a station.

ter res tri al (tə-rĕs′ trē-əl) adj.: Living on the earth; ground-dwelling.

terse (tûrs) adj.: Short and clipped; using few words.

tes ta ment (tĕs′ tə-mənt) n.: A statement or will.

teth er (tĕth′ ər) v.: To tie up; to restrain.

the sis (thē′ sĭs) n.: **1.** An idea or proposal which must be examined and proven. **2.** A long, formal essay, as written by a candidate for a university degree.

thresh (thrĕsh) v.: To beat against; to pound out.

tou sle (tou′ zəl) *v.*: To rumple; to put in disorder. —**tou sled,** *adj.*

trans form (trăns-fôrm′) *v.*: To change; to become something else.

trans for ma tion (trăns′fər-mā′ shən) *n.*: A total change; a reversal.

treb le (trĕb′ əl) *n.*: A high-ranged singing voice.

tre men dous (trĭ-mĕn′ dəs) *adj.*: Huge; gigantic.

trem u lous (trĕm′ yə-ləs) *adj.*: Shaky; quivering. —**trem u lous ly,** adv.

tuft (tŭft) *n.*: A clump or bunch.

tu nic (tōō′ nĭk, tyōō′ nĭk) *n.*: A long, shirt-like garment. (In "The Rising of the Moon," part of a policeman's uniform.)

turf (tûrf) *n.*: Grass or other ground covering.

tur ret (tûr′ ĭt) *n.*: A tower-like structure usually found on castles.

tyr an ny (tĭr′ ə-nē) *n.*: Absolute power or control, especially when imposed unjustly or cruelly.

U

un der priv i leged (ŭn′dər-prĭv′ ə-lĭjd) *adj.*: Not having the same opportunities that others do; poor.

un en dur a ble (ŭn-ĕn-dōōr′ ə-bəl, ŭn-ĕn-dyōōr′ ə-bəl) *adj.*: Impossible to bear; horrible.

un prec e dent ed (ŭn′prĕs′ ə-dĕn′tĭd) *adj.*: Having no earlier instance or example of; completely unheard of.

un yield ing (ŭn-yēl′ dĭng) *adj.*: Inflexible; firm.

V

vac u um (văk′ yōō-əm, văk′ yōōm) *n.*: Void or emptiness (an area empty of matter, as is outerspace).

va lise (və-lēs′) *n.*: A suitcase; a satchel.

val or (văl′ ər) *n.*: Strength and worth; bravery.

van dal ism (vănd′ l-ĭz′əm) *n.*: Willful destruction of public or private property, usually for no apparent reason.

van quish (văng′ kwĭsh, văn′ kwĭsh) *v.*: To conquer; to defeat.

ven er a ble (vĕn′ ər-ə-bəl) *adj.*: Old and respected.

ven ture some (vĕn′ chər-səm) *adj.*: Adventurous; willing to try new things.

ves tige (vĕs′ tĭj) *n.*: A trace; a tiny bit.

vi bra to (vĭ-brä′ tō, vē-brä′ tō) *n.*: A wavering quality of sound in music.

vir tu o so (vûr′chōō-ō′ sō) *n.*: An accomplished musician.

vo cif er ous (vō-sĭf′ ər-əs) *adj.*: **1.** Loud and outspoken; noisy. **2.** Wholehearted. —**vo cif er ous ly,** *adv.*

void (void) *n.*: Empty space; nothingness.

W

war y (wâr′ ē) *adj.*: Cautious; mistrustful. —**war i ly,** *adv.*

wend (wĕnd) *v.*: To walk; to make one's way.

wharf (hwôrf) *n.*: A dock or pier.

wisp y (wĭsp′ ē) *adj.*: Thin and fragile; frail; insubstantial.

wraith (rāth) *n.*: A ghost or spirit.

wraith like (rāth′ līk) *adj.*: Like a spirit; ghostly.

Y

yore (yôr, yōr) *n.*: Oldentimes; days gone by.

INDEX OF CONTENTS BY TYPE

ILLUSTRATION AND PHOTO CREDITS

Illustration

Cheng, Judith, pp. 86, 90–91, 379, 380–381, 383
Cummins, Jim, pp. 68, 73
Friedman, Jon, pp. 180–181, 184–185, 268–269, 272–273, 280–281
Geiger, Paul, pp. 2–3, 398–399, 401, 405
Hicinbothem, Ron, pp. 78–79, 81, 209, 210–211, 370–371, 374
Leamon, Tom, pp. 38, 42–43, 44–45, 308–309, 313, 317, 320, 324–325
Lorenz, Al, pp. 111, 114, 411, 414–415
Maccabe, Richard, pp. 32–33, 190–191, 194, 332–333, 336–337, 338
McDaniel, Jerry, pp. 8, 12, 15, 286, 290–291, 293
Munger, Nancy, pp. 451, 454, 456, 462, 465
Owen, Ralph, pp. 96–97, 100, 103, 352, 434, 438, 441, 443, 447
Rabinowitz, Sandy, pp. 248, 250, 342, 346
Raymond, Larry, pp. 200, 203

Photo

Page xviii - 1, Rainbow © Hank Morgan; 20, Taurus © Melvin West; 26–27, De Wys © C. Lutman; 54–55, Wide World Photos; 58–59, The Bettmann Archive; 62, Culver; 66–67, Photo Researchers © Fred Maroon; 109, National Museum of American Art, Smithsonian Institution; 118–131, © Jan Esteves; 136, Nancy Palmer © Le Clair Bissell; 138, Peter Arnold © H. Gritscher; 140, Peter Arnold © James Karales; 143, © Shostal Associates; 145, Peter Arnold © James Karales; 154, © Richard Rowan; 159, © John Bottomley; 162–163, Joan Kramer © David Stahl; 164, © Robin Lee Graham; 167, Shostal Associates © Ray Manley, (inset) © Shostal Associates; 168, 171, © Shostal Associates; 178, H. Armstrong Roberts © J. Hohmann, (insert) Photo Researchers © Ronny Jacques; 222, Reprinted from PSYCHOLOGY TODAY Magazine, © 1976, Ziff-Davis Publishing Co.; 225, Wide World Photos, (insert) Culver; 228, Culver; 230–231, Joan Kramer © Edward Young; 232, © H. Armstrong Roberts; 234–235, © H. Armstrong Roberts; 236, Peter Arnold © S. J. Krasemann; 239, H. Armstrong Roberts © A. McWhirter; 240, © Taurus; 243, "The Little White Girl" by James McNeill Whistler, The Tate Gallery, London; 244, Photo Trends © Victoria Beller-Smith; 247, Bruce Coleman © Fritz Prenzel; 255, Culver; 258–259, © Joan Menschenfreund; 263, © Milt & Joan Mann; 266, Bruce Coleman © Jane Burton; 299, © Shostal Asso-

INDEX OF AUTHORS AND TITLES

A 1
B 2
C 3
D 4
E 5
F 6
G 7
H 8
I 9
J 0